דברי הימים

THE
ISRAEL
BIBLE

CHRONICLES

EDITED BY

Rabbi Tuly Weisz

The Israel Bible: Chronicles

First Edition, 2021

The Israel Bible was produced by Israel365 in cooperation with Teach for Israel and is used with permission from Teach for Israel. All rights reserved. The English translation was adapted by Israel365 from the JPS Tanakh. Copyright © 1985 by the Jewish Publication Society. All rights reserved.

Cover image used under license from Shutterstock.com

ISBN 978-1-957109-45-9

A CIP catalogue record for this title is available from the British Library

The Israel Bible: Chronicles is a holy book that contains the name of God and should be treated with respect.

Table of Contents

Introduction

The Hebrew Bible is commonly known as the *Tanakh* which stands for *Torah* (the Five Books of Moses), *Neviim* (the Prophets) and *Ketuvim* (the Writings). The *Tanakh* consists of 24 books that are considered by Jews to be the word of God. While these books have been referred to as the "Old Testament," many Jews reject this label since it implies the replacement of the Hebrew Bible with something newer and prefer the more authentic Jewish name.

The *Tanakh* is not only the most important book known to man, it is God's word that is perfect and absolute. It is therefore a daunting undertaking to publish an edition of the *Tanakh*, and the responsibilities are awesome. There is no room for error or carelessness in dealing with the eternal word of God. Further, upon embarking on such a serious initiative, we ask ourselves if our efforts are gratuitous. Considering the many editions of the Bible in print, is there truly a need for yet another one?

While there are numerous Bibles in circulation today, its most central aspect – the Land of Israel – has often been overlooked. References to Israel appear on nearly every page, and the city of Jerusalem is specifically referred to hundreds of times throughout the Bible. The essential link between Israel and *Torah* is emphasized repeatedly in verses such as, "For instruction (*Torah*) shall come forth from *Tzion*, the word of *Hashem* from *Yerushalayim*" (Micah 4:2).

The miraculous return of the People of Israel to the Land of Israel in our own generation provides the perfect moment for a new volume to fill this void in biblical literature. *The Israel Bible* includes many special features elucidating God's focus on Israel throughout *Tanakh* and there are many additional, multimedia features available on our website **www.theisraelbible.com**.

Ordering and Presentation – In presenting *The Israel Bible*, our goal is to spread awareness of the biblical significance of the Land of Israel as well as the Jewish people's eternal connection to the land, based on the text of the *Tanakh*, the Hebrew Bible. We aim to honor "the God, the People and the Land of Israel" from an Orthodox Jewish perspective. To that end, *The Israel Bible* follows the traditional Jewish ordering of the books and the customary Hebrew division of chapters. Therefore, for example, we count 24 books of *Tanakh* with *Sefer Divrei Hayamim* (Chronicles) appearing last. It is our hope that our rich content will speak to all Jews and non-Jews who appreciate Israel as the God given land of the Jewish people.

English Translation – Throughout history, Jews have studied the Bible in Hebrew, as any form of translation would miss much of the nuance of the original holy tongue in which *Torah* has been transmitted since the days of Moses. However, as many Jews settled in America in the 19th Century, the need for an English translation became necessary. To be sure, there were already English translations prepared over the centuries by Christians, but in the words of the original editors of the Jewish Publication Society (JPS), "The Jew cannot afford to have his Bible translation prepared for him by others. He cannot have it as a gift, even as he cannot borrow his soul from others."

JPS set out in the late 1800s to publish an authoritative English translation "in the spirit of Jewish tradition." It was compiled over decades by some of the leading Jewish scholars of the time. They formed committees and subcommittees to compare existing English versions, considering medieval and modern Jewish commentators. The monumental JPS translation, originally published in 1917, has been updated in recent years, and *The Israel Bible* is proud to utilize the 1984 New Jewish Publication Society (NJPS) version with its modern, clear language, as well as its wide-ranging acceptance as an accurate and high-quality translation. We applied the NJPS translation verbatim, except for a select list of nouns which we replaced with their traditional Hebrew names. This is true even when we found the NJPS translation to be different than the popular translation of a word or phrase and when the NJPS switched the order of the text for the sake of clarity (see, for example, Ezekiel 24:22–24).

Hebrew Transliteration – To give our readers an authentic *Tanakh* experience, every verse that has commentary is transliterated from Hebrew into English. The Hebrew alphabet chart includes our standards for transliteration and pronunciation of Hebrew verses, enabling readers of *The Israel Bible* to decipher key biblical passages in the holy language. Readers can hear the entire Bible read in Hebrew on our website **www.theisraelbible.com**.

There are various standards when it comes to transliterating Hebrew words into English letters. While we have relied primarily on the classical Hebrew transliteration, we have occasionally deviated for the sake of simplicity, clarity and to reflect common usage.

In addition to whole verses, we have also transliterated many proper nouns in the English translation so that our readers can learn the names of key biblical figures and locations in their Hebrew form. As a rule, we chose to transliterate names of people that were central in the establishment and functioning of the nation of Israel, as well as significant places in the Holy Land. Therefore, regarding Adam's sons, for example, only *Shet* (Seth) is transliterated since it was from him that *Noach* (Noah), and ultimately *Avraham* (Abraham), descended. For this reason, there might be verses or sections of *The Israel Bible* that contains multiple names and only some of them are transliterated.

For the same reason, we have transliterated the names of the books of *Tanakh* when referring to them in our introductions and commentary. When referencing a specific chapter or verse, however, we use the English names of the books in our citations for clarity. We also transliterated ideas and concepts that are central to Judaism such as *Shabbat* (Sabbath), the names of the Jewish holidays and the *Beit Hamikdash* (Temple), as well as biblical measurements. Finally, the name of God is transliterated. Out of respect, Orthodox Jews generally refer to the Lord as *Hashem*, which literally means 'the Name.' Referring to God as *Hashem* reminds us that we feel close to Him but also recognize our distance at the same time. To stress this moniker, we transliterated both the Tetragrammaton as well as the name *Elohim* as *Hashem*.

Study Notes – Our unique commentary was compiled by Orthodox Jewish scholars who live in Israel. It is an anthology in the sense that most of the commentary is not original, but draws from traditional teachings of early Jewish Sages and modern rabbinic commentators. We also include quotations from individuals who have played a significant part in the past century of modern Israeli history including Israeli prime ministers, poets and military leaders.

Our commentary can be broken into four categories, three of which are identified by an icon at the beginning of the study note:

 Israel lessons are indicated with an icon bearing the map of Israel and focus on the Land of Israel and the modern State of Israel.

 Jewish lessons are indicated with a *Torah* scroll and teach a concept in Judaism or a classic idea from rabbinic thought.

 Hebrew lessons are represented by an icon bearing the letter *aleph* and focus on the meaning of a Hebrew word or phrase.

All other comments are considered general comments and are not assigned an icon.

Supplemental Material – In addition to our unique translation and original commentary, *The Israel Bible* offers supplementary material to enrich the learning experience of our readers. Before every book of *Tanakh,* we provide an introduction, as well as information, generally in the form of a map, a chart or a list, which is central to the specific book.

Maps – As the purpose of *The Israel Bible* is to highlight the biblical significance of the Land of Israel, significant time was spent researching and preparing maps to bring the physical contours of the holy land to life with great accuracy. However, since there is a lack of information regarding the precise locations of certain ancient cities, some of the places on our maps are approximate or subject to debate. In these cases, we followed the opinion that we are most comfortable with, but acknowledge that there is room for disagreement. We continue to produce new maps, which are available on our website **www.theisraelbible.com/maps.**

Torah **Readings** – The *Torah* is not just a work that is studied privately, it is also read out loud in synagogue. Every *Shabbat* and holiday a portion of the *Torah* is read, as well as a related section from *Neviim,* the prophets, called the *haftarah.* We included the blessings recited before and after the reading of the *Torah,* a list of the weekly *Torah* portions and their corresponding *haftarot,* and a chart of the *Torah* readings for special days with their corresponding *haftarot.* Readers can always find the current week's *Torah* portion by visiting **www.theisraelbible.com/weekly-torah-portion.** In this volume, we indicate where a new *Torah* portion begins by highlighting the Hebrew verse number with a gray box so readers can follow along with the communal *Torah* readings. Furthermore, we have included prayers for the State of Israel and the soldiers of the Israel Defense Forces (IDF) that are generally recited following the *Torah* reading in synagogue. It is our constant prayer that God watch over the State of Israel and the members of the IDF, who defend Israel every hour of every day.

In 1948, the State of Israel was created providing a modern answer to Isaiah's ancient question, "Is a nation born all at once?" (Isaiah 66:8). *The Israel Bible* was first published in the 70th year of God's miraculous restoration of the People of Israel to the Land of Israel. Jewish wisdom teaches that 70 is a significant number: *Moshe* (Moses) translated the *Torah* into 70 languages for all 70 nations of the world. From our very origins, the Jewish people were meant to be a light unto the 70 nations, spreading God's truth to the masses.

In the seven decades since the modern rebirth of the State of Israel, God's plan has been unfolding with unprecedented speed, dramatic highs and heartbreaking lows. Never has Israel been at the forefront of the world's attention as it is in our generation. Efforts to vilify the Jewish State seem to spread every day across the globe. At the same time, so does the growing movement of millions of non-Jewish biblical Zionists who stand with the nation of Israel as an expression of their commitment to God's word. As we seek to understand the clash of these two conflicting worldviews, the need for *The Israel Bible* has never been so important.

Standing on the great shoulders of those who came before us and emanating from the land that has always served as the birthplace for the Bible, we conclude with a heartfelt prayer: May the Almighty bless our efforts in offering this *Tanakh* to influence the hearts, minds and actions of its readers. In this way, it is our hope to spread God's name so that the publication of *The Israel Bible* brings us one step closer to the final redemption of Israel and the entire world.

Rabbi Tuly Weisz
Editor, *The Israel Bible*

Foreword

The mandate to study God's word daily is interestingly not found in the Five Books of Moses (Pentateuch), but rather in the first book of our prophetic writings: "Let not this Book of the Teaching cease from your lips, but recite it day and night, so that you may observe faithfully all that is written in it. Only then will you prosper in your undertakings and only then will you be successful" (Joshua 1:8). Charged with bringing the Israelites into the land covenantally promised to Abraham, Isaac and Jacob, God ensures Joshua of His protection if the nation observes His ways as dictated in the Divine constitution known as the *Torah*.

In Jewish tradition, Joshua (1:8) is directly linked with Deuteronomy (11:14), "You shall gather in your new grain and wine, and oil."[1] Our Sages deduced from this scriptural combination the importance of merging *Torah* study with a profession. Completely dedicating oneself to the study of *Torah* without having the financial means to sustain this lifestyle can lead one to eventually straying from observance of God's will. Poverty and crime can have an intimate relationship.

We must also be careful that our work does not affect our daily study of Scripture. The addiction of becoming a workaholic and not making *Torah* study a priority can also lead one into temptations that can violate our personal relationship with Him as well as our fellow human beings. The goal is to achieve a healthy balance between our study of God's word and our daily work.

The Deuteronomic verse quoted above is part of the second section of the Shema[2] that discusses the concept of reward and punishment. Sanctifying God by fulfilling His commandments results in the Land of Israel practically benefitting from rains that occur in the right season and reaping the abundance from the fields. However, if the nation follows pagan gods and practices, the consequences are devastating – famine and death. The Land of Israel is intrinsically linked with the keeping of the *Torah*. Covenant Land comes with covenant responsibility.

---

1   Talmud Bavli Berachot 35b

2   Consisting of three sections within the Five Books of Moses (Deut. 6:4–8; 11:13–22 and Numbers 15:37–42), the *Shema* is proclamation of accepting God's Kingdom in our lives, loyalty to His commandments and remembering His redemptive act of liberating us from Egypt. Jews recite the *Shema* twice a day as stated in Deut. 6:7.

Born into slavery, Joshua is now leading His people into the Promised Land. More than 500 years separates him from his ancestral forefather Abraham. The historical narratives that took place between Abraham leaving everything behind to follow God in Genesis 12 and the death of Moses in the last chapter of Deuteronomy are filled with intrigue, suspense, joy, sorrow and hope. What began as a family is now a nation actualizing its mission to be a kingdom of priests to the world. However, for the Israelites to succeed in the Land of Israel, they must see the *Torah* as the only compass to direct their lives.

The biblical episodes after our first entry into the land are well known. Our ancestors' triumphs and sins are all on public record. We learned the harsh reality of Leviticus (18:28) "So let not the land spew you out for defiling it as it spewed out the nation that came before you." Twice, we lost the privilege to be stewards of the Land of Israel and to fulfill our nation state mandate to be a light to the world. However, when the annals of history were ready to archive the Jewish people after the Holocaust, God kept His covenantal promise and gathered us from the four corners of the globe to come home. The year 1948 was a game changer. Biblical prophecies were and are being realized. We are now living in the birth pangs of the messianic era.

In our morning prayers, we recite a series of blessings over the *Torah* that include petitioning God to have a sweet tooth for His word, to study it without any ulterior motive and to have Him to teach it to us. They are some congregations that invoke the following liturgical prayer after the completion of these blessings: *May the Torah be my faith and El Shaddai my help. Blessed be the name of His glorious kingdom forever and all time.*

According to Jewish tradition, the neglect of not blessing the *Torah* before engaging in its study was one of the reasons for the destruction of the Temple.[3] This is deduced from the redundancy of words in Jeremiah (9:12) that talks about Israel not following God: "... Because they forsook the teaching I had set before them. They did not obey Me and they did not follow it [did not make a blessing before studying it]." Our inability to properly cherish God's greatest gift to the world, the *Torah*, led to our eventual exile from our land.

On Israel's Independence Day, Jews around the world recite Psalms 113–118 to express our gratitude to God for His Divine hand in helping establish the State of Israel. We have learned from our past and realize the privilege to see firsthand the land, people and *Torah* operating all together in our generation.

---

3 Babylonian Talmud Nedarim 81a

When Rabbi Tuly Weisz approached me about his intent to publish *The Israel Bible* that would highlight commentary about the special relationship between the land and people, I saw this project as another way to publicly demonstrate our appreciation to God for having the State of Israel. In addition, it is another educational tool to ensure biblical literacy. If we are to truly enjoy the Land of Israel, it is incumbent upon us to continually study the *Torah*. Isaiah once prophesied that the Jewish people would return to Zion with songs, "crowned with everlasting joy" (35:10). *The Israel Bible* provides us the lyrical content to express our joy in living in the land that God calls holy.

Rabbi Shlomo Riskin
Chief Rabbi of Efrat
Founder of the Center for Jewish-Christian
Understanding & Cooperation (CJCUC)

Introduction to Sefer Divrei Hayamim
The Book of Chronicles

Introduction and commentary by Alexander Jacob Tsykin

Sefer Divrei Hayamim (Chronicles) is the final book of *Tanakh*, the Hebrew Bible. Like the books of *Shmuel* and *Melachim*, *Divrei Hayamim* is divided into two sections which together form a single book. It is traditionally attributed to *Ezra* the scribe. The first nine chapters of the book contain a series of genealogies, tracing the lineage of the Jews who returned from Babylon to *Eretz Yisrael*, starting from the time of creation. The second part of the book is mainly a review of events previously detailed in the books of *Shmuel* and *Melachim*, starting with the death of *Shaul* and focusing primarily on the kingdom of *Yehuda*. The book ends with a brief epilogue mentioning the proclamation of Cyrus allowing the Jews to return to *Eretz Yisrael* and rebuild the *Beit Hamikdash*, as described in the books of *Ezra* and *Nechemya*.

What is the connection between the genealogies and the rest of the book, and what is the purpose of the book which is, to a large extent, a repetition of other books of *Tanach*?

Perhaps part of the reason *Ezra* chose to include the genealogies in *Sefer Divrei Hayamim* is to demonstrate the legitimacy of Jewish settlement in *Eretz Yisrael* during the return from Babylonian exile. By enumerating the genealogies of so many people involved in the resettlement of the land and the re-construction of the *Beit Hamikdash* in *Yerushalayim*, *Ezra* sought to emphasize that the people who had come to Israel were not interlopers trying to seize the Holy Land and its trade routes. Rather, they were natives who had returned to their homeland as a matter of right. Additionally, these lists legitimized the status of the *Kohanim* and *Leviim* of that time, as these roles are hereditary, by showing that they were descendants of the original *Kohanim* and *Leviim* of the first Temple period.

Even though the return to the Land of Israel took place only several decades after the final exiles had left the land with the destruction of the first Temple, their claim to the land had already come under question. As described in *Sefer Ezra* chapter 4, the new inhabitants of the land were angry that the Jews were returning to reclaim some of their territory and rebuild the *Beit Hamikdash,* and they repeatedly tried to prevent that from occurring. As such, we can see why *Ezra* felt the need to prove the legitimacy of their claim to the land. This might also be the reason that *Sefer Divrei Hayamim* ends with the permission granted by Cyrus, king of Persia, for the Jews to return to Israel. This provided additional confirmation to the new residents of the land, and to the returning Jews, that *Eretz Yisrael* is indeed the property of the Jewish people.

Since the purpose of the book is to justify the Jewish claim to Israel, *Ezra* felt it necessary to repeat much of the history of the kingdom of *Yehuda.* In doing so, he sometimes repeated verbatim what it says in *Shmuel* and *Melachim,* and other times wrote about the events differently than the other books of *Tanakh,* in a way that reflects the purpose and messages of *Sefer Divrei Hayamim.* This historical account further strengthens the Jews' claim to the land. Additionally, the first leader of the return from exile, *Zerubavel,* descended from the Davidic dynasty (see 1 Chronicles 3:19). This fact further bolsters the legitimacy of the Jewish resettlement and sovereignty, as *Sefer Divrei Hayamim* continuously stresses that the Davidic line has an eternal claim to kingship in the Land of Israel. Finally, the accounts of the repeated sins of the Davidic monarchs, their repentance and *Hashem's* forgiveness, shows that God did not give up on the Jewish people when he exiled them from *Eretz Yisrael.* Rather, He intended for the Jewish claim over the land to be everlasting.

Today, as in the time of *Ezra,* there are those who seek to delegitimize the Jewish people's claim to *Eretz Yisrael.* Like the "adversaries of *Yehuda* and *Binyamin*" in *Sefer Ezra* (Ezra 4:1), they contend that the Jews are no longer the rightful inhabitants of the land, that others have an equal or superior claim and that the Jews should be prevented from building and expanding Israel. The message of *Sefer Divrei Hayamim,* justifying the eternal Jewish claim to the Land of Israel, is therefore as relevant today as it was at the time it was written. Concluding *Tanakh* with *Sefer Divrei Hayamim,* which strongly supports the Jewish people's connection to their ancient homeland, confirms the centrality of the Land of Israel, which appears prominently in so many chapters of the Hebrew Bible, in the history and destiny of the Jewish people.

List of the Generations from *Adam* to King *David*

According to Rabbi Yitzchak Abrabanel, *Sefer Divrei Hayamim* was written to promote the stature of King *David* and the Davidic dynasty. It is from this lineage that *Mashiach* will come. *Divrei Hayamim* begins with a list of genealogies, starting with *Adam*, and then focuses on King *David* and the kingdom of *Yehuda*, whose kings were all descendants of *David*. The following is a list of generations from *Adam* through *David*.

Name	Years of life	Biblical Verse
Adam	930	Genesis 5:3–5
Shet	912	Genesis 5:6–8
Enosh	905	Genesis 5:9–11
Keinan	910	Genesis 5:12–14
Mahalalel	895	Genesis 5:15–17
Yered	962	Genesis 5:18–20
Enosh	365	Genesis 5:21–24
Metushelach	969	Genesis 5:25–27
Lemech	777	Genesis 5:28–31
Noach	950	Genesis 9:28–29
Shem	600	Genesis 11:10–11
Arpachshad	438	Genesis 11:12–13
Sheila	433	Genesis 11:14–15
Ever	464	Genesis 11:16–17
Peleg	239	Genesis 11:18–19
Re'u	239	Genesis 11:20–21
Serug	230	Genesis 11:22–23
Nachor	148	Genesis 11:24–25
Terach	205	Genesis 11:26–32
Avraham	175	Genesis 11:26, 25:7–10
Yitzchak	180	Genesis 25:19–20 Genesis 35:28–29
Yaakov	147	Genesis 47:28
Yehuda	119*	Genesis 29:35
Peretz	Unknown	Genesis 38
Chetzron	Unknown	Ruth 4:18
Ram	Unknown	Ruth 4:19
Aminadav	Unknown	Ruth 4:19
Nachshon	Unknown	Ruth 4:20

* Number based on the calculation of the Sages

Name	Years of life	Biblical Verse
Salma	Unknown	Ruth 4:20
Boaz	80*	Ruth 4:21
Oved	Unknown	Ruth 4:21
Yishai	Unknown	Ruth 4:22
David	70	Ruth 4:22

* Number based on the calculation of the Sages

1 ¹ *Adam, Shet, Enosh;*

אָדָם שֵׁת אֱנוֹשׁ: א

² *Keinan, Mehalalel, Yered;*

קֵינָן מַהֲלַלְאֵל יָרֶד: ב

³ *Chanoch, Metushelach, Lemech;*

חֲנוֹךְ מְתוּשֶׁלַח לָמֶךְ: ג

⁴ *Noach, Shem,* Ham, and Japheth.

נֹחַ שֵׁם חָם וָיָפֶת: ד

⁵ The sons of Japheth: Gomer, Magog, Media, Javan, Tubal, Meshech, and Tiras.

בְּנֵי יֶפֶת גֹּמֶר וּמָגוֹג וּמָדַי וְיָוָן וְתֻבָל וּמֶשֶׁךְ וְתִירָס: ה

⁶ The sons of Gomer: Ashkenaz, Diphath, and Togarmah.

וּבְנֵי גֹּמֶר אַשְׁכְּנַז וְדִיפַת וְתוֹגַרְמָה: ו

⁷ The sons of Javan: Elishah, Tarshish, Kittim, and Rodanim.

וּבְנֵי יָוָן אֱלִישָׁה וְתַרְשִׁישָׁה כִּתִּים וְרוֹדָנִים: ז

⁸ The sons of Ham: Cush, Mizraim, Put, and Canaan.

בְּנֵי חָם כּוּשׁ וּמִצְרַיִם פּוּט וּכְנָעַן: ח

⁹ The sons of Cush: Seba, Havilah, Sabta, Raama, and Sabteca. The sons of Raama: Sheba and Dedan.

וּבְנֵי כוּשׁ סְבָא וַחֲוִילָה וְסַבְתָּא וְרַעְמָא וְסַבְתְּכָא וּבְנֵי רַעְמָא שְׁבָא וּדְדָן: ט

¹⁰ Cush begot Nimrod; he was the first mighty one on earth.

וְכוּשׁ יָלַד אֶת־נִמְרוֹד הוּא הֵחֵל לִהְיוֹת גִּבּוֹר בָּאָרֶץ: י

¹¹ Mizraim begot the Ludim, the Anamim, the Lehabim, the Naphtuhim,

וּמִצְרַיִם יָלַד אֶת־לוּדִיים [לוּדִים] וְאֶת־עֲנָמִים וְאֶת־לְהָבִים וְאֶת־נַפְתֻּחִים: יא

¹² the Pathrusim, the Casluhim (whence the Philistines came forth), and the Caphtorim.

וְאֶת־פַּתְרֻסִים וְאֶת־כַּסְלֻחִים אֲשֶׁר יָצְאוּ מִשָּׁם פְּלִשְׁתִּים וְאֶת־כַּפְתֹּרִים: יב

¹³ Canaan begot Sidon his first-born, and Heth,

וּכְנַעַן יָלַד אֶת־צִידוֹן בְּכֹרוֹ וְאֶת־חֵת: יג

¹⁴ and the Jebusites, the Amorites, the Girgashites,

וְאֶת־הַיְבוּסִי וְאֶת־הָאֱמֹרִי וְאֵת הַגִּרְגָּשִׁי: יד

¹⁵ the Hivites, the Arkites, the Sinites,

וְאֶת־הַחִוִּי וְאֶת־הַעַרְקִי וְאֶת־הַסִּינִי: טו

¹⁶ the Arvadites, the Zemarites, and the Hamathites.

וְאֶת־הָאַרְוָדִי וְאֶת־הַצְּמָרִי וְאֶת־הַחֲמָתִי: טז

¹⁷ The sons of *Shem:* Elam, Assyria, *Arpachshad,* Lud, Aram, Uz, Hul, Gether, and Meshech.

בְּנֵי שֵׁם עֵילָם וְאַשּׁוּר וְאַרְפַּכְשַׁד וְלוּד וַאֲרָם וְעוּץ וְחוּל וְגֶתֶר וָמֶשֶׁךְ: יז

¹⁸ *Arpachshad* begot *Shelach;* and *Shelach* begot *Ever.*

וְאַרְפַּכְשַׁד יָלַד אֶת־שָׁלַח וְשֶׁלַח יָלַד אֶת־עֵבֶר: יח

¹⁹ Two sons were born to *Ever:* the name of the one was Peleg (for in his days the earth was divided), and the name of his brother Joktan.

וּלְעֵבֶר יֻלַּד שְׁנֵי בָנִים שֵׁם הָאֶחָד פֶּלֶג כִּי בְיָמָיו נִפְלְגָה הָאָרֶץ וְשֵׁם אָחִיו יָקְטָן: יט

²⁰ Joktan begot Almodad, Sheleph, Hazarmaveth, Jerah,

וְיָקְטָן יָלַד אֶת־אַלְמוֹדָד וְאֶת־שָׁלֶף וְאֶת־חֲצַרְמָוֶת וְאֶת־יָרַח: כ

²¹ Hadoram, Uzal, Diklah,

וְאֶת־הֲדוֹרָם וְאֶת־אוּזָל וְאֶת־דִּקְלָה: כא

²² Ebal, Abimael, Sheba,

וְאֶת־עֵיבָל וְאֶת־אֲבִימָאֵל וְאֶת־שְׁבָא: כב

²³ Ophir, Havilah, and Jobab; all these were the sons of Joktan.

וְאֶת־אוֹפִיר וְאֶת־חֲוִילָה וְאֶת־יוֹבָב כָּל־אֵלֶּה בְּנֵי יָקְטָן: כג

24	*Shem, Arpachshad, Shelach;*	כד שֵׁם אַרְפַּכְשַׁד שָׁלַח:
25	*Ever, Peleg, Re'u;*	כה עֵבֶר פֶּלֶג רְעוּ:
26	*Serug, Nachor, Terach;*	כו שְׂרוּג נָחוֹר תָּרַח:
27	*Avram, that is, Avraham.*	כז אַבְרָם הוּא אַבְרָהָם:
28	The sons of *Avraham: Yitzchak* and Ishmael.	כח בְּנֵי אַבְרָהָם יִצְחָק וְיִשְׁמָעֵאל:
29	This is their line: The first-born of Ishmael, Nebaioth; and Kedar, Abdeel, Mibsam,	כט אֵלֶּה תֹּלְדוֹתָם בְּכוֹר יִשְׁמָעֵאל נְבָיוֹת וְקֵדָר וְאַדְבְּאֵל וּמִבְשָׂם:
30	Mishma, Dumah, Massa, Hadad, Tema,	ל מִשְׁמָע וְדוּמָה מַשָּׂא חֲדַד וְתֵימָא:
31	Jetur, Naphish, and Kedmah. These are the sons of Ishmael.	לא יְטוּר נָפִישׁ וָקֵדְמָה אֵלֶּה הֵם בְּנֵי יִשְׁמָעֵאל:
32	The sons of Keturah, *Avraham*'s concubine: she bore Zimran, Jokshan, Medan, Midian, Ishbak, and Shuah. The sons of Jokshan: Sheba and Dedan.	לב וּבְנֵי קְטוּרָה פִּילֶגֶשׁ אַבְרָהָם יָלְדָה אֶת־זִמְרָן וְיָקְשָׁן וּמְדָן וּמִדְיָן וְיִשְׁבָּק וְשׁוּחַ וּבְנֵי יָקְשָׁן שְׁבָא וּדְדָן:
33	The sons of Midian: Ephah, Epher, Enoch, Abida, and Eldaah. All these were the descendants of Keturah.	לג וּבְנֵי מִדְיָן עֵיפָה וָעֵפֶר וַחֲנוֹךְ וַאֲבִידָע וְאֶלְדָּעָה כָּל־אֵלֶּה בְּנֵי קְטוּרָה:
34	*Avraham* begot *Yitzchak.* The sons of *Yitzchak:* Esau and *Yisrael.*	לד וַיּוֹלֶד אַבְרָהָם אֶת־יִצְחָק בְּנֵי יִצְחָק עֵשָׂו וְיִשְׂרָאֵל:
35	The sons of Esau: Eliphaz, Reuel, Jeush, Jalam, and Korah.	לה בְּנֵי עֵשָׂו אֱלִיפַז רְעוּאֵל וִיעוּשׁ וְיַעְלָם וְקֹרַח:
36	The sons of Eliphaz: Teman, Omar, Zephi, Gatam, Kenaz, Timna, and Amalek.	לו בְּנֵי אֱלִיפָז תֵּימָן וְאוֹמָר צְפִי וְגַעְתָּם קְנַז וְתִמְנָע וַעֲמָלֵק:
37	The sons of Reuel: Nahath, Zerah, Shammah, and Mizzah.	לז בְּנֵי רְעוּאֵל נַחַת זֶרַח שַׁמָּה וּמִזָּה:
38	The sons of Seir: Lotan, Shobal, Zibeon, Anah, Dishon, Ezer, and Dishan.	לח וּבְנֵי שֵׂעִיר לוֹטָן וְשׁוֹבָל וְצִבְעוֹן וַעֲנָה וְדִישֹׁן וְאֵצֶר וְדִישָׁן:
39	The sons of Lotan: Hori and Homam; and Lotan's sister was Timna.	לט וּבְנֵי לוֹטָן חֹרִי וְהוֹמָם וַאֲחוֹת לוֹטָן תִּמְנָע:
40	The sons of Shobal: Alian, Manahath, Ebal, Shephi, and Onam. The sons of Zibeon: Aiah and Anah.	מ בְּנֵי שׁוֹבָל עַלְיָן וּמָנַחַת וְעֵיבָל שְׁפִי וְאוֹנָם וּבְנֵי צִבְעוֹן אַיָּה וַעֲנָה:
41	The sons of Anah: Dishon. The sons of Dishon: Hamran, Eshban, Ithran, and Cheran.	מא בְּנֵי עֲנָה דִּישׁוֹן וּבְנֵי דִישׁוֹן חַמְרָן וְאֶשְׁבָּן וְיִתְרָן וּכְרָן:
42	The sons of Ezer: Bilhan, Zaavan, and Jaakan. The sons of Dishan: Uz and Aran.	מב בְּנֵי־אֵצֶר בִּלְהָן וְזַעֲוָן יַעֲקָן בְּנֵי דִישׁוֹן עוּץ וַאֲרָן:

⁴³ These are the kings who reigned in the land of Edom before any king reigned over the Israelites: Bela son of Beor, and the name of his city was Dinhabah.

מג וְאֵלֶּה הַמְּלָכִים אֲשֶׁר מָלְכוּ בְּאֶרֶץ אֱדוֹם לִפְנֵי מְלָךְ־מֶלֶךְ לִבְנֵי יִשְׂרָאֵל בֶּלַע בֶּן־בְּעוֹר וְשֵׁם עִירוֹ דִּנְהָבָה:

*v'-AY-leh ha-m'-la-KHEEM a-SHER ma-l'-KHU b'-E-retz e-DOM lif-NAY m'-lokh
ME-lekh liv-NAY yis-ra-AYL BE-la ben b'-OR v'-SHAYM ee-RO din-HA-vah*

⁴⁴ When Bela died, Jobab son of Zerah from Bozrah succeeded him as king.

מד וַיָּמָת בָּלַע וַיִּמְלֹךְ תַּחְתָּיו יוֹבָב בֶּן־זֶרַח מִבָּצְרָה:

⁴⁵ When Jobab died, Husham of the land of the Temanites succeeded him as king.

מה וַיָּמָת יוֹבָב וַיִּמְלֹךְ תַּחְתָּיו חוּשָׁם מֵאֶרֶץ הַתֵּימָנִי:

⁴⁶ When Husham died, Hadad son of Bedad, who defeated the Midianites in the country of Moab, succeeded him as king, and the name of his city was Avith.

מו וַיָּמָת חוּשָׁם וַיִּמְלֹךְ תַּחְתָּיו הֲדַד בֶּן־בְּדַד הַמַּכֶּה אֶת־מִדְיָן בִּשְׂדֵה מוֹאָב וְשֵׁם עִירוֹ עֲיוֹת [עֲוִית]:

⁴⁷ When Hadad died, Samlah of Masrekah succeeded him as king.

מז וַיָּמָת הֲדָד וַיִּמְלֹךְ תַּחְתָּיו שַׂמְלָה מִמַּשְׂרֵקָה:

⁴⁸ When Samlah died, Saul of Rehoboth-on-the-River succeeded him as king.

מח וַיָּמָת שַׂמְלָה וַיִּמְלֹךְ תַּחְתָּיו שָׁאוּל מֵרְחֹבוֹת הַנָּהָר:

⁴⁹ When Saul died, Baal-hanan son of Achbor succeeded him as king.

מט וַיָּמָת שָׁאוּל וַיִּמְלֹךְ תַּחְתָּיו בַּעַל חָנָן בֶּן־עַכְבּוֹר:

⁵⁰ When Baal-hanan died, Hadad succeeded him as king; and the name of his city was Pai, and his wife's name Mehetabel daughter of Matred daughter of Me-zahab.

נ וַיָּמָת בַּעַל חָנָן וַיִּמְלֹךְ תַּחְתָּיו הֲדַד וְשֵׁם עִירוֹ פָּעִי וְשֵׁם אִשְׁתּוֹ מְהֵיטַבְאֵל בַּת־מַטְרֵד בַּת מֵי זָהָב:

⁵¹ And Hadad died. The clans of Edom were the clans of Timna, Alvah, Jetheth,

נא וַיָּמָת הֲדָד וַיִּהְיוּ אַלּוּפֵי אֱדוֹם אַלּוּף תִּמְנָע אַלּוּף עַלְיָה [עַלְוָה] אַלּוּף יְתֵת:

⁵² Oholibamah, Elah, Pinon,

נב אַלּוּף אָהֳלִיבָמָה אַלּוּף אֵלָה אַלּוּף פִּינֹן:

⁵³ Kenaz, Teman, Mibzar,

נג אַלּוּף קְנַז אַלּוּף תֵּימָן אַלּוּף מִבְצָר:

⁵⁴ Magdiel, and Iram; these are the clans of Edom.

נד אַלּוּף מַגְדִּיאֵל אַלּוּף עִירָם אֵלֶּה אַלּוּפֵי אֱדוֹם:

The Arava Valley with the Edom Mountains in the background

1:43 These are the kings who reigned in the land of Edom
Sefer Divrei Hayamim begins with a record of the generations from *Adam* through the descendants of *Yaakov*. This verse introduces the leaders of the children of Esau, also known as Edom. By listing the heads of the family of Esau, the text confirms that *Hashem* fulfilled his promise to *Rivka* that she and *Yitzchak* would be the parents of two great nations (Genesis 25:23). Since God promised that both their sons would be become great nations, we are shown that *Hashem* kept his assurances and blessed Esau, regardless of Esau's choice to reject God and His covenant. The lesson is obvious. If God even keeps His promise with Esau, who rejected the path of his father *Yitzchak*, how much more so will *Hashem* keep His promise to *Yaakov*, who maintained the covenant.

2 ¹ These are the sons of *Yisrael*: *Reuven, Shimon, Levi, Yehuda, Yissachar, Zevulun,*

ב א אֵ֚לֶּה בְּנֵ֣י יִשְׂרָאֵ֔ל רְאוּבֵ֥ן שִׁמְע֖וֹן לֵוִ֑י וִיהוּדָ֖ה יִשָׂשכָ֥ר וּזְבֻלֽוּן׃

² *Dan, Yosef, Binyamin, Naftali, Gad,* and *Asher.*

ב דָּ֚ן יוֹסֵ֣ף וּבִנְיָמִ֔ן נַפְתָּלִ֖י גָּ֥ד וְאָשֵֽׁר׃

³ The sons of *Yehuda: Er, Onan,* and *Sheila;* these three, Bath-shua the Canaanite woman bore to him. But *Er, Yehuda's* first-born, was displeasing to *Hashem,* and He took his life.

ג בְּנֵ֣י יְהוּדָ֗ה עֵ֤ר וְאוֹנָן֙ וְשֵׁלָ֔ה שְׁלוֹשָׁה֙ נֽוֹלַד־ל֔וֹ מִבַּת־שׁ֖וּעַ הַכְּנַעֲנִ֑ית וַיְהִ֞י עֵ֣ר ׀ בְּכ֣וֹר יְהוּדָ֗ה רַ֛ע בְּעֵינֵ֥י יְהוָ֖ה וַיְמִיתֵֽהוּ׃

⁴ His daughter-in-law *Tamar* also bore him *Peretz* and *Zerach. Yehuda's* sons were five in all.

ד וְתָמָר֙ כַּלָּת֔וֹ יָ֥לְדָה לּ֖וֹ אֶת־פֶּ֣רֶץ וְאֶת־זָ֑רַח כָּל־בְּנֵ֥י יְהוּדָ֖ה חֲמִשָּֽׁה׃

v'-ta-MAR ka-la-TO ya-l'-DAH LO et PE-retz v'-et ZA-rakh kol b'-NAY y'-hu-DAH kha-mi-SHAH

⁵ The sons of *Peretz: Chetzron* and Hamul.

ה בְּנֵי־פֶ֖רֶץ חֶצְר֥וֹן וְחָמֽוּל׃

⁶ The sons of *Zerach: Zimri,* Ethan, *Hayman,* Calcol, and Dara, five in all.

ו וּבְנֵ֣י זֶ֗רַח זִמְרִ֧י וְאֵיתָ֛ן וְהֵימָ֥ן וְכַלְכֹּ֖ל וָדָ֑רַע כֻּלָּ֖ם חֲמִשָּֽׁה׃

⁷ The sons of Carmi: Achar, the troubler of *Yisrael,* who committed a trespass against the proscribed thing;

ז וּבְנֵ֖י כַּרְמִ֑י עָכָר֙ עוֹכֵ֣ר יִשְׂרָאֵ֔ל אֲשֶׁ֥ר מָעַ֖ל בַּחֵֽרֶם׃

⁸ and Ethan's son was *Azarya.*

ח וּבְנֵ֥י אֵיתָ֖ן עֲזַרְיָֽה׃

⁹ The sons of *Chetzron* that were born to him: Jerahmeel, *Ram,* and Chelubai.

ט וּבְנֵ֥י חֶצְר֖וֹן אֲשֶׁ֣ר נֽוֹלַד־ל֑וֹ אֶת־יְרַחְמְאֵ֥ל וְאֶת־רָ֖ם וְאֶת־כְּלוּבָֽי׃

¹⁰ *Ram* begot *Aminadav,* and *Aminadav* begot *Nachshon,* prince of the sons of *Yehuda.*

י וְרָ֖ם הוֹלִ֣יד אֶת־עַמִּינָדָ֑ב וְעַמִּינָדָב֙ הוֹלִ֣יד אֶת־נַחְשׁ֔וֹן נְשִׂ֖יא בְּנֵ֥י יְהוּדָֽה׃

¹¹ *Nachshon* was the father of *Salma, Salma* of *Boaz,*

יא וְנַחְשׁוֹן֙ הוֹלִ֣יד אֶת־שַׂלְמָ֔א וְשַׂלְמָ֖א הוֹלִ֥יד אֶת־בֹּֽעַז׃

¹² *Boaz* of *Oved, Oved* of *Yishai.*

יב וּבֹ֙עַז֙ הוֹלִ֣יד אֶת־עוֹבֵ֔ד וְעוֹבֵ֖ד הוֹלִ֥יד אֶת־יִשָֽׁי׃

¹³ *Yishai* begot *Eliav* his first-born, *Avinadav* the second, Shimea the third,

יג וְאִישַׁ֛י הוֹלִ֥יד אֶת־בְּכֹר֖וֹ אֶת־אֱלִיאָ֑ב וַאֲבִינָדָב֙ הַשֵּׁנִ֔י וְשִׁמְעָ֖א הַשְּׁלִשִֽׁי׃

¹⁴ Nethanel the fourth, Raddai the fifth,

יד נְתַנְאֵל֙ הָרְבִיעִ֔י רַדַּ֖י הַחֲמִישִֽׁי׃

2:4 His daughter-in-law *Tamar* also bore him *Peretz* and *Zerach* *Rashi* wonders why *Ezra* mentions the seemingly shameful incident of *Yehuda* and *Tamar.* Perhaps the answer is that rather than bringing shame upon *Yehuda,* this incident actually reveals his true greatness. Everyone, even the great heroes of the Bible, makes mistakes. However, it is to *Yehuda's* credit that he recognizes, admits and takes responsibility for his error rather than trying to cover it up, and also refrains from repeating his mistake (Genesis 38:26). This quality of humility is necessary in the forefather of the Davidic dynasty and, ultimately, the *Mashiach.* Many other nations would have chosen a king with an unblem-ished background and impeccable lineage, yet king *David* was a product of a troubling relationship. A powerful lesson can be learned from king *David's* humble origins: No matter what one's background is, all people have the ability to overcome their shortcomings and make a difference in the world.

Rabbi Tuly Weisz and Israel365 bring *Purim* joy to orphans in *Yerushalayim*

¹⁵ Ozem the sixth, *David* the seventh;

טו אֹצֶם הַשִּׁשִּׁי דָּוִיד הַשְּׁבִעִי:

¹⁶ their sisters were *Tzeruya* and *Avigail*. The sons of *Tzeruya*: *Avishai, Yoav,* and *Asael,* three.

טז וְאַחְיֹתֵיהֶם [וְאַחְיוֹתֵיהֶם] צְרוּיָה וַאֲבִיגָיִל וּבְנֵי צְרוּיָה אַבְשַׁי וְיוֹאָב וַעֲשָׂה־אֵל שְׁלֹשָׁה:

¹⁷ *Avigail* bore Amasa, and the father of Amasa was Jether the Ishmaelite.

יז וַאֲבִיגַיִל יָלְדָה אֶת־עֲמָשָׂא וַאֲבִי עֲמָשָׂא יֶתֶר הַיִּשְׁמְעֵאלִי:

¹⁸ *Kalev* son of *Chetzron* had children by his wife Azubah, and by Jerioth; these were her sons: Jesher, Shobab, and Ardon.

יח וְכָלֵב בֶּן־חֶצְרוֹן הוֹלִיד אֶת־עֲזוּבָה אִשָּׁה וְאֶת־יְרִיעוֹת וְאֵלֶּה בָנֶיהָ יֵשֶׁר וְשׁוֹבָב וְאַרְדּוֹן:

¹⁹ When Azubah died, *Kalev* married *Efrat,* who bore him *Chur.*

יט וַתָּמָת עֲזוּבָה וַיִּקַּח־לוֹ כָלֵב אֶת־אֶפְרָת וַתֵּלֶד לוֹ אֶת־חוּר:

²⁰ *Chur* begot *Uri,* and *Uri* begot *Betzalel.*

כ וְחוּר הוֹלִיד אֶת־אוּרִי וְאוּרִי הוֹלִיד אֶת־בְּצַלְאֵל:

²¹ Afterward *Chetzron* had relations with the daughter of Machir father of *Gilad* – he had married her when he was sixty years old – and she bore him Segub;

כא וְאַחַר בָּא חֶצְרוֹן אֶל־בַּת־מָכִיר אֲבִי גִלְעָד וְהוּא לְקָחָהּ וְהוּא בֶּן־שִׁשִּׁים שָׁנָה וַתֵּלֶד לוֹ אֶת־שְׂגוּב:

²² and Segub begot *Yair;* he had twenty-three cities in the land of *Gilad.*

כב וּשְׂגוּב הוֹלִיד אֶת־יָאִיר וַיְהִי־לוֹ עֶשְׂרִים וְשָׁלוֹשׁ עָרִים בְּאֶרֶץ הַגִּלְעָד:

²³ But Geshur and Aram took from them Havvoth-jair, Kenath and its dependencies, sixty towns. All these were the sons of Machir, the father of *Gilad.*

כג וַיִּקַּח גְּשׁוּר־וַאֲרָם אֶת־חַוֹּת יָאִיר מֵאִתָּם אֶת־קְנָת וְאֶת־בְּנֹתֶיהָ שִׁשִּׁים עִיר כָּל־אֵלֶּה בְּנֵי מָכִיר אֲבִי־גִלְעָד:

²⁴ After the death of *Chetzron,* in Caleb-ephrathah, *Aviya,* wife of *Chetzron,* bore Ashhur, the father of Tekoa.

כד וְאַחַר מוֹת־חֶצְרוֹן בְּכָלֵב אֶפְרָתָה וְאֵשֶׁת חֶצְרוֹן אֲבִיָּה וַתֵּלֶד לוֹ אֶת־אַשְׁחוּר אֲבִי תְקוֹעַ:

²⁵ The sons of Jerahmeel the first-born of *Chetzron:* *Ram* his first-born, Bunah, Oren, Ozem, and *Achiya.*

כה וַיִּהְיוּ בְנֵי־יְרַחְמְאֵל בְּכוֹר חֶצְרוֹן הַבְּכוֹר רָם וּבוּנָה וָאֹרֶן וָאֹצֶם אֲחִיָּה:

²⁶ Jerahmeel had another wife, whose name was Atarah; she was the mother of Onam.

כו וַתְּהִי אִשָּׁה אַחֶרֶת לִירַחְמְאֵל וּשְׁמָהּ עֲטָרָה הִיא אֵם אוֹנָם:

²⁷ The sons of *Ram* the first-born of Jerahmeel: Maaz, Jamin, and Eker.

כז וַיִּהְיוּ בְנֵי־רָם בְּכוֹר יְרַחְמְאֵל מַעַץ וְיָמִין וָעֵקֶר:

²⁸ The sons of Onam: Shammai and Jada. The sons of Shammai: *Nadav* and Abishur.

כח וַיִּהְיוּ בְנֵי־אוֹנָם שַׁמַּי וְיָדָע וּבְנֵי שַׁמַּי נָדָב וַאֲבִישׁוּר:

²⁹ The name of Abishur's wife was *Avichayil,* and she bore him Ahban and Molid.

כט וְשֵׁם אֵשֶׁת אֲבִישׁוּר אֲבִיהָיִל וַתֵּלֶד לוֹ אֶת־אַחְבָּן וְאֶת־מוֹלִיד:

³⁰ The sons of *Nadav:* Seled and Appaim; Seled died childless.

ל וּבְנֵי נָדָב סֶלֶד וְאַפָּיִם וַיָּמָת סֶלֶד לֹא בָנִים:

³¹ The sons of Appaim: Ishi. The sons of Ishi: Sheshan. The sons of Sheshan: Ahlai.

לא וּבְנֵי אַפַּיִם יִשְׁעִי וּבְנֵי יִשְׁעִי שֵׁשָׁן וּבְנֵי שֵׁשָׁן אַחְלָי:

³² The sons of Jada, Shammai's brother: Jether and *Yonatan*; Jether died childless.

לב וּבְנֵי יָדָע אֲחִי שַׁמַּי יֶתֶר וְיוֹנָתָן וַיָּמָת יֶתֶר לֹא בָנִים:

³³ The sons of *Yonatan*: Peleth and Zaza. These were the descendants of Jerahmeel.

לג וּבְנֵי יוֹנָתָן פֶּלֶת וְזָזָא אֵלֶּה הָיוּ בְּנֵי יְרַחְמְאֵל:

³⁴ Sheshan had no sons, only daughters; Sheshan had an Egyptian slave, whose name was Jarha.

לד וְלֹא־הָיָה לְשֵׁשָׁן בָּנִים כִּי אִם־בָּנוֹת וּלְשֵׁשָׁן עֶבֶד מִצְרִי וּשְׁמוֹ יַרְחָע:

³⁵ So Sheshan gave his daughter in marriage to Jarha his slave; and she bore him Attai.

לה וַיִּתֵּן שֵׁשָׁן אֶת־בִּתּוֹ לְיַרְחָע עַבְדּוֹ לְאִשָּׁה וַתֵּלֶד לוֹ אֶת־עַתָּי:

³⁶ Attai begot *Natan*, and *Natan* begot Zabad.

לו וְעַתַּי הֹלִיד אֶת־נָתָן וְנָתָן הוֹלִיד אֶת־זָבָד:

³⁷ Zabad begot Ephlal, and Ephlal begot Oved.

לז וְזָבָד הוֹלִיד אֶת־אֶפְלָל וְאֶפְלָל הוֹלִיד אֶת־עוֹבֵד:

³⁸ Oved begot *Yehu*, and *Yehu* begot *Azarya*.

לח וְעוֹבֵד הוֹלִיד אֶת־יֵהוּא וְיֵהוּא הוֹלִיד אֶת־עֲזַרְיָה:

³⁹ *Azarya* begot Helez, and Helez begot Eleasah.

לט וַעֲזַרְיָה הֹלִיד אֶת־חָלֶץ וְחֶלֶץ הֹלִיד אֶת־אֶלְעָשָׂה:

⁴⁰ Eleasah begot Sisamai, and Sisamai begot *Shalum*.

מ וְאֶלְעָשָׂה הֹלִיד אֶת־סִסְמַי וְסִסְמַי הֹלִיד אֶת־שַׁלּוּם:

⁴¹ *Shalum* begot Jekamiah, and Jekamiah begot Elishama.

מא וְשַׁלּוּם הוֹלִיד אֶת־יְקַמְיָה וִיקַמְיָה הֹלִיד אֶת־אֱלִישָׁמָע:

⁴² The sons of *Kalev* brother of Jerahmeel: Meshah his first-born, who was the father of Ziph. The sons of Mareshah father of *Chevron*.

מב וּבְנֵי כָלֵב אֲחִי יְרַחְמְאֵל מֵישָׁע בְּכֹרוֹ הוּא אֲבִי־זִיף וּבְנֵי מָרֵשָׁה אֲבִי חֶבְרוֹן:

⁴³ The sons of *Chevron*: Korach, Tappuah, Rekem, and Shema.

מג וּבְנֵי חֶבְרוֹן קֹרַח וְתַפֻּחַ וְרֶקֶם וָשָׁמַע:

⁴⁴ Shema begot Raham the father of Jorkeam, and Rekem begot Shammai.

מד וְשֶׁמַע הוֹלִיד אֶת־רַחַם אֲבִי יָרְקֳעָם וְרֶקֶם הוֹלִיד אֶת־שַׁמָּי:

⁴⁵ The son of Shammai: Maon, and Maon begot Bethzur.

מה וּבֶן־שַׁמַּי מָעוֹן וּמָעוֹן אֲבִי בֵית־צוּר:

⁴⁶ Ephah, *Kalev*'s concubine, bore Haran, Moza, and Gazez; Haran begot Gazez.

מו וְעֵיפָה פִּילֶגֶשׁ כָּלֵב יָלְדָה אֶת־חָרָן וְאֶת־מוֹצָא וְאֶת־גָּזֵז וְחָרָן הֹלִיד אֶת־גָּזֵז:

⁴⁷ The sons of Jahdai: Regem, *Yotam*, Geshan, Pelet, Ephah, and Shaaph.

מז וּבְנֵי יָהְדָּי רֶגֶם וְיוֹתָם וְגֵישָׁן וָפֶלֶט וְעֵיפָה וָשָׁעַף:

⁴⁸ Maacah, *Kalev*'s concubine, bore Sheber and Tirhanah.

מח פִּלֶגֶשׁ כָּלֵב מַעֲכָה יָלַד שֶׁבֶר וְאֶת־תִּרְחֲנָה:

⁴⁹ She also bore Shaaph father of Madmannah, Sheva father of Machbenah and father of Gibea; the daughter of *Kalev* was Achsah.

מט וַתֵּלֶד שַׁעַף אֲבִי מַדְמַנָּה אֶת־שְׁוָא אֲבִי מַכְבֵּנָה וַאֲבִי גִבְעָא וּבַת־כָּלֵב עַכְסָה:

50 These were the descendants of *Kalev*. The sons of *Chur* the first-born of *Efrat*: Shobal father of *Kiryat Ye'arim*,

נ אֵלֶּה הָיוּ בְּנֵי כָלֵב בֶּן־חוּר בְּכוֹר אֶפְרָתָה שׁוֹבָל אֲבִי קִרְיַת יְעָרִים:

51 Salma father of *Beit Lechem*, Hareph father of Beth-gader.

נא שַׂלְמָא אֲבִי בֵית־לָחֶם חָרֵף אֲבִי בֵית־גָּדֵר:

52 Shobal father of *Kiryat Ye'arim* had sons: Haroeh, half of the Menuhoth.

נב וַיִּהְיוּ בָנִים לְשׁוֹבָל אֲבִי קִרְיַת יְעָרִים הָרֹאֶה חֲצִי הַמְּנֻחוֹת:

53 And the families of *Kiryat Ye'arim*: the Ithrites, the Puthites, the Shumathites, and the Mishraites; from these came the Zorathites and the Eshtaolites.

נג וּמִשְׁפְּחוֹת קִרְיַת יְעָרִים הַיִּתְרִי וְהַפּוּתִי וְהַשֻּׁמָתִי וְהַמִּשְׁרָעִי מֵאֵלֶּה יָצְאוּ הַצָּרְעָתִי וְהָאֶשְׁתָּאֻלִי:

54 The sons of Salma: *Beit Lechem*, the Netophathites, Atroth-beth-joab, and half of the Manahathites, the Zorites.

נד בְּנֵי שַׂלְמָא בֵּית לֶחֶם וּנְטוֹפָתִי עַטְרוֹת בֵּית יוֹאָב וַחֲצִי הַמָּנַחְתִּי הַצָּרְעִי:

55 The families of the scribes that dwelt at Jabez: the Tirathites, the Shimeathites, the Sucathites; these are the Kenites who came from Hammath, father of the house of Rechab.

נה וּמִשְׁפְּחוֹת סֹפְרִים ישבו [יֹשְׁבֵי] יַעְבֵּץ תִּרְעָתִים שִׁמְעָתִים שׂוּכָתִים הֵמָּה הַקֵּינִים הַבָּאִים מֵחַמַּת אֲבִי בֵית־רֵכָב:

3 1 These are the sons of *David* who were born to him in *Chevron*: the first-born *Amnon*, by Ahinoam the Yizraelite; the second *Daniel*, by *Avigail* the Carmelite;

ג א וְאֵלֶּה הָיוּ בְּנֵי דָוִיד אֲשֶׁר נוֹלַד־לוֹ בְּחֶבְרוֹן הַבְּכוֹר אַמְנֹן לַאֲחִינֹעַם הַיִּזְרְעֵאלִית שֵׁנִי דָּנִיֵּאל לַאֲבִיגַיִל הַכַּרְמְלִית:

2 the third *Avshalom*, son of Maacah daughter of King Talmai of Geshur; the fourth *Adoniyahu*, son of Haggith;

ב הַשְּׁלִשִׁי לְאַבְשָׁלוֹם בֶּן־מַעֲכָה בַּת־תַּלְמַי מֶלֶךְ גְּשׁוּר הָרְבִיעִי אֲדֹנִיָּה בֶן־חַגִּית:

3 the fifth Shephatiah, by Abital; the sixth Ithream, by his wife Eglah;

ג הַחֲמִישִׁי שְׁפַטְיָה לַאֲבִיטָל הַשִּׁשִּׁי יִתְרְעָם לְעֶגְלָה אִשְׁתּוֹ:

4 six were born to him in *Chevron*. He reigned there seven years and six months, and in *Yerushalayim* he reigned thirty-three years.

ד שִׁשָּׁה נוֹלַד־לוֹ בְחֶבְרוֹן וַיִּמְלָךְ־שָׁם שֶׁבַע שָׁנִים וְשִׁשָּׁה חֳדָשִׁים וּשְׁלֹשִׁים וְשָׁלוֹשׁ שָׁנָה מָלַךְ בִּירוּשָׁלָ͏ִם:

*shi-SHAH no-lad LO v'-khev-RON va-YIM-lokh SHAM SHE-va
sha-NEEM v'-shi-SHAH kho-da-SHEEM ush-lo-SHEEM
v'-sha-LOSH sha-NAH ma-LAKH bee-ru-sha-LA-im*

Chaim Weizmann
(1874–1952)

3:4 And in *Yerushalayim* he reigned thirty-three years The text delineates exactly how many years of *David*'s reign were spent ruling in *Chevron*, and how many in *Yerushalayim*, because ruling in *Yerushalayim*, *Hashem*'s chosen city, is qualitatively different than ruling anywhere else, even another city in *Eretz Yisrael*. *Yerushalayim* is the center of the world and the holiest place on earth. In December 1948, the first president of Israel, Chaim Weizmann, passionately de-

clared: "Jerusalem holds a unique place in the heart of every Jew. Jerusalem is to us the quintessence of the Palestine idea. Its restoration symbolizes the redemption of Israel … To us Jerusalem has both a spiritual and a temporal significance. It is the City of God, the seat of our ancient sanctuary. But it is also the capital of David and Solomon, the City of the Great King, the metropolis of our ancient commonwealth … It is the center of our ancient national glory. It was our lodestar in all our wanderings. It

⁵ These were born to him in *Yerushalayim*: Shimea, Shobab, *Natan*, and *Shlomo*, four by Bathshua daughter of Ammiel;

ה וְאֵלֶּה נוּלְּדוּ־לוֹ בִּירוּשָׁלָיִם שִׁמְעָא וְשׁוֹבָב וְנָתָן וּשְׁלֹמֹה אַרְבָּעָה לְבַת־שׁוּעַ בַּת־עַמִּיאֵל:

⁶ then Ibhar, Elishama, Eliphelet,

ו וְיִבְחָר וֶאֱלִישָׁמָע וֶאֱלִיפָלֶט:

⁷ Nogah, Nepheg, Japhia,

ז וְנֹגַהּ וְנֶפֶג וְיָפִיעַ:

⁸ Elishama, Eliada, and Eliphelet – nine.

ח וֶאֱלִישָׁמָע וְאֶלְיָדָע וֶאֱלִיפָלֶט תִּשְׁעָה:

⁹ All were *David*'s sons, besides the sons of the concubines; and *Tamar* was their sister.

ט כָּל בְּנֵי דָוִיד מִלְּבַד בְּנֵי־פִילַגְשִׁים וְתָמָר אֲחוֹתָם:

¹⁰ The son of *Shlomo*: *Rechovam*; his son *Aviya*, his son *Asa*, his son *Yehoshafat*,

י וּבֶן־שְׁלֹמֹה רְחַבְעָם אֲבִיָּה בְנוֹ אָסָא בְנוֹ יְהוֹשָׁפָט בְּנוֹ:

¹¹ his son *Yoram*, his son *Achazyahu*, his son *Yoash*,

יא יוֹרָם בְּנוֹ אֲחַזְיָהוּ בְנוֹ יוֹאָשׁ בְּנוֹ:

¹² his son *Amatzya*, his son *Azarya*, his son *Yotam*,

יב אֲמַצְיָהוּ בְנוֹ עֲזַרְיָה בְנוֹ יוֹתָם בְּנוֹ:

¹³ his son *Achaz*, his son *Chizkiyahu*, his son *Menashe*,

יג אָחָז בְּנוֹ חִזְקִיָּהוּ בְנוֹ מְנַשֶּׁה בְּנוֹ:

¹⁴ his son *Amon*, and his son *Yoshiyahu*.

יד אָמוֹן בְּנוֹ יֹאשִׁיָּהוּ בְנוֹ:

¹⁵ The sons of *Yoshiyahu*: *Yochanan* the first-born, the second *Yehoyakim*, the third *Tzidkiyahu*, the fourth *Shalum*.

טו וּבְנֵי יֹאשִׁיָּהוּ הַבְּכוֹר יוֹחָנָן הַשֵּׁנִי יְהוֹיָקִים הַשְּׁלִשִׁי צִדְקִיָּהוּ הָרְבִיעִי שַׁלּוּם:

¹⁶ The descendants of *Yehoyakim*: his son *Yechonya*, his son *Tzidkiyahu*;

טז וּבְנֵי יְהוֹיָקִים יְכָנְיָה בְנוֹ צִדְקִיָּה בְנוֹ:

¹⁷ and the sons of *Yechonya*, the captive: *Shealtiel* his son,

יז וּבְנֵי יְכָנְיָה אַסִּר שְׁאַלְתִּיאֵל בְּנוֹ:

¹⁸ MalHiram, Pedaiah, Shenazzar, Jekamiah, Hoshama, and Nedabiah;

יח וּמַלְכִּירָם וּפְדָיָה וְשֶׁנְאַצַּר יְקַמְיָה הוֹשָׁמָע וּנְדַבְיָה:

¹⁹ the sons of Pedaiah: *Zerubavel* and *Shim'i*; the sons of *Zerubavel*: Meshullam and *Chananya*, and Shelomith was their sister;

יט וּבְנֵי פְדָיָה זְרֻבָּבֶל וְשִׁמְעִי וּבֶן־זְרֻבָּבֶל מְשֻׁלָּם וַחֲנַנְיָה וּשְׁלֹמִית אֲחוֹתָם:

²⁰ Hashubah, Ohel, *Berechya*, Hasadiah, and Jushabhesed – five.

כ וַחֲשֻׁבָה וָאֹהֶל וּבֶרֶכְיָה וַחֲסַדְיָה יוּשַׁב חֶסֶד חָמֵשׁ:

²¹ And the sons of *Chananya*: Pelatiah and Jeshaiah; the sons of [Jeshaiah]: Rephaiah; the sons of [Rephaiah]: Arnan; the sons of [Arnan]: *Ovadya*; the sons of [*Ovadya*]: Shechanya.

כא וּבֶן־חֲנַנְיָה פְּלַטְיָה וִישַׁעְיָה בְּנֵי רְפָיָה בְּנֵי אַרְנָן בְּנֵי עֹבַדְיָה בְּנֵי שְׁכַנְיָה:

embodies all that is noblest in our hopes for the future. Jerusalem is the eternal mother of the Jewish people, precious and beloved even in its desolation. When David made Jerusalem the capital of Judea, on that day there began the Jewish Commonwealth … It seems inconceivable that the establishment of a Jewish State in Palestine should be accompanied by the detachment from it of its spiritual center and historical capital."

²² And the sons of *Shechanya*: *Shemaya*; and the sons of *Shemaya*: Hattush, and Igal, and Bariah, and Neariah, and *Shafat* – six.

²³ And the sons of Neariah: Elioenai, and Hizkiah, and Azrikam – three.

²⁴ And the sons of Elioenai: Hodaviah, and *Elyashiv*, and Pelaiah, and Akkub, and *Yochanan*, and Delaiah, and Anani – seven.

4 ¹ The sons of *Yehuda*: *Peretz, Chetzron*, Carmi, *Chur*, and Shobal.

² Reaiah son of Shobal begot Jahath, and Jahath begot Ahumai and Lahad. These were the families of the Zorathites.

³ These were [the sons of] the father of Etam: *Yizrael*, Ishma, and Idbash; and the name of their sister was Hazlelponi,

⁴ and Penuel was the father of Gedor, and Ezer the father of Hushah. These were the sons of *Chur*, the first-born of *Efrat*, the father of *Beit Lechem*.

⁵ Ashhur the father of Tekoa had two wives, Helah and Naarah;

⁶ Naarah bore him Ahuzam, Hepher, Temeni, and Ahashtari. These were the sons of Naarah.

⁷ The sons of Helah: Zereth, Zohar, and Ethnan.

⁸ Koz was the father of Anub, Zobebah, and the families of Aharhel son of Harum.

⁹ Jabez was more esteemed than his brothers; and his mother named him Jabez, "Because," she said, "I bore him in pain."

¹⁰ Jabez invoked the God of *Yisrael*, saying, "Oh, bless me, enlarge my territory, stand by me, and make me not suffer pain from misfortune!" And *Hashem* granted what he asked.

¹¹ Chelub the brother of Shuhah begot Mehir, who was the father of Eshton.

¹² Eshton begot Bethrapha, Paseah, and Tehinnah father of Ir-nahash. These were the men of Recah.

¹³ The sons of Kenaz: *Otniel* and *Seraya*; and the sons of *Otniel*:

כב וּבְנֵי שְׁכַנְיָה שְׁמַעְיָה וּבְנֵי שְׁמַעְיָה חַטּוּשׁ וְיִגְאָל וּבָרִיחַ וּנְעַרְיָה וְשָׁפָט שִׁשָּׁה:

כג וּבֶן־נְעַרְיָה אֶלְיוֹעֵינַי וְחִזְקִיָּה וְעַזְרִיקָם שְׁלֹשָׁה:

כד וּבְנֵי אֶלְיוֹעֵינַי הדיוהו [הוֹדַוְיָהוּ] וְאֶלְיָשִׁיב וּפְלָיָה וְעַקּוּב וְיוֹחָנָן וּדְלָיָה וַעֲנָנִי שִׁבְעָה:

ד א בְּנֵי יְהוּדָה פֶּרֶץ חֶצְרוֹן וְכַרְמִי וְחוּר וְשׁוֹבָל:

ב וּרְאָיָה בֶן־שׁוֹבָל הוֹלִיד אֶת־יַחַת וְיַחַת הֹלִיד אֶת־אֲחוּמַי וְאֶת־לָהַד אֵלֶּה מִשְׁפְּחוֹת הַצָּרְעָתִי:

ג וְאֵלֶּה אֲבִי עֵיטָם יִזְרְעֶאל וְיִשְׁמָא וְיִדְבָּשׁ וְשֵׁם אֲחוֹתָם הַצְלֶלְפּוֹנִי:

ד וּפְנוּאֵל אֲבִי גְדֹר וְעֵזֶר אֲבִי חוּשָׁה אֵלֶּה בְנֵי־חוּר בְּכוֹר אֶפְרָתָה אֲבִי בֵּית לָחֶם:

ה וּלְאַשְׁחוּר אֲבִי תְקוֹעַ הָיוּ שְׁתֵּי נָשִׁים חֶלְאָה וְנַעֲרָה:

ו וַתֵּלֶד לוֹ נַעֲרָה אֶת־אֲחֻזָּם וְאֶת־חֵפֶר וְאֶת־תֵּימְנִי וְאֶת־הָאֲחַשְׁתָּרִי אֵלֶּה בְּנֵי נַעֲרָה:

ז וּבְנֵי חֶלְאָה צֶרֶת יצחר [וְצֹחַר] וְאֶתְנָן:

ח וְקוֹץ הוֹלִיד אֶת־עָנוּב וְאֶת־הַצֹּבֵבָה וּמִשְׁפְּחוֹת אֲחַרְחֵל בֶּן־הָרוּם:

ט וַיְהִי יַעְבֵּץ נִכְבָּד מֵאֶחָיו וְאִמּוֹ קָרְאָה שְׁמוֹ יַעְבֵּץ לֵאמֹר כִּי יָלַדְתִּי בְּעֹצֶב:

י וַיִּקְרָא יַעְבֵּץ לֵאלֹהֵי יִשְׂרָאֵל לֵאמֹר אִם־בָּרֵךְ תְּבָרֲכֵנִי וְהִרְבִּיתָ אֶת־גְּבוּלִי וְהָיְתָה יָדְךָ עִמִּי וְעָשִׂיתָ מֵּרָעָה לְבִלְתִּי עָצְבִּי וַיָּבֵא אֱלֹהִים אֵת אֲשֶׁר־שָׁאָל:

יא וּכְלוּב אֲחִי־שׁוּחָה הוֹלִיד אֶת־מְחִיר הוּא אֲבִי אֶשְׁתּוֹן:

יב וְאֶשְׁתּוֹן הוֹלִיד אֶת־בֵּית רָפָא וְאֶת־פָּסֵחַ וְאֶת־תְּחִנָּה אֲבִי עִיר נָחָשׁ אֵלֶּה אַנְשֵׁי רֵכָה:

יג וּבְנֵי קְנַז עָתְנִיאֵל וּשְׂרָיָה וּבְנֵי עָתְנִיאֵל חֲתַת:

¹⁴ Hathath and Meonothai. He begot Ophrah. *Seraya* begot *Yoav* father of Ge-harashim, so-called because they were craftsmen.

יד וּמְעוֹנֹתַי הוֹלִיד אֶת־עׇפְרָה וּשְׂרָיָה הוֹלִיד אֶת־יוֹאָב אֲבִי גֵּיא חֲרָשִׁים כִּי חֲרָשִׁים הָיוּ׃

¹⁵ The sons of *Kalev* son of Jephunneh: Iru, Elah, and Naam; and the sons of Elah: Kenaz.

טו וּבְנֵי כָּלֵב בֶּן־יְפֻנֶּה עִירוּ אֵלָה וָנָעַם וּבְנֵי אֵלָה וּקְנַז׃

¹⁶ The sons of Jehallelel: Ziph, Ziphah, Tiria, and Asarel.

טז וּבְנֵי יְהַלֶּלְאֵל זִיף וְזִיפָה תִּירְיָא וַאֲשַׂרְאֵל׃

¹⁷ The sons of Ezrah: Jether, Mered, Epher, and Jalon. She conceived and bore *Miriam*, Shammai, and Ishbah father of Eshtemoa.

יז וּבֶן־עֶזְרָה יֶתֶר וּמֶרֶד וְעֵפֶר וְיָלוֹן וַתַּהַר אֶת־מִרְיָם וְאֶת־שַׁמַּי וְאֶת־יִשְׁבָּח אֲבִי אֶשְׁתְּמֹעַ׃

¹⁸ And his Judahite wife bore Jered father of Gedor, *Chever* father of Soco, and Jekuthiel father of *Zanoach*. These were the sons of Bithiah daughter of Pharaoh, whom Mered married.

יח וְאִשְׁתּוֹ הַיְהֻדִיָּה יָלְדָה אֶת־יֶרֶד אֲבִי גְדוֹר וְאֶת־חֶבֶר אֲבִי שׂוֹכוֹ וְאֶת־יְקוּתִיאֵל אֲבִי זָנוֹחַ וְאֵלֶּה בְּנֵי בִּתְיָה בַת־פַּרְעֹה אֲשֶׁר לָקַח מָרֶד׃

¹⁹ The sons of the wife of Hodiah sister of Naham were the fathers of Keilah the Garmite and Eshtemoa the Maacathite.

יט וּבְנֵי אֵשֶׁת הוֹדִיָּה אֲחוֹת נַחַם אֲבִי קְעִילָה הַגַּרְמִי וְאֶשְׁתְּמֹעַ הַמַּעֲכָתִי׃

²⁰ The sons of *Shimon*: *Amnon*, Rinnah, Ben-hanan, and Tilon. The sons of Ishi: Zoheth and Ben-zoheth.

כ וּבְנֵי שִׁימוֹן אַמְנוֹן וְרִנָּה בֶּן־חָנָן וְתוֹלוֹן [וְתִילוֹן] וּבְנֵי יִשְׁעִי זוֹחֵת וּבֶן־זוֹחֵת׃

²¹ The sons of *Sheila* son of *Yehuda*: Er father of Lecah, Laadah father of Mareshah, and the families of the linen factory at Beth-ashbea;

כא בְּנֵי שֵׁלָה בֶן־יְהוּדָה עֵר אֲבִי לֵכָה וְלַעְדָּה אֲבִי מָרֵשָׁה וּמִשְׁפְּחוֹת בֵּית־עֲבֹדַת הַבֻּץ לְבֵית אַשְׁבֵּעַ׃

²² and Jokim, and the men of Cozeba and *Yoash*, and Saraph, who married into Moab and Yashuvi Lehem (the records are ancient).

כב וְיוֹקִים וְאַנְשֵׁי כֹזֵבָא וְיוֹאָשׁ וְשָׂרָף אֲשֶׁר־בָּעֲלוּ לְמוֹאָב וְיָשֻׁבִי לָחֶם וְהַדְּבָרִים עַתִּיקִים׃

²³ These were the potters who dwelt at Netaim and Gedera; they dwelt there in the king's service.

כג הֵמָּה הַיּוֹצְרִים וְיֹשְׁבֵי נְטָעִים וּגְדֵרָה עִם־הַמֶּלֶךְ בִּמְלַאכְתּוֹ יָשְׁבוּ שָׁם׃

²⁴ The sons of *Shimon*: Nemuel, Jamin, Jarib, *Zerach*, *Shaul*;

כד בְּנֵי שִׁמְעוֹן נְמוּאֵל וְיָמִין יָרִיב זֶרַח שָׁאוּל׃

²⁵ his son *Shalum*, his son Mibsam, his son Mishma.

כה שַׁלֻּם בְּנוֹ מִבְשָׂם בְּנוֹ מִשְׁמָע בְּנוֹ׃

²⁶ The sons of Mishma: his son Hammuel, his son Zaccur, his son *Shim'i*.

כו וּבְנֵי מִשְׁמָע חַמּוּאֵל בְּנוֹ זַכּוּר בְּנוֹ שִׁמְעִי בְּנוֹ׃

²⁷ *Shim'i* had sixteen sons and six daughters; but his brothers had not many children; in all, their families were not as prolific as the Judahites.

כז וּלְשִׁמְעִי בָּנִים שִׁשָּׁה עָשָׂר וּבָנוֹת שֵׁשׁ וּלְאֶחָיו אֵין בָּנִים רַבִּים וְכֹל מִשְׁפַּחְתָּם לֹא הִרְבּוּ עַד־בְּנֵי יְהוּדָה׃

²⁸ They dwelt in *Be'er Sheva*, Moladah, Hazar-shual,

כח וַיֵּשְׁבוּ בִּבְאֵר־שֶׁבַע וּמוֹלָדָה וַחֲצַר שׁוּעָל׃

²⁹ Bilhah, Ezem, Tolad,

כט וּבְבִלְהָה וּבְעֶצֶם וּבְתוֹלָד׃

³⁰ Bethuel, Hormah, *Tziklag*,

ל וּבִבְתוּאֵל וּבְחׇרְמָה וּבְצִיקְלָג׃

³¹ Beth-marcaboth, Hazar-susim, Beth-biri, and *Shaarayim*. These were their towns until *David* became king,

לא וּבְבֵית מַרְכָּבוֹת וּבַחֲצַר סוּסִים וּבְבֵית בִּרְאִי וּבְשַׁעֲרָיִם אֵלֶּה עָרֵיהֶם עַד־מְלֹךְ דָּוִיד:

³² together with their villages, Etam, Ain, Rimmon, Tochen, and Ashan – five towns,

לב וְחַצְרֵיהֶם עֵיטָם וָעַיִן רִמּוֹן וְתֹכֶן וְעָשָׁן עָרִים חָמֵשׁ:

³³ along with all their villages that were around these towns as far as Baal; such were their settlements. Registered in their genealogy were:

לג וְכָל־חַצְרֵיהֶם אֲשֶׁר סְבִיבוֹת הֶעָרִים הָאֵלֶּה עַד־בָּעַל זֹאת מוֹשְׁבֹתָם וְהִתְיַחְשָׂם לָהֶם:

³⁴ Meshobab, Jamlech, Joshah son of *Amatzya*,

לד וּמְשׁוֹבָב וְיַמְלֵךְ וְיוֹשָׁה בֶּן־אֲמַצְיָה:

³⁵ *Yoel*, *Yehu* son of Joshibiah son of *Seraya* son of Asiel.

לה וְיוֹאֵל וְיֵהוּא בֶּן־יוֹשִׁבְיָה בֶּן־שְׂרָיָה בֶּן־עֲשִׂיאֵל:

³⁶ Elioenai, Jaakobah, Jeshohaiah, Asaiah, Adiel, Jesimiel, Benaiah,

לו וְאֶלְיוֹעֵינַי וְיַעֲקֹבָה וִישׁוֹחָיָה וַעֲשָׂיָה וַעֲדִיאֵל וִישִׂימִאֵל וּבְנָיָה:

³⁷ Ziza son of Shiphi son of Allon son of Jedaiah son of Shimri son of *Shemaya* –

לז וְזִיזָא בֶן־שִׁפְעִי בֶּן־אַלּוֹן בֶּן־יְדָיָה בֶּן־שִׁמְרִי בֶּן־שְׁמַעְיָה:

³⁸ these mentioned by name were chiefs in their families, and their clans increased greatly.

לח אֵלֶּה הַבָּאִים בְּשֵׁמוֹת נְשִׂיאִים בְּמִשְׁפְּחוֹתָם וּבֵית אֲבוֹתֵיהֶם פָּרְצוּ לָרוֹב:

³⁹ They went to the approaches to Gedor, to the eastern side of the valley, in search of pasture for their flocks.

לט וַיֵּלְכוּ לִמְבוֹא גְדֹר עַד לְמִזְרַח הַגָּיְא לְבַקֵּשׁ מִרְעֶה לְצֹאנָם:

⁴⁰ They found rich, good pasture, and the land was ample, quiet, and peaceful. The former inhabitants were of Ham;

מ וַיִּמְצְאוּ מִרְעֶה שָׁמֵן וָטוֹב וְהָאָרֶץ רַחֲבַת יָדַיִם וְשֹׁקֶטֶת וּשְׁלֵוָה כִּי מִן־חָם הַיֹּשְׁבִים שָׁם לְפָנִים:

va-yim-tz'-U mir-EH sha-MAYN va-TOV v'-ha-A-retz ra-kha-VAT ya-DA-yim v'-sho-KE-tet ush-lay-VAH KEE min KHAM ha-yo-sh'-VEEM sham l'-fa-NEEM

⁴¹ those recorded by name came in the days of King *Chizkiyahu* of *Yehuda*, and attacked their encampments and the Meunim who were found there, and wiped them out forever, and settled in their place, because there was pasture there for their flocks.

מא וַיָּבֹאוּ אֵלֶּה הַכְּתוּבִים בְּשֵׁמוֹת בִּימֵי יְחִזְקִיָּהוּ מֶלֶךְ־יְהוּדָה וַיַּכּוּ אֶת־אָהֳלֵיהֶם וְאֶת־הַמְּעִינִים [הַמְּעוּנִים] אֲשֶׁר נִמְצְאוּ־שָׁמָּה וַיַּחֲרִימֻם עַד־הַיּוֹם הַזֶּה וַיֵּשְׁבוּ תַּחְתֵּיהֶם כִּי־מִרְעֶה לְצֹאנָם שָׁם:

שלוה
שלום

4:40 The land was ample, quiet, and peaceful The Hebrew word for 'peaceful' in this verse is *shalva* (שלוה), rather than the more common word 'shalom' (שלום). What is the difference between *shalom* and *shalva*? The 19th-century commentator *Malbim* explains that *shalom* refers an external peace, meaning that one is free from threats or harm. *Shalva*, on the other hand, refers to internal har-

A prayer for peace at the Western Wall

mony. Accordingly, this verse teaches that the inhabitants of the cities of *Shimon* experienced not only a quiet security from outside threats, but also enjoyed peaceful coexistence with their brethren and neighbors. In his prayer for the peace of Jerusalem (Psalm 122:6) the Psalmist includes both terms: "Pray for the well-being (*shalom*) of *Yerushalayim*; may those who love you be at peace (*shalva*)."

⁴² And some of them, five hundred of the Simeonites, went to Mount Seir, with Pelatiah, Neariah, Rephaiah, and Uzziel, sons of Ishi, at their head,

מב וּמֵהֶם מִן־בְּנֵי שִׁמְעוֹן הָלְכוּ לְהַר שֵׂעִיר אֲנָשִׁים חֲמֵשׁ מֵאוֹת וּפְלַטְיָה וּנְעַרְיָה וּרְפָיָה וְעֻזִּיאֵל בְּנֵי יִשְׁעִי בְּרֹאשָׁם:

⁴³ and they destroyed the last surviving Amalekites, and they live there to this day.

מג וַיַּכּוּ אֶת־שְׁאֵרִית הַפְּלֵטָה לַעֲמָלֵק וַיֵּשְׁבוּ שָׁם עַד הַיּוֹם הַזֶּה:

5 ¹ The sons of *Reuven* the first-born of *Yisrael*. (He was the first-born; but when he defiled his father's bed, his birthright was given to the sons of *Yosef* son of *Yisrael*, so he is not reckoned as first-born in the genealogy;

ה א וּבְנֵי רְאוּבֵן בְּכוֹר־יִשְׂרָאֵל כִּי הוּא הַבְּכוֹר וּבְחַלְּלוֹ יְצוּעֵי אָבִיו נִתְּנָה בְּכֹרָתוֹ לִבְנֵי יוֹסֵף בֶּן־יִשְׂרָאֵל וְלֹא לְהִתְיַחֵשׂ לַבְּכֹרָה:

² though *Yehuda* became more powerful than his brothers and a leader came from him, yet the birthright belonged to *Yosef*.)

ב כִּי יְהוּדָה גָּבַר בְּאֶחָיו וּלְנָגִיד מִמֶּנּוּ וְהַבְּכֹרָה לְיוֹסֵף:

³ The sons of *Reuven*, the first-born of *Yisrael*: Enoch, Pallu, *Chetzron*, and Carmi.

ג בְּנֵי רְאוּבֵן בְּכוֹר יִשְׂרָאֵל חֲנוֹךְ וּפַלּוּא חֶצְרוֹן וְכַרְמִי:

⁴ The sons of *Yoel*: his son *Shemaya*, his son Gog, his son *Shim'i*,

ד בְּנֵי יוֹאֵל שְׁמַעְיָה בְנוֹ גּוֹג בְּנוֹ שִׁמְעִי בְנוֹ:

⁵ his son *Micha*, his son Reaiah, his son Baal,

ה מִיכָה בְנוֹ רְאָיָה בְנוֹ בַּעַל בְּנוֹ:

⁶ his son Beerah – whom King Tillegath-pilneser of Assyria exiled – was chieftain of the Rebenites.

ו בְּאֵרָה בְנוֹ אֲשֶׁר הֶגְלָה תִּלְּגַת פִּלְנְאֶסֶר מֶלֶךְ אַשֻּׁר הוּא נָשִׂיא לָראוּבֵנִי:

⁷ And his kinsmen, by their families, according to their lines in the genealogy: the head, Jeiel, and *Zecharya*,

ז וְאֶחָיו לְמִשְׁפְּחֹתָיו בְּהִתְיַחֵשׂ לְתֹלְדוֹתָם הָרֹאשׁ יְעִיאֵל וּזְכַרְיָהוּ:

⁸ and Bela son of Azaz son of Shema son of *Yoel*; he dwelt in Aroer as far as Nebo and Baal-meon.

ח וּבֶלַע בֶּן־עָזָז בֶּן־שֶׁמַע בֶּן־יוֹאֵל הוּא יוֹשֵׁב בַּעֲרֹעֵר וְעַד־נְבוֹ וּבַעַל מְעוֹן:

⁹ He also dwelt to the east as far as the fringe of the wilderness this side of the Euphrates, because their cattle had increased in the land of *Gilad*.

ט וְלַמִּזְרָח יָשַׁב עַד־לְבוֹא מִדְבָּרָה לְמִן־הַנָּהָר פְּרָת כִּי מִקְנֵיהֶם רָבוּ בְּאֶרֶץ גִּלְעָד:

¹⁰ And in the days of *Shaul* they made war on the Hagrites, who fell by their hand; and they occupied their tents throughout all the region east of *Gilad*.

י וּבִימֵי שָׁאוּל עָשׂוּ מִלְחָמָה עִם־הַהַגְרִאִים וַיִּפְּלוּ בְּיָדָם וַיֵּשְׁבוּ בְּאָהֳלֵיהֶם עַל־כָּל־פְּנֵי מִזְרָח לַגִּלְעָד:

¹¹ The sons of *Gad* dwelt facing them in the land of Bashan as far as Salcah:

יא וּבְנֵי־גָד לְנֶגְדָּם יָשְׁבוּ בְּאֶרֶץ הַבָּשָׁן עַד־סַלְכָה:

¹² *Yoel* the chief, Shapham the second, Janai, and *Shafat* in Bashan.

יב יוֹאֵל הָרֹאשׁ וְשָׁפָם הַמִּשְׁנֶה וְיַעְנַי וְשָׁפָט בַּבָּשָׁן:

¹³ And by clans: *Michael*, Meshullam, Sheba, Jorai, Jacan, Zia, and *Ever* – seven.

יג וַאֲחֵיהֶם לְבֵית אֲבוֹתֵיהֶם מִיכָאֵל וּמְשֻׁלָּם וְשֶׁבַע וְיוֹרַי וְיַעְכָּן וְזִיעַ וָעֵבֶר שִׁבְעָה:

¹⁴ These were the sons of *Avichayil* son of Huri son of Jaroah son of *Gilad* son of *Michael* son of Jeshishai son of Jahdo son of Buz;

יד אֵלֶּה בְּנֵי אֲבִיחַיִל בֶּן־חוּרִי בֶּן־יָרוֹחַ בֶּן־גִּלְעָד בֶּן־מִיכָאֵל בֶּן־יְשִׁישַׁי בֶּן־יַחְדּוֹ בֶּן־בּוּז:

¹⁵ Ahi son of Abdiel son of Guni was chief of their clan,

טו אֲחִי בֶן־עַבְדִּיאֵל בֶּן־גּוּנִי רֹאשׁ לְבֵית אֲבוֹתָם:

¹⁶ and they dwelt in *Gilad*, in Bashan, and in its dependencies, and in all the pasturelands of Sharon, to their limits.

טז וַיֵּשְׁבוּ בַּגִּלְעָד בַּבָּשָׁן וּבִבְנֹתֶיהָ וּבְכָל־מִגְרְשֵׁי שָׁרוֹן עַל־תּוֹצְאוֹתָם:

¹⁷ All of them were registered by genealogies in the days of King *Yotam* of *Yehuda*, and in the days of King *Yerovam* of *Yisrael*.

יז כֻּלָּם הִתְיַחְשׂוּ בִּימֵי יוֹתָם מֶלֶךְ־יְהוּדָה וּבִימֵי יָרָבְעָם מֶלֶךְ־יִשְׂרָאֵל:

¹⁸ The Reubenites, the Gadites, and the half-tribe of *Menashe* had warriors who carried shield and sword, drew the bow, and were experienced at war – 44,760, ready for service.

יח בְּנֵי־רְאוּבֵן וְגָדִי וַחֲצִי שֵׁבֶט־מְנַשֶּׁה מִן־בְּנֵי־חַיִל אֲנָשִׁים נֹשְׂאֵי מָגֵן וְחֶרֶב וְדֹרְכֵי קֶשֶׁת וּלְמוּדֵי מִלְחָמָה אַרְבָּעִים וְאַרְבָּעָה אֶלֶף וּשְׁבַע־מֵאוֹת וְשִׁשִּׁים יֹצְאֵי צָבָא:

¹⁹ They made war on the Hagrites – Jetur, Naphish, and Nodab.

יט וַיַּעֲשׂוּ מִלְחָמָה עִם־הַהַגְרִיאִים וִיטוּר וְנָפִישׁ וְנוֹדָב:

²⁰ They prevailed against them; the Hagrites and all who were with them were delivered into their hands, for they cried to *Hashem* in the battle, and He responded to their entreaty because they trusted in Him.

כ וַיֵּעָזְרוּ עֲלֵיהֶם וַיִּנָּתְנוּ בְיָדָם הַהַגְרִיאִים וְכֹל שֶׁעִמָּהֶם כִּי לֵאלֹהִים זָעֲקוּ בַּמִּלְחָמָה וְנַעְתּוֹר לָהֶם כִּי־בָטְחוּ בוֹ:

va-yay-a-z'-RU a-lay-HEM va-yi-na-t'-NU v'-ya-DAM ha-hag-ree-EEM v'-KHOL she-i-ma-HEM KEE lay-lo-HEEM za-a-KU ba-mil-kha-MAH v'-na-TOR la-HEM kee VA-t'-khu VO

²¹ They carried off their livestock: 50,000 of their camels, 250,000 sheep, 2,000 asses, and 100,000 people.

כא וַיִּשְׁבּוּ מִקְנֵיהֶם גְּמַלֵּיהֶם חֲמִשִּׁים אֶלֶף וְצֹאן מָאתַיִם וַחֲמִשִּׁים אֶלֶף וַחֲמוֹרִים אַלְפָּיִם וְנֶפֶשׁ אָדָם מֵאָה אָלֶף:

²² For many fell slain, because it was *Hashem*'s battle. And they dwelt in their place until the exile.

כב כִּי־חֲלָלִים רַבִּים נָפָלוּ כִּי מֵהָאֱלֹהִים הַמִּלְחָמָה וַיֵּשְׁבוּ תַחְתֵּיהֶם עַד־הַגֹּלָה:

²³ The members of the half-tribe of *Menashe* dwelt in the land; they were very numerous from Bashan to Baal-hermon, Senir, and Mount *Chermon*.

כג וּבְנֵי חֲצִי שֵׁבֶט מְנַשֶּׁה יָשְׁבוּ בָּאָרֶץ מִבָּשָׁן עַד־בַּעַל חֶרְמוֹן וּשְׂנִיר וְהַר־חֶרְמוֹן הֵמָּה רָבוּ:

²⁴ These were the chiefs of their clans: Epher, Ishi, Eliel, Azriel, *Yirmiyahu*, Hodaviah, and Jahdiel, men of substance, famous men, chiefs of their clans.

כד וְאֵלֶּה רָאשֵׁי בֵית־אֲבוֹתָם וְעֵפֶר וְיִשְׁעִי וֶאֱלִיאֵל וְעַזְרִיאֵל וְיִרְמְיָה וְהוֹדַוְיָה וְיַחְדִּיאֵל אֲנָשִׁים גִּבּוֹרֵי חַיִל אַנְשֵׁי שֵׁמוֹת רָאשִׁים לְבֵית אֲבוֹתָם:

A woman crying to *Hashem* at the Western Wall

5:20 For they cried to *Hashem* in the battle In the previous verses, we are told that the combined forces of the tribes of *Reuven*, *Gad* and *Menashe* numbered an impressive 44,760 troops of exceptional quality. And yet, we are told that the reason they were victorious in battle is because they trusted in *Hashem* and believed that He would help them and save them. As we have seen numerous times throughout *Tanakh*, success in the Land of Israel is not tied to physical capability and effort alone, though these are very important, but also to faith and trust in God.

25 But they trespassed against the God of their fathers by going astray after the gods of the peoples of the land, whom *Hashem* had destroyed before them.

כה וַיִּמְעֲלוּ בֵּאלֹהֵי אֲבוֹתֵיהֶם וַיִּזְנוּ אַחֲרֵי אֱלֹהֵי עַמֵּי־הָאָרֶץ אֲשֶׁר־הִשְׁמִיד אֱלֹהִים מִפְּנֵיהֶם:

26 So the God of *Yisrael* roused the spirit of King Pul of Assyria – the spirit of King Tillegath-pilneser of Assyria – and he carried them away, namely, the Reubenites, the Gadites, and the half-tribe of *Menashe*, and brought them to Halah, Habor, Hara, and the river Gozan, to this day.

כו וַיָּעַר אֱלֹהֵי יִשְׂרָאֵל אֶת־רוּחַ פּוּל מֶלֶךְ־אַשּׁוּר וְאֶת־רוּחַ תִּלְּגַת פִּלְנֶסֶר מֶלֶךְ אַשּׁוּר וַיַּגְלֵם לָראוּבֵנִי וְלַגָּדִי וְלַחֲצִי שֵׁבֶט מְנַשֶּׁה וַיְבִיאֵם לַחְלַח וְחָבוֹר וְהָרָא וּנְהַר גּוֹזָן עַד הַיּוֹם הַזֶּה:

27 The sons of *Levi: Gershon, Kehat*, and *Merari*.

כז בְּנֵי לֵוִי גֵּרְשׁוֹן קְהָת וּמְרָרִי:

28 The sons of *Kehat: Amram*, Izhar, *Chevron*, and Uzziel.

כח וּבְנֵי קְהָת עַמְרָם יִצְהָר וְחֶבְרוֹן וְעֻזִּיאֵל:

29 The children of *Amram: Aharon, Moshe*, and *Miriam*. The sons of *Aharon: Nadav, Avihu, Elazar*, and *Itamar*.

כט וּבְנֵי עַמְרָם אַהֲרֹן וּמֹשֶׁה וּמִרְיָם וּבְנֵי אַהֲרֹן נָדָב וַאֲבִיהוּא אֶלְעָזָר וְאִיתָמָר:

30 *Elazar* begot *Pinchas, Pinchas* begot Abishua,

ל אֶלְעָזָר הוֹלִיד אֶת־פִּינְחָס פִּינְחָס הוֹלִיד אֶת־אֲבִישׁוּעַ:

31 Abishua begot Bukki, Bukki begot Uzzi,

לא וַאֲבִישׁוּעַ הוֹלִיד אֶת־בֻּקִּי וּבֻקִּי הוֹלִיד אֶת־עֻזִּי:

32 Uzzi begot Zerahiah, Zerahiah begot Meraioth,

לב וְעֻזִּי הוֹלִיד אֶת־זְרַחְיָה וּזְרַחְיָה הוֹלִיד אֶת־מְרָיוֹת:

33 Meraioth begot Amariah, Amariah begot *Achituv*,

לג מְרָיוֹת הוֹלִיד אֶת־אֲמַרְיָה וַאֲמַרְיָה הוֹלִיד אֶת־אֲחִיטוּב:

34 *Achituv* begot *Tzadok, Tzadok* begot Ahimaaz,

לד וַאֲחִיטוּב הוֹלִיד אֶת־צָדוֹק וְצָדוֹק הוֹלִיד אֶת־אֲחִימָעַץ:

35 Ahimaaz begot *Azarya, Azarya* begot *Yochanan*,

לה וַאֲחִימַעַץ הוֹלִיד אֶת־עֲזַרְיָה וַעֲזַרְיָה הוֹלִיד אֶת־יוֹחָנָן:

36 and *Yochanan* begot *Azarya* (it was he who served as *Kohen* in the House that *Shlomo* built in *Yerushalayim*).

לו וְיוֹחָנָן הוֹלִיד אֶת־עֲזַרְיָה הוּא אֲשֶׁר כִּהֵן בַּבַּיִת אֲשֶׁר־בָּנָה שְׁלֹמֹה בִּירוּשָׁלָםִ:

37 *Azarya* begot Amariah, Amariah begot *Achituv*,

לז וַיּוֹלֶד עֲזַרְיָה אֶת־אֲמַרְיָה וַאֲמַרְיָה הוֹלִיד אֶת־אֲחִיטוּב:

38 *Achituv* begot *Tzadok, Tzadok* begot *Shalum*,

לח וַאֲחִיטוּב הוֹלִיד אֶת־צָדוֹק וְצָדוֹק הוֹלִיד אֶת־שַׁלּוּם:

39 *Shalum* begot *Chilkiyahu, Chilkiyahu* begot *Azarya*,

לט וְשַׁלּוּם הוֹלִיד אֶת־חִלְקִיָּה וְחִלְקִיָּה הוֹלִיד אֶת־עֲזַרְיָה:

40 *Azarya* begot Seraya, Seraya begot *Yehotzadak*;

מ וַעֲזַרְיָה הוֹלִיד אֶת־שְׂרָיָה וּשְׂרָיָה הוֹלִיד אֶת־יְהוֹצָדָק:

41 and *Yehotzadak* went into exile when *Hashem* exiled *Yehuda* and *Yerushalayim* by the hand of Nebuchadnezzar.

מא וִיהוֹצָדָק הָלַךְ בְּהַגְלוֹת יְהֹוָה אֶת־יְהוּדָה וִירוּשָׁלָםִ בְּיַד נְבֻכַדְנֶאצַּר:

6 ¹ The sons of *Levi: Gershom, Kehat,* and *Merari.*

א בְּנֵי לֵוִי גֵּרְשֹׁם קְהָת וּמְרָרִי:

² And these are the names of the sons of *Gershom:* Libni and *Shim'i.*

ב וְאֵלֶּה שְׁמוֹת בְּנֵי־גֵרְשׁוֹם לִבְנִי וְשִׁמְעִי:

³ The sons of *Kehat: Amram,* Izhar, *Chevron,* and Uzziel.

ג וּבְנֵי קְהָת עַמְרָם וְיִצְהָר וְחֶבְרוֹן וְעֻזִּיאֵל:

⁴ The sons of *Merari:* Mahli and Mushi. These were the families of the *Leviim* according to their clans.

ד בְּנֵי מְרָרִי מַחְלִי וּמֻשִׁי וְאֵלֶּה מִשְׁפְּחוֹת הַלֵּוִי לַאֲבוֹתֵיהֶם:

⁵ Of *Gershom:* his son Libni, his son Jahath, his son Zimmah,

ה לְגֵרְשׁוֹם לִבְנִי בְנוֹ יַחַת בְּנוֹ זִמָּה בְנוֹ:

⁶ his son Joah, his son *Ido,* his son *Zerach,* his son Jeatherai.

ו יוֹאָח בְּנוֹ עִדּוֹ בְנוֹ זֶרַח בְּנוֹ יְאָתְרַי בְּנוֹ:

⁷ The sons of *Kehat:* his son *Aminadav,* his son *Korach,* his son Assir,

ז בְּנֵי קְהָת עַמִּינָדָב בְּנוֹ קֹרַח בְּנוֹ אַסִּיר בְּנוֹ:

⁸ his son *Elkana,* his son Ebiasaph, his son Assir,

ח אֶלְקָנָה בְנוֹ וְאֶבְיָסָף בְּנוֹ וְאַסִּיר בְּנוֹ:

⁹ his son Tahath, his son Uriel, his son *Uzziyahu,* and his son *Shaul.*

ט תַּחַת בְּנוֹ אוּרִיאֵל בְּנוֹ עֻזִּיָּה בְנוֹ וְשָׁאוּל בְּנוֹ:

¹⁰ The sons of *Elkana:* Amasai and Ahimoth,

י וּבְנֵי אֶלְקָנָה עֲמָשַׂי וַאֲחִימוֹת:

¹¹ his son *Elkana,* his son Zophai, his son Nahath,

יא אֶלְקָנָה בנו [בְּנֵי] אֶלְקָנָה צוֹפַי בְּנוֹ וְנַחַת בְּנוֹ:

¹² his son *Eliav,* his son Jeroham, his son *Elkana.*

יב אֱלִיאָב בְּנוֹ יְרֹחָם בְּנוֹ אֶלְקָנָה בְנוֹ:

¹³ The sons of *Shmuel:* his first-born Vashni, and *Aviya.*

יג וּבְנֵי שְׁמוּאֵל הַבְּכֹר וַשְׁנִי וַאֲבִיָּה:

¹⁴ The sons of *Merari:* Mahli, his son Libni, his son *Shim'i,* his son Uzzah,

יד בְּנֵי מְרָרִי מַחְלִי לִבְנִי בְנוֹ שִׁמְעִי בְנוֹ עֻזָּה בְנוֹ:

¹⁵ his son Shimea, his son Haggiah, and his son Asaiah.

טו שִׁמְעָא בְנוֹ חַגִּיָּה בְנוֹ עֲשָׂיָה בְנוֹ:

¹⁶ These were appointed by *David* to be in charge of song in the House of *Hashem,* from the time the *Aron* came to rest.

טז וְאֵלֶּה אֲשֶׁר הֶעֱמִיד דָּוִיד עַל־יְדֵי־שִׁיר בֵּית יְהֹוָה מִמְּנוֹחַ הָאָרוֹן:

v'-AY-leh a-SHER he-e-MEED da-VEED al y'-day SHEER
BAYT a-do-NAI mi-m'-NO-akh ha-a-RON

6:16 From the time the *Aron* came to rest King *David* gives the *Leviim* their roles as singers after he brought the *Aron HaBrit* to rest in its eternal home, the holy city of *Yerushalayim.* Just as one does not assign chores in a temporary residence, it was not meaningful to set permanent tasks surrounding the Ark of the Covenant until it had been brought to its proper place. Only in *Yerushalayim,* the resting place of *Hashem*'s presence in the world and the source of His continuous revelation, could the *Aron* be deemed to have reached its permanent home.

The Temple Mount in *Yerushalayim*

Chronicles

17 They served at the *Mishkan* of the Tent of Meeting with song until *Shlomo* built the House of *Hashem* in *Yerushalayim*; and they carried out their duties as prescribed for them.

יז וַיִּהְיוּ מְשָׁרְתִים לִפְנֵי מִשְׁכַּן אֹהֶל־מוֹעֵד בַּשִּׁיר עַד־בְּנוֹת שְׁלֹמֹה אֶת־בֵּית יְהֹוָה בִּירוּשָׁלָ͏ִם וַיַּעַמְדוּ כְמִשְׁפָּטָם עַל־עֲבוֹדָתָם׃

18 Those were the appointed men; and their sons were: the Kohathites: *Hayman* the singer, son of *Yoel* son of *Shmuel*

יח וְאֵלֶּה הָעֹמְדִים וּבְנֵיהֶם מִבְּנֵי הַקְּהָתִי הֵימָן הַמְשׁוֹרֵר בֶּן־יוֹאֵל בֶּן־שְׁמוּאֵל׃

19 son of *Elkana* son of Jeroham son of Eliel son of Toah

יט בֶּן־אֶלְקָנָה בֶּן־יְרֹחָם בֶּן־אֱלִיאֵל בֶּן־תּוֹחַ׃

20 son of Zuph son of *Elkana* son of Mahath son of Amasai

כ בֶּן־[צִיף] צוּף בֶּן־אֶלְקָנָה בֶּן־מַחַת בֶּן־עֲמָשָׂי׃

21 son of *Elkana* son of *Yoel* son of *Azarya* son of *Tzefanya*

כא בֶּן־אֶלְקָנָה בֶּן־יוֹאֵל בֶּן־עֲזַרְיָה בֶּן־צְפַנְיָה׃

22 son of Tahath son of Assir son of Ebiasaph son of *Korach*

כב בֶּן־תַּחַת בֶּן־אַסִּיר בֶּן־אֶבְיָסָף בֶּן־קֹרַח׃

23 son of Izhar son of *Kehat* son of *Levi* son of *Yisrael*;

כג בֶּן־יִצְהָר בֶּן־קְהָת בֶּן־לֵוִי בֶּן־יִשְׂרָאֵל׃

24 and his kinsman *Asaf*, who stood on his right, namely, *Asaf* son of *Berechya* son of Shimea

כד וְאָחִיו אָסָף הָעֹמֵד עַל־יְמִינוֹ אָסָף בֶּן־בֶּרֶכְיָהוּ בֶּן־שִׁמְעָא׃

25 son of *Michael* son of Baaseiah son of Malchijah

כה בֶּן־מִיכָאֵל בֶּן־בַּעֲשֵׂיָה בֶּן־מַלְכִּיָּה׃

26 son of Ethni son of *Zerach* son of Adaiah

כו בֶּן־אֶתְנִי בֶּן־זֶרַח בֶּן־עֲדָיָה׃

27 son of Ethan son of Zimmah son of *Shim'i*

כז בֶּן־אֵיתָן בֶּן־זִמָּה בֶּן־שִׁמְעִי׃

28 son of Jahath son of *Gershom* son of *Levi*.

כח בֶּן־יַחַת בֶּן־גֵּרְשֹׁם בֶּן־לֵוִי׃

29 On the left were their kinsmen: the sons of *Merari*: Ethan son of Kishi son of Abdi son of Malluch

כט וּבְנֵי מְרָרִי אֲחֵיהֶם עַל־הַשְּׂמֹאול אֵיתָן בֶּן־קִישִׁי בֶּן־עַבְדִּי בֶּן־מַלּוּךְ׃

30 son of Hashabiah son of *Amatzya* son of *Chilkiyahu*

ל בֶּן־חֲשַׁבְיָה בֶּן־אֲמַצְיָה בֶּן־חִלְקִיָּה׃

31 son of Amzi son of Bani son of Shemer

לא בֶּן־אַמְצִי בֶּן־בָּנִי בֶּן־שָׁמֶר׃

32 son of Mahli son of Mushi son of *Merari* son of *Levi*;

לב בֶּן־מַחְלִי בֶּן־מוּשִׁי בֶּן־מְרָרִי בֶּן־לֵוִי׃

33 and their kinsmen the *Leviim* were appointed for all the service of the *Mishkan* of the House of *Hashem*.

לג וַאֲחֵיהֶם הַלְוִיִּם נְתוּנִים לְכָל־עֲבוֹדַת מִשְׁכַּן בֵּית הָאֱלֹהִים׃

34 But *Aharon* and his sons made offerings upon the *Mizbayach* of burnt offering and upon the *Mizbayach* of incense, performing all the tasks of the most holy place, to make atonement for *Yisrael*, according to all that *Moshe* the servant of *Hashem* had commanded.

לד וְאַהֲרֹן וּבָנָיו מַקְטִירִים עַל־מִזְבַּח הָעוֹלָה וְעַל־מִזְבַּח הַקְּטֹרֶת לְכֹל מְלֶאכֶת קֹדֶשׁ הַקֳּדָשִׁים וּלְכַפֵּר עַל־יִשְׂרָאֵל כְּכֹל אֲשֶׁר צִוָּה מֹשֶׁה עֶבֶד הָאֱלֹהִים׃

35 These are the sons of *Aharon*: his son *Elazar*, his son *Pinchas*, his son Abishua,

לה וְאֵלֶּה בְּנֵי אַהֲרֹן אֶלְעָזָר בְּנוֹ פִּינְחָס בְּנוֹ אֲבִישׁוּעַ בְּנוֹ׃

36 his son Bukki, his son Uzzi, his son Zerahiah,

לו בֻּקִּי בְנוֹ עֻזִּי בְנוֹ זְרַחְיָה בְנוֹ׃

37 his son Meraioth, his son Amariah, his son *Achituv*,

לז מְרָיוֹת בְּנוֹ אֲמַרְיָה בְנוֹ אֲחִיטוּב בְּנוֹ:

38 his son *Tzadok*, his son Ahimaaz.

לח צָדוֹק בְּנוֹ אֲחִימַעַץ בְּנוֹ:

39 These are their dwelling-places according to their settlements within their borders: to the sons of *Aharon* of the families of Kohathites, for theirs was the [first] lot;

לט וְאֵלֶּה מוֹשְׁבוֹתָם לְטִירוֹתָם בִּגְבוּלָם לִבְנֵי אַהֲרֹן לְמִשְׁפַּחַת הַקְּהָתִי כִּי לָהֶם הָיָה הַגּוֹרָל:

40 they gave them *Chevron* in the land of *Yehuda* and its surrounding pasturelands,

מ וַיִּתְּנוּ לָהֶם אֶת־חֶבְרוֹן בְּאֶרֶץ יְהוּדָה וְאֶת־מִגְרָשֶׁיהָ סְבִיבֹתֶיהָ:

41 but the fields of the city and its villages they gave to *Kalev* son of Jephunneh.

מא וְאֶת־שְׂדֵה הָעִיר וְאֶת־חֲצֵרֶיהָ נָתְנוּ לְכָלֵב בֶּן־יְפֻנֶּה:

42 To the sons of *Aharon* they gave the cities of refuge: *Chevron* and Libnah with its pasturelands, Jattir and Eshtemoa with its pasturelands,

מב וְלִבְנֵי אַהֲרֹן נָתְנוּ אֶת־עָרֵי הַמִּקְלָט אֶת־חֶבְרוֹן וְאֶת־לִבְנָה וְאֶת־מִגְרָשֶׁיהָ וְאֶת־יַתִּר וְאֶת־אֶשְׁתְּמֹעַ וְאֶת־מִגְרָשֶׁיהָ:

43 Hilen with its pasturelands, Debir with its pasturelands,

מג וְאֶת־חִילֵז וְאֶת־מִגְרָשֶׁיהָ אֶת־דְּבִיר וְאֶת־מִגְרָשֶׁיהָ:

44 Ashan with its pasturelands, and *Beit Shemesh* with its pasturelands.

מד וְאֶת־עָשָׁן וְאֶת־מִגְרָשֶׁיהָ וְאֶת־בֵּית שֶׁמֶשׁ וְאֶת־מִגְרָשֶׁיהָ:

45 From the tribe of *Binyamin*, Geba with its pasturelands, Alemeth with its pasturelands, and *Anatot* with its pasturelands. All their cities throughout their families were thirteen.

מה וּמִמַּטֵּה בִנְיָמִן אֶת־גֶּבַע וְאֶת־מִגְרָשֶׁיהָ וְאֶת־עָלֶמֶת וְאֶת־מִגְרָשֶׁיהָ וְאֶת־עֲנָתוֹת וְאֶת־מִגְרָשֶׁיהָ כָּל־עָרֵיהֶם שְׁלֹשׁ־עֶשְׂרֵה עִיר בְּמִשְׁפְּחוֹתֵיהֶם:

46 To the remaining Kohathites were given by lot out of the family of the tribe, out of the half-tribe, the half of *Menashe*, ten cities.

מו וְלִבְנֵי קְהָת הַנּוֹתָרִים מִמִּשְׁפַּחַת הַמַּטֶּה מִמַּחֲצִית מַטֵּה חֲצִי מְנַשֶּׁה בַּגּוֹרָל עָרִים עָשֶׂר:

47 To the Gershomites according to their families were allotted thirteen cities out of the tribes of *Yissachar, Asher, Naftali,* and *Menashe* in Bashan.

מז וְלִבְנֵי גֵרְשׁוֹם לְמִשְׁפְּחוֹתָם מִמַּטֵּה יִשָּׂשכָר וּמִמַּטֵּה אָשֵׁר וּמִמַּטֵּה נַפְתָּלִי וּמִמַּטֵּה מְנַשֶּׁה בַּבָּשָׁן עָרִים שְׁלֹשׁ עֶשְׂרֵה:

48 To the Merarites according to their families were allotted twelve cities out of the tribes of *Reuven, Gad,* and *Zevulun.*

מח לִבְנֵי מְרָרִי לְמִשְׁפְּחוֹתָם מִמַּטֵּה רְאוּבֵן וּמִמַּטֵּה־גָד וּמִמַּטֵּה זְבוּלֻן בַּגּוֹרָל עָרִים שְׁתֵּים עֶשְׂרֵה:

49 So the people of *Yisrael* gave the *Leviim* the cities with their pasturelands.

מט וַיִּתְּנוּ בְנֵי־יִשְׂרָאֵל לַלְוִיִּם אֶת־הֶעָרִים וְאֶת־מִגְרְשֵׁיהֶם:

50 They gave them by lot out of the tribe of the Judahites these cities that are mentioned by name, and out of the tribe of the Simeon, and out of the tribe of the Benjaminites.

נ וַיִּתְּנוּ בַגּוֹרָל מִמַּטֵּה בְנֵי־יְהוּדָה וּמִמַּטֵּה בְנֵי־שִׁמְעוֹן וּמִמַּטֵּה בְּנֵי בִנְיָמִן אֵת הֶעָרִים הָאֵלֶּה אֲשֶׁר־יִקְרְאוּ אֶתְהֶם בְּשֵׁמוֹת:

51 And some of the families of the sons of *Kehat* had cities of their territory out of the tribe of *Efraim.*

נא וּמִמִּשְׁפְּחוֹת בְּנֵי קְהָת וַיְהִי עָרֵי גְבוּלָם מִמַּטֵּה אֶפְרָיִם:

52 They gave them the cities of refuge: *Shechem* with its pasturelands in the hill country of *Efraim*, Gezer with its pasturelands,

נב וַיִּתְּנוּ לָהֶם אֶת־עָרֵי הַמִּקְלָט אֶת־שְׁכֶם וְאֶת־מִגְרָשֶׁיהָ בְּהַר אֶפְרָיִם וְאֶת־גֶּזֶר וְאֶת־מִגְרָשֶׁיהָ:

53 Jokmeam with its pasturelands, Beth-horon with its pasturelands,

נג וְאֶת־יׇקְמְעָם וְאֶת־מִגְרָשֶׁיהָ וְאֶת־בֵּית חוֹרוֹן וְאֶת־מִגְרָשֶׁיהָ:

54 Aijalon with its pasturelands, Gath-rimmon with its pasturelands;

נד וְאֶת־אַיָּלוֹן וְאֶת־מִגְרָשֶׁיהָ וְאֶת־גַּת־רִמּוֹן וְאֶת־מִגְרָשֶׁיהָ:

55 and out of the half-tribe of *Menashe*: Aner with its pasturelands, and Bileam with its pasturelands, for the rest of the families of the Kohathites.

נה וּמִמַּחֲצִית מַטֵּה מְנַשֶּׁה אֶת־עָנֵר וְאֶת־מִגְרָשֶׁיהָ וְאֶת־בִּלְעָם וְאֶת־מִגְרָשֶׁיהָ לְמִשְׁפַּחַת לִבְנֵי־קְהָת הַנּוֹתָרִים:

56 To the Gershomites; out of the half-tribe of *Menashe*: Golan in Bashan with its pasturelands and Ashtaroth with its pasturelands;

נו לִבְנֵי גֵרְשׁוֹם מִמִּשְׁפַּחַת חֲצִי מַטֵּה מְנַשֶּׁה אֶת־גּוֹלָן בַּבָּשָׁן וְאֶת־מִגְרָשֶׁיהָ וְאֶת־עַשְׁתָּרוֹת וְאֶת־מִגְרָשֶׁיהָ:

57 and out of the tribe of *Yissachar*: Kedesh with its pasturelands, Dobrath with its pasturelands,

נז וּמִמַּטֵּה יִשָּׂשכָר אֶת־קֶדֶשׁ וְאֶת־מִגְרָשֶׁיהָ אֶת־דׇּבְרַת וְאֶת־מִגְרָשֶׁיהָ:

58 Ramoth with its pasturelands, and Anem with its pasturelands;

נח וְאֶת־רָאמוֹת וְאֶת־מִגְרָשֶׁיהָ וְאֶת־עָנֵם וְאֶת־מִגְרָשֶׁיהָ:

59 out of the tribe of *Asher*: Mashal with its pasturelands, *Avdon* with its pasturelands,

נט וּמִמַּטֵּה אָשֵׁר אֶת־מָשָׁל וְאֶת־מִגְרָשֶׁיהָ וְאֶת־עַבְדּוֹן וְאֶת־מִגְרָשֶׁיהָ:

60 Hukok with its pasturelands, and Rehob with its pasturelands;

ס וְאֶת־חוּקֹק וְאֶת־מִגְרָשֶׁיהָ וְאֶת־רְחֹב וְאֶת־מִגְרָשֶׁיהָ:

61 and out of the tribe of *Naftali*: Kedesh in Galilee with its pasturelands; Hammon with its pasturelands, and Kiriathaim with its pasturelands.

סא וּמִמַּטֵּה נַפְתָּלִי אֶת־קֶדֶשׁ בַּגָּלִיל וְאֶת־מִגְרָשֶׁיהָ וְאֶת־חַמּוֹן וְאֶת־מִגְרָשֶׁיהָ וְאֶת־קִרְיָתַיִם וְאֶת־מִגְרָשֶׁיהָ:

62 To the rest of the Merarites, out of the tribe of *Zevulun*: Rimmono with its pasturelands, *Tavor* with its pasturelands;

סב לִבְנֵי מְרָרִי הַנּוֹתָרִים מִמַּטֵּה זְבוּלֻן אֶת־רִמּוֹנוֹ וְאֶת־מִגְרָשֶׁיהָ אֶת־תָּבוֹר וְאֶת־מִגְרָשֶׁיהָ:

63 and beyond the *Yarden* at *Yericho*, on the east side of the *Yarden*, out of the tribe of *Reuven*: Bezer in the wilderness with its pasturelands, Jahaz with its pasturelands,

סג וּמֵעֵבֶר לְיַרְדֵּן יְרֵחוֹ לְמִזְרַח הַיַּרְדֵּן מִמַּטֵּה רְאוּבֵן אֶת־בֶּצֶר בַּמִּדְבָּר וְאֶת־מִגְרָשֶׁיהָ וְאֶת־יַהְצָה וְאֶת־מִגְרָשֶׁיהָ:

64 Kedemoth with its pasturelands, and Mephaath with its pasture lands;

סד וְאֶת־קְדֵמוֹת וְאֶת־מִגְרָשֶׁיהָ וְאֶת־מֵיפַעַת וְאֶת־מִגְרָשֶׁיהָ:

65 and out of the tribe of *Gad*: Ramoth in *Gilad* with its pasturelands, Mahanaim with its pasturelands,

סה וּמִמַּטֵּה גָד אֶת־רָאמוֹת בַּגִּלְעָד וְאֶת־מִגְרָשֶׁיהָ וְאֶת־מַחֲנַיִם וְאֶת־מִגְרָשֶׁיהָ:

66 Heshbon with its pasturelands, and Jazer with its pasturelands.

סו וְאֶת־חֶשְׁבּוֹן וְאֶת־מִגְרָשֶׁיהָ וְאֶת־יַעְזֵיר וְאֶת־מִגְרָשֶׁיהָ:

7 1 The sons of *Yissachar*: *Tola*, Puah, Yashuv, and Shimron – four.

ז א וְלִבְנֵי יִשָּׂשכָר תּוֹלָע וּפוּאָה יָשִׁיב [יָשׁוּב] וְשִׁמְרוֹן אַרְבָּעָה:

2 The sons of *Tola*: Uzzi, Rephaiah, Jeriel, Jahmai, Ibsam, Shemuel, chiefs of their clans, men of substance according to their lines; their number in the days of *David* was 22,600.

ב וּבְנֵי תוֹלָע עֻזִּי וּרְפָיָה וִירִיאֵל וְיַחְמַי וְיִבְשָׂם וּשְׁמוּאֵל רָאשִׁים לְבֵית־אֲבוֹתָם לְתוֹלָע גִּבּוֹרֵי חַיִל לְתֹלְדוֹתָם מִסְפָּרָם בִּימֵי דָוִיד עֶשְׂרִים־וּשְׁנַיִם אֶלֶף וְשֵׁשׁ מֵאוֹת:

3 The sons of Uzzi: Izrahiah. And the sons of Izrahiah: *Michael, Ovadya, Yoel,* and Isshiah – five. All of them were chiefs.

ג וּבְנֵי עֻזִּי יִזְרַחְיָה וּבְנֵי יִזְרַחְיָה מִיכָאֵל וְעֹבַדְיָה וְיוֹאֵל יִשִּׁיָּה חֲמִשָּׁה רָאשִׁים כֻּלָּם:

4 And together with them, by their lines, according to their clans, were units of the fighting force, 36,000, for they had many wives and sons.

ד וַעֲלֵיהֶם לְתֹלְדוֹתָם לְבֵית אֲבוֹתָם גְּדוּדֵי צְבָא מִלְחָמָה שְׁלֹשִׁים וְשִׁשָּׁה אָלֶף כִּי־הִרְבּוּ נָשִׁים וּבָנִים:

5 Their kinsmen belonging to all the families of *Yissachar* were in all 87,000 men of substance; they were all registered by genealogy.

ה וַאֲחֵיהֶם לְכֹל מִשְׁפְּחוֹת יִשָּׂשכָר גִּבּוֹרֵי חֲיָלִים שְׁמוֹנִים וְשִׁבְעָה אֶלֶף הִתְיַחְשָׂם לַכֹּל:

6 [The sons of] *Binyamin*: Bela, Becher, and Jediael – three.

ו בִּנְיָמִן בֶּלַע וָבֶכֶר וִידִיעֲאֵל שְׁלֹשָׁה:

7 The sons of Bela: Ezbon, Uzzi, Uzziel, Jerimoth, and Iri – five, chiefs of clans, men of substance, registered by genealogy – 22,034.

ז וּבְנֵי בֶלַע אֶצְבּוֹן וְעֻזִּי וְעֻזִּיאֵל וִירִימוֹת וְעִירִי חֲמִשָּׁה רָאשֵׁי בֵּית אָבוֹת גִּבּוֹרֵי חֲיָלִים וְהִתְיַחְשָׂם עֶשְׂרִים וּשְׁנַיִם אֶלֶף וּשְׁלֹשִׁים וְאַרְבָּעָה:

8 The sons of Becher: Zemirah, *Yoash, Eliezer,* Elioenai, *Omri,* Jeremoth, *Aviya, Anatot,* and Alemeth. All these were the sons of Becher;

ח וּבְנֵי בֶכֶר זְמִירָה וְיוֹעָשׁ וֶאֱלִיעֶזֶר וְאֶלְיוֹעֵינַי וְעָמְרִי וִירֵמוֹת וַאֲבִיָּה וַעֲנָתוֹת וָעָלָמֶת כָּל־אֵלֶּה בְּנֵי־בָכֶר:

9 and they were registered by genealogy according to their lines, as chiefs of their clans, men of substance – 20,200.

ט וְהִתְיַחְשָׂם לְתֹלְדוֹתָם רָאשֵׁי בֵּית אֲבוֹתָם גִּבּוֹרֵי חָיִל עֶשְׂרִים אֶלֶף וּמָאתָיִם:

10 The sons of Jediael: Bilhan. And the sons of Bilhan: Jeush, *Binyamin, Ehud,* Chenaanah, Zethan, Tarshish, and Ahishahar.

י וּבְנֵי יְדִיעֲאֵל בִּלְהָן וּבְנֵי בִלְהָן יעיש [יְעוּשׁ] וּבִנְיָמִן וְאֵהוּד וּכְנַעֲנָה וְזֵיתָן וְתַרְשִׁישׁ וַאֲחִישָׁחַר:

11 All these were the sons of Jediael, chiefs of the clans, men of substance – 17,200, who made up the fighting force.

יא כָּל־אֵלֶּה בְּנֵי יְדִיעֲאֵל לְרָאשֵׁי הָאָבוֹת גִּבּוֹרֵי חֲיָלִים שִׁבְעָה־עָשָׂר אֶלֶף וּמָאתַיִם יֹצְאֵי צָבָא לַמִּלְחָמָה:

12 And Shuppim and Huppim were the sons of Ir; Hushim the sons of Aher.

יב וְשֻׁפִּם וְחֻפִּם בְּנֵי עִיר חֻשִׁם בְּנֵי אַחֵר:

13 The sons of *Naftali*: Jahziel, Guni, Jezer, and *Shalum*, the descendants of *Bilha*.

יג בְּנֵי נַפְתָּלִי יַחֲצִיאֵל וְגוּנִי וְיֵצֶר וְשַׁלּוּם בְּנֵי בִלְהָה:

14 The sons of *Menashe*: Asriel, whom his Aramean concubine bore; she bore Machir the father of *Gilad*.

יד בְּנֵי מְנַשֶּׁה אַשְׂרִיאֵל אֲשֶׁר יָלָדָה פִּילַגְשׁוֹ הָאֲרַמִּיָּה יָלְדָה אֶת־מָכִיר אֲבִי גִלְעָד:

15 And Machir took wives for Huppim and for Shuppim. The name of his sister was Maacah. And the name of the second was *Tzelofchad*; and *Tzelofchad* had daughters.

טו וּמָכִיר לָקַח אִשָּׁה לְחֻפִּים וּלְשֻׁפִּים וְשֵׁם אֲחֹתוֹ מַעֲכָה וְשֵׁם הַשֵּׁנִי צְלָפְחָד וַתִּהְיֶינָה לִצְלָפְחָד בָּנוֹת:

16 And Maacah the wife of Machir bore a son, and she named him Peresh; and the name of his brother was Sheresh; and his sons were Ulam and Rekem.

טז וַתֵּלֶד מַעֲכָה אֵשֶׁת־מָכִיר בֵּן וַתִּקְרָא שְׁמוֹ פֶּרֶשׁ וְשֵׁם אָחִיו שָׁרֶשׁ וּבָנָיו אוּלָם וָרָקֶם:

17 The sons of Ulam: Bedan. These were the sons of *Gilad* son of Machir son of *Menashe*.

יז וּבְנֵי אוּלָם בְּדָן אֵלֶּה בְּנֵי גִלְעָד בֶּן־מָכִיר בֶּן־מְנַשֶּׁה:

18 And his sister Hammolecheth bore Ishhod, Abiezer, and *Machla*.

יח וַאֲחֹתוֹ הַמֹּלֶכֶת יָלְדָה אֶת־אִישְׁהוֹד וְאֶת־אֲבִיעֶזֶר וְאֶת־מַחְלָה:

19 The sons of Shemida were Ahian, *Shechem*, Likhi, and Aniam.

יט וַיִּהְיוּ בְּנֵי שְׁמִידָע אַחְיָן וָשֶׁכֶם וְלִקְחִי וַאֲנִיעָם:

20 The sons of *Efraim*: Shuthelah, his son Bered, his son Tahath, his son Eleadah, his son Tahath,

כ וּבְנֵי אֶפְרַיִם שׁוּתָלַח וּבֶרֶד בְּנוֹ וְתַחַת בְּנוֹ וְאֶלְעָדָה בְנוֹ וְתַחַת בְּנוֹ:

21 his son Zabad, his son Shuthelah, also Ezer and Elead. The men of Gath, born in the land, killed them because they had gone down to take their cattle.

כא וְזָבָד בְּנוֹ וְשׁוּתֶלַח בְּנוֹ וְעֵזֶר וְאֶלְעָד וַהֲרָגוּם אַנְשֵׁי־גַת הַנּוֹלָדִים בָּאָרֶץ כִּי יָרְדוּ לָקַחַת אֶת־מִקְנֵיהֶם:

22 And *Efraim* their father mourned many days, and his brothers came to comfort him.

כב וַיִּתְאַבֵּל אֶפְרַיִם אֲבִיהֶם יָמִים רַבִּים וַיָּבֹאוּ אֶחָיו לְנַחֲמוֹ:

23 He cohabited with his wife, who conceived and bore a son; and she named him Beriah, because it occurred when there was misfortune in his house.

כג וַיָּבֹא אֶל־אִשְׁתּוֹ וַתַּהַר וַתֵּלֶד בֵּן וַיִּקְרָא אֶת־שְׁמוֹ בְּרִיעָה כִּי בְרָעָה הָיְתָה בְּבֵיתוֹ:

24 His daughter was Sheerah, who built both Lower and Upper Beth-horon, and Uzzen-sheerah.

כד וּבִתּוֹ שֶׁאֱרָה וַתִּבֶן אֶת־בֵּית־חוֹרוֹן הַתַּחְתּוֹן וְאֶת־הָעֶלְיוֹן וְאֵת אֻזֵּן שֶׁאֱרָה:

25 His son Rephah, his son Resheph, his son Telah, his son Tahan,

כה וְרֶפַח בְּנוֹ וְרֶשֶׁף וְתֶלַח בְּנוֹ וְתַחַן בְּנוֹ:

26 his son Ladan, his son Ammihud, his son Elishama,

כו לַעְדָּן בְּנוֹ עַמִּיהוּד בְּנוֹ אֱלִישָׁמָע בְּנוֹ:

27 his son Non, his son *Yehoshua*.

כז נוֹן בְּנוֹ יְהוֹשֻׁעַ בְּנוֹ:

28 Their possessions and settlements were *Beit El* and its dependencies, and on the east Naaran, and on the west Gezer and its dependencies, *Shechem* and its dependencies, and Aiah and its dependencies;

כח וַאֲחֻזָּתָם וּמֹשְׁבוֹתָם בֵּית־אֵל וּבְנֹתֶיהָ וְלַמִּזְרָח נַעֲרָן וְלַמַּעֲרָב גֶּזֶר וּבְנֹתֶיהָ וּשְׁכֶם וּבְנֹתֶיהָ עַד־עַיָּה וּבְנֹתֶיהָ:

29 also along the borders of the Manassites, *Beit-Shean* and its dependencies, Taanach and its dependencies, Megiddo and its dependencies, Dor and its dependencies. In these dwelt the sons of *Yosef* son of *Yisrael*.

כט וְעַל־יְדֵי בְנֵי־מְנַשֶּׁה בֵּית־שְׁאָן וּבְנֹתֶיהָ תַּעְנַךְ וּבְנֹתֶיהָ מְגִדּוֹ וּבְנוֹתֶיהָ דּוֹר וּבְנוֹתֶיהָ בְּאֵלֶּה יָשְׁבוּ בְּנֵי יוֹסֵף בֶּן־יִשְׂרָאֵל:

30 The sons of *Asher*: Imnah, Ishvah, Ishvi, Beriah, and their sister Serah.

ל בְּנֵי אָשֵׁר יִמְנָה וְיִשְׁוָה וְיִשְׁוִי וּבְרִיעָה וְשֶׂרַח אֲחוֹתָם:

³¹ The sons of Beriah: *Chever* and Malchiel, who was the father of Birzaith.

לא וּבְנֵי בְרִיעָה חֶבֶר וּמַלְכִּיאֵל הוּא אֲבִי ברזות [בִרְזָיִת:]

uv-NAY v'-ree-AH KHE-ver u-mal-kee-AYL HU a-VEE vir-ZA-yit

³² *Chever* begot Japhlet, Shomer, Hotham, and their sister, Shua.

לב וְחֶבֶר הוֹלִיד אֶת־יַפְלֵט וְאֶת־שׁוֹמֵר וְאֶת־חוֹתָם וְאֵת שׁוּעָא אֲחוֹתָם:

³³ The sons of Japhlet: Pasach, Bimhal, and Ashvath. These were the sons of Japhlet.

לג וּבְנֵי יַפְלֵט פָּסַךְ וּבִמְהָל וְעַשְׁוָת אֵלֶּה בְּנֵי יַפְלֵט:

³⁴ The sons of Shemer: Ahi, Rohgah, Hubbah, and Aram.

לד וּבְנֵי שֶׁמֶר אֲחִי וְרוֹהֲגָה [וְרָהְגָּה] יחבה [וְחֻבָּה] וַאֲרָם:

³⁵ The sons of Helem his brother: Zophah, Imna, Shelesh, and Amal.

לה וּבֶן־הֵלֶם אָחִיו צוֹפַח וְיִמְנָע וְשֵׁלֶשׁ וְעָמָל:

³⁶ The sons of Zophah: Suah, Harnepher, Shual, Beri, Imrah,

לו בְּנֵי צוֹפָח סוּחַ וְחַרְנֶפֶר וְשׁוּעָל וּבֵרִי וְיִמְרָה:

³⁷ Bezer, Hod, Shamma, Shilshah, Ithran, and Beera.

לז בֶּצֶר וָהוֹד וְשַׁמָּא וְשִׁלְשָׁה וְיִתְרָן וּבְאֵרָא:

³⁸ The sons of Jether: Jephunneh, Pispa, and Ara.

לח וּבְנֵי יֶתֶר יְפֻנֶּה וּפִסְפָּה וַאֲרָא:

³⁹ The sons of Ulla: Arah, Hanniel, and Rizia.

לט וּבְנֵי עֻלָּא אָרַח וְחַנִּיאֵל וְרִצְיָא:

⁴⁰ All of these men of *Asher*, chiefs of the clans, select men, men of substance, heads of the chieftains. And they were registered by genealogy according to fighting force; the number of the men was 26,000 men.

מ כָּל־אֵלֶּה בְנֵי־אָשֵׁר רָאשֵׁי בֵית־הָאָבוֹת בְּרוּרִים גִּבּוֹרֵי חֲיָלִים רָאשֵׁי הַנְּשִׂיאִים וְהִתְיַחְשָׂם בַּצָּבָא בַּמִּלְחָמָה מִסְפָּרָם אֲנָשִׁים עֶשְׂרִים וְשִׁשָּׁה אָלֶף:

8 ¹ *Binyamin* begot Bela his first-born, Ashbel the second, Aharah the third,

ח א וּבִנְיָמִן הוֹלִיד אֶת־בֶּלַע בְּכֹרוֹ אַשְׁבֵּל הַשֵּׁנִי וְאַחְרַח הַשְּׁלִישִׁי:

² Nohah the fourth, and Rapha the fifth.

ב נוֹחָה הָרְבִיעִי וְרָפָא הַחֲמִישִׁי:

³ And Bela had sons: Addar, Gera, *Avihud*,

ג וַיִּהְיוּ בָנִים לְבָלַע אַדָּר וְגֵרָא וַאֲבִיהוּד:

⁴ Abishua, Naaman, Ahoah,

ד וַאֲבִישׁוּעַ וְנַעֲמָן וַאֲחוֹחַ:

⁵ Gera, Shephuphan, and Huram.

ה וְגֵרָא וּשְׁפוּפָן וְחוּרָם:

7:31 Birzaith In the list of the children of *Asher*, the name Birzaith (בִרְזָיִת), which literally means 'of the oil,' appears. The Sages debate the significance of this name. Some say it means that this man's daughters were so beautiful that they married the High Priests, or the kings, who were anointed with the sacred oil made by *Moshe*. Other interpretations suggest that this is not the name of a person, rather the name of a place found in the tribe of *Asher*. Either way, the connection between the tribe of *Asher* and the sacred oil is celebrated in this verse. Indeed, *Asher* is blessed by both *Yaakov* and *Moshe* with an abundance of oil in his territory (see Genesis 49:20 and Deuteronomy 33:24). The Sages state (*Menachot* 85b) that olive oil would flow like a fountain in the lands of *Asher*, and its quality was so superior that people in search of high quality oil were sent to the tribe of *Asher*. Furthermore, they state that *Asher*'s land was so fertile that in times of shortage, such as during the Sabbatical year when it is prohibited to work the land, *Asher* would provide olive oil for the entire Nation of Israel.

Olives from the Upper Galilee, part of the land of the tribe of *Asher*

⁶ These were the sons of *Ehud* – they were chiefs of clans of the inhabitants of Geba, and they were exiled to Manahath:

ו וְאֵלֶּה בְּנֵי אֵחוּד אֵלֶּה הֵם רָאשֵׁי אָבוֹת לְיוֹשְׁבֵי גֶבַע וַיַּגְלוּם אֶל־מָנָחַת:

⁷ Naaman, *Achiya*, and Gera – he exiled them and begot Uzza and Ahihud.

ז וְנַעֲמָן וַאֲחִיָּה וְגֵרָא הוּא הֶגְלָם וְהוֹלִיד אֶת־עֻזָּא וְאֶת־אֲחִיחֻד:

⁸ And Shaharaim had sons in the country of Moab after he had sent away Hushim and Baara his wives.

ח וְשַׁחֲרַיִם הוֹלִיד בִּשְׂדֵה מוֹאָב מִן־שִׁלְחוֹ אֹתָם חוּשִׁים וְאֶת־בַּעֲרָא נָשָׁיו:

⁹ He had sons by Hodesh his wife: Jobab, Zibia, Mesha, Malcam,

ט וַיּוֹלֶד מִן־חֹדֶשׁ אִשְׁתּוֹ אֶת־יוֹבָב וְאֶת־צִבְיָא וְאֶת־מֵישָׁא וְאֶת־מַלְכָּם:

¹⁰ Jeuz, Sachiah, and Mirmah. These were his sons, chiefs of clans.

י וְאֶת־יְעוּץ וְאֶת־שָׂכְיָה וְאֶת־מִרְמָה אֵלֶּה בָנָיו רָאשֵׁי אָבוֹת:

¹¹ He also begot by Hushim: Abitub and Elpaal.

יא וּמֵחֻשִׁים הוֹלִיד אֶת־אֲבִיטוּב וְאֶת־אֶלְפָּעַל:

¹² The sons of Elpaal: *Ever*, Misham, and Shemed, who built Ono and Lod with its dependencies,

יב וּבְנֵי אֶלְפַּעַל עֵבֶר וּמִשְׁעָם וָשָׁמֶד הוּא בָּנָה אֶת־אוֹנוֹ וְאֶת־לֹד וּבְנֹתֶיהָ:

¹³ and Beriah and Shema – they were chiefs of clans of the inhabitants of Aijalon, who put to flight the inhabitants of Gath;

יג וּבְרִעָה וָשֶׁמַע הֵמָּה רָאשֵׁי הָאָבוֹת לְיוֹשְׁבֵי אַיָּלוֹן הֵמָּה הִבְרִיחוּ אֶת־יוֹשְׁבֵי גַת:

¹⁴ and Ahio, Shashak, and Jeremoth.

יד וְאַחְיוֹ שָׁשָׁק וִירֵמוֹת:

¹⁵ Zebadiah, Arad, Eder,

טו וּזְבַדְיָה וַעֲרָד וָעָדֶר:

¹⁶ *Michael*, Ishpah, and Joha were sons of Beriah.

טז וּמִיכָאֵל וְיִשְׁפָּה וְיוֹחָא בְּנֵי בְרִיעָה:

¹⁷ Zebadiah, Meshullam, Hizki, *Chever*,

יז וּזְבַדְיָה וּמְשֻׁלָּם וְחִזְקִי וָחָבֶר:

¹⁸ Ishmerai, Izliah, and Jobab were the sons of Elpaal.

יח וְיִשְׁמְרַי וְיִזְלִיאָה וְיוֹבָב בְּנֵי אֶלְפָּעַל:

¹⁹ Jakim, Zichri, Zabdi,

יט וְיָקִים וְזִכְרִי וְזַבְדִּי:

²⁰ Elienai, Zillethai, Eliel,

כ וֶאֱלִיעֵנַי וְצִלְּתַי וֶאֱלִיאֵל:

²¹ Adaiah, Beraiah, and Shimrath were the sons of *Shim'i*.

כא וַעֲדָיָה וּבְרָאיָה וְשִׁמְרָת בְּנֵי שִׁמְעִי:

²² Ishpan, *Ever*, Eliel,

כב וְיִשְׁפָּן וָעֵבֶר וֶאֱלִיאֵל:

²³ *Avdon*, Zichri, Hanan,

כג וְעַבְדּוֹן וְזִכְרִי וְחָנָן:

²⁴ *Chananya*, Elam, Anthothiah,

כד וַחֲנַנְיָה וְעֵילָם וְעַנְתֹתִיָּה:

²⁵ Iphdeiah, and Penuel were the sons of Shashak.

כה וְיִפְדְיָה וּפְנִיאֵל [וּפְנוּאֵל] בְּנֵי שָׁשָׁק:

²⁶ Shamsherai, Shehariah, *Atalya*,

כו וְשַׁמְשְׁרַי וּשְׁחַרְיָה וַעֲתַלְיָה:

²⁷ Jaareshiah, *Eliyahu*, and Zichri were the sons of Jeroham.

כז וְיַעֲרֶשְׁיָה וְאֵלִיָּה וְזִכְרִי בְּנֵי יְרֹחָם:

28 These were the chiefs of the clans, according to their lines. These chiefs dwelt in *Yerushalayim.*

כח אֵלֶּה רָאשֵׁי אָבוֹת לְתֹלְדוֹתָם רָאשִׁים אֵלֶּה יָשְׁבוּ בִירוּשָׁלָֽם׃

AY-leh ra-SHAY a-VOT l'-to-l'-do-TAM ra-SHEEM
AY-leh ya-sh'-VU vee-ru-sha-LA-im

29 The father of *Givon* dwelt in *Givon*, and the name of his wife was Maacah.

כט וּבְגִבְעוֹן יָשְׁבוּ אֲבִי גִבְעוֹן וְשֵׁם אִשְׁתּוֹ מַעֲכָֽה׃

30 His first-born son: *Avdon*; then Zur, *Keesh*, Baal, Nadav,

ל וּבְנוֹ הַבְּכוֹר עַבְדּוֹן וְצוּר וְקִישׁ וּבַעַל וְנָדָֽב׃

31 Gedor, Ahio, Zecher.

לא וּגְדוֹר וְאַחְיוֹ וָזָֽכֶר׃

32 Mikloth begot Shimeah. And they dwelt in *Yerushalayim* opposite their kinsmen, with their kinsmen.

לב וּמִקְלוֹת הוֹלִיד אֶת־שִׁמְאָה וְאַף־הֵמָּה נֶגֶד אֲחֵיהֶם יָשְׁבוּ בִירוּשָׁלַ͏ִם עִם־אֲחֵיהֶֽם׃

33 Ner begot *Keesh*, *Keesh* begot *Shaul*, *Shaul* begot *Yehonatan*, Malchi-shua, *Avinadav*, and Eshbaal;

לג וְנֵר הוֹלִיד אֶת־קִישׁ וְקִישׁ הוֹלִיד אֶת־שָׁאוּל וְשָׁאוּל הוֹלִיד אֶת־יְהוֹנָתָן וְאֶת־מַלְכִּי־שׁוּעַ וְאֶת־אֲבִינָדָב וְאֶת־אֶשְׁבָּֽעַל׃

34 and the son of *Yehonatan* was Merib-baal; and Merib-baal begot *Micha.*

לד וּבֶן־יְהוֹנָתָן מְרִיב בָּעַל וּמְרִיב בַּעַל הוֹלִיד אֶת־מִיכָֽה׃

35 The sons of *Micha*: Pithon, Melech, Taarea, and *Achaz.*

לה וּבְנֵי מִיכָה פִּיתוֹן וָמֶלֶךְ וְתַאְרֵעַ וְאָחָֽז׃

36 *Achaz* begot Jehoaddah; and Jehoaddah begot Alemeth, Azmaveth, and *Zimri*; *Zimri* begot Moza.

לו וְאָחָז הוֹלִיד אֶת־יְהוֹעַדָּה וִיהוֹעַדָּה הוֹלִיד אֶת־עָלֶמֶת וְאֶת־עַזְמָוֶת וְאֶת־זִמְרִי וְזִמְרִי הוֹלִיד אֶת־מוֹצָֽא׃

37 Moza begot Binea; his son Raphah; his son Eleasah, his son Azel.

לז וּמוֹצָא הוֹלִיד אֶת־בִּנְעָא רָפָה בְנוֹ אֶלְעָשָׂה בְנוֹ אָצֵל בְּנֽוֹ׃

38 Azel had six sons, and these are their names: Azrikam, Bocheru, Ishmael, Sheariah, *Ovadya*, and Hanan. All these were the sons of Azel.

לח וּלְאָצֵל שִׁשָּׁה בָנִים וְאֵלֶּה שְׁמוֹתָם עַזְרִיקָם בֹּכְרוּ וְיִשְׁמָעֵאל וּשְׁעַרְיָה וְעֹבַדְיָה וְחָנָן כָּל־אֵלֶּה בְּנֵי אָצַֽל׃

39 The sons of Eshek his brother: Ulam his first-born, Jeush the second, and Eliphelet the third.

לט וּבְנֵי עֵשֶׁק אָחִיו אוּלָם בְּכֹרוֹ יְעוּשׁ הַשֵּׁנִי וֶאֱלִיפֶלֶט הַשְּׁלִשִֽׁי׃

40 The descendants of Ulam – men of substance, who drew the bow, had many children and grandchildren – one hundred and fifty; all these were Benjaminites.

מ וַיִּהְיוּ בְנֵי־אוּלָם אֲנָשִׁים גִּבּוֹרֵי־חַיִל דֹּרְכֵי קֶשֶׁת וּמַרְבִּים בָּנִים וּבְנֵי בָנִים מֵאָה וַחֲמִשִּׁים כָּל־אֵלֶּה מִבְּנֵי בִנְיָמִֽן׃

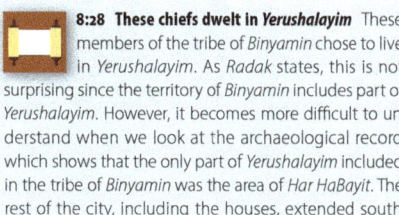

8:28 These chiefs dwelt in *Yerushalayim* These members of the tribe of *Binyamin* chose to live in *Yerushalayim*. As *Radak* states, this is not surprising since the territory of *Binyamin* includes part of *Yerushalayim*. However, it becomes more difficult to understand when we look at the archaeological record, which shows that the only part of *Yerushalayim* included in the tribe of *Binyamin* was the area of *Har HaBayit*. The rest of the city, including the houses, extended southwards into the territory of *Yehuda*. Nevertheless, these Benjaminites chose to live outside their tribal lands since *Yerushalayim* was so beloved to them.

Yerushalayim

9 **¹** All *Yisrael* was registered by genealogies; and these are in the book of the kings of *Yisrael*. And *Yehuda* was taken into exile in Babylon because of their trespass.

ט **א** וְכָל־יִשְׂרָאֵל הִתְיַחְשׂוּ וְהִנָּם כְּתוּבִים עַל־סֵפֶר מַלְכֵי יִשְׂרָאֵל וִיהוּדָה הָגְלוּ לְבָבֶל בְּמַעֲלָם:

² The first to settle in their towns, on their property, were Israelites, *Kohanim*, *Leviim*, and temple servants,

ב וְהַיּוֹשְׁבִים הָרִאשֹׁנִים אֲשֶׁר בַּאֲחֻזָּתָם בְּעָרֵיהֶם יִשְׂרָאֵל הַכֹּהֲנִים הַלְוִיִּם וְהַנְּתִינִים:

³ while some of the Judahites and some of the Benjaminites and some of the Ephraimites and Manassehites settled in *Yerushalayim*;

ג וּבִירוּשָׁלַםִ יָשְׁבוּ מִן־בְּנֵי יְהוּדָה וּמִן־בְּנֵי בִנְיָמִן וּמִן־בְּנֵי אֶפְרַיִם וּמְנַשֶּׁה:

u-vee-ru-sha-LA-im ya-sh'-VU min b'-NAY y'-hu-DAH u-min b'-NAY vin-ya-MIN u-min b'-NAY ef-RA-yim um-na-SHEH

⁴ Uthai son of Ammihud son of *Omri* son of Imri son of Bani, from the sons of *Peretz* son of *Yehuda*;

ד עוּתַי בֶּן־עַמִּיהוּד בֶּן־עָמְרִי בֶּן־אִמְרִי בֶּן־ [בָּנִי] [מִן־] בְּנֵי־פֶרֶץ בֶּן־יְהוּדָה:

⁵ and of the Shilonites: Asaiah the first-born and his sons.

ה וּמִן־הַשִּׁילוֹנִי עֲשָׂיָה הַבְּכוֹר וּבָנָיו:

⁶ Of the sons of *Zerach*: Jeuel and their kinsmen – 690.

ו וּמִן־בְּנֵי־זֶרַח יְעוּאֵל וַאֲחֵיהֶם שֵׁשׁ־מֵאוֹת וְתִשְׁעִים:

⁷ Of the Benjaminites: Sallu son of Meshullam son of Hodaviah son of Hassenuah,

ז וּמִן־בְּנֵי בִּנְיָמִן סַלּוּא בֶּן־מְשֻׁלָּם בֶּן־הוֹדַוְיָה בֶּן־הַסְּנֻאָה:

⁸ Ibneiah son of Jeroham, Elah son of Uzzi son of Michri, and Meshullam son of Shephatiah son of Reuel son of Ibneiah;

ח וְיִבְנְיָה בֶּן־יְרֹחָם וְאֵלָה בֶן־עֻזִּי בֶּן־מִכְרִי וּמְשֻׁלָּם בֶּן־שְׁפַטְיָה בֶּן־רְעוּאֵל בֶּן־יִבְנִיָּה:

⁹ and their kinsmen, according to their lines – 956. All these were chiefs of their ancestral clans.

ט וַאֲחֵיהֶם לְתֹלְדוֹתָם תְּשַׁע מֵאוֹת וַחֲמִשִּׁים וְשִׁשָּׁה כָּל־אֵלֶּה אֲנָשִׁים רָאשֵׁי אָבוֹת לְבֵית אֲבֹתֵיהֶם:

¹⁰ Of the *Kohanim*: Jedaiah, Jehoiarib, Jachin,

י וּמִן־הַכֹּהֲנִים יְדַעְיָה וִיהוֹיָרִיב וְיָכִין:

¹¹ and *Azarya* son of *Chilkiyahu* son of Meshullam son of *Tzadok* son of Meraioth son of *Achituv*, chief officer of the House of *Hashem*;

יא וַעֲזַרְיָה בֶן־חִלְקִיָּה בֶּן־מְשֻׁלָּם בֶּן־צָדוֹק בֶּן־מְרָיוֹת בֶּן־אֲחִיטוּב נְגִיד בֵּית הָאֱלֹהִים:

Chronicles

9:3 Manassehites settled in *Yerushalayim* In *Sefer Nechemya* (chapter 11) we are told that the exiles who had returned from Babylonia drew lots to see which individuals would settle in *Yerushalayim*. Even though *Yerushalayim* did not belong to the territories of *Ephraim* and *Menashe*, it was important to have more people inhabiting the Holy City so that it would be secure and defensible. By bringing additional people to *Yerushalayim*, they also sought to fulfill the prophecy: "There shall yet be old men and women in the squares of *Yerushalayim*, each with staff in hand because of their great age. And the squares of the city shall be crowded with boys and girls playing in the squares" (Zechariah 8:4–5). Perhaps the fact that these members of the tribe of *Menashe* inhabited the city together with people from other tribes reflects the opinion in the Talmud (*Yoma* 12a) that the city of *Yerushalayim* was not divided among the tribes. Rather, everyone has a claim to the holiest city on earth.

Former President Reuven Rivlin plays soccer with children in *Yerushalayim*

24

12 and Adaiah son of Jeroham son of Pashhur son of Malchijah, and Maasai son of Adiel son of Jahzerah son of Meshullam son of Meshillemith son of Immer,

יב וַעֲדָיָה בֶּן־יְרֹחָם בֶּן־פַּשְׁחוּר בֶּן־מַלְכִּיָּה וּמַעְשַׂי בֶּן־עֲדִיאֵל בֶּן־יַחְזֵרָה בֶּן־מְשֻׁלָּם בֶּן־מְשִׁלֵּמִית בֶּן־אִמֵּר:

13 together with their kinsmen, chiefs of their clans – 1,760, men of substance for the work of the service of the House of *Hashem*.

יג וַאֲחֵיהֶם רָאשִׁים לְבֵית אֲבוֹתָם אֶלֶף וּשְׁבַע מֵאוֹת וְשִׁשִּׁים גִּבּוֹרֵי חֵיל מְלֶאכֶת עֲבוֹדַת בֵּית־הָאֱלֹהִים:

14 Of the *Leviim*: Shemaya son of Hasshub son of Azrikam son of Hashabiah, of the sons of *Merari*;

יד וּמִן־הַלְוִיִּם שְׁמַעְיָה בֶן־חַשּׁוּב בֶּן־עַזְרִיקָם בֶּן־חֲשַׁבְיָה מִן־בְּנֵי מְרָרִי:

15 and Bakbakkar, Heresh, Galal, and Mattaniah son of Mica son of Zichri son of *Asaf*;

טו וּבַקְבַּקַּר חֶרֶשׁ וְגָלָל וּמַתַּנְיָה בֶּן־מִיכָא בֶּן־זִכְרִי בֶּן־אָסָף:

16 and *Ovadya* son of *Shemaya* son of Galal son of *Yedutun*, and *Berechya* son of *Asa* son of *Elkana*, who dwelt in the villages of the Netophathites.

טז וְעֹבַדְיָה בֶּן־שְׁמַעְיָה בֶּן־גָּלָל בֶּן־יְדוּתוּן וּבֶרֶכְיָה בֶן־אָסָא בֶּן־אֶלְקָנָה הַיּוֹשֵׁב בְּחַצְרֵי נְטוֹפָתִי:

17 The gatekeepers were: *Shalum*, Akkub, Talmon, Ahiman; and their kinsman *Shalum* was the chief

יז וְהַשֹּׁעֲרִים שַׁלּוּם וְעַקּוּב וְטַלְמֹן וַאֲחִימָן וַאֲחִיהֶם שַׁלּוּם הָרֹאשׁ:

18 hitherto in the King's Gate on the east. They were the keepers belonging to the Levite camp.

יח וְעַד־הֵנָּה בְּשַׁעַר הַמֶּלֶךְ מִזְרָחָה הֵמָּה הַשֹּׁעֲרִים לְמַחֲנוֹת בְּנֵי לֵוִי:

19 *Shalum* son of Kore son of Ebiasaph son of *Korach*, and his kinsmen of his clan, the Korahites, were in charge of the work of the service, guards of the threshold of the Tent; their fathers had been guards of the entrance to the camp of *Hashem*.

יט וְשַׁלּוּם בֶּן־קוֹרֵא בֶּן־אֶבְיָסָף בֶּן־קֹרַח וְאֶחָיו לְבֵית־אָבִיו הַקָּרְחִים עַל מְלֶאכֶת הָעֲבוֹדָה שֹׁמְרֵי הַסִּפִּים לָאֹהֶל וַאֲבֹתֵיהֶם עַל־מַחֲנֵה יְהֹוָה שֹׁמְרֵי הַמָּבוֹא:

20 And *Pinchas* son of *Elazar* was the chief officer over them in time past; *Hashem* was with him.

כ וּפִינְחָס בֶּן־אֶלְעָזָר נָגִיד הָיָה עֲלֵיהֶם לְפָנִים יְהֹוָה עִמּוֹ:

21 *Zecharya* the son of Meshelemiah was gatekeeper at the entrance of the Tent of Meeting.

כא זְכַרְיָה בֶּן־מְשֶׁלֶמְיָה שֹׁעֵר פֶּתַח לְאֹהֶל מוֹעֵד:

22 All these, who were selected as gatekeepers at the thresholds, were 212. They were selected by genealogies in their villages. *David* and *Shmuel* the seer established them in their office of trust.

כב כֻּלָּם הַבְּרוּרִים לְשֹׁעֲרִים בַּסִּפִּים מָאתַיִם וּשְׁנֵים עָשָׂר הֵמָּה בְחַצְרֵיהֶם הִתְיַחְשָׂם הֵמָּה יִסַּד דָּוִיד וּשְׁמוּאֵל הָרֹאֶה בֶּאֱמוּנָתָם:

23 They and their descendants were in charge of the gates of the House of *Hashem*, that is, the House of the Tent, as guards.

כג וְהֵם וּבְנֵיהֶם עַל־הַשְּׁעָרִים לְבֵית־יְהֹוָה לְבֵית־הָאֹהֶל לְמִשְׁמָרוֹת:

24 The gatekeepers were on the four sides, east, west, north, and south;

כד לְאַרְבַּע רוּחוֹת יִהְיוּ הַשֹּׁעֲרִים מִזְרָח יָמָּה צָפוֹנָה וָנֶגְבָּה:

25 and their kinsmen in their villages were obliged to join them every seven days, according to a fixed schedule.

כה וַאֲחֵיהֶם בְּחַצְרֵיהֶם לָבוֹא לְשִׁבְעַת הַיָּמִים מֵעֵת אֶל־עֵת עִם־אֵלֶּה:

26 The four chief gatekeepers, who were *Leviim*, were entrusted to be over the chambers and the treasuries of the House of *Hashem*.

כו כִּי בֶאֱמוּנָה הֵמָּה אַרְבַּעַת גִּבֹּרֵי הַשֹּׁעֲרִים הֵם הַלְוִיִּם וְהָיוּ עַל־הַלְּשָׁכוֹת וְעַל הָאֹצְרוֹת בֵּית הָאֱלֹהִים:

27 They spent the night near the House of *Hashem*; for they had to do guard duty, and they were in charge of opening it every morning.

כז וּסְבִיבוֹת בֵּית־הָאֱלֹהִים יָלִינוּ כִּי־עֲלֵיהֶם מִשְׁמֶרֶת וְהֵם עַל־הַמַּפְתֵּחַ וְלַבֹּקֶר לַבֹּקֶר:

28 Some of them had charge of the service vessels, for they were counted when they were brought back and taken out.

כח וּמֵהֶם עַל־כְּלֵי הָעֲבוֹדָה כִּי־בְמִסְפָּר יְבִיאוּם וּבְמִסְפָּר יוֹצִיאוּם:

29 Some of them were in charge of the vessels and all the holy vessels, and of the flour, wine, oil, incense, and spices.

כט וּמֵהֶם מְמֻנִּים עַל־הַכֵּלִים וְעַל כָּל־כְּלֵי הַקֹּדֶשׁ וְעַל־הַסֹּלֶת וְהַיַּיִן וְהַשֶּׁמֶן וְהַלְּבוֹנָה וְהַבְּשָׂמִים:

30 Some of the *Kohanim* blended the compound of spices.

ל וּמִן־בְּנֵי הַכֹּהֲנִים רֹקְחֵי הַמִּרְקַחַת לַבְּשָׂמִים:

31 Mattithiah, one of the *Leviim*, the first-born of *Shalum* the Korahite, was entrusted with making the flat cakes.

לא וּמַתִּתְיָה מִן־הַלְוִיִּם הוּא הַבְּכוֹר לְשַׁלֻּם הַקָּרְחִי בֶּאֱמוּנָה עַל מַעֲשֵׂה הַחֲבִתִּים:

32 Also some of their Kohathite kinsmen had charge of the rows of bread, to prepare them for each *Shabbat*.

לב וּמִן־בְּנֵי הַקְּהָתִי מִן־אֲחֵיהֶם עַל־לֶחֶם הַמַּעֲרָכֶת לְהָכִין שַׁבַּת שַׁבָּת:

33 Now these are the singers, the chiefs of Levitical clans who remained in the chambers free of other service, for they were on duty day and night.

לג וְאֵלֶּה הַמְשֹׁרְרִים רָאשֵׁי אָבוֹת לַלְוִיִּם בַּלְּשָׁכֹת פְּטִירִים [פְּטוּרִים] כִּי־יוֹמָם וָלַיְלָה עֲלֵיהֶם בַּמְּלָאכָה:

34 These were chiefs of Levitical clans, according to their lines; these chiefs lived in *Yerushalayim*.

לד אֵלֶּה רָאשֵׁי הָאָבוֹת לַלְוִיִּם לְתֹלְדוֹתָם רָאשִׁים אֵלֶּה יָשְׁבוּ בִירוּשָׁלָם:

35 The father of *Givon*, Jeiel, lived in *Givon*, and the name of his wife was Maacah.

לה וּבְגִבְעוֹן יָשְׁבוּ אֲבִי־גִבְעוֹן יְעוּאֵל [יְעִיאֵל] וְשֵׁם אִשְׁתּוֹ מַעֲכָה:

36 His first-born son, *Avdon*; then Zur, *Keesh*, Baal, Ner, *Nadav*,

לו וּבְנוֹ הַבְּכוֹר עַבְדּוֹן וְצוּר וְקִישׁ וּבַעַל וְנֵר וְנָדָב:

37 Gedor, Ahio, *Zecharya*, and Mikloth;

לז וּגְדוֹר וְאַחְיוֹ וּזְכַרְיָה וּמִקְלוֹת:

38 Mikloth begot Shimeam; and they lived in *Yerushalayim* opposite their kinsmen, with their kinsmen.

לח וּמִקְלוֹת הוֹלִיד אֶת־שִׁמְאָם וְאַף־הֵם נֶגֶד אֲחֵיהֶם יָשְׁבוּ בִירוּשָׁלַם עִם־אֲחֵיהֶם:

39 Ner begot *Keesh*, Keesh begot *Shaul*, Shaul begot *Yehonatan*, Malchi-shua, *Avinadav*, and Eshbaal;

לט וְנֵר הוֹלִיד אֶת־קִישׁ וְקִישׁ הוֹלִיד אֶת־שָׁאוּל וְשָׁאוּל הוֹלִיד אֶת־יְהוֹנָתָן וְאֶת־מַלְכִּי־שׁוּעַ וְאֶת־אֲבִינָדָב וְאֶת־אֶשְׁבָּעַל:

40 and the son of *Yehonatan* was Merib-baal; and Merib-baal begot *Micha*.

מ וּבֶן־יְהוֹנָתָן מְרִיב בָּעַל וּמְרִי־בַעַל הוֹלִיד אֶת־מִיכָה:

41 The sons of *Micha*: Pithon, Melech, Taharea;

מא וּבְנֵי מִיכָה פִּיתוֹן וָמֶלֶךְ וְתַחְרֵעַ:

42 *Achaz* begot Jarah, and Jarah begot Alemeth, Azmaveth, and *Zimri*; Zimri begot Moza.

מב וְאָחָז הוֹלִיד אֶת־יַעְרָה וְיַעְרָה הוֹלִיד אֶת־עָלֶמֶת וְאֶת־עַזְמָוֶת וְאֶת־זִמְרִי וְזִמְרִי הוֹלִיד אֶת־מוֹצָא:

⁴³ Moza begot Binea; his son was Rephaiah, his son Eleasah, his son Azel.

מג וּמוֹצָא הוֹלִיד אֶת־בִּנְעָא וּרְפָיָה בְנוֹ אֶלְעָשָׂה בְנוֹ אָצֵל בְּנוֹ:

⁴⁴ Azel had six sons and these were their names: Azrikam, Bocheru, Ishmael, Sheariah, *Ovadya*, and Hanan. These were the sons of Azel.

מד וּלְאָצֵל שִׁשָּׁה בָנִים וְאֵלֶּה שְׁמוֹתָם עַזְרִיקָם בֹּכְרוּ וְיִשְׁמָעֵאל וּשְׁעַרְיָה וְעֹבַדְיָה וְחָנָן אֵלֶּה בְּנֵי אָצַל:

10 ¹ The Philistines attacked *Yisrael*, and the men of *Yisrael* fled before the Philistines and [many] fell on Mount Gilboa.

א וּפְלִשְׁתִּים נִלְחֲמוּ בְיִשְׂרָאֵל וַיָּנָס אִישׁ־יִשְׂרָאֵל מִפְּנֵי פְלִשְׁתִּים וַיִּפְּלוּ חֲלָלִים בְּהַר גִּלְבֹּעַ:

² The Philistines pursued *Shaul* and his sons, and the Philistines struck down *Yonatan*, *Avinadav*, and Malchishua, sons of *Shaul*.

ב וַיַּדְבְּקוּ פְלִשְׁתִּים אַחֲרֵי שָׁאוּל וְאַחֲרֵי בָנָיו וַיַּכּוּ פְלִשְׁתִּים אֶת־יוֹנָתָן וְאֶת־אֲבִינָדָב וְאֶת־מַלְכִּי־שׁוּעַ בְּנֵי שָׁאוּל:

³ The battle raged around *Shaul*, and the archers hit him, and he was wounded by the archers.

ג וַתִּכְבַּד הַמִּלְחָמָה עַל־שָׁאוּל וַיִּמְצָאֻהוּ הַמּוֹרִים בַּקָּשֶׁת וַיָּחֶל מִן־הַיּוֹרִים:

⁴ *Shaul* said to his arms-bearer, "Draw your sword and run me through, so that these uncircumcised may not come and make sport of me." But his arms-bearer, out of great awe, refused; whereupon *Shaul* grasped the sword and fell upon it.

ד וַיֹּאמֶר שָׁאוּל אֶל־נֹשֵׂא כֵלָיו שְׁלֹף חַרְבְּךָ וְדָקְרֵנִי בָהּ פֶּן־יָבֹאוּ הָעֲרֵלִים הָאֵלֶּה וְהִתְעַלְּלוּ־בִי וְלֹא אָבָה נֹשֵׂא כֵלָיו כִּי יָרֵא מְאֹד וַיִּקַּח שָׁאוּל אֶת־הַחֶרֶב וַיִּפֹּל עָלֶיהָ:

⁵ When the arms-bearer saw that *Shaul* was dead, he too fell on his sword and died.

ה וַיַּרְא נֹשֵׂא־כֵלָיו כִּי מֵת שָׁאוּל וַיִּפֹּל גַּם־הוּא עַל־הַחֶרֶב וַיָּמֹת:

⁶ Thus *Shaul* and his three sons and his entire house died together.

ו וַיָּמָת שָׁאוּל וּשְׁלֹשֶׁת בָּנָיו וְכָל־בֵּיתוֹ יַחְדָּו מֵתוּ:

⁷ And when all the men of *Yisrael* who were in the valley saw that they had fled and that *Shaul* and his sons were dead, they abandoned their towns and fled; the Philistines then came and occupied them.

ז וַיִּרְאוּ כָּל־אִישׁ יִשְׂרָאֵל אֲשֶׁר־בָּעֵמֶק כִּי נָסוּ וְכִי־מֵתוּ שָׁאוּל וּבָנָיו וַיַּעַזְבוּ עָרֵיהֶם וַיָּנֻסוּ וַיָּבֹאוּ פְלִשְׁתִּים וַיֵּשְׁבוּ בָּהֶם:

⁸ The next day the Philistines came to strip the slain, and they found *Shaul* and his sons lying on Mount Gilboa.

ח וַיְהִי מִמָּחֳרָת וַיָּבֹאוּ פְלִשְׁתִּים לְפַשֵּׁט אֶת־הַחֲלָלִים וַיִּמְצְאוּ אֶת־שָׁאוּל וְאֶת־בָּנָיו נֹפְלִים בְּהַר גִּלְבֹּעַ:

⁹ They stripped him, and carried off his head and his armor, and sent them throughout the land of the Philistines to spread the news to their idols and among the people.

ט וַיַּפְשִׁיטֻהוּ וַיִּשְׂאוּ אֶת־רֹאשׁוֹ וְאֶת־כֵּלָיו וַיְשַׁלְּחוּ בְאֶרֶץ־פְּלִשְׁתִּים סָבִיב לְבַשֵּׂר אֶת־עֲצַבֵּיהֶם וְאֶת־הָעָם:

¹⁰ They placed his armor in the temple of their god, and they impaled his head in the temple of Dagan.

י וַיָּשִׂימוּ אֶת־כֵּלָיו בֵּית אֱלֹהֵיהֶם וְאֶת־גֻּלְגָּלְתּוֹ תָקְעוּ בֵּית דָּגוֹן:

¹¹ When all Jabesh-gilead heard everything that the Philistines had done to *Shaul*,

יא וַיִּשְׁמְעוּ כֹּל יָבֵישׁ גִּלְעָד אֵת כָּל־אֲשֶׁר־עָשׂוּ פְלִשְׁתִּים לְשָׁאוּל:

¹² all their stalwart men set out, removed the bodies of *Shaul* and his sons, and brought them to Jabesh. They buried the bones under the oak tree in Jabesh, and they fasted for seven days.

יב וַיָּקוּמוּ כָּל־אִישׁ חַיִל וַיִּשְׂאוּ אֶת־גּוּפַת שָׁאוּל וְאֵת גּוּפֹת בָּנָיו וַיְבִיאוּם יָבֵישָׁה וַיִּקְבְּרוּ אֶת־עַצְמוֹתֵיהֶם תַּחַת הָאֵלָה בְּיָבֵשׁ וַיָּצוּמוּ שִׁבְעַת יָמִים:

13 *Shaul* died for the trespass that he had committed against *Hashem* in not having fulfilled the command of *Hashem*; moreover, he had consulted a ghost to seek advice,

יג וַיָּמָת שָׁאוּל בְּמַעֲלוֹ אֲשֶׁר מָעַל בַּיהוָה עַל־דְּבַר יְהוָה אֲשֶׁר לֹא־שָׁמָר וְגַם־לִשְׁאוֹל בָּאוֹב לִדְרוֹשׁ:

14 and did not seek advice of *Hashem*; so He had him slain and the kingdom transferred to *David* son of *Yishai*.

יד וְלֹא־דָרַשׁ בַּיהוָה וַיְמִיתֵהוּ וַיַּסֵּב אֶת־הַמְּלוּכָה לְדָוִיד בֶּן־יִשָׁי:

v'-LO da-RASH ba-do-NAI vai-mee-TAY-hu va-ya-SAYV et ha-m'-lu-KHAH l'-da-VEED ben yi-SHAI

11 1 All *Yisrael* gathered to *David* at *Chevron* and said, "We are your own flesh and blood.

יא א וַיִּקָּבְצוּ כָל־יִשְׂרָאֵל אֶל־דָּוִיד חֶבְרוֹנָה לֵאמֹר הִנֵּה עַצְמְךָ וּבְשָׂרְךָ אֲנָחְנוּ:

2 Long before now, even when *Shaul* was king, you were the leader of *Yisrael*; and *Hashem* your God said to you: You shall shepherd My people *Yisrael*; you shall be ruler of My people *Yisrael*."

ב גַּם־תְּמוֹל גַּם־שִׁלְשׁוֹם גַּם בִּהְיוֹת שָׁאוּל מֶלֶךְ אַתָּה הַמּוֹצִיא וְהַמֵּבִיא אֶת־יִשְׂרָאֵל וַיֹּאמֶר יְהוָה אֱלֹהֶיךָ לְךָ אַתָּה תִרְעֶה אֶת־עַמִּי אֶת־יִשְׂרָאֵל וְאַתָּה תִּהְיֶה נָגִיד עַל עַמִּי יִשְׂרָאֵל:

3 All the elders of *Yisrael* came to the king at *Chevron*, and *David* made a pact with them in *Chevron* before *Hashem*. And they anointed *David* king over *Yisrael*, according to the word of *Hashem* through *Shmuel*.

ג וַיָּבֹאוּ כָּל־זִקְנֵי יִשְׂרָאֵל אֶל־הַמֶּלֶךְ חֶבְרוֹנָה וַיִּכְרֹת לָהֶם דָּוִיד בְּרִית בְּחֶבְרוֹן לִפְנֵי יְהוָה וַיִּמְשְׁחוּ אֶת־דָּוִיד לְמֶלֶךְ עַל־יִשְׂרָאֵל כִּדְבַר יְהוָה בְּיַד־שְׁמוּאֵל:

4 *David* and all *Yisrael* set out for *Yerushalayim*, that is Jebus, where the Jebusite inhabitants of the land lived.

ד וַיֵּלֶךְ דָּוִיד וְכָל־יִשְׂרָאֵל יְרוּשָׁלַם הִיא יְבוּס וְשָׁם הַיְבוּסִי יֹשְׁבֵי הָאָרֶץ:

va-YAY-lekh da-VEED v'-khol yis-ra-AYL y'-ru-sha-LA-yim hee y'-VUS v'-SHAM hai-vu-SEE yo-sh'-VAY ha-A-retz

5 *David* was told by the inhabitants of Jebus, "You will never get in here!" But *David* captured the stronghold of *Tzion*; it is now the City of *David*.

ה וַיֹּאמְרוּ יֹשְׁבֵי יְבוּס לְדָוִיד לֹא תָבוֹא הֵנָּה וַיִּלְכֹּד דָּוִיד אֶת־מְצֻדַת צִיּוֹן הִיא עִיר דָּוִיד:

Chronicles

10:14 The kingdom transferred to *David* son of *Yishai* *Shaul* was given a double punishment for the sins he had committed, which included consulting *Shmuel's* spirit in contravention of *Torah* law (I Samuel 28): He died, and his kingdom was transferred to *David*. Consulting a spirit is a crime labeled as an abomination (Deuteronomy 18:9–12). Only someone with an outstanding record of righteousness is truly fit to lead the People of Israel in the Land of Israel.

11:4 *David* and all *Yisrael* set out for *Yerushalayim* This first action that the text informs us *David* took after becoming king was to capture *Yerushalayim* and establish it as his capital. However, this actually occurred several years into *David's* reign, as he ruled in *Chevron* for seven years before moving to *Yerushalayim* (I Kings 2:11). Nonetheless, *Divrei Hayamim* does not record any of his accomplishments during those years. Conquering the Holy City from the idolatrous Jebusites and establishing his capital there was the most meaningful event of David's reign until that point. By doing so, he began the process that would lead to the construction of the *Beit Hamikdash* and service of God in "the site that *Hashem* your God will choose amidst all your tribes as His habitation, to establish His name there" (Deuteronomy 12:5).

Ruins from the City of David in *Yerushalayim*

6 *David* said, "Whoever attacks the Jebusites first will be the chief officer"; *Yoav* son of *Tzeruya* attacked first, and became the chief.

ו וַיֹּאמֶר דָּוִיד כָּל־מַכֵּה יְבוּסִי בָּרִאשׁוֹנָה יִהְיֶה לְרֹאשׁ וּלְשָׂר וַיַּעַל בָּרִאשׁוֹנָה יוֹאָב בֶּן־צְרוּיָה וַיְהִי לְרֹאשׁ:

7 *David* occupied the stronghold; therefore it was renamed the City of *David*.

ז וַיֵּשֶׁב דָּוִיד בַּמְצָד עַל־כֵּן קָרְאוּ־לוֹ עִיר דָּוִיד:

8 *David* also fortified the surrounding area, from the Millo roundabout, and *Yoav* rebuilt the rest of the city.

ח וַיִּבֶן הָעִיר מִסָּבִיב מִן־הַמִּלּוֹא וְעַד־הַסָּבִיב וְיוֹאָב יְחַיֶּה אֶת־שְׁאָר הָעִיר:

9 *David* kept growing stronger, for the Lord of Hosts was with him.

ט וַיֵּלֶךְ דָּוִיד הָלוֹךְ וְגָדוֹל וַיהוָה צְבָאוֹת עִמּוֹ:

10 And these were *David*'s chief warriors who strongly supported him in his kingdom, together with all *Yisrael*, to make him king, according to the word of *Hashem* concerning *Yisrael*.

י וְאֵלֶּה רָאשֵׁי הַגִּבּוֹרִים אֲשֶׁר לְדָוִיד הַמִּתְחַזְּקִים עִמּוֹ בְמַלְכוּתוֹ עִם־כָּל־יִשְׂרָאֵל לְהַמְלִיכוֹ כִּדְבַר יְהוָה עַל־יִשְׂרָאֵל:

11 This is the list of *David*'s warriors: Jashobeam son of Hachmoni, the chief officer; he wielded his spear against three hundred and slew them all on one occasion.

יא וְאֵלֶּה מִסְפַּר הַגִּבֹּרִים אֲשֶׁר לְדָוִיד יָשָׁבְעָם בֶּן־חַכְמוֹנִי רֹאשׁ הַשְּׁלוֹשִׁים [הַשָּׁלִישִׁים] הוּא־עוֹרֵר אֶת־חֲנִיתוֹ עַל־שְׁלֹשׁ־מֵאוֹת חָלָל בְּפַעַם אֶחָת:

12 Next to him was *Elazar* son of Dodo, the Ahohite; he was one of the three warriors.

יב וְאַחֲרָיו אֶלְעָזָר בֶּן־דּוֹדוֹ הָאֲחוֹחִי הוּא בִּשְׁלוֹשָׁה הַגִּבֹּרִים:

13 He was with *David* at Pas Dammim when the Philistines gathered there for battle. There was a plot of ground full of barley there; the troops had fled from the Philistines,

יג הוּא־הָיָה עִם־דָּוִיד בַּפַּס דַּמִּים וְהַפְּלִשְׁתִּים נֶאֶסְפוּ־שָׁם לַמִּלְחָמָה וַתְּהִי חֶלְקַת הַשָּׂדֶה מְלֵאָה שְׂעוֹרִים וְהָעָם נָסוּ מִפְּנֵי פְלִשְׁתִּים:

14 but they took their stand in the middle of the plot and defended it, and they routed the Philistines. Thus *Hashem* wrought a great victory.

יד וַיִּתְיַצְּבוּ בְתוֹךְ־הַחֶלְקָה וַיַּצִּילוּהָ וַיַּכּוּ אֶת־פְּלִשְׁתִּים וַיּוֹשַׁע יְהוָה תְּשׁוּעָה גְדוֹלָה:

15 Three of the thirty chiefs went down to the rock to *David*, at the cave of *Adulam*, while a force of Philistines was encamped in the Valley of Rephaim.

טו וַיֵּרְדוּ שְׁלוֹשָׁה מִן־הַשְּׁלוֹשִׁים רֹאשׁ עַל־הַצֻּר אֶל־דָּוִיד אֶל־מְעָרַת עֲדֻלָּם וּמַחֲנֵה פְלִשְׁתִּים חֹנָה בְּעֵמֶק רְפָאִים:

16 *David* was then in the stronghold, and a Philistine garrison was then at *Beit Lechem*.

טז וְדָוִיד אָז בַּמְצוּדָה וּנְצִיב פְּלִשְׁתִּים אָז בְּבֵית לָחֶם:

17 *David* felt a craving and said, "If only I could get a drink of water from the cistern which is by the gate of *Beit Lechem*!"

יז וַיִּתְאַו [וַיִּתְאָיו] דָּוִיד וַיֹּאמַר מִי יַשְׁקֵנִי מַיִם מִבּוֹר בֵּית־לֶחֶם אֲשֶׁר בַּשָּׁעַר:

18 So the three got through the Philistine camp, and drew water from the cistern which is by the gate of *Beit Lechem*, and they carried it back to *David*. But *David* would not drink it, and he poured it out as a libation to *Hashem*.

יח וַיִּבְקְעוּ הַשְּׁלֹשָׁה בְּמַחֲנֵה פְלִשְׁתִּים וַיִּשְׁאֲבוּ־מַיִם מִבּוֹר בֵּית־לֶחֶם אֲשֶׁר בַּשַּׁעַר וַיִּשְׂאוּ וַיָּבִאוּ אֶל־דָּוִיד וְלֹא־אָבָה דָוִיד לִשְׁתּוֹתָם וַיְנַסֵּךְ אֹתָם לַיהוָה:

¹⁹ For he said, "*Hashem* forbid that I should do this! Can I drink the blood of these men who risked their lives?" – for they had brought it at the risk of their lives, and he would not drink it. Such were the exploits of the three warriors.

יט וַיֹּאמֶר חָלִילָה לִּי מֵאֱלֹהַי מֵעֲשׂוֹת זֹאת הֲדַם הָאֲנָשִׁים הָאֵלֶּה אֶשְׁתֶּה בְנַפְשׁוֹתָם כִּי בְנַפְשׁוֹתָם הֱבִיאוּם וְלֹא אָבָה לִשְׁתּוֹתָם אֵלֶּה עָשׂוּ שְׁלֹשֶׁת הַגִּבּוֹרִים:

²⁰ Abshai, the brother of *Yoav*, was head of another three. He once wielded his spear against three hundred and slew them. He won a name among the three;

כ וְאַבְשַׁי אֲחִי־יוֹאָב הוּא הָיָה רֹאשׁ הַשְּׁלוֹשָׁה וְהוּא עוֹרֵר אֶת־חֲנִיתוֹ עַל־שְׁלֹשׁ מֵאוֹת חָלָל וְלֹא־[וְלוֹ־] שֵׁם בַּשְּׁלוֹשָׁה:

²¹ among the three he was more highly regarded than the other two, and so he became their commander. However, he did not attain to the other three.

כא מִן־הַשְּׁלוֹשָׁה בַשְּׁנַיִם נִכְבָּד וַיְהִי לָהֶם לְשָׂר וְעַד־הַשְּׁלוֹשָׁה לֹא־בָא:

²² Benaiah son of *Yehoyada* from Kabzeel was a brave soldier who performed great deeds. He killed the two [sons] of Ariel of Moab. Once, on a snowy day, he went down into a pit and killed a lion.

כב בְּנָיָה בֶן־יְהוֹיָדָע בֶּן־אִישׁ־חַיִל רַב־פְּעָלִים מִן־קַבְצְאֵל הוּא הִכָּה אֵת שְׁנֵי אֲרִיאֵל מוֹאָב וְהוּא יָרַד וְהִכָּה אֶת־הָאֲרִי בְּתוֹךְ הַבּוֹר בְּיוֹם הַשָּׁלֶג:

²³ He also killed an Egyptian, a giant of a man five *amot* tall. The Egyptian had a spear in his hand, like a weaver's beam, yet [Benaiah] went down against him with a club, wrenched the spear out of the Egyptian's hand, and killed him with his own spear.

כג וְהוּא־הִכָּה אֶת־הָאִישׁ הַמִּצְרִי אִישׁ מִדָּה חָמֵשׁ בָּאַמָּה וּבְיַד הַמִּצְרִי חֲנִית כִּמְנוֹר אֹרְגִים וַיֵּרֶד אֵלָיו בַּשָּׁבֶט וַיִּגְזֹל אֶת־הַחֲנִית מִיַּד הַמִּצְרִי וַיַּהַרְגֵהוּ בַּחֲנִיתוֹ:

²⁴ Such were the exploits of Benaiah son of *Yehoyada*; and he won a name among the three warriors.

כד אֵלֶּה עָשָׂה בְּנָיָהוּ בֶּן־יְהוֹיָדָע וְלוֹ־שֵׁם בִּשְׁלוֹשָׁה הַגִּבֹּרִים:

²⁵ He was highly regarded among the thirty, but he did not attain to the three. *David* put him in charge of his bodyguard.

כה מִן־הַשְּׁלוֹשִׁים הִנּוֹ נִכְבָּד הוּא וְאֶל־הַשְּׁלוֹשָׁה לֹא־בָא וַיְשִׂימֵהוּ דָוִיד עַל־מִשְׁמַעְתּוֹ:

²⁶ The valiant warriors: *Asael* brother of *Yoav*, *Elchanan* son of Dodo from *Beit Lechem*,

כו וְגִבּוֹרֵי הַחֲיָלִים עֲשָׂה־אֵל אֲחִי יוֹאָב אֶלְחָנָן בֶּן־דּוֹדוֹ מִבֵּית לָחֶם:

²⁷ Shammoth the Harorite, Helez the Pelonite,

כז שַׁמּוֹת הַהֲרוֹרִי חֶלֶץ הַפְּלוֹנִי:

²⁸ Ira son of Ikkesh from *Tekoa*, Abiezer of *Anatot*,

כח עִירָא בֶן־עִקֵּשׁ הַתְּקוֹעִי אֲבִיעֶזֶר הָעֲנְּתוֹתִי:

²⁹ Sibbecai the Hushathite, Ilai the Ahohite,

כט סִבְּכַי הַחֻשָׁתִי עִילַי הָאֲחוֹחִי:

³⁰ Mahrai the Netophathite, Heled son of Baanah the Netophathite,

ל מַהְרַי הַנְּטֹפָתִי חֵלֶד בֶּן־בַּעֲנָה הַנְּטוֹפָתִי:

³¹ Ittai son of Ribai from *Giva* of the Benjaminites, Benaiah of Pirathon,

לא אִיתַי בֶּן־רִיבַי מִגִּבְעַת בְּנֵי בִנְיָמִן בְּנָיָה הַפִּרְעָתֹנִי:

³² Hurai of Nahale-gaash, Abiel the Arbathite,

לב חוּרַי מִנַּחֲלֵי גָעַשׁ אֲבִיאֵל הָעַרְבָתִי:

³³ Azmaveth the Bahrumite, Eliahba of Shaalbon,

לג עַזְמָוֶת הַבַּחֲרוּמִי אֶלְיַחְבָּא הַשַּׁעַלְבֹנִי:

³⁴ the sons of *Hashem* the Gizonite, *Yonatan* son of Shageh the Hararite,

לד בְּנֵי הָשֵׁם הַגִּזוֹנִי יוֹנָתָן בֶּן־שָׁגֵה הַהֲרָרִי:

³⁵ Ahiam son of Sacar the Hararite, Eliphal son of Ur,

לה אֲחִיאָם בֶּן־שָׂכָר הַהֲרָרִי אֱלִיפַל בֶּן־אוּר:

³⁶ Hepher the Mecherathite, *Achiya* the Pelonite,

לו חֵפֶר הַמְּכֵרָתִי אֲחִיָּה הַפְּלֹנִי:

³⁷ Hezro the Carmelite, Naarai son of Ezbai,

לז חֶצְרוֹ הַכַּרְמְלִי נַעֲרַי בֶּן־אֶזְבָּי:

³⁸ *Yoel* brother of *Natan*, Mibhar son of Hagri,

לח יוֹאֵל אֲחִי נָתָן מִבְחָר בֶּן־הַגְרִי:

³⁹ Zelek the Ammonite, Naharai the Berothite – the arms-bearer of *Yoav* son of *Tzeruya* –

לט צֶלֶק הָעַמּוֹנִי נַחְרַי הַבֵּרֹתִי נֹשֵׂא כְּלֵי יוֹאָב בֶּן־צְרוּיָה:

⁴⁰ Ira the Ithrite, Gareb the Ithrite,

מ עִירָא הַיִּתְרִי גָּרֵב הַיִּתְרִי:

⁴¹ *Uriya* the Hittite, Zabad son of Ahlai.

מא אוּרִיָּה הַחִתִּי זָבָד בֶּן־אַחְלָי:

⁴² Adina son of Shiza the Reubenite, a chief of the Reubenites, and thirty with him;

מב עֲדִינָא בֶן־שִׁיזָא הָראוּבֵנִי רֹאשׁ לָראוּבֵנִי וְעָלָיו שְׁלוֹשִׁים:

⁴³ Hanan son of Maacah, and Joshaphat the Mithnite;

מג חָנָן בֶּן־מַעֲכָה וְיוֹשָׁפָט הַמִּתְנִי:

⁴⁴ *Uzziyahu* the Ashterathite, Shama and Jeiel sons of Hotham the Aroerite;

מד עֻזִּיָּא הָעַשְׁתְּרָתִי שָׁמָע וִיעוּאֵל [וִיעִיאֵל] בְּנֵי חוֹתָם הָעֲרֹעֵרִי:

⁴⁵ Jedaiael son of Shimri, and Joha his brother, the Tizite;

מה יְדִיעֲאֵל בֶּן־שִׁמְרִי וְיֹחָא אָחִיו הַתִּיצִי:

⁴⁶ Eliel the Mahavite, and Jeribai and Joshaviah sons of Elnaam, and Ithmah the Moabite;

מו אֱלִיאֵל הַמַּחֲוִים וִירִיבַי וְיוֹשַׁוְיָה בְּנֵי אֶלְנָעַם וְיִתְמָה הַמּוֹאָבִי:

⁴⁷ Eliel, Oved, and Jaassiel the Mezobaite.

מז אֱלִיאֵל וְעוֹבֵד וְיַעֲשִׂיאֵל הַמְּצֹבָיָה:

12 ¹ The following joined *David* at *Tziklag* while he was still in hiding from *Shaul* son of *Keesh*; these were the warriors who gave support in battle;

יב א וְאֵלֶּה הַבָּאִים אֶל־דָּוִיד לְצִיקְלַג עוֹד עָצוּר מִפְּנֵי שָׁאוּל בֶּן־קִישׁ וְהֵמָּה בַּגִּבּוֹרִים עֹזְרֵי הַמִּלְחָמָה:

² they were armed with the bow and could use both right hand and left hand to sling stones or shoot arrows with the bow; they were kinsmen of *Shaul* from *Binyamin.*

ב נֹשְׁקֵי קֶשֶׁת מַיְמִינִים וּמַשְׂמִאלִים בָּאֲבָנִים וּבַחִצִּים בַּקָּשֶׁת מֵאֲחֵי שָׁאוּל מִבִּנְיָמִן:

³ At the head were Ahiezer and *Yoash*, sons of Shemaah of *Giva*; and Jeziel and Pelet, sons of Azmaveth; and Beracah and *Yehu* of *Anatot*;

ג הָראשׁ אֲחִיעֶזֶר וְיוֹאָשׁ בְּנֵי הַשְּׁמָעָה הַגִּבְעָתִי וִיזוּאֵל [וִיזִיאֵל] וָפֶלֶט בְּנֵי עַזְמָוֶת וּבְרָכָה וְיֵהוּא הָעֲנְתֹתִי:

⁴ Ishmaiah of *Givon*, a warrior among the thirty, leading the thirty;

ד וְיִשְׁמַעְיָה הַגִּבְעוֹנִי גִּבּוֹר בַּשְּׁלֹשִׁים וְעַל־הַשְּׁלֹשִׁים:

⁵ *Yirmiyahu, Yachaziel, Yochanan,* and *Yozavad* of Gedera;

ה וְיִרְמְיָה וְיַחֲזִיאֵל וְיוֹחָנָן וְיוֹזָבָד הַגְּדֵרָתִי:

⁶ Eluzai, Jerimoth, Bealiah, Shemariah, and Shephatiah the Hariphite;

ו אֶלְעוּזַי וִירִימוֹת וּבְעַלְיָה וּשְׁמַרְיָהוּ וּשְׁפַטְיָהוּ הַחֲרִיפִי [הַחֲרוּפִי]:

⁷ *Elkana*, Isshiah, Azarel, Joezer, and Jashobeam the Korahites;

ז אֶלְקָנָה וְיִשִּׁיָּהוּ וַעֲזַרְאֵל וְיוֹעֶזֶר וְיָשָׁבְעָם הַקָּרְחִים:

⁸ Yoelah and Zebadiah, sons of Jeroham of Gedor.

ח וְיוֹעֵאלָה וּזְבַדְיָה בְּנֵי יְרֹחָם מִן־הַגְּדוֹר:

9 Of the Gadites, there withdrew to follow *David* to the wilderness stronghold valiant men, fighters fit for battle, armed with shield and spear; they had the appearance of lions, and were as swift as gazelles upon the mountains:

ט וּמִן־הַגָּדִי נִבְדְּלוּ אֶל־דָּוִיד לַמְצַד מִדְבָּרָה גִּבֹּרֵי הַחַיִל אַנְשֵׁי צָבָא לַמִּלְחָמָה עֹרְכֵי צִנָּה וָרֹמַח וּפְנֵי אַרְיֵה פְּנֵיהֶם וְכִצְבָאִים עַל־הֶהָרִים לְמַהֵר:

10 Ezer the chief, *Ovadya* the second, *Eliav* the third,

י עֵזֶר הָרֹאשׁ עֹבַדְיָה הַשֵּׁנִי אֱלִיאָב הַשְּׁלִשִׁי:

11 Mashmannah the fourth, *Yirmiyahu* the fifth,

יא מִשְׁמַנָּה הָרְבִיעִי יִרְמְיָה הַחֲמִשִׁי:

12 Attai the sixth, Eliel the seventh,

יב עַתַּי הַשִּׁשִּׁי אֱלִיאֵל הַשְּׁבִעִי:

13 *Yochanan* the eighth, Elzabad the ninth,

יג יוֹחָנָן הַשְּׁמִינִי אֶלְזָבָד הַתְּשִׁיעִי:

14 *Yirmiyahu* the tenth, Machbannai the eleventh.

יד יִרְמְיָהוּ הָעֲשִׂירִי מַכְבַּנַּי עַשְׁתֵּי עָשָׂר:

15 Those were the Gadites, heads of the army. The least was equal to a hundred, the greatest to a thousand.

טו אֵלֶּה מִבְּנֵי־גָד רָאשֵׁי הַצָּבָא אֶחָד לְמֵאָה הַקָּטָן וְהַגָּדוֹל לְאָלֶף:

16 These were the ones who crossed the *Yarden* in the first month, when it was at its crest, and they put to flight all the lowlanders to the east and west.

טז אֵלֶּה הֵם אֲשֶׁר עָבְרוּ אֶת־הַיַּרְדֵּן בַּחֹדֶשׁ הָרִאשׁוֹן וְהוּא מְמַלֵּא עַל־כָּל־גְּדִיתָיו [גְּדוֹתָיו] וַיַּבְרִיחוּ אֶת־כָּל־הָעֲמָקִים לַמִּזְרָח וְלַמַּעֲרָב:

AY-leh HAYM a-SHER a-v'-RU et ha-yar-DAYN ba-KHO-desh ha-ri-SHON v'-HU m'-ma-LAY al kol g'-do-TAV va-yav-REE-khu et kol HA-a-ma-KEEM la-miz-RAKH v'-la-ma-a-RAV

17 Some of the Benjaminites and Judahites came to the stronghold to *David*,

יז וַיָּבֹאוּ מִן־בְּנֵי בִנְיָמִן וִיהוּדָה עַד־לַמְצָד לְדָוִיד:

18 and *David* went out to meet them, saying to them, "If you come on a peaceful errand, to support me, then I will make common cause with you, but if to betray me to my foes, for no injustice on my part, then let the God of our fathers take notice and give judgment."

יח וַיֵּצֵא דָוִיד לִפְנֵיהֶם וַיַּעַן וַיֹּאמֶר לָהֶם אִם־לְשָׁלוֹם בָּאתֶם אֵלַי לְעָזְרֵנִי יִהְיֶה־לִּי עֲלֵיכֶם לֵבָב לְיָחַד וְאִם־לְרַמּוֹתַנִי לְצָרַי בְּלֹא חָמָס בְּכַפַּי יֵרֶא אֱלֹהֵי אֲבוֹתֵינוּ וְיוֹכַח:

19 Then the spirit seized Amasai, chief of the captains "We are yours, *David* On your side, son of *Yishai*

יט וְרוּחַ לָבְשָׁה אֶת־עֲמָשַׂי רֹאשׁ השלושים [הַשָּׁלִישִׁים] לְךָ דָוִיד וְעִמְּךָ

12:16 They put to flight all the lowlanders to the east and west The simple meaning of this verse is that the warriors who crossed the Jordan river routed all enemies from the nearby valleys. However, *Rashi* offers an alternative interpretation of this phrase. He suggests that the soldiers used their shields to push the water away, so that they could cross on dry land. This is reminiscent of two similar crossings recorded in the *Tanakh*: *Moshe* split the Sea of Reeds, rendering the area dry for the children of Israel to pass through (Exodus 14:21), and the waters of the Jordan river were also stopped so that the Children of Israel could cross on dry land into the Land of Israel under the leadership of *Yehoshua* (Joshua 3:16). By stating that *David*'s warriors did something similar, *Rashi* is telling us that *David* was the next link in a chain of great leaders which stretched back to *Moshe* and *Yehoshua*.

Sunset over the Jordan River

At peace, at peace with you And at peace with him who supports you For your God supports you. So *David* accepted them, and placed them at the head of his band.

בֶּן־יִשַׁי שָׁלוֹם שָׁלוֹם לְךָ וְשָׁלוֹם לְעֹזְרֶךָ כִּי עֲזָרְךָ אֱלֹהֶיךָ וַיְקַבְּלֵם דָּוִיד וַיִּתְּנֵם בְּרָאשֵׁי הַגְּדוּד:

20 Some Manassites went over to *David*'s side when he came with the Philistines to make war against *Shaul*, but they were of no help to them, because the lords of the Philistines in council dismissed him, saying, "He will go over to the side of his lord, *Shaul*, and it will cost us our heads";

כ וּמִמְּנַשֶּׁה נָפְלוּ עַל־דָּוִיד בְּבֹאוֹ עִם־ פְּלִשְׁתִּים עַל־שָׁאוּל לַמִּלְחָמָה וְלֹא עֲזָרֻם כִּי בְעֵצָה שִׁלְּחֻהוּ סַרְנֵי פְלִשְׁתִּים לֵאמֹר בְּרָאשֵׁינוּ יִפּוֹל אֶל־אֲדֹנָיו שָׁאוּל:

21 when he went to *Tziklag*, these Manassites went over to his side – Adnah, *Yozavad*, Jediael, *Michael*, *Yozavad*, Elihu, and Zillethai, chiefs of the clans of *Menashe*.

כא בְּלֶכְתּוֹ אֶל־צִיקְלַג נָפְלוּ עָלָיו מִמְּנַשֶּׁה עַדְנַח וְיוֹזָבָד וִידִיעֲאֵל וּמִיכָאֵל וְיוֹזָבָד וֶאֱלִיהוּא וְצִלְּתָי רָאשֵׁי הָאֲלָפִים אֲשֶׁר לִמְנַשֶּׁה:

22 It was they who gave support to *David* against the band, for all were valiant men; and they were officers of the force.

כב וְהֵמָּה עָזְרוּ עִם־דָּוִיד עַל־הַגְּדוּד כִּי־ גִבּוֹרֵי חַיִל כֻּלָּם וַיִּהְיוּ שָׂרִים בַּצָּבָא:

23 Day in day out, people came to *David* to give him support, until there was an army as vast as the army of *Hashem*.

כג כִּי לְעֶת־יוֹם בְּיוֹם יָבֹאוּ עַל־דָּוִיד לְעָזְרוֹ עַד־לְמַחֲנֶה גָדוֹל כְּמַחֲנֵה אֱלֹהִים:

24 These are the numbers of the [men of the] armed bands who joined *David* at *Chevron* to transfer *Shaul*'s kingdom to him, in accordance with the word of *Hashem*:

כד וְאֵלֶּה מִסְפְּרֵי רָאשֵׁי הֶחָלוּץ לַצָּבָא בָּאוּ עַל־דָּוִיד חֶבְרוֹנָה לְהָסֵב מַלְכוּת שָׁאוּל אֵלָיו כְּפִי יְהֹוָה:

25 Judahites, equipped with shield and spear – 6,800 armed men;

כה בְּנֵי יְהוּדָה נֹשְׂאֵי צִנָּה וָרֹמַח שֵׁשֶׁת אֲלָפִים וּשְׁמוֹנֶה מֵאוֹת חֲלוּצֵי צָבָא:

26 Simeonites, valiant men, fighting troops – 7,100;

כו מִן־בְּנֵי שִׁמְעוֹן גִּבּוֹרֵי חַיִל לַצָּבָא שִׁבְעַת אֲלָפִים וּמֵאָה:

27 of the *Leviim* – 4,600;

כז מִן־בְּנֵי הַלֵּוִי אַרְבַּעַת אֲלָפִים וְשֵׁשׁ מֵאוֹת:

28 *Yehoyada*, chief officer of the Aaronides; with him, 3,700;

כח וִיהוֹיָדָע הַנָּגִיד לְאַהֲרֹן וְעִמּוֹ שְׁלֹשֶׁת אֲלָפִים וּשְׁבַע מֵאוֹת:

29 *Tzadok*, a young valiant man, with his clan – 22 officers;

כט וְצָדוֹק נַעַר גִּבּוֹר חָיִל וּבֵית־אָבִיו שָׂרִים עֶשְׂרִים וּשְׁנָיִם:

30 of the Benjaminites, kinsmen of *Shaul*, 3,000 in their great numbers, hitherto protecting the interests of the house of *Shaul*;

ל וּמִן־בְּנֵי בִנְיָמִן אֲחֵי שָׁאוּל שְׁלֹשֶׁת אֲלָפִים וְעַד־הֵנָּה מַרְבִּיתָם שֹׁמְרִים מִשְׁמֶרֶת בֵּית שָׁאוּל:

31 of the Ephraimites, 20,800 valiant men, famous in their clans;

לא וּמִן־בְּנֵי אֶפְרַיִם עֶשְׂרִים אֶלֶף וּשְׁמוֹנֶה מֵאוֹת גִּבּוֹרֵי חָיִל אַנְשֵׁי שֵׁמוֹת לְבֵית אֲבוֹתָם:

32 of the half-tribe of *Menashe*, 18,000, who were designated by name to come and make *David* king;

לב וּמֵחֲצִי מַטֵּה מְנַשֶּׁה שְׁמוֹנָה עָשָׂר אָלֶף אֲשֶׁר נִקְּבוּ בְּשֵׁמוֹת לָבוֹא לְהַמְלִיךְ אֶת־דָּוִיד׃

33 of the Issacharites, men who knew how to interpret the signs of the times, to determine how *Yisrael* should act; their chiefs were 200, and all their kinsmen followed them;

לג וּמִבְּנֵי יִשָּׂשכָר יוֹדְעֵי בִינָה לַעִתִּים לָדַעַת מַה־יַּעֲשֶׂה יִשְׂרָאֵל רָאשֵׁיהֶם מָאתַיִם וְכָל־אֲחֵיהֶם עַל־פִּיהֶם׃

34 of *Zevulun*, those ready for service, able to man a battle line with all kinds of weapons, 50,000, giving support wholeheartedly;

לד מִזְּבֻלוּן יוֹצְאֵי צָבָא עֹרְכֵי מִלְחָמָה בְּכָל־כְּלֵי מִלְחָמָה חֲמִשִּׁים אָלֶף וְלַעֲדֹר בְּלֹא־לֵב וָלֵב׃

35 of *Naftali*, 1,000 chieftains with their shields and lances – 37,000;

לה וּמִנַּפְתָּלִי שָׂרִים אָלֶף וְעִמָּהֶם בְּצִנָּה וַחֲנִית שְׁלֹשִׁים וְשִׁבְעָה אָלֶף׃

36 of the Danites, able to man the battle line – 28,600;

לו וּמִן־הַדָּנִי עֹרְכֵי מִלְחָמָה עֶשְׂרִים־וּשְׁמוֹנָה אֶלֶף וְשֵׁשׁ מֵאוֹת׃

37 of *Asher*, those ready for service to man the battle line – 40,000;

לז וּמֵאָשֵׁר יוֹצְאֵי צָבָא לַעֲרֹךְ מִלְחָמָה אַרְבָּעִים אָלֶף׃

38 from beyond the *Yarden*, of the Reubenites, the Gadites, and the half-tribe of *Menashe*, together with all kinds of military weapons – 120,000.

לח וּמֵעֵבֶר לַיַּרְדֵּן מִן־הָראוּבֵנִי וְהַגָּדִי וַחֲצִי שֵׁבֶט מְנַשֶּׁה בְּכֹל כְּלֵי צְבָא מִלְחָמָה מֵאָה וְעֶשְׂרִים אָלֶף׃

39 All these, fighting men, manning the battle line with whole heart, came to *Chevron* to make *David* king over all *Yisrael*. Likewise, all the rest of *Yisrael* was of one mind to make *David* king.

לט כָּל־אֵלֶּה אַנְשֵׁי מִלְחָמָה עֹדְרֵי מַעֲרָכָה בְּלֵבָב שָׁלֵם בָּאוּ חֶבְרוֹנָה לְהַמְלִיךְ אֶת־דָּוִיד עַל־כָּל־יִשְׂרָאֵל וְגַם כָּל־שֵׁרִית יִשְׂרָאֵל לֵב אֶחָד לְהַמְלִיךְ אֶת־דָּוִיד׃

40 They were there with *David* three days, eating and drinking, for their kinsmen had provided for them.

מ וַיִּהְיוּ־שָׁם עִם־דָּוִיד יָמִים שְׁלוֹשָׁה אֹכְלִים וְשׁוֹתִים כִּי־הֵכִינוּ לָהֶם אֲחֵיהֶם׃

41 And also, their relatives as far away as *Yissachar*, *Zevulun*, and *Naftali* brought food by ass, camel, mule, and ox – provisions of flour, cakes of figs, raisin cakes, wine, oil, cattle, and sheep in abundance, for there was joy in *Yisrael*.

מא וְגַם הַקְּרוֹבִים־אֲלֵיהֶם עַד־יִשָּׂשכָר וּזְבֻלוּן וְנַפְתָּלִי מְבִיאִים לֶחֶם בַּחֲמוֹרִים וּבַגְּמַלִּים וּבַפְּרָדִים וּבַבָּקָר מַאֲכָל קֶמַח דְּבֵלִים וְצִמּוּקִים וְיַיִן־וְשֶׁמֶן וּבָקָר וְצֹאן לָרֹב כִּי שִׂמְחָה בְּיִשְׂרָאֵל׃

13 1 Then *David* consulted with the officers of the thousands and the hundreds, with every chief officer.

יג א וַיִּוָּעַץ דָּוִיד עִם־שָׂרֵי הָאֲלָפִים וְהַמֵּאוֹת לְכָל־נָגִיד׃

2 *David* said to the entire assembly of *Yisrael*, "If you approve, and if *Hashem* our God concurs, let us send far and wide to our remaining kinsmen throughout the territories of *Yisrael*, including the *Kohanim* and *Leviim* in the towns where they have pasturelands, that they should gather together to us

ב וַיֹּאמֶר דָּוִיד לְכֹל קְהַל יִשְׂרָאֵל אִם־עֲלֵיכֶם טוֹב וּמִן־יְהוָה אֱלֹהֵינוּ נִפְרְצָה נִשְׁלְחָה עַל־אַחֵינוּ הַנִּשְׁאָרִים בְּכֹל אַרְצוֹת יִשְׂרָאֵל וְעִמָּהֶם הַכֹּהֲנִים וְהַלְוִיִּם בְּעָרֵי מִגְרְשֵׁיהֶם וְיִקָּבְצוּ אֵלֵינוּ׃

va-YO-mer da-VEED l'-KHOL k'-HAL yis-ra-AYL im a-lay-KHEM TOV
u-min a-do-NAI e-lo-HAY-nu nif-r'-TZAH nish-l'-KHAH al a-KHAY-nu
ha-nish-a-REEM b'-KHOL ar-TZOT yis-ra-AYL v'-i-ma-HEM ha-ko-ha-NEEM
v'-hal-vi-YIM b'-a-RAY mig-r'-shay-HEM v'-yi-ka-v'-TZU ay-LAY-nu

3 in order to transfer the *Aron* of our God to us, for throughout the days of *Shaul* we paid no regard to it."

ג וְנָסֵבָּה אֶת־אֲרוֹן אֱלֹהֵינוּ אֵלֵינוּ כִּי־לֹא דְרַשְׁנֻהוּ בִּימֵי שָׁאוּל:

4 The entire assembly agreed to do so, for the proposal pleased all the people.

ד וַיֹּאמְרוּ כָל־הַקָּהָל לַעֲשׂוֹת כֵּן כִּי־יָשַׁר הַדָּבָר בְּעֵינֵי כָל־הָעָם:

5 *David* then assembled all *Yisrael* from Shihor of Egypt to Lebo-hamath, in order to bring the *Aron* of *Hashem* from *Kiryat Ye'arim*.

ה וַיַּקְהֵל דָּוִיד אֶת־כָּל־יִשְׂרָאֵל מִן־שִׁיחוֹר מִצְרַיִם וְעַד־לְבוֹא חֲמָת לְהָבִיא אֶת־אֲרוֹן הָאֱלֹהִים מִקִּרְיַת יְעָרִים:

6 *David* and all *Yisrael* went up to Baalah, *Kiryat Ye'arim* of *Yehuda*, to bring up from there the *Aron* of *Hashem*, *Hashem*, Enthroned on the *Keruvim*, to which the Name was attached.

ו וַיַּעַל דָּוִיד וְכָל־יִשְׂרָאֵל בַּעֲלָתָה אֶל־קִרְיַת יְעָרִים אֲשֶׁר לִיהוּדָה לְהַעֲלוֹת מִשָּׁם אֵת אֲרוֹן הָאֱלֹהִים יְהוָה יוֹשֵׁב הַכְּרוּבִים אֲשֶׁר־נִקְרָא שֵׁם:

7 They transported the *Aron* of *Hashem* on a new cart from the house of *Avinadav*; Uzza and Ahio guided the cart,

ז וַיַּרְכִּיבוּ אֶת־אֲרוֹן הָאֱלֹהִים עַל־עֲגָלָה חֲדָשָׁה מִבֵּית אֲבִינָדָב וְעֻזָּא וְאַחְיוֹ נֹהֲגִים בָּעֲגָלָה:

8 and *David* and all *Yisrael* danced before *Hashem* with all their might – with songs, lyres, harps, timbrels, cymbals, and trumpets.

ח וְדָוִיד וְכָל־יִשְׂרָאֵל מְשַׂחֲקִים לִפְנֵי הָאֱלֹהִים בְּכָל־עֹז וּבְשִׁירִים וּבְכִנֹּרוֹת וּבִנְבָלִים וּבְתֻפִּים וּבִמְצִלְתַּיִם וּבַחֲצֹצְרוֹת:

9 But when they came to the threshing floor of Chidon, Uzza put out his hand to hold the *Aron* of *Hashem* because the oxen had stumbled.

ט וַיָּבֹאוּ עַד־גֹּרֶן כִּידֹן וַיִּשְׁלַח עֻזָּא אֶת־יָדוֹ לֶאֱחֹז אֶת־הָאָרוֹן כִּי שָׁמְטוּ הַבָּקָר:

10 *Hashem* was incensed at Uzza, and struck him down, because he laid a hand on the *Aron*; and so he died there before *Hashem*.

י וַיִּחַר־אַף יְהוָה בְּעֻזָּא וַיַּכֵּהוּ עַל אֲשֶׁר־שָׁלַח יָדוֹ עַל־הָאָרוֹן וַיָּמָת שָׁם לִפְנֵי אֱלֹהִים:

11 *David* was distressed because *Hashem* had burst out against Uzza; and that place was named Perez-uzzah, as it is still called.

יא וַיִּחַר לְדָוִיד כִּי־פָרַץ יְהוָה פֶּרֶץ בְּעֻזָּא וַיִּקְרָא לַמָּקוֹם הַהוּא פֶּרֶץ עֻזָּא עַד הַיּוֹם הַזֶּה:

A large crowd gathers at the Western Wall to celebrate the Jewish festivals

13:2 That they should gather together to us King *David* assembled the People of Israel before bringing the *Aron HaBrit* to its resting place in *Yerushalayim*. The Ark is the symbol of the covenant between the Children of Israel and God, as it says, "And deposit in the *Aron* [the tablets of] the Pact which I will give you" (Exodus 25:16). The verses in Exodus continue to elaborate about the function of the *Aron*: "There I will meet with you, and I will impart to you – from above the cover, from between the two cherubim that are on top of the *Aron HaBrit*" (Exodus 25:22). Since the Lord continues to communicate with the people from above the *Aron* after the revelation at Sinai, this means that the Ark is the means through which He expresses His continued commitment to the covenant and His closeness with the people. *David* therefore felt that the entire nation should take part in the ceremony marking the transference of the Ark to *Yerushalayim*.

¹² *David* was afraid of *Hashem* that day; he said, "How can I bring the *Aron* of *Hashem* here?"

יב וַיִּירָא דָוִיד אֶת־הָאֱלֹהִים בַּיּוֹם הַהוּא לֵאמֹר הֵיךְ אָבִיא אֵלַי אֵת אֲרוֹן הָאֱלֹהִים:

¹³ So *David* did not remove the *Aron* to his place in the City of *David*; instead, he diverted it to the house of *Oved Edom* the Gittite.

יג וְלֹא־הֵסִיר דָוִיד אֶת־הָאָרוֹן אֵלָיו אֶל־עִיר דָוִיד וַיַּטֵּהוּ אֶל־בֵּית עֹבֵד־אֱדֹם הַגִּתִּי:

¹⁴ The *Aron* of *Hashem* remained in the house of *Oved Edom*, in its own abode, three months, and *Hashem* blessed the house of *Oved Edom* and all he had.

יד וַיֵּשֶׁב אֲרוֹן הָאֱלֹהִים עִם־בֵּית עֹבֵד אֱדֹם בְּבֵיתוֹ שְׁלֹשָׁה חֳדָשִׁים וַיְבָרֶךְ יְהֹוָה אֶת־בֵּית עֹבֵד־אֱדֹם וְאֶת־כָּל־אֲשֶׁר־לוֹ:

14

¹ King Hiram of Tyre sent envoys to *David* with cedar logs, stonemasons, and carpenters to build a palace for him.

יד א וַיִּשְׁלַח חִירָם [חוּרָם] מֶלֶךְ־צֹר מַלְאָכִים אֶל־דָוִיד וַעֲצֵי אֲרָזִים וְחָרָשֵׁי קִיר וְחָרָשֵׁי עֵצִים לִבְנוֹת לוֹ בָּיִת:

² Thus *David* knew that *Hashem* had established him as king over *Yisrael*, and that his kingship was highly exalted for the sake of His people *Yisrael*.

ב וַיֵּדַע דָוִיד כִּי־הֱכִינוֹ יְהֹוָה לְמֶלֶךְ עַל־יִשְׂרָאֵל כִּי־נִשֵּׂאת לְמַעְלָה מַלְכוּתוֹ בַּעֲבוּר עַמּוֹ יִשְׂרָאֵל:

³ *David* took more wives in *Yerushalayim*, and *David* begot more sons and daughters.

ג וַיִּקַּח דָוִיד עוֹד נָשִׁים בִּירוּשָׁלָםִ וַיּוֹלֶד דָוִיד עוֹד בָּנִים וּבָנוֹת:

⁴ These are the names of the children born to him in *Yerushalayim*: Shammua, Shobab, *Natan*, and *Shlomo*;

ד וְאֵלֶּה שְׁמוֹת הַיְלוּדִים אֲשֶׁר הָיוּ־לוֹ בִּירוּשָׁלָםִ שַׁמּוּעַ וְשׁוֹבָב נָתָן וּשְׁלֹמֹה:

⁵ Ibhar, Elishua, and Elpelet;

ה וְיִבְחָר וֶאֱלִישׁוּעַ וְאֶלְפָּלֶט:

⁶ Nogah, Nepheg, and Japhia;

ו וְנֹגַהּ וְנֶפֶג וְיָפִיעַ:

⁷ Elishama, Beeliada, and Eliphelet.

ז וֶאֱלִישָׁמָע וּבְעֶלְיָדָע וֶאֱלִיפָלֶט:

⁸ When the Philistines heard that *David* had been anointed king over all *Yisrael*, all the Philistines went up in search of *David*; but *David* heard of it, and he went out to them.

ח וַיִּשְׁמְעוּ פְלִשְׁתִּים כִּי־נִמְשַׁח דָוִיד לְמֶלֶךְ עַל־כָּל־יִשְׂרָאֵל וַיַּעֲלוּ כָל־פְּלִשְׁתִּים לְבַקֵּשׁ אֶת־דָוִיד וַיִּשְׁמַע דָוִיד וַיֵּצֵא לִפְנֵיהֶם:

⁹ The Philistines came and raided the Valley of Rephaim.

ט וּפְלִשְׁתִּים בָּאוּ וַיִּפְשְׁטוּ בְּעֵמֶק רְפָאִים:

¹⁰ *David* inquired of *Hashem*, "Shall I go up against the Philistines? Will You deliver them into my hands?" And *Hashem* answered him, "Go up, and I will deliver them into your hands."

י וַיִּשְׁאַל דָוִיד בֵּאלֹהִים לֵאמֹר הַאֶעֱלֶה עַל־פְּלִשְׁתִּיִּים [פְּלִשְׁתִּים] וּנְתַתָּם בְּיָדִי וַיֹּאמֶר לוֹ יְהֹוָה עֲלֵה וּנְתַתִּים בְּיָדֶךָ:

*va-yish-AL da-VEED bay-lo-HEEM lay-MOR ha-e-e-LEH al p'-lish-TEEM
un-ta-TAM b'-ya-DEE va-YO-mer LO a-do-NAI a-LAY un-ta-TEEM b'-ya-DE-kha*

14:10 Shall I go up against the Philistines *David* understood that success is dependent upon God's consent and aid. Therefore, although he is a superior warrior and general, he asks the Almighty if he should proceed before attacking the Philistines. By doing so, *David* teaches a crucial lesson about the importance of acting within the bounds of divine consent, especially in God's chosen land.

Sunrise over Masada

11 Thereupon *David* ascended Baal-perazim, and *David* defeated them there. *David* said, "*Hashem* burst out against my enemies by my hands as waters burst out." That is why that place was named Baal-perazim.

יא וַיַּעֲלוּ בְּבַעַל־פְּרָצִים וַיַּכֵּם שָׁם דָּוִיד וַיֹּאמֶר דָּוִיד פָּרַץ הָאֱלֹהִים אֶת־אוֹיְבַי בְּיָדִי כְּפֶרֶץ מָיִם עַל־כֵּן קָרְאוּ שֵׁם־הַמָּקוֹם הַהוּא בַּעַל פְּרָצִים:

12 They abandoned their gods there, and *David* ordered these to be burned.

יב וַיַּעַזְבוּ־שָׁם אֶת־אֱלֹהֵיהֶם וַיֹּאמֶר דָּוִיד וַיִּשָּׂרְפוּ בָּאֵשׁ:

13 Once again the Philistines raided the valley.

יג וַיֹּסִיפוּ עוֹד פְּלִשְׁתִּים וַיִּפְשְׁטוּ בָּעֵמֶק:

14 *David* inquired of *Hashem* once more, and *Hashem* answered, "Do not go up after them, but circle around them and confront them at the baca trees.

יד וַיִּשְׁאַל עוֹד דָּוִיד בֵּאלֹהִים וַיֹּאמֶר לוֹ הָאֱלֹהִים לֹא תַעֲלֶה אַחֲרֵיהֶם הָסֵב מֵעֲלֵיהֶם וּבָאתָ לָהֶם מִמּוּל הַבְּכָאִים:

15 And when you hear the sound of marching in the tops of the baca trees, then go out to battle, for *Hashem* will be going in front of you to attack the Philistine forces."

טו וִיהִי כְּשָׁמְעֲךָ אֶת־קוֹל הַצְּעָדָה בְּרָאשֵׁי הַבְּכָאִים אָז תֵּצֵא בַמִּלְחָמָה כִּי־יָצָא הָאֱלֹהִים לְפָנֶיךָ לְהַכּוֹת אֶת־מַחֲנֵה פְלִשְׁתִּים:

16 *David* did as *Hashem* had commanded him; and they routed the Philistines from *Givon* all the way to Gezer.

טז וַיַּעַשׂ דָּוִיד כַּאֲשֶׁר צִוָּהוּ הָאֱלֹהִים וַיַּכּוּ אֶת־מַחֲנֵה פְלִשְׁתִּים מִגִּבְעוֹן וְעַד־גָּזְרָה:

17 *David* became famous throughout the lands, and *Hashem* put the fear of him in all the nations.

יז וַיֵּצֵא שֵׁם־דָּוִיד בְּכָל־הָאֲרָצוֹת וַיהֹוָה נָתַן אֶת־פַּחְדּוֹ עַל־כָּל־הַגּוֹיִם:

15

1 He had houses made for himself in the City of *David*, and he prepared a place for the *Aron* of *Hashem*, and pitched a tent for it.

א וַיַּעַשׂ־לוֹ בָתִּים בְּעִיר דָּוִיד וַיָּכֶן מָקוֹם לַאֲרוֹן הָאֱלֹהִים וַיֶּט־לוֹ אֹהֶל: טו

2 Then *David* gave orders that none but the *Leviim* were to carry the *Aron* of *Hashem*, for *Hashem* had chosen them to carry the *Aron* of *Hashem* and to minister to Him forever.

ב אָז אָמַר דָּוִיד לֹא לָשֵׂאת אֶת־אֲרוֹן הָאֱלֹהִים כִּי אִם־הַלְוִיִּם כִּי־בָם בָּחַר יְהֹוָה לָשֵׂאת אֶת־אֲרוֹן יְהֹוָה וּלְשָׁרְתוֹ עַד־עוֹלָם:

3 *David* assembled all *Yisrael* in *Yerushalayim* to bring up the *Aron* of *Hashem* to its place, which he had prepared for it.

ג וַיַּקְהֵל דָּוִיד אֶת־כָּל־יִשְׂרָאֵל אֶל־יְרוּשָׁלִָם לְהַעֲלוֹת אֶת־אֲרוֹן יְהֹוָה אֶל־מְקוֹמוֹ אֲשֶׁר־הֵכִין לוֹ:

va-yak-HAYL da-VEED et kol yis-ra-AYL el y'-ru-sha-LA-im l'-ha-a-LOT et a-RON a-do-NAI el m'-ko-MO a-sher hay-KHEEN LO

4 Then *David* gathered together the Aaronides and the *Leviim*:

ד וַיֶּאֱסֹף דָּוִיד אֶת־בְּנֵי אַהֲרֹן וְאֶת־הַלְוִיִּם:

The Western Wall in *Yerushalayim*

15:3 *David* assembled all *Yisrael* in *Yerushalayim* *David* summoned the entire Nation of Israel to bring the *Aron HaBrit* to its place in the heart of *Yerushalayim*. Such a public demonstration was necessary because this was a truly momentous event: King *David* was bringing the spiritual center, or focal point, of the people to the spiritual center of the land. This highlights the never-ending bond between the People of Israel and the Land of Israel, which is cemented by their covenant with the God of Israel.

5 the sons of *Kehat*: Uriel the officer and his kinsmen – 120;

ה לִבְנֵי קְהָת אוּרִיאֵל הַשָּׂר וְאֶחָיו מֵאָה וְעֶשְׂרִים:

6 the sons of *Merari*: Asaiah the officer and his kinsmen – 220;

ו לִבְנֵי מְרָרִי עֲשָׂיָה הַשָּׂר וְאֶחָיו מָאתַיִם וְעֶשְׂרִים:

7 the sons of *Gershom*: *Yoel* the officer and his kinsmen – 130;

ז לִבְנֵי גֵרְשׁוֹם יוֹאֵל הַשָּׂר וְאֶחָיו מֵאָה וּשְׁלֹשִׁים:

8 the sons of Elizaphan: *Shemaya* the officer and his kinsmen – 200;

ח לִבְנֵי אֱלִיצָפָן שְׁמַעְיָה הַשָּׂר וְאֶחָיו מָאתָיִם:

9 the sons of *Chevron*: Eliel the officer and his kinsmen – 80;

ט לִבְנֵי חֶבְרוֹן אֱלִיאֵל הַשָּׂר וְאֶחָיו שְׁמוֹנִים:

10 the sons of Uzziel: *Aminadav* the officer and his kinsmen – 112.

י לִבְנֵי עֻזִּיאֵל עַמִּינָדָב הַשָּׂר וְאֶחָיו מֵאָה וּשְׁנֵים עָשָׂר:

11 *David* sent for *Tzadok* and *Evyatar* the *Kohanim*, and for the *Leviim*: Uriel, Asaiah, *Yoel*, Shemaya, Eliel, and *Aminadav*.

יא וַיִּקְרָא דָוִיד לְצָדוֹק וּלְאֶבְיָתָר הַכֹּהֲנִים וְלַלְוִיִּם לְאוּרִיאֵל עֲשָׂיָה וְיוֹאֵל שְׁמַעְיָה וֶאֱלִיאֵל וְעַמִּינָדָב:

12 He said to them, "You are the heads of the clans of the *Leviim*; sanctify yourselves, you and your kinsmen, and bring up the *Aron* of *Hashem* God of *Yisrael* to [the place] I have prepared for it.

יב וַיֹּאמֶר לָהֶם אַתֶּם רָאשֵׁי הָאָבוֹת לַלְוִיִּם הִתְקַדְּשׁוּ אַתֶּם וַאֲחֵיכֶם וְהַעֲלִיתֶם אֵת אֲרוֹן יְהוָה אֱלֹהֵי יִשְׂרָאֵל אֶל־הֲכִינוֹתִי לוֹ:

13 Because you were not there the first time, *Hashem* our God burst out against us, for we did not show due regard for Him."

יג כִּי לְמַבָּרִאשׁוֹנָה לֹא אַתֶּם פָּרַץ יְהוָה אֱלֹהֵינוּ בָּנוּ כִּי־לֹא דְרַשְׁנֻהוּ כַּמִּשְׁפָּט:

14 The *Kohanim* and *Leviim* sanctified themselves in order to bring up the *Aron* of *Hashem* God of *Yisrael*.

יד וַיִּתְקַדְּשׁוּ הַכֹּהֲנִים וְהַלְוִיִּם לְהַעֲלוֹת אֶת־אֲרוֹן יְהוָה אֱלֹהֵי יִשְׂרָאֵל:

15 The *Leviim* carried the *Aron* of *Hashem* by means of poles on their shoulders, as *Moshe* had commanded in accordance with the word of *Hashem*.

טו וַיִּשְׂאוּ בְנֵי־הַלְוִיִּם אֵת אֲרוֹן הָאֱלֹהִים כַּאֲשֶׁר צִוָּה מֹשֶׁה כִּדְבַר יְהוָה בִּכְתֵפָם בַּמֹּטוֹת עֲלֵיהֶם:

16 *David* ordered the officers of the *Leviim* to install their kinsmen, the singers, with musical instruments, harps, lyres, and cymbals, joyfully making their voices heard.

טז וַיֹּאמֶר דָּוִיד לְשָׂרֵי הַלְוִיִּם לְהַעֲמִיד אֶת־אֲחֵיהֶם הַמְשֹׁרְרִים בִּכְלֵי־שִׁיר נְבָלִים וְכִנֹּרוֹת וּמְצִלְתָּיִם מַשְׁמִעִים לְהָרִים־בְּקוֹל לְשִׂמְחָה:

17 So the *Leviim* installed *Hayman* son of *Yoel* and, of his kinsmen, *Asaf* son of *Berechya*; and, of the sons of *Merari* their kinsmen, Ethan son of Kushaiah.

יז וַיַּעֲמִידוּ הַלְוִיִּם אֵת הֵימָן בֶּן־יוֹאֵל וּמִן־אֶחָיו אָסָף בֶּן־בֶּרֶכְיָהוּ וּמִן־בְּנֵי מְרָרִי אֲחֵיהֶם אֵיתָן בֶּן־קוּשָׁיָהוּ:

18 Together with them were their kinsmen of second rank, *Zecharya*, Ben, Jaaziel, Shemiramoth, *Yechiel*, Unni, *Eliav*, Benaiah, Maaseiah, Mattithiah, Eliphalehu, Mikneiah, *Oved Edom* and Jeiel the gatekeepers.

יח וְעִמָּהֶם אֲחֵיהֶם הַמִּשְׁנִים זְכַרְיָהוּ בֵּן וְיַעֲזִיאֵל וּשְׁמִירָמוֹת וִיחִיאֵל וְעֻנִּי אֱלִיאָב וּבְנָיָהוּ וּמַעֲשֵׂיָהוּ וּמַתִּתְיָהוּ וֶאֱלִיפְלֵהוּ וּמִקְנֵיָהוּ וְעֹבֵד אֱדֹם וִיעִיאֵל הַשֹּׁעֲרִים:

19 Also the singers *Hayman*, *Asaf*, and Ethan to sound the bronze cymbals,

יט וְהַמְשֹׁרְרִים הֵימָן אָסָף וְאֵיתָן בִּמְצִלְתַּיִם נְחֹשֶׁת לְהַשְׁמִיעַ:

²⁰ and *Zecharya*, Aziel, Shemiramoth, *Yechiel*, Unni, *Eliav*, Maaseiah, and Benaiah with harps on alamoth;

²¹ also Mattithiah, Eliphalehu, Mikneiah, Obededom, Jeiel, and Azaziah, with lyres to lead on the sheminith;

²² also Chenaniah, officer of the *Leviim* in song; he was in charge of the song because he was a master.

²³ *Berechya* and *Elkana* were gatekeepers for the *Aron*.

²⁴ Shebaniah, Joshaphat, Nethanel, Amasai, *Zecharya*, Benaiah, and *Eliezer* the *Kohanim* sounded the trumpets before the *Aron* of *Hashem*, and Obededom and Jehiah were gatekeepers for the *Aron*.

²⁵ Then *David* and the elders of *Yisrael* and the officers of the thousands who were going to bring up the *Aron Brit Hashem* from the house of *Oved Edom* were joyful.

²⁶ Since *Hashem* helped the *Leviim* who were carrying the *Aron Brit Hashem*, they sacrificed seven bulls and seven rams.

²⁷ Now *David* and all the *Leviim* who were carrying the *Aron*, and the singers and Chenaniah, officer of song of the singers, were wrapped in robes of fine linen, and *David* wore a linen ephod.

²⁸ All *Yisrael* brought up the *Aron Brit Hashem* with shouts and with blasts of the *shofar*, with trumpets and cymbals, playing on harps and lyres.

²⁹ As the *Aron Brit Hashem* arrived at the City of *David*, *Michal* daughter of *Shaul* looked out of the window and saw King *David* leaping and dancing, and she despised him for it.

16 ¹ They brought in the *Aron* of *Hashem* and set it up inside the tent that *David* had pitched for it, and they sacrificed burnt offerings and offerings of well-being before *Hashem*.

² When *David* finished sacrificing the burnt offerings and the offerings of well-being, he blessed the people in the name of *Hashem*.

³ And he distributed to every person in *Yisrael* – man and woman alike – to each a loaf of bread, a cake made in a pan, and a raisin cake.

כ וּזְכַרְיָה וַעֲזִיאֵל וּשְׁמִירָמוֹת וִיחִיאֵל וְעֻנִּי וֶאֱלִיאָב וּמַעֲשֵׂיָהוּ וּבְנָיָהוּ בִּנְבָלִים עַל־עֲלָמוֹת:

כא וּמַתִּתְיָהוּ וֶאֱלִיפְלֵהוּ וּמִקְנֵיָהוּ וְעֹבֵד אֱדֹם וִיעִיאֵל וַעֲזַזְיָהוּ בְּכִנֹּרוֹת עַל־הַשְּׁמִינִית לְנַצֵּחַ:

כב וּכְנַנְיָהוּ שַׂר־הַלְוִיִּם בְּמַשָּׂא יָסֹר בַּמַּשָּׂא כִּי מֵבִין הוּא:

כג וּבֶרֶכְיָה וְאֶלְקָנָה שֹׁעֲרִים לָאָרוֹן:

כד וּשְׁבַנְיָהוּ וְיוֹשָׁפָט וּנְתַנְאֵל וַעֲמָשַׂי וּזְכַרְיָהוּ וּבְנָיָהוּ וֶאֱלִיעֶזֶר הַכֹּהֲנִים מַחְצְרִים [מַחְצְרִים] בַּחֲצֹצְרוֹת לִפְנֵי אֲרוֹן הָאֱלֹהִים וְעֹבֵד אֱדֹם וִיחִיָּה שֹׁעֲרִים לָאָרוֹן:

כה וַיְהִי דָוִיד וְזִקְנֵי יִשְׂרָאֵל וְשָׂרֵי הָאֲלָפִים הַהֹלְכִים לְהַעֲלוֹת אֶת־אֲרוֹן בְּרִית־יהוה מִן־בֵּית עֹבֵד־אֱדֹם בְּשִׂמְחָה:

כו וַיְהִי בֶּעְזֹר הָאֱלֹהִים אֶת־הַלְוִיִּם נֹשְׂאֵי אֲרוֹן בְּרִית־יהוה וַיִּזְבְּחוּ שִׁבְעָה־פָרִים וְשִׁבְעָה אֵילִים:

כז וְדָוִיד מְכֻרְבָּל בִּמְעִיל בּוּץ וְכָל־הַלְוִיִּם הַנֹּשְׂאִים אֶת־הָאָרוֹן וְהַמְשֹׁרְרִים וּכְנַנְיָה הַשַּׂר הַמַּשָּׂא הַמְשֹׁרְרִים וְעַל־דָּוִיד אֵפוֹד בָּד:

כח וְכָל־יִשְׂרָאֵל מַעֲלִים אֶת־אֲרוֹן בְּרִית־יהוה בִּתְרוּעָה וּבְקוֹל שׁוֹפָר וּבַחֲצֹצְרוֹת וּבִמְצִלְתָּיִם מַשְׁמִעִים בִּנְבָלִים וְכִנֹּרוֹת:

כט וַיְהִי אֲרוֹן בְּרִית יהוה בָּא עַד־עִיר דָּוִיד וּמִיכַל בַּת־שָׁאוּל נִשְׁקְפָה בְּעַד הַחַלּוֹן וַתֵּרֶא אֶת־הַמֶּלֶךְ דָּוִיד מְרַקֵּד וּמְשַׂחֵק וַתִּבֶז לוֹ בְּלִבָּהּ:

טז א וַיָּבִיאוּ אֶת־אֲרוֹן הָאֱלֹהִים וַיַּצִּיגוּ אֹתוֹ בְּתוֹךְ הָאֹהֶל אֲשֶׁר נָטָה־לוֹ דָּוִיד וַיַּקְרִיבוּ עֹלוֹת וּשְׁלָמִים לִפְנֵי הָאֱלֹהִים:

ב וַיְכַל דָּוִיד מֵהַעֲלוֹת הָעֹלָה וְהַשְּׁלָמִים וַיְבָרֶךְ אֶת־הָעָם בְּשֵׁם יהוה:

ג וַיְחַלֵּק לְכָל־אִישׁ יִשְׂרָאֵל מֵאִישׁ וְעַד־אִשָּׁה לְאִישׁ כִּכַּר־לֶחֶם וְאֶשְׁפָּר וַאֲשִׁישָׁה:

⁴ He appointed *Leviim* to minister before the *Aron* of *Hashem*, to invoke, to praise, and to extol God of *Yisrael*:

ד וַיִּתֵּן לִפְנֵי אֲרוֹן יְהוָה מִן־הַלְוִיִּם מְשָׁרְתִים וּלְהַזְכִּיר וּלְהוֹדוֹת וּלְהַלֵּל לַיהוָה אֱלֹהֵי יִשְׂרָאֵל:

⁵ *Asaf* the chief, *Zecharya* second in rank, Jeiel, Shemiramoth, *Yechiel*, Mattithiah, *Eliav*, Benaiah, *Oved Edom*, and Jeiel, with harps and lyres, and *Asaf* sounding the cymbals,

ה אָסָף הָרֹאשׁ וּמִשְׁנֵהוּ זְכַרְיָה יְעִיאֵל וּשְׁמִירָמוֹת וִיחִיאֵל וּמַתִּתְיָה וֶאֱלִיאָב וּבְנָיָהוּ וְעֹבֵד אֱדֹם וִיעִיאֵל בִּכְלֵי נְבָלִים וּבְכִנֹּרוֹת וְאָסָף בַּמְצִלְתַּיִם מַשְׁמִיעַ:

⁶ and Benaiah and *Yachaziel* the *Kohanim*, with trumpets, regularly before the *Aron Brit Hashem*.

ו וּבְנָיָהוּ וְיַחֲזִיאֵל הַכֹּהֲנִים בַּחֲצֹצְרוֹת תָּמִיד לִפְנֵי אֲרוֹן בְּרִית־הָאֱלֹהִים:

⁷ Then, on that day, *David* first commissioned *Asaf* and his kinsmen to give praise to *Hashem*:

ז בַּיּוֹם הַהוּא אָז נָתַן דָּוִיד בָּרֹאשׁ לְהֹדוֹת לַיהוָה בְּיַד־אָסָף וְאֶחָיו:

⁸ "Praise *Hashem*; call on His name; proclaim His deeds among the peoples.

ח הוֹדוּ לַיהוָה קִרְאוּ בִשְׁמוֹ הוֹדִיעוּ בָעַמִּים עֲלִילֹתָיו:

⁹ Sing praises unto Him; speak of all His wondrous acts.

ט שִׁירוּ לוֹ זַמְּרוּ־לוֹ שִׂיחוּ בְּכָל־נִפְלְאֹתָיו:

¹⁰ Exult in His holy name; let all who seek *Hashem* rejoice.

י הִתְהַלְלוּ בְּשֵׁם קָדְשׁוֹ יִשְׂמַח לֵב מְבַקְשֵׁי יְהוָה:

¹¹ Turn to *Hashem*, to His might; seek His presence constantly.

יא דִּרְשׁוּ יְהוָה וְעֻזּוֹ בַּקְּשׁוּ פָנָיו תָּמִיד:

¹² Remember the wonders He has done; His portents and the judgments He has pronounced,

יב זִכְרוּ נִפְלְאֹתָיו אֲשֶׁר עָשָׂה מֹפְתָיו וּמִשְׁפְּטֵי־פִיהוּ:

¹³ O offspring of *Yisrael*, His servant, O descendants of *Yaakov*, His chosen ones.

יג זֶרַע יִשְׂרָאֵל עַבְדּוֹ בְּנֵי יַעֲקֹב בְּחִירָיו:

¹⁴ He is *Hashem* our God; His judgments are throughout the earth.

יד הוּא יְהוָה אֱלֹהֵינוּ בְּכָל־הָאָרֶץ מִשְׁפָּטָיו:

¹⁵ Be ever mindful of His covenant, the promise He gave for a thousand generations,

טו זִכְרוּ לְעוֹלָם בְּרִיתוֹ דָּבָר צִוָּה לְאֶלֶף דּוֹר:

¹⁶ that He made with *Avraham*, swore to *Yitzchak*,

טז אֲשֶׁר כָּרַת אֶת־אַבְרָהָם וּשְׁבוּעָתוֹ לְיִצְחָק:

¹⁷ and confirmed in a decree for *Yaakov*, for *Yisrael*, as an eternal covenant,

יז וַיַּעֲמִידֶהָ לְיַעֲקֹב לְחֹק לְיִשְׂרָאֵל בְּרִית עוֹלָם:

¹⁸ saying, 'To you I will give the land of Canaan as your allotted heritage.'

יח לֵאמֹר לְךָ אֶתֵּן אֶרֶץ־כְּנָעַן חֶבֶל נַחֲלַתְכֶם:

lay-MOR l'-KHA e-TAYN E-retz k'-NA-an KHE-vel na-kha-lat-KHEM

¹⁹ You were then few in number, a handful, merely sojourning there,

יט בִּהְיוֹתְכֶם מְתֵי מִסְפָּר כִּמְעַט וְגָרִים בָּהּ:

²⁰ wandering from nation to nation, from one kingdom to another.

כ וַיִּתְהַלְּכוּ מִגּוֹי אֶל־גּוֹי וּמִמַּמְלָכָה אֶל־עַם אַחֵר:

²¹ He allowed no one to oppress them; He reproved kings on their account,

כא לֹא־הִנִּיחַ לְאִישׁ לְעָשְׁקָם וַיּוֹכַח עֲלֵיהֶם מְלָכִים:

22 'Do not touch My anointed ones; do not harm My *Neviim*.'

כב אַל־תִּגְּעוּ בִּמְשִׁיחָי וּבִנְבִיאַי אַל־תָּרֵעוּ:

23 "Sing to *Hashem*, all the earth. proclaim His victory day after day.

כג שִׁירוּ לַיהֹוָה כָּל־הָאָרֶץ בַּשְּׂרוּ מִיּוֹם־אֶל־יוֹם יְשׁוּעָתוֹ:

24 Tell of His glory among the nations, His wondrous deeds among all peoples.

כד סַפְּרוּ בַגּוֹיִם אֶת־כְּבוֹדוֹ בְּכָל־הָעַמִּים נִפְלְאֹתָיו:

25 For *Hashem* is great and much acclaimed, He is held in awe by all divine beings.

כה כִּי גָדוֹל יְהֹוָה וּמְהֻלָּל מְאֹד וְנוֹרָא הוּא עַל־כָּל־אֱלֹהִים:

26 All the gods of the peoples are mere idols, but *Hashem* made the heavens.

כו כִּי כָּל־אֱלֹהֵי הָעַמִּים אֱלִילִים וַיהֹוָה שָׁמַיִם עָשָׂה:

27 Glory and majesty are before Him; strength and joy are in His place.

כז הוֹד וְהָדָר לְפָנָיו עֹז וְחֶדְוָה בִּמְקֹמוֹ:

28 "Ascribe to *Hashem*, O families of the peoples, ascribe to *Hashem* glory and strength.

כח הָבוּ לַיהֹוָה מִשְׁפְּחוֹת עַמִּים הָבוּ לַיהֹוָה כָּבוֹד וָעֹז:

29 Ascribe to *Hashem* the glory of His name, bring tribute and enter before Him, bow down to *Hashem* majestic in holiness.

כט הָבוּ לַיהֹוָה כְּבוֹד שְׁמוֹ שְׂאוּ מִנְחָה וּבֹאוּ לְפָנָיו הִשְׁתַּחֲווּ לַיהֹוָה בְּהַדְרַת־קֹדֶשׁ:

30 Tremble in His presence, all the earth! The world stands firm; it cannot be shaken.

ל חִילוּ מִלְּפָנָיו כָּל־הָאָרֶץ אַף־תִּכּוֹן תֵּבֵל בַּל־תִּמּוֹט:

31 Let the heavens rejoice and the earth exult; let them declare among the nations, "*Hashem* is King!"

לא יִשְׂמְחוּ הַשָּׁמַיִם וְתָגֵל הָאָרֶץ וְיֹאמְרוּ בַגּוֹיִם יְהֹוָה מָלָךְ:

32 Let the sea and all within it thunder, the fields and everything in them exult;

לב יִרְעַם הַיָּם וּמְלוֹאוֹ יַעֲלֹץ הַשָּׂדֶה וְכָל־אֲשֶׁר־בּוֹ:

33 then shall all the trees of the forest shout for joy at the presence of *Hashem*, for He is coming to rule the earth.

לג אָז יְרַנְּנוּ עֲצֵי הַיָּעַר מִלִּפְנֵי יְהֹוָה כִּי־בָא לִשְׁפּוֹט אֶת־הָאָרֶץ:

34 Praise *Hashem* for He is good; His steadfast love is eternal.

לד הוֹדוּ לַיהֹוָה כִּי טוֹב כִּי לְעוֹלָם חַסְדּוֹ:

35 Declare: Deliver us, O *Hashem*, our deliverer, and gather us and save us from the nations, to acclaim Your holy name, to glory in Your praise.

לה וְאִמְרוּ הוֹשִׁיעֵנוּ אֱלֹהֵי יִשְׁעֵנוּ וְקַבְּצֵנוּ וְהַצִּילֵנוּ מִן־הַגּוֹיִם לְהֹדוֹת לְשֵׁם קָדְשֶׁךָ לְהִשְׁתַּבֵּחַ בִּתְהִלָּתֶךָ:

36 Blessed is *Hashem*, God of *Yisrael*, from eternity to eternity." And all the people said "*Amen*" and "Praise *Hashem*."

לו בָּרוּךְ יְהֹוָה אֱלֹהֵי יִשְׂרָאֵל מִן־הָעוֹלָם וְעַד הָעֹלָם וַיֹּאמְרוּ כָל־הָעָם אָמֵן וְהַלֵּל לַיהֹוָה:

37 He left *Asaf* and his kinsmen there before the *Aron Brit Hashem* to minister before the *Aron* regularly as each day required,

לז וַיַּעֲזָב־שָׁם לִפְנֵי אֲרוֹן בְּרִית־יְהֹוָה לְאָסָף וּלְאֶחָיו לְשָׁרֵת לִפְנֵי הָאָרוֹן תָּמִיד לִדְבַר־יוֹם בְּיוֹמוֹ:

38 as well as *Oved Edom* with their kinsmen – 68; also *Oved Edom* son of Jedithun and Hosah as gatekeepers;

לח וְעֹבֵד אֱדֹם וַאֲחֵיהֶם שִׁשִּׁים וּשְׁמוֹנָה וְעֹבֵד אֱדֹם בֶּן־יְדִיתוּן וְחֹסָה לְשֹׁעֲרִים:

³⁹ also *Tzadok* the *Kohen* and his fellow *Kohanim* before the *Mishkan* of *Hashem* at the shrine which was in *Givon*;

לט וְאֵת צָדוֹק הַכֹּהֵן וְאֶחָיו הַכֹּהֲנִים לִפְנֵי מִשְׁכַּן יְהֹוָה בַּבָּמָה אֲשֶׁר בְּגִבְעוֹן:

⁴⁰ to sacrifice burnt offerings to *Hashem* on the *Mizbayach* of the burnt offering regularly, morning and evening, in accordance with what was prescribed in the Teaching of *Hashem* with which He charged *Yisrael*.

מ לְהַעֲלוֹת עֹלוֹת לַיהֹוָה עַל־מִזְבַּח הָעֹלָה תָּמִיד לַבֹּקֶר וְלָעָרֶב וּלְכָל־הַכָּתוּב בְּתוֹרַת יְהֹוָה אֲשֶׁר צִוָּה עַל־יִשְׂרָאֵל:

⁴¹ With them were *Hayman* and *Yedutun* and the other selected men designated by name to give praise to *Hashem*, "For His steadfast love is eternal."

מא וְעִמָּהֶם הֵימָן וִידוּתוּן וּשְׁאָר הַבְּרוּרִים אֲשֶׁר נִקְּבוּ בְּשֵׁמוֹת לְהֹדוֹת לַיהֹוָה כִּי לְעוֹלָם חַסְדּוֹ:

⁴² *Hayman* and *Yedutun* had with them trumpets and cymbals to sound, and instruments for the songs of *Hashem*; and the sons of *Yedutun* were to be at the gate.

מב וְעִמָּהֶם הֵימָן וִידוּתוּן חֲצֹצְרוֹת וּמְצִלְתַּיִם לְמַשְׁמִיעִים וּכְלֵי שִׁיר הָאֱלֹהִים וּבְנֵי יְדוּתוּן לַשָּׁעַר:

*v'-i-ma-HEM hay-MAN vee-du-TUN kha-tzo-tz'-ROT um-tzil-TA-yim
l'-mash-mee-EEM ukh-LAY SHEER ha-e-lo-HEEM uv-NAY y'-du-TUN la-SHA-ar*

⁴³ Then all the people went every one to his home, and *David* returned to greet his household.

מג וַיֵּלְכוּ כָל־הָעָם אִישׁ לְבֵיתוֹ וַיִּסֹּב דָּוִיד לְבָרֵךְ אֶת־בֵּיתוֹ:

17 ¹ When *David* settled in his palace, *David* said to the *Navi Natan*, "Here I am dwelling in a house of cedar, while the *Aron Brit Hashem* is under tent-cloths."

יז א וַיְהִי כַּאֲשֶׁר יָשַׁב דָּוִיד בְּבֵיתוֹ וַיֹּאמֶר דָּוִיד אֶל־נָתָן הַנָּבִיא הִנֵּה אָנֹכִי יוֹשֵׁב בְּבֵית הָאֲרָזִים וַאֲרוֹן בְּרִית־יְהֹוָה תַּחַת יְרִיעוֹת:

² *Natan* said to *David*, "Do whatever you have in mind, for *Hashem* is with you."

ב וַיֹּאמֶר נָתָן אֶל־דָּוִיד כֹּל אֲשֶׁר בִּלְבָבְךָ עֲשֵׂה כִּי הָאֱלֹהִים עִמָּךְ:

³ But that same night the word of *Hashem* came to *Natan*:

ג וַיְהִי בַּלַּיְלָה הַהוּא וַיְהִי דְּבַר־אֱלֹהִים אֶל־נָתָן לֵאמֹר:

⁴ "Go and say to My servant *David*: Thus said *Hashem*: You are not the one to build a house for Me to dwell in.

ד לֵךְ וְאָמַרְתָּ אֶל־דָּוִיד עַבְדִּי כֹּה אָמַר יְהֹוָה לֹא אַתָּה תִּבְנֶה־לִּי הַבַּיִת לָשָׁבֶת:

⁵ From the day that I brought out *Yisrael* to this day, I have not dwelt in a house, but have [gone] from tent to tent and from one *Mishkan* [to another].

ה כִּי לֹא יָשַׁבְתִּי בְּבַיִת מִן־הַיּוֹם אֲשֶׁר הֶעֱלֵיתִי אֶת־יִשְׂרָאֵל עַד הַיּוֹם הַזֶּה וָאֶהְיֶה מֵאֹהֶל אֶל־אֹהֶל וּמִמִּשְׁכָּן:

16:42 Instruments for the songs of *Hashem* This verse describes how when *David* brought the *Aron* to *Yerushalayim*, he offered prayers of thanksgiving to God, accompanied by various musical instruments. The trumpets and cymbals mentioned in this verse, along with the lyres and harps mentioned in *Sefer Divrei Hayamim* I 15:16, were also used during worship in the *Beit Hamikdash*. The music of the Levitical choir and orchestra was an integral part of the divine service of the Holy Temple every day of the year, and was the sweet-est music on earth, as it was the Levitical expression of the music of heaven. In today's Jerusalem, musicologists and expert craftsman work closely with the scholars at the Temple Institute to recreate the "musical instruments of *Hashem*" to be used when the Third Temple will be built.

Statue of a Levite blowing a trumpet, Temple Institute in *Yerushalayim*

6 As I moved about wherever *Yisrael* went, did I ever reproach any of the judges of *Yisrael* whom I appointed to care for My people *Yisrael*: Why have you not built Me a house of cedar?

ו בְּכֹל אֲשֶׁר־הִתְהַלַּכְתִּי בְּכָל־יִשְׂרָאֵל הֲדָבָר דִּבַּרְתִּי אֶת־אַחַד שֹׁפְטֵי יִשְׂרָאֵל אֲשֶׁר צִוִּיתִי לִרְעוֹת אֶת־עַמִּי לֵאמֹר לָמָּה לֹא־בְנִיתֶם לִי בֵּית אֲרָזִים:

7 "Further, say thus to My servant *David*: Thus said the Lord of Hosts: I took you from the pasture, from following the flock, to be ruler of My people *Yisrael*,

ז וְעַתָּה כֹּה־תֹאמַר לְעַבְדִּי לְדָוִיד כֹּה אָמַר יְהוָה צְבָאוֹת אֲנִי לְקַחְתִּיךָ מִן־הַנָּוֶה מִן־אַחֲרֵי הַצֹּאן לִהְיוֹת נָגִיד עַל עַמִּי יִשְׂרָאֵל:

8 and I have been with you wherever you went, and have cut down all your enemies before you. Moreover, I will give you renown like that of the greatest men on earth.

ח וָאֶהְיֶה עִמְּךָ בְּכֹל אֲשֶׁר הָלַכְתָּ וָאַכְרִית אֶת־כָּל־אוֹיְבֶיךָ מִפָּנֶיךָ וְעָשִׂיתִי לְךָ שֵׁם כְּשֵׁם הַגְּדוֹלִים אֲשֶׁר בָּאָרֶץ:

9 I will establish a home for My people *Yisrael* and will plant them firm, so that they shall dwell secure and shall tremble no more. Evil men shall not wear them down anymore as in the past,

ט וְשַׂמְתִּי מָקוֹם לְעַמִּי יִשְׂרָאֵל וּנְטַעְתִּיהוּ וְשָׁכַן תַּחְתָּיו וְלֹא יִרְגַּז עוֹד וְלֹא־יוֹסִיפוּ בְנֵי־עַוְלָה לְבַלֹּתוֹ כַּאֲשֶׁר בָּרִאשׁוֹנָה:

10 ever since I appointed judges over My people *Yisrael*. I will subdue all your enemies. And I declare to you: *Hashem* will build a house for you.

י וּלְמִיָּמִים אֲשֶׁר צִוִּיתִי שֹׁפְטִים עַל־עַמִּי יִשְׂרָאֵל וְהִכְנַעְתִּי אֶת־כָּל־אוֹיְבֶיךָ וָאַגִּד לָךְ וּבַיִת יִבְנֶה־לְּךָ יְהוָה:

11 When your days are done and you follow your fathers, I will raise up your offspring after you, one of your own sons, and I will establish his kingship.

יא וְהָיָה כִּי־מָלְאוּ יָמֶיךָ לָלֶכֶת עִם־אֲבֹתֶיךָ וַהֲקִימוֹתִי אֶת־זַרְעֲךָ אַחֲרֶיךָ אֲשֶׁר יִהְיֶה מִבָּנֶיךָ וַהֲכִינוֹתִי אֶת־מַלְכוּתוֹ:

12 He shall build a house for Me, and I will establish his throne forever.

יב הוּא יִבְנֶה־לִּי בָּיִת וְכֹנַנְתִּי אֶת־כִּסְאוֹ עַד־עוֹלָם:

HU yiv-neh LEE BA-yit v'-kho-nan-TEE et kis-O ad o-LAM

13 I will be a father to him, and he shall be a son to Me, but I will never withdraw My favor from him as I withdrew it from your predecessor.

יג אֲנִי אֶהְיֶה־לּוֹ לְאָב וְהוּא יִהְיֶה־לִּי לְבֵן וְחַסְדִּי לֹא־אָסִיר מֵעִמּוֹ כַּאֲשֶׁר הֲסִירוֹתִי מֵאֲשֶׁר הָיָה לְפָנֶיךָ:

14 I will install him in My house and in My kingship forever, and his throne shall be established forever."

יד וְהַעֲמַדְתִּיהוּ בְּבֵיתִי וּבְמַלְכוּתִי עַד־הָעוֹלָם וְכִסְאוֹ יִהְיֶה נָכוֹן עַד־עוֹלָם:

שלמה

17:12 He shall build a house for me King *David* wants to build the Holy Temple. However, *Hashem* tells him that his son, not he, will be the one to build the *Beit Hamikdash*. As the king who helps conquer the Land of Israel, fights Amalek and solidifies the monarchy, *David* plays an important part in the process of establishing the Israelites in their land. He is even able to make the preparations for the building of the Temple. However, as a warrior, he is not able to build the actual *Beit Hamikdash*, which is intended to promote peace and harmony among the Children of Israel as well as all the nations of the world. In contrast to *David*, his son *Shlomo* (שלמה) is a man of peace, as reflected in his name which derives from the Hebrew word for 'peace,' *shalom* (שלום). *Shlomo*, therefore, is God's choice for the king who will build the Temple. For this same reason, instruments of war and violence were not used in the construction of The *Beit Hamikdash*, so that peace would be built into its very foundation (I Kings 6:7).

Model of the second *Beit Hamikdash* in *Yerushalayim*

15 *Natan* spoke to *David* in accordance with all these words and all this prophecy.

טו כְּכֹל הַדְּבָרִים הָאֵלֶּה וּכְכֹל הֶחָזוֹן הַזֶּה כֵּן דִּבֶּר נָתָן אֶל־דָּוִיד:

16 Then King *David* came and sat before *Hashem*, and he said, "What am I, O *Hashem*, and what is my family, that You have brought me thus far?

טז וַיָּבֹא הַמֶּלֶךְ דָּוִיד וַיֵּשֶׁב לִפְנֵי יְהֹוָה וַיֹּאמֶר מִי־אֲנִי יְהֹוָה אֱלֹהִים וּמִי בֵיתִי כִּי הֲבִיאֹתַנִי עַד־הֲלֹם:

17 Yet even this, O *Hashem*, has seemed too little to You; for You have spoken of Your servant's house for the future. You regard me as a man of distinction, O *Hashem*.

יז וַתִּקְטַן זֹאת בְּעֵינֶיךָ אֱלֹהִים וַתְּדַבֵּר עַל־בֵּית־עַבְדְּךָ לְמֵרָחוֹק וּרְאִיתַנִי כְּתוֹר הָאָדָם הַמַּעֲלָה יְהֹוָה אֱלֹהִים:

18 What more can *David* add regarding the honoring of Your servant? You know Your servant.

יח מַה־יּוֹסִיף עוֹד דָּוִיד אֵלֶיךָ לְכָבוֹד אֶת־עַבְדֶּךָ וְאַתָּה אֶת־עַבְדְּךָ יָדָעְתָּ:

19 *Hashem*, for Your servant's sake, and of Your own accord, You have wrought this great thing, and made known all these great things.

יט יְהֹוָה בַּעֲבוּר עַבְדְּךָ וּכְלִבְּךָ עָשִׂיתָ אֵת כָּל־הַגְּדוּלָּה הַזֹּאת לְהֹדִיעַ אֶת־כָּל־הַגְּדֻלּוֹת:

20 *Hashem*, there is none like You, and there is no other God but You, as we have always heard.

כ יְהֹוָה אֵין כָּמוֹךָ וְאֵין אֱלֹהִים זוּלָתֶךָ בְּכֹל אֲשֶׁר־שָׁמַעְנוּ בְּאָזְנֵינוּ:

21 And who is like Your people *Yisrael*, a unique nation on earth, whom *Hashem* went and redeemed as His people, winning renown for Yourself for great and marvelous deeds, driving out nations before Your people whom You redeemed from Egypt.

כא וּמִי כְּעַמְּךָ יִשְׂרָאֵל גּוֹי אֶחָד בָּאָרֶץ אֲשֶׁר הָלַךְ הָאֱלֹהִים לִפְדּוֹת לוֹ עָם לָשׂוּם לְךָ שֵׁם גְּדֻלּוֹת וְנֹרָאוֹת לְגָרֵשׁ מִפְּנֵי עַמְּךָ אֲשֶׁר־פָּדִיתָ מִמִּצְרַיִם גּוֹיִם:

u-MEE k'-a-m'-KHA yis-ra-AYL GOY e-KHAD ba-A-retz a-SHER ha-LAKH ha-e-lo-HEEM lif-DOT LO AM la-SUM l'-KHA shaym g'-du-LOT v'-no-ra-OT l'-ga-RAYSH mi-p'-NAY a-m'-KHA a-sher pa-DEE-ta mi-mitz-RA-yim go-YIM

22 You have established Your people *Yisrael* as Your very own people forever; and You, *Hashem*, have become their God.

כב וַתִּתֵּן אֶת־עַמְּךָ יִשְׂרָאֵל לְךָ לְעָם עַד־עוֹלָם וְאַתָּה יְהֹוָה הָיִיתָ לָהֶם לֵאלֹהִים:

23 "And now, *Hashem*, let Your promise concerning Your servant and his house be fulfilled forever; and do as You have promised.

כג וְעַתָּה יְהֹוָה הַדָּבָר אֲשֶׁר דִּבַּרְתָּ עַל־עַבְדְּךָ וְעַל־בֵּיתוֹ יֵאָמֵן עַד־עוֹלָם וַעֲשֵׂה כַּאֲשֶׁר דִּבַּרְתָּ:

24 Let it be fulfilled that Your name be glorified forever, in that men will say, 'the Lord of Hosts, God of *Yisrael*, is *Yisrael*'s God'; and may the house of Your servant *David* be established before You.

כד וְיֵאָמֵן וְיִגְדַּל שִׁמְךָ עַד־עוֹלָם לֵאמֹר יְהֹוָה צְבָאוֹת אֱלֹהֵי יִשְׂרָאֵל אֱלֹהִים לְיִשְׂרָאֵל וּבֵית־דָּוִיד עַבְדְּךָ נָכוֹן לְפָנֶיךָ:

17:21 And who is like Your people *Yisrael* In this verse, Israel is referred to not only as a "people" but as a "singular nation on earth." Throughout history, the unique character of the Jewish people has been variously described, by friend and foe alike, as a people, a nation, a religion and even a race. It is hard to pin down the exact nature of the Jewish people, but it certainly seems to contain elements of both nationality and spirituality that deeply connect Jews with one another. During the first bloody week of the Yom Kippur War, a soldier stationed on the Golan Heights asked Prime Minister Golda Meir about the many casualties Israel had suffered, "I know we will win, but is all our sacrifice worthwhile?" The Prime Minister replied, "If our sacrifices are for ourselves, then no. But if for the sake of the whole Jewish people, then I believe with all my heart that any price is worthwhile." Her message was that the State of Israel would serve as a safe haven not only for Israelis, but for the entire People of Israel all over the world. Indeed, "who is like Your people *Yisrael*"?

Prime Minister
Golda Meir
(1898–1978)

44

25 Because You, my God, have revealed to Your
servant that You will build a house for him, Your
servant has ventured to pray to You.

26 And now, *Hashem*, You are *Hashem* and You have
made this gracious promise to Your servant.

27 Now, it has pleased You to bless Your servant's
house, that it abide before You forever; for You,
Hashem, have blessed and are blessed forever."

18 1 Sometime afterward, *David* attacked the Philistines
and subdued them; and *David* took Gath and its
dependencies from the Philistines.

2 He also defeated the Moabites; the Moabites
became tributary vassals of *David*.

3 *David* defeated Hadadezer, king of Zobahhamath,
who was on his way to set up his monument at the
Euphrates River.

4 *David* captured 1,000 chariots and 7,000 horsemen
and 20,000 foot soldiers of his force; and *David*
hamstrung all the chariot horses except for 100,
which he retained.

5 And when the Arameans of Damascus came to the
aid of King Hadadezer of Zobah-hamath, *David*
struck down 22,000 of the Arameans.

6 *David* stationed [garrisons] in Aram of Damascus,
and the Arameans became tributary vassals of *David*.
Hashem gave *David* victory wherever he went.

7 *David* took the gold shields carried by Hadadezer's
retinue and brought them to *Yerushalayim*;

8 and from Tibbath and Cun, towns of Hadadezer,
David took a vast amount of copper, from which
Shlomo made the bronze tank, the columns, and
the bronze vessels.

9 When King Tou of Hamath heard that *David* had
defeated the entire army of King Hadadezer of
Zobah,

10 he sent his son Hadoram to King *David* to greet
him and to congratulate him on his military victory
over Hadadezer – for Hadadezer had been at war
with Tou; [he brought with him] all manner of
gold, silver, and copper objects.

11 King *David* dedicated these to *Hashem*, along with
the other silver and gold that he had taken from all
the nations: from Edom, Moab, and Ammon; from
the Philistines and the Amalekites.

כה כִּי אַתָּה אֱלֹהַי גָּלִיתָ אֶת־אֹזֶן עַבְדְּךָ
לִבְנוֹת לוֹ בָּיִת עַל־כֵּן מָצָא עַבְדְּךָ
לְהִתְפַּלֵּל לְפָנֶיךָ׃

כו וְעַתָּה יְהוָה אַתָּה־הוּא הָאֱלֹהִים וַתְּדַבֵּר
עַל־עַבְדְּךָ הַטּוֹבָה הַזֹּאת׃

כז וְעַתָּה הוֹאַלְתָּ לְבָרֵךְ אֶת־בֵּית עַבְדְּךָ
לִהְיוֹת לְעוֹלָם לְפָנֶיךָ כִּי־אַתָּה יְהוָה
בֵּרַכְתָּ וּמְבֹרָךְ לְעוֹלָם׃

יח א וַיְהִי אַחֲרֵי־כֵן וַיַּךְ דָּוִיד אֶת־פְּלִשְׁתִּים
וַיַּכְנִיעֵם וַיִּקַּח אֶת־גַּת וּבְנֹתֶיהָ מִיַּד
פְּלִשְׁתִּים׃

ב וַיַּךְ אֶת־מוֹאָב וַיִּהְיוּ מוֹאָב עֲבָדִים
לְדָוִיד נֹשְׂאֵי מִנְחָה׃

ג וַיַּךְ דָּוִיד אֶת־הֲדַדְעֶזֶר מֶלֶךְ־צוֹבָה
חֲמָתָה בְּלֶכְתּוֹ לְהַצִּיב יָדוֹ בִּנְהַר־פְּרָת׃

ד וַיִּלְכֹּד דָּוִיד מִמֶּנּוּ אֶלֶף רֶכֶב וְשִׁבְעַת
אֲלָפִים פָּרָשִׁים וְעֶשְׂרִים אֶלֶף אִישׁ
רַגְלִי וַיְעַקֵּר דָּוִיד אֶת־כָּל־הָרֶכֶב וַיּוֹתֵר
מִמֶּנּוּ מֵאָה רָכֶב׃

ה וַיָּבֹא אֲרַם דַּרְמֶשֶׂק לַעְזוֹר לַהֲדַדְעֶזֶר
מֶלֶךְ צוֹבָה וַיַּךְ דָּוִיד בַּאֲרָם עֶשְׂרִים־
וּשְׁנַיִם אֶלֶף אִישׁ׃

ו וַיָּשֶׂם דָּוִיד בַּאֲרַם דַּרְמֶשֶׂק וַיְהִי אֲרָם
לְדָוִיד עֲבָדִים נֹשְׂאֵי מִנְחָה וַיּוֹשַׁע יְהוָה
לְדָוִיד בְּכֹל אֲשֶׁר הָלָךְ׃

ז וַיִּקַּח דָּוִיד אֵת שִׁלְטֵי הַזָּהָב אֲשֶׁר הָיוּ
עַל עַבְדֵי הֲדַדְעָזֶר וַיְבִיאֵם יְרוּשָׁלִָם׃

ח וּמִטִּבְחַת וּמִכּוּן עָרֵי הֲדַדְעֶזֶר לָקַח דָּוִיד
נְחֹשֶׁת רַבָּה מְאֹד בָּהּ עָשָׂה שְׁלֹמֹה אֶת־
יָם הַנְּחֹשֶׁת וְאֶת־הָעַמּוּדִים וְאֵת כְּלֵי
הַנְּחֹשֶׁת׃

ט וַיִּשְׁמַע תֹּעוּ מֶלֶךְ חֲמָת כִּי הִכָּה דָּוִיד
אֶת־כָּל־חֵיל הֲדַדְעֶזֶר מֶלֶךְ־צוֹבָה׃

י וַיִּשְׁלַח אֶת־הֲדוֹרָם־בְּנוֹ אֶל־הַמֶּלֶךְ־דָּוִיד
לִשְׁאָול־[לִשְׁאָל־] לוֹ לְשָׁלוֹם וּלְבָרְכוֹ
עַל אֲשֶׁר נִלְחַם בַּהֲדַדְעֶזֶר וַיַּכֵּהוּ כִּי־
אִישׁ מִלְחֲמוֹת תֹּעוּ הָיָה הֲדַדְעָזֶר וְכֹל
כְּלֵי זָהָב וָכֶסֶף וּנְחֹשֶׁת׃

יא גַּם־אֹתָם הִקְדִּישׁ דָּוִיד הַמֶּלֶךְ לַיהוָה
עִם־הַכֶּסֶף וְהַזָּהָב אֲשֶׁר נָשָׂא מִכָּל־
הַגּוֹיִם מֵאֱדוֹם וּמִמּוֹאָב וּמִבְּנֵי עַמּוֹן
וּמִפְּלִשְׁתִּים וּמֵעֲמָלֵק׃

¹² Abshai son of *Tzeruya* struck down Edom in the Valley of Salt, 18,000 in all.

יב וְאַבְשַׁי בֶּן־צְרוּיָה הִכָּה אֶת־אֱדוֹם בְּגֵיא הַמֶּלַח שְׁמוֹנָה עָשָׂר אָלֶף:

¹³ He stationed garrisons in Edom, and all the Edomites became vassals of *David*. *Hashem* gave *David* victory wherever he went.

יג וַיָּשֶׂם בֶּאֱדוֹם נְצִיבִים וַיִּהְיוּ כָל־אֱדוֹם עֲבָדִים לְדָוִיד וַיּוֹשַׁע יְהוָה אֶת־דָּוִיד בְּכֹל אֲשֶׁר הָלָךְ:

¹⁴ *David* reigned over all *Yisrael*, and *David* executed true justice among all his people.

יד וַיִּמְלֹךְ דָּוִיד עַל־כָּל־יִשְׂרָאֵל וַיְהִי עֹשֶׂה מִשְׁפָּט וּצְדָקָה לְכָל־עַמּוֹ:

va-yim-LOKH da-VEED al kol yis-ra-AYL vai-HEE
o-SEH mish-PAT utz-da-KÁH l'-khol a-MO

¹⁵ *Yoav* son of *Tzeruya* was commander of the army; *Yehoshafat* son of *Achilud* was recorder;

טו וְיוֹאָב בֶּן־צְרוּיָה עַל־הַצָּבָא וִיהוֹשָׁפָט בֶּן־אֲחִילוּד מַזְכִּיר:

¹⁶ *Tzadok* son of *Achituv* and *Avimelech* son of *Evyatar* were *Kohanim*; Shavsha was scribe;

טז וְצָדוֹק בֶּן־אֲחִיטוּב וַאֲבִימֶלֶךְ בֶּן־אֶבְיָתָר כֹּהֲנִים וְשַׁוְשָׁא סוֹפֵר:

¹⁷ Benaiah son of *Yehoyada* was commander of the Cherethites and the Pelethites; and *David*'s sons were first ministers of the king.

יז וּבְנָיָהוּ בֶּן־יְהוֹיָדָע עַל־הַכְּרֵתִי וְהַפְּלֵתִי וּבְנֵי־דָוִיד הָרִאשֹׁנִים לְיַד הַמֶּלֶךְ:

19 ¹ Sometime afterward, Nahash the king of the Ammonites died, and his son succeeded him as king.

יט א וַיְהִי אַחֲרֵי־כֵן וַיָּמָת נָחָשׁ מֶלֶךְ בְּנֵי־עַמּוֹן וַיִּמְלֹךְ בְּנוֹ תַּחְתָּיו:

² *David* said, "I will keep faith with Hanun son of Nahash, since his father kept faith with me." *David* sent messengers with condolences to him over his father. But when *David*'s courtiers came to the land of Ammon to Hanun, with condolences,

ב וַיֹּאמֶר דָּוִיד אֶעֱשֶׂה־חֶסֶד עִם־חָנוּן בֶּן־נָחָשׁ כִּי־עָשָׂה אָבִיו עִמִּי חֶסֶד וַיִּשְׁלַח דָּוִיד מַלְאָכִים לְנַחֲמוֹ עַל־אָבִיו וַיָּבֹאוּ עַבְדֵי דָוִיד אֶל־אֶרֶץ בְּנֵי־עַמּוֹן אֶל־חָנוּן לְנַחֲמוֹ:

va-YO-mer da-VEED e-e-seh KHE-sed im kha-NUN ben na-KHASH
kee a-SAH a-VEEV i-MEE KHE-sed va-yish-LAKH da-VEED
mal-a-KHEEM l'-na-kha-MO al a-VEEV va-ya-vo-U av-DAY
da-VEED el E-retz b'-NAY a-MON el kha-NUN l'-na-kha-MO

Yerushalayim, City of Righteousness

18:14 *David* executed true justice among all his people
King *David*'s rule over Israel is defined by justice and righteousness. As emphasized by the prophets, executing justice and righteousness is the charge of the Jewish people and their leaders in the Land of Israel (see Ezekiel 45:9). In this sense, *David* was an ideal king. While he did conduct several wars, his reign is ultimately defined not by violence, but justice. He was a just king, providing a model for all to follow. Following in King *David*'s path will bring the ultimate redemption, as the prophet *Yeshayahu* says, "*Tzion* shall be saved in the judgment, her repentant ones, in the retribution." (Isaiah 1:27).

19:2 I will keep faith with Hanun son of Nahash *David* sends messages to comfort Hanun over the death of his father, even though he is a rival king. With this action, *David* shows that he understood that when it comes to relations between nations, there are considerations that go beyond mere politics. By disgracing *David*'s emissaries, though, Hanun shows that he does not believe in the possibility of friendship or gratitude between kings. *David*'s first instinct, however, is that statecraft doesn't nullify the necessity for kindness. By behaving in this manner, *David* shows what makes the kings of Israel who reign in *Yerushalayim* unique. After all, *Yerushalayim* is called "City of Righteousness, Faithful City" (Isaiah 1:26).

3 the Ammonite officials said to Hanun, "Do you think *David* is really honoring your father just because he sent you men with condolences? Why, it is to explore, to subvert, and to spy out the land that his courtiers have come to you."

ג וַיֹּאמְרוּ שָׂרֵי בְנֵי־עַמּוֹן לְחָנוּן הַמְכַבֵּד דָּוִיד אֶת־אָבִיךָ בְּעֵינֶיךָ כִּי־שָׁלַח לְךָ מְנַחֲמִים הֲלֹא בַּעֲבוּר לַחְקֹר וְלַהֲפֹךְ וּלְרַגֵּל הָאָרֶץ בָּאוּ עֲבָדָיו אֵלֶיךָ:

4 So Hanun seized *David*'s courtiers, shaved them, and cut away half of their garments up to the buttocks, and sent them off.

ד וַיִּקַּח חָנוּן אֶת־עַבְדֵי דָוִיד וַיְגַלְּחֵם וַיִּכְרֹת אֶת־מַדְוֵיהֶם בַּחֵצִי עַד־הַמִּפְשָׂעָה וַיְשַׁלְּחֵם:

5 When *David* was told about the men, he dispatched others to meet them, for the men were greatly embarrassed. And the king gave orders, "Stay in *Yericho* until your beards grow back; then you can return."

ה וַיֵּלְכוּ וַיַּגִּידוּ לְדָוִיד עַל־הָאֲנָשִׁים וַיִּשְׁלַח לִקְרָאתָם כִּי־הָיוּ הָאֲנָשִׁים נִכְלָמִים מְאֹד וַיֹּאמֶר הַמֶּלֶךְ שְׁבוּ בִירֵחוֹ עַד אֲשֶׁר־יְצַמַּח זְקַנְכֶם וְשַׁבְתֶּם:

6 The Ammonites realized that they had incurred the wrath of *David*; so Hanun and the Ammonites sent 1,000 silver *kikarim* to hire chariots and horsemen from Aram-Naharaim, Aram-maacah, and Zobah.

ו וַיִּרְאוּ בְּנֵי עַמּוֹן כִּי הִתְבָּאֲשׁוּ עִם־דָּוִיד וַיִּשְׁלַח חָנוּן וּבְנֵי עַמּוֹן אֶלֶף כִּכַּר־כֶּסֶף לִשְׂכֹּר לָהֶם מִן־אֲרַם נַהֲרַיִם וּמִן־אֲרַם מַעֲכָה וּמִצּוֹבָה רֶכֶב וּפָרָשִׁים:

7 They hired 32,000 chariots, the king of Maacah, and his army, who came and encamped before Medeba. The Ammonites were mobilized from their cities and came to do battle.

ז וַיִּשְׂכְּרוּ לָהֶם שְׁנַיִם וּשְׁלֹשִׁים אֶלֶף רֶכֶב וְאֶת־מֶלֶךְ מַעֲכָה וְאֶת־עַמּוֹ וַיָּבֹאוּ וַיַּחֲנוּ לִפְנֵי מֵידְבָא וּבְנֵי עַמּוֹן נֶאֶסְפוּ מֵעָרֵיהֶם וַיָּבֹאוּ לַמִּלְחָמָה:

8 On learning this, *David* sent out *Yoav* and the whole army, [including] the professional fighters.

ח וַיִּשְׁמַע דָּוִיד וַיִּשְׁלַח אֶת־יוֹאָב וְאֵת כָּל־צְבָא הַגִּבּוֹרִים:

9 The Ammonites marched out and took up their battle position at the entrance of the city, while the kings who came [took their stand] separately in the open.

ט וַיֵּצְאוּ בְּנֵי עַמּוֹן וַיַּעַרְכוּ מִלְחָמָה פֶּתַח הָעִיר וְהַמְּלָכִים אֲשֶׁר־בָּאוּ לְבַדָּם בַּשָּׂדֶה:

10 *Yoav* saw that there was a battle line against him both front and rear. So he made a selection from all the picked men of *Yisrael* and arrayed them against the Arameans,

י וַיַּרְא יוֹאָב כִּי־הָיְתָה פְנֵי־הַמִּלְחָמָה אֵלָיו פָּנִים וְאָחוֹר וַיִּבְחַר מִכָּל־בָּחוּר בְּיִשְׂרָאֵל וַיַּעֲרֹךְ לִקְרַאת אֲרָם:

11 and the rest of the troops he put under the command of his brother Abishai and arrayed them against the Ammonites.

יא וְאֵת יֶתֶר הָעָם נָתַן בְּיַד אַבְשַׁי אָחִיו וַיַּעַרְכוּ לִקְרַאת בְּנֵי עַמּוֹן:

12 *Yoav* said, "If the Arameans prove too strong for me, you come to my aid; and if the Ammonites prove too strong for you, I will come to your aid.

יב וַיֹּאמֶר אִם־תֶּחֱזַק מִמֶּנִּי אֲרָם וְהָיִיתָ לִּי לִתְשׁוּעָה וְאִם־בְּנֵי עַמּוֹן יֶחֶזְקוּ מִמְּךָ וְהוֹשַׁעְתִּיךָ:

13 Let us be strong and resolute for the sake of our people and the towns of our God; and *Hashem* will do what He deems right."

יג חֲזַק וְנִתְחַזְּקָה בְּעַד־עַמֵּנוּ וּבְעַד עָרֵי אֱלֹהֵינוּ וַיהוָה הַטּוֹב בְּעֵינָיו יַעֲשֶׂה:

14 *Yoav* and the troops with him marched into battle against the Arameans, who fled before him.

יד וַיִּגַּשׁ יוֹאָב וְהָעָם אֲשֶׁר־עִמּוֹ לִפְנֵי אֲרָם לַמִּלְחָמָה וַיָּנוּסוּ מִפָּנָיו:

¹⁵ And when the Ammonites saw that the Arameans had fled, they too fled before his brother Abishai, and withdrew into the city. So *Yoav* went to *Yerushalayim*.

טו וּבְנֵי עַמּוֹן רָאוּ כִּי־נָס אֲרָם וַיָּנֻסוּ גַם־הֵם מִפְּנֵי אַבְשַׁי אָחִיו וַיָּבֹאוּ הָעִירָה וַיָּבֹא יוֹאָב יְרוּשָׁלָ͏ִם׃

¹⁶ When the Arameans saw that they had been routed by *Yisrael*, they sent messengers to bring out the Arameans from across the Euphrates; Shophach, Hadadezer's army commander, led them.

טז וַיַּרְא אֲרָם כִּי נִגְּפוּ לִפְנֵי יִשְׂרָאֵל וַיִּשְׁלְחוּ מַלְאָכִים וַיּוֹצִיאוּ אֶת־אֲרָם אֲשֶׁר מֵעֵבֶר הַנָּהָר וְשׁוֹפַךְ שַׂר־צְבָא הֲדַדְעֶזֶר לִפְנֵיהֶם׃

¹⁷ *David* was informed of it; he assembled all *Yisrael*, crossed the *Yarden*, and came and took up positions against them. *David* drew up his forces against Aram; and they fought with him.

יז וַיֻּגַּד לְדָוִיד וַיֶּאֱסֹף אֶת־כָּל־יִשְׂרָאֵל וַיַּעֲבֹר הַיַּרְדֵּן וַיָּבֹא אֲלֵהֶם וַיַּעֲרֹךְ אֲלֵהֶם וַיַּעֲרֹךְ דָּוִיד לִקְרַאת אֲרָם מִלְחָמָה וַיִּלָּחֲמוּ עִמּוֹ׃

¹⁸ But the Arameans were put to flight by *Yisrael*. *David* killed 7,000 Aramean charioteers and 40,000 footmen; he also killed Shophach, the army commander.

יח וַיָּנָס אֲרָם מִלִּפְנֵי יִשְׂרָאֵל וַיַּהֲרֹג דָּוִיד מֵאֲרָם שִׁבְעַת אֲלָפִים רֶכֶב וְאַרְבָּעִים אֶלֶף אִישׁ רַגְלִי וְאֵת שׁוֹפַךְ שַׂר־הַצָּבָא הֵמִית׃

¹⁹ And when all the vassals of Hadadezer saw that they had been routed by *Yisrael*, they submitted to *David* and became his vassals. And the Arameans would not help the Ammonites anymore.

יט וַיִּרְאוּ עַבְדֵי הֲדַדְעֶזֶר כִּי נִגְּפוּ לִפְנֵי יִשְׂרָאֵל וַיַּשְׁלִימוּ עִם־דָּוִיד וַיַּעַבְדֻהוּ וְלֹא־אָבָה אֲרָם לְהוֹשִׁיעַ אֶת־בְּנֵי־עַמּוֹן עוֹד׃

20 ¹ At the turn of the year, the season when kings go out [to battle], *Yoav* led out the army force and devastated the land of Ammon, and then besieged Rabbah, while *David* remained in *Yerushalayim*; *Yoav* reduced Rabbah and left it in ruins.

כ א וַיְהִי לְעֵת תְּשׁוּבַת הַשָּׁנָה לְעֵת צֵאת הַמְּלָכִים וַיִּנְהַג יוֹאָב אֶת־חֵיל הַצָּבָא וַיַּשְׁחֵת אֶת־אֶרֶץ בְּנֵי־עַמּוֹן וַיָּבֹא וַיָּצַר אֶת־רַבָּה וְדָוִיד יֹשֵׁב בִּירוּשָׁלָ͏ִם וַיַּךְ יוֹאָב אֶת־רַבָּה וַיֶּהֶרְסֶהָ׃

vai-HEE l'-AYT t'-shu-VAT ha-sha-NAH l'-AYT TZAYT ha-m'-la-KHEEM
va-yin-HAG yo-AV et KHAYL ha-tza-VA va-yash-KHAYT et E-retz
b'-NAY a-MON va-ya-VO va-YA-tzar et ra-BAH v'-da-VEED yo-SHAYV
bee-ru-sha-LA-im va-YAKH yo-AV et ra-BAH va-ye-her-SE-ha

² *David* took the crown from the head of their king; he found that it weighed a *kikar* of gold, and in it were precious stones. It was placed on *David's* head. He also carried off a vast amount of booty from the city.

ב וַיִּקַּח דָּוִיד אֶת־עֲטֶרֶת־מַלְכָּם מֵעַל רֹאשׁוֹ וַיִּמְצָאָהּ מִשְׁקַל כִּכַּר־זָהָב וּבָהּ אֶבֶן יְקָרָה וַתְּהִי עַל־רֹאשׁ דָּוִיד וּשְׁלַל הָעִיר הוֹצִיא הַרְבֵּה מְאֹד׃

Blowing the *shofar*, a call to repent

20:1 The turn of the year In this verse, the beginning of the year is called *teshuvat hashanah,* (תשובת השנה) which literally means "the turn of the year." The year is cyclical in nature, and the holidays, which are the focus of the Jewish year, are repeated at the same time each year. In a certain sense, the beginning of a new year is in fact a return to previous years, going back to the times of *Moshe* and the Exodus from Egypt which many of the holidays commemorate. Furthermore, the Jewish New Year focuses on God's judgement and man's repentance. The word *teshuva* (תשובה), which means 'return', also means 'repentance'. Hence, the expression *"Teshuvat Hashanah"* also refers to the time of year when we are obligated to repent.

תשובת השנה

³ He led out the people who lived there and he hacked them with saws and iron threshing boards and axes; *David* did thus to all the towns of Ammon. Then *David* and all the troops returned to *Yerushalayim.*

ג וְאֶת־הָעָם אֲשֶׁר־בָּהּ הוֹצִיא וַיָּשַׂר בַּמְּגֵרָה וּבַחֲרִיצֵי הַבַּרְזֶל וּבַמְּגֵרוֹת וְכֵן יַעֲשֶׂה דָוִיד לְכֹל עָרֵי בְנֵי־עַמּוֹן וַיָּשָׁב דָּוִיד וְכָל־הָעָם יְרוּשָׁלָ͏ִם:

⁴ After this, fighting broke out with the Philistines at Gezer; that was when Sibbecai the Hushathite killed Sippai, a descendant of the Rephaim, and they were humbled.

ד וַיְהִי אַחֲרֵיכֵן וַתַּעֲמֹד מִלְחָמָה בְּגֶזֶר עִם־פְּלִשְׁתִּים אָז הִכָּה סִבְּכַי הַחֻשָׁתִי אֶת־סִפַּי מִילִדֵי הָרְפָאִים וַיִּכָּנֵעוּ:

⁵ Again there was fighting with the Philistines, and *Elchanan* son of *Yair* killed Lahmi, the brother of Goliath the Gittite; his spear had a shaft like a weaver's beam.

ה וַתְּהִי־עוֹד מִלְחָמָה אֶת־פְּלִשְׁתִּים וַיַּךְ אֶלְחָנָן בֶּן־[יָעוּר] אֶת־לַחְמִי אֲחִי גָּלְיָת הַגִּתִּי וְעֵץ חֲנִיתוֹ כִּמְנוֹר אֹרְגִים:

⁶ Once again there was fighting at Gath. There was a giant of a man who had twenty-four fingers [and toes], six [on each hand] and six [on each foot]; he too was descended from the Raphah.

ו וַתְּהִי־עוֹד מִלְחָמָה בְּגַת וַיְהִי אִישׁ מִדָּה וְאֶצְבְּעֹתָיו שֵׁשׁ־וָשֵׁשׁ עֶשְׂרִים וְאַרְבַּע וְגַם־הוּא נוֹלַד לְהָרָפָא:

⁷ When he taunted *Yisrael, Yehonatan* son of *David's* brother Shimea killed him.

ז וַיְחָרֵף אֶת־יִשְׂרָאֵל וַיַּכֵּהוּ יְהוֹנָתָן בֶּן־שִׁמְעָא אֲחִי דָוִיד:

⁸ These were descended from the Raphah in Gath, and they fell by the hands of *David* and his men.

ח אֵל נוּלְּדוּ לְהָרָפָא בְּגַת וַיִּפְּלוּ בְיַד־דָּוִיד וּבְיַד־עֲבָדָיו:

21 ¹ Satan arose against *Yisrael* and incited *David* to number *Yisrael.*

כא א וַיַּעֲמֹד שָׂטָן עַל־יִשְׂרָאֵל וַיָּסֶת אֶת־דָּוִיד לִמְנוֹת אֶת־יִשְׂרָאֵל:

² *David* said to *Yoav* and to the commanders of the army, "Go and count *Yisrael* from *Be'er Sheva* to *Dan* and bring me information as to their number."

ב וַיֹּאמֶר דָּוִיד אֶל־יוֹאָב וְאֶל־שָׂרֵי הָעָם לְכוּ סִפְרוּ אֶת־יִשְׂרָאֵל מִבְּאֵר שֶׁבַע וְעַד־דָּן וְהָבִיאוּ אֵלַי וְאֵדְעָה אֶת־מִסְפָּרָם:

³ *Yoav* answered, "May *Hashem* increase His people a hundredfold; my lord king, are they not all subjects of my lord? Why should my lord require this? Why should it be a cause of guilt for *Yisrael*?"

ג וַיֹּאמֶר יוֹאָב יוֹסֵף יְהֹוָה עַל־עַמּוֹ כָּהֵם מֵאָה פְעָמִים הֲלֹא אֲדֹנִי הַמֶּלֶךְ כֻּלָּם לַאדֹנִי לַעֲבָדִים לָמָּה יְבַקֵּשׁ זֹאת אֲדֹנִי לָמָּה יִהְיֶה לְאַשְׁמָה לְיִשְׂרָאֵל:

⁴ However, the king's command to *Yoav* remained firm, so *Yoav* set out and traversed all *Yisrael;* he then came to *Yerushalayim.*

ד וּדְבַר־הַמֶּלֶךְ חָזַק עַל־יוֹאָב וַיֵּצֵא יוֹאָב וַיִּתְהַלֵּךְ בְּכָל־יִשְׂרָאֵל וַיָּבֹא יְרוּשָׁלָ͏ִם:

⁵ *Yoav* reported to *David* the number of the people that had been recorded. All *Yisrael* comprised 1,100,000 ready to draw the sword, while in *Yehuda* there were 470,000 men ready to draw the sword.

ה וַיִּתֵּן יוֹאָב אֶת־מִסְפַּר מִפְקַד־הָעָם אֶל־דָּוִיד וַיְהִי כָל־יִשְׂרָאֵל אֶלֶף אֲלָפִים וּמֵאָה אֶלֶף אִישׁ שֹׁלֵף חֶרֶב וִיהוּדָה אַרְבַּע מֵאוֹת וְשִׁבְעִים אֶלֶף אִישׁ שֹׁלֵף חָרֶב:

⁶ He did not record among them *Levi* and *Binyamin,* because the king's command had become repugnant to *Yoav.*

ו וְלֵוִי וּבִנְיָמִן לֹא פָקַד בְּתוֹכָם כִּי־נִתְעַב דְּבַר־הַמֶּלֶךְ אֶת־יוֹאָב:

7 *Hashem* was displeased about this matter and He struck *Yisrael.*

8 *David* said to *Hashem,* "I have sinned grievously in having done this thing; please remit the guilt of Your servant, for I have acted foolishly."

9 *Hashem* ordered *Gad, David's* seer:

10 "Go and tell *David:* Thus said *Hashem:* I offer you three things; choose one of them and I will bring it upon you."

11 *Gad* came to *David* and told him, "Thus said *Hashem:* Select for yourself

12 a three-year famine; or that you be swept away three months before your adversaries with the sword of your enemies overtaking you; or three days of the sword of *Hashem,* pestilence in the land, the angel of *Hashem* wreaking destruction throughout the territory of *Yisrael.* Now consider what reply I shall take back to Him who sent me."

13 *David* said to *Gad,* "I am in great distress. Let me fall into the hands of *Hashem,* for His compassion is very great; and let me not fall into the hands of men."

14 *Hashem* sent a pestilence upon *Yisrael,* and 70,000 men fell in *Yisrael.*

15 *Hashem* sent an angel to *Yerushalayim* to destroy it, but as he was about to wreak destruction, *Hashem* saw and renounced further punishment and said to the destroying angel, "Enough! Stay your hand!" The angel of *Hashem* was then standing by the threshing floor of Ornan the Jebusite.

16 *David* looked up and saw the angel of *Hashem* standing between heaven and earth, with a drawn sword in his hand directed against *Yerushalayim. David* and the elders, covered in sackcloth, threw themselves on their faces.

17 *David* said to *Hashem,* "Was it not I alone who ordered the numbering of the people? I alone am guilty, and have caused severe harm; but these sheep, what have they done? *Hashem* my God, let Your hand fall upon me and my father's house, and let not Your people be plagued!"

ז וַיֵּרַע בְּעֵינֵי הָאֱלֹהִים עַל־הַדָּבָר הַזֶּה וַיַּךְ אֶת־יִשְׂרָאֵל:

ח וַיֹּאמֶר דָּוִיד אֶל־הָאֱלֹהִים חָטָאתִי מְאֹד אֲשֶׁר עָשִׂיתִי אֶת־הַדָּבָר הַזֶּה וְעַתָּה הַעֲבֶר־נָא אֶת־עֲוֹן עַבְדְּךָ כִּי נִסְכַּלְתִּי מְאֹד:

ט וַיְדַבֵּר יְהֹוָה אֶל־גָּד חֹזֵה דָוִיד לֵאמֹר:

י לֵךְ וְדִבַּרְתָּ אֶל־דָּוִיד לֵאמֹר כֹּה אָמַר יְהֹוָה שָׁלוֹשׁ אֲנִי נֹטֶה עָלֶיךָ בְּחַר־לְךָ אַחַת מֵהֵנָּה וְאֶעֱשֶׂה־לָּךְ:

יא וַיָּבֹא גָד אֶל־דָּוִיד וַיֹּאמֶר לוֹ כֹּה־אָמַר יְהֹוָה קַבֶּל־לָךְ:

יב אִם־שָׁלוֹשׁ שָׁנִים רָעָב וְאִם־שְׁלֹשָׁה חֳדָשִׁים נִסְפֶּה מִפְּנֵי־צָרֶיךָ וְחֶרֶב אוֹיְבֶךָ לְמַשֶּׂגֶת וְאִם־שְׁלֹשֶׁת יָמִים חֶרֶב יְהֹוָה וְדֶבֶר בָּאָרֶץ וּמַלְאַךְ יְהֹוָה מַשְׁחִית בְּכָל־גְּבוּל יִשְׂרָאֵל וְעַתָּה רְאֵה מָה־אָשִׁיב אֶת־שֹׁלְחִי דָּבָר:

יג וַיֹּאמֶר דָּוִיד אֶל־גָּד צַר־לִי מְאֹד אֶפְּלָה־נָּא בְיַד־יְהֹוָה כִּי־רַבִּים רַחֲמָיו מְאֹד וּבְיַד־אָדָם אַל־אֶפֹּל:

יד וַיִּתֵּן יְהֹוָה דֶּבֶר בְּיִשְׂרָאֵל וַיִּפֹּל מִיִּשְׂרָאֵל שִׁבְעִים אֶלֶף אִישׁ:

טו וַיִּשְׁלַח הָאֱלֹהִים מַלְאָךְ לִירוּשָׁלַ͏ִם לְהַשְׁחִיתָהּ וּכְהַשְׁחִית רָאָה יְהֹוָה וַיִּנָּחֶם עַל־הָרָעָה וַיֹּאמֶר לַמַּלְאָךְ הַמַּשְׁחִית רַב עַתָּה הֶרֶף יָדֶךָ וּמַלְאַךְ יְהֹוָה עֹמֵד עִם־גֹּרֶן אָרְנָן הַיְבוּסִי:

טז וַיִּשָּׂא דָוִיד אֶת־עֵינָיו וַיַּרְא אֶת־מַלְאַךְ יְהֹוָה עֹמֵד בֵּין הָאָרֶץ וּבֵין הַשָּׁמַיִם וְחַרְבּוֹ שְׁלוּפָה בְּיָדוֹ נְטוּיָה עַל־יְרוּשָׁלָ͏ִם וַיִּפֹּל דָּוִיד וְהַזְּקֵנִים מְכֻסִּים בַּשַּׂקִּים עַל־פְּנֵיהֶם:

יז וַיֹּאמֶר דָּוִיד אֶל־הָאֱלֹהִים הֲלֹא אֲנִי אָמַרְתִּי לִמְנוֹת בָּעָם וַאֲנִי־הוּא אֲשֶׁר־חָטָאתִי וְהָרֵעַ הֲרֵעוֹתִי וְאֵלֶּה הַצֹּאן מֶה עָשׂוּ יְהֹוָה אֱלֹהַי תְּהִי נָא יָדְךָ בִּי וּבְבֵית אָבִי וּבְעַמְּךָ לֹא לְמַגֵּפָה:

18 The angel of *Hashem* told *Gad* to inform *David* that *David* should go and set up a *Mizbayach* to *Hashem* on the threshing floor of Ornan the Jebusite.

יח וּמַלְאַךְ יְהֹוָה אָמַר אֶל־גָּד לֵאמֹר לְדָוִיד כִּי יַעֲלֶה דָוִיד לְהָקִים מִזְבֵּחַ לַיהֹוָה בְּגֹרֶן אָרְנָן הַיְבֻסִי:

19 *David* went up, following *Gad*'s instructions, which he had delivered in the name of *Hashem*.

יט וַיַּעַל דָּוִיד בִּדְבַר־גָּד אֲשֶׁר דִּבֶּר בְּשֵׁם יְהֹוָה:

20 Ornan too saw the angel; his four sons who were with him hid themselves while Ornan kept on threshing wheat.

כ וַיָּשָׁב אָרְנָן וַיַּרְא אֶת־הַמַּלְאָךְ וְאַרְבַּעַת בָּנָיו עִמּוֹ מִתְחַבְּאִים וְאָרְנָן דָּשׁ חִטִּים:

21 *David* came to Ornan; when Ornan looked up, he saw *David* and came off the threshing floor and bowed low to *David*, with his face to the ground.

כא וַיָּבֹא דָוִיד עַד־אָרְנָן וַיַּבֵּט אָרְנָן וַיַּרְא אֶת־דָּוִיד וַיֵּצֵא מִן־הַגֹּרֶן וַיִּשְׁתַּחוּ לְדָוִיד אַפַּיִם אָרְצָה:

22 *David* said to Ornan, "Sell me the site of the threshing floor, that I may build on it a *Mizbayach* to *Hashem*. Sell it to me at the full price, that the plague against the people will be checked."

כב וַיֹּאמֶר דָּוִיד אֶל־אָרְנָן תְּנָה־לִּי מְקוֹם הַגֹּרֶן וְאֶבְנֶה־בּוֹ מִזְבֵּחַ לַיהֹוָה בְּכֶסֶף מָלֵא תְּנֵהוּ לִי וְתֵעָצַר הַמַּגֵּפָה מֵעַל הָעָם:

23 Ornan said to *David*, "Take it and let my lord the king do whatever he sees fit. See, I donate oxen for burnt offerings, and the threshing boards for wood, as well as wheat for a meal offering – I donate all of it."

כג וַיֹּאמֶר אָרְנָן אֶל־דָּוִיד קַח־לָךְ וְיַעַשׂ אֲדֹנִי הַמֶּלֶךְ הַטּוֹב בְּעֵינָיו רְאֵה נָתַתִּי הַבָּקָר לָעֹלוֹת וְהַמּוֹרִגִּים לָעֵצִים וְהַחִטִּים לַמִּנְחָה הַכֹּל נָתָתִּי:

24 But King *David* replied to Ornan, "No, I will buy them at the full price. I cannot make a present to God of what belongs to you, or sacrifice a burnt offering that has cost me nothing."

כד וַיֹּאמֶר הַמֶּלֶךְ דָּוִיד לְאָרְנָן לֹא כִּי־קָנֹה אֶקְנֶה בְּכֶסֶף מָלֵא כִּי לֹא־אֶשָּׂא אֲשֶׁר־לְךָ לַיהֹוָה וְהַעֲלוֹת עוֹלָה חִנָּם:

*va-YO-mer ha-ME-lekh da-VEED l'-or-NAN LO kee ka-NOH ek-NEH b'-KHE-sef
ma-LAY KEE lo e-SA a-sher l-KHA la-do-NAI v'-ha-a-LOT o-LAH khi-NAM*

25 So *David* paid Ornan for the site 600 *shekalim* worth of gold.

כה וַיִּתֵּן דָּוִיד לְאָרְנָן בַּמָּקוֹם שִׁקְלֵי זָהָב מִשְׁקָל שֵׁשׁ מֵאוֹת:

26 And *David* built there a *Mizbayach* to *Hashem* and sacrificed burnt offerings and offerings of well-being. He invoked *Hashem*, who answered him with fire from heaven on the *Mizbayach* of burnt offerings.

כו וַיִּבֶן שָׁם דָּוִיד מִזְבֵּחַ לַיהֹוָה וַיַּעַל עֹלוֹת וּשְׁלָמִים וַיִּקְרָא אֶל־יְהֹוָה וַיַּעֲנֵהוּ בָאֵשׁ מִן־הַשָּׁמַיִם עַל מִזְבַּח הָעֹלָה:

21:24 I will buy them at the full price King *David* refuses to receive the land upon which he would build the altar as a gift. Instead, he insists on paying full price for it. The first verse of the next chapter reveals that this land *David* purchased would become the permanent location of the *Beit Hamikdash*, the spiritual center of the Jewish people. As such, the ownership of the land must be beyond dispute. When something is given as a gift, the previous owner maintains some small moral claim to it, as he gave it without recompense. By buying the land, as *Avraham* had bought the Cave of Machpelah, *David* guarantees that the Jewish people's claim to the Temple Mount in *Yerushalayim* would be indisputable for all time.

The Temple Mount in *Yerushalayim*

²⁷ *Hashem* ordered the angel to return his sword to its sheath.

כז וַיֹּאמֶר יְהֹוָה לַמַּלְאָךְ וַיָּשֶׁב חַרְבּוֹ אֶל־נְדָנָהּ:

²⁸ At that time, when *David* saw that *Hashem* answered him at the threshing floor of Ornan the Jebusite, then he sacrificed there –

כח בָּעֵת הַהִיא בִּרְאוֹת דָּוִיד כִּי־עָנָהוּ יְהֹוָה בְּגֹרֶן אָרְנָן הַיְבוּסִי וַיִּזְבַּח שָׁם:

²⁹ for the *Mishkan* of *Hashem*, which *Moshe* had made in the wilderness, and the *Mizbayach* of burnt offerings, were at that time in the shrine at *Givon*,

כט וּמִשְׁכַּן יְהֹוָה אֲשֶׁר־עָשָׂה מֹשֶׁה בַמִּדְבָּר וּמִזְבַּח הָעוֹלָה בָּעֵת הַהִיא בַּבָּמָה בְּגִבְעוֹן:

³⁰ and *David* was unable to go to it to worship *Hashem* because he was terrified by the sword of the angel of *Hashem*.

ל וְלֹא־יָכֹל דָּוִיד לָלֶכֶת לְפָנָיו לִדְרֹשׁ אֱלֹהִים כִּי נִבְעַת מִפְּנֵי חֶרֶב מַלְאַךְ יְהֹוָה:

22 ¹ *David* said, "Here will be the House of *Hashem* and here the *Mizbayach* of burnt offerings for *Yisrael*."

כב א וַיֹּאמֶר דָּוִיד זֶה הוּא בֵּית יְהֹוָה הָאֱלֹהִים וְזֶה־מִּזְבֵּחַ לְעֹלָה לְיִשְׂרָאֵל:

² *David* gave orders to assemble the aliens living in the land of *Yisrael*, and assigned them to be hewers, to quarry and dress stones for building the House of *Hashem*.

ב וַיֹּאמֶר דָּוִיד לִכְנוֹס אֶת־הַגֵּרִים אֲשֶׁר בְּאֶרֶץ יִשְׂרָאֵל וַיַּעֲמֵד חֹצְבִים לַחְצוֹב אַבְנֵי גָזִית לִבְנוֹת בֵּית הָאֱלֹהִים:

³ Much iron for nails for the doors of the gates and for clasps did *David* lay aside, and so much copper it could not be weighed,

ג וּבַרְזֶל לָרֹב לַמִּסְמְרִים לְדַלְתוֹת הַשְּׁעָרִים וְלַמְחַבְּרוֹת הֵכִין דָּוִיד וּנְחֹשֶׁת לָרֹב אֵין מִשְׁקָל:

⁴ and cedar logs without number – for the Sidonians and the Tyrians brought many cedar logs to *David*.

ד וַעֲצֵי אֲרָזִים לְאֵין מִסְפָּר כִּי הֵבִיאוּ הַצִּידֹנִים וְהַצֹּרִים עֲצֵי אֲרָזִים לָרֹב לְדָוִיד:

⁵ For *David* thought, "My son *Shlomo* is an untried youth, and the House to be built for *Hashem* is to be made exceedingly great to win fame and glory throughout all the lands; let me then lay aside material for him." So *David* laid aside much material before he died.

ה וַיֹּאמֶר דָּוִיד שְׁלֹמֹה בְנִי נַעַר וָרָךְ וְהַבַּיִת לִבְנוֹת לַיהֹוָה לְהַגְדִּיל לְמַעְלָה לְשֵׁם וּלְתִפְאֶרֶת לְכָל־הָאֲרָצוֹת אָכִינָה נָּא לוֹ וַיָּכֶן דָּוִיד לָרֹב לִפְנֵי מוֹתוֹ:

va-YO-mer da-VEED sh'-lo-MOH v'-NEE NA-ar va-RAKH v'-ha-BA-yit liv-NOT la-do-NAI l'-hag-DEEL l'-MA-lah l'-SHAYM ul-tif-E-ret l'-khol HA-a-ra-TZOT a-KHEE-nah NA LO va-YA-khen da-VEED la-ROV lif-NAY mo-TO

⁶ Then he summoned his son *Shlomo* and charged him with building the House for God of *Yisrael*.

ו וַיִּקְרָא לִשְׁלֹמֹה בְנוֹ וַיְצַוֵּהוּ לִבְנוֹת בַּיִת לַיהֹוָה אֱלֹהֵי יִשְׂרָאֵל:

Stones that were once part of the outer wall of the Second Temple

22:5 Let me then lay aside material for him Even though he has not been instructed to do so, King *David* begins preparations for the construction of the Temple. He feels that if he would leave all of the preparation to *Shlomo*, who was still young at the time, the building project would be delayed significantly. In addition, it is likely that *David* feels an overpowering urge to do whatever he can for God's glory. While he has been told that he will not be able to build the *Beit Hamikdash*, there is nothing stopping him from preparing for its construction. He simply cannot ignore his concern that God's honor is impugned by the lack of a permanent home.

7 *David* said to *Shlomo*, "My son, I wanted to build a House for the name of *Hashem* my God.

וַיֹּאמֶר דָּוִיד לִשְׁלֹמֹה בנו [בְּנִי] אֲנִי הָיָה עִם־לְבָבִי לִבְנוֹת בַּיִת לְשֵׁם יְהוָה אֱלֹהָי: ז

8 But the word of *Hashem* came to me, saying, 'You have shed much blood and fought great battles; you shall not build a House for My name for you have shed much blood on the earth in My sight.

וַיְהִי עָלַי דְּבַר־יְהוָה לֵאמֹר דָּם לָרֹב שָׁפַכְתָּ וּמִלְחָמוֹת גְּדֹלוֹת עָשִׂיתָ לֹא־תִבְנֶה בַיִת לִשְׁמִי כִּי דָּמִים רַבִּים שָׁפַכְתָּ אַרְצָה לְפָנָי: ח

9 But you will have a son who will be a man at rest, for I will give him rest from all his enemies on all sides; *Shlomo* will be his name and I shall confer peace and quiet on *Yisrael* in his time.

הִנֵּה־בֵן נוֹלָד לָךְ הוּא יִהְיֶה אִישׁ מְנוּחָה וַהֲנִחוֹתִי לוֹ מִכָּל־אוֹיְבָיו מִסָּבִיב כִּי שְׁלֹמֹה יִהְיֶה שְׁמוֹ וְשָׁלוֹם וָשֶׁקֶט אֶתֵּן עַל־יִשְׂרָאֵל בְּיָמָיו: ט

10 He will build a House for My name; he shall be a son to Me and I to him a father, and I will establish his throne of kingship over *Yisrael* forever.'

הוּא־יִבְנֶה בַיִת לִשְׁמִי וְהוּא יִהְיֶה־ לִי לְבֵן וַאֲנִי־לוֹ לְאָב וַהֲכִינוֹתִי כִּסֵּא מַלְכוּתוֹ עַל־יִשְׂרָאֵל עַד־עוֹלָם: י

11 Now, my son, may *Hashem* be with you, and may you succeed in building the House of *Hashem* your God as He promised you would.

עַתָּה בְנִי יְהִי יְהוָה עִמָּךְ וְהִצְלַחְתָּ וּבָנִיתָ בֵּית יְהוָה אֱלֹהֶיךָ כַּאֲשֶׁר דִּבֶּר עָלֶיךָ: יא

12 Only let *Hashem* give you sense and understanding and put you in charge of *Yisrael* and the observance of the Teaching of *Hashem* your God.

אַךְ יִתֶּן־לְךָ יְהוָה שֵׂכֶל וּבִינָה וִיצַוְּךָ עַל־יִשְׂרָאֵל וְלִשְׁמוֹר אֶת־תּוֹרַת יְהוָה אֱלֹהֶיךָ: יב

13 Then you shall succeed, if you observantly carry out the laws and the rules that *Hashem* charged *Moshe* to lay upon *Yisrael*. Be strong and of good courage; do not be afraid or dismayed.

אָז תַּצְלִיחַ אִם־תִּשְׁמוֹר לַעֲשׂוֹת אֶת־ הַחֻקִּים וְאֶת־הַמִּשְׁפָּטִים אֲשֶׁר צִוָּה יְהוָה אֶת־מֹשֶׁה עַל־יִשְׂרָאֵל חֲזַק וֶאֱמָץ אַל־תִּירָא וְאַל־תֵּחָת: יג

14 See, by denying myself, I have laid aside for the House of *Hashem* one hundred thousand *kikarim* of gold and one million *kikarim* of silver, and so much copper and iron it cannot be weighed; I have also laid aside wood and stone, and you shall add to them.

וְהִנֵּה בְעָנְיִי הֲכִינוֹתִי לְבֵית־יְהוָה זָהָב כִּכָּרִים מֵאָה־אֶלֶף וְכֶסֶף אֶלֶף אֲלָפִים כִּכָּרִים וְלַנְּחֹשֶׁת וְלַבַּרְזֶל אֵין מִשְׁקָל כִּי לָרֹב הָיָה וְעֵצִים וַאֲבָנִים הֲכִינוֹתִי וַעֲלֵיהֶם תּוֹסִיף: יד

15 An abundance of workmen is at your disposal – hewers, workers in stone and wood, and every kind of craftsman in every kind of material –

וְעִמְּךָ לָרֹב עֹשֵׂי מְלָאכָה חֹצְבִים וְחָרָשֵׁי אֶבֶן וָעֵץ וְכָל־חָכָם בְּכָל־מְלָאכָה: טו

16 gold, silver, copper, and iron without limit. Go and do it, and may *Hashem* be with you."

לַזָּהָב לַכֶּסֶף וְלַנְּחֹשֶׁת וְלַבַּרְזֶל אֵין מִסְפָּר קוּם וַעֲשֵׂה וִיהִי יְהוָה עִמָּךְ: טז

17 *David* charged all the officers of *Yisrael* to support his son *Shlomo*,

וַיְצַו דָּוִיד לְכָל־שָׂרֵי יִשְׂרָאֵל לַעְזֹר לִשְׁלֹמֹה בְנוֹ: יז

18 "See, *Hashem* your God is with you, and He will give you rest on every side, for He delivered the inhabitants of the land into my hand so that the land lies conquered before *Hashem* and before His people.

הֲלֹא יְהוָה אֱלֹהֵיכֶם עִמָּכֶם וְהֵנִיחַ לָכֶם מִסָּבִיב כִּי נָתַן בְּיָדִי אֵת יֹשְׁבֵי הָאָרֶץ וְנִכְבְּשָׁה הָאָרֶץ לִפְנֵי יְהוָה וְלִפְנֵי עַמּוֹ: יח

19 Now, set your minds and hearts on worshiping *Hashem* your God, and go build the Sanctuary of *Hashem* your God so that you may bring the *Aron Brit Hashem* and the holy vessels of *Hashem* to the house that is built for the name of *Hashem*."

יט עַתָּה תְּנוּ לְבַבְכֶם וְנַפְשְׁכֶם לִדְרוֹשׁ לַיהֹוָה אֱלֹהֵיכֶם וְקוּמוּ וּבְנוּ אֶת־מִקְדַּשׁ יְהֹוָה הָאֱלֹהִים לְהָבִיא אֶת־אֲרוֹן בְּרִית־יְהֹוָה וּכְלֵי קֹדֶשׁ הָאֱלֹהִים לַבַּיִת הַנִּבְנֶה לְשֵׁם־יְהֹוָה:

23 1 When *David* reached a ripe old age, he made his son *Shlomo* king over *Yisrael*.

כג א וְדָוִיד זָקֵן וְשָׂבַע יָמִים וַיַּמְלֵךְ אֶת־שְׁלֹמֹה בְנוֹ עַל־יִשְׂרָאֵל:

2 Then *David* assembled all the officers of *Yisrael* and the *Kohanim* and the *Leviim*.

ב וַיֶּאֱסֹף אֶת־כָּל־שָׂרֵי יִשְׂרָאֵל וְהַכֹּהֲנִים וְהַלְוִיִּם:

3 The *Leviim*, from the age of thirty and upward, were counted; the head-count of their males was 38,000:

ג וַיִּסָּפְרוּ הַלְוִיִּם מִבֶּן שְׁלֹשִׁים שָׁנָה וָמָעְלָה וַיְהִי מִסְפָּרָם לְגֻלְגְּלֹתָם לִגְבָרִים שְׁלֹשִׁים וּשְׁמוֹנָה אָלֶף:

4 of these there were 24,000 in charge of the work of the House of *Hashem*, 6,000 officers and magistrates,

ד מֵאֵלֶּה לְנַצֵּחַ עַל־מְלֶאכֶת בֵּית־יְהֹוָה עֶשְׂרִים וְאַרְבָּעָה אָלֶף וְשֹׁטְרִים וְשֹׁפְטִים שֵׁשֶׁת אֲלָפִים:

5 4,000 gatekeepers, and 4,000 for praising *Hashem* "with instruments I devised for singing praises."

ה וְאַרְבַּעַת אֲלָפִים שֹׁעֲרִים וְאַרְבַּעַת אֲלָפִים מְהַלְלִים לַיהֹוָה בַּכֵּלִים אֲשֶׁר עָשִׂיתִי לְהַלֵּל:

6 *David* formed them into divisions: The sons of *Levi*: Gershon, Kehat, and *Merari*.

ו וַיֶּחָלְקֵם דָּוִיד מַחְלְקוֹת לִבְנֵי לֵוִי לְגֵרְשׁוֹן קְהָת וּמְרָרִי:

7 The Gershonites: Ladan and *Shim'i*.

ז לַגֵּרְשֻׁנִּי לַעְדָּן וְשִׁמְעִי:

8 The sons of Ladan: *Yechiel* the chief, Zetham, and *Yoel* – 3.

ח בְּנֵי לַעְדָּן הָרֹאשׁ יְחִיאֵל וְזֵתָם וְיוֹאֵל שְׁלֹשָׁה:

9 The sons of *Shim'i*: Shelomith, Haziel, and Haran – 3. These were the chiefs of the clans of the Ladanites.

ט בְּנֵי שִׁמְעִי שְׁלֹמִית [שְׁלוֹמִית] וַחֲזִיאֵל וְהָרָן שְׁלֹשָׁה אֵלֶּה רָאשֵׁי הָאָבוֹת לְלַעְדָּן:

10 And the sons of *Shim'i*: Jahath, Zina, Jeush, and Beriah; these were the sons of *Shim'i* – 4.

י וּבְנֵי שִׁמְעִי יַחַת זִינָא וִיעוּשׁ וּבְרִיעָה אֵלֶּה בְנֵי־שִׁמְעִי אַרְבָּעָה:

11 Jahath was the chief and Zizah the second, but Jeush and Beriah did not have many children, so they were enrolled together as a single clan.

יא וַיְהִי־יַחַת הָרֹאשׁ וְזִיזָה הַשֵּׁנִי וִיעוּשׁ וּבְרִיעָה לֹא־הִרְבּוּ בָנִים וַיִּהְיוּ לְבֵית אָב לִפְקֻדָּה אֶחָת:

12 The sons of *Kehat*: Amram, Izhar, *Chevron*, and Uzziel – 4.

יב בְּנֵי קְהָת עַמְרָם יִצְהָר חֶבְרוֹן וְעֻזִּיאֵל אַרְבָּעָה:

13 The sons of *Amram*: Aharon and *Moshe*. Aharon was set apart, he and his sons, forever, to be consecrated as most holy, to make burnt offerings to *Hashem* and serve Him and pronounce blessings in His name forever.

יג בְּנֵי עַמְרָם אַהֲרֹן וּמֹשֶׁה וַיִּבָּדֵל אַהֲרֹן לְהַקְדִּישׁוֹ קֹדֶשׁ קָדָשִׁים הוּא־וּבָנָיו עַד־עוֹלָם לְהַקְטִיר לִפְנֵי יְהֹוָה לְשָׁרְתוֹ וּלְבָרֵךְ בִּשְׁמוֹ עַד־עוֹלָם:

14 As for *Moshe*, the man of *Hashem*, his sons were named after the tribe of *Levi*.

יד וּמֹשֶׁה אִישׁ הָאֱלֹהִים בָּנָיו יִקָּרְאוּ עַל־שֵׁבֶט הַלֵּוִי:

15 The sons of *Moshe*: Gershom and *Eliezer*.

טו בְּנֵי מֹשֶׁה גֵּרְשֹׁם וֶאֱלִיעֶזֶר:

16 The sons of *Gershom*: Shebuel the chief.

טז בְּנֵי גֵרְשׁוֹם שְׁבוּאֵל הָרֹאשׁ׃

17 And the sons of *Eliezer* were: Rehabiah the chief. *Eliezer* had no other sons, but the sons of Rehabiah were very numerous.

יז וַיִּהְיוּ בְנֵי־אֱלִיעֶזֶר רְחַבְיָה הָרֹאשׁ וְלֹא־
הָיָה לֶאֱלִיעֶזֶר בָּנִים אֲחֵרִים וּבְנֵי רְחַבְיָה
רָבוּ לְמָעְלָה׃

18 The sons of Izhar: Shelomith the chief.

יח בְּנֵי יִצְהָר שְׁלֹמִית הָרֹאשׁ׃

19 The sons of *Chevron*: Jeriah the chief, Amariah the second, *Yachaziel* the third, and Jekameam the fourth.

יט בְּנֵי חֶבְרוֹן יְרִיָּהוּ הָרֹאשׁ אֲמַרְיָה הַשֵּׁנִי
יַחֲזִיאֵל הַשְּׁלִישִׁי וִיקַמְעָם הָרְבִיעִי׃

20 The sons of Uzziel: *Micha* the chief and Isshiah the second.

כ בְּנֵי עֻזִּיאֵל מִיכָה הָרֹאשׁ וְיִשִּׁיָּה הַשֵּׁנִי׃

21 The sons of *Merari*: Mahli and Mushi. The sons of Mahli: *Elazar* and *Keesh*.

כא בְּנֵי מְרָרִי מַחְלִי וּמוּשִׁי בְּנֵי מַחְלִי
אֶלְעָזָר וְקִישׁ׃

22 *Elazar* died having no sons but only daughters; the sons of *Keesh*, their kinsmen, married them.

כב וַיָּמָת אֶלְעָזָר וְלֹא־הָיוּ לוֹ בָּנִים כִּי אִם־
בָּנוֹת וַיִּשָּׂאוּם בְּנֵי־קִישׁ אֲחֵיהֶם׃

23 The sons of Mushi: Mahli, Eder, and Jeremoth – 3.

כג בְּנֵי מוּשִׁי מַחְלִי וְעֵדֶר וִירֵמוֹת שְׁלֹשָׁה׃

24 These are the sons of *Levi* by clans, with their clan chiefs as they were enrolled, with a list of their names by heads, who did the work of the service of the House of *Hashem* from the age of twenty and upward.

כד אֵלֶּה בְנֵי־לֵוִי לְבֵית אֲבֹתֵיהֶם רָאשֵׁי
הָאָבוֹת לִפְקוּדֵיהֶם בְּמִסְפַּר שֵׁמוֹת
לְגֻלְגְּלֹתָם עֹשֵׂה הַמְּלָאכָה לַעֲבֹדַת בֵּית
יְהֹוָה מִבֶּן עֶשְׂרִים שָׁנָה וָמָעְלָה׃

25 For *David* said, "God of *Yisrael* has given rest to His people and made His dwelling in *Yerushalayim* forever.

כה כִּי אָמַר דָּוִיד הֵנִיחַ יְהֹוָה אֱלֹהֵי־יִשְׂרָאֵל
לְעַמּוֹ וַיִּשְׁכֹּן בִּירוּשָׁלַ‍ִם עַד־לְעוֹלָם׃

26 Therefore the *Leviim* need not carry the *Mishkan* and all its various service vessels."

כו וְגַם לַלְוִיִּם אֵין־לָשֵׂאת אֶת־הַמִּשְׁכָּן
וְאֶת־כָּל־כֵּלָיו לַעֲבֹדָתוֹ׃

v'-GAM lal-vi-YIM ayn la-SAYT et ha-mish-KAN v'-et kol kay-LAV la-a-vo-da-TO

23:26 Therefore the *Leviim* need not carry the *Mishkan* In anticipation of the construction of the *Beit Hamikdash* in *Yerushalayim*, *David* counts the *Leviim* and assigns them a new role. Now that the house of God will find its permanent resting place in *Yerushalayim*, the job of carrying the *Mishkan* and the holy vessels, which had been assigned to the *Leviim* in the desert, is no longer relevant. They are therefore assigned other tasks; they are to assist the priests in the Temple service, serve as the gatekeepers for the Temple, and sing daily praises to the Lord. However, each *Levi* is to serve in the *Beit Hamikdash* for only one week out of every twenty-four (see chapter 25). The rest of their time, the members of the tribe of *Levi* have another highly significant job. They are to become the spiritual leaders of the Children of Israel by serving as officers, judges and teachers. As *Moshe* had blessed the tribe of *Levi* before his death, "They shall teach Your laws to *Yaakov* And Your instructions to *Yisrael*" (Deuteronomy 33:10). It is for this reason that they are not given their own portion in the Land of Israel, but instead are scattered among all the other tribes (see Joshua chapter 21). In this way, they are able to have an impact on the entire nation, providing the spiritual guidance essential for the Children of Israel to accurately represent God to the rest of the world.

A rabbi teaches *Torah* to his young students in *Meah She'arim*

27 Among the last acts of *David* was the counting of the *Leviim* from the age of twenty and upward.

כז כִּי בְדִבְרֵי דָוִיד הָאַחֲרֹנִים הֵמָּה מִסְפַּר בְּנֵי־לֵוִי מִבֶּן עֶשְׂרִים שָׁנָה וּלְמָעְלָה:

28 For their appointment was alongside the Aaronites for the service of the House of *Hashem*, to look after the courts and the chambers, and the purity of all the holy things, and the performance of the service of the House of *Hashem*,

כח כִּי מַעֲמָדָם לְיַד־בְּנֵי אַהֲרֹן לַעֲבֹדַת בֵּית יְהוָה עַל־הַחֲצֵרוֹת וְעַל־הַלְּשָׁכוֹת וְעַל־טָהֳרַת לְכָל־קֹדֶשׁ וּמַעֲשֵׂה עֲבֹדַת בֵּית הָאֱלֹהִים:

29 and the rows of bread, and the fine flour for the meal offering, and the unleavened wafers, and the cakes made on the griddle and soaked, and every measure of capacity and length;

כט וּלְלֶחֶם הַמַּעֲרֶכֶת וּלְסֹלֶת לְמִנְחָה וְלִרְקִיקֵי הַמַּצּוֹת וְלַמַּחֲבַת וְלַמֻּרְבָּכֶת וּלְכָל־מְשׂוּרָה וּמִדָּה:

30 and to be present every morning to praise and extol *Hashem*, and at evening too,

ל וְלַעֲמֹד בַּבֹּקֶר בַּבֹּקֶר לְהֹדוֹת וּלְהַלֵּל לַיהוָה וְכֵן לָעָרֶב:

31 and whenever offerings were made to *Hashem*, according to the quantities prescribed for them, on *Shabbatot*, new moons and holidays, regularly, before *Hashem*;

לא וּלְכֹל הַעֲלוֹת עֹלוֹת לַיהוָה לַשַּׁבָּתוֹת לֶחֳדָשִׁים וְלַמֹּעֲדִים בְּמִסְפָּר כְּמִשְׁפָּט עֲלֵיהֶם תָּמִיד לִפְנֵי יְהוָה:

32 and so to keep watch over the Tent of Meeting, over the holy things, and over the Aaronites their kinsmen, for the service of the House of *Hashem*.

לב וְשָׁמְרוּ אֶת־מִשְׁמֶרֶת אֹהֶל־מוֹעֵד וְאֵת מִשְׁמֶרֶת הַקֹּדֶשׁ וּמִשְׁמֶרֶת בְּנֵי אַהֲרֹן אֲחֵיהֶם לַעֲבֹדַת בֵּית יְהוָה:

24 1 The divisions of the Aaronites were: The sons of *Aharon*: *Nadav* and *Avihu*, *Elazar* and *Itamar*.

כד א וְלִבְנֵי אַהֲרֹן מַחְלְקוֹתָם בְּנֵי אַהֲרֹן נָדָב וַאֲבִיהוּא אֶלְעָזָר וְאִיתָמָר:

2 *Nadav* and *Avihu* died in the lifetime of their father, and they had no children, so *Elazar* and *Itamar* served as *Kohanim*.

ב וַיָּמָת נָדָב וַאֲבִיהוּא לִפְנֵי אֲבִיהֶם וּבָנִים לֹא־הָיוּ לָהֶם וַיְכַהֲנוּ אֶלְעָזָר וְאִיתָמָר:

va-YA-mot na-DAV va-a-vee-HU lif-NAY a-vee-HEM u-va-NEEM
lo ha-YU la-HEM vai-kha-ha-NU el-a-ZAR v'-ee-ta-MAR

24:2 *Nadav* and *Avihu* died in the lifetime of their father The *Torah* tells us that *Nadav* and *Avihu* died during the joyous dedication ceremony of the *Mishkan*. After a heavenly fire descended and consumed the sacrificial offerings, revealing the Divine Presence, the verse states that these two of *Aharon's* sons "offered before *Hashem* alien fire, which He had not enjoined upon them" (Leviticus 10:1). The severe consequence of this act was that they were then consumed as well, also by heavenly fire. The *Netziv* suggests that their motivation for bringing the forbidden fire was the closeness that they felt to God at the moment of revelation; they were so overcome with this feeling that they desired to get even closer with an offering of their own, which they brought into the Holy of Holies. Though their intentions were pure, the offering was unauthorized and entry into the Holy sanctuary was forbidden, so they were punished. *Nadav* and *Avihu* were indeed close to God, as *Moshe* says of them "Through those near to Me I show Myself holy, and gain glory before all the people" (Leviticus 10:3), but such closeness does not grant a license to bend the rules. *Nadav* and *Avihu* teach us that holy places must be approached with awe and trepidation, and that holy people are held to a higher standard. One of the lessons for our generation is that the Children of Israel, living in the Land of Israel, must be especially careful to respect its sanctity and to behave in a way that will bring glory to God's name.

A fiery sky over the Mediterranean Sea

³ *David, Tzadok* of the sons of *Elazar,* and *Achimelech* of the sons of *Itamar* divided them into offices by their tasks.

ג וַיֶּחְלְקֵם דָּוִיד וְצָדוֹק מִן־בְּנֵי אֶלְעָזָר וַאֲחִימֶלֶךְ מִן־בְּנֵי אִיתָמָר לִפְקֻדָּתָם בַּעֲבֹדָתָם:

⁴ The sons of *Elazar* turned out to be more numerous by male heads than the sons of *Itamar,* so they divided the sons of *Elazar* into sixteen chiefs of clans and the sons of *Itamar* into eight clans.

ד וַיִּמָּצְאוּ בְנֵי־אֶלְעָזָר רַבִּים לְרָאשֵׁי הַגְּבָרִים מִן־בְּנֵי אִיתָמָר וַיַּחְלְקוּם לִבְנֵי אֶלְעָזָר רָאשִׁים לְבֵית־אָבוֹת שִׁשָּׁה עָשָׂר וְלִבְנֵי אִיתָמָר לְבֵית אֲבוֹתָם שְׁמוֹנָה:

⁵ They divided them by lot, both on an equal footing, since they were all sanctuary officers and officers of *Hashem* – the sons of *Elazar* and the sons of *Itamar.*

ה וַיַּחְלְקוּם בְּגוֹרָלוֹת אֵלֶּה עִם־אֵלֶּה כִּי־הָיוּ שָׂרֵי־קֹדֶשׁ וְשָׂרֵי הָאֱלֹהִים מִבְּנֵי אֶלְעָזָר וּבִבְנֵי אִיתָמָר:

⁶ *Shemaya* son of Nathanel, the scribe, who was of the *Leviim,* registered them under the eye of the king, the officers, and *Tzadok* the *Kohen,* and *Achimelech* son of *Evyatar,* and the chiefs of clans of the *Kohanim* and *Leviim* – one clan more taken for *Elazar* for each one taken of *Itamar.*

ו וַיִּכְתְּבֵם שְׁמַעְיָה בֶן־נְתַנְאֵל הַסּוֹפֵר מִן־הַלֵּוִי לִפְנֵי הַמֶּלֶךְ וְהַשָּׂרִים וְצָדוֹק הַכֹּהֵן וַאֲחִימֶלֶךְ בֶּן־אֶבְיָתָר וְרָאשֵׁי הָאָבוֹת לַכֹּהֲנִים וְלַלְוִיִּם בֵּית־אָב אֶחָד אָחֻז לְאֶלְעָזָר וְאָחֻז אָחֻז לְאִיתָמָר:

⁷ The first lot fell on Jehoiarib; the second on Jedaiah;

ז וַיֵּצֵא הַגּוֹרָל הָרִאשׁוֹן לִיהוֹיָרִיב לִידַעְיָה הַשֵּׁנִי:

⁸ the third on Harim; the fourth on Seorim;

ח לְחָרִם הַשְּׁלִישִׁי לִשְׂעֹרִים הָרְבִעִי:

⁹ the fifth on Malchijah; the sixth on Mijamin;

ט לְמַלְכִּיָּה הַחֲמִישִׁי לְמִיָּמִן הַשִּׁשִּׁי:

¹⁰ the seventh on Hakkoz; the eighth on *Aviya;*

י לְהַקּוֹץ הַשְּׁבִעִי לַאֲבִיָּה הַשְּׁמִינִי:

¹¹ the ninth on *Yeshua;* the tenth on *Shechanya;*

יא לְיֵשׁוּעַ הַתְּשִׁעִי לִשְׁכַנְיָהוּ הָעֲשִׂרִי:

¹² the eleventh on *Elyashiv;* the twelfth on Jakim;

יב לְאֶלְיָשִׁיב עַשְׁתֵּי עָשָׂר לְיָקִים שְׁנֵים עָשָׂר:

¹³ the thirteenth on Huppah; the fourteenth on Jeshebeab;

יג לְחֻפָּה שְׁלֹשָׁה עָשָׂר לְיֶשֶׁבְאָב אַרְבָּעָה עָשָׂר:

¹⁴ the fifteenth on Bilgah; the sixteenth on Immer;

יד לְבִלְגָּה חֲמִשָּׁה עָשָׂר לְאִמֵּר שִׁשָּׁה עָשָׂר:

¹⁵ the seventeenth on Hezir; the eighteenth on Happizzez;

טו לְחֵזִיר שִׁבְעָה עָשָׂר לְהַפִּצֵּץ שְׁמוֹנָה עָשָׂר:

¹⁶ the nineteenth on Pethahiah; the twentieth on Jehezkel;

טז לִפְתַחְיָה תִּשְׁעָה עָשָׂר לִיחֶזְקֵאל הָעֶשְׂרִים:

¹⁷ the twenty-first on Jachin; the twenty-second on Gamul;

יז לְיָכִין אֶחָד וְעֶשְׂרִים לְגָמוּל שְׁנַיִם וְעֶשְׂרִים:

¹⁸ the twenty-third on Delaiah; the twenty-fourth on Maaziah.

יח לִדְלָיָהוּ שְׁלֹשָׁה וְעֶשְׂרִים לְמַעַזְיָהוּ אַרְבָּעָה וְעֶשְׂרִים:

¹⁹ According to this allocation of offices by tasks, they were to enter the House of *Hashem* as was laid down for them by *Aharon* their father, as God of *Yisrael* had commanded him.

יט אֵלֶּה פְקֻדָּתָם לַעֲבֹדָתָם לָבוֹא לְבֵית־יְהֹוָה כְּמִשְׁפָּטָם בְּיַד אַהֲרֹן אֲבִיהֶם כַּאֲשֶׁר צִוָּהוּ יְהֹוָה אֱלֹהֵי יִשְׂרָאֵל:

²⁰ The remaining *Leviim*: the sons of *Amram*: Shubael; the sons of Shubael: Jehdeiah;

כ וְלִבְנֵי לֵוִי הַנּוֹתָרִים לִבְנֵי עַמְרָם שׁוּבָאֵל לִבְנֵי שׁוּבָאֵל יֶחְדְּיָהוּ:

²¹ Rehabiah. The sons of Rehabiah: Isshiah, the chief.

כא לִרְחַבְיָהוּ לִבְנֵי רְחַבְיָהוּ הָרֹאשׁ יִשִּׁיָּה:

²² Izharites: Shelomoth. The sons of Shelomoth: Jahath

כב לַיִּצְהָרִי שְׁלֹמוֹת לִבְנֵי שְׁלֹמוֹת יָחַת:

²³ and Benai, Jeriah; the second, Amariah; the third, *Yachaziel*; the fourth, Jekameam.

כג וּבְנֵי יְרִיָּהוּ אֲמַרְיָהוּ הַשֵּׁנִי יַחֲזִיאֵל הַשְּׁלִישִׁי יְקַמְעָם הָרְבִיעִי:

²⁴ The sons of Uzziel: *Micha*. The sons of *Micha*: Shamir.

כד בְּנֵי עֻזִּיאֵל מִיכָה לִבְנֵי מִיכָה שָׁמוֹר [שָׁמִיר:]

²⁵ The brother of *Micha*: Isshiah. The sons of Isshiah: *Zecharya*.

כה אֲחִי מִיכָה יִשִּׁיָּה לִבְנֵי יִשִּׁיָּה זְכַרְיָהוּ:

²⁶ The sons of *Merari*: Mahli and Mushi. The sons of Jaazaiah, his son –

כו בְּנֵי מְרָרִי מַחְלִי וּמוּשִׁי בְּנֵי יַעֲזִיָּהוּ בְנוֹ:

²⁷ the sons of *Merari* by Jaazaiah his son: Shoham, Zakkur, and Ibri.

כז בְּנֵי מְרָרִי לְיַעֲזִיָּהוּ בְנוֹ וְשֹׁהַם וְזַכּוּר וְעִבְרִי:

²⁸ Mahli: *Elazar*; he had no sons.

כח לְמַחְלִי אֶלְעָזָר וְלֹא־הָיָה לוֹ בָּנִים:

²⁹ *Keesh*: the sons of *Keesh*: Jerahmeel.

כט לְקִישׁ בְּנֵי־קִישׁ יְרַחְמְאֵל:

³⁰ The sons of Mushi: Mahli, Eder, and Jerimoth. These were the sons of the *Leviim* by their clans.

ל וּבְנֵי מוּשִׁי מַחְלִי וְעֵדֶר וִירִימוֹת אֵלֶּה בְּנֵי הַלְוִיִּם לְבֵית אֲבֹתֵיהֶם:

³¹ These too cast lots corresponding to their kinsmen, the sons of *Aharon*, under the eye of King *David* and *Tzadok* and *Achimelech* and the chiefs of the clans of the *Kohanim* and *Leviim*, on the principle of "chief and youngest brother alike."

לא וַיַּפִּילוּ גַם־הֵם גּוֹרָלוֹת לְעֻמַּת אֲחֵיהֶם בְּנֵי־אַהֲרֹן לִפְנֵי דָוִיד הַמֶּלֶךְ וְצָדוֹק וַאֲחִימֶלֶךְ וְרָאשֵׁי הָאָבוֹת לַכֹּהֲנִים וְלַלְוִיִּם אָבוֹת הָרֹאשׁ לְעֻמַּת אָחִיו הַקָּטָן:

25 ¹ *David* and the officers of the army set apart for service the sons of *Asaf*, of *Hayman*, and of *Yedutun*, who prophesied to the accompaniment of lyres, harps, and cymbals. The list of men who performed this work, according to their service, was:

כה א וַיַּבְדֵּל דָּוִיד וְשָׂרֵי הַצָּבָא לַעֲבֹדָה לִבְנֵי אָסָף וְהֵימָן וִידוּתוּן הַנְּבִיאִים [הַנִּבְּאִים] בְּכִנֹּרוֹת בִּנְבָלִים וּבִמְצִלְתָּיִם וַיְהִי מִסְפָּרָם אַנְשֵׁי מְלָאכָה לַעֲבֹדָתָם:

² Sons of *Asaf*: Zaccur, *Yosef*, Nethaniah, and Asarelah – sons of *Asaf* under the charge of *Asaf*, who prophesied by order of the king.

ב לִבְנֵי אָסָף זַכּוּר וְיוֹסֵף וּנְתַנְיָה וַאֲשַׂרְאֵלָה בְּנֵי אָסָף עַל יַד־אָסָף הַנִּבָּא עַל־יְדֵי הַמֶּלֶךְ:

³ *Yedutun* – the sons of *Yedutun*: *Gedalia*, Zeri, Jeshaiah, Hashabiah, Mattithiah – 6, under the charge of their father *Yedutun*, who, accompanied on the harp, prophesied, praising and extolling *Hashem*.

ג לִידוּתוּן בְּנֵי יְדוּתוּן גְּדַלְיָהוּ וּצְרִי וִישַׁעְיָהוּ חֲשַׁבְיָהוּ וּמַתִּתְיָהוּ שִׁשָּׁה עַל־יְדֵי אֲבִיהֶם יְדוּתוּן בַּכִּנּוֹר הַנִּבָּא עַל־הֹדוֹת וְהַלֵּל לַיהֹוָה:

⁴ *Hayman* – the sons of *Hayman*: Bukkiah, Mattaniah, Uzziel, Shebuel, Jerimoth, *Chananya*, *Chanani*, Eliathah, Giddalti, Romamti-ezer, Joshbekashah, Mallothi, Hothir, and Mahazioth;

ד לְהֵימָן בְּנֵי הֵימָן בֻּקִּיָּהוּ מַתַּנְיָהוּ עֻזִּיאֵל שְׁבוּאֵל וִירִימוֹת חֲנַנְיָה חֲנָנִי אֱלִיאָתָה גִּדַּלְתִּי וְרֹמַמְתִּי עֶזֶר יָשְׁבְּקָשָׁה מַלּוֹתִי הוֹתִיר מַחֲזִיאוֹת:

⁵ all these were sons of *Hayman*, the seer of the king, [who uttered] prophecies of *Hashem* for His greater glory. *Hashem* gave *Hayman* fourteen sons and three daughters;

ה כָּל־אֵלֶּה בָנִים לְהֵימָן חֹזֵה הַמֶּלֶךְ בְּדִבְרֵי הָאֱלֹהִים לְהָרִים קָרֶן וַיִּתֵּן הָאֱלֹהִים לְהֵימָן בָּנִים אַרְבָּעָה עָשָׂר וּבָנוֹת שָׁלוֹשׁ:

⁶ all these were under the charge of their father for the singing in the House of *Hashem*, to the accompaniment of cymbals, harps, and lyres, for the service of the House of *Hashem* by order of the king. *Asaf*, *Yedutun*, and *Hayman* –

ו כָּל־אֵלֶּה עַל־יְדֵי אֲבִיהֶם בַּשִּׁיר בֵּית יְהֹוָה בִּמְצִלְתַּיִם נְבָלִים וְכִנֹּרוֹת לַעֲבֹדַת בֵּית הָאֱלֹהִים עַל יְדֵי הַמֶּלֶךְ אָסָף וִידוּתוּן וְהֵימָן:

⁷ their total number with their kinsmen, trained singers of *Hashem* – all the masters, 288.

ז וַיְהִי מִסְפָּרָם עִם־אֲחֵיהֶם מְלֻמְּדֵי־שִׁיר לַיהֹוָה כָּל־הַמֵּבִין מָאתַיִם שְׁמוֹנִים וּשְׁמוֹנָה:

⁸ They cast lots for shifts on the principle of "small and great alike, like master like apprentice."

ח וַיַּפִּילוּ גּוֹרָלוֹת מִשְׁמֶרֶת לְעֻמַּת כַּקָּטֹן כַּגָּדוֹל מֵבִין עִם־תַּלְמִיד:

va-ya-PEE-lu go-ra-LOT mish-ME-ret l'-u-MAT ka-ka-TON ka-ga-DOL may-VEEN im tal-MEED

⁹ The first lot fell to *Asaf* – to *Yosef*; the second, to *Gedalia*, he and his brothers and his sons – 12;

ט וַיֵּצֵא הַגּוֹרָל הָרִאשׁוֹן לְאָסָף לְיוֹסֵף גְּדַלְיָהוּ הַשֵּׁנִי הוּא וְאֶחָיו וּבָנָיו שְׁנֵים עָשָׂר:

¹⁰ the third, to Zaccur: his sons and his brothers – 12;

י הַשְּׁלִשִׁי זַכּוּר בָּנָיו וְאֶחָיו שְׁנֵים עָשָׂר:

¹¹ the fourth, to Izri: his sons and his brothers – 12;

יא הָרְבִיעִי לַיִּצְרִי בָּנָיו וְאֶחָיו שְׁנֵים עָשָׂר:

Prime Minister Benjamin Netanyahu sings with Holocaust survivor in *Yerushalayim*

25:8 They cast lots The *Leviim* are to sing and prepare the sacrifices in the *Beit Hamikdash* in *Yerushalayim*. Just as the *Kohanim*, who actually perform the sacrificial order, are divided into twenty-four separate groups and then ordered by lot, so too the *Leviim*, who sing praises of God as accompaniment to the sacrifices, are also divided into twenty-four groups and ordered by lot. The Sages (*Rosh Hashana* 31a) enumerate the particular Psalms the *Leviim* would sing each day while the daily sacrifices were offered. As a remembrance of this recitation by the *Leviim*, Jews recite these same psalms, referred to as the "Song of the Day," at the conclusion of the morning prayers. The Sages (*Sofrim* 18:2) further teach that anyone one who mentions these verses on the proper day is considered as having built a new altar and offered a sacrifice on it.

12 the fifth, to Nethaniah: his sons and his brothers – 12;	יג הַחֲמִישִׁי נְתַנְיָהוּ בָּנָיו וְאֶחָיו שְׁנֵים עָשָׂר:
13 the sixth, to Bukkiah: his sons and his brothers – 12;	יג הַשִּׁשִּׁי בֻקִּיָּהוּ בָּנָיו וְאֶחָיו שְׁנֵים עָשָׂר:
14 the seventh, to Jesarelah: his sons and his brothers – 12;	יד הַשְּׁבִעִי יְשַׂרְאֵלָה בָּנָיו וְאֶחָיו שְׁנֵים עָשָׂר:
15 the eighth, to Jeshaiah: his sons and his brothers – 12;	טו הַשְּׁמִינִי יְשַׁעְיָהוּ בָּנָיו וְאֶחָיו שְׁנֵים עָשָׂר:
16 the ninth, to Mattaniah: his sons and his brothers – 12;	טז הַתְּשִׁיעִי מַתַּנְיָהוּ בָּנָיו וְאֶחָיו שְׁנֵים עָשָׂר:
17 the tenth, to *Shim'i*: his sons and his brothers – 12;	יז הָעֲשִׂירִי שִׁמְעִי בָּנָיו וְאֶחָיו שְׁנֵים עָשָׂר:
18 the eleventh to Azarel: his sons and his brothers – 12;	יח עַשְׁתֵּי־עָשָׂר עֲזַרְאֵל בָּנָיו וְאֶחָיו שְׁנֵים עָשָׂר:
19 the twelfth, to Hashabiah: his sons and his brothers – 12;	יט הַשְּׁנֵים עָשָׂר לַחֲשַׁבְיָה בָּנָיו וְאֶחָיו שְׁנֵים עָשָׂר:
20 the thirteenth, to Shubael: his sons and his brothers – 12;	כ לִשְׁלֹשָׁה עָשָׂר שׁוּבָאֵל בָּנָיו וְאֶחָיו שְׁנֵים עָשָׂר:
21 the fourteenth, to Mattithiah: his sons and his brothers – 12;	כא לְאַרְבָּעָה עָשָׂר מַתִּתְיָהוּ בָּנָיו וְאֶחָיו שְׁנֵים עָשָׂר:
22 the fifteenth, to Jeremoth: his sons and his brothers – 12;	כב לַחֲמִשָּׁה עָשָׂר לִירֵמוֹת בָּנָיו וְאֶחָיו שְׁנֵים עָשָׂר:
23 the sixteenth, to *Chananya*: his sons and his brothers – 12;	כג לְשִׁשָּׁה עָשָׂר לַחֲנַנְיָהוּ בָּנָיו וְאֶחָיו שְׁנֵים עָשָׂר:
24 the seventeenth, to Joshbekashah: his sons and his brothers – 12;	כד לְשִׁבְעָה עָשָׂר לְיָשְׁבְּקָשָׁה בָּנָיו וְאֶחָיו שְׁנֵים עָשָׂר:
25 the eighteenth, to *Chanani*: his sons and his brothers – 12;	כה לִשְׁמוֹנָה עָשָׂר לַחֲנָנִי בָּנָיו וְאֶחָיו שְׁנֵים עָשָׂר:
26 the nineteenth, to Mallothi: his sons and his brothers – 12;	כו לְתִשְׁעָה עָשָׂר לְמַלּוֹתִי בָּנָיו וְאֶחָיו שְׁנֵים עָשָׂר:
27 the twentieth, to Eliathah: his sons and his brothers – 12;	כז לְעֶשְׂרִים לֶאֱלִיָּתָה בָּנָיו וְאֶחָיו שְׁנֵים עָשָׂר:
28 the twenty-first, to Hothir: his sons and his brothers – 12;	כח לְאֶחָד וְעֶשְׂרִים לְהוֹתִיר בָּנָיו וְאֶחָיו שְׁנֵים עָשָׂר:
29 the twenty-second, to Giddalti: his sons and his brothers – 12;	כט לִשְׁנַיִם וְעֶשְׂרִים לְגִדַּלְתִּי בָּנָיו וְאֶחָיו שְׁנֵים עָשָׂר:
30 the twenty-third, to Mahazioth: his sons and his brothers – 12;	ל לִשְׁלֹשָׁה וְעֶשְׂרִים לְמַחֲזִיאוֹת בָּנָיו וְאֶחָיו שְׁנֵים עָשָׂר:

³¹ the twenty-fourth, to Romamti-ezer: his sons and his brothers – 12.

לא לְאַרְבָּעָה וְעֶשְׂרִים לְרוֹמַמְתִּי עֶזֶר בָּנָיו וְאֶחָיו שְׁנֵים עָשָׂר:

26 ¹ The divisions of the gatekeepers: Korahites: Meshelemiah son of Kore, of the sons of *Asaf.*

כו א לְמַחְלְקוֹת לְשֹׁעֲרִים לַקָּרְחִים מְשֶׁלֶמְיָהוּ בֶן־קֹרֵא מִן־בְּנֵי אָסָף:

l'-makh-l'-KOT l'-sho-a-REEM la-kor-KHEEM
m'-she-lem-YA-hu ven ko-RAY min b'-NAY a-SAF

² Sons of Meshelemiah: *Zecharya* the firstborn, Jediael the second, Zebadiah the third, Jathniel the fourth,

ב וְלִמְשֶׁלֶמְיָהוּ בָּנִים זְכַרְיָהוּ הַבְּכוֹר יְדִיעֵאֵל הַשֵּׁנִי זְבַדְיָהוּ הַשְּׁלִישִׁי יַתְנִיאֵל הָרְבִיעִי:

³ Elam the fifth, *Yehochanan* the sixth, Eliehoenai the seventh.

ג עֵילָם הַחֲמִישִׁי יְהוֹחָנָן הַשִּׁשִּׁי אֶלְיְהוֹעֵינַי הַשְּׁבִיעִי:

⁴ Sons of *Oved Edom*: *Shemaya* the first-born, Jehozabad the second, Joah the third, Sacar the fourth, Nethanel the fifth,

ד וּלְעֹבֵד אֱדֹם בָּנִים שְׁמַעְיָה הַבְּכוֹר יְהוֹזָבָד הַשֵּׁנִי יוֹאָח הַשְּׁלִשִׁי וְשָׂכָר הָרְבִיעִי וּנְתַנְאֵל הַחֲמִישִׁי:

⁵ Ammiel the sixth, *Yissachar* the seventh, Peullethai the eighth – for *Hashem* had blessed him.

ה עַמִּיאֵל הַשִּׁשִּׁי יִשָּׂשכָר הַשְּׁבִיעִי פְּעֻלְּתַי הַשְּׁמִינִי כִּי בֵרֲכוֹ אֱלֹהִים:

⁶ To his son *Shemaya* were born sons who exercised authority in their clans because they were men of substance.

ו וְלִשְׁמַעְיָה בְנוֹ נוֹלַד בָּנִים הַמִּמְשָׁלִים לְבֵית אֲבִיהֶם כִּי־גִבּוֹרֵי חַיִל הֵמָּה:

⁷ The sons of *Shemaya*: Othni, Rephael, Oved, Elzabad – his brothers, men of ability, were Elihu and Semachiah.

ז בְּנֵי שְׁמַעְיָה עָתְנִי וּרְפָאֵל וְעוֹבֵד אֶלְזָבָד אֶחָיו בְּנֵי־חָיִל אֱלִיהוּ וּסְמַכְיָהוּ:

⁸ All these, sons of Obededom; they and their sons and brothers, strong and able men for the service – 62 of Obededom.

ח כָּל־אֵלֶּה מִבְּנֵי עֹבֵד אֱדֹם הֵמָּה וּבְנֵיהֶם וַאֲחֵיהֶם אִישׁ־חַיִל בַּכֹּחַ לַעֲבֹדָה שִׁשִּׁים וּשְׁנַיִם לְעֹבֵד אֱדֹם:

⁹ Meshelemiah had sons and brothers, able men – 18.

ט וְלִמְשֶׁלֶמְיָהוּ בָּנִים וְאַחִים בְּנֵי־חָיִל שְׁמוֹנָה עָשָׂר:

¹⁰ Hosah of the Merarites had sons: Shimri the chief (he was not the first-born, but his father designated him chief),

י וּלְחֹסָה מִן־בְּנֵי־מְרָרִי בָּנִים שִׁמְרִי הָרֹאשׁ כִּי לֹא־הָיָה בְכוֹר וַיְשִׂימֵהוּ אָבִיהוּ לְרֹאשׁ:

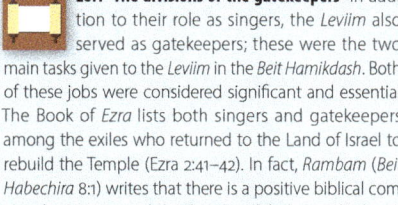

26:1 The divisions of the gatekeepers In addition to their role as singers, the *Leviim* also served as gatekeepers; these were the two main tasks given to the *Leviim* in the *Beit Hamikdash*. Both of these jobs were considered significant and essential. The Book of *Ezra* lists both singers and gatekeepers among the exiles who returned to the Land of Israel to rebuild the Temple (Ezra 2:41–42). In fact, *Rambam* (*Beit Habechira* 8:1) writes that there is a positive biblical commandment to guard the *Beit Hamikdash* as a display of honor to the Temple, and to *Hashem*. He writes, "Even though there is no concern of enemies or robbers entering the *Beit Hamikdash*, guarding it is a show of honor. There is no comparison between a palace with guards to a palace without them." The Temple, and by extension all of *Eretz Yisrael*, is the King's palace, and we must treat it with the proper awe and respect.

Zion gate, gate to the Old City of *Yerushalayim*

11 *Chilkiyahu* the second, Tebaliah the third, *Zecharya* the fourth. All the sons and brothers of Hosah – 13.

12 These are the divisions of the gatekeepers, by their chief men, [who worked in] shifts corresponding to their kinsmen, ministering in the House of *Hashem*.

13 They cast lots, small and great alike, by clans, for each gate.

14 The lot for the east [gate] fell to Shelemiah. Then they cast lots [for] *Zecharya* his son, a prudent counselor, and his lot came out to be the north [gate].

15 For *Oved Edom*, the south [gate], and for his sons, the vestibule.

16 For Shuppim and for Hosah, the west [gate], with the Shallecheth gate on the ascending highway. Watch corresponded to watch:

17 At the east – six *Leviim*; at the north – four daily; at the south – four daily; at the vestibule – two by two;

18 at the colonnade on the west – four at the causeway and two at the colonnade.

19 These were the divisions of the gatekeepers of the sons of *Korach* and the sons of *Merari*.

20 And the *Leviim*: *Achiya* over the treasuries of the House of *Hashem* and the treasuries of the dedicated things.

21 The sons of Ladan: the sons of the Gershonites belonging to Ladan; the chiefs of the clans of Ladan, the Gershonite – Yechieli.

22 The sons of Yechieli: Zetham and *Yoel*; his brother was over the treasuries of the House of *Hashem*.

23 Of the Amramites, the Izharites, the Chevronites, the Uzzielites:

24 Shebuel son of *Gershom* son of *Moshe* was the chief officer over the treasuries.

25 And his brothers: *Eliezer*, his son Rehabiah, his son Jeshaiah, his son *Yoram*, his son Zichri, his son Shelomith –

יא חִלְקִיָּהוּ הַשֵּׁנִי טְבַלְיָהוּ הַשְּׁלִשִׁי זְכַרְיָהוּ הָרְבִעִי כָּל־בָּנִים וְאַחִים לְחֹסָה שְׁלֹשָׁה עָשָׂר:

יב לְאֵלֶּה מַחְלְקוֹת הַשֹּׁעֲרִים לְרָאשֵׁי הַגְּבָרִים מִשְׁמָרוֹת לְעֻמַּת אֲחֵיהֶם לְשָׁרֵת בְּבֵית יְהֹוָה:

יג וַיַּפִּילוּ גוֹרָלוֹת כַּקָּטֹן כַּגָּדוֹל לְבֵית אֲבוֹתָם לְשַׁעַר וָשָׁעַר:

יד וַיִּפֹּל הַגּוֹרָל מִזְרָחָה לְשֶׁלֶמְיָהוּ וּזְכַרְיָהוּ בְנוֹ יוֹעֵץ בְּשֵׂכֶל הִפִּילוּ גוֹרָלוֹת וַיֵּצֵא גוֹרָלוֹ צָפוֹנָה:

טו לְעֹבֵד אֱדֹם נֶגְבָּה וּלְבָנָיו בֵּית הָאֲסֻפִּים:

טז לְשֻׁפִּים וּלְחֹסָה לַמַּעֲרָב עִם שַׁעַר שַׁלֶּכֶת בַּמְסִלָּה הָעוֹלָה מִשְׁמָר לְעֻמַּת מִשְׁמָר:

יז לַמִּזְרָח הַלְוִיִּם שִׁשָּׁה לַצָּפוֹנָה לַיּוֹם אַרְבָּעָה לַנֶּגְבָּה לַיּוֹם אַרְבָּעָה וְלָאֲסֻפִּים שְׁנַיִם שְׁנָיִם:

יח לַפַּרְבָּר לַמַּעֲרָב אַרְבָּעָה לַמְסִלָּה שְׁנַיִם לַפַּרְבָּר:

יט אֵלֶּה מַחְלְקוֹת הַשֹּׁעֲרִים לִבְנֵי הַקָּרְחִי וְלִבְנֵי מְרָרִי:

כ וְהַלְוִיִּם אֲחִיָּה עַל־אוֹצְרוֹת בֵּית הָאֱלֹהִים וּלְאֹצְרוֹת הַקֳּדָשִׁים:

כא בְּנֵי לַעְדָּן בְּנֵי הַגֵּרְשֻׁנִּי לְלַעְדָּן רָאשֵׁי הָאָבוֹת לְלַעְדָּן הַגֵּרְשֻׁנִּי יְחִיאֵלִי:

כב בְּנֵי יְחִיאֵלִי זֵתָם וְיוֹאֵל אָחִיו עַל־אֹצְרוֹת בֵּית יְהֹוָה:

כג לַעַמְרָמִי לַיִּצְהָרִי לַחֶבְרוֹנִי לָעָזִּיאֵלִי:

כד וּשְׁבֻאֵל בֶּן־גֵּרְשׁוֹם בֶּן־מֹשֶׁה נָגִיד עַל־הָאֹצָרוֹת:

כה וְאֶחָיו לֶאֱלִיעֶזֶר רְחַבְיָהוּ בְנוֹ וִישַׁעְיָהוּ בְנוֹ וְיֹרָם בְּנוֹ וְזִכְרִי בְנוֹ וּשְׁלֹמוֹת [וּשְׁלֹמִית] בְּנוֹ:

26 that Shelomith and his brothers were over all the treasuries of dedicated things that were dedicated by King *David* and the chiefs of the clans, and the officers of thousands and hundreds and the other army officers;

כו הוּא שְׁלֹמוֹת וְאֶחָיו עַל כָּל־אֹצְרוֹת הַקֳּדָשִׁים אֲשֶׁר הִקְדִּישׁ דָּוִיד הַמֶּלֶךְ וְרָאשֵׁי הָאָבוֹת לְשָׂרֵי־הָאֲלָפִים וְהַמֵּאוֹת וְשָׂרֵי הַצָּבָא:

27 they dedicated some of the booty of the wars to maintain the House of *Hashem*.

כז מִן־הַמִּלְחָמוֹת וּמִן־הַשָּׁלָל הִקְדִּישׁוּ לְחַזֵּק לְבֵית יְהוָה:

28 All that *Shmuel* the seer had dedicated, and *Shaul* son of *Keesh*, and *Avner* son of Ner, and *Yoav* son of *Tzeruya* – or [what] any other man had dedicated, was under the charge of Shelomith and his brothers.

כח וְכֹל הַהִקְדִּישׁ שְׁמוּאֵל הָרֹאֶה וְשָׁאוּל בֶּן־קִישׁ וְאַבְנֵר בֶּן־נֵר וְיוֹאָב בֶּן־צְרוּיָה כֹּל הַמַּקְדִּישׁ עַל יַד־שְׁלֹמִית וְאֶחָיו:

29 The Izharites: Chenaniah and his sons were over *Yisrael* as clerks and magistrates for affairs outside [the sanctuary].

כט לַיִּצְהָרִי כְּנַנְיָהוּ וּבָנָיו לַמְּלָאכָה הַחִיצוֹנָה עַל־יִשְׂרָאֵל לְשֹׁטְרִים וּלְשֹׁפְטִים:

30 The Chevronites: Hashabiah and his brothers, capable men, 1,700, supervising *Yisrael* on the west side of the *Yarden* in all matters of *Hashem* and the service of the king.

ל לַחֶבְרוֹנִי חֲשַׁבְיָהוּ וְאֶחָיו בְּנֵי־חַיִל אֶלֶף וּשְׁבַע־מֵאוֹת עַל פְּקֻדַּת יִשְׂרָאֵל מֵעֵבֶר לַיַּרְדֵּן מַעְרָבָה לְכֹל מְלֶאכֶת יְהוָה וְלַעֲבֹדַת הַמֶּלֶךְ:

31 The Chevronites: Jeriah, the chief of the Chevronites – they were investigated in the fortieth year of *David*'s reign by clans of all their lines, and men of substance were found among them in Jazer-gilead.

לא לַחֶבְרוֹנִי יְרִיָּה הָרֹאשׁ לַחֶבְרוֹנִי לְתֹלְדֹתָיו לְאָבוֹת בִּשְׁנַת הָאַרְבָּעִים לְמַלְכוּת דָּוִיד נִדְרָשׁוּ וַיִּמָּצֵא בָהֶם גִּבּוֹרֵי חַיִל בְּיַעְזֵיר גִּלְעָד:

32 His brothers, able men, 2,700, chiefs of clans – *David* put them in charge of the Reubenites, the Gadites, and the half-tribe of *Menashe* in all matters of *Hashem* and matters of the king.

לב וְאֶחָיו בְּנֵי־חַיִל אַלְפַּיִם וּשְׁבַע מֵאוֹת רָאשֵׁי הָאָבוֹת וַיַּפְקִידֵם דָּוִיד הַמֶּלֶךְ עַל־הָראוּבֵנִי וְהַגָּדִי וַחֲצִי שֵׁבֶט הַמְנַשִּׁי לְכָל־דְּבַר הָאֱלֹהִים וּדְבַר הַמֶּלֶךְ:

27 1 The number of Israelites – chiefs of clans, officers of thousands and hundreds and their clerks, who served the king in all matters of the divisions, who worked in monthly shifts during all the months of the year – each division, 24,000.

כז א וּבְנֵי יִשְׂרָאֵל לְמִסְפָּרָם רָאשֵׁי הָאָבוֹת וְשָׂרֵי הָאֲלָפִים וְהַמֵּאוֹת וְשֹׁטְרֵיהֶם הַמְשָׁרְתִים אֶת־הַמֶּלֶךְ לְכֹל דְּבַר הַמַּחְלְקוֹת הַבָּאָה וְהַיֹּצֵאת חֹדֶשׁ בְּחֹדֶשׁ לְכֹל חָדְשֵׁי הַשָּׁנָה הַמַּחֲלֹקֶת הָאַחַת עֶשְׂרִים וְאַרְבָּעָה אָלֶף:

*uv-NAY yis-ra-AYL l'-mis-pa-RAM ra-SHAY ha-a-VOT v'-sa-RAY ha-a-la-FEEM
v'-ha-may-OT v'-sho-t'-ray-HEM ha-m'-sha-r'-TEEM et ha-ME-lekh l'-KHOL d'-VAR
ha-makh-l'-KOT ha-ba-AH v'-ha-yo-TZAYT KHO-desh b'-KHO-desh l'-KHOL
khod-SHAY ha-sha-NAH ha-ma-kha-LO-ket ha-KHAT es-REEM v'-ar-ba-AH A-lef*

27:1 The number of Israelites After listing the jobs of the *Kohahim* and *Leviim*, we are told that the rest of the Children of Israel also have an important task: They must perform national army service. While the tribe of *Levi* is entrusted with the job of spiritually fortifying the nation, the rest of the people are charged with the responsibility of physical protection and defense. In contemporary Israel as well, every citizen is required to perform national army

Israeli soldiers with arms raised in a salute

63

² Over the first division for the first month –
Jashobeam son of Zabdiel; his division had 24,000.

ב עַל הַמַּחֲלֹקֶת הָרִאשׁוֹנָה לַחֹדֶשׁ
הָרִאשׁוֹן יָשָׁבְעָם בֶּן־זַבְדִּיאֵל וְעַל
מַחֲלֻקְתּוֹ עֶשְׂרִים וְאַרְבָּעָה אָלֶף:

³ Of the sons of *Peretz*, he, the chief of all the officers
of the army, [served] for the first month.

ג מִן־בְּנֵי־פֶרֶץ הָרֹאשׁ לְכָל־שָׂרֵי הַצְּבָאוֹת
לַחֹדֶשׁ הָרִאשׁוֹן:

⁴ Over the division of the second month – Dodai the
Ahohite; Mikloth was chief officer of his division;
his division had 24,000.

ד וְעַל מַחֲלֹקֶת הַחֹדֶשׁ הַשֵּׁנִי דּוֹדַי
הָאֲחוֹחִי וּמַחֲלֻקְתּוֹ וּמִקְלוֹת הַנָּגִיד וְעַל
מַחֲלֻקְתּוֹ עֶשְׂרִים וְאַרְבָּעָה אָלֶף:

⁵ The third army officer for the third month –
Benaiah son of *Yehoyada*, the chief *Kohen*; his
division had 24,000.

ה שַׂר הַצָּבָא הַשְּׁלִישִׁי לַחֹדֶשׁ הַשְּׁלִישִׁי
בְּנָיָהוּ בֶן־יְהוֹיָדָע הַכֹּהֵן רֹאשׁ וְעַל
מַחֲלֻקְתּוֹ עֶשְׂרִים וְאַרְבָּעָה אָלֶף:

⁶ That was Benaiah, one of the warriors of the thirty
and over the thirty; and [over] his division was
Ammizabad his son.

ו הוּא בְנָיָהוּ גִּבּוֹר הַשְּׁלֹשִׁים וְעַל־
הַשְּׁלֹשִׁים וּמַחֲלֻקְתּוֹ עַמִּיזָבָד בְּנוֹ:

⁷ The fourth, for the fourth month, *Asael* brother of
Yoav, and his son Zebadiah after him; his division
had 24,000.

ז הָרְבִיעִי לַחֹדֶשׁ הָרְבִיעִי עֲשָׂה־אֵל אֲחִי
יוֹאָב וּזְבַדְיָה בְנוֹ אַחֲרָיו וְעַל מַחֲלֻקְתּוֹ
עֶשְׂרִים וְאַרְבָּעָה אָלֶף:

⁸ The fifth, for the fifth month, the officer Shamhut
the Izrahite; his division had 24,000.

ח הַחֲמִישִׁי לַחֹדֶשׁ הַחֲמִישִׁי הַשַּׂר
שַׁמְהוּת הַיִּזְרָח וְעַל מַחֲלֻקְתּוֹ עֶשְׂרִים
וְאַרְבָּעָה אָלֶף:

⁹ The sixth, for the sixth month, Ira son of Ikkesh the
Tekoite; his division had 24,000.

ט הַשִּׁשִּׁי לַחֹדֶשׁ הַשִּׁשִּׁי עִירָא בֶן־עִקֵּשׁ
הַתְּקוֹעִי וְעַל מַחֲלֻקְתּוֹ עֶשְׂרִים
וְאַרְבָּעָה אָלֶף:

¹⁰ The seventh, for the seventh month, Helez the
Pelonite, of the Ephraimites; his division had
24,000.

י הַשְּׁבִיעִי לַחֹדֶשׁ הַשְּׁבִיעִי חֶלֶץ הַפְּלוֹנִי
מִן־בְּנֵי אֶפְרָיִם וְעַל מַחֲלֻקְתּוֹ עֶשְׂרִים
וְאַרְבָּעָה אָלֶף:

¹¹ The eighth, for the eighth month, Sibbecai the
Hushathite, of *Zerach*; his division had 24,000.

יא הַשְּׁמִינִי לַחֹדֶשׁ הַשְּׁמִינִי סִבְּכַי הַחֻשָׁתִי
לַזַּרְחִי וְעַל מַחֲלֻקְתּוֹ עֶשְׂרִים וְאַרְבָּעָה
אָלֶף:

¹² The ninth, for the ninth month, Abiezer the
Anatotite, of *Binyamin*; his division had 24,000.

יב הַתְּשִׁיעִי לַחֹדֶשׁ הַתְּשִׁיעִי אֲבִיעֶזֶר
הָעֲנְּתֹתִי לבנימיני [לַבֶּן] [יְמִינִי] וְעַל
מַחֲלֻקְתּוֹ עֶשְׂרִים וְאַרְבָּעָה אָלֶף:

¹³ The tenth, for the tenth month, Mahrai the
Netophathite, of *Zerach*; his division had 24,000.

יג הָעֲשִׂירִי לַחֹדֶשׁ הָעֲשִׂירִי מַהְרַי
הַנְּטוֹפָתִי לַזַּרְחִי וְעַל מַחֲלֻקְתּוֹ עֶשְׂרִים
וְאַרְבָּעָה אָלֶף:

service in the IDF, except those engaged in full time *Torah* study. In the early 1950s, Prime Minister David Ben Gurion reached an agreement with the leaders of the religious parties, exempting full time *Torah* scholars from serving in the IDF. Since its earliest days, Israel has affirmed the fact that just as the army strengthens the *Torah*, the *Torah* strengthens the army.

14 The eleventh, for the eleventh month, Benaiah the Pirathonite, of the Ephraimites; his division had 24,000.

יד עַשְׁתֵּי־עָשָׂר לְעַשְׁתֵּי־עָשָׂר הַחֹדֶשׁ בְּנָיָה הַפִּרְעָתוֹנִי מִן־בְּנֵי אֶפְרָיִם וְעַל מַחֲלֻקְתּוֹ עֶשְׂרִים וְאַרְבָּעָה אָלֶף:

15 The twelfth, for the twelfth month, Heldai the Netophathite, of *Otniel*; his division had 24,000.

טו הַשְּׁנֵים עָשָׂר לִשְׁנֵים עָשָׂר הַחֹדֶשׁ חֶלְדַּי הַנְּטוֹפָתִי לְעָתְנִיאֵל וְעַל מַחֲלֻקְתּוֹ עֶשְׂרִים וְאַרְבָּעָה אָלֶף:

16 Over the tribes of *Yisrael*: *Reuven*: the chief officer, *Eliezer* son of Zichri. *Shimon*: Shephatiah son of Maaca.

טז וְעַל שִׁבְטֵי יִשְׂרָאֵל לָרֻאוּבֵנִי נָגִיד אֱלִיעֶזֶר בֶּן־זִכְרִי לַשִּׁמְעוֹנִי שְׁפַטְיָהוּ בֶּן־מַעֲכָה:

17 *Levi*: Hashabiah son of Kemuel. *Aharon*: *Tzadok*.

יז לְלֵוִי חֲשַׁבְיָה בֶּן־קְמוּאֵל לְאַהֲרֹן צָדוֹק:

18 *Yehuda*: Elihu, of the brothers of *David*. *Yissachar*: Omri son of *Michael*.

יח לִיהוּדָה אֱלִיהוּ מֵאֲחֵי דָוִיד לְיִשָׂשכָר עָמְרִי בֶּן־מִיכָאֵל:

19 *Zevulun*: Ishmaiah son of *Ovadya*. *Naftali*: Jerimoth son of Azriel.

יט לִזְבוּלֻן יִשְׁמַעְיָהוּ בֶּן־עֹבַדְיָהוּ לְנַפְתָּלִי יְרִימוֹת בֶּן־עַזְרִיאֵל:

20 Ephraimites: *Hoshea* son of Azaziah. The half-tribe of *Menashe*: *Yoel* son of Pedaiah.

כ לִבְנֵי אֶפְרַיִם הוֹשֵׁעַ בֶּן־עֲזַזְיָהוּ לַחֲצִי שֵׁבֶט מְנַשֶּׁה יוֹאֵל בֶּן־פְּדָיָהוּ:

21 Half *Menashe* in Gilad: *Ido* son of *Zecharya*. *Binyamin*: Jaasiel son of *Avner*.

כא לַחֲצִי הַמְנַשֶּׁה גִּלְעָדָה יִדּוֹ בֶּן־זְכַרְיָהוּ לְבִנְיָמִן יַעֲשִׂיאֵל בֶּן־אַבְנֵר:

22 *Dan*: Azarel son of Jeroham. These were the officers of the tribes of *Yisrael*.

כב לְדָן עֲזַרְאֵל בֶּן־יְרֹחָם אֵלֶּה שָׂרֵי שִׁבְטֵי יִשְׂרָאֵל:

23 *David* did not take a census of those under twenty years of age, for *Hashem* had promised to make *Yisrael* as numerous as the stars of heaven.

כג וְלֹא־נָשָׂא דָוִיד מִסְפָּרָם לְמִבֶּן עֶשְׂרִים שָׁנָה וּלְמָטָּה כִּי אָמַר יְהֹוָה לְהַרְבּוֹת אֶת־יִשְׂרָאֵל כְּכוֹכְבֵי הַשָּׁמָיִם:

24 *Yoav* son of *Tzeruya* did begin to count them, but he did not finish; wrath struck *Yisrael* on account of this, and the census was not entered into the account of the chronicles of King *David*.

כד יוֹאָב בֶּן־צְרוּיָה הֵחֵל לִמְנוֹת וְלֹא כִלָּה וַיְהִי בָזֹאת קֶצֶף עַל־יִשְׂרָאֵל וְלֹא עָלָה הַמִּסְפָּר בְּמִסְפַּר דִּבְרֵי־הַיָּמִים לַמֶּלֶךְ דָּוִיד:

25 Over the royal treasuries: Azmaveth son of Adiel. Over the treasuries in the country – in the towns, the hamlets, and the citadels: *Yehonatan* son of Uzziyahu.

כה וְעַל אֹצְרוֹת הַמֶּלֶךְ עַזְמָוֶת בֶּן־עֲדִיאֵל וְעַל הָאֹצָרוֹת בַּשָּׂדֶה בֶּעָרִים וּבַכְּפָרִים וּבַמִּגְדָּלוֹת יְהוֹנָתָן בֶּן־עֻזִּיָּהוּ:

26 Over the field laborers in agricultural work: Ezri son of Chelub.

כו וְעַל עֹשֵׂי מְלֶאכֶת הַשָּׂדֶה לַעֲבֹדַת הָאֲדָמָה עֶזְרִי בֶּן־כְּלוּב:

27 Over the vineyards: *Shim'i* the Ramathite. And over the produce in the vineyards for wine cellars: Zabdi the Shiphmite.

כז וְעַל־הַכְּרָמִים שִׁמְעִי הָרָמָתִי וְעַל שֶׁבַּכְּרָמִים לְאֹצְרוֹת הַיַּיִן זַבְדִּי הַשִּׁפְמִי:

28 Over the olive trees and the sycamores in the Shephelah: Baal-hanan the Gederite. Over the oil-stores: *Yoash*.

כח וְעַל־הַזֵּיתִים וְהַשִּׁקְמִים אֲשֶׁר בַּשְּׁפֵלָה בַּעַל חָנָן הַגְּדֵרִי וְעַל־אֹצְרוֹת הַשֶּׁמֶן יוֹעָשׁ:

29 Over the cattle pasturing in Sharon: Shirtai the Sharonite. And over the cattle in the valleys: *Shafat* son of Adlai.

כט וְעַל־הַבָּקָר הָרֹעִים בַּשָּׁרוֹן שִׁטְרַי [שִׁרְטַי] הַשָּׁרוֹנִי וְעַל־הַבָּקָר בָּעֲמָקִים שָׁפָט בֶּן־עַדְלָי:

30 Over the camels: Obil the Ishmaelite. And over the she-asses: Jehdeiah the Meronothite.

ל וְעַל־הַגְּמַלִּים אוֹבִיל הַיִּשְׁמְעֵלִי וְעַל־הָאֲתֹנוֹת יֶחְדְּיָהוּ הַמֵּרֹנֹתִי:

31 Over the flocks: Jaziz the Hagrite. All these were stewards of the property of King *David*.

לא וְעַל־הַצֹּאן יָזִיז הַהַגְרִי כָּל־אֵלֶּה שָׂרֵי הָרְכוּשׁ אֲשֶׁר לַמֶּלֶךְ דָּוִיד:

32 *Yehonatan, David*'s uncle, was a counselor, a master, and a scribe: *Yechiel* son of Hachmoni was with the king's sons.

לב וִיהוֹנָתָן דּוֹד־דָּוִיד יוֹעֵץ אִישׁ־מֵבִין וְסוֹפֵר הוּא וִיחִיאֵל בֶּן־חַכְמוֹנִי עִם־בְּנֵי הַמֶּלֶךְ:

33 *Achitofel* was a counselor to the king. Hushai the Archite was the king's friend.

לג וַאֲחִיתֹפֶל יוֹעֵץ לַמֶּלֶךְ וְחוּשַׁי הָאַרְכִּי רֵעַ הַמֶּלֶךְ:

34 After *Achitofel* were *Yehoyada* son of Benaiah and *Evyatar*. The commander of the king's army was Yoav.

לד וְאַחֲרֵי אֲחִיתֹפֶל יְהוֹיָדָע בֶּן־בְּנָיָהוּ וְאֶבְיָתָר וְשַׂר־צָבָא לַמֶּלֶךְ יוֹאָב:

28 1 *David* assembled all the officers of *Yisrael* – the tribal officers, the divisional officers who served the king, the captains of thousands and the captains of hundreds, and the stewards of all the property and cattle of the king and his sons, with the eunuchs and the warriors, all the men of substance – to *Yerushalayim*.

כח א וַיַּקְהֵל דָּוִיד אֶת־כָּל־שָׂרֵי יִשְׂרָאֵל שָׂרֵי הַשְּׁבָטִים וְשָׂרֵי הַמַּחְלְקוֹת הַמְשָׁרְתִים אֶת־הַמֶּלֶךְ וְשָׂרֵי הָאֲלָפִים וְשָׂרֵי הַמֵּאוֹת וְשָׂרֵי כָל־רְכוּשׁ־וּמִקְנֶה לַמֶּלֶךְ וּלְבָנָיו עִם־הַסָּרִיסִים וְהַגִּבּוֹרִים וּלְכָל־גִּבּוֹר חָיִל אֶל־יְרוּשָׁלָ͏ִם:

2 King *David* rose to his feet and said, "Hear me, my brothers, my people! I wanted to build a resting-place for the *Aron Brit Hashem*, for the footstool of our God, and I laid aside material for building.

ב וַיָּקָם דָּוִיד הַמֶּלֶךְ עַל־רַגְלָיו וַיֹּאמֶר שְׁמָעוּנִי אַחַי וְעַמִּי אֲנִי עִם־לְבָבִי לִבְנוֹת בֵּית מְנוּחָה לַאֲרוֹן בְּרִית־יְהֹוָה וְלַהֲדֹם רַגְלֵי אֱלֹהֵינוּ וַהֲכִינוֹתִי לִבְנוֹת:

3 But *Hashem* said to me, 'You will not build a house for My name, for you are a man of battles and have shed blood.'

ג וְהָאֱלֹהִים אָמַר לִי לֹא־תִבְנֶה בַיִת לִשְׁמִי כִּי אִישׁ מִלְחָמוֹת אַתָּה וְדָמִים שָׁפָכְתָּ:

4 God of *Yisrael* chose me of all my father's house to be king over *Yisrael* forever. For He chose *Yehuda* to be ruler, and of the family of *Yehuda*, my father's house; and of my father's sons, He preferred to make me king over all *Yisrael*;

ד וַיִּבְחַר יְהֹוָה אֱלֹהֵי יִשְׂרָאֵל בִּי מִכֹּל בֵּית־אָבִי לִהְיוֹת לְמֶלֶךְ עַל־יִשְׂרָאֵל לְעוֹלָם כִּי בִיהוּדָה בָּחַר לְנָגִיד וּבְבֵית יְהוּדָה בֵּית אָבִי וּבִבְנֵי אָבִי בִּי רָצָה לְהַמְלִיךְ עַל־כָּל־יִשְׂרָאֵל:

5 and of all my sons – for many are the sons *Hashem* gave me – He chose my son *Shlomo* to sit on the throne of the kingdom of *Hashem* over *Yisrael*.

ה וּמִכָּל־בָּנַי כִּי רַבִּים בָּנִים נָתַן לִי יְהֹוָה וַיִּבְחַר בִּשְׁלֹמֹה בְנִי לָשֶׁבֶת עַל־כִּסֵּא מַלְכוּת יְהֹוָה עַל־יִשְׂרָאֵל:

6 He said to me, 'It will be your son *Shlomo* who will build My House and My courts, for I have chosen him to be a son to Me, and I will be a father to him.

ו וַיֹּאמֶר לִי שְׁלֹמֹה בִנְךָ הוּא־יִבְנֶה בֵיתִי וַחֲצֵרוֹתָי כִּי־בָחַרְתִּי בוֹ לִי לְבֵן וַאֲנִי אֶהְיֶה־לּוֹ לְאָב:

va-YO-mer LEE sh'-lo-MOH vin-KHA hu yiv-NEH vay-TEE va-kha-tzay-ro-TAI kee va-KHAR-tee VO LEE v'-VAYN va-a-NEE eh-yeh LO l'-AV

7 I will establish his kingdom forever, if he keeps firmly to the observance of My commandments and rules as he does now.'

ז וַהֲכִינוֹתִי אֶת־מַלְכוּתוֹ עַד־לְעוֹלָם אִם־יֶחֱזַק לַעֲשׂוֹת מִצְוֺתַי וּמִשְׁפָּטַי כַּיּוֹם הַזֶּה:

8 And now, in the sight of all *Yisrael*, the congregation of *Hashem*, and in the hearing of our God, [I say:] Observe and apply yourselves to all the commandments of *Hashem* your God in order that you may possess this good land and bequeath it to your children after you forever.

ח וְעַתָּה לְעֵינֵי כָל־יִשְׂרָאֵל קְהַל־יְהֹוָה וּבְאָזְנֵי אֱלֹהֵינוּ שִׁמְרוּ וְדִרְשׁוּ כָּל־מִצְוֺת יְהֹוָה אֱלֹהֵיכֶם לְמַעַן תִּירְשׁוּ אֶת־הָאָרֶץ הַטּוֹבָה וְהִנְחַלְתֶּם לִבְנֵיכֶם אַחֲרֵיכֶם עַד־עוֹלָם:

9 "And you, my son *Shlomo*, know the God of your father, and serve Him with single mind and fervent heart, for *Hashem* searches all minds and discerns the design of every thought; if you seek Him He will be available to you, but if you forsake Him He will abandon you forever.

ט וְאַתָּה שְׁלֹמֹה־בְנִי דַּע אֶת־אֱלֹהֵי אָבִיךָ וְעָבְדֵהוּ בְּלֵב שָׁלֵם וּבְנֶפֶשׁ חֲפֵצָה כִּי כָל־לְבָבוֹת דּוֹרֵשׁ יְהֹוָה וְכָל־יֵצֶר מַחֲשָׁבוֹת מֵבִין אִם־תִּדְרְשֶׁנּוּ יִמָּצֵא לָךְ וְאִם־תַּעַזְבֶנּוּ יַזְנִיחֲךָ לָעַד:

10 See then, *Hashem* chose you to build a house as the sanctuary; be strong and do it."

י רְאֵה עַתָּה כִּי־יְהֹוָה בָּחַר בְּךָ לִבְנוֹת־בַּיִת לַמִּקְדָּשׁ חֲזַק וַעֲשֵׂה:

11 *David* gave his son *Shlomo* the plan of the porch and its houses, its storerooms and its upper chambers and inner chambers; and of the place of the *Aron*-cover;

יא וַיִּתֵּן דָּוִיד לִשְׁלֹמֹה בְנוֹ אֶת־תַּבְנִית הָאוּלָם וְאֶת־בָּתָּיו וְגַנְזַכָּיו וַעֲלִיֹּתָיו וַחֲדָרָיו הַפְּנִימִים וּבֵית הַכַּפֹּרֶת:

12 and the plan of all that he had by the spirit: of the courts of the House of *Hashem* and all its surrounding chambers, and of the treasuries of the House of *Hashem* and of the treasuries of the holy things;

יב וְתַבְנִית כֹּל אֲשֶׁר הָיָה בָרוּחַ עִמּוֹ לְחַצְרוֹת בֵּית־יְהֹוָה וּלְכָל־הַלְּשָׁכוֹת סָבִיב לְאֹצְרוֹת בֵּית הָאֱלֹהִים וּלְאֹצְרוֹת הַקֳּדָשִׁים:

Sunburst over the Old City of *Yerushalayim*

 28:6 For I have chosen him to be a son to Me, and I will be a father to him King *David's* son *Shlomo* is chosen by God as the heir to his father's throne and the eternal monarchy of the People of Israel. In addition to the name *Shlomo*, he is also known as *Yedidya*, which means 'beloved of God' (II Samuel 12:25). *Radak* suggests that *Hashem* wants his name to be *Shlomo* (שלמה), from the Hebrew word *shalom* (שלום), meaning 'peace', because during his reign God would bless him and the People of Israel with peace. But *Shlomo* is also *Yedidya*, the beloved of God, as reflected in this verse. Indeed, both of his names accurately describe his accomplishments. During King *Shlomo's* reign, the Nation of Israel achieves the greatest heights, peace with the other nations, as well closeness to *Hashem* through service in the *Beit Hamikdash*.

13 the divisions of *Kohanim* and *Leviim* for all the work of the service of the House of *Hashem* and all the vessels of the service of the House of *Hashem*;

יג וּלְמַחְלְקוֹת הַכֹּהֲנִים וְהַלְוִיִּם וּלְכָל־מְלֶאכֶת עֲבוֹדַת בֵּית־יְהֹוָה וּלְכָל־כְּלֵי עֲבוֹדַת בֵּית־יְהֹוָה:

14 and gold, the weight of gold for vessels of every sort of use; silver for all the vessels of silver by weight, for all the vessels of every kind of service;

יד לַזָּהָב בַּמִּשְׁקָל לַזָּהָב לְכָל־כְּלֵי עֲבוֹדָה וַעֲבוֹדָה לְכֹל כְּלֵי הַכֶּסֶף בְּמִשְׁקָל לְכָל־כְּלֵי עֲבוֹדָה וַעֲבוֹדָה:

15 the weight of the gold *menorah*s and their gold lamps, and the weight of the silver *menorah*s, each *menorah* and its silver lamps, according to the use of every *menorah*;

טו וּמִשְׁקָל לִמְנֹרוֹת הַזָּהָב וְנֵרֹתֵיהֶם זָהָב בְּמִשְׁקָל־מְנוֹרָה וּמְנוֹרָה וְנֵרֹתֶיהָ וְלִמְנֹרוֹת הַכֶּסֶף בְּמִשְׁקָל לִמְנוֹרָה וְנֵרֹתֶיהָ כַּעֲבוֹדַת מְנוֹרָה וּמְנוֹרָה:

16 and the weight of gold for the tables of the rows of bread, for each table, and of silver for the silver tables;

טז וְאֶת־הַזָּהָב מִשְׁקָל לְשֻׁלְחֲנוֹת הַמַּעֲרֶכֶת לְשֻׁלְחַן וְשֻׁלְחָן וְכֶסֶף לְשֻׁלְחֲנוֹת הַכָּסֶף:

17 and of the pure gold for the forks and the basins and the jars; and the weight of the gold bowls, every bowl; and the weight of the silver bowls, each and every bowl;

יז וְהַמִּזְלָגוֹת וְהַמִּזְרָקוֹת וְהַקְּשָׂוֹת זָהָב טָהוֹר וְלִכְפוֹרֵי הַזָּהָב בְּמִשְׁקָל לִכְפוֹר וּכְפוֹר וְלִכְפוֹרֵי הַכֶּסֶף בְּמִשְׁקָל לִכְפוֹר וּכְפוֹר:

18 the weight of refined gold for the incense *Mizbayach* and the gold for the figure of the chariot – the cherubs – those with outspread wings screening the *Aron Brit Hashem*.

יח וּלְמִזְבַּח הַקְּטֹרֶת זָהָב מְזֻקָּק בַּמִּשְׁקָל וּלְתַבְנִית הַמֶּרְכָּבָה הַכְּרֻבִים זָהָב לְפֹרְשִׂים וְסֹכְכִים עַל־אֲרוֹן בְּרִית־יְהֹוָה:

19 "All this that *Hashem* made me understand by His hand on me, I give you in writing – the plan of all the works."

יט הַכֹּל בִּכְתָב מִיַּד יְהֹוָה עָלַי הִשְׂכִּיל כֹּל מַלְאֲכוֹת הַתַּבְנִית:

20 *David* said to his son *Shlomo*, "Be strong and of good courage and do it; do not be afraid or dismayed, for *Hashem* my God is with you; He will not fail you or forsake you till all the work on the House of *Hashem* is done.

כ וַיֹּאמֶר דָּוִיד לִשְׁלֹמֹה בְנוֹ חֲזַק וֶאֱמָץ וַעֲשֵׂה אַל־תִּירָא וְאַל־תֵּחָת כִּי יְהֹוָה אֱלֹהִים אֱלֹהַי עִמָּךְ לֹא יַרְפְּךָ וְלֹא יַעַזְבֶךָּ עַד־לִכְלוֹת כָּל־מְלֶאכֶת עֲבוֹדַת בֵּית־יְהֹוָה:

21 Here are the divisions of the *Kohanim* and *Leviim* for all kinds of service of the House of *Hashem*, and with you in all the work are willing men, skilled in all sorts of tasks; also the officers and all the people are at your command."

כא וְהִנֵּה מַחְלְקוֹת הַכֹּהֲנִים וְהַלְוִיִּם לְכָל־עֲבוֹדַת בֵּית הָאֱלֹהִים וְעִמְּךָ בְכָל־מְלָאכָה לְכָל־נָדִיב בַּחָכְמָה לְכָל־עֲבוֹדָה וְהַשָּׂרִים וְכָל־הָעָם לְכָל־דְּבָרֶיךָ:

כט 29 1 King *David* said to the entire assemblage, "*Hashem* has chosen my son *Shlomo* alone, an untried lad, although the work to be done is vast – for the temple is not for a man but for *Hashem*.

כט א וַיֹּאמֶר דָּוִיד הַמֶּלֶךְ לְכָל־הַקָּהָל שְׁלֹמֹה בְנִי אֶחָד בָּחַר־בּוֹ אֱלֹהִים נַעַר וָרָךְ וְהַמְּלָאכָה גְדוֹלָה כִּי לֹא לְאָדָם הַבִּירָה כִּי לַיהֹוָה אֱלֹהִים:

2 I have spared no effort to lay up for the House of my God gold for golden objects, silver for silver, copper for copper, iron for iron, wood for wooden, onyx-stone and inlay-stone, stone of antimony and variegated colors – every kind of precious stone and much marble.

ב וּכְכָל־כֹּחִי הֲכִינוֹתִי לְבֵית־אֱלֹהַי הַזָּהָב לַזָּהָב וְהַכֶּסֶף לַכֶּסֶף וְהַנְּחֹשֶׁת לַנְּחֹשֶׁת הַבַּרְזֶל לַבַּרְזֶל וְהָעֵצִים לָעֵצִים אַבְנֵי־שֹׁהַם וּמִלּוּאִים אַבְנֵי־פוּךְ וְרִקְמָה וְכֹל אֶבֶן יְקָרָה וְאַבְנֵי־שַׁיִשׁ לָרֹב:

³ Besides, out of my solicitude for the House of my God, I gave over my private hoard of gold and silver to the House of my God – in addition to all that I laid aside for the holy House:

ג וְעוֹד בִּרְצוֹתִי בְּבֵית אֱלֹהַי יֶשׁ־לִי סְגֻלָּה זָהָב וָכָסֶף נָתַתִּי לְבֵית־אֱלֹהַי לְמַעְלָה מִכָּל־הֲכִינוֹתִי לְבֵית הַקֹּדֶשׁ:

⁴ 3,000 gold *kikarim* of Ophir gold, and 7,000 *kikarim* of refined silver for covering the walls of the houses

ד שְׁלֹשֶׁת אֲלָפִים כִּכְּרֵי זָהָב מִזְּהַב אוֹפִיר וְשִׁבְעַת אֲלָפִים כִּכַּר־כֶּסֶף מְזֻקָּק לָטוּחַ קִירוֹת הַבָּתִּים:

⁵ (gold for golden objects, silver for silver for all the work) – into the hands of craftsmen. Now who is going to make a freewill offering and devote himself today to *Hashem*?"

ה לַזָּהָב לַזָּהָב וְלַכֶּסֶף לַכֶּסֶף וּלְכָל־מְלָאכָה בְּיַד חָרָשִׁים וּמִי מִתְנַדֵּב לְמַלֹּאות יָדוֹ הַיּוֹם לַיהוָה:

⁶ The officers of the clans and the officers of the tribes of *Yisrael* and the captains of thousands and hundreds and the supervisors of the king's work made freewill offerings,

ו וַיִּתְנַדְּבוּ שָׂרֵי הָאָבוֹת וְשָׂרֵי שִׁבְטֵי יִשְׂרָאֵל וְשָׂרֵי הָאֲלָפִים וְהַמֵּאוֹת וּלְשָׂרֵי מְלֶאכֶת הַמֶּלֶךְ:

⁷ giving for the work of the House of *Hashem*: 5,000 *kikarim* of gold, 10,000 darics, 10,000 *kikarim* of silver, 18,000 *kikarim* of copper, 100,000 *kikarim* of iron.

ז וַיִּתְּנוּ לַעֲבוֹדַת בֵּית־הָאֱלֹהִים זָהָב כִּכָּרִים חֲמֵשֶׁת־אֲלָפִים וַאֲדַרְכֹנִים רִבּוֹ וְכֶסֶף כִּכָּרִים עֲשֶׂרֶת אֲלָפִים וּנְחֹשֶׁת רִבּוֹ וּשְׁמוֹנַת אֲלָפִים כִּכָּרִים וּבַרְזֶל מֵאָה־אֶלֶף כִּכָּרִים:

⁸ Whoever had stones in his possession gave them to the treasury of the House of *Hashem* in the charge of *Yechiel* the Gershonite.

ח וְהַנִּמְצָא אִתּוֹ אֲבָנִים נָתְנוּ לְאוֹצַר בֵּית־יְהוָה עַל יַד־יְחִיאֵל הַגֵּרְשֻׁנִּי:

⁹ The people rejoiced over the freewill offerings they made, for with a whole heart they made freewill offerings to *Hashem*; King *David* also rejoiced very much.

ט וַיִּשְׂמְחוּ הָעָם עַל־הִתְנַדְּבָם כִּי בְּלֵב שָׁלֵם הִתְנַדְּבוּ לַיהוָה וְגַם דָּוִיד הַמֶּלֶךְ שָׂמַח שִׂמְחָה גְדוֹלָה:

¹⁰ *David* blessed *Hashem* in front of all the assemblage; *David* said, "Blessed are You, *Hashem*, God of *Yisrael* our father, from eternity to eternity.

י וַיְבָרֶךְ דָּוִיד אֶת־יְהוָה לְעֵינֵי כָּל־הַקָּהָל וַיֹּאמֶר דָּוִיד בָּרוּךְ אַתָּה יְהוָה אֱלֹהֵי יִשְׂרָאֵל אָבִינוּ מֵעוֹלָם וְעַד־עוֹלָם:

¹¹ Yours, *Hashem*, are greatness, might, splendor, triumph, and majesty – yes, all that is in heaven and on earth; to You, *Hashem*, belong kingship and preeminence above all.

יא לְךָ יְהוָה הַגְּדֻלָּה וְהַגְּבוּרָה וְהַתִּפְאֶרֶת וְהַנֵּצַח וְהַהוֹד כִּי־כֹל בַּשָּׁמַיִם וּבָאָרֶץ לְךָ יְהוָה הַמַּמְלָכָה וְהַמִּתְנַשֵּׂא לְכֹל לְרֹאשׁ:

¹² Riches and honor are Yours to dispense; You have dominion over all; with You are strength and might, and it is in Your power to make anyone great and strong.

יב וְהָעֹשֶׁר וְהַכָּבוֹד מִלְּפָנֶיךָ וְאַתָּה מוֹשֵׁל בַּכֹּל וּבְיָדְךָ כֹּחַ וּגְבוּרָה וּבְיָדְךָ לְגַדֵּל וּלְחַזֵּק לַכֹּל:

¹³ Now, *Hashem*, we praise You and extol Your glorious name.

יג וְעַתָּה אֱלֹהֵינוּ מוֹדִים אֲנַחְנוּ לָךְ וּמְהַלְלִים לְשֵׁם תִּפְאַרְתֶּךָ:

¹⁴ Who am I and who are my people, that we should have the means to make such a freewill offering; but all is from You, and it is Your gift that we have given to You.

יד וְכִי מִי אֲנִי וּמִי עַמִּי כִּי־נַעְצֹר כֹּחַ לְהִתְנַדֵּב כָּזֹאת כִּי־מִמְּךָ הַכֹּל וּמִיָּדְךָ נָתַנּוּ לָךְ:

15 For we are sojourners with You, mere transients like our fathers; our days on earth are like a shadow, with nothing in prospect.

טו כִּי־גֵרִים אֲנַחְנוּ לְפָנֶיךָ וְתוֹשָׁבִים כְּכָל־אֲבֹתֵינוּ כַּצֵּל יָמֵינוּ עַל־הָאָרֶץ וְאֵין מִקְוֶה:

16 *Hashem* our God, all this great mass that we have laid aside to build You a House for Your holy name is from You, and it is all Yours.

טז יְהֹוָה אֱלֹהֵינוּ כֹל הֶהָמוֹן הַזֶּה אֲשֶׁר הֲכִינֹנוּ לִבְנוֹת־לְךָ בַיִת לְשֵׁם קָדְשֶׁךָ מִיָּדְךָ הִיא [הוּא] וּלְךָ הַכֹּל:

17 I know, *Hashem*, that You search the heart and desire uprightness; I, with upright heart, freely offered all these things; now Your people, who are present here – I saw them joyously making freewill offerings.

יז וְיָדַעְתִּי אֱלֹהַי כִּי אַתָּה בֹּחֵן לֵבָב וּמֵישָׁרִים תִּרְצֶה אֲנִי בְּיֹשֶׁר לְבָבִי הִתְנַדַּבְתִּי כָל־אֵלֶּה וְעַתָּה עַמְּךָ הַנִּמְצְאוּ־פֹה רָאִיתִי בְשִׂמְחָה לְהִתְנַדֶּב־לָךְ:

18 O God of *Avraham*, *Yitzchak*, and *Yisrael*, our fathers, remember this to the eternal credit of the thoughts of Your people's hearts, and make their hearts constant toward You.

יח יְהֹוָה אֱלֹהֵי אַבְרָהָם יִצְחָק וְיִשְׂרָאֵל אֲבֹתֵינוּ שָׁמְרָה־זֹּאת לְעוֹלָם לְיֵצֶר מַחְשְׁבוֹת לְבַב עַמֶּךָ וְהָכֵן לְבָבָם אֵלֶיךָ:

19 As to my son *Shlomo*, give him a whole heart to observe Your commandments, Your admonitions, and Your laws, and to fulfill them all, and to build this temple for which I have made provision."

יט וְלִשְׁלֹמֹה בְנִי תֵּן לֵבָב שָׁלֵם לִשְׁמוֹר מִצְוֹתֶיךָ עֵדְוֹתֶיךָ וְחֻקֶּיךָ וְלַעֲשׂוֹת הַכֹּל וְלִבְנוֹת הַבִּירָה אֲשֶׁר־הֲכִינוֹתִי:

20 *David* said to the whole assemblage, "Now bless *Hashem* your God." All the assemblage blessed God of their fathers, and bowed their heads low to *Hashem* and the king.

כ וַיֹּאמֶר דָּוִיד לְכָל־הַקָּהָל בָּרְכוּ־נָא אֶת־יְהֹוָה אֱלֹהֵיכֶם וַיְבָרְכוּ כָל־הַקָּהָל לַיהֹוָה אֱלֹהֵי אֲבֹתֵיהֶם וַיִּקְּדוּ וַיִּשְׁתַּחֲווּ לַיהֹוָה וְלַמֶּלֶךְ:

21 They offered sacrifices to *Hashem* and made burnt offerings to *Hashem* on the morrow of that day: 1,000 bulls, 1,000 rams, 1,000 lambs, with their libations; [they made] sacrifices in great number for all *Yisrael*,

כא וַיִּזְבְּחוּ לַיהֹוָה זְבָחִים וַיַּעֲלוּ עֹלוֹת לַיהֹוָה לְמָחֳרַת הַיּוֹם הַהוּא פָּרִים אֶלֶף אֵילִים אֶלֶף כְּבָשִׂים אֶלֶף וְנִסְכֵּיהֶם וּזְבָחִים לָרֹב לְכָל־יִשְׂרָאֵל:

22 and they ate and drank in the presence of *Hashem* on that day with great joy. They again proclaimed *Shlomo* son of *David* king, and they anointed him as ruler before *Hashem*, and *Tzadok* as *Kohen Gadol*.

כב וַיֹּאכְלוּ וַיִּשְׁתּוּ לִפְנֵי יְהֹוָה בַּיּוֹם הַהוּא בְּשִׂמְחָה גְדוֹלָה וַיַּמְלִיכוּ שֵׁנִית לִשְׁלֹמֹה בֶן־דָּוִיד וַיִּמְשְׁחוּ לַיהֹוָה לְנָגִיד וּלְצָדוֹק לְכֹהֵן:

*va-yo-kh'-LU va-yish-TU lif-NAY a-do-NAI ba-YOM ha-HU b'-sim-KHAH
g'-do-LAH va-yam-LEE-khu shay-NEET lish-lo-MOH ven da-VEED
va-yim-sh'-KHU la-do-NAI l'-na-GEED ul-tza-DOK l'-kho-HAYN*

29:22 **Tzadok as Kohen Gadol**
The name *Tzadok* (צדוק) comes from the Hebrew word *tzedek* (צדק) which means 'justice' or 'righteousness'. *Tzadok* was a righteous priest who served in the times of King *David* and King *Shlomo*. After King *Shlomo*

The Garden of the Righteous at Yad Vashem

built the *Beit Hamikdash*, *Tzadok* was the first to serve as its High Priest. *Tzadok* and his descendants displayed loyalty and commitment to *Hashem*, and 'the house of *Tzadok*' is thus considered dear to God (see Ezekiel 44:15).

צדוק

23 *Shlomo* successfully took over the throne of *Hashem* as king instead of his father *David*, and all went well with him. All *Yisrael* accepted him;

כג וַיֵּשֶׁב שְׁלֹמֹה עַל־כִּסֵּא יְהֹוָה לְמֶלֶךְ תַּחַת־דָּוִיד אָבִיו וַיַּצְלַח וַיִּשְׁמְעוּ אֵלָיו כָּל־יִשְׂרָאֵל׃

24 all the officials and the warriors, and the sons of King *David* as well, gave their hand in support of King *Shlomo*.

כד וְכָל־הַשָּׂרִים וְהַגִּבֹּרִים וְגַם כָּל־בְּנֵי הַמֶּלֶךְ דָּוִיד נָתְנוּ יָד תַּחַת שְׁלֹמֹה הַמֶּלֶךְ׃

25 *Hashem* made *Shlomo* exceedingly great in the eyes of all *Yisrael*, and endowed him with a regal majesty that no king of *Yisrael* before him ever had.

כה וַיְגַדֵּל יְהֹוָה אֶת־שְׁלֹמֹה לְמַעְלָה לְעֵינֵי כָּל־יִשְׂרָאֵל וַיִּתֵּן עָלָיו הוֹד מַלְכוּת אֲשֶׁר לֹא־הָיָה עַל־כָּל־מֶלֶךְ לְפָנָיו עַל־יִשְׂרָאֵל׃

26 Thus *David* son of *Yishai* reigned over all *Yisrael*;

כו וְדָוִיד בֶּן־יִשָׁי מָלַךְ עַל־כָּל־יִשְׂרָאֵל׃

27 the length of his reign over *Yisrael* was forty years: he reigned seven years in *Chevron* and thirty-three years in *Yerushalayim*.

כז וְהַיָּמִים אֲשֶׁר מָלַךְ עַל־יִשְׂרָאֵל אַרְבָּעִים שָׁנָה בְּחֶבְרוֹן מָלַךְ שֶׁבַע שָׁנִים וּבִירוּשָׁלַיִם מָלַךְ שְׁלֹשִׁים וְשָׁלוֹשׁ׃

28 He died at a ripe old age, having enjoyed long life, riches and honor, and his son *Shlomo* reigned in his stead.

כח וַיָּמָת בְּשֵׂיבָה טוֹבָה שְׂבַע יָמִים עֹשֶׁר וְכָבוֹד וַיִּמְלֹךְ שְׁלֹמֹה בְנוֹ תַּחְתָּיו׃

29 The acts of King *David*, early and late, are recorded in the history of *Shmuel* the seer, the history of *Natan* the Navi, and the history of *Gad* the seer,

כט וְדִבְרֵי דָּוִיד הַמֶּלֶךְ הָרִאשֹׁנִים וְהָאַחֲרֹנִים הִנָּם כְּתוּבִים עַל־דִּבְרֵי שְׁמוּאֵל הָרֹאֶה וְעַל־דִּבְרֵי נָתָן הַנָּבִיא וְעַל־דִּבְרֵי גָּד הַחֹזֶה׃

30 together with all the mighty deeds of his kingship and the events that befell him and *Yisrael* and all the kingdoms of the earth.

ל עִם כָּל־מַלְכוּתוֹ וּגְבוּרָתוֹ וְהָעִתִּים אֲשֶׁר עָבְרוּ עָלָיו וְעַל־יִשְׂרָאֵל וְעַל כָּל־מַמְלְכוֹת הָאֲרָצוֹת׃

1 ¹ *Shlomo* son of *David* took firm hold of his kingdom, for *Hashem* his God was with him and made him exceedingly great.

א וַיִּתְחַזֵּק שְׁלֹמֹה בֶן־דָּוִיד עַל־מַלְכוּתוֹ וַיהֹוָה אֱלֹהָיו עִמּוֹ וַיְגַדְּלֵהוּ לְמָעְלָה:

² *Shlomo* summoned all *Yisrael* – the officers of thousands and of hundreds, and the judges, and all the chiefs of all *Yisrael*, the heads of the clans.

ב וַיֹּאמֶר שְׁלֹמֹה לְכָל־יִשְׂרָאֵל לְשָׂרֵי הָאֲלָפִים וְהַמֵּאוֹת וְלַשֹּׁפְטִים וּלְכֹל נָשִׂיא לְכָל־יִשְׂרָאֵל רָאשֵׁי הָאָבוֹת:

³ Then *Shlomo*, and all the assemblage with him, went to the shrine at *Givon*, for the Tent of Meeting, which *Moshe* the servant of *Hashem* had made in the wilderness, was there.

ג וַיֵּלְכוּ שְׁלֹמֹה וְכָל־הַקָּהָל עִמּוֹ לַבָּמָה אֲשֶׁר בְּגִבְעוֹן כִּי־שָׁם הָיָה אֹהֶל מוֹעֵד הָאֱלֹהִים אֲשֶׁר עָשָׂה מֹשֶׁה עֶבֶד־יְהֹוָה בַּמִּדְבָּר:

⁴ But the *Aron* of *Hashem David* had brought up from *Kiryat Ye'arim* to the place which *David* had prepared for it; for he had pitched a tent for it in *Yerushalayim*.)

ד אֲבָל אֲרוֹן הָאֱלֹהִים הֶעֱלָה דָוִיד מִקִּרְיַת יְעָרִים בַּהֵכִין לוֹ דָּוִיד כִּי נָטָה־לוֹ אֹהֶל בִּירוּשָׁלָ͏ִם:

⁵ The bronze *Mizbayach*, which *Betzalel* son of *Uri* son of *Chur* had made, was also there before the *Mishkan* of *Hashem*, and *Shlomo* and the assemblage resorted to it.

ה וּמִזְבַּח הַנְּחֹשֶׁת אֲשֶׁר עָשָׂה בְּצַלְאֵל בֶּן־אוּרִי בֶן־חוּר שָׂם לִפְנֵי מִשְׁכַּן יְהֹוָה וַיִּדְרְשֵׁהוּ שְׁלֹמֹה וְהַקָּהָל:

⁶ There *Shlomo* ascended the bronze *Mizbayach* before *Hashem*, which was at the Tent of Meeting, and on it sacrificed a thousand burnt offerings.

ו וַיַּעַל שְׁלֹמֹה שָׁם עַל־מִזְבַּח הַנְּחֹשֶׁת לִפְנֵי יְהֹוָה אֲשֶׁר לְאֹהֶל מוֹעֵד וַיַּעַל עָלָיו עֹלוֹת אָלֶף:

⁷ That night, *Hashem* appeared to *Shlomo* and said to him, "Ask, what shall I grant you?"

ז בַּלַּיְלָה הַהוּא נִרְאָה אֱלֹהִים לִשְׁלֹמֹה וַיֹּאמֶר לוֹ שְׁאַל מָה אֶתֶּן־לָךְ:

⁸ *Shlomo* said to *Hashem*, "You dealt most graciously with my father *David*, and now You have made me king in his stead.

ח וַיֹּאמֶר שְׁלֹמֹה לֵאלֹהִים אַתָּה עָשִׂיתָ עִם־דָּוִיד אָבִי חֶסֶד גָּדוֹל וְהִמְלַכְתַּנִי תַּחְתָּיו:

⁹ Now, O *Hashem*, let Your promise to my father *David* be fulfilled; for You have made me king over a people as numerous as the dust of the earth.

ט עַתָּה יְהֹוָה אֱלֹהִים יֵאָמֵן דְּבָרְךָ עִם דָּוִיד אָבִי כִּי אַתָּה הִמְלַכְתַּנִי עַל־עַם רַב כַּעֲפַר הָאָרֶץ:

¹⁰ Grant me then the wisdom and the knowledge to lead this people, for who can govern Your great people?"

י עַתָּה חָכְמָה וּמַדָּע תֶּן־לִי וְאֵצְאָה לִפְנֵי הָעָם־הַזֶּה וְאָבוֹאָה כִּי־מִי יִשְׁפֹּט אֶת־עַמְּךָ הַזֶּה הַגָּדוֹל:

a-TAH khokh-MAH u-ma-DA ten LEE v'-AY-tz'-AH lif-NAY ha-am ha-ZEH v'-a-VO-ah kee MEE yish-POT et a-m'-KHA ha-ZEH ha-ga-DOL

1:10 For who can govern Your great people When given the opportunity to make a request of *Hashem*, *Shlomo* asks for wisdom and understanding to be able to judge the nation properly. Just as *David* his father "executed true justice among all his people" (I Chronicles 18:14) though he was "a man of battles and have shed blood" (Chronicles 28:3), *Shlomo*'s reign will be similarly char- acterized by justice. While the wars to secure Israel's borders are significant, what personifies the Land of Israel in general, and the city of *Yerushalayim* in particular, is justice and righteousness (see, for example, Isaiah 33:5). Thus, *Eretz*

Supreme court in *Yerushalayim*

¹¹ *Hashem* said to *Shlomo*, "Because you want this, and have not asked for wealth, property, and glory, nor have you asked for the life of your enemy, or long life for yourself, but you have asked for the wisdom and the knowledge to be able to govern My people over whom I have made you king,

יא וַיֹּאמֶר־אֱלֹהִים לִשְׁלֹמֹה יַעַן אֲשֶׁר הָיְתָה זֹאת עִם־לְבָבֶךָ וְלֹא־שָׁאַלְתָּ עֹשֶׁר נְכָסִים וְכָבוֹד וְאֵת נֶפֶשׁ שֹׂנְאֶיךָ וְגַם־יָמִים רַבִּים לֹא שָׁאָלְתָּ וַתִּשְׁאַל־לְךָ חׇכְמָה וּמַדָּע אֲשֶׁר תִּשְׁפּוֹט אֶת־עַמִּי אֲשֶׁר הִמְלַכְתִּיךָ עָלָיו:

¹² wisdom and knowledge are granted to you, and I grant you also wealth, property, and glory, the like of which no king before you has had, nor shall any after you have."

יב הַחׇכְמָה וְהַמַּדָּע נָתוּן לָךְ וְעֹשֶׁר וּנְכָסִים וְכָבוֹד אֶתֶּן־לָךְ אֲשֶׁר לֹא־הָיָה כֵן לַמְּלָכִים אֲשֶׁר לְפָנֶיךָ וְאַחֲרֶיךָ לֹא יִהְיֶה־כֵּן:

¹³ From the shrine at *Givon*, from the Tent of Meeting, *Shlomo* went to *Yerushalayim* and reigned over *Yisrael*.

יג וַיָּבֹא שְׁלֹמֹה לַבָּמָה אֲשֶׁר־בְּגִבְעוֹן יְרוּשָׁלַ͏ִם מִלִּפְנֵי אֹהֶל מוֹעֵד וַיִּמְלֹךְ עַל־יִשְׂרָאֵל:

¹⁴ *Shlomo* assembled chariots and horsemen; he had 1,400 chariots and 12,000 horses that he stationed in the chariot towns and with the king in *Yerushalayim*.

יד וַיֶּאֱסֹף שְׁלֹמֹה רֶכֶב וּפָרָשִׁים וַיְהִי־לוֹ אֶלֶף וְאַרְבַּע־מֵאוֹת רֶכֶב וּשְׁנֵים־עָשָׂר אֶלֶף פָּרָשִׁים וַיַּנִּיחֵם בְּעָרֵי הָרֶכֶב וְעִם־הַמֶּלֶךְ בִּירוּשָׁלָ͏ִם:

¹⁵ The king made silver and gold as plentiful in *Yerushalayim* as stones, and cedars as plentiful as the sycamores in the Shephelah.

טו וַיִּתֵּן הַמֶּלֶךְ אֶת־הַכֶּסֶף וְאֶת־הַזָּהָב בִּירוּשָׁלַ͏ִם כָּאֲבָנִים וְאֵת הָאֲרָזִים נָתַן כַּשִּׁקְמִים אֲשֶׁר־בַּשְּׁפֵלָה לָרֹב:

¹⁶ *Shlomo*'s horses were imported from Egypt and from *Que*; the king's traders would buy them from *Que* at the market price.

טז וּמוֹצָא הַסּוּסִים אֲשֶׁר לִשְׁלֹמֹה מִמִּצְרָיִם וּמִקְוֵא סֹחֲרֵי הַמֶּלֶךְ מִקְוֵא יִקְחוּ בִּמְחִיר:

¹⁷ A chariot imported from Egypt cost 600 *shekalim* of silver, and a horse 150. These in turn were exported by them to all the kings of the Hittites and the kings of the Arameans.

יז וַיַּעֲלוּ וַיּוֹצִיאוּ מִמִּצְרַיִם מֶרְכָּבָה בְּשֵׁשׁ מֵאוֹת כֶּסֶף וְסוּס בַּחֲמִשִּׁים וּמֵאָה וְכֵן לְכׇל־מַלְכֵי הַחִתִּים וּמַלְכֵי אֲרָם בְּיָדָם יוֹצִיאוּ:

¹⁸ Then *Shlomo* resolved to build a House for the name of *Hashem* and a royal palace for himself.

יח וַיֹּאמֶר שְׁלֹמֹה לִבְנוֹת בַּיִת לְשֵׁם יְהֹוָה וּבַיִת לְמַלְכוּתוֹ:

2 ¹ *Shlomo* mustered 70,000 basket carriers and 80,000 quarriers in the hills, with 3,600 men supervising them.

ב א וַיִּסְפֹּר שְׁלֹמֹה שִׁבְעִים אֶלֶף אִישׁ סַבָּל וּשְׁמוֹנִים אֶלֶף אִישׁ חֹצֵב בָּהָר וּמְנַצְּחִים עֲלֵיהֶם שְׁלֹשֶׁת אֲלָפִים וְשֵׁשׁ מֵאוֹת:

Yisrael is inherited through justice (Deuteronomy 16:20), justice allows for the land to flourish, and conversely, a lack of justice leads to its downfall and destruction. The *Beit Hamikdash*, built by *Shlomo*, is the seat of justice (Deuteronomy 17:8–10), and it is where the High Court would meet. In making this request of God, *Shlomo* sought to ensure that he would lead the Nation of Israel, in the Land of Israel, in justice and truth. Today, the State of Israel has an established judicial system which continues to pursue justice in the Holy Land, ensuring that the population is law-abiding and protecting the rights of its citizens. Like the High Court of old, Israel's Supreme Court is located in *Yerushalayim*.

² *Shlomo* sent this message to King Huram of Tyre, "In view of what you did for my father *David* in sending him cedars to build a palace for his residence –

ב וַיִּשְׁלַח שְׁלֹמֹה אֶל־חוּרָם מֶלֶךְ־צֹר לֵאמֹר כַּאֲשֶׁר עָשִׂיתָ עִם־דָּוִיד אָבִי וַתִּשְׁלַח־לוֹ אֲרָזִים לִבְנוֹת־לוֹ בַיִת לָשֶׁבֶת בּוֹ:

³ see, I intend to build a House for the name of *Hashem* my God; I will dedicate it to Him for making incense offering of sweet spices in His honor, for the regular rows of bread, and for the morning and evening burnt offerings on *Shabbatot*, new moons, and festivals, as is *Yisrael*'s eternal duty.

ג הִנֵּה אֲנִי בוֹנֶה־בַּיִת לְשֵׁם יְהֹוָה אֱלֹהָי לְהַקְדִּישׁ לוֹ לְהַקְטִיר לְפָנָיו קְטֹרֶת־סַמִּים וּמַעֲרֶכֶת תָּמִיד וְעֹלוֹת לַבֹּקֶר וְלָעֶרֶב לַשַּׁבָּתוֹת וְלֶחֳדָשִׁים וּלְמוֹעֲדֵי יְהֹוָה אֱלֹהֵינוּ לְעוֹלָם זֹאת עַל־יִשְׂרָאֵל:

> hi-NAY a-NEE vo-neh BA-yit l'-SHAYM a-do-NAI e-lo-HAI l'-hak-DEESH
> LO l'-hak-TEER l'-fa-NAV k'-TO-ret sa-MEEM u-ma-a-RE-khet ta-MEED
> v'-o-LOT la-BO-ker v'-la-E-rev la-sha-ba-TOT v'-le-kho-da-SHEEM
> ul-mo-a-DAY a-do-NAI e-lo-HAY-nu l'-o-LAM ZOT al yis-ra-AYL

⁴ The House that I intend to build will be great, inasmuch as our God is greater than all gods.

ד וְהַבַּיִת אֲשֶׁר־אֲנִי בוֹנֶה גָּדוֹל כִּי־גָדוֹל אֱלֹהֵינוּ מִכָּל־הָאֱלֹהִים:

⁵ Who indeed is capable of building a House for Him! Even the heavens to their uttermost reaches cannot contain Him, and who am I that I should build Him a House – except as a place for making burnt offerings to Him?

ה וּמִי יַעֲצָר־כֹּחַ לִבְנוֹת־לוֹ בַיִת כִּי הַשָּׁמַיִם וּשְׁמֵי הַשָּׁמַיִם לֹא יְכַלְכְּלֻהוּ וּמִי אֲנִי אֲשֶׁר אֶבְנֶה־לּוֹ בַיִת כִּי אִם־לְהַקְטִיר לְפָנָיו:

⁶ Now send me a craftsman to work in gold, silver, bronze, and iron, and in purple, crimson, and blue yarn, and who knows how to engrave, alongside the craftsmen I have here in *Yehuda* and in *Yerushalayim*, whom my father *David* provided.

ו וְעַתָּה שְׁלַח־לִי אִישׁ־חָכָם לַעֲשׂוֹת בַּזָּהָב וּבַכֶּסֶף וּבַנְּחֹשֶׁת וּבַבַּרְזֶל וּבָאַרְגְּוָן וְכַרְמִיל וּתְכֵלֶת וְיֹדֵעַ לְפַתֵּחַ פִּתּוּחִים עִם־הַחֲכָמִים אֲשֶׁר עִמִּי בִּיהוּדָה וּבִירוּשָׁלַם אֲשֶׁר הֵכִין דָּוִיד אָבִי:

⁷ Send me cedars, cypress, and algum wood from the Lebanon, for I know that your servants are skilled at cutting the trees of Lebanon. My servants will work with yours

ז וּשְׁלַח־לִי עֲצֵי אֲרָזִים בְּרוֹשִׁים וְאַלְגּוּמִּים מֵהַלְּבָנוֹן כִּי אֲנִי יָדַעְתִּי אֲשֶׁר עֲבָדֶיךָ יוֹדְעִים לִכְרוֹת עֲצֵי לְבָנוֹן וְהִנֵּה עֲבָדַי עִם־עֲבָדֶיךָ:

⁸ to provide me with a great stock of timber; for the House that I intend to build will be singularly great.

ח וּלְהָכִין לִי עֵצִים לָרֹב כִּי הַבַּיִת אֲשֶׁר־אֲנִי בוֹנֶה גָּדוֹל וְהַפְלֵא:

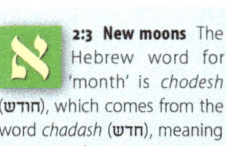

2:3 New moons The Hebrew word for 'month' is *chodesh* (חודש), which comes from the word *chadash* (חדש), meaning 'new'. Sanctifying the new moon each month is the very first biblical commandment given collectively to the People of Israel (Exodus 12:2). As opposed to pagan worship, which requires a steady force such as the sun to venerate, the People of Israel were told

New moon over Be'er Sheva

to sanctify the moon which waxes and wanes on a monthly basis. The message is that no matter how dark life may seem, societies, nations and individuals can always change for the better. Our optimistic scanning of the black-blue skies for the first sliver of the new moon every month is our testimony to the possibility of growth, change and development. We must learn to sanctify that change.

חודש

9 I have allocated for your servants, the wood-cutters who fell the trees, 20,000 *kor* of crushed wheat and 20,000 *kor* of barley, 20,000 *batim* of wine and 20,000 *batim* of oil."

ט וְהִנֵּה לַחֹטְבִים לְכֹרְתֵי הָעֵצִים נָתַתִּי חִטִּים מַכּוֹת לַעֲבָדֶיךָ כֹּרִים עֶשְׂרִים אֶלֶף וּשְׂעֹרִים כֹּרִים עֶשְׂרִים אָלֶף וְיַיִן בַּתִּים עֶשְׂרִים אֶלֶף וְשֶׁמֶן בַּתִּים עֶשְׂרִים אָלֶף:

10 Huram, king of Tyre, sent *Shlomo* this written message in reply, "Because *Hashem* loved His people, He made you king over them."

י וַיֹּאמֶר חוּרָם מֶלֶךְ־צֹר בִּכְתָב וַיִּשְׁלַח אֶל־שְׁלֹמֹה בְּאַהֲבַת יְהוָה אֶת־עַמּוֹ נְתָנְךָ עֲלֵיהֶם מֶלֶךְ:

11 Huram continued, "Blessed is *Hashem*, God of *Yisrael*, who made the heavens and the earth, who gave King *David* a wise son, endowed with intelligence and understanding, to build a House for *Hashem* and a royal palace for himself.

יא וַיֹּאמֶר חוּרָם בָּרוּךְ יְהוָה אֱלֹהֵי יִשְׂרָאֵל אֲשֶׁר עָשָׂה אֶת־הַשָּׁמַיִם וְאֶת־הָאָרֶץ אֲשֶׁר נָתַן לְדָוִיד הַמֶּלֶךְ בֵּן חָכָם יוֹדֵעַ שֵׂכֶל וּבִינָה אֲשֶׁר יִבְנֶה־בַּיִת לַיהוָה וּבַיִת לְמַלְכוּתוֹ:

12 Now I am sending you a skillful and intelligent man, my master Huram,

יב וְעַתָּה שָׁלַחְתִּי אִישׁ־חָכָם יוֹדֵעַ בִּינָה לְחוּרָם אָבִי:

13 the son of a Danite woman, his father a Tyrian. He is skilled at working in gold, silver, bronze, iron, precious stones, and wood; in purple, blue, and crimson yarn and in fine linen; and at engraving and designing whatever will be required of him, alongside your craftsmen and the craftsmen of my lord, your father *David*.

יג בֶּן־אִשָּׁה מִן־בְּנוֹת דָּן וְאָבִיו אִישׁ־צֹרִי יוֹדֵעַ לַעֲשׂוֹת בַּזָּהָב־וּבַכֶּסֶף בַּנְּחֹשֶׁת בַּבַּרְזֶל בָּאֲבָנִים וּבָעֵצִים בָּאַרְגָּמָן בַּתְּכֵלֶת וּבַבּוּץ וּבַכַּרְמִיל וּלְפַתֵּחַ כָּל־פִּתּוּחַ וְלַחְשֹׁב כָּל־מַחֲשָׁבֶת אֲשֶׁר יִנָּתֶן־לוֹ עִם־חֲכָמֶיךָ וְחַכְמֵי אֲדֹנִי דָּוִיד אָבִיךָ:

14 As to the wheat, barley, oil, and wine which my lord mentioned, let him send them to his servants.

יד וְעַתָּה הַחִטִּים וְהַשְּׂעֹרִים הַשֶּׁמֶן וְהַיַּיִן אֲשֶׁר אָמַר אֲדֹנִי יִשְׁלַח לַעֲבָדָיו:

15 We undertake to cut down as many trees of Lebanon as you need, and deliver them to you as rafts by sea to Jaffa; you will transport them to *Yerushalayim*."

טו וַאֲנַחְנוּ נִכְרֹת עֵצִים מִן־הַלְּבָנוֹן כְּכָל־צָרְכֶּךָ וּנְבִיאֵם לְךָ רַפְסֹדוֹת עַל־יָם יָפוֹ וְאַתָּה תַּעֲלֶה אֹתָם יְרוּשָׁלָ͏ִם:

16 *Shlomo* took a census of all the aliens who were in the land of *Yisrael*, besides the census taken by his father *David*, and they were found to be 153,600.

טז וַיִּסְפֹּר שְׁלֹמֹה כָּל־הָאֲנָשִׁים הַגֵּירִים אֲשֶׁר בְּאֶרֶץ יִשְׂרָאֵל אַחֲרֵי הַסְּפָר אֲשֶׁר סְפָרָם דָּוִיד אָבִיו וַיִּמָּצְאוּ מֵאָה וַחֲמִשִּׁים אֶלֶף וּשְׁלֹשֶׁת אֲלָפִים וְשֵׁשׁ מֵאוֹת:

17 He made 70,000 of them basket carriers, and 80,000 of them quarriers, with 3,600 supervisors to see that the people worked.

יז וַיַּעַשׂ מֵהֶם שִׁבְעִים אֶלֶף סַבָּל וּשְׁמֹנִים אֶלֶף חֹצֵב בָּהָר וּשְׁלֹשֶׁת אֲלָפִים וְשֵׁשׁ מֵאוֹת מְנַצְּחִים לְהַעֲבִיד אֶת־הָעָם:

3 1 Then *Shlomo* began to build the House of *Hashem* in *Yerushalayim* on Mount *Moriah*, where [*Hashem*] had appeared to his father *David*, at the place which *David* had designated, at the threshing floor of Ornan the Jebusite.

ג א וַיָּחֶל שְׁלֹמֹה לִבְנוֹת אֶת־בֵּית־יְהוָה בִּירוּשָׁלַ͏ִם בְּהַר הַמּוֹרִיָּה אֲשֶׁר נִרְאָה לְדָוִיד אָבִיהוּ אֲשֶׁר הֵכִין בִּמְקוֹם דָּוִיד בְּגֹרֶן אָרְנָן הַיְבוּסִי:

2 He began to build on the second day of the second month of the fourth year of his reign.

ב וַיָּחֶל לִבְנוֹת בַּחֹדֶשׁ הַשֵּׁנִי בַּשֵּׁנִי בִּשְׁנַת אַרְבַּע לְמַלְכוּתוֹ:

3 These were the dimensions *Shlomo* established for building the House of *Hashem*: its length in *amot*, by the former measure, was 60, and its breadth was 20.

ג וְאֵלֶּה הוּסַד שְׁלֹמֹה לִבְנוֹת אֶת־בֵּית הָאֱלֹהִים הָאֹרֶךְ אַמּוֹת בַּמִּדָּה הָרִאשׁוֹנָה אַמּוֹת שִׁשִּׁים וְרֹחַב אַמּוֹת עֶשְׂרִים:

4 The length of the porch in front [was equal] to the breadth of the House – 20 *amot*, and its height was 120. Inside he overlaid it with pure gold.

ד וְהָאוּלָם אֲשֶׁר עַל־פְּנֵי הָאֹרֶךְ עַל־פְּנֵי רֹחַב־הַבַּיִת אַמּוֹת עֶשְׂרִים וְהַגֹּבַהּ מֵאָה וְעֶשְׂרִים וַיְצַפֵּהוּ מִפְּנִימָה זָהָב טָהוֹר:

5 The House itself he paneled with cypress wood. He overlaid it with fine gold and embossed on it palms and chains.

ה וְאֵת הַבַּיִת הַגָּדוֹל חִפָּה עֵץ בְּרוֹשִׁים וַיְחַפֵּהוּ זָהָב טוֹב וַיַּעַל עָלָיו תִּמֹרִים וְשַׁרְשְׁרוֹת:

6 He studded the House with precious stones for decoration; the gold was from Parvaim.

ו וַיְצַף אֶת־הַבַּיִת אֶבֶן יְקָרָה לְתִפְאָרֶת וְהַזָּהָב זְהַב פַּרְוָיִם:

7 He overlaid the House with gold – the beams, the thresholds, its walls and doors; he carved cherubim on the walls.

ז וַיְחַף אֶת־הַבַּיִת הַקֹּרוֹת הַסִּפִּים וְקִירוֹתָיו וְדַלְתוֹתָיו זָהָב וּפִתַּח כְּרוּבִים עַל־הַקִּירוֹת:

8 He made the Holy of Holies: its length was [equal to] the breadth of the house – 20 *amot*, and its breadth was 20 *amot*. He overlaid it with 600 *kikarim* of fine gold.

ח וַיַּעַשׂ אֶת־בֵּית־קֹדֶשׁ הַקֳּדָשִׁים אָרְכּוֹ עַל־פְּנֵי רֹחַב־הַבַּיִת אַמּוֹת עֶשְׂרִים וְרָחְבּוֹ אַמּוֹת עֶשְׂרִים וַיְחַפֵּהוּ זָהָב טוֹב לְכִכָּרִים שֵׁשׁ מֵאוֹת:

9 The weight of the nails was 50 *shekalim* of gold; the upper chambers he overlaid with gold.

ט וּמִשְׁקָל לְמִסְמְרוֹת לִשְׁקָלִים חֲמִשִּׁים זָהָב וְהָעֲלִיּוֹת חִפָּה זָהָב:

10 He made two sculptured cherubim in the Holy of Holies, and they were overlaid with gold.

י וַיַּעַשׂ בְּבֵית־קֹדֶשׁ הַקֳּדָשִׁים כְּרוּבִים שְׁנַיִם מַעֲשֵׂה צַעֲצֻעִים וַיְצַפּוּ אֹתָם זָהָב:

va-YA-as b'-VAYT KO-desh ha-ko-da-SHEEM k'-ru-VEEM sh'-NA-yim ma-a-SAY tza-a-tzu-EEM vai-tza-PU o-TAM za-HAV

11 The outspread wings of the cherubim were 20 *amot* across: one wing 5 *amot* long touching one wall of the House, and the other wing 5 *amot* long touching the wing of the other cherub;

יא וְכַנְפֵי הַכְּרוּבִים אָרְכָּם אַמּוֹת עֶשְׂרִים כְּנַף הָאֶחָד לְאַמּוֹת חָמֵשׁ מַגַּעַת לְקִיר הַבַּיִת וְהַכָּנָף הָאַחֶרֶת אַמּוֹת חָמֵשׁ מַגִּיעַ לִכְנַף הַכְּרוּב הָאַחֵר:

12 one wing of the other [cherub] 5 *amot* long extending to the other wall of the House, and its other wing 5 *amot* long touching the wing of the first cherub.

יב וּכְנַף הַכְּרוּב הָאֶחָד אַמּוֹת חָמֵשׁ מַגִּיעַ לְקִיר הַבָּיִת וְהַכָּנָף הָאַחֶרֶת אַמּוֹת חָמֵשׁ דְּבֵקָה לִכְנַף הַכְּרוּב הָאַחֵר:

3:10 He made two sculptured cherubim *Shlomo* builds two great cherubim in the Holy of Holies, paralleling the cherubim which God placed in front of the Garden of Eden "to guard the way to the tree of life" (Genesis 3:24). *Shlomo's* cherubim symbolize these guardians, showing that what lies behind them, the *Aron HaBrit*, holds the roots to the tree of life. The *Torah*, which is contained in the Ark, and the commandments therein are the pathway to life. As King *Shlomo* writes about the wisdom of the *Torah* "For they will bestow on you length of days, years of life and well-being," and, "she is a tree of life to those who grasp her" (Proverbs 3:2,18).

IDF artillery corps reading from the *Torah* near Gaza

Chronicles

¹³ The wingspread of these cherubim was thus 20 *amot* across, and they were standing up facing the House.

יג כַּנְפֵי הַכְּרוּבִים הָאֵלֶּה פֹּרְשִׂים אַמּוֹת עֶשְׂרִים וְהֵם עֹמְדִים עַל־רַגְלֵיהֶם וּפְנֵיהֶם לַבָּיִת:

¹⁴ He made the curtain of blue, purple, and crimson yarn and fine linen, and he worked cherubim into it.

יד וַיַּעַשׂ אֶת־הַפָּרֹכֶת תְּכֵלֶת וְאַרְגָּמָן וְכַרְמִיל וּבוּץ וַיַּעַל עָלָיו כְּרוּבִים:

¹⁵ At the front of the House he made two columns 35 *amot* high; the capitals on top of them were 5 *amot* high.

טו וַיַּעַשׂ לִפְנֵי הַבַּיִת עַמּוּדִים שְׁנַיִם אַמּוֹת שְׁלֹשִׁים וְחָמֵשׁ אֹרֶךְ וְהַצֶּפֶת אֲשֶׁר־עַל־רֹאשׁוֹ אַמּוֹת חָמֵשׁ:

¹⁶ He made chainwork in the inner Sanctuary and set it on the top of the columns; he made a hundred pomegranates and set them into the chainwork.

טז וַיַּעַשׂ שַׁרְשְׁרוֹת בַּדְּבִיר וַיִּתֵּן עַל־רֹאשׁ הָעַמֻּדִים וַיַּעַשׂ רִמּוֹנִים מֵאָה וַיִּתֵּן בַּשַּׁרְשְׁרוֹת:

¹⁷ He erected the columns in front of the Great Hall, one to its right and one to its left; the one to the right was called Jachin, and the one to the left, *Boaz.*

יז וַיָּקֶם אֶת־הָעַמּוּדִים עַל־פְּנֵי הַהֵיכָל אֶחָד מִיָּמִין וְאֶחָד מֵהַשְּׂמֹאול וַיִּקְרָא שֵׁם־הַיְמִינִי [הַיְמָנִי] יָכִין וְשֵׁם הַשְּׂמָאלִי בֹּעַז:

4 ¹ He made a *Mizbayach* of bronze 20 *amot* long, 20 *amot* wide, and 10 *amot* high.

ד א וַיַּעַשׂ מִזְבַּח נְחֹשֶׁת עֶשְׂרִים אַמָּה אָרְכּוֹ וְעֶשְׂרִים אַמָּה רָחְבּוֹ וְעֶשֶׂר אַמּוֹת קוֹמָתוֹ:

² He made the sea of cast metal 10 *amot* across from brim to brim, perfectly round; it was 5 *amot* high, and its circumference was 30 *amot.*

ב וַיַּעַשׂ אֶת־הַיָּם מוּצָק עֶשֶׂר בָּאַמָּה מִשְּׂפָתוֹ אֶל־שְׂפָתוֹ עָגוֹל סָבִיב וְחָמֵשׁ בָּאַמָּה קוֹמָתוֹ וְקָו שְׁלֹשִׁים בָּאַמָּה יָסֹב אֹתוֹ סָבִיב:

³ Beneath were figures of oxen set all around it, of 10 *amot*, encircling the sea; the oxen were in two rows, cast in one piece with it.

ג וּדְמוּת בְּקָרִים תַּחַת לוֹ סָבִיב סָבִיב סוֹבְבִים אֹתוֹ עֶשֶׂר בָּאַמָּה מַקִּיפִים אֶת־הַיָּם סָבִיב שְׁנַיִם טוּרִים הַבָּקָר יְצוּקִים בְּמֻצַקְתּוֹ:

⁴ It stood upon twelve oxen: three faced north, three faced west, three faced south, and three faced east, with the sea resting upon them; their haunches were all turned inward.

ד עוֹמֵד עַל־שְׁנֵים עָשָׂר בָּקָר שְׁלֹשָׁה פֹנִים צָפוֹנָה וּשְׁלוֹשָׁה פֹנִים יָמָּה וּשְׁלֹשָׁה פֹּנִים נֶגְבָּה וּשְׁלֹשָׁה פֹּנִים מִזְרָחָה וְהַיָּם עֲלֵיהֶם מִלְמָעְלָה וְכָל־אֲחֹרֵיהֶם בָּיְתָה:

⁵ It was a *tefach* thick, and its brim was made like that of a cup, like the petals of a lily. It held 3,000 *batim.*

ה וְעָבְיוֹ טֶפַח וּשְׂפָתוֹ כְּמַעֲשֵׂה שְׂפַת־כּוֹס פֶּרַח שׁוֹשַׁנָּה מַחֲזִיק בַּתִּים שְׁלֹשֶׁת אֲלָפִים יָכִיל:

⁶ He made ten bronze lavers for washing; he set five on the right and five on the left; they would rinse off in them the parts of the burnt offering; but the sea served the *Kohanim* for washing.

ו וַיַּעַשׂ כִּיּוֹרִים עֲשָׂרָה וַיִּתֵּן חֲמִשָּׁה מִיָּמִין וַחֲמִשָּׁה מִשְּׂמֹאול לְרָחְצָה בָהֶם אֶת־מַעֲשֵׂה הָעוֹלָה יָדִיחוּ בָם וְהַיָּם לְרָחְצָה לַכֹּהֲנִים בּוֹ:

⁷ He made ten *menorah*s of gold as prescribed, and placed them in the Great Hall, five on the right and five on the left.

ז וַיַּעַשׂ אֶת־מְנֹרוֹת הַזָּהָב עֶשֶׂר כְּמִשְׁפָּטָם וַיִּתֵּן בַּהֵיכָל חָמֵשׁ מִיָּמִין וְחָמֵשׁ מִשְּׂמֹאול:

8 He made ten tables and placed them in the Great Hall, five on the right and five on the left. He made one hundred gold basins.

ח וַיַּעַשׂ שֻׁלְחָנוֹת עֲשָׂרָה וַיַּנַּח בַּהֵיכָל חֲמִשָּׁה מִיָּמִין וַחֲמִשָּׁה מִשְּׂמֹאול וַיַּעַשׂ מִזְרְקֵי זָהָב מֵאָה:

9 He built the court of the *Kohanim* and the great court, and doors for the great court; he overlaid the doors with bronze.

ט וַיַּעַשׂ חֲצַר הַכֹּהֲנִים וְהָעֲזָרָה הַגְּדוֹלָה וּדְלָתוֹת לָעֲזָרָה וְדַלְתוֹתֵיהֶם צִפָּה נְחֹשֶׁת:

10 He set the sea on the right side, at the southeast corner.

י וְאֶת־הַיָּם נָתַן מִכֶּתֶף הַיְמָנִית קֵדְמָה מִמּוּל נֶגְבָּה:

11 Huram made the pails, the shovels, and the basins. With that Huram completed the work he had undertaken for King *Shlomo* in the House of *Hashem*:

יא וַיַּעַשׂ חוּרָם אֶת־הַסִּירוֹת וְאֶת־הַיָּעִים וְאֶת־הַמִּזְרָקוֹת וַיְכַל חִירָם [חוּרָם] לַעֲשׂוֹת אֶת־הַמְּלָאכָה אֲשֶׁר עָשָׂה לַמֶּלֶךְ שְׁלֹמֹה בְּבֵית הָאֱלֹהִים:

12 the two columns, the globes, and the two capitals on top of the columns; and the two pieces of network to cover the two globes of the capitals on top of the columns;

יב עַמּוּדִים שְׁנַיִם וְהַגֻּלּוֹת וְהַכֹּתָרוֹת עַל־רֹאשׁ הָעַמּוּדִים שְׁתָּיִם וְהַשְּׂבָכוֹת שְׁתַּיִם לְכַסּוֹת אֶת־שְׁתֵּי גֻּלּוֹת הַכֹּתָרוֹת אֲשֶׁר עַל־רֹאשׁ הָעַמּוּדִים:

13 the four hundred pomegranates for the two pieces of network, two rows of pomegranates for each network, to cover the two globes of the capitals on top of the columns;

יג וְאֶת־הָרִמּוֹנִים אַרְבַּע מֵאוֹת לִשְׁתֵּי הַשְּׂבָכוֹת שְׁנַיִם טוּרִים רִמּוֹנִים לַשְּׂבָכָה הָאֶחָת לְכַסּוֹת אֶת־שְׁתֵּי גֻּלּוֹת הַכֹּתָרוֹת אֲשֶׁר עַל־פְּנֵי הָעַמּוּדִים:

14 he made the stands and the lavers upon the stands;

יד וְאֶת־הַמְּכֹנוֹת עָשָׂה וְאֶת־הַכִּיֹּרוֹת עָשָׂה עַל־הַמְּכֹנוֹת:

15 one sea with the twelve oxen beneath it;

טו אֶת־הַיָּם אֶחָד וְאֶת־הַבָּקָר שְׁנֵים־עָשָׂר תַּחְתָּיו:

16 the pails, the shovels, and the bowls. And all the vessels made for King *Shlomo* for the House of *Hashem* by Huram his master were of burnished bronze.

טז וְאֶת־הַסִּירוֹת וְאֶת־הַיָּעִים וְאֶת־הַמִּזְלָגוֹת וְאֶת־כָּל־כְּלֵיהֶם עָשָׂה חוּרָם אָבִיו לַמֶּלֶךְ שְׁלֹמֹה לְבֵית יְהֹוָה נְחֹשֶׁת מָרוּק:

17 The king had them cast in molds dug out of the earth, in the plain of the *Yarden* between Succoth and Zeredah.

יז בְּכִכַּר הַיַּרְדֵּן יְצָקָם הַמֶּלֶךְ בַּעֲבִי הָאֲדָמָה בֵּין סֻכּוֹת וּבֵין צְרֵדָתָה:

18 *Shlomo* made a very large number of vessels; the weight of the bronze used could not be reckoned.

יח וַיַּעַשׂ שְׁלֹמֹה כָּל־הַכֵּלִים הָאֵלֶּה לָרֹב מְאֹד כִּי לֹא נֶחְקַר מִשְׁקַל הַנְּחֹשֶׁת:

19 And *Shlomo* made all the furn3ishings that were in the House of *Hashem*: the *Mizbayach* of gold; the tables for the bread of display;

יט וַיַּעַשׂ שְׁלֹמֹה אֵת כָּל־הַכֵּלִים אֲשֶׁר בֵּית הָאֱלֹהִים וְאֵת מִזְבַּח הַזָּהָב וְאֶת־הַשֻּׁלְחָנוֹת וַעֲלֵיהֶם לֶחֶם הַפָּנִים:

20 the *menorah*s and their lamps, to burn as prescribed in front of the inner Sanctuary, of solid gold;

כ וְאֶת־הַמְּנֹרוֹת וְנֵרֹתֵיהֶם לְבַעֲרָם כַּמִּשְׁפָּט לִפְנֵי הַדְּבִיר זָהָב סָגוּר:

v'-et ha-m'-no-ROT v'-nay-ro-tay-HEM l'-va-a-RAM
ka-mish-PAT lif-NAY ha-d'-VEER za-HAV sa-GUR

21 and the petals, lamps, and tongs, of purest gold;

כא וְהַפֶּרַח וְהַנֵּרוֹת וְהַמֶּלְקָחַיִם זָהָב הוּא מִכְלוֹת זָהָב:

22 the snuffers, basins, ladles, and fire pans, of solid gold; and the entrance to the House: the doors of the innermost part of the House, the Holy of Holies, and the doors of the Great Hall of the House, of gold.

כב וְהַמְזַמְּרוֹת וְהַמִּזְרָקוֹת וְהַכַּפּוֹת וְהַמַּחְתּוֹת זָהָב סָגוּר וּפֶתַח הַבַּיִת דַּלְתוֹתָיו הַפְּנִימִיּוֹת לְקֹדֶשׁ הַקֳּדָשִׁים וְדַלְתֵי הַבַּיִת לַהֵיכָל זָהָב:

ה 5 1 When all the work that King *Shlomo* undertook for the House of *Hashem* was completed, *Shlomo* brought the things that his father *David* had consecrated – the silver, the gold, and the utensils – and deposited them in the treasury of the House of *Hashem*.

א וַתִּשְׁלַם כָּל־הַמְּלָאכָה אֲשֶׁר־עָשָׂה שְׁלֹמֹה לְבֵית יְהֹוָה וַיָּבֵא שְׁלֹמֹה אֶת־קָדְשֵׁי דָּוִיד אָבִיו וְאֶת־הַכֶּסֶף וְאֶת־הַזָּהָב וְאֶת־כָּל־הַכֵּלִים נָתַן בְּאֹצְרוֹת בֵּית הָאֱלֹהִים:

2 Then *Shlomo* convoked the elders of *Yisrael* – all the heads of the tribes and the ancestral chiefs of the Israelites – in *Yerushalayim*, to bring up the *Aron Brit Hashem* from the City of *David*, that is, *Tzion*.

ב אָז יַקְהֵיל שְׁלֹמֹה אֶת־זִקְנֵי יִשְׂרָאֵל וְאֶת־כָּל־רָאשֵׁי הַמַּטּוֹת נְשִׂיאֵי הָאָבוֹת לִבְנֵי יִשְׂרָאֵל אֶל־יְרוּשָׁלָ͏ִם לְהַעֲלוֹת אֶת־אֲרוֹן בְּרִית־יְהֹוָה מֵעִיר דָּוִיד הִיא צִיּוֹן:

3 All the men of *Yisrael* assembled before the king at the Feast, in the seventh month.

ג וַיִּקָּהֲלוּ אֶל־הַמֶּלֶךְ כָּל־אִישׁ יִשְׂרָאֵל בֶּחָג הוּא הַחֹדֶשׁ הַשְּׁבִעִי:

4 When all the elders of *Yisrael* had come, the *Leviim* carried the *Aron*.

ד וַיָּבֹאוּ כֹּל זִקְנֵי יִשְׂרָאֵל וַיִּשְׂאוּ הַלְוִיִּם אֶת־הָאָרוֹן:

5 They brought up the *Aron* and the Tent of Meeting and all the holy vessels that were in the Tent – the Levite *Kohanim* brought them up.

ה וַיַּעֲלוּ אֶת־הָאָרוֹן וְאֶת־אֹהֶל מוֹעֵד וְאֶת־כָּל־כְּלֵי הַקֹּדֶשׁ אֲשֶׁר בָּאֹהֶל הֶעֱלוּ אֹתָם הַכֹּהֲנִים הַלְוִיִּם:

6 Meanwhile, King *Shlomo* and the whole community of *Yisrael*, who had gathered to him before the *Aron*, were sacrificing sheep and oxen in such abundance that they could not be numbered or counted.

ו וְהַמֶּלֶךְ שְׁלֹמֹה וְכָל־עֲדַת יִשְׂרָאֵל הַנּוֹעָדִים עָלָיו לִפְנֵי הָאָרוֹן מְזַבְּחִים צֹאן וּבָקָר אֲשֶׁר לֹא־יִסָּפְרוּ וְלֹא יִמָּנוּ מֵרֹב:

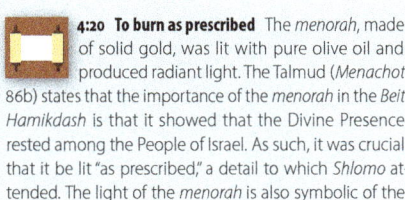

4:20 To burn as prescribed The *menorah*, made of solid gold, was lit with pure olive oil and produced radiant light. The Talmud (*Menachot* 86b) states that the importance of the *menorah* in the *Beit Hamikdash* is that it showed that the Divine Presence rested among the People of Israel. As such, it was crucial that it be lit "as prescribed," a detail to which *Shlomo* attended. The light of the *menorah* is also symbolic of the Jewish Nation's duty to spread the light of *Torah* and God's will. The pure gold and olive oil are reflective of the pure intentions necessary to have a meaningful influence upon the entire world, for the sake of Heaven.

Replica of the Temple *Menorah*

7 The *Kohanim* brought the *Aron Brit Hashem* to its place in the inner Sanctuary of the House, in the Holy of Holies, beneath the wings of the cherubim;

ז וַיָּבִיאוּ הַכֹּהֲנִים אֶת־אֲרוֹן בְּרִית־יְהֹוָה אֶל־מְקוֹמוֹ אֶל־דְּבִיר הַבַּיִת אֶל־קֹדֶשׁ הַקֳּדָשִׁים אֶל־תַּחַת כַּנְפֵי הַכְּרוּבִים:

8 for the cherubim had their wings spread out over the place of the *Aron* so that the cherubim covered the *Aron* and its poles from above.

ח וַיִּהְיוּ הַכְּרוּבִים פֹּרְשִׂים כְּנָפַיִם עַל־מְקוֹם הָאָרוֹן וַיְכַסּוּ הַכְּרוּבִים עַל־הָאָרוֹן וְעַל־בַּדָּיו מִלְמָעְלָה:

9 The poles projected beyond the *Aron* and the ends of the poles were visible from the front of the inner Sanctuary, but they could not be seen from the outside; and there they remain to this day.

ט וַיַּאֲרִיכוּ הַבַּדִּים וַיֵּרָאוּ רָאשֵׁי הַבַּדִּים מִן־הָאָרוֹן עַל־פְּנֵי הַדְּבִיר וְלֹא יֵרָאוּ הַחוּצָה וַיְהִי־שָׁם עַד הַיּוֹם הַזֶּה:

10 There was nothing inside the *Aron* but the two tablets that *Moshe* placed [there] at Horeb, when *Hashem* made [a Covenant] with the Israelites after their departure from Egypt.

י אֵין בָּאָרוֹן רַק שְׁנֵי הַלֻּחוֹת אֲשֶׁר־נָתַן מֹשֶׁה בְּחֹרֵב אֲשֶׁר כָּרַת יְהֹוָה עִם־בְּנֵי יִשְׂרָאֵל בְּצֵאתָם מִמִּצְרָיִם:

11 When the *Kohanim* came out of the Sanctuary – all the *Kohanim* present had sanctified themselves, without keeping to the set divisions –

יא וַיְהִי בְּצֵאת הַכֹּהֲנִים מִן־הַקֹּדֶשׁ כִּי כָּל־הַכֹּהֲנִים הַנִּמְצְאִים הִתְקַדָּשׁוּ אֵין לִשְׁמוֹר לְמַחְלְקוֹת:

12 all the Levite singers, *Asaf, Hayman, Yedutun,* their sons and their brothers, dressed in fine linen, holding cymbals, harps, and lyres, were standing to the east of the *Mizbayach,* and with them were 120 *Kohanim* who blew trumpets.

יב וְהַלְוִיִּם הַמְשֹׁרֲרִים לְכֻלָּם לְאָסָף לְהֵימָן לִידֻתוּן וְלִבְנֵיהֶם וְלַאֲחֵיהֶם מְלֻבָּשִׁים בּוּץ בִּמְצִלְתַּיִם וּבִנְבָלִים וְכִנֹּרוֹת עֹמְדִים מִזְרָח לַמִּזְבֵּחַ וְעִמָּהֶם כֹּהֲנִים לְמֵאָה וְעֶשְׂרִים מַחְצְרִרים [מַחְצְרִים] בַּחֲצֹצְרוֹת:

13 The trumpeters and the singers joined in unison to praise and extol *Hashem*; and as the sound of the trumpets, cymbals, and other musical instruments, and the praise of *Hashem*, "For He is good, for His steadfast love is eternal," grew louder, the House, the House of *Hashem*, was filled with a cloud.

יג וַיְהִי כְאֶחָד לִמְחַצְרִרים [לַמְחַצְרִים] וְלַמְשֹׁרֲרִים לְהַשְׁמִיעַ קוֹל־אֶחָד לְהַלֵּל וּלְהֹדוֹת לַיהֹוָה וּכְהָרִים קוֹל בַּחֲצֹצְרוֹת וּבִמְצִלְתַּיִם וּבִכְלֵי הַשִּׁיר וּבְהַלֵּל לַיהֹוָה כִּי טוֹב כִּי לְעוֹלָם חַסְדּוֹ וְהַבַּיִת מָלֵא עָנָן בֵּית יְהֹוָה:

14 The *Kohanim* could not stay and perform the service because of the cloud, for the glory of *Hashem* filled the House of *Hashem*.

יד וְלֹא־יָכְלוּ הַכֹּהֲנִים לַעֲמוֹד לְשָׁרֵת מִפְּנֵי הֶעָנָן כִּי־מָלֵא כְבוֹד־יְהֹוָה אֶת־בֵּית הָאֱלֹהִים:

v'-lo ya-kh'-LU ha-ko-ha-NEEM la-a-MOD l'-sha-RAYT mi-p'-NAY he-a-NAN kee ma-LAY kh'-VOD a-do-NAI et BAYT ha-e-lo-HEEM

Cloudy sky over the Temple Mount

5:14 For the glory of *Hashem* filled the house of *Hashem* This description closely resembles that of the completion of the construction of the *Mishkan*: "Moshe could not enter the Tent of Meeting, because the cloud had settled upon it and the presence of *Hashem* filled the *Mishkan*" (Exodus 40:35). In both cases, a resting place for the Lord is built in the heart of the nation, and God's glory comes down to reside within it. In the desert, the *Mishkan* rests at the center of the Israelite camp. Here, the *Beit Hamikdash* is built on hallowed ground in the city of *Yerushalayim*. The concentration of His presence is a reminder that *Hashem* continuously dwells among His people.

6 ¹ Then *Shlomo* declared: "*Hashem* has chosen To abide in a thick cloud;

² I have built for You A stately House, And a place where You May dwell forever."

³ Then, as the whole congregation of *Yisrael* stood, the king turned and blessed the whole congregation of *Yisrael*.

⁴ He said, "Blessed is God of *Yisrael*, who made a promise to my father *David* and fulfilled it. For He said,

⁵ 'From the time I brought My people out of the land of Egypt, I never chose a city from among all the tribes of *Yisrael* to build a House where My name might abide; nor did I choose anyone to be the leader of my people *Yisrael*.

⁶ But then I chose *Yerushalayim* for My name to abide there, and I chose *David* to rule My people *Yisrael*.'

⁷ "Now my father *David* had wanted to build a House for the name of God of *Yisrael*.

⁸ But *Hashem* said to my father *David*, 'As for your wanting to build a House for My name, you do well to want that.

⁹ However, you shall not build the House; your son, the issue of your loins, he shall build the House for My name.'

¹⁰ Now *Hashem* has fulfilled the promise that He made. I have succeeded my father *David* and have ascended the throne of *Yisrael*, as *Hashem* promised. I have built the House for the name of God of *Yisrael*,

¹¹ and there I have set the *Aron* containing the Covenant that *Hashem* made with the Israelites."

¹² Then, standing before the *Mizbayach* of *Hashem* in front of the whole congregation of *Yisrael*, he spread forth his hands.

¹³ *Shlomo* had made a bronze platform and placed it in the midst of the Great Court; it was 5 *amot* long and 5 *amot* wide and 3 *amot* high. He stood on it; then, kneeling in front of the whole congregation of *Yisrael*, he spread forth his hands to heaven

א אָז אָמַר שְׁלֹמֹה יְהוָה אָמַר לִשְׁכּוֹן בָּעֲרָפֶל:

ב וַאֲנִי בָּנִיתִי בֵית־זְבֻל לָךְ וּמָכוֹן לְשִׁבְתְּךָ עוֹלָמִים:

ג וַיַּסֵּב הַמֶּלֶךְ אֶת־פָּנָיו וַיְבָרֶךְ אֵת כָּל־קְהַל יִשְׂרָאֵל וְכָל־קְהַל יִשְׂרָאֵל עוֹמֵד:

ד וַיֹּאמֶר בָּרוּךְ יְהוָה אֱלֹהֵי יִשְׂרָאֵל אֲשֶׁר דִּבֶּר בְּפִיו אֵת דָּוִיד אָבִי וּבְיָדָיו מִלֵּא לֵאמֹר:

ה מִן־הַיּוֹם אֲשֶׁר הוֹצֵאתִי אֶת־עַמִּי מֵאֶרֶץ מִצְרַיִם לֹא־בָחַרְתִּי בְעִיר מִכֹּל שִׁבְטֵי יִשְׂרָאֵל לִבְנוֹת בַּיִת לִהְיוֹת שְׁמִי שָׁם וְלֹא־בָחַרְתִּי בְאִישׁ לִהְיוֹת נָגִיד עַל־עַמִּי יִשְׂרָאֵל:

ו וָאֶבְחַר בִּירוּשָׁלַם לִהְיוֹת שְׁמִי שָׁם וָאֶבְחַר בְּדָוִיד לִהְיוֹת עַל־עַמִּי יִשְׂרָאֵל:

ז וַיְהִי עִם־לְבַב דָּוִיד אָבִי לִבְנוֹת בָּיִת לְשֵׁם יְהוָה אֱלֹהֵי יִשְׂרָאֵל:

ח וַיֹּאמֶר יְהוָה אֶל־דָּוִיד אָבִי יַעַן אֲשֶׁר הָיָה עִם־לְבָבְךָ לִבְנוֹת בַּיִת לִשְׁמִי הֱטִיבוֹתָ כִּי הָיָה עִם־לְבָבֶךָ:

ט רַק אַתָּה לֹא תִבְנֶה הַבָּיִת כִּי בִנְךָ הַיּוֹצֵא מֵחֲלָצֶיךָ הוּא־יִבְנֶה הַבַּיִת לִשְׁמִי:

י וַיָּקֶם יְהוָה אֶת־דְּבָרוֹ אֲשֶׁר דִּבֵּר וָאָקוּם תַּחַת דָּוִיד אָבִי וָאֵשֵׁב עַל־כִּסֵּא יִשְׂרָאֵל כַּאֲשֶׁר דִּבֶּר יְהוָה וָאֶבְנֶה הַבַּיִת לְשֵׁם יְהוָה אֱלֹהֵי יִשְׂרָאֵל:

יא וָאָשִׂים שָׁם אֶת־הָאָרוֹן אֲשֶׁר־שָׁם בְּרִית יְהוָה אֲשֶׁר כָּרַת עִם־בְּנֵי יִשְׂרָאֵל:

יב וַיַּעֲמֹד לִפְנֵי מִזְבַּח יְהוָה נֶגֶד כָּל־קְהַל יִשְׂרָאֵל וַיִּפְרֹשׂ כַּפָּיו:

יג כִּי־עָשָׂה שְׁלֹמֹה כִּיּוֹר נְחֹשֶׁת וַיִּתְּנֵהוּ בְּתוֹךְ הָעֲזָרָה חָמֵשׁ אַמּוֹת אָרְכּוֹ וְחָמֵשׁ אַמּוֹת רָחְבּוֹ וְאַמּוֹת שָׁלוֹשׁ קוֹמָתוֹ וַיַּעֲמֹד עָלָיו וַיִּבְרַךְ עַל־בִּרְכָּיו נֶגֶד כָּל־קְהַל יִשְׂרָאֵל וַיִּפְרֹשׂ כַּפָּיו הַשָּׁמָיְמָה:

14 and said, "O God of *Yisrael*, there is no god like You in the heavens and on the earth, You who steadfastly maintain the Covenant with Your servants who walk before You with all their heart;

יד וַיֹּאמַר יְהוָה אֱלֹהֵי יִשְׂרָאֵל אֵין־כָּמוֹךָ אֱלֹהִים בַּשָּׁמַיִם וּבָאָרֶץ שֹׁמֵר הַבְּרִית וְהַחֶסֶד לַעֲבָדֶיךָ הַהֹלְכִים לְפָנֶיךָ בְּכָל־לִבָּם:

15 You who have kept the promises You made to Your servant, my father *David*; You made a promise and have fulfilled it – as is now the case.

טו אֲשֶׁר שָׁמַרְתָּ לְעַבְדְּךָ דָּוִיד אָבִי אֵת אֲשֶׁר־דִּבַּרְתָּ לוֹ וַתְּדַבֵּר בְּפִיךָ וּבְיָדְךָ מִלֵּאתָ כַּיּוֹם הַזֶּה:

16 And now, O God of *Yisrael*, keep that promise that You made to Your servant, my father *David*, 'You shall never lack a descendant in My sight sitting on the throne of *Yisrael* if only your children will look to their way and walk in the [path] of My teachings as you have walked before Me.'

טז וְעַתָּה יְהוָה אֱלֹהֵי יִשְׂרָאֵל שְׁמֹר לְעַבְדְּךָ דָוִיד אָבִי אֵת אֲשֶׁר דִּבַּרְתָּ לּוֹ לֵאמֹר לֹא־יִכָּרֵת לְךָ אִישׁ מִלְּפָנַי יוֹשֵׁב עַל־כִּסֵּא יִשְׂרָאֵל רַק אִם־יִשְׁמְרוּ בָנֶיךָ אֶת־דַּרְכָּם לָלֶכֶת בְּתוֹרָתִי כַּאֲשֶׁר הָלַכְתָּ לְפָנָי:

17 Now, therefore, O God of *Yisrael*, let the promise that You made to Your servant, my father *David*, be confirmed.

יז וְעַתָּה יְהוָה אֱלֹהֵי יִשְׂרָאֵל יֵאָמֵן דְּבָרְךָ אֲשֶׁר דִּבַּרְתָּ לְעַבְדְּךָ לְדָוִיד:

18 "Does *Hashem* really dwell with man on earth? Even the heavens to their uttermost reaches cannot contain You; how much less this House that I have built!

יח כִּי הַאֻמְנָם יֵשֵׁב אֱלֹהִים אֶת־הָאָדָם עַל־הָאָרֶץ הִנֵּה שָׁמַיִם וּשְׁמֵי הַשָּׁמַיִם לֹא יְכַלְכְּלוּךָ אַף כִּי־הַבַּיִת הַזֶּה אֲשֶׁר בָּנִיתִי:

19 Yet turn, *Hashem* my God, to the prayer and supplication of Your servant, and hear the cry and the prayer that Your servant offers to You.

יט וּפָנִיתָ אֶל־תְּפִלַּת עַבְדְּךָ וְאֶל־תְּחִנָּתוֹ יְהוָה אֱלֹהָי לִשְׁמֹעַ אֶל־הָרִנָּה וְאֶל־הַתְּפִלָּה אֲשֶׁר עַבְדְּךָ מִתְפַּלֵּל לְפָנֶיךָ:

20 May Your eyes be open day and night toward this House, toward the place where You have resolved to make Your name abide; may You heed the prayers that Your servant offers toward this place.

כ לִהְיוֹת עֵינֶיךָ פְתֻחוֹת אֶל־הַבַּיִת הַזֶּה יוֹמָם וָלַיְלָה אֶל־הַמָּקוֹם אֲשֶׁר אָמַרְתָּ לָשׂוּם שִׁמְךָ שָׁם לִשְׁמוֹעַ אֶל־הַתְּפִלָּה אֲשֶׁר יִתְפַּלֵּל עַבְדְּךָ אֶל־הַמָּקוֹם הַזֶּה:

21 And when You hear the supplications that Your servant and Your people *Yisrael* offer toward this place, give heed in Your heavenly abode – give heed and pardon.

כא וְשָׁמַעְתָּ אֶל־תַּחֲנוּנֵי עַבְדְּךָ וְעַמְּךָ יִשְׂרָאֵל אֲשֶׁר יִתְפַּלְלוּ אֶל־הַמָּקוֹם הַזֶּה וְאַתָּה תִּשְׁמַע מִמְּקוֹם שִׁבְתְּךָ מִן־הַשָּׁמַיִם וְשָׁמַעְתָּ וְסָלָחְתָּ:

22 "If a man commits an offense against his fellow, and an oath is exacted from him, causing him to utter an imprecation against himself, and he comes with his imprecation before Your *Mizbayach* in this House,

כב אִם־יֶחֱטָא אִישׁ לְרֵעֵהוּ וְנָשָׁא־בוֹ אָלָה לְהַאֲלֹתוֹ וּבָא אָלָה לִפְנֵי מִזְבַּחֲךָ בַּבַּיִת הַזֶּה:

23 may You hear in heaven and take action to judge Your servants, requiting him who is in the wrong by bringing down the punishment of his conduct on his head, vindicating him who is in the right by rewarding him according to his righteousness.

כג וְאַתָּה תִּשְׁמַע מִן־הַשָּׁמַיִם וְעָשִׂיתָ וְשָׁפַטְתָּ אֶת־עֲבָדֶיךָ לְהָשִׁיב לְרָשָׁע לָתֵת דַּרְכּוֹ בְּרֹאשׁוֹ וּלְהַצְדִּיק צַדִּיק לָתֶת לוֹ כְּצִדְקָתוֹ:

²⁴ "Should Your people *Yisrael* be defeated by an enemy because they have sinned against You, and then once again acknowledge Your name and offer prayer and supplication to You in this House,

כד וְאִם־יִנָּגֵף עַמְּךָ יִשְׂרָאֵל לִפְנֵי אוֹיֵב כִּי יֶחֶטְאוּ־לָךְ וְשָׁבוּ וְהוֹדוּ אֶת־שְׁמֶךָ וְהִתְפַּלְלוּ וְהִתְחַנְּנוּ לְפָנֶיךָ בַּבַּיִת הַזֶּה:

²⁵ may You hear in heaven and pardon the sin of Your people *Yisrael*, and restore them to the land that You gave to them and to their fathers.

כה וְאַתָּה תִּשְׁמַע מִן־הַשָּׁמַיִם וְסָלַחְתָּ לְחַטַּאת עַמְּךָ יִשְׂרָאֵל וַהֲשֵׁיבוֹתָם אֶל־הָאֲדָמָה אֲשֶׁר־נָתַתָּה לָהֶם וְלַאֲבֹתֵיהֶם:

²⁶ "Should the heavens be shut up and there be no rain because they have sinned against You, and then they pray toward this place and acknowledge Your name and repent of their sins, because You humbled them,

כו בְּהֵעָצֵר הַשָּׁמַיִם וְלֹא־יִהְיֶה מָטָר כִּי יֶחֶטְאוּ־לָךְ וְהִתְפַּלְלוּ אֶל־הַמָּקוֹם הַזֶּה וְהוֹדוּ אֶת־שְׁמֶךָ מֵחַטָּאתָם יְשׁוּבוּן כִּי תַעֲנֵם:

²⁷ may You hear in heaven and pardon the sin of Your servants, Your people *Yisrael*, when You have shown them the proper way in which they are to walk, and send down rain upon the land that You gave to Your people as their heritage.

כז וְאַתָּה תִּשְׁמַע הַשָּׁמַיִם וְסָלַחְתָּ לְחַטַּאת עֲבָדֶיךָ וְעַמְּךָ יִשְׂרָאֵל כִּי תוֹרֵם אֶל־הַדֶּרֶךְ הַטּוֹבָה אֲשֶׁר יֵלְכוּ־בָהּ וְנָתַתָּה מָטָר עַל־אַרְצְךָ אֲשֶׁר־נָתַתָּה לְעַמְּךָ לְנַחֲלָה:

*v'-a-TAH tish-MA ha-sha-MA-yim v'-SA-lakh-TA l'-kha-TAT
a-va-DE-kha v'-a-m'-KHA yis-ra-AYL KEE to-RAYM el ha-DE-rekh
ha-to-VAH a-SHER yay-l'-khu VAH v'-na-ta-TAH ma-TAR al
ar-tz'-KHA a-sher na-TA-tah l'-a-m'-KHA l'-na-kha-LAH*

²⁸ So, too, if there is a famine in the land, if there is pestilence, blight, mildew, locusts, or caterpillars, or if an enemy oppresses them in any of the settlements of their land. "In any plague and in any disease,

כח רָעָב כִּי־יִהְיֶה בָאָרֶץ דֶּבֶר כִּי־יִהְיֶה שִׁדָּפוֹן וְיֵרָקוֹן אַרְבֶּה וְחָסִיל כִּי יִהְיֶה כִּי יָצַר־לוֹ אוֹיְבָיו בְּאֶרֶץ שְׁעָרָיו כָּל־נֶגַע וְכָל־מַחֲלָה:

²⁹ any prayer or supplication offered by any person among all Your people *Yisrael* – each of whom knows his affliction and his pain – when he spreads forth his hands toward this House,

כט כָּל־תְּפִלָּה כָל־תְּחִנָּה אֲשֶׁר יִהְיֶה לְכָל־הָאָדָם וּלְכֹל עַמְּךָ יִשְׂרָאֵל אֲשֶׁר יֵדְעוּ אִישׁ נִגְעוֹ וּמַכְאֹבוֹ וּפָרַשׂ כַּפָּיו אֶל־הַבַּיִת הַזֶּה:

³⁰ may You hear in Your heavenly abode, and pardon. Deal with each man according to his ways as You know his heart to be – for You alone know the hearts of all men –

ל וְאַתָּה תִּשְׁמַע מִן־הַשָּׁמַיִם מְכוֹן שִׁבְתֶּךָ וְסָלַחְתָּ וְנָתַתָּה לָאִישׁ כְּכָל־דְּרָכָיו אֲשֶׁר תֵּדַע אֶת־לְבָבוֹ כִּי אַתָּה לְבַדְּךָ יָדַעְתָּ אֶת־לְבַב בְּנֵי הָאָדָם:

6:27 Pardon the sin of Your servants, Your people Yisrael In his prayer at the dedication of the *Beit Hamikdash*, *Shlomo* acknowledges that over time, the people will sin and will be punished, both as individuals and as a nation. He calls upon *Hashem* to bestow forgiveness on anyone who directs their prayers towards the *Beit Hamikdash* in *Yerushalayim*. The way to solve the problems of the Children of Israel and the Land of Israel is to face its spiritual center and pray to the true Owner of the land to forgive its inhabitants and inheritors. This is also the key to bringing salvation and redemption, as it says in verse 25, "restore them to the land that You gave to them and to their fathers." Throughout the ages, Jews have maintained the tradition of praying facing *Yerushalayim*, showing their eternal connection with their holy city and their belief in the fulfillment of *Shlomo's* prayer. God responds to *Shlomo* in the next chapter: "When My people, who bear My name, humble themselves, pray, and seek My favor and turn from their evil ways, I will hear in My heavenly abode and forgive their sins and heal their land" (7:14).

A man prays towards the site of the *Beit Hamikdash* in *Yerushalayim*

31 so that they may revere You all the days that they live on the land that You gave to our fathers.

לא לְמַעַן יִירָאוּךָ לָלֶכֶת בִּדְרָכֶיךָ כָּל־הַיָּמִים אֲשֶׁר־הֵם חַיִּים עַל־פְּנֵי הָאֲדָמָה אֲשֶׁר נָתַתָּה לַאֲבֹתֵינוּ:

32 "Or if a foreigner who is not of Your people *Yisrael* comes from a distant land for the sake of Your great name, Your mighty hand, and Your outstretched arm, if he comes to pray toward this House,

לב וְגַם אֶל־הַנָּכְרִי אֲשֶׁר לֹא מֵעַמְּךָ יִשְׂרָאֵל הוּא וּבָא מֵאֶרֶץ רְחוֹקָה לְמַעַן שִׁמְךָ הַגָּדוֹל וְיָדְךָ הַחֲזָקָה וּזְרוֹעֲךָ הַנְּטוּיָה וּבָאוּ וְהִתְפַּלְלוּ אֶל־הַבַּיִת הַזֶּה:

33 may You hear in Your heavenly abode and grant whatever the foreigner appeals to You for. Thus all the peoples of the earth will know Your name and revere You, as does Your people *Yisrael*; and they will recognize that Your name is attached to this House that I have built.

לג וְאַתָּה תִּשְׁמַע מִן־הַשָּׁמַיִם מִמְּכוֹן שִׁבְתֶּךָ וְעָשִׂיתָ כְּכֹל אֲשֶׁר־יִקְרָא אֵלֶיךָ הַנָּכְרִי לְמַעַן יֵדְעוּ כָל־עַמֵּי הָאָרֶץ אֶת־שְׁמֶךָ וּלְיִרְאָה אֹתְךָ כְּעַמְּךָ יִשְׂרָאֵל וְלָדַעַת כִּי־שִׁמְךָ נִקְרָא עַל־הַבַּיִת הַזֶּה אֲשֶׁר בָּנִיתִי:

34 "When Your people take the field against their enemies in a campaign on which You send them, and they pray to You in the direction of the city which You have chosen and the House which I have built to Your name,

לד כִּי־יֵצֵא עַמְּךָ לַמִּלְחָמָה עַל־אוֹיְבָיו בַּדֶּרֶךְ אֲשֶׁר תִּשְׁלָחֵם וְהִתְפַּלְלוּ אֵלֶיךָ דֶּרֶךְ הָעִיר הַזֹּאת אֲשֶׁר בָּחַרְתָּ בָּהּ וְהַבַּיִת אֲשֶׁר־בָּנִיתִי לִשְׁמֶךָ:

35 may You hear in heaven their prayer and supplication and uphold their cause.

לה וְשָׁמַעְתָּ מִן־הַשָּׁמַיִם אֶת־תְּפִלָּתָם וְאֶת־תְּחִנָּתָם וְעָשִׂיתָ מִשְׁפָּטָם:

36 "When they sin against You – for there is no person who does not sin – and You are angry with them and deliver them to the enemy, and their captors carry them off to an enemy land, near or far;

לו כִּי יֶחֶטְאוּ־לָךְ כִּי אֵין אָדָם אֲשֶׁר לֹא־יֶחֱטָא וְאָנַפְתָּ בָם וּנְתַתָּם לִפְנֵי אוֹיֵב וְשָׁבוּם שׁוֹבֵיהֶם אֶל־אֶרֶץ רְחוֹקָה אוֹ קְרוֹבָה:

37 and they take it to heart in the land to which they have been carried off, and repent and make supplication to You in the land of their captivity, saying, 'We have sinned, we have acted perversely, we have acted wickedly,'

לז וְהֵשִׁיבוּ אֶל־לְבָבָם בָּאָרֶץ אֲשֶׁר נִשְׁבּוּ־שָׁם וְשָׁבוּ וְהִתְחַנְּנוּ אֵלֶיךָ בְּאֶרֶץ שִׁבְיָם לֵאמֹר חָטָאנוּ הֶעֱוִינוּ וְרָשָׁעְנוּ:

38 and they turn back to You with all their heart and soul, in the land of their captivity where they were carried off, and pray in the direction of their land which You gave to their fathers and the city which You have chosen, and toward the House which I have built for Your name –

לח וְשָׁבוּ אֵלֶיךָ בְּכָל־לִבָּם וּבְכָל־נַפְשָׁם בְּאֶרֶץ שִׁבְיָם אֲשֶׁר־שָׁבוּ אֹתָם וְהִתְפַּלְלוּ דֶּרֶךְ אַרְצָם אֲשֶׁר נָתַתָּה לַאֲבוֹתָם וְהָעִיר אֲשֶׁר בָּחַרְתָּ וְלַבַּיִת אֲשֶׁר־בָּנִיתִי לִשְׁמֶךָ:

39 may You hear their prayer and supplication in Your heavenly abode, uphold their cause, and pardon Your people who have sinned against You.

לט וְשָׁמַעְתָּ מִן־הַשָּׁמַיִם מִמְּכוֹן שִׁבְתְּךָ אֶת־תְּפִלָּתָם וְאֶת־תְּחִנֹּתֵיהֶם וְעָשִׂיתָ מִשְׁפָּטָם וְסָלַחְתָּ לְעַמְּךָ אֲשֶׁר חָטְאוּ־לָךְ:

40 Now My *Hashem*, may Your eyes be open and Your ears attentive to prayer from this place, and now,

מ עַתָּה אֱלֹהַי יִהְיוּ־נָא עֵינֶיךָ פְּתֻחוֹת וְאָזְנֶיךָ קַשֻּׁבוֹת לִתְפִלַּת הַמָּקוֹם הַזֶּה:

41 Advance, O *Hashem*, to your resting-place, You and Your mighty *Aron*. Your *Kohanim*, O *Hashem*, are clothed in triumph; Your loyal ones will rejoice in [Your] goodness.

מא וְעַתָּה קוּמָה יְהֹוָה אֱלֹהִים לְנוּחֶךָ אַתָּה וַאֲרוֹן עֻזֶּךָ כֹּהֲנֶיךָ יְהֹוָה אֱלֹהִים יִלְבְּשׁוּ תְשׁוּעָה וַחֲסִידֶיךָ יִשְׂמְחוּ בַטּוֹב:

42 O *Hashem*, do not reject Your anointed one; remember the loyalty of Your servant *David*."

מב יְהֹוָה אֱלֹהִים אַל־תָּשֵׁב פְּנֵי מְשִׁיחֶיךָ זָכְרָה לְחַסְדֵי דָּוִיד עַבְדֶּךָ:

7 1 When *Shlomo* finished praying, fire descended from heaven and consumed the burnt offering and the sacrifices, and the glory of *Hashem* filled the House.

ז א וּכְכַלּוֹת שְׁלֹמֹה לְהִתְפַּלֵּל וְהָאֵשׁ יָרְדָה מֵהַשָּׁמַיִם וַתֹּאכַל הָעֹלָה וְהַזְּבָחִים וּכְבוֹד יְהֹוָה מָלֵא אֶת־הַבָּיִת:

2 The *Kohanim* could not enter the House of *Hashem*, for the glory of *Hashem* filled the House of *Hashem*.

ב וְלֹא יָכְלוּ הַכֹּהֲנִים לָבוֹא אֶל־בֵּית יְהֹוָה כִּי־מָלֵא כְבוֹד־יְהֹוָה אֶת־בֵּית יְהֹוָה:

3 All the Israelites witnessed the descent of the fire and the glory of *Hashem* on the House; they knelt with their faces to the ground and prostrated themselves, praising *Hashem*, "For He is good, for His steadfast love is eternal."

ג וְכֹל בְּנֵי יִשְׂרָאֵל רֹאִים בְּרֶדֶת הָאֵשׁ וּכְבוֹד יְהֹוָה עַל־הַבָּיִת וַיִּכְרְעוּ אַפַּיִם אַרְצָה עַל־הָרִצְפָה וַיִּשְׁתַּחֲווּ וְהוֹדוֹת לַיהֹוָה כִּי טוֹב כִּי לְעוֹלָם חַסְדּוֹ:

4 Then the king and all the people offered sacrifices before *Hashem*.

ד וְהַמֶּלֶךְ וְכָל־הָעָם זֹבְחִים זֶבַח לִפְנֵי יְהֹוָה:

5 King *Shlomo* offered as sacrifices 22,000 oxen and 120,000 sheep; thus the king and all the people dedicated the House of *Hashem*.

ה וַיִּזְבַּח הַמֶּלֶךְ שְׁלֹמֹה אֶת־זֶבַח הַבָּקָר עֶשְׂרִים וּשְׁנַיִם אֶלֶף וְצֹאן מֵאָה וְעֶשְׂרִים אָלֶף וַיַּחְנְכוּ אֶת־בֵּית הָאֱלֹהִים הַמֶּלֶךְ וְכָל־הָעָם:

6 The *Kohanim* stood at their watches; the *Leviim* with the instruments for *Hashem*'s music that King *David* had made to praise *Hashem*, "For His steadfast love is eternal," by means of the psalms of *David* that they knew. The *Kohanim* opposite them blew trumpets while all *Yisrael* were standing.

ו וְהַכֹּהֲנִים עַל־מִשְׁמְרוֹתָם עֹמְדִים וְהַלְוִיִּם בִּכְלֵי־שִׁיר יְהֹוָה אֲשֶׁר עָשָׂה דָּוִיד הַמֶּלֶךְ לְהֹדוֹת לַיהֹוָה כִּי־לְעוֹלָם חַסְדּוֹ בְּהַלֵּל דָּוִיד בְּיָדָם וְהַכֹּהֲנִים מַחְצְרִים [מַחְצְצְרִים] נֶגְדָּם וְכָל־יִשְׂרָאֵל עֹמְדִים:

7 *Shlomo* consecrated the center of the court in front of the House of *Hashem*, because he presented there the burnt offerings and the fat parts of the offerings of well-being, since the bronze *Mizbayach* that *Shlomo* had made was not able to hold the burnt offerings, the meal offerings, and the fat parts.

ז וַיְקַדֵּשׁ שְׁלֹמֹה אֶת־תּוֹךְ הֶחָצֵר אֲשֶׁר לִפְנֵי בֵית־יְהֹוָה כִּי־עָשָׂה שָׁם הָעֹלוֹת וְאֵת חֶלְבֵי הַשְּׁלָמִים כִּי־מִזְבַּח הַנְּחֹשֶׁת אֲשֶׁר עָשָׂה שְׁלֹמֹה לֹא יָכוֹל לְהָכִיל אֶת־הָעֹלָה וְאֶת־הַמִּנְחָה וְאֶת־הַחֲלָבִים:

8 At that time *Shlomo* kept the Feast for seven days – all *Yisrael* with him – a great assemblage from Lebo-hamath to the Wadi of Egypt.

ח וַיַּעַשׂ שְׁלֹמֹה אֶת־הֶחָג בָּעֵת הַהִיא שִׁבְעַת יָמִים וְכָל־יִשְׂרָאֵל עִמּוֹ קָהָל גָּדוֹל מְאֹד מִלְּבוֹא חֲמָת עַד־נַחַל מִצְרָיִם:

9 On the eighth day they held a solemn gathering; they observed the dedication of the *Mizbayach* seven days, and the Feast seven days.

ט וַיַּעֲשׂוּ בַּיּוֹם הַשְּׁמִינִי עֲצָרֶת כִּי חֲנֻכַּת הַמִּזְבֵּחַ עָשׂוּ שִׁבְעַת יָמִים וְהֶחָג שִׁבְעַת יָמִים:

10 On the twenty-third day of the seventh month he dismissed the people to their homes, rejoicing and in good spirits over the goodness that *Hashem* had shown to *David* and *Shlomo* and His people *Yisrael*.

י וּבְיוֹם עֶשְׂרִים וּשְׁלֹשָׁה לַחֹדֶשׁ הַשְּׁבִיעִי שִׁלַּח אֶת־הָעָם לְאָהֳלֵיהֶם שְׂמֵחִים וְטוֹבֵי לֵב עַל־הַטּוֹבָה אֲשֶׁר עָשָׂה יְהֹוָה לְדָוִיד וְלִשְׁלֹמֹה וּלְיִשְׂרָאֵל עַמּוֹ:

11 Thus *Shlomo* finished building the House of *Hashem* and the royal palace; *Shlomo* succeeded in everything he had set his heart on accomplishing with regard to the House of *Hashem* and his palace.

יא וַיְכַל שְׁלֹמֹה אֶת־בֵּית יְהֹוָה וְאֶת־בֵּית הַמֶּלֶךְ וְאֵת כָּל־הַבָּא עַל־לֵב שְׁלֹמֹה לַעֲשׂוֹת בְּבֵית־יְהֹוָה וּבְבֵיתוֹ הִצְלִיחַ:

12 *Hashem* appeared to *Shlomo* at night and said to him, "I have heard your prayer and have chosen this site as My House of sacrifice.

יב וַיֵּרָא יְהֹוָה אֶל־שְׁלֹמֹה בַּלָּיְלָה וַיֹּאמֶר לוֹ שָׁמַעְתִּי אֶת־תְּפִלָּתֶךָ וּבָחַרְתִּי בַּמָּקוֹם הַזֶּה לִי לְבֵית זָבַח:

13 If I shut up the heavens and there is no rain; if I command the locusts to ravage the land; or if I let loose pestilence against My people,

יג הֵן אֶעֱצֹר הַשָּׁמַיִם וְלֹא־יִהְיֶה מָטָר וְהֵן־אֲצַוֶּה עַל־חָגָב לֶאֱכוֹל הָאָרֶץ וְאִם־אֲשַׁלַּח דֶּבֶר בְּעַמִּי:

14 when My people, who bear My name, humble themselves, pray, and seek My favor and turn from their evil ways, I will hear in My heavenly abode and forgive their sins and heal their land.

יד וְיִכָּנְעוּ עַמִּי אֲשֶׁר נִקְרָא־שְׁמִי עֲלֵיהֶם וְיִתְפַּלְלוּ וִיבַקְשׁוּ פָנַי וְיָשֻׁבוּ מִדַּרְכֵיהֶם הָרָעִים וַאֲנִי אֶשְׁמַע מִן־הַשָּׁמַיִם וְאֶסְלַח לְחַטָּאתָם וְאֶרְפָּא אֶת־אַרְצָם:

v'-yi-ka-n'-U a-MEE a-SHER nik-ra sh'-MEE a-lay-HEM v'-yit-pa-l'-LU vee-vak-SHU fa-NAI v'-ya-SHU-vu mi-dar-khay-HEM ha-ra-EEM va-a-NEE esh-MA min ha-sha-MA-yim v'-es-LAKH l'-kha-ta-TAM v'-er-PA et ar-TZAM

15 Now My eyes will be open and My ears attentive to the prayers from this place.

טו עַתָּה עֵינַי יִהְיוּ פְתֻחוֹת וְאָזְנַי קַשֻּׁבוֹת לִתְפִלַּת הַמָּקוֹם הַזֶּה:

16 And now I have chosen and consecrated this House that My name be there forever. My eyes and My heart shall always be there.

טז וְעַתָּה בָּחַרְתִּי וְהִקְדַּשְׁתִּי אֶת־הַבַּיִת הַזֶּה לִהְיוֹת־שְׁמִי שָׁם עַד־עוֹלָם וְהָיוּ עֵינַי וְלִבִּי שָׁם כָּל־הַיָּמִים:

17 As for you, if you walk before Me as your father *David* walked before Me, doing all that I have commanded you, keeping My laws and rules,

יז וְאַתָּה אִם־תֵּלֵךְ לְפָנַי כַּאֲשֶׁר הָלַךְ דָּוִיד אָבִיךָ וְלַעֲשׂוֹת כְּכֹל אֲשֶׁר צִוִּיתִיךָ וְחֻקַּי וּמִשְׁפָּטַי תִּשְׁמוֹר:

18 then I will establish your royal throne over *Yisrael* forever, in accordance with the Covenant I made with your father *David*, saying, 'You shall never lack a descendant ruling over *Yisrael*.'

יח וַהֲקִימוֹתִי אֵת כִּסֵּא מַלְכוּתֶךָ כַּאֲשֶׁר כָּרַתִּי לְדָוִיד אָבִיךָ לֵאמֹר לֹא־יִכָּרֵת לְךָ אִישׁ מוֹשֵׁל בְּיִשְׂרָאֵל:

19 But if you turn away from Me and forsake My laws and commandments that I set before you, and go and serve other gods and worship them,

יט וְאִם־תְּשׁוּבוּן אַתֶּם וַעֲזַבְתֶּם חֻקּוֹתַי וּמִצְוֹתַי אֲשֶׁר נָתַתִּי לִפְנֵיכֶם וַהֲלַכְתֶּם וַעֲבַדְתֶּם אֱלֹהִים אֲחֵרִים וְהִשְׁתַּחֲוִיתֶם לָהֶם:

7:14 Forgive their sins and heal their land The Children of Israel are God's chosen people, and the Land of Israel is His chosen land. The people's conduct directly influences what happens in the land, since *Hashem* responds to them with reward or

Israeli children picking buttercups

punishment as appropriate. As such, the people feel a great attachment to the land, since it is through the land that God communicates whether or not His people are following His will.

20 then I will uproot them from My land that I gave them, and this House that I consecrated to My name I shall cast out of my sight, and make it a proverb and a byword among all peoples.

21 And as for this House, once so exalted, everyone passing by it shall be appalled and say, 'Why did *Hashem* do thus to this land and to this House?'

22 And the reply will be, 'It is because they forsook God of their fathers who freed them from the land of Egypt, and adopted other gods and worshiped them and served them; therefore He brought all this calamity upon them.'"

8 1 At the end of twenty years, during which *Shlomo* constructed the House of *Hashem* and his palace –

2 *Shlomo* also rebuilt the cities that Huram had given to him, and settled Israelites in them –

3 *Shlomo* marched against Hamath-zobah and overpowered it.

4 He built Tadmor in the desert and all the garrison towns that he built in Hamath.

5 He built Upper Beth-horon and Lower Beth-horon as fortified cities with walls, gates, and bars,

6 as well as Baalath and all of *Shlomo*'s garrison towns, chariot towns, and cavalry towns – everything that *Shlomo* desired to build in *Yerushalayim* and in the Lebanon, and throughout the territory that he ruled.

7 All the people that were left of the Hittites, Amorites, Perizzites, Hivites, and Jebusites, none of whom were of Israelite stock –

8 those of their descendants who were left after them in the land, whom the Israelites had not annihilated – these *Shlomo* subjected to forced labor, as is still the case.

9 But the Israelites, none of whom *Shlomo* enslaved for his works, served as soldiers and as his chief officers, and as commanders of his chariotry and cavalry.

10 These were King *Shlomo*'s prefects – 250 foremen over the people.

כ וּנְתַשְׁתִּים מֵעַל אַדְמָתִי אֲשֶׁר נָתַתִּי לָהֶם וְאֶת־הַבַּיִת הַזֶּה אֲשֶׁר הִקְדַּשְׁתִּי לִשְׁמִי אַשְׁלִיךְ מֵעַל פָּנָי וְאֶתְּנֶנּוּ לְמָשָׁל וְלִשְׁנִינָה בְּכָל־הָעַמִּים:

כא וְהַבַּיִת הַזֶּה אֲשֶׁר הָיָה עֶלְיוֹן לְכָל־עֹבֵר עָלָיו יִשֹּׁם וְאָמַר בַּמֶּה עָשָׂה יְהֹוָה כָּכָה לָאָרֶץ הַזֹּאת וְלַבַּיִת הַזֶּה:

כב וְאָמְרוּ עַל אֲשֶׁר עָזְבוּ אֶת־יְהֹוָה אֱלֹהֵי אֲבֹתֵיהֶם אֲשֶׁר הוֹצִיאָם מֵאֶרֶץ מִצְרַיִם וַיַּחֲזִיקוּ בֵּאלֹהִים אֲחֵרִים וַיִּשְׁתַּחֲווּ לָהֶם וַיַּעַבְדוּם עַל־כֵּן הֵבִיא עֲלֵיהֶם אֵת כָּל־הָרָעָה הַזֹּאת:

ח א וַיְהִי מִקֵּץ עֶשְׂרִים שָׁנָה אֲשֶׁר בָּנָה שְׁלֹמֹה אֶת־בֵּית יְהֹוָה וְאֶת־בֵּיתוֹ:

ב וְהֶעָרִים אֲשֶׁר נָתַן חוּרָם לִשְׁלֹמֹה בָּנָה שְׁלֹמֹה אֹתָם וַיּוֹשֶׁב שָׁם אֶת־בְּנֵי יִשְׂרָאֵל:

ג וַיֵּלֶךְ שְׁלֹמֹה חֲמָת צוֹבָה וַיֶּחֱזַק עָלֶיהָ:

ד וַיִּבֶן אֶת־תַּדְמֹר בַּמִּדְבָּר וְאֵת כָּל־עָרֵי הַמִּסְכְּנוֹת אֲשֶׁר בָּנָה בַּחֲמָת:

ה וַיִּבֶן אֶת־בֵּית חוֹרוֹן הָעֶלְיוֹן וְאֶת־בֵּית חוֹרוֹן הַתַּחְתּוֹן עָרֵי מָצוֹר חוֹמוֹת דְּלָתַיִם וּבְרִיחַ:

ו וְאֶת־בַּעֲלָת וְאֵת כָּל־עָרֵי הַמִּסְכְּנוֹת אֲשֶׁר הָיוּ לִשְׁלֹמֹה וְאֵת כָּל־עָרֵי הָרֶכֶב וְאֵת עָרֵי הַפָּרָשִׁים וְאֵת כָּל־חֵשֶׁק שְׁלֹמֹה אֲשֶׁר חָשַׁק לִבְנוֹת בִּירוּשָׁלַﬦ וּבַלְּבָנוֹן וּבְכֹל אֶרֶץ מֶמְשַׁלְתּוֹ:

ז כָּל־הָעָם הַנּוֹתָר מִן־הַחִתִּי וְהָאֱמֹרִי וְהַפְּרִזִּי וְהַחִוִּי וְהַיְבוּסִי אֲשֶׁר לֹא מִיִּשְׂרָאֵל הֵמָּה:

ח מִן־בְּנֵיהֶם אֲשֶׁר נוֹתְרוּ אַחֲרֵיהֶם בָּאָרֶץ אֲשֶׁר לֹא־כִלּוּם בְּנֵי יִשְׂרָאֵל וַיַּעֲלֵם שְׁלֹמֹה לְמַס עַד הַיּוֹם הַזֶּה:

ט וּמִן־בְּנֵי יִשְׂרָאֵל אֲשֶׁר לֹא־נָתַן שְׁלֹמֹה לַעֲבָדִים לִמְלַאכְתּוֹ כִּי־הֵמָּה אַנְשֵׁי מִלְחָמָה וְשָׂרֵי שָׁלִישָׁיו וְשָׂרֵי רִכְבּוֹ וּפָרָשָׁיו:

י וְאֵלֶּה שָׂרֵי הַנְּצִיבִים [הַנִּצָּבִים] אֲשֶׁר־לַמֶּלֶךְ שְׁלֹמֹה חֲמִשִּׁים וּמָאתָיִם הָרֹדִים בָּעָם:

11 *Shlomo* brought up Pharaoh's daughter from the City of *David* to the palace that he had built for her, for he said, "No wife of mine shall dwell in a palace of King *David* of *Yisrael*, for [the area] is sacred since the *Aron* of *Hashem* has entered it."

יא וְאֶת־בַּת־פַּרְעֹה הֶעֱלָה שְׁלֹמֹה מֵעִיר דָּוִיד לַבַּיִת אֲשֶׁר בָּנָה־לָהּ כִּי אָמַר לֹא־תֵשֵׁב אִשָּׁה לִי בְּבֵית דָּוִיד מֶלֶךְ־יִשְׂרָאֵל כִּי־קֹדֶשׁ הֵמָּה אֲשֶׁר־בָּאָה אֲלֵיהֶם אֲרוֹן יְהוָֹה:

12 At that time, *Shlomo* offered burnt offerings on the *Mizbayach* that he had built in front of the porch.

יב אָז הֶעֱלָה שְׁלֹמֹה עֹלוֹת לַיהוָֹה עַל מִזְבַּח יְהוָֹה אֲשֶׁר בָּנָה לִפְנֵי הָאוּלָם:

*AZ he-e-LAH sh'-lo-MOH o-LOT la-do-NAI AL miz-BAKH
a-do-NAI a-SHER ba-NAH lif-NAY ha-u-LAM*

13 What was due for each day he sacrificed according to the commandment of *Moshe* for the *Shabbatot*, the new moons, and the thrice-yearly festivals – the festival of *Pesach*, the festival of *Shavuot*, and the festival of *Sukkot*.

יג וּבִדְבַר־יוֹם בְּיוֹם לְהַעֲלוֹת כְּמִצְוַת מֹשֶׁה לַשַּׁבָּתוֹת וְלֶחֳדָשִׁים וְלַמּוֹעֲדוֹת שָׁלוֹשׁ פְּעָמִים בַּשָּׁנָה בְּחַג הַמַּצּוֹת וּבְחַג הַשָּׁבֻעוֹת וּבְחַג הַסֻּכּוֹת:

14 Following the prescription of his father *David*, he set up the divisions of the *Kohanim* for their duties, and the *Leviim* for their watches, to praise and to serve alongside the *Kohanim*, according to each day's requirement, and the gatekeepers in their watches, gate by gate, for such was the commandment of *David*, the man of *Hashem*.

יד וַיַּעֲמֵד כְּמִשְׁפַּט דָּוִיד־אָבִיו אֶת־מַחְלְקוֹת הַכֹּהֲנִים עַל־עֲבֹדָתָם וְהַלְוִיִּם עַל־מִשְׁמְרוֹתָם לְהַלֵּל וּלְשָׁרֵת נֶגֶד הַכֹּהֲנִים לִדְבַר־יוֹם בְּיוֹמוֹ וְהַשּׁוֹעֲרִים בְּמַחְלְקוֹתָם לְשַׁעַר וָשָׁעַר כִּי כֵן מִצְוַת דָּוִיד אִישׁ־הָאֱלֹהִים:

15 They did not depart from the commandment of the king relating to the *Kohanim* and the *Leviim* in all these matters and also relating to the treasuries.

טו וְלֹא סָרוּ מִצְוַת הַמֶּלֶךְ עַל־הַכֹּהֲנִים וְהַלְוִיִּם לְכָל־דָּבָר וְלָאֹצָרוֹת:

16 And all of *Shlomo*'s work was well executed from the day the House of *Hashem* was founded until the House of *Hashem* was completed to perfection.

טז וַתִּכֹּן כָּל־מְלֶאכֶת שְׁלֹמֹה עַד־הַיּוֹם מוּסַד בֵּית־יְהוָֹה וְעַד־כְּלֹתוֹ שָׁלֵם בֵּית יְהוָֹה:

17 At that time *Shlomo* went to Ezion-geber and to Eloth on the seacoast of the land of Edom.

יז אָז הָלַךְ שְׁלֹמֹה לְעֶצְיוֹן־גֶּבֶר וְאֶל־אֵילוֹת עַל־שְׂפַת הַיָּם בְּאֶרֶץ אֱדוֹם:

The Temple Mount

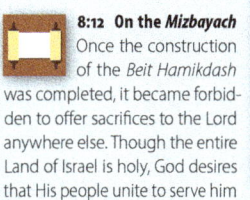
8:12 On the *Mizbayach*
Once the construction of the *Beit Hamikdash* was completed, it became forbidden to offer sacrifices to the Lord anywhere else. Though the entire Land of Israel is holy, God desires that His people unite to serve him in one single center of worship. It is in *Yerushalayim* that the daily offerings, as well as individual offerings and the communal offerings of the *Shabbat* and festivals, are to be brought. According to Rabbi Yitzchak Abrabanel, having one central place of worship is a constant reminder of the unity of God. In his words, "The oneness of the altar and the Temple point to the oneness of *Hashem*, Who governs and watches over them." This was especially important in the ancient pagan world in which the Israelites lived. Indeed, when *Yerovam* established alternate places of worship to prevent his subjects in the northern Kingdom from worshipping in the *Beit Hamikdash*, this quickly led to idolatry (I Kings 12:28–30). Today, in the absence of the Temple, we may pray to *Hashem* wherever we find ourselves. But our prayers are always directed towards the *Har HaBayit*, the place where the *Beit Hamikdash* once stood and will again stand in the future.

88

¹⁸ Huram sent him, under the charge of servants, a fleet with a crew of expert seamen; they went with *Shlomo*'s men to Ophir, and obtained gold there in the amount of 450 *kikarim*, which they brought to King *Shlomo*.

יח וַיִּשְׁלַח־לוֹ חוּרָם בְּיַד־עֲבָדָיו אוֹנִיּוֹת [אֳנִיּוֹת] וַעֲבָדִים יוֹדְעֵי יָם וַיָּבֹאוּ עִם־עַבְדֵי שְׁלֹמֹה אוֹפִירָה וַיִּקְחוּ מִשָּׁם אַרְבַּע־מֵאוֹת וַחֲמִשִּׁים כִּכַּר זָהָב וַיָּבִיאוּ אֶל־הַמֶּלֶךְ שְׁלֹמֹה:

9 ¹ The queen of Sheba heard of *Shlomo*'s fame, and came to *Yerushalayim* to test *Shlomo* with hard questions, accompanied by a very large retinue, including camels bearing spices, a great quantity of gold, and precious stones. When she came to *Shlomo*, she spoke to him of all that she had on her mind.

ט א וּמַלְכַּת־שְׁבָא שָׁמְעָה אֶת־שֵׁמַע שְׁלֹמֹה וַתָּבוֹא לְנַסּוֹת אֶת־שְׁלֹמֹה בְחִידוֹת בִּירוּשָׁלַם בְּחַיִל כָּבֵד מְאֹד וּגְמַלִּים נֹשְׂאִים בְּשָׂמִים וְזָהָב לָרֹב וְאֶבֶן יְקָרָה וַתָּבוֹא אֶל־שְׁלֹמֹה וַתְּדַבֵּר עִמּוֹ אֵת כָּל־אֲשֶׁר הָיָה עִם־לְבָבָהּ:

u-mal-kat sh'-VA sha-m'-AH et SHAY-ma sh'-lo-MOH va-ta-VO l'-na-SOT et sh'-lo-MOH v'-khee-DOT bee-ru-sha-LA-im b'-KHA-yil ka-VAYD m'-OD ug-ma-LEEM no-s'-EEM b'-sa-MEEM v'-za-HAV la-ROV v'-E-ven y'-ka-RAH va-ta-VO el sh'-lo-MOH va-t'-da-BAYR i-MO AYT kol a-SHER ha-YAH im l'-va-VAH

² *Shlomo* had answers for all her questions; there was nothing that *Shlomo* did not know, nothing to which he could not give her an answer.

ב וַיַּגֶּד־לָהּ שְׁלֹמֹה אֶת־כָּל־דְּבָרֶיהָ וְלֹא־נֶעְלַם דָּבָר מִשְּׁלֹמֹה אֲשֶׁר לֹא הִגִּיד לָהּ:

³ When the queen of Sheba saw how wise *Shlomo* was and the palace he had built,

ג וַתֵּרֶא מַלְכַּת־שְׁבָא אֵת חָכְמַת שְׁלֹמֹה וְהַבַּיִת אֲשֶׁר בָּנָה:

⁴ the fare of his table, the seating of his courtiers, the service and attire of his attendants, his butlers and their attire, and the procession with which he went up to the House of *Hashem*, it took her breath away.

ד וּמַאֲכַל שֻׁלְחָנוֹ וּמוֹשַׁב עֲבָדָיו וּמַעֲמַד מְשָׁרְתָיו וּמַלְבּוּשֵׁיהֶם וּמַשְׁקָיו וּמַלְבּוּשֵׁיהֶם וַעֲלִיָּתוֹ אֲשֶׁר יַעֲלֶה בֵּית יְהוָה וְלֹא־הָיָה עוֹד בָּהּ רוּחַ:

⁵ She said to the king, "What I heard in my own land about you and your wisdom was true.

ה וַתֹּאמֶר אֶל־הַמֶּלֶךְ אֱמֶת הַדָּבָר אֲשֶׁר שָׁמַעְתִּי בְּאַרְצִי עַל־דְּבָרֶיךָ וְעַל־חָכְמָתֶךָ:

⁶ I did not believe what they said until I came and saw with my own eyes that not even the half of your great wisdom had been described to me; you surpass the report that I heard.

ו וְלֹא־הֶאֱמַנְתִּי לְדִבְרֵיהֶם עַד אֲשֶׁר־בָּאתִי וַתִּרְאֶינָה עֵינַי וְהִנֵּה לֹא הֻגַּד־לִי חֲצִי מַרְבִּית חָכְמָתֶךָ יָסַפְתָּ עַל־הַשְּׁמוּעָה אֲשֶׁר שָׁמָעְתִּי:

Israel365 staff with Christian tourists in *Chevron*

9:1 The queen of Sheba heard of *Shlomo*'s fame King *Shlomo*'s reign can be described as the glory days of the Kingdom of Israel. *Shlomo* creates a kingdom that is characterized by peace and security, wealth and prosperity, wisdom and knowledge, justice and righteousness, spiritual devotion and international recognition. One of *Shlomo*'s goals in building the *Beit Hamikdash* is for the gentile nations of the world to also come to recognize the greatness and oneness of God, as he says "Thus all the peoples of the earth will know Your name and revere You, as does Your people *Yisrael*" (6:33). Perhaps this is why *Shlomo* made a point of making his kingdom so grand and establishing political connections and alliances. Indeed, in addition to his renowned reputation and vast impact, he succeeds in his mission to spread recognition of God, as demonstrated by the queen of Sheba's visit. She is so impressed with *Shlomo* and his kingdom, yet her reaction to her visit is, "Blessed is *Hashem* your God, who favored you and set you on His throne as a king before *Hashem*" (verse 8). The Nation of Israel continues to be charged with the same mission of spreading God's great name and His Oneness throughout the entire world.

7 How fortunate are your men and how fortunate are these courtiers of yours who are always in attendance on you and can hear your wisdom!

ז אַשְׁרֵי אֲנָשֶׁיךָ וְאַשְׁרֵי עֲבָדֶיךָ אֵלֶּה הָעֹמְדִים לְפָנֶיךָ תָּמִיד וְשֹׁמְעִים אֶת־חָכְמָתֶךָ:

8 Blessed is *Hashem* your God, who favored you and set you on His throne as a king before *Hashem*. It is because of your God's love for *Yisrael* and in order to establish them forever that He made you king over them to execute righteous justice."

ח יְהִי יְהֹוָה אֱלֹהֶיךָ בָּרוּךְ אֲשֶׁר חָפֵץ בְּךָ לְתִתְּךָ עַל־כִּסְאוֹ לְמֶלֶךְ לַיהֹוָה אֱלֹהֶיךָ בְּאַהֲבַת אֱלֹהֶיךָ אֶת־יִשְׂרָאֵל לְהַעֲמִידוֹ לְעוֹלָם וַיִּתֶּנְךָ עֲלֵיהֶם לְמֶלֶךְ לַעֲשׂוֹת מִשְׁפָּט וּצְדָקָה:

9 She presented the king with 120 *kikarim* of gold, and a vast quantity of spices and precious stones. There were no such spices as those which the queen of Sheba gave to King *Shlomo* –

ט וַתִּתֵּן לַמֶּלֶךְ מֵאָה וְעֶשְׂרִים כִּכַּר זָהָב וּבְשָׂמִים לָרֹב מְאֹד וְאֶבֶן יְקָרָה וְלֹא הָיָה כַּבֹּשֶׂם הַהוּא אֲשֶׁר־נָתְנָה מַלְכַּת־שְׁבָא לַמֶּלֶךְ שְׁלֹמֹה:

10 also, the servants of Huram and *Shlomo* who brought gold from Ophir brought algum-wood and precious stones.

י וְגַם־עַבְדֵי חִירָם [חוּרָם] וְעַבְדֵי שְׁלֹמֹה אֲשֶׁר־הֵבִיאוּ זָהָב מֵאוֹפִיר הֵבִיאוּ עֲצֵי אַלְגּוּמִּים וְאֶבֶן יְקָרָה:

11 The king made of the algum-wood ramps for the House of *Hashem* and for the royal palace, and lyres and harps for the musicians, whose like had never before been seen in the land of *Yehuda* –

יא וַיַּעַשׂ הַמֶּלֶךְ אֶת־עֲצֵי הָאַלְגּוּמִּים מְסִלּוֹת לְבֵית־יְהֹוָה וּלְבֵית הַמֶּלֶךְ וְכִנֹּרוֹת וּנְבָלִים לַשָּׁרִים וְלֹא־נִרְאוּ כָהֵם לְפָנִים בְּאֶרֶץ יְהוּדָה:

12 King *Shlomo*, in turn, gave the queen of Sheba everything she expressed a desire for, exceeding a return for what she had brought to the king. Then she and her courtiers left and returned to her own land.

יב וְהַמֶּלֶךְ שְׁלֹמֹה נָתַן לְמַלְכַּת־שְׁבָא אֶת־כָּל־חֶפְצָהּ אֲשֶׁר שָׁאָלָה מִלְּבַד אֲשֶׁר־הֵבִיאָה אֶל־הַמֶּלֶךְ וַתַּהֲפֹךְ וַתֵּלֶךְ לְאַרְצָהּ הִיא וַעֲבָדֶיהָ:

13 The gold that *Shlomo* received every year weighed 666 gold *kikarim*,

יג וַיְהִי מִשְׁקַל הַזָּהָב אֲשֶׁר־בָּא לִשְׁלֹמֹה בְּשָׁנָה אֶחָת שֵׁשׁ מֵאוֹת וְשִׁשִּׁים וָשֵׁשׁ כִּכְּרֵי זָהָב:

14 besides what traders and merchants brought, and the gold and silver that all the kings of Arabia and governors of the regions brought to *Shlomo*.

יד לְבַד מֵאַנְשֵׁי הַתָּרִים וְהַסֹּחֲרִים מְבִיאִים וְכָל־מַלְכֵי עֲרַב וּפַחוֹת הָאָרֶץ מְבִיאִים זָהָב וָכֶסֶף לִשְׁלֹמֹה:

15 King *Shlomo* made 200 shields of beaten gold – 600 *shekalim* of beaten gold for each shield,

טו וַיַּעַשׂ הַמֶּלֶךְ שְׁלֹמֹה מָאתַיִם צִנָּה זָהָב שָׁחוּט שֵׁשׁ מֵאוֹת זָהָב שָׁחוּט יַעֲלֶה עַל־הַצִּנָּה הָאֶחָת:

16 and 300 bucklers of beaten gold – 300 [*shekalim*] of gold for each buckler. The king placed them in the Lebanon Forest House.

טז וּשְׁלֹשׁ־מֵאוֹת מָגִנִּים זָהָב שָׁחוּט שְׁלֹשׁ מֵאוֹת זָהָב יַעֲלֶה עַל־הַמָּגֵן הָאֶחָת וַיִּתְּנֵם הַמֶּלֶךְ בְּבֵית יַעַר הַלְּבָנוֹן:

17 The king also made a large throne of ivory, overlaid with pure gold.

יז וַיַּעַשׂ הַמֶּלֶךְ כִּסֵּא־שֵׁן גָּדוֹל וַיְצַפֵּהוּ זָהָב טָהוֹר:

18 Six steps led up to the throne; and the throne had a golden footstool attached to it, and arms on either side of the seat. Two lions stood beside the arms,

יח וְשֵׁשׁ מַעֲלוֹת לַכִּסֵּא וְכֶבֶשׁ בַּזָּהָב לַכִּסֵּא מָאֳחָזִים וְיָדוֹת מִזֶּה וּמִזֶּה עַל־מְקוֹם הַשָּׁבֶת וּשְׁנַיִם אֲרָיוֹת עֹמְדִים אֵצֶל הַיָּדוֹת:

19 and twelve lions stood on the six steps, six on either side. None such was ever made for any other kingdom.

20 All of King *Shlomo*'s drinking vessels were of gold, and all the utensils of the Lebanon Forest House were of pure gold; silver counted for nothing in *Shlomo*'s days.

21 The king's fleet traveled to Tarshish with Huram's servants. Once every three years, the Tarshish fleet came in, bearing gold and silver, ivory, apes, and peacocks.

22 King *Shlomo* surpassed all the kings of the earth in wealth and wisdom.

23 All the kings of the earth came to pay homage to *Shlomo* and to listen to the wisdom with which *Hashem* had endowed him.

24 Each brought his tribute – silver and gold objects, robes, weapons, and spices, horses and mules – in the amount due each year.

25 *Shlomo* had 4,000 stalls for horses and chariots, and 12,000 horsemen, which he stationed in the chariot towns and with the king in *Yerushalayim*.

26 He ruled over all the kings from the Euphrates to the land of the Philistines and to the border of Egypt.

27 The king made silver as plentiful in *Yerushalayim* as stones, and cedars as plentiful as sycamores in the Shephelah.

28 Horses were brought for *Shlomo* from Egypt and all the lands.

29 The other events of *Shlomo*'s reign, early and late, are recorded in the chronicle of the *Navi Natan* and in the prophecies of *Achiya* the Shilonite and in the visions of Jedo the seer concerning *Yerovam* son of Nebat.

30 *Shlomo* reigned forty years over all *Yisrael* in *Yerushalayim*.

31 *Shlomo* slept with his fathers and was buried in the city of his father *David*; his son *Rechovam* succeeded him as king.

יט וּשְׁנֵים עָשָׂר אֲרָיוֹת עֹמְדִים שָׁם עַל־שֵׁשׁ הַמַּעֲלוֹת מִזֶּה וּמִזֶּה לֹא־נַעֲשָׂה כֵן לְכָל־מַמְלָכָה:

כ וְכֹל כְּלֵי מַשְׁקֵה הַמֶּלֶךְ שְׁלֹמֹה זָהָב וְכֹל כְּלֵי בֵּית־יַעַר הַלְּבָנוֹן זָהָב סָגוּר אֵין כֶּסֶף נֶחְשָׁב בִּימֵי שְׁלֹמֹה לִמְאוּמָה:

כא כִּי־אֳנִיּוֹת לַמֶּלֶךְ הֹלְכוֹת תַּרְשִׁישׁ עִם עַבְדֵי חוּרָם אַחַת לְשָׁלוֹשׁ שָׁנִים תָּבוֹאנָה אֳנִיּוֹת תַּרְשִׁישׁ נֹשְׂאוֹת זָהָב וָכֶסֶף שֶׁנְהַבִּים וְקוֹפִים וְתֻכִּיִּים:

כב וַיִּגְדַּל הַמֶּלֶךְ שְׁלֹמֹה מִכֹּל מַלְכֵי הָאָרֶץ לְעֹשֶׁר וְחָכְמָה:

כג וְכֹל מַלְכֵי הָאָרֶץ מְבַקְשִׁים אֶת־פְּנֵי שְׁלֹמֹה לִשְׁמֹעַ אֶת־חָכְמָתוֹ אֲשֶׁר־נָתַן הָאֱלֹהִים בְּלִבּוֹ:

כד וְהֵם מְבִיאִים אִישׁ מִנְחָתוֹ כְּלֵי כֶסֶף וּכְלֵי זָהָב וּשְׂלָמוֹת נֵשֶׁק וּבְשָׂמִים סוּסִים וּפְרָדִים דְּבַר־שָׁנָה בְּשָׁנָה:

כה וַיְהִי לִשְׁלֹמֹה אַרְבַּעַת אֲלָפִים אֻרְיוֹת סוּסִים וּמַרְכָּבוֹת וּשְׁנֵים־עָשָׂר אֶלֶף פָּרָשִׁים וַיַּנִּיחֵם בְּעָרֵי הָרֶכֶב וְעִם־הַמֶּלֶךְ בִּירוּשָׁלָם:

כו וַיְהִי מוֹשֵׁל בְּכָל־הַמְּלָכִים מִן־הַנָּהָר וְעַד־אֶרֶץ פְּלִשְׁתִּים וְעַד גְּבוּל מִצְרָיִם:

כז וַיִּתֵּן הַמֶּלֶךְ אֶת־הַכֶּסֶף בִּירוּשָׁלַם כָּאֲבָנִים וְאֵת הָאֲרָזִים נָתַן כַּשִּׁקְמִים אֲשֶׁר־בַּשְּׁפֵלָה לָרֹב:

כח וּמוֹצִיאִים סוּסִים מִמִּצְרַיִם לִשְׁלֹמֹה וּמִכָּל־הָאֲרָצוֹת:

כט וּשְׁאָר דִּבְרֵי שְׁלֹמֹה הָרִאשֹׁנִים וְהָאַחֲרוֹנִים הֲלֹא־הֵם כְּתוּבִים עַל־דִּבְרֵי נָתָן הַנָּבִיא וְעַל־נְבוּאַת אֲחִיָּה הַשִּׁילוֹנִי וּבַחֲזוֹת יֶעְדִּי [יֶעְדּוֹ] הַחֹזֶה עַל־יָרָבְעָם בֶּן־נְבָט:

ל וַיִּמְלֹךְ שְׁלֹמֹה בִירוּשָׁלַם עַל־כָּל־יִשְׂרָאֵל אַרְבָּעִים שָׁנָה:

לא וַיִּשְׁכַּב שְׁלֹמֹה עִם־אֲבֹתָיו וַיִּקְבְּרֻהוּ בְּעִיר דָּוִיד אָבִיו וַיִּמְלֹךְ רְחַבְעָם בְּנוֹ תַּחְתָּיו:

Chronicles

10 1 *Rechovam* went to *Shechem*, for all *Yisrael* had come to *Shechem* to acclaim him king.

2 *Yerovam* son of Nebat learned of it while he was in Egypt where he had fled from King *Shlomo*, and *Yerovam* returned from Egypt.

3 They sent for him; and *Yerovam* and all *Yisrael* came and spoke to *Rechovam* as follows:

4 "Your father made our yoke heavy. Now lighten the harsh labor and the heavy yoke that your father laid on us, and we will serve you."

5 He answered them, "Come back to me in three days." So the people went away.

6 King *Rechovam* took counsel with the elders who had served during the lifetime of his father *Shlomo*. He said, "What answer do you counsel to give these people?"

va-yi-va-ATZ ha-ME-lekh r'-khav-AM et ha-z'-kay-NEEM a-sher ha-YU
o-m'-DEEM lif-NAY sh'-lo-MOH a-VEEV bih-yo-TO KHAI lay-MOR
AYKH a-TEM no-a-TZEEM l'-ha-SHEEV la-AM ha-ZEH da-VAR

7 They answered him, "If you will be good to these people and appease them and speak to them with kind words, they will be your servants always."

8 But he ignored the counsel that the elders gave him, and took counsel with the young men who had grown up with him and were serving him.

9 "What," he asked, "do you counsel that we reply to these people who said to me, 'Lighten the yoke that your father laid on us'?"

י א וַיֵּלֶךְ רְחַבְעָם שְׁכֶמָה כִּי שְׁכֶם בָּאוּ כָל־יִשְׂרָאֵל לְהַמְלִיךְ אֹתוֹ:

ב וַיְהִי כִּשְׁמֹעַ יָרָבְעָם בֶּן־נְבָט וְהוּא בְמִצְרַיִם אֲשֶׁר בָּרַח מִפְּנֵי שְׁלֹמֹה הַמֶּלֶךְ וַיָּשָׁב יָרָבְעָם מִמִּצְרָיִם:

ג וַיִּשְׁלְחוּ וַיִּקְרְאוּ־לוֹ וַיָּבֹא יָרָבְעָם וְכָל־יִשְׂרָאֵל וַיְדַבְּרוּ אֶל־רְחַבְעָם לֵאמֹר:

ד אָבִיךָ הִקְשָׁה אֶת־עֻלֵּנוּ וְעַתָּה הָקֵל מֵעֲבֹדַת אָבִיךָ הַקָּשָׁה וּמֵעֻלּוֹ הַכָּבֵד אֲשֶׁר־נָתַן עָלֵינוּ וְנַעַבְדֶךָ:

ה וַיֹּאמֶר אֲלֵהֶם עוֹד שְׁלֹשֶׁת יָמִים וְשׁוּבוּ אֵלָי וַיֵּלֶךְ הָעָם:

ו וַיִּוָּעַץ הַמֶּלֶךְ רְחַבְעָם אֶת־הַזְּקֵנִים אֲשֶׁר־הָיוּ עֹמְדִים לִפְנֵי שְׁלֹמֹה אָבִיו בִּהְיֹתוֹ חַי לֵאמֹר אֵיךְ אַתֶּם נוֹעָצִים לְהָשִׁיב לָעָם־הַזֶּה דָּבָר:

ז וַיְדַבְּרוּ אֵלָיו לֵאמֹר אִם־תִּהְיֶה לְטוֹב לְהָעָם הַזֶּה וּרְצִיתָם וְדִבַּרְתָּ אֲלֵהֶם דְּבָרִים טוֹבִים וְהָיוּ לְךָ עֲבָדִים כָּל־הַיָּמִים:

ח וַיַּעֲזֹב אֶת־עֲצַת הַזְּקֵנִים אֲשֶׁר יְעָצֻהוּ וַיִּוָּעַץ אֶת־הַיְלָדִים אֲשֶׁר גָּדְלוּ אִתּוֹ הָעֹמְדִים לְפָנָיו:

ט וַיֹּאמֶר אֲלֵהֶם מָה אַתֶּם נוֹעָצִים וְנָשִׁיב דָּבָר אֶת־הָעָם הַזֶּה אֲשֶׁר דִּבְּרוּ אֵלַי לֵאמֹר הָקֵל מִן־הָעֹל אֲשֶׁר־נָתַן אָבִיךָ עָלֵינוּ:

10:6 Who had served during the lifetime of his father *Shlomo* Upon assuming the throne after his father's death, *Rechovam* is approached by representatives of the nation who request an easing of the tax burden that had been placed upon them by King *Shlomo*. *Rechovam* first consults the elders who had advised his father, but not liking the counsel they give, he instead turns to the younger people, his own contemporaries. This was a breach of the principle, "Ask your father, he will inform you, Your elders, they will tell you" (Deuteronomy 32:7). *Rechovam* follows the advice of his young friends, and this leads to the split in the kingdom, setting the ten tribes of the kingdom of *Yisrael* on a very negative path of idolatry and sin. Had *Rechovam* appreciated the meaning and importance of history and tradition, instead of trying to assert himself and his reign over the nation, much evil might have been averted.

Three generations celebrating the Passover seder

10 And the young men who had grown up with him answered, "Speak thus to the people who said to you, 'Your father made our yoke heavy, now you make it lighter for us.' Say to them, 'My little finger is thicker than my father's loins.

י וַיְדַבְּרוּ אִתּוֹ הַיְלָדִים אֲשֶׁר גָּדְלוּ אִתּוֹ לֵאמֹר כֹּה־תֹאמַר לָעָם אֲשֶׁר־דִּבְּרוּ אֵלֶיךָ לֵאמֹר אָבִיךָ הִכְבִּיד אֶת־עֻלֵּנוּ וְאַתָּה הָקֵל מֵעָלֵינוּ כֹּה תֹּאמַר אֲלֵהֶם קָטָנִּי עָבָה מִמָּתְנֵי אָבִי:

11 My father imposed a heavy yoke on you, and I will add to your yoke; my father flogged you with whips, but I [will do so] with scorpions.'"

יא וְעַתָּה אָבִי הֶעְמִיס עֲלֵיכֶם עֹל כָּבֵד וַאֲנִי אֹסִיף עַל־עֻלְּכֶם אָבִי יִסַּר אֶתְכֶם בַּשּׁוֹטִים וַאֲנִי בָּעַקְרַבִּים:

12 Yerovam and all the people came to Rechovam on the third day, since the king had told them, "Come back on the third day."

יב וַיָּבֹא יָרָבְעָם וְכָל־הָעָם אֶל־רְחַבְעָם בַּיּוֹם הַשְּׁלִשִׁי כַּאֲשֶׁר דִּבֶּר הַמֶּלֶךְ לֵאמֹר שׁוּבוּ אֵלַי בַּיּוֹם הַשְּׁלִשִׁי:

13 The king answered them harshly; thus King Rechovam ignored the elders' counsel.

יג וַיַּעֲנֵם הַמֶּלֶךְ קָשָׁה וַיַּעֲזֹב הַמֶּלֶךְ רְחַבְעָם אֵת עֲצַת הַזְּקֵנִים:

14 He spoke to them in accordance with the counsel of the young men, and said, "I will make your yoke heavy, and I will add to it; my father flogged you with whips, but I [will do so] with scorpions."

יד וַיְדַבֵּר אֲלֵהֶם כַּעֲצַת הַיְלָדִים לֵאמֹר אַכְבִּיד אֶת־עֻלְּכֶם וַאֲנִי אֹסִיף עָלָיו אָבִי יִסַּר אֶתְכֶם בַּשּׁוֹטִים וַאֲנִי בָּעַקְרַבִּים:

15 The king did not listen to the people, for *Hashem* had brought it about in order that *Hashem* might fulfill the promise that He had made through *Achiya* the Shilonite to *Yerovam* son of Nebat.

טו וְלֹא־שָׁמַע הַמֶּלֶךְ אֶל־הָעָם כִּי־הָיְתָה נְסִבָּה מֵעִם הָאֱלֹהִים לְמַעַן הָקִים יְהֹוָה אֶת־דְּבָרוֹ אֲשֶׁר דִּבֶּר בְּיַד אֲחִיָּהוּ הַשִּׁלוֹנִי אֶל־יָרָבְעָם בֶּן־נְבָט:

16 When all *Yisrael* [saw] that the king had not listened to them, the people answered the king: "We have no portion in *David*, No share in *Yishai's* son! To your tents, O *Yisrael*! Now look to your own house, O *David*." So all *Yisrael* returned to their homes.

טז וְכָל־יִשְׂרָאֵל כִּי לֹא־שָׁמַע הַמֶּלֶךְ לָהֶם וַיָּשִׁיבוּ הָעָם אֶת־הַמֶּלֶךְ לֵאמֹר מַה־לָּנוּ חֵלֶק בְּדָוִיד וְלֹא־נַחֲלָה בְּבֶן־יִשַׁי אִישׁ לְאֹהָלֶיךָ יִשְׂרָאֵל עַתָּה רְאֵה בֵיתְךָ דָּוִיד וַיֵּלֶךְ כָּל־יִשְׂרָאֵל לְאֹהָלָיו:

17 But *Rechovam* continued to reign over the Israelites who lived in the towns of *Yehuda*.

יז וּבְנֵי יִשְׂרָאֵל הַיֹּשְׁבִים בְּעָרֵי יְהוּדָה וַיִּמְלֹךְ עֲלֵיהֶם רְחַבְעָם:

18 King *Rechovam* sent out Hadoram, who was in charge of the forced labor, but the Israelites pelted him to death with stones. Thereupon, King *Rechovam* hurriedly mounted his chariot and fled to *Yerushalayim*.

יח וַיִּשְׁלַח הַמֶּלֶךְ רְחַבְעָם אֶת־הֲדֹרָם אֲשֶׁר עַל־הַמַּס וַיִּרְגְּמוּ־בוֹ בְנֵי־יִשְׂרָאֵל אֶבֶן וַיָּמֹת וְהַמֶּלֶךְ רְחַבְעָם הִתְאַמֵּץ לַעֲלוֹת בַּמֶּרְכָּבָה לָנוּס יְרוּשָׁלָ͏ִם:

19 *Yisrael* has been in revolt against the house of *David* to this day.

יט וַיִּפְשְׁעוּ יִשְׂרָאֵל בְּבֵית דָּוִיד עַד הַיּוֹם הַזֶּה:

11 1 When *Rechovam* arrived in *Yerushalayim*, he mustered the house of *Yehuda* and *Binyamin*, 180,000 picked fighting men, to make war with *Yisrael* in order to restore the kingdom to *Rechovam*.

יא א וַיָּבֹא רְחַבְעָם יְרוּשָׁלַ͏ִם וַיַּקְהֵל אֶת־בֵּית יְהוּדָה וּבִנְיָמִן מֵאָה וּשְׁמוֹנִים אֶלֶף בָּחוּר עֹשֵׂה מִלְחָמָה לְהִלָּחֵם עִם־יִשְׂרָאֵל לְהָשִׁיב אֶת־הַמַּמְלָכָה לִרְחַבְעָם:

² But the word of *Hashem* came to *Shemaya*, the man of *Hashem*:

ב וַיְהִי דְּבַר־יְהֹוָה אֶל־שְׁמַעְיָהוּ אִישׁ־הָאֱלֹהִים לֵאמֹר׃

³ "Say to *Rechovam* son of *Shlomo* king of *Yehuda*, and to all *Yisrael* in *Yehuda* and *Binyamin*:

ג אֱמֹר אֶל־רְחַבְעָם בֶּן־שְׁלֹמֹה מֶלֶךְ יְהוּדָה וְאֶל כָּל־יִשְׂרָאֵל בִּיהוּדָה וּבִנְיָמִן לֵאמֹר׃

⁴ Thus said *Hashem*: You shall not set out to make war on your kinsmen. Let every man return to his home, for this thing has been brought about by Me." They heeded the words of *Hashem* and refrained from marching against *Yerovam*.

ד כֹּה אָמַר יְהֹוָה לֹא־תַעֲלוּ וְלֹא־תִלָּחֲמוּ עִם־אֲחֵיכֶם שׁוּבוּ אִישׁ לְבֵיתוֹ כִּי מֵאִתִּי נִהְיָה הַדָּבָר הַזֶּה וַיִּשְׁמְעוּ אֶת־דִּבְרֵי יְהֹוָה וַיָּשֻׁבוּ מִלֶּכֶת אֶל־יָרָבְעָם׃

> KOH a-MAR a-do-NAI lo ta-a-LU v'-lo ti-LA-kha-MU im a-khay-KHEM
> SHU-vu EESH l'-vay-TO KEE may-i-TEE nih-YAH ha-da-VAR ha-ZEH
> va-yish-m'-U et div-RAY a-do-NAI va-ya-SHU-vu mi-LE-khet el ya-rov-AM

⁵ *Rechovam* dwelt in *Yerushalayim* and built fortified towns in *Yehuda*.

ה וַיֵּשֶׁב רְחַבְעָם בִּירוּשָׁלָ͏ִם וַיִּבֶן עָרִים לְמָצוֹר בִּיהוּדָה׃

⁶ He built up *Beit Lechem*, and Etam, and *Tekoa*,

ו וַיִּבֶן אֶת־בֵּית־לֶחֶם וְאֶת־עֵיטָם וְאֶת־תְּקוֹעַ׃

⁷ and Beth-zur, and Soco, and *Adulam*,

ז וְאֶת־בֵּית־צוּר וְאֶת־שׂוֹכוֹ וְאֶת־עֲדֻלָּם׃

⁸ and Gath, and Mareshah, and Ziph,

ח וְאֶת־גַּת וְאֶת־מָרֵשָׁה וְאֶת־זִיף׃

⁹ and Adoraim, and *Lachish*, and *Azeika*,

ט וְאֶת־אֲדוֹרַיִם וְאֶת־לָכִישׁ וְאֶת־עֲזֵקָה׃

¹⁰ and *Tzora*, and Aijalon, and *Chevron*, which are in *Yehuda* and in *Binyamin*, as fortified towns.

י וְאֶת־צָרְעָה וְאֶת־אַיָּלוֹן וְאֶת־חֶבְרוֹן אֲשֶׁר בִּיהוּדָה וּבְנְיָמִן עָרֵי מְצֻרוֹת׃

¹¹ He strengthened the fortified towns and put commanders in them, along with stores of food, oil, and wine,

יא וַיְחַזֵּק אֶת־הַמְּצֻרוֹת וַיִּתֵּן בָּהֶם נְגִידִים וְאֹצְרוֹת מַאֲכָל וְשֶׁמֶן וָיָיִן׃

¹² and shields and spears in every town. He strengthened them exceedingly; thus *Yehuda* and *Binyamin* were his.

יב וּבְכָל־עִיר וָעִיר צִנּוֹת וּרְמָחִים וַיְחַזְּקֵם לְהַרְבֵּה מְאֹד וַיְהִי־לוֹ יְהוּדָה וּבִנְיָמִן׃

¹³ The *Kohanim* and the *Leviim*, from all their territories throughout *Yisrael*, presented themselves to him.

יג וְהַכֹּהֲנִים וְהַלְוִיִּם אֲשֶׁר בְּכָל־יִשְׂרָאֵל הִתְיַצְּבוּ עָלָיו מִכָּל־גְּבוּלָם׃

11:4 You shall not set out to make war on your kinsmen Though the kingdom has split and ten tribes have rejected *Rechovam* and the house of *David*, God does not want there to be a war between the two kingdoms. He reminds the southern tribes of *Yehuda* and *Binyamin* that despite the rift, the members of both kingdoms are brothers, and they should therefore treat each other with peace and brotherhood. The split in the kingdom is not ideal, and it pains *Hashem* to see different members of the Nation of Israel at odds with each other. Instead, He longs for the time when once again "one king shall be king of them all. Never again shall they be two nations, and never again shall they be divided into two kingdoms" (Ezekiel 37:22). With the establishment of the State of Israel, the ingathering of the exiles and the return of some of the ten tribes, we are beginning to witness the miraculous fulfilment of the unity between the kingdom of *Yisrael* and the kingdom of *Yehuda*.

Two brothers at the beach in Haifa

14 The *Leviim* had left their pasturelands and their holdings and had set out for *Yehuda* and *Yerushalayim*, for *Yerovam* and his sons had prevented them from serving *Hashem*,

יד כִּי־עָזְבוּ הַלְוִיִּם אֶת־מִגְרְשֵׁיהֶם וַאֲחֻזָּתָם וַיֵּלְכוּ לִיהוּדָה וְלִירוּשָׁלָ͏ִם כִּי־הִזְנִיחָם יָרָבְעָם וּבָנָיו מִכַּהֵן לַיהוָה:

15 having appointed his own *Kohanim* for the shrines, goat-demons, and calves which he had made.

טו וַיַּעֲמֶד־לוֹ כֹּהֲנִים לַבָּמוֹת וְלַשְּׂעִירִים וְלָעֲגָלִים אֲשֶׁר עָשָׂה:

16 From all the tribes of *Yisrael*, those intent on seeking God of *Yisrael* followed them to *Yerushalayim*, to sacrifice to God of their fathers.

טז וְאַחֲרֵיהֶם מִכֹּל שִׁבְטֵי יִשְׂרָאֵל הַנֹּתְנִים אֶת־לְבָבָם לְבַקֵּשׁ אֶת־יְהוָה אֱלֹהֵי יִשְׂרָאֵל בָּאוּ יְרוּשָׁלַ͏ִם לִזְבּוֹחַ לַיהוָה אֱלֹהֵי אֲבוֹתֵיהֶם:

17 They strengthened the kingdom of *Yehuda*, and supported *Rechovam* son of *Shlomo* for three years, for they followed the ways of *David* and *Shlomo* for three years.

יז וַיְחַזְּקוּ אֶת־מַלְכוּת יְהוּדָה וַיְאַמְּצוּ אֶת־רְחַבְעָם בֶּן־שְׁלֹמֹה לְשָׁנִים שָׁלוֹשׁ כִּי הָלְכוּ בְּדֶרֶךְ דָּוִיד וּשְׁלֹמֹה לְשָׁנִים שָׁלוֹשׁ:

18 *Rechovam* married Mahalath daughter of Jerimoth son of *David*, and *Avichayil* daughter of *Eliav* son of *Yishai*.

יח וַיִּקַּח־לוֹ רְחַבְעָם אִשָּׁה אֶת־מָחֲלַת בֶּן־[בַּת־] יְרִימוֹת בֶּן־דָּוִיד אֲבִיהַיִל בַּת־אֱלִיאָב בֶּן־יִשָׁי:

19 She bore him sons: Jeush, Shemariah, and Zaham.

יט וַתֵּלֶד לוֹ בָּנִים אֶת־יְעוּשׁ וְאֶת־שְׁמַרְיָה וְאֶת־זָהַם:

20 He then took Maacah daughter of *Avshalom*; she bore him *Aviya*, Attai, Ziza, and Shelomith.

כ וְאַחֲרֶיהָ לָקַח אֶת־מַעֲכָה בַּת־אַבְשָׁלוֹם וַתֵּלֶד לוֹ אֶת־אֲבִיָּה וְאֶת־עַתַּי וְאֶת־זִיזָא וְאֶת־שְׁלֹמִית:

21 *Rechovam* loved Maacah daughter of *Avshalom* more than his other wives and concubines – for he took eighteen wives and sixty concubines; he begot twenty-eight sons and sixty daughters.

כא וַיֶּאֱהַב רְחַבְעָם אֶת־מַעֲכָה בַת־אַבְשָׁלוֹם מִכָּל־נָשָׁיו וּפִילַגְשָׁיו כִּי נָשִׁים שְׁמוֹנֶה־עֶשְׂרֵה נָשָׂא וּפִילַגְשִׁים שִׁשִּׁים וַיּוֹלֶד עֶשְׂרִים וּשְׁמוֹנָה בָּנִים וְשִׁשִּׁים בָּנוֹת:

22 *Rechovam* designated *Aviya* son of Maacah as chief and leader among his brothers, for he intended him to be his successor.

כב וַיַּעֲמֵד לָרֹאשׁ רְחַבְעָם אֶת־אֲבִיָּה בֶן־מַעֲכָה לְנָגִיד בְּאֶחָיו כִּי לְהַמְלִיכוֹ:

23 He prudently distributed all his sons throughout the regions of *Yehuda* and *Binyamin* and throughout the fortified towns; he provided them with abundant food, and he sought many wives for them.

כג וַיָּבֶן וַיִּפְרֹץ מִכָּל־בָּנָיו לְכָל־אַרְצוֹת יְהוּדָה וּבִנְיָמִן לְכֹל עָרֵי הַמְּצֻרוֹת וַיִּתֵּן לָהֶם הַמָּזוֹן לָרֹב וַיִּשְׁאַל הֲמוֹן נָשִׁים:

12 1 When the kingship of *Rechovam* was firmly established, and he grew strong, he abandoned the Teaching of *Hashem*, he and all *Yisrael* with him.

יב א וַיְהִי כְּהָכִין מַלְכוּת רְחַבְעָם וּכְחֶזְקָתוֹ עָזַב אֶת־תּוֹרַת יְהוָה וְכָל־יִשְׂרָאֵל עִמּוֹ:

2 In the fifth year of King *Rechovam*, King Shishak of Egypt marched against *Yerushalayim* – for they had trespassed against *Hashem* –

ב וַיְהִי בַּשָּׁנָה הַחֲמִישִׁית לַמֶּלֶךְ רְחַבְעָם עָלָה שִׁישַׁק מֶלֶךְ־מִצְרַיִם עַל־יְרוּשָׁלָ͏ִם כִּי מָעֲלוּ בַּיהוָה:

3 with 1,200 chariots, 60,000 horsemen and innumerable troops who came with him from Egypt: Lybians, Sukkites, and Kushites.

ג בְּאֶלֶף וּמָאתַיִם רֶכֶב וּבְשִׁשִּׁים אֶלֶף פָּרָשִׁים וְאֵין מִסְפָּר לָעָם אֲשֶׁר־בָּאוּ עִמּוֹ מִמִּצְרַיִם לוּבִים סֻכִּיִּים וְכוּשִׁים:

4 He took the fortified towns of *Yehuda* and advanced on *Yerushalayim*.

ד וַיִּלְכֹּד אֶת־עָרֵי הַמְּצֻרוֹת אֲשֶׁר לִיהוּדָה וַיָּבֹא עַד־יְרוּשָׁלָ͏ִם:

5 The *Navi Shemaya* came to *Rechovam* and the officers of *Yehuda*, who had assembled in *Yerushalayim* because of Shishak, and said to them, "Thus said *Hashem*: You have abandoned Me, so I am abandoning you to Shishak."

ה וּשְׁמַעְיָה הַנָּבִיא בָּא אֶל־רְחַבְעָם וְשָׂרֵי יְהוּדָה אֲשֶׁר־נֶאֶסְפוּ אֶל־יְרוּשָׁלַ͏ִם מִפְּנֵי שִׁישָׁק וַיֹּאמֶר לָהֶם כֹּה־אָמַר יְהוָה אַתֶּם עֲזַבְתֶּם אֹתִי וְאַף־אֲנִי עָזַבְתִּי אֶתְכֶם בְּיַד־שִׁישָׁק:

6 Then the officers of *Yisrael* and the king humbled themselves and declared, "*Hashem* is in the right."

ו וַיִּכָּנְעוּ שָׂרֵי־יִשְׂרָאֵל וְהַמֶּלֶךְ וַיֹּאמְרוּ צַדִּיק יְהוָה:

7 When *Hashem* saw that they had submitted, the word of *Hashem* came to *Shemaya*, saying, "Since they have humbled themselves, I will not destroy them but will grant them some measure of deliverance, and My wrath will not be poured out on *Yerushalayim* through Shishak.

ז וּבִרְאוֹת יְהוָה כִּי נִכְנָעוּ הָיָה דְבַר־יְהוָה אֶל־שְׁמַעְיָה לֵאמֹר נִכְנְעוּ לֹא אַשְׁחִיתֵם וְנָתַתִּי לָהֶם כִּמְעַט לִפְלֵיטָה וְלֹא־תִתַּךְ חֲמָתִי בִּירוּשָׁלַ͏ִם בְּיַד־שִׁישָׁק:

8 They will be subject to him, and they will know the difference between serving Me and serving the kingdoms of the earth." King Shishak of Egypt marched against *Yerushalayim*.

ח כִּי יִהְיוּ־לוֹ לַעֲבָדִים וְיֵדְעוּ עֲבוֹדָתִי וַעֲבוֹדַת מַמְלְכוֹת הָאֲרָצוֹת:

9 He took away the treasures of the House of *Hashem* and the treasures of the royal palace; he took away everything; he took away the golden shields that *Shlomo* had made.

ט וַיַּעַל שִׁישַׁק מֶלֶךְ־מִצְרַיִם עַל־יְרוּשָׁלַ͏ִם וַיִּקַּח אֶת־אֹצְרוֹת בֵּית־יְהוָה וְאֶת־אֹצְרוֹת בֵּית הַמֶּלֶךְ אֶת־הַכֹּל לָקָח וַיִּקַּח אֶת־מָגִנֵּי הַזָּהָב אֲשֶׁר עָשָׂה שְׁלֹמֹה:

10 King *Rechovam* had bronze shields made in their place, and entrusted them to the officers of the guard who guarded the entrance to the royal palace.

י וַיַּעַשׂ הַמֶּלֶךְ רְחַבְעָם תַּחְתֵּיהֶם מָגִנֵּי נְחֹשֶׁת וְהִפְקִיד עַל־יַד שָׂרֵי הָרָצִים הַשֹּׁמְרִים פֶּתַח בֵּית הַמֶּלֶךְ:

11 Whenever the king entered the House of *Hashem*, the guards would carry them and then bring them back to the armory of the guards.

יא וַיְהִי מִדֵּי־בוֹא הַמֶּלֶךְ בֵּית יְהוָה בָּאוּ הָרָצִים וּנְשָׂאוּם וֶהֱשִׁבוּם אֶל־תָּא הָרָצִים:

12 After he had humbled himself, the anger of *Hashem* was averted and He did not destroy him entirely; in *Yehuda*, too, good things were found.

יב וּבְהִכָּנְעוֹ שָׁב מִמֶּנּוּ אַף־יְהוָה וְלֹא לְהַשְׁחִית לְכָלָה וְגַם בִּיהוּדָה הָיָה דְּבָרִים טוֹבִים:

13 King *Rechovam* grew strong in *Yerushalayim* and exercised kingship. *Rechovam* was forty-one years old when he became king, and he reigned seventeen years in *Yerushalayim* – the city *Hashem* had chosen out of all the tribes of *Yisrael* to establish His name there. His mother's name was Naamah the Ammonitess.

יג וַיִּתְחַזֵּק הַמֶּלֶךְ רְחַבְעָם בִּירוּשָׁלַ͏ִם וַיִּמְלֹךְ כִּי בֶן־אַרְבָּעִים וְאַחַת שָׁנָה רְחַבְעָם בְּמָלְכוֹ וּשְׁבַע עֶשְׂרֵה שָׁנָה מָלַךְ בִּירוּשָׁלַ͏ִם הָעִיר אֲשֶׁר־בָּחַר יְהוָה לָשׂוּם אֶת־שְׁמוֹ שָׁם מִכֹּל שִׁבְטֵי יִשְׂרָאֵל וְשֵׁם אִמּוֹ נַעֲמָה הָעַמֹּנִית:

va-yit-kha-ZAYK ha-ME-lekh r'-khav-AM bee-ru-sha-LA-im va-yim-LOKH
KEE ven ar-ba-EEM v'-a-KHAT sha-NAH r'-khav-AM b'-mol-KHO
ush-VA es-RAY sha-NAH ma-LAKH bee-ru-sha-LA-im ha-EER a-sher
ba-KHAR a-do-NAI la-SUM et sh'-MO SHAM mi-KOL shiv-TAY
yis-ra-AYL v'-SHAYM i-MO na-a-MAH ha-a-mo-NEET

14 He did what was wrong, for he had not set his heart to seek *Hashem*.

יד וַיַּעַשׂ הָרַע כִּי לֹא הֵכִין לִבּוֹ לִדְרוֹשׁ אֶת־יְהֹוָה:

15 The deeds of *Rechovam*, early and late, are recorded in the chronicles of the *Navi Shemaya* and *Ido* the seer, in the manner of genealogy. There was continuous war between *Rechovam* and *Yerovam*.

טו וְדִבְרֵי רְחַבְעָם הָרִאשֹׁנִים וְהָאַחֲרוֹנִים הֲלֹא־הֵם כְּתוּבִים בְּדִבְרֵי שְׁמַעְיָה הַנָּבִיא וְעִדּוֹ הַחֹזֶה לְהִתְיַחֵשׂ וּמִלְחֲמוֹת רְחַבְעָם וְיָרָבְעָם כָּל־הַיָּמִים:

16 *Rechovam* slept with his fathers and was buried in the City of *David*. His son *Aviya* succeeded him as king.

טז וַיִּשְׁכַּב רְחַבְעָם עִם־אֲבֹתָיו וַיִּקָּבֵר בְּעִיר דָּוִיד וַיִּמְלֹךְ אֲבִיָּה בְנוֹ תַּחְתָּיו:

13 1 In the eighteenth year of King *Yerovam*, *Aviya* became king over *Yehuda*.

יג א בִּשְׁנַת שְׁמוֹנֶה עֶשְׂרֵה לַמֶּלֶךְ יָרָבְעָם וַיִּמְלֹךְ אֲבִיָּה עַל־יְהוּדָה:

2 He reigned three years in *Yerushalayim*; his mother's name was *Michaihu* daughter of Uriel of *Giva*. There was war between *Aviya* and *Yerovam*.

ב שָׁלוֹשׁ שָׁנִים מָלַךְ בִּירוּשָׁלָ͏ִם וְשֵׁם אִמּוֹ מִיכָיָהוּ בַת־אוּרִיאֵל מִן־גִּבְעָה וּמִלְחָמָה הָיְתָה בֵּין אֲבִיָּה וּבֵין יָרָבְעָם:

3 *Aviya* joined battle with a force of warriors, 400,000 picked men. *Yerovam* arrayed for battle against him 800,000 picked men, warriors.

ג וַיֶּאְסֹר אֲבִיָּה אֶת־הַמִּלְחָמָה בְּחַיִל גִּבּוֹרֵי מִלְחָמָה אַרְבַּע־מֵאוֹת אֶלֶף אִישׁ בָּחוּר וְיָרָבְעָם עָרַךְ עִמּוֹ מִלְחָמָה בִּשְׁמוֹנֶה מֵאוֹת אֶלֶף אִישׁ בָּחוּר גִּבּוֹר חָיִל:

4 *Aviya* stood on top of Mount Zemaraim in the hill country of *Efraim* and said, "Listen to me, *Yerovam* and all *Yisrael*.

ד וַיָּקָם אֲבִיָּה מֵעַל לְהַר צְמָרַיִם אֲשֶׁר בְּהַר אֶפְרָיִם וַיֹּאמֶר שְׁמָעוּנִי יָרָבְעָם וְכָל־יִשְׂרָאֵל:

5 Surely you know that God of *Yisrael* gave *David* kingship over *Yisrael* forever – to him and his sons – by a covenant of salt.

ה הֲלֹא לָכֶם לָדַעַת כִּי יְהֹוָה אֱלֹהֵי יִשְׂרָאֵל נָתַן מַמְלָכָה לְדָוִיד עַל־יִשְׂרָאֵל לְעוֹלָם לוֹ וּלְבָנָיו בְּרִית מֶלַח:

6 *Yerovam* son of Nebat had been in the service of *Shlomo* son of *David*, but he rose up and rebelled against his master.

ו וַיָּקָם יָרָבְעָם בֶּן־נְבָט עֶבֶד שְׁלֹמֹה בֶן־דָּוִיד וַיִּמְרֹד עַל־אֲדֹנָיו:

Prime Minister
Benjamin
Netanyahu
(b. 1949)

12:13 To establish His name there At an event celebrating Jerusalem Day in 2012, Prime Minister Benjamin Netanyahu stated: "Our generation had a great privilege – we saw the words of the prophets come true. We saw the rise of Zion, the return of Jewish sovereignty in the Land of Israel, the ingathering of exiles and our return to Jerusalem. We will make sure Jerusalem's golden light will shine on our people, and spread the light of Jerusalem to the whole world. We will protect Jerusalem, because Israel without Jerusalem is like a body without a heart." *Yerushalayim* is central to Israel, to Judaism and to the entire world, and this is not because any individual declared it special. It is so significant and beloved to man because, as this verse states, it is the place chosen by God "to establish His name there."

7 Riff-raff and scoundrels gathered around him and pressed hard upon *Rechovam* son of *Shlomo*. *Rechovam* was inexperienced and fainthearted and could not stand up to them.

ז וַיִּקָּבְצוּ עָלָיו אֲנָשִׁים רֵקִים בְּנֵי בְלִיַּעַל וַיִּתְאַמְּצוּ עַל־רְחַבְעָם בֶּן־שְׁלֹמֹה וּרְחַבְעָם הָיָה נַעַר וְרַךְ־לֵבָב וְלֹא הִתְחַזַּק לִפְנֵיהֶם:

8 Now you are bent on opposing the kingdom of *Hashem*, which is in the charge of the sons of *David*, because you are a great multitude and possess the golden calves that *Yerovam* made for you as gods.

ח וְעַתָּה אַתֶּם אֹמְרִים לְהִתְחַזֵּק לִפְנֵי מַמְלֶכֶת יְהוָה בְּיַד בְּנֵי דָוִיד וְאַתֶּם הָמוֹן רָב וְעִמָּכֶם עֶגְלֵי זָהָב אֲשֶׁר עָשָׂה לָכֶם יָרָבְעָם לֵאלֹהִים:

v'-a-TAH a-TEM o-m'-REEM l'-hit-kha-ZAYK lif-NAY mam-LE-khet a-do-NAI b'-YAD b'-NAY da-VEED v'-a-TEM ha-MON RAV v'-i-ma-KHEM eg-LAY za-HAV a-SHER a-SAH la-KHEM ya-rov-AM lay-lo-HEEM

9 Did you not banish the *Kohanim* of *Hashem*, the sons of *Aharon* and the *Leviim*, and, like the peoples of the land, appoint your own *Kohanim*? Anyone who offered himself for ordination with a young bull of the herd and seven rams became a *Kohen* of no-gods!

ט הֲלֹא הִדַּחְתֶּם אֶת־כֹּהֲנֵי יְהוָה אֶת־בְּנֵי אַהֲרֹן וְהַלְוִיִּם וַתַּעֲשׂוּ לָכֶם כֹּהֲנִים כְּעַמֵּי הָאֲרָצוֹת כָּל־הַבָּא לְמַלֵּא יָדוֹ בְּפַר בֶּן־בָּקָר וְאֵילִם שִׁבְעָה וְהָיָה כֹהֵן לְלֹא אֱלֹהִים:

10 As for us, *Hashem* is our God, and we have not forsaken Him. The *Kohanim* who minister to *Hashem* are the sons of *Aharon*, and the *Leviim* are at their tasks.

י וַאֲנַחְנוּ יְהוָה אֱלֹהֵינוּ וְלֹא עֲזַבְנֻהוּ וְכֹהֲנִים מְשָׁרְתִים לַיהוָה בְּנֵי אַהֲרֹן וְהַלְוִיִּם בַּמְּלָאכֶת:

11 They offer burnt offerings in smoke each morning and each evening, and the aromatic incense, the rows of bread on the pure table; they kindle the golden *menorah* with its lamps burning each evening, for we keep the charge of *Hashem* our God, while you have forsaken it.

יא וּמַקְטִרִים לַיהוָה עֹלוֹת בַּבֹּקֶר־בַּבֹּקֶר וּבָעֶרֶב־בָּעֶרֶב וּקְטֹרֶת־סַמִּים וּמַעֲרֶכֶת לֶחֶם עַל־הַשֻּׁלְחָן הַטָּהוֹר וּמְנוֹרַת הַזָּהָב וְנֵרֹתֶיהָ לְבָעֵר בָּעֶרֶב־בָּעֶרֶב כִּי־שֹׁמְרִים אֲנַחְנוּ אֶת־מִשְׁמֶרֶת יְהוָה אֱלֹהֵינוּ וְאַתֶּם עֲזַבְתֶּם אֹתוֹ:

12 See, *Hashem* is with us as our chief, and His *Kohanim* have the trumpets for sounding blasts against you. O children of *Yisrael*, do not fight God of your fathers, because you will not succeed."

יב וְהִנֵּה עִמָּנוּ בָרֹאשׁ הָאֱלֹהִים וְכֹהֲנָיו וַחֲצֹצְרוֹת הַתְּרוּעָה לְהָרִיעַ עֲלֵיכֶם בְּנֵי יִשְׂרָאֵל אַל־תִּלָּחֲמוּ עִם־יְהוָה אֱלֹהֵי־אֲבֹתֵיכֶם כִּי־לֹא תַצְלִיחוּ:

13 *Yerovam*, however, had directed the ambush to go around and come from the rear, thus the main body was in front of *Yehuda*, while the ambush was behind them.

יג וְיָרָבְעָם הֵסֵב אֶת־הַמַּאְרָב לָבוֹא מֵאַחֲרֵיהֶם וַיִּהְיוּ לִפְנֵי יְהוּדָה וְהַמַּאְרָב מֵאַחֲרֵיהֶם:

Chronicles

13:8 The kingdom of *Hashem*, which is in the charge of the sons of *David* *Aviya* understands that the reason he has arisen to the throne is to serve God. He tells *Yerovam* that he rules the "kingdom of *Hashem*," as the kings of *Yehuda* are from the line of *David*, and they maintain the service of God in the *Beit Hamikdash* in *Yerushalayim*. *Aviya* sees himself as the emissary of the Lord, the caretaker of His people who is expected to lead them in the service of *Hashem*. Because he understands this, God grants him victory; the triumph which was denied to his father *Rechovam*, who was motivated by pride, not piety. This is an example of how success in the Land of Israel is dependent upon recognition of *Hashem*, as *Asa* declares in the next chapter: "While the land is at our disposal because we turned to *Hashem* our God" (14:6).

Israeli flag at the beach in *Tel Aviv*

14 When *Yehuda* turned around and saw that the fighting was before and behind them, they cried out to *Hashem*, and the *Kohanim* blew the trumpets.

יד וַיִּפְנוּ יְהוּדָה וְהִנֵּה לָהֶם הַמִּלְחָמָה פָּנִים וְאָחוֹר וַיִּצְעֲקוּ לַיהֹוָה וְהַכֹּהֲנִים מַחְצְרִים [מַחְצְרִים] בַּחֲצֹצְרוֹת:

15 The men of *Yehuda* raised a shout; and when the men of *Yehuda* raised a shout, *Hashem* routed *Yerovam* and all *Yisrael* before *Aviya* and *Yehuda*.

טו וַיָּרִיעוּ אִישׁ יְהוּדָה וַיְהִי בְּהָרִיעַ אִישׁ יְהוּדָה וְהָאֱלֹהִים נָגַף אֶת־יָרָבְעָם וְכָל־ יִשְׂרָאֵל לִפְנֵי אֲבִיָּה וִיהוּדָה:

16 The Israelites fled before *Yehuda*, and *Hashem* delivered them into their hands.

טז וַיָּנוּסוּ בְנֵי־יִשְׂרָאֵל מִפְּנֵי יְהוּדָה וַיִּתְּנֵם אֱלֹהִים בְּיָדָם:

17 *Aviya* and his army inflicted a severe defeat on them; 500,000 men of *Yisrael* fell slain.

יז וַיַּכּוּ בָהֶם אֲבִיָּה וְעַמּוֹ מַכָּה רַבָּה וַיִּפְּלוּ חֲלָלִים מִיִּשְׂרָאֵל חֲמֵשׁ־מֵאוֹת אֶלֶף אִישׁ בָּחוּר:

18 The Israelites were crushed at that time, while the people of *Yehuda* triumphed because they relied on God of their fathers.

יח וַיִּכָּנְעוּ בְנֵי־יִשְׂרָאֵל בָּעֵת הַהִיא וַיֶּאֶמְצוּ בְּנֵי יְהוּדָה כִּי נִשְׁעֲנוּ עַל־יְהֹוָה אֱלֹהֵי אֲבוֹתֵיהֶם:

19 *Aviya* pursued *Yerovam* and captured some of his cities – *Beit El* with its dependencies, Jeshanah with its dependencies, and Ephrain with its dependencies.

יט וַיִּרְדֹּף אֲבִיָּה אַחֲרֵי יָרָבְעָם וַיִּלְכֹּד מִמֶּנּוּ עָרִים אֶת־בֵּית־אֵל וְאֶת־בְּנוֹתֶיהָ וְאֶת־ יְשָׁנָה וְאֶת־בְּנוֹתֶיהָ וְאֶת־עֶפְרוֹן [עֶפְרַיִן] וּבְנֹתֶיהָ:

20 *Yerovam* could not muster strength again during the days of *Aviya*. *Hashem* struck him down and he died.

כ וְלֹא־עָצַר כֹּחַ־יָרָבְעָם עוֹד בִּימֵי אֲבִיָּהוּ וַיִּגְּפֵהוּ יְהֹוָה וַיָּמֹת:

21 But *Aviya* grew powerful; he married fourteen wives and begat twenty-two sons and sixteen daughters.

כא וַיִּתְחַזֵּק אֲבִיָּהוּ וַיִּשָּׂא־לוֹ נָשִׁים אַרְבַּע עֶשְׂרֵה וַיּוֹלֶד עֶשְׂרִים וּשְׁנַיִם בָּנִים וְשֵׁשׁ עֶשְׂרֵה בָּנוֹת:

22 The other events of *Aviya*'s reign, his conduct and his acts, are recorded in the story of the *Navi Ido*.

כב וְיֶתֶר דִּבְרֵי אֲבִיָּה וּדְרָכָיו וּדְבָרָיו כְּתוּבִים בְּמִדְרַשׁ הַנָּבִיא עִדּוֹ:

23 *Aviya* slept with his fathers and was buried in the City of *David*; his son *Asa* succeeded him as king. The land was untroubled for ten years.

כג וַיִּשְׁכַּב אֲבִיָּה עִם־אֲבֹתָיו וַיִּקְבְּרוּ אֹתוֹ בְּעִיר דָּוִיד וַיִּמְלֹךְ אָסָא בְנוֹ תַּחְתָּיו בְּיָמָיו שָׁקְטָה הָאָרֶץ עֶשֶׂר שָׁנִים:

14 1 *Asa* did what was good and pleasing to *Hashem* his God.

יד א וַיַּעַשׂ אָסָא הַטּוֹב וְהַיָּשָׁר בְּעֵינֵי יְהֹוָה אֱלֹהָיו:

2 He abolished the alien altars and shrines; he smashed the pillars and cut down the sacred posts.

ב וַיָּסַר אֶת־מִזְבְּחוֹת הַנֵּכָר וְהַבָּמוֹת וַיְשַׁבֵּר אֶת־הַמַּצֵּבוֹת וַיְגַדַּע אֶת־ הָאֲשֵׁרִים:

3 He ordered *Yehuda* to turn to God of their fathers and to observe the Teaching and the Commandment.

ג וַיֹּאמֶר לִיהוּדָה לִדְרוֹשׁ אֶת־יְהֹוָה אֱלֹהֵי אֲבוֹתֵיהֶם וְלַעֲשׂוֹת הַתּוֹרָה וְהַמִּצְוָה:

4 He abolished the shrines and the incense stands throughout the cities of *Yehuda*, and the kingdom was untroubled under him.

ד וַיָּסַר מִכָּל־עָרֵי יְהוּדָה אֶת־הַבָּמוֹת וְאֶת־הַחַמָּנִים וַתִּשְׁקֹט הַמַּמְלָכָה לְפָנָיו:

⁵ He built fortified towns in *Yehuda*, since the land was untroubled and he was not engaged in warfare during those years, for *Hashem* had granted him respite.

ה וַיִּבֶן עָרֵי מְצוּרָה בִּיהוּדָה כִּי־שָׁקְטָה הָאָרֶץ וְאֵין־עִמּוֹ מִלְחָמָה בַּשָּׁנִים הָאֵלֶּה כִּי־הֵנִיחַ יְהֹוָה לוֹ:

⁶ He said to *Yehuda*, "Let us build up these cities and surround them with walls and towers, gates and bars, while the land is at our disposal because we turned to *Hashem* our God – we turned [to Him] and He gave us respite on all sides." They were successful in their building.

ו וַיֹּאמֶר לִיהוּדָה נִבְנֶה אֶת־הֶעָרִים הָאֵלֶּה וְנָסֵב חוֹמָה וּמִגְדָּלִים דְּלָתַיִם וּבְרִיחִים עוֹדֶנּוּ הָאָרֶץ לְפָנֵינוּ כִּי דָרַשְׁנוּ אֶת־יְהֹוָה אֱלֹהֵינוּ דָּרַשְׁנוּ וַיָּנַח לָנוּ מִסָּבִיב וַיִּבְנוּ וַיַּצְלִיחוּ:

⁷ *Asa* had an army of 300,000 men from *Yehuda* bearing shields and spears, and 280,000 from *Binyamin* bearing bucklers and drawing the bow; all these were valiant men.

ז וַיְהִי לְאָסָא חַיִל נֹשֵׂא צִנָּה וָרֹמַח מִיהוּדָה שְׁלֹשׁ מֵאוֹת אֶלֶף וּמִבִּנְיָמִן נֹשְׂאֵי מָגֵן וְדֹרְכֵי קֶשֶׁת מָאתַיִם וּשְׁמוֹנִים אָלֶף כָּל־אֵלֶּה גִּבּוֹרֵי חָיִל:

⁸ Zerah the Cushite marched out against them with an army of a thousand thousand and 300 chariots. When he reached Mareshah

ח וַיֵּצֵא אֲלֵיהֶם זֶרַח הַכּוּשִׁי בְּחַיִל אֶלֶף אֲלָפִים וּמַרְכָּבוֹת שְׁלֹשׁ מֵאוֹת וַיָּבֹא עַד־מָרֵשָׁה:

⁹ *Asa* confronted him, and the battle lines were drawn in the valley of Zephat by Mareshah.

ט וַיֵּצֵא אָסָא לְפָנָיו וַיַּעַרְכוּ מִלְחָמָה בְּגֵיא צְפַתָה לְמָרֵשָׁה:

¹⁰ *Asa* called to *Hashem* his God, and said, "*Hashem*, it is all the same to You to help the numerous and the powerless. Help us, *Hashem* our God, for we rely on You, and in Your name we have come against this great multitude. You are *Hashem* our God. Let no mortal hinder You."

י וַיִּקְרָא אָסָא אֶל־יְהֹוָה אֱלֹהָיו וַיֹּאמַר יְהֹוָה אֵין־עִמְּךָ לַעְזוֹר בֵּין רַב לְאֵין כֹּחַ עָזְרֵנוּ יְהֹוָה אֱלֹהֵינוּ כִּי־עָלֶיךָ נִשְׁעַנּוּ וּבְשִׁמְךָ בָאנוּ עַל־הֶהָמוֹן הַזֶּה יְהֹוָה אֱלֹהֵינוּ אַתָּה אַל־יַעְצֹר עִמְּךָ אֱנוֹשׁ:

va-yik-RA a-SA el a-do-NAI e-lo-HAV va-yo-MAR a-do-NAI ayn i-m'-KHA la-ZOR BAYN RAV l'-AYN KO-akh oz-RAY-nu a-do-NAI e-lo-HAY-nu kee a-LE-kha nish-A-nu uv-shim-KHA VA-nu al he-ha-MON ha-ZEH a-do-NAI e-lo-HAY-nu A-tah al ya-TZOR i-m'-KHA e-NOSH

¹¹ So *Hashem* routed the Cushites before *Asa* and *Yehuda*, and the Cushites fled.

יא וַיִּגֹּף יְהֹוָה אֶת־הַכּוּשִׁים לִפְנֵי אָסָא וְלִפְנֵי יְהוּדָה וַיָּנֻסוּ הַכּוּשִׁים:

¹² *Asa* and the army with him pursued them as far as Gerar. Many of the Cushites fell wounded beyond recovery, for they broke before *Hashem* and His camp. Very much spoil was taken.

יב וַיִּרְדְּפֵם אָסָא וְהָעָם אֲשֶׁר־עִמּוֹ עַד־לִגְרָר וַיִּפֹּל מִכּוּשִׁים לְאֵין לָהֶם מִחְיָה כִּי־נִשְׁבְּרוּ לִפְנֵי־יְהֹוָה וְלִפְנֵי מַחֲנֵהוּ וַיִּשְׂאוּ שָׁלָל הַרְבֵּה מְאֹד:

14:10 In Your name we have come against this great multitude Since the kingdom of *Yehuda* is the "kingdom of *Hashem*" (13:8), when it is attacked by a foreign enemy, it is fighting for God and His holy name. If the enemy wins, then in the enemy's mind, they have defeated not only the Nation of Israel but also *Hashem*. This is one reason why throughout Jewish history, so many empires sought to conquer the Land of Israel and the city of *Yerushalayim*. This is also why it was so important to foreign powers to destroy the *Beit Hamikdash*, as a sign that they had overpowered the God of Israel. Just as *Asa* fought to defend God's honor, so should we all.

A new IDF recruit holding a *Tanakh* and a gun

¹³ All the cities in the vicinity of Gerar were ravaged, for a terror of *Hashem* seized them. All the cities were plundered, and they yielded much booty.

יג וַיַּכּוּ אֵת כָּל־הֶעָרִים סְבִיבוֹת גְּרָר כִּי־הָיָה פַחַד־יהוה עֲלֵיהֶם וַיָּבֹזּוּ אֶת־כָּל־הֶעָרִים כִּי־בִזָּה רַבָּה הָיְתָה בָהֶם:

¹⁴ They also ravaged the encampment of herdsmen, capturing much sheep and camels. Then they returned to *Yerushalayim*.

יד וְגַם־אָהֳלֵי מִקְנֶה הִכּוּ וַיִּשְׁבּוּ צֹאן לָרֹב וּגְמַלִּים וַיָּשֻׁבוּ יְרוּשָׁלָ͏ִם:

15 ¹ The spirit of *Hashem* came upon *Azarya* son of *Oded*.

טו א וַעֲזַרְיָהוּ בֶּן־עוֹדֵד הָיְתָה עָלָיו רוּחַ אֱלֹהִים:

² He came to *Asa* and said to him, "Listen to me, *Asa* and all *Yehuda* and *Binyamin*; *Hashem* is with you as long as you are with Him. If you turn to Him, He will respond to you, but if you forsake Him, He will forsake you.

ב וַיֵּצֵא לִפְנֵי אָסָא וַיֹּאמֶר לוֹ שְׁמָעוּנִי אָסָא וְכָל־יְהוּדָה וּבִנְיָמִן יהוה עִמָּכֶם בִּהְיוֹתְכֶם עִמּוֹ וְאִם־תִּדְרְשֻׁהוּ יִמָּצֵא לָכֶם וְאִם־תַּעַזְבֻהוּ יַעֲזֹב אֶתְכֶם:

³ *Yisrael* has gone many days without the true *Hashem*, without a *Kohen* to give instruction and without Teaching.

ג וְיָמִים רַבִּים לְיִשְׂרָאֵל לְלֹא אֱלֹהֵי אֱמֶת וּלְלֹא כֹּהֵן מוֹרֶה וּלְלֹא תוֹרָה:

⁴ But in distress it returned to God of *Yisrael*, and sought Him, and He responded to them.

ד וַיָּשָׁב בַּצַּר־לוֹ עַל־יהוה אֱלֹהֵי יִשְׂרָאֵל וַיְבַקְשֻׁהוּ וַיִּמָּצֵא לָהֶם:

⁵ At those times, no wayfarer was safe, for there was much tumult among all the inhabitants of the lands.

ה וּבָעִתִּים הָהֵם אֵין שָׁלוֹם לַיּוֹצֵא וְלַבָּא כִּי מְהוּמֹת רַבּוֹת עַל כָּל־יוֹשְׁבֵי הָאֲרָצוֹת:

⁶ Nation was crushed by nation and city by city, for *Hashem* threw them into panic with every kind of trouble.

ו וְכֻתְּתוּ גוֹי־בְּגוֹי וְעִיר בְּעִיר כִּי־אֱלֹהִים הֲמָמָם בְּכָל־צָרָה:

⁷ As for you, be strong, do not be disheartened, for there is reward for your labor."

ז וְאַתֶּם חִזְקוּ וְאַל־יִרְפּוּ יְדֵיכֶם כִּי יֵשׁ שָׂכָר לִפְעֻלַּתְכֶם:

⁸ When *Asa* heard these words, the prophecy of *Oded* the *Navi*, he took courage and removed the abominations from the entire land of *Yehuda* and *Binyamin* and from the cities that he had captured in the hill country of *Efraim*. He restored the *Mizbayach* of *Hashem* in front of the porch of *Hashem*.

ח וְכִשְׁמֹעַ אָסָא הַדְּבָרִים הָאֵלֶּה וְהַנְּבוּאָה עֹדֵד הַנָּבִיא הִתְחַזַּק וַיַּעֲבֵר הַשִּׁקּוּצִים מִכָּל־אֶרֶץ יְהוּדָה וּבִנְיָמִן וּמִן־הֶעָרִים אֲשֶׁר לָכַד מֵהַר אֶפְרָיִם וַיְחַדֵּשׁ אֶת־מִזְבַּח יהוה אֲשֶׁר לִפְנֵי אוּלָם יהוה:

⁹ He assembled all the people of *Yehuda* and *Binyamin* and those people of *Efraim*, *Menashe*, and *Shimon* who sojourned among them, for many in *Yisrael* had thrown in their lot with him when they saw that *Hashem* his God was with him.

ט וַיִּקְבֹּץ אֶת־כָּל־יְהוּדָה וּבִנְיָמִן וְהַגָּרִים עִמָּהֶם מֵאֶפְרַיִם וּמְנַשֶּׁה וּמִשִּׁמְעוֹן כִּי־נָפְלוּ עָלָיו מִיִּשְׂרָאֵל לָרֹב בִּרְאֹתָם כִּי־יהוה אֱלֹהָיו עִמּוֹ:

¹⁰ They were assembled in *Yerushalayim* in the third month of the fifteenth year of the reign of *Asa*.

י וַיִּקָּבְצוּ יְרוּשָׁלַ͏ִם בַּחֹדֶשׁ הַשְּׁלִישִׁי לִשְׁנַת חֲמֵשׁ־עֶשְׂרֵה לְמַלְכוּת אָסָא:

¹¹ They brought sacrifices to *Hashem* on that day; they brought 700 oxen and 7,000 sheep of the spoil.

יא וַיִּזְבְּחוּ לַיהוה בַּיּוֹם הַהוּא מִן־הַשָּׁלָל הֵבִיאוּ בָּקָר שְׁבַע מֵאוֹת וְצֹאן שִׁבְעַת אֲלָפִים:

12 They entered into a covenant to worship God of their fathers with all their heart and with all their soul.

יב וַיָּבֹאוּ בַבְּרִית לִדְרוֹשׁ אֶת־יְהֹוָה אֱלֹהֵי אֲבוֹתֵיהֶם בְּכָל־לְבָבָם וּבְכָל־נַפְשָׁם:

13 Whoever would not worship God of *Yisrael* would be put to death, whether small or great, whether man or woman.

יג וְכֹל אֲשֶׁר לֹא־יִדְרֹשׁ לַיהֹוָה אֱלֹהֵי־יִשְׂרָאֵל יוּמָת לְמִן־קָטֹן וְעַד־גָּדוֹל לְמֵאִישׁ וְעַד־אִשָּׁה:

14 So they took an oath to *Hashem* in a loud voice and with shouts, with trumpeting and blasts of the *shofar*.

יד וַיִּשָּׁבְעוּ לַיהֹוָה בְּקוֹל גָּדוֹל וּבִתְרוּעָה וּבַחֲצֹצְרוֹת וּבְשׁוֹפָרוֹת:

15 All *Yehuda* rejoiced over the oath, for they swore with all their heart and sought Him with all their will. He responded to them and gave them respite on every side.

טו וַיִּשְׂמְחוּ כָל־יְהוּדָה עַל־הַשְּׁבוּעָה כִּי בְכָל־לְבָבָם נִשְׁבָּעוּ וּבְכָל־רְצוֹנָם בִּקְשֻׁהוּ וַיִּמָּצֵא לָהֶם וַיָּנַח יְהֹוָה לָהֶם מִסָּבִיב:

va-yis-m'-KHU khol y'-hu-DAH al ha-sh'-vu-AH KEE v'-khol
l'-va-VAM nish-BA-u uv-khol r'-tzo-NAM bik-SHU-hu va-yi-ma-TZAY
la-HEM va-YA-nakh a-do-NAI la-HEM mi-sa-VEEV

16 He also deposed Maacah mother of King *Asa* from the rank of queen mother, because she had made an abominable thing for [the goddess] Asherah. *Asa* cut down her abominable thing, reduced it to dust, and burned it in the Wadi Kidron.

טז וְגַם־מַעֲכָה אֵם אָסָא הַמֶּלֶךְ הֱסִירָהּ מִגְּבִירָה אֲשֶׁר־עָשְׂתָה לַאֲשֵׁרָה מִפְלָצֶת וַיִּכְרֹת אָסָא אֶת־מִפְלַצְתָּהּ וַיָּדֶק וַיִּשְׂרֹף בְּנַחַל קִדְרוֹן:

17 The shrines, indeed, were not abolished in *Yisrael*; however, *Asa* was wholehearted [with *Hashem*] all his life.

יז וְהַבָּמוֹת לֹא־סָרוּ מִיִּשְׂרָאֵל רַק לְבַב־אָסָא הָיָה שָׁלֵם כָּל־יָמָיו:

18 He brought into the House of *Hashem* the things that he and his father had consecrated – silver, gold, and utensils.

יח וַיָּבֵא אֶת־קָדְשֵׁי אָבִיו וְקָדָשָׁיו בֵּית הָאֱלֹהִים כֶּסֶף וְזָהָב וְכֵלִים:

19 There was no war until the thirty-fifth year of the reign of *Asa*.

יט וּמִלְחָמָה לֹא הָיָתָה עַד שְׁנַת־שְׁלֹשִׁים וְחָמֵשׁ לְמַלְכוּת אָסָא:

16 1 In the thirty-sixth year of the reign of *Asa*, King *Basha* of *Yisrael* marched against *Yehuda* and built up *Rama* to block all movement of King *Asa* of *Yehuda*.

טז א בִּשְׁנַת שְׁלֹשִׁים וָשֵׁשׁ לְמַלְכוּת אָסָא עָלָה בַּעְשָׁא מֶלֶךְ־יִשְׂרָאֵל עַל־יְהוּדָה וַיִּבֶן אֶת־הָרָמָה לְבִלְתִּי תֵּת יוֹצֵא וָבָא לְאָסָא מֶלֶךְ יְהוּדָה:

2 *Asa* took all the silver and gold from the treasuries of the House of *Hashem* and the royal palace, and sent them to King Ben-hadad of Aram, who resided in Damascus, with this message:

ב וַיֹּצֵא אָסָא כֶּסֶף וְזָהָב מֵאֹצְרוֹת בֵּית יְהֹוָה וּבֵית הַמֶּלֶךְ וַיִּשְׁלַח אֶל־בֶּן־הֲדַד מֶלֶךְ אֲרָם הַיּוֹשֵׁב בְּדַרְמֶשֶׂק לֵאמֹר:

15:15 For they swore with all their heart *Asa* leads the people of *Yehuda* and *Binyamin* to recommit themselves wholeheartedly to God. They understand that to find *Hashem*, and for Him to remain with them, they must swear their absolute loyalty to Him. As such, *Asa* gathers the people together in *Yerushalayim* where they make an oath to serve *Hashem*, renewing the covenant first established by *Moshe* at Mount Sinai. In turn, God makes Himself available to them and grants them peace in the land.

The Old City of *Yerushalayim*

³ "There is a pact between me and you, as there was between my father and your father. I herewith send you silver and gold; go and break your pact with King *Basha* of *Yisrael* so that he may withdraw from me."

ג בְּרִית בֵּינִי וּבֵינֶךָ וּבֵין אָבִי וּבֵין אָבִיךָ הִנֵּה שָׁלַחְתִּי לְךָ כֶּסֶף וְזָהָב לֵךְ הָפֵר בְּרִיתְךָ אֶת־בַּעְשָׁא מֶלֶךְ יִשְׂרָאֵל וְיַעֲלֶה מֵעָלָי:

⁴ Ben-hadad acceded to King *Asa*'s request; he sent his army commanders against the towns of *Yisrael* and ravaged Ijon, *Dan*, Abel-maim, and all the garrison towns of *Naftali*.

ד וַיִּשְׁמַע בֶּן הֲדַד אֶל־הַמֶּלֶךְ אָסָא וַיִּשְׁלַח אֶת־שָׂרֵי הַחֲיָלִים אֲשֶׁר־לוֹ אֶל־עָרֵי יִשְׂרָאֵל וַיַּכּוּ אֶת־עִיּוֹן וְאֶת־דָּן וְאֵת אָבֵל מָיִם וְאֵת כָּל־מִסְכְּנוֹת עָרֵי נַפְתָּלִי:

⁵ When *Basha* heard about it, he stopped building up *Rama* and put an end to the work on it.

ה וַיְהִי כִּשְׁמֹעַ בַּעְשָׁא וַיֶּחְדַּל מִבְּנוֹת אֶת־הָרָמָה וַיַּשְׁבֵּת אֶת־מְלַאכְתּוֹ:

⁶ Then King *Asa* mustered all *Yehuda*, and they carried away the stones and timber with which *Basha* had built up *Rama*; with these King *Asa* built up Geba and *Mitzpa*.

ו וְאָסָא הַמֶּלֶךְ לָקַח אֶת־כָּל־יְהוּדָה וַיִּשְׂאוּ אֶת־אַבְנֵי הָרָמָה וְאֶת־עֵצֶיהָ אֲשֶׁר בָּנָה בַּעְשָׁא וַיִּבֶן בָּהֶם אֶת־גֶּבַע וְאֶת־הַמִּצְפָּה:

⁷ At that time, *Chanani* the seer came to King *Asa* of *Yehuda* and said to him, "Because you relied on the king of Aram and did not rely on *Hashem* your God, therefore the army of the king of Aram has slipped out of your hands.

ז וּבָעֵת הַהִיא בָּא חֲנָנִי הָרֹאֶה אֶל־אָסָא מֶלֶךְ יְהוּדָה וַיֹּאמֶר אֵלָיו בְּהִשָּׁעֶנְךָ עַל־מֶלֶךְ אֲרָם וְלֹא נִשְׁעַנְתָּ עַל־יְהוָה אֱלֹהֶיךָ עַל־כֵּן נִמְלַט חֵיל מֶלֶךְ־אֲרָם מִיָּדֶךָ:

u-va-AYT ha-HEE BA kha-NA-nee ha-ro-EH el a-SA ME-lekh y'-hu-DAH
va-YO-mer ay-LAV b'-hi-SHA-en-KHA al ME-lekh a-RAM v'-LO nish-AN-ta al
a-do-NAI e-lo-HE-kha al KAYN nim-LAT KHAYL ME-lekh a-RAM mi-ya-DE-kha

⁸ The Cushites and Lybians were a mighty army with chariots and horsemen in very great numbers, yet because you relied on *Hashem* He delivered them into your hands.

ח הֲלֹא הַכּוּשִׁים וְהַלּוּבִים הָיוּ לְחַיִל לָרֹב לְרֶכֶב וּלְפָרָשִׁים לְהַרְבֵּה מְאֹד וּבְהִשָּׁעֶנְךָ עַל־יְהוָה נְתָנָם בְּיָדֶךָ:

⁹ For the eyes of *Hashem* range over the entire earth, to give support to those who are wholeheartedly with Him. You have acted foolishly in this matter, and henceforth you will be beset by wars."

ט כִּי יְהוָה עֵינָיו מְשֹׁטְטוֹת בְּכָל־הָאָרֶץ לְהִתְחַזֵּק עִם־לְבָבָם שָׁלֵם אֵלָיו נִסְכַּלְתָּ עַל־זֹאת כִּי מֵעַתָּה יֵשׁ עִמְּךָ מִלְחָמוֹת:

¹⁰ *Asa* was vexed at the seer and put him into the stocks, for he was furious with him because of that. *Asa* inflicted cruelties on some of the people at that time.

י וַיִּכְעַס אָסָא אֶל־הָרֹאֶה וַיִּתְּנֵהוּ בֵּית הַמַּהְפֶּכֶת כִּי־בְזַעַף עִמּוֹ עַל־זֹאת וַיְרַצֵּץ אָסָא מִן־הָעָם בָּעֵת הַהִיא:

Man lifting up his hands to Heaven in prayer

16:7 Because you relied on the king of Aram *Asa* is criticized for the way he enlists assistance to help him defeat *Basha*, king of *Yisrael*. Instead of appealing to *Hashem* for help, he appeals to the king of Aram. In addition, he pays Aram with gold and silver taken from the treasuries of the *Beit Hamikdash*. While acting to protect oneself is praiseworthy, this is only true when it is accompanied by faith in God and prayer to *Hashem*.

11 The acts of *Asa*, early and late, are recorded in the annals of the kings of *Yehuda* and *Yisrael*.

יא וְהִנֵּה דִּבְרֵי אָסָא הָרִאשׁוֹנִים וְהָאַחֲרוֹנִים הִנָּם כְּתוּבִים עַל־סֵפֶר הַמְּלָכִים לִיהוּדָה וְיִשְׂרָאֵל:

12 In the thirty-ninth year of his reign, *Asa* suffered from an acute foot ailment; but ill as he was, he still did not turn to *Hashem* but to physicians.

יב וַיֶּחֱלָא אָסָא בִּשְׁנַת שְׁלוֹשִׁים וָתֵשַׁע לְמַלְכוּתוֹ בְּרַגְלָיו עַד־לְמַעְלָה חָלְיוֹ וְגַם־בְּחָלְיוֹ לֹא־דָרַשׁ אֶת־יְהֹוָה כִּי בָּרֹפְאִים:

13 *Asa* slept with his fathers. He died in the forty-first year of his reign

יג וַיִּשְׁכַּב אָסָא עִם־אֲבֹתָיו וַיָּמָת בִּשְׁנַת אַרְבָּעִים וְאַחַת לְמָלְכוֹ:

14 and was buried in the grave that he had made for himself in the City of *David*. He was laid in his resting-place, which was filled with spices of all kinds, expertly blended; a very great fire was made in his honor.

יד וַיִּקְבְּרֻהוּ בְקִבְרֹתָיו אֲשֶׁר כָּרָה־לוֹ בְּעִיר דָּוִיד וַיַּשְׁכִּיבֻהוּ בַּמִּשְׁכָּב אֲשֶׁר מִלֵּא בְּשָׂמִים וּזְנִים מְרֻקָּחִים בְּמִרְקַחַת מַעֲשֶׂה וַיִּשְׂרְפוּ־לוֹ שְׂרֵפָה גְּדוֹלָה עַד־לִמְאֹד:

17 1 His son *Yehoshafat* succeeded him as king, and took firm hold of *Yisrael*.

יז א וַיִּמְלֹךְ יְהוֹשָׁפָט בְּנוֹ תַּחְתָּיו וַיִּתְחַזֵּק עַל־יִשְׂרָאֵל:

2 He stationed troops in all the fortified towns of *Yehuda*, and stationed garrisons throughout the land of *Yehuda* and the cities of *Efraim* which his father *Asa* had captured.

ב וַיִּתֶּן־חַיִל בְּכָל־עָרֵי יְהוּדָה הַבְּצֻרוֹת וַיִּתֵּן נְצִיבִים בְּאֶרֶץ יְהוּדָה וּבְעָרֵי אֶפְרַיִם אֲשֶׁר לָכַד אָסָא אָבִיו:

3 *Hashem* was with *Yehoshafat* because he followed the earlier ways of his father *David*, and did not worship the Baalim,

ג וַיְהִי יְהֹוָה עִם־יְהוֹשָׁפָט כִּי הָלַךְ בְּדַרְכֵי דָּוִיד אָבִיו הָרִאשֹׁנִים וְלֹא דָרַשׁ לַבְּעָלִים:

4 but worshiped the God of his father and followed His commandments – unlike the behavior of *Yisrael*.

ד כִּי לֵאלֹהֵי אָבִיו דָּרָשׁ וּבְמִצְוֹתָיו הָלָךְ וְלֹא כְּמַעֲשֵׂה יִשְׂרָאֵל:

5 So *Hashem* established the kingdom in his hands, and all *Yehuda* gave presents to *Yehoshafat*. He had wealth and glory in abundance.

ה וַיָּכֶן יְהֹוָה אֶת־הַמַּמְלָכָה בְּיָדוֹ וַיִּתְּנוּ כָל־יְהוּדָה מִנְחָה לִיהוֹשָׁפָט וַיְהִי־לוֹ עֹשֶׁר־וְכָבוֹד לָרֹב:

6 His mind was elevated in the ways of *Hashem*. Moreover, he abolished the shrines and the sacred posts from *Yehuda*.

ו וַיִּגְבַּהּ לִבּוֹ בְּדַרְכֵי יְהֹוָה וְעוֹד הֵסִיר אֶת־הַבָּמוֹת וְאֶת־הָאֲשֵׁרִים מִיהוּדָה:

7 In the third year of his reign he sent his officers Ben-hail, *Ovadya*, *Zecharya*, Nethanel, and *Michaihu* throughout the cities of *Yehuda* to offer instruction.

ז וּבִשְׁנַת שָׁלוֹשׁ לְמָלְכוֹ שָׁלַח לְשָׂרָיו לְבֶן־חַיִל וּלְעֹבַדְיָה וְלִזְכַרְיָה וְלִנְתַנְאֵל וּלְמִיכָיָהוּ לְלַמֵּד בְּעָרֵי יְהוּדָה:

8 With them were the *Leviim*, *Shemaya*, Nethaniah, Zebadiah, *Asael*, Shemiramoth, Jehonathan, *Adoniyahu*, Tobijah and Tob-*Adoniyahu* the *Leviim*; with them were Elishama and *Yehoram* the *Kohanim*.

ח וְעִמָּהֶם הַלְוִיִּם שְׁמַעְיָהוּ וּנְתַנְיָהוּ וּזְבַדְיָהוּ וַעֲשָׂהאֵל וּשְׁמִרִימוֹת [וּשְׁמִרָמוֹת] וִיהוֹנָתָן וַאֲדֹנִיָּהוּ וְטוֹבִיָּהוּ וְטוֹב אֲדוֹנִיָּה הַלְוִיִּם וְעִמָּהֶם אֱלִישָׁמָע וִיהוֹרָם הַכֹּהֲנִים:

9 They offered instruction throughout *Yehuda*, having with them the Book of the Teaching of *Hashem*. They made the rounds of all the cities of *Yehuda* and instructed the people.

ט וַיְלַמְּדוּ בִּיהוּדָה וְעִמָּהֶם סֵפֶר תּוֹרַת יְהֹוָה וַיָּסֹבּוּ בְּכָל־עָרֵי יְהוּדָה וַיְלַמְּדוּ בָּעָם:

10 A terror of *Hashem* seized all the kingdoms of the lands around *Yehuda*, and they did not go to war with *Yehoshafat*.

י וַיְהִי פַּחַד יְהֹוָה עַל כָּל־מַמְלְכוֹת הָאֲרָצוֹת אֲשֶׁר סְבִיבוֹת יְהוּדָה וְלֹא נִלְחֲמוּ עִם־יְהוֹשָׁפָט:

vai-HEE PA-khad a-do-NAI AL kol mam-l'-KHOT ha-a-ra-TZOT a-SHER s'-vee-VOT y'-hu-DAH v'-LO nil-kha-MU im y'-ho-sha-FAT

11 From Philistia a load of silver was brought to *Yehoshafat* as tribute. The Arabs, too, brought him flocks: 7,700 rams and 7,700 he-goats.

יא וּמִן־פְּלִשְׁתִּים מְבִיאִים לִיהוֹשָׁפָט מִנְחָה וְכֶסֶף מַשָּׂא גַּם הָעַרְבִיאִים מְבִיאִים לוֹ צֹאן אֵילִים שִׁבְעַת אֲלָפִים וּשְׁבַע מֵאוֹת וּתְיָשִׁים שִׁבְעַת אֲלָפִים וּשְׁבַע מֵאוֹת:

12 *Yehoshafat* grew greater and greater, and he built up fortresses and garrison towns in *Yehuda*.

יב וַיְהִי יְהוֹשָׁפָט הֹלֵךְ וְגָדֵל עַד־לְמָעְלָה וַיִּבֶן בִּיהוּדָה בִּירָנִיּוֹת וְעָרֵי מִסְכְּנוֹת:

13 He carried out extensive works in the towns of *Yehuda*, and had soldiers, valiant men, in *Yerushalayim*.

יג וּמְלָאכָה רַבָּה הָיָה לוֹ בְּעָרֵי יְהוּדָה וְאַנְשֵׁי מִלְחָמָה גִּבּוֹרֵי חַיִל בִּירוּשָׁלָ͏ִם:

14 They were enrolled according to their clans. *Yehuda*: chiefs of thousands, Adnah the chief, who had 300,000 valiant men;

יד וְאֵלֶּה פְקֻדָּתָם לְבֵית אֲבוֹתֵיהֶם לִיהוּדָה שָׂרֵי אֲלָפִים עַדְנָה הַשָּׂר וְעִמּוֹ גִּבּוֹרֵי חַיִל שְׁלֹשׁ מֵאוֹת אָלֶף:

15 next to him was *Yehochanan* the captain, who had 280,000;

טו וְעַל־יָדוֹ יְהוֹחָנָן הַשָּׂר וְעִמּוֹ מָאתַיִם וּשְׁמוֹנִים אָלֶף:

16 next to him was Amasiah son of Zichri, who made a freewill offering to *Hashem*. He had 200,000 valiant men.

טז וְעַל־יָדוֹ עֲמַסְיָה בֶן־זִכְרִי הַמִּתְנַדֵּב לַיהֹוָה וְעִמּוֹ מָאתַיִם אָלֶף גִּבּוֹר חָיִל:

17 *Binyamin*: Eliada, a valiant man, who had 200,000 men armed with bow and buckler;

יז וּמִן־בִּנְיָמִן גִּבּוֹר חַיִל אֶלְיָדָע וְעִמּוֹ נֹשְׁקֵי־קֶשֶׁת וּמָגֵן מָאתַיִם אָלֶף:

18 next to him was Jehozabad, who had 180,000 armed men.

יח וְעַל־יָדוֹ יְהוֹזָבָד וְעִמּוֹ מֵאָה־וּשְׁמוֹנִים אֶלֶף חֲלוּצֵי צָבָא:

19 These served the king, besides those whom the king assigned to the fortified towns throughout *Yehuda*.

יט אֵלֶּה הַמְשָׁרְתִים אֶת־הַמֶּלֶךְ מִלְּבַד אֲשֶׁר־נָתַן הַמֶּלֶךְ בְּעָרֵי הַמִּבְצָר בְּכָל־יְהוּדָה:

US Ambassodar to Israel studies Torah with students at the Mir Yeshiva in *Yerushalayim*

17:10 A terror of *Hashem* seized all the kingdoms *Yehoshafat* is one of the greatest kings of the kingdom of *Yehuda*. He continues to remove idol worship from the kingdom and ensures that the people engage in *Torah* study. In response, the nations who surround *Yehuda* fear the God of Israel and do not wage war on His people. Furthermore, the Philistines even send gifts to *Yehoshafat*. This demonstrates that the combination of the People of Israel studying the *Torah* in the Land of Israel brings respect from their adversaries, and brings faith and peace to the world.

Chronicles

18 ¹ So *Yehoshafat* had wealth and honor in abundance, and he allied himself by marriage to *Achav*.

² After some years had passed, he came to visit *Achav* at *Shomron*. *Achav* slaughtered sheep and oxen in abundance for him and for the people with him, and persuaded him to march against Ramoth-gilead.

> va-YAY-red l'-KAYTZ sha-NEEM el akh-AV l'-SHO-m'-RON
> va-yiz-bakh LO akh-AV TZON u-va-KAR la-ROV v'-la-AM
> a-SHER i-MO vai-see-TAY-hu la-a-LOT el ra-MOT gil-AD

³ King *Achav* of *Yisrael* said to King *Yehoshafat* of *Yehuda*, "Will you accompany me to Ramoth-gilead?" He answered him, "I will do what you do; my troops shall be your troops and shall accompany you in battle."

⁴ *Yehoshafat* then said to the king of *Yisrael*, "But first inquire for the word of *Hashem*."

⁵ So the king of *Yisrael* gathered the *Neviim*, four hundred men, and asked them, "Shall I march upon Ramoth-gilead for battle, or shall I not?" "March," they said, "and *Hashem* will deliver it into the king's hands."

⁶ Then *Yehoshafat* asked, "Is there not another *Navi* of *Hashem* here through whom we can inquire?"

⁷ And the king of *Yisrael* answered *Yehoshafat*, "There is one more man through whom we can inquire of *Hashem*; but I hate him, because he never prophesies anything good for me but always misfortune. He is *Michaihu* son of Imlah." *Yehoshafat* replied, "Let the king not say such a thing."

⁸ So the king of *Yisrael* summoned an officer and said, "Bring *Michaihu* son of Imlah at once."

יח א וַיְהִי לִיהוֹשָׁפָט עֹשֶׁר וְכָבוֹד לָרֹב וַיִּתְחַתֵּן לְאַחְאָב:

ב וַיֵּרֶד לְקֵץ שָׁנִים אֶל־אַחְאָב לְשֹׁמְרוֹן וַיִּזְבַּח־לוֹ אַחְאָב צֹאן וּבָקָר לָרֹב וְלָעָם אֲשֶׁר עִמּוֹ וַיְסִיתֵהוּ לַעֲלוֹת אֶל־רָמוֹת גִּלְעָד:

ג וַיֹּאמֶר אַחְאָב מֶלֶךְ־יִשְׂרָאֵל אֶל־יְהוֹשָׁפָט מֶלֶךְ יְהוּדָה הֲתֵלֵךְ עִמִּי רָמֹת גִּלְעָד וַיֹּאמֶר לוֹ כָּמוֹנִי כָמוֹךָ וּכְעַמְּךָ עַמִּי וְעִמְּךָ בַּמִּלְחָמָה:

ד וַיֹּאמֶר יְהוֹשָׁפָט אֶל־מֶלֶךְ יִשְׂרָאֵל דְּרָשׁ־נָא כַיּוֹם אֶת־דְּבַר יְהוָה:

ה וַיִּקְבֹּץ מֶלֶךְ־יִשְׂרָאֵל אֶת־הַנְּבִאִים אַרְבַּע מֵאוֹת אִישׁ וַיֹּאמֶר אֲלֵהֶם הֲנֵלֵךְ אֶל־רָמֹת גִּלְעָד לַמִּלְחָמָה אִם־אֶחְדָּל וַיֹּאמְרוּ עֲלֵה וְיִתֵּן הָאֱלֹהִים בְּיַד הַמֶּלֶךְ:

ו וַיֹּאמֶר יְהוֹשָׁפָט הַאֵין פֹּה נָבִיא לַיהוָה עוֹד וְנִדְרְשָׁה מֵאֹתוֹ:

ז וַיֹּאמֶר מֶלֶךְ־יִשְׂרָאֵל אֶל־יְהוֹשָׁפָט עוֹד אִישׁ־אֶחָד לִדְרוֹשׁ אֶת־יְהוָה מֵאֹתוֹ וַאֲנִי שְׂנֵאתִיהוּ כִּי־אֵינֶנּוּ מִתְנַבֵּא עָלַי לְטוֹבָה כִּי כָל־יָמָיו לְרָעָה הוּא מִיכָיְהוּ בֶן־יִמְלָא וַיֹּאמֶר יְהוֹשָׁפָט אַל־יֹאמַר הַמֶּלֶךְ כֵּן:

ח וַיִּקְרָא מֶלֶךְ יִשְׂרָאֵל אֶל־סָרִיס אֶחָד וַיֹּאמֶר מַהֵר מיכהו [מִיכָיְהוּ] בֶן־יִמְלָא:

Chronicles

18:2 *After some years had passed, he came to visit Achav at Shomron* *Yehoshafat* visits *Achav* in Samaria, known in Hebrew as *Shomron* (שומרון). The city of Samaria was purchased by *Achav's* father *Omri* to be the capital of the kingdom of *Yisrael* (I Kings 16:24), and is an important part of both the biblical and the modern State of Israel. Today, the area known as Samaria comprises over 11% of the modern State of Israel and is home to many vibrant communities including *Ariel, Karnei Shomron, Elon Moreh* and *Itamar*. Since it is located in the middle of Israel, Samaria plays a vital role in the spirituality, economics and security of the country. Though *Omri* sinned greatly in his religious conduct, his acquisition of the *Shomron* was of great national importance both in his time and today.

View of the *Shomron*

9 The king of *Yisrael* and King *Yehoshafat* of *Yehuda*, wearing their robes, were seated on their thrones situated in the threshing floor at the entrance of the gate of *Shomron*; and all the *Neviim* were prophesying before them.

ט וּמֶלֶךְ יִשְׂרָאֵל וִיהוֹשָׁפָט מֶלֶךְ־יְהוּדָה יוֹשְׁבִים אִישׁ עַל־כִּסְאוֹ מְלֻבָּשִׁים בְּגָדִים וְיֹשְׁבִים בְּגֹרֶן פֶּתַח שַׁעַר שֹׁמְרוֹן וְכָל־הַנְּבִיאִים מִתְנַבְּאִים לִפְנֵיהֶם:

10 *Tzidkiyahu* son of Chenaanah had provided himself with iron horns; and he said, "Thus said *Hashem*: With these you shall gore the Arameans till you make an end of them."

י וַיַּעַשׂ לוֹ צִדְקִיָּהוּ בֶן־כְּנַעֲנָה קַרְנֵי בַרְזֶל וַיֹּאמֶר כֹּה־אָמַר יְהֹוָה בְּאֵלֶּה תְּנַגַּח אֶת־אֲרָם עַד־כַּלּוֹתָם:

11 All the other *Neviim* were prophesying similarly, "March against Ramoth-gilead and be victorious! *Hashem* will deliver it into Your Majesty's hands."

יא וְכָל־הַנְּבִאִים נִבְּאִים כֵּן לֵאמֹר עֲלֵה רָמֹת גִּלְעָד וְהַצְלַח וְנָתַן יְהֹוָה בְּיַד הַמֶּלֶךְ:

12 The messenger who had gone to summon *Michaihu* said to him, "Look, the words of the *Neviim* are unanimously favorable to the king. Let your word be like that of the rest of them; speak a favorable word."

יב וְהַמַּלְאָךְ אֲשֶׁר־הָלַךְ לִקְרֹא לְמִיכָיְהוּ דִּבֶּר אֵלָיו לֵאמֹר הִנֵּה דִּבְרֵי הַנְּבִאִים פֶּה־אֶחָד טוֹב אֶל־הַמֶּלֶךְ וִיהִי־נָא דְבָרְךָ כְּאַחַד מֵהֶם וְדִבַּרְתָּ טּוֹב:

13 "By the life of *Hashem*," *Michaihu* answered, "I will speak only what my God tells me."

יג וַיֹּאמֶר מִיכָיְהוּ חַי־יְהֹוָה כִּי אֶת־אֲשֶׁר־יֹאמַר אֱלֹהַי אֹתוֹ אֲדַבֵּר:

14 When he came before the king, the king said to him, "*Micha*, shall we march against Ramoth-gilead for battle or shall we not?" He answered him, "March and be victorious! They will be delivered into your hands."

יד וַיָּבֹא אֶל־הַמֶּלֶךְ וַיֹּאמֶר הַמֶּלֶךְ אֵלָיו מִיכָה הֲנֵלֵךְ אֶל־רָמֹת גִּלְעָד לַמִּלְחָמָה אִם־אֶחְדָּל וַיֹּאמֶר עֲלוּ וְהַצְלִיחוּ וְיִנָּתְנוּ בְּיֶדְכֶם:

15 The king said to him, "How many times must I adjure you to tell me nothing but the truth in the name of *Hashem*?"

טו וַיֹּאמֶר אֵלָיו הַמֶּלֶךְ עַד־כַּמֶּה פְעָמִים אֲנִי מַשְׁבִּיעֶךָ אֲשֶׁר לֹא־תְדַבֵּר אֵלַי רַק־אֱמֶת בְּשֵׁם יְהֹוָה:

16 Then he said, "I saw all *Yisrael* scattered over the hills like sheep without a shepherd; and *Hashem* said, 'These have no master; let everyone return to his home in safety.'"

טז וַיֹּאמֶר רָאִיתִי אֶת־כָּל־יִשְׂרָאֵל נְפוֹצִים עַל־הֶהָרִים כַּצֹּאן אֲשֶׁר אֵין־לָהֶן רֹעֶה וַיֹּאמֶר יְהֹוָה לֹא־אֲדֹנִים לָאֵלֶּה יָשׁוּבוּ אִישׁ־לְבֵיתוֹ בְּשָׁלוֹם:

17 The king of *Yisrael* said to *Yehoshafat*, "Did I not tell you that he would not prophesy good fortune for me, but only misfortune?"

יז וַיֹּאמֶר מֶלֶךְ־יִשְׂרָאֵל אֶל־יְהוֹשָׁפָט הֲלֹא אָמַרְתִּי אֵלֶיךָ לֹא־יִתְנַבֵּא עָלַי טוֹב כִּי אִם־לְרָע:

18 Then [*Michaihu*] said, "Indeed, hear now the word of *Hashem*! I saw *Hashem* seated upon His throne, with all the host of heaven standing in attendance to the right and to the left of Him.

יח וַיֹּאמֶר לָכֵן שִׁמְעוּ דְבַר־יְהֹוָה רָאִיתִי אֶת־יְהֹוָה יוֹשֵׁב עַל־כִּסְאוֹ וְכָל־צְבָא הַשָּׁמַיִם עֹמְדִים עַל־יְמִינוֹ וּשְׂמֹאלוֹ:

19 *Hashem* asked, 'Who will entice King *Achav* of *Yisrael* so that he will march and fall at Ramoth-gilead?' Then one said this and another said that,

יט וַיֹּאמֶר יְהֹוָה מִי יְפַתֶּה אֶת־אַחְאָב מֶלֶךְ־יִשְׂרָאֵל וְיַעַל וְיִפֹּל בְּרָמוֹת גִּלְעָד וַיֹּאמֶר זֶה אֹמֵר כָּכָה וְזֶה אֹמֵר כָּכָה:

20 until a certain spirit came forward and stood before *Hashem* and said, 'I will entice him.' 'How?' said *Hashem* to him.

כ וַיֵּצֵא הָרוּחַ וַיַּעֲמֹד לִפְנֵי יְהֹוָה וַיֹּאמֶר אֲנִי אֲפַתֶּנּוּ וַיֹּאמֶר יְהֹוָה אֵלָיו בַּמָּה:

21 And he replied, 'I will go forth and become a lying spirit in the mouth of all his *Neviim*.' Then He said, 'You will entice with success. Go forth and do it.'

כא וַיֹּאמֶר אֵצֵא וְהָיִיתִי לְרוּחַ שֶׁקֶר בְּפִי כָּל־נְבִיאָיו וַיֹּאמֶר תְּפַתֶּה וְגַם־תּוּכָל צֵא וַעֲשֵׂה־כֵן:

22 Thus *Hashem* has put a lying spirit in the mouth of all these *Neviim* of yours; for *Hashem* has decreed misfortune for you."

כב וְעַתָּה הִנֵּה נָתַן יְהֹוָה רוּחַ שֶׁקֶר בְּפִי נְבִיאֶיךָ אֵלֶּה וַיהֹוָה דִּבֶּר עָלֶיךָ רָעָה:

23 Thereupon *Tzidkiyahu* son of Chenaanah came up and struck *Michaihu* on the cheek, and exclaimed, "However did the spirit of *Hashem* pass from me to speak with you!"

כג וַיִּגַּשׁ צִדְקִיָּהוּ בֶן־כְּנַעֲנָה וַיַּךְ אֶת־מִיכָיְהוּ עַל־הַלֶּחִי וַיֹּאמֶר אֵי זֶה הַדֶּרֶךְ עָבַר רוּחַ־יְהֹוָה מֵאִתִּי לְדַבֵּר אֹתָךְ:

24 *Michaihu* replied, "You will see on the day when you try to hide in the innermost room."

כד וַיֹּאמֶר מִיכָיְהוּ הִנְּךָ רֹאֶה בַּיּוֹם הַהוּא אֲשֶׁר תָּבוֹא חֶדֶר בְּחֶדֶר לְהֵחָבֵא:

25 Then the king of *Yisrael* said, "Take *Michaihu* and turn him over to *Amon*, the governor of the city, and to Prince *Yoash*,

כה וַיֹּאמֶר מֶלֶךְ יִשְׂרָאֵל קְחוּ אֶת־מִיכָיְהוּ וַהֲשִׁיבֻהוּ אֶל־אָמוֹן שַׂר־הָעִיר וְאֶל־יוֹאָשׁ בֶּן־הַמֶּלֶךְ:

26 and say, 'The king's orders are: Put this fellow in prison, and let his fare be scant bread and scant water until I come home safe.'"

כו וַאֲמַרְתֶּם כֹּה אָמַר הַמֶּלֶךְ שִׂימוּ זֶה בֵּית הַכֶּלֶא וְהַאֲכִלֻהוּ לֶחֶם לַחַץ וּמַיִם לַחַץ עַד שׁוּבִי בְשָׁלוֹם:

27 To which *Michaihu* retorted, "If you ever come home safe, *Hashem* has not spoken through me." He said further, "Listen, all you peoples!"

כז וַיֹּאמֶר מִיכָיְהוּ אִם־שׁוֹב תָּשׁוּב בְּשָׁלוֹם לֹא־דִבֶּר יְהֹוָה בִּי וַיֹּאמֶר שִׁמְעוּ עַמִּים כֻּלָּם:

28 The king of *Yisrael* and King *Yehoshafat* of Yehuda marched against Ramoth-gilead.

כח וַיַּעַל מֶלֶךְ־יִשְׂרָאֵל וִיהוֹשָׁפָט מֶלֶךְ־יְהוּדָה אֶל־רָמֹת גִּלְעָד:

29 The king of *Yisrael* said to *Yehoshafat*, "I will disguise myself and go into the battle, but you, wear your robes." So the king of *Yisrael* disguised himself, and they went into the battle.

כט וַיֹּאמֶר מֶלֶךְ יִשְׂרָאֵל אֶל־יְהוֹשָׁפָט הִתְחַפֵּשׂ וָבוֹא בַמִּלְחָמָה וְאַתָּה לְבַשׁ בְּגָדֶיךָ וַיִּתְחַפֵּשׂ מֶלֶךְ יִשְׂרָאֵל וַיָּבֹאוּ בַּמִּלְחָמָה:

30 The king of Aram had given these instructions to his chariot officers: "Do not attack anyone, small or great, except the king of *Yisrael*."

ל וּמֶלֶךְ אֲרָם צִוָּה אֶת־שָׂרֵי הָרֶכֶב אֲשֶׁר־לוֹ לֵאמֹר לֹא תִּלָּחֲמוּ אֶת־הַקָּטֹן אֶת־הַגָּדוֹל כִּי אִם־אֶת־מֶלֶךְ יִשְׂרָאֵל לְבַדּוֹ:

31 When the chariot officers saw *Yehoshafat*, whom they took for the king of *Yisrael*, they wheeled around to attack him, and *Yehoshafat* cried out and *Hashem* helped him, and *Hashem* diverted them from him.

לא וַיְהִי כִּרְאוֹת שָׂרֵי הָרֶכֶב אֶת־יְהוֹשָׁפָט וְהֵמָּה אָמְרוּ מֶלֶךְ יִשְׂרָאֵל הוּא וַיָּסֹבּוּ עָלָיו לְהִלָּחֵם וַיִּזְעַק יְהוֹשָׁפָט וַיהֹוָה עֲזָרוֹ וַיְסִיתֵם אֱלֹהִים מִמֶּנּוּ:

32 And when the chariot officers realized that he was not the king of *Yisrael*, they gave up the pursuit.

לב וַיְהִי כִּרְאוֹת שָׂרֵי הָרֶכֶב כִּי לֹא־הָיָה מֶלֶךְ יִשְׂרָאֵל וַיָּשֻׁבוּ מֵאַחֲרָיו:

33 Then a man drew his bow at random and hit the king of *Yisrael* between the plates of the armor and he said to his charioteer, "Turn around and get me behind the lines; I am wounded."

לג וְאִישׁ מָשַׁךְ בַּקֶּשֶׁת לְתֻמּוֹ וַיַּךְ אֶת־מֶלֶךְ יִשְׂרָאֵל בֵּין הַדְּבָקִים וּבֵין הַשִּׁרְיָן וַיֹּאמֶר לָרַכָּב הֲפֹךְ יָדְךָ [יָדֶיךָ] וְהוֹצֵאתַנִי מִן־הַמַּחֲנֶה כִּי הָחֳלֵיתִי:

Chronicles

108

³⁴ The battle raged all day long, and the king remained propped up in the chariot facing Aram until dusk; he died as the sun was setting.

לד וַתַּעַל הַמִּלְחָמָה בַּיּוֹם הַהוּא וּמֶלֶךְ יִשְׂרָאֵל הָיָה מַעֲמִיד בַּמֶּרְכָּבָה נֹכַח אֲרָם עַד־הָעֶרֶב וַיָּמָת לְעֵת בּוֹא הַשָּׁמֶשׁ:

19 ¹ King *Yehoshafat* of *Yehuda* returned safely to his palace, to *Yerushalayim*.

ט *יט* ¹ וַיָּשָׁב יְהוֹשָׁפָט מֶלֶךְ־יְהוּדָה אֶל־בֵּיתוֹ בְּשָׁלוֹם לִירוּשָׁלָ͏ִם:

² *Yehu* son of *Chanani* the seer went out to meet King *Yehoshafat* and said to him, "Should one give aid to the wicked and befriend those who hate *Hashem*? For this, wrath is upon you from *Hashem*.

ב וַיֵּצֵא אֶל־פָּנָיו יֵהוּא בֶן־חֲנָנִי הַחֹזֶה וַיֹּאמֶר אֶל־הַמֶּלֶךְ יְהוֹשָׁפָט הֲלָרָשָׁע לַעְזֹר וּלְשֹׂנְאֵי יְהוָה תֶּאֱהָב וּבָזֹאת עָלֶיךָ קֶּצֶף מִלִּפְנֵי יְהוָה:

³ However, there is some good in you, for you have purged the land of the sacred posts and have dedicated yourself to worship *Hashem*."

ג אֲבָל דְּבָרִים טוֹבִים נִמְצְאוּ עִמָּךְ כִּי־בִעַרְתָּ הָאֲשֵׁרוֹת מִן־הָאָרֶץ וַהֲכִינוֹתָ לְבָבְךָ לִדְרֹשׁ הָאֱלֹהִים:

⁴ *Yehoshafat* remained in *Yerushalayim* a while and then went out among the people from *Be'er Sheva* to the hill country of *Efraim*; he brought them back to God of their fathers.

ד וַיֵּשֶׁב יְהוֹשָׁפָט בִּירוּשָׁלָ͏ִם וַיָּשָׁב וַיֵּצֵא בָעָם מִבְּאֵר שֶׁבַע עַד־הַר אֶפְרַיִם וַיְשִׁיבֵם אֶל־יְהוָה אֱלֹהֵי אֲבוֹתֵיהֶם:

⁵ He appointed judges in the land in all the fortified towns of *Yehuda*, in each and every town.

ה וַיַּעֲמֵד שֹׁפְטִים בָּאָרֶץ בְּכָל־עָרֵי יְהוּדָה הַבְּצֻרוֹת לְעִיר וָעִיר:

va-ya-a-MAYD sho-f'-TEEM ba-A-ratz b'-khol a-RAY y'-hu-DAH ha-b'-tzu-ROT l'-EER va-EER

⁶ He charged the judges: "Consider what you are doing, for you judge not on behalf of man, but on behalf of *Hashem*, and He is with you when you pass judgment.

ו וַיֹּאמֶר אֶל־הַשֹּׁפְטִים רְאוּ מָה־אַתֶּם עֹשִׂים כִּי לֹא לְאָדָם תִּשְׁפְּטוּ כִּי לַיהוָה וְעִמָּכֶם בִּדְבַר מִשְׁפָּט:

⁷ Now let the dread of *Hashem* be upon you; act with care, for there is no injustice or favoritism or bribe-taking with *Hashem* our God."

ז וְעַתָּה יְהִי פַחַד־יְהוָה עֲלֵיכֶם שִׁמְרוּ וַעֲשׂוּ כִּי־אֵין עִם־יְהוָה אֱלֹהֵינוּ עַוְלָה וּמַשֹּׂא פָנִים וּמִקַּח־שֹׁחַד:

⁸ *Yehoshafat* also appointed in *Yerushalayim* some *Leviim* and *Kohanim* and heads of the clans of Israelites for rendering judgment in matters of *Hashem*, and for disputes. Then they returned to *Yerushalayim*.

ח וְגַם בִּירוּשָׁלַ͏ִם הֶעֱמִיד יְהוֹשָׁפָט מִן־הַלְוִיִּם וְהַכֹּהֲנִים וּמֵרָאשֵׁי הָאָבוֹת לְיִשְׂרָאֵל לְמִשְׁפַּט יְהוָה וְלָרִיב וַיָּשֻׁבוּ יְרוּשָׁלָ͏ִם:

A modern courthouse in *Beersheva*

19:5 He appointed judges in the land *Yehoshafat* understands the importance of justice in the land. As he has dedicated himself to worship *Hashem* (verse 3) he not only prays and offers sacrifices, but also places a strong emphasis on seeking justice. He appoints judges throughout the land to judge "on behalf of *Hashem*" (verse 6), and warns them about being honest and against taking bribes. He understands that part of serving God in the Land of Israel is pursuing justice and righteousness. In fact, the prophets emphasize that it was when the Jewish people stopped acting with justice that their troubles in the land, culminating with the destruction and exile, really began. Therefore, as part of the ultimate redemption, *Yeshayahu* teaches that *Hashem* "will restore your magistrates as of old, and your counselors as of yore. After that you shall be called City of Righteousness, Faithful City." He continues, "*Tzion* shall be saved in the judgment, her repentant ones, in the retribution" (Isaiah 1:26–27).

9 He charged them, "This is how you shall act: in fear of *Hashem*, with fidelity, and with whole heart.

10 When a dispute comes before you from your brothers living in their towns, whether about homicide, or about ritual, or laws or rules, you must instruct them so that they do not incur guilt before *Hashem* and wrath be upon you and your brothers. Act so and you will not incur guilt.

11 See, Amariah the chief *Kohen* is over you in all cases concerning *Hashem*, and Zebadiah son of Ishmael is the commander of the house of *Yehuda* in all cases concerning the king; the Levitical officials are at your disposal; act with resolve and *Hashem* be with the good."

20 1 After that, Moabites, Ammonites, together with some Ammonites, came against *Yehoshafat* to wage war.

2 The report was brought to *Yehoshafat*: "A great multitude is coming against you from beyond the sea, from Aram, and is now in Hazazon-tamar" – that is, Ein-gedi.

3 *Yehoshafat* was afraid; he decided to resort to *Hashem* and proclaimed a fast for all *Yehuda*.

4 *Yehuda* assembled to beseech *Hashem*. They also came from all the towns of *Yehuda* to seek *Hashem*.

5 *Yehoshafat* stood in the congregation of *Yehuda* and *Yerushalayim* in the House of *Hashem* at the front of the new court.

6 He said, "God of our fathers, truly You are the God in heaven and You rule over the kingdoms of the nations; power and strength are Yours; none can oppose You.

7 O our God, you dispossessed the inhabitants of this land before Your people *Yisrael*, and You gave it to the descendants of Your friend *Avraham* forever.

8 They settled in it and in it built for You a House for Your name. They said,

9 'Should misfortune befall us – the punishing sword, pestilence, or famine, we shall stand before this House and before You – for Your name is in this House – and we shall cry out to You in our distress, and You will listen and deliver us.'

ט וַיְצַו עֲלֵיהֶם לֵאמֹר כֹּה תַעֲשׂוּן בְּיִרְאַת יְהֹוָה בֶּאֱמוּנָה וּבְלֵבָב שָׁלֵם:

י וְכָל־רִיב אֲשֶׁר־יָבוֹא עֲלֵיכֶם מֵאֲחֵיכֶם הַיֹּשְׁבִים בְּעָרֵיהֶם בֵּין־דָּם לְדָם בֵּין־תּוֹרָה לְמִצְוָה לְחֻקִּים וּלְמִשְׁפָּטִים וְהִזְהַרְתֶּם אֹתָם וְלֹא יֶאְשְׁמוּ לַיהֹוָה וְהָיָה־קֶצֶף עֲלֵיכֶם וְעַל־אֲחֵיכֶם כֹּה תַעֲשׂוּן וְלֹא תֶאְשָׁמוּ:

יא וְהִנֵּה אֲמַרְיָהוּ כֹהֵן הָרֹאשׁ עֲלֵיכֶם לְכֹל דְּבַר־יְהֹוָה וּזְבַדְיָהוּ בֶן־יִשְׁמָעֵאל הַנָּגִיד לְבֵית־יְהוּדָה לְכֹל דְּבַר־הַמֶּלֶךְ וְשֹׁטְרִים הַלְוִיִּם לִפְנֵיכֶם חִזְקוּ וַעֲשׂוּ וִיהִי יְהֹוָה עִם־הַטּוֹב:

כ א וַיְהִי אַחֲרֵיכֵן בָּאוּ בְנֵי־מוֹאָב וּבְנֵי עַמּוֹן וְעִמָּהֶם מֵהָעַמּוֹנִים עַל־יְהוֹשָׁפָט לַמִּלְחָמָה:

ב וַיָּבֹאוּ וַיַּגִּידוּ לִיהוֹשָׁפָט לֵאמֹר בָּא עָלֶיךָ הָמוֹן רָב מֵעֵבֶר לַיָּם מֵאֲרָם וְהִנָּם בְּחַצְצוֹן תָּמָר הִיא עֵין גֶּדִי:

ג וַיִּרָא וַיִּתֵּן יְהוֹשָׁפָט אֶת־פָּנָיו לִדְרוֹשׁ לַיהֹוָה וַיִּקְרָא־צוֹם עַל־כָּל־יְהוּדָה:

ד וַיִּקָּבְצוּ יְהוּדָה לְבַקֵּשׁ מֵיְהֹוָה גַּם מִכָּל־עָרֵי יְהוּדָה בָּאוּ לְבַקֵּשׁ אֶת־יְהֹוָה:

ה וַיַּעֲמֹד יְהוֹשָׁפָט בִּקְהַל יְהוּדָה וִירוּשָׁלַ͏ִם בְּבֵית יְהֹוָה לִפְנֵי הֶחָצֵר הַחֲדָשָׁה:

ו וַיֹּאמַר יְהֹוָה אֱלֹהֵי אֲבֹתֵינוּ הֲלֹא אַתָּה־הוּא אֱלֹהִים בַּשָּׁמַיִם וְאַתָּה מוֹשֵׁל בְּכֹל מַמְלְכוֹת הַגּוֹיִם וּבְיָדְךָ כֹּחַ וּגְבוּרָה וְאֵין עִמְּךָ לְהִתְיַצֵּב:

ז הֲלֹא אַתָּה אֱלֹהֵינוּ הוֹרַשְׁתָּ אֶת־יֹשְׁבֵי הָאָרֶץ הַזֹּאת מִלִּפְנֵי עַמְּךָ יִשְׂרָאֵל וַתִּתְּנָהּ לְזֶרַע אַבְרָהָם אֹהַבְךָ לְעוֹלָם:

ח וַיֵּשְׁבוּ־בָהּ וַיִּבְנוּ לְךָ בָּהּ מִקְדָּשׁ לְשִׁמְךָ לֵאמֹר:

ט אִם־תָּבוֹא עָלֵינוּ רָעָה חֶרֶב שְׁפוֹט וְדֶבֶר וְרָעָב נַעַמְדָה לִפְנֵי הַבַּיִת הַזֶּה וּלְפָנֶיךָ כִּי שִׁמְךָ בַּבַּיִת הַזֶּה וְנִזְעַק אֵלֶיךָ מִצָּרָתֵנוּ וְתִשְׁמַע וְתוֹשִׁיעַ:

10 Now the people of Ammon, Moab, and the hill country of Seir, into whose [land] You did not let *Yisrael* come when they came from Egypt, but they turned aside from them and did not wipe them out,

יֹ וְעַתָּה הִנֵּה בְנֵי־עַמּוֹן וּמוֹאָב וְהַר־שֵׂעִיר אֲשֶׁר לֹא־נָתַתָּה לְיִשְׂרָאֵל לָבוֹא בָהֶם בְּבֹאָם מֵאֶרֶץ מִצְרָיִם כִּי סָרוּ מֵעֲלֵיהֶם וְלֹא הִשְׁמִידוּם:

11 these now repay us by coming to expel us from Your possession which You gave us as ours.

יא וְהִנֵּה־הֵם גֹּמְלִים עָלֵינוּ לָבוֹא לְגָרְשֵׁנוּ מִיְּרֻשָּׁתְךָ אֲשֶׁר הוֹרַשְׁתָּנוּ:

12 O our God, surely You will punish them, for we are powerless before this great multitude that has come against us, and do not know what to do, but our eyes are on You."

יב אֱלֹהֵינוּ הֲלֹא תִשְׁפָּט־בָּם כִּי אֵין בָּנוּ כֹּחַ לִפְנֵי הֶהָמוֹן הָרָב הַזֶּה הַבָּא עָלֵינוּ וַאֲנַחְנוּ לֹא נֵדַע מַה־נַּעֲשֶׂה כִּי עָלֶיךָ עֵינֵינוּ:

13 All *Yehuda* stood before *Hashem* with their little ones, their womenfolk, and their children.

יג וְכָל־יְהוּדָה עֹמְדִים לִפְנֵי יְהוָה גַּם־טַפָּם נְשֵׁיהֶם וּבְנֵיהֶם:

14 Then in the midst of the congregation the spirit of *Hashem* came upon *Yachaziel* son of *Zecharya* son of Benaiah son of Jeiel son of Mattaniah the *Levi*, of the sons of *Asaf*,

יד וְיַחֲזִיאֵל בֶּן־זְכַרְיָהוּ בֶּן־בְּנָיָה בֶּן־יְעִיאֵל בֶּן־מַתַּנְיָה הַלֵּוִי מִן־בְּנֵי אָסָף הָיְתָה עָלָיו רוּחַ יְהוָה בְּתוֹךְ הַקָּהָל:

15 and he said, "Give heed, all *Yehuda* and the inhabitants of *Yerushalayim* and King *Yehoshafat*; thus said *Hashem* to you, 'Do not fear or be dismayed by this great multitude, for the battle is *Hashem*'s, not yours.

טו וַיֹּאמֶר הַקְשִׁיבוּ כָל־יְהוּדָה וְיֹשְׁבֵי יְרוּשָׁלַם וְהַמֶּלֶךְ יְהוֹשָׁפָט כֹּה־אָמַר יְהוָה לָכֶם אַתֶּם אַל־תִּירְאוּ וְאַל־תֵּחַתּוּ מִפְּנֵי הֶהָמוֹן הָרָב הַזֶּה כִּי לֹא לָכֶם הַמִּלְחָמָה כִּי לֵאלֹהִים:

16 March down against them tomorrow as they come up by the Ascent of Ziz; you will find them at the end of the wadi in the direction of the wilderness of Jeruel.

טז מָחָר רְדוּ עֲלֵיהֶם הִנָּם עֹלִים בְּמַעֲלֵה הַצִּיץ וּמְצָאתֶם אֹתָם בְּסוֹף הַנַּחַל פְּנֵי מִדְבַּר יְרוּאֵל:

17 It is not for you to fight this battle; stand by, wait, and witness your deliverance by *Hashem*, O *Yehuda* and *Yerushalayim*; do not fear or be dismayed; go forth to meet them tomorrow and *Hashem* will be with you.'"

יז לֹא לָכֶם לְהִלָּחֵם בָּזֹאת הִתְיַצְּבוּ עִמְדוּ וּרְאוּ אֶת־יְשׁוּעַת יְהוָה עִמָּכֶם יְהוּדָה וִירוּשָׁלַם אַל־תִּירְאוּ וְאַל־תֵּחַתּוּ מָחָר צְאוּ לִפְנֵיהֶם וַיהוָה עִמָּכֶם:

18 *Yehoshafat* bowed low with his face to the ground, and all *Yehuda* and the inhabitants of *Yerushalayim* threw themselves down before *Hashem* to worship *Hashem*.

יח וַיִּקֹּד יְהוֹשָׁפָט אַפַּיִם אָרְצָה וְכָל־יְהוּדָה וְיֹשְׁבֵי יְרוּשָׁלַם נָפְלוּ לִפְנֵי יְהוָה לְהִשְׁתַּחֲוֹת לַיהוָה:

19 *Leviim* of the sons of *Kehat* and of the sons of *Korach* got up to extol God of *Yisrael* at the top of their voices.

יט וַיָּקֻמוּ הַלְוִיִּם מִן־בְּנֵי הַקְּהָתִים וּמִן־בְּנֵי הַקָּרְחִים לְהַלֵּל לַיהוָה אֱלֹהֵי יִשְׂרָאֵל בְּקוֹל גָּדוֹל לְמָעְלָה:

20 Early the next morning they arose and went forth to the wilderness of *Tekoa*. As they went forth, *Yehoshafat* stood and said, "Listen to me, O *Yehuda* and inhabitants of *Yerushalayim*: Trust firmly in *Hashem* your God and you will stand firm; trust firmly in His *Neviim* and you will succeed."

כ וַיַּשְׁכִּימוּ בַבֹּקֶר וַיֵּצְאוּ לְמִדְבַּר תְּקוֹעַ וּבְצֵאתָם עָמַד יְהוֹשָׁפָט וַיֹּאמֶר שְׁמָעוּנִי יְהוּדָה וְיֹשְׁבֵי יְרוּשָׁלַם הַאֲמִינוּ בַּיהוָה אֱלֹהֵיכֶם וְתֵאָמֵנוּ הַאֲמִינוּ בִנְבִיאָיו וְהַצְלִיחוּ:

21 After taking counsel with the people, he stationed singers to *Hashem* extolling the One majestic in holiness as they went forth ahead of the vanguard, saying, "Praise *Hashem*, for His steadfast love is eternal."

כא וַיִּוָּעַץ אֶל־הָעָם וַיַּעֲמֵד מְשֹׁרְרִים לַיהֹוָה וּמְהַלְלִים לְהַדְרַת־קֹדֶשׁ בְּצֵאת לִפְנֵי הֶחָלוּץ וְאֹמְרִים הוֹדוּ לַיהֹוָה כִּי לְעוֹלָם חַסְדּוֹ:

22 As they began their joyous shouts and hymns, *Hashem* set ambushes for the men of Ammon, Moab, and the hill country of Seir, who were marching against *Yehuda*, and they were routed.

כב וּבְעֵת הֵחֵלּוּ בְרִנָּה וּתְהִלָּה נָתַן יְהֹוָה מְאָרְבִים עַל־בְּנֵי עַמּוֹן מוֹאָב וְהַר־שֵׂעִיר הַבָּאִים לִיהוּדָה וַיִּנָּגֵפוּ:

23 The Ammonites and Moabites turned against the men of the hill country of Seir to exterminate and annihilate them. When they had made an end of the men of Seir, each helped to destroy his fellow.

כג וַיַּעַמְדוּ בְּנֵי עַמּוֹן וּמוֹאָב עַל־יֹשְׁבֵי הַר־שֵׂעִיר לְהַחֲרִים וּלְהַשְׁמִיד וּכְכַלּוֹתָם בְּיוֹשְׁבֵי שֵׂעִיר עָזְרוּ אִישׁ־בְּרֵעֵהוּ לְמַשְׁחִית:

24 When *Yehuda* reached the lookout in the wilderness and looked for the multitude, they saw them lying on the ground as corpses; not one had survived.

כד וִיהוּדָה בָּא עַל־הַמִּצְפֶּה לַמִּדְבָּר וַיִּפְנוּ אֶל־הֶהָמוֹן וְהִנָּם פְּגָרִים נֹפְלִים אַרְצָה וְאֵין פְּלֵיטָה:

25 *Yehoshafat* and his army came to take the booty, and found an abundance of goods, corpses, and precious objects, which they pillaged, more than they could carry off. For three days they were taking booty, there was so much of it.

כה וַיָּבֹא יְהוֹשָׁפָט וְעַמּוֹ לָבֹז אֶת־שְׁלָלָם וַיִּמְצְאוּ בָהֶם לָרֹב וּרְכוּשׁ וּפְגָרִים וּכְלֵי חֲמֻדוֹת וַיְנַצְּלוּ לָהֶם לְאֵין מַשָּׂא וַיִּהְיוּ יָמִים שְׁלוֹשָׁה בֹּזְזִים אֶת־הַשָּׁלָל כִּי רַב־הוּא:

26 On the fourth day they assembled in the Valley of Blessing – for there they blessed *Hashem*; that is why that place is called the Valley of Blessing to this day.

כו וּבַיּוֹם הָרְבִעִי נִקְהֲלוּ לְעֵמֶק בְּרָכָה כִּי־שָׁם בֵּרְכוּ אֶת־יְהֹוָה עַל־כֵּן קָרְאוּ אֶת־שֵׁם הַמָּקוֹם הַהוּא עֵמֶק בְּרָכָה עַד־הַיּוֹם:

u-va-YOM ha-r'-vi-EE nik-ha-LU l'-AY-mek b'-ra-KHAH KEE
SHAM bay-r'-KHU et a-do-NAI al KAYN ka-r'-U et SHAYM
ha-ma-KOM ha-HU AY-mek b'-ra-KHAH ad ha-YOM

27 All the men of *Yehuda* and *Yerushalayim* with *Yehoshafat* at their head returned joyfully to *Yerushalayim*, for *Hashem* had given them cause for rejoicing over their enemies.

כז וַיָּשֻׁבוּ כָּל־אִישׁ יְהוּדָה וִירוּשָׁלַ͏ִם וִיהוֹשָׁפָט בְּרֹאשָׁם לָשׁוּב אֶל־יְרוּשָׁלַ͏ִם בְּשִׂמְחָה כִּי־שִׂמְּחָם יְהֹוָה מֵאוֹיְבֵיהֶם:

28 They came to *Yerushalayim* to the House of *Hashem*, to the accompaniment of harps, lyres, and trumpets.

כח וַיָּבֹאוּ יְרוּשָׁלַ͏ִם בִּנְבָלִים וּבְכִנֹּרוֹת וּבַחֲצֹצְרוֹת אֶל־בֵּית יְהֹוָה:

Chronicles

20:26 That place is called the Valley of Blessing to this day After God miraculously defeats his enemies, *Yehoshafat* gathers the people together to bless *Hashem*. The site of this blessing is named 'the Valley of Blessing,' or *Emek HaBeracha* (עמק ברכה) since *beracha* is the Hebrew word for blessing. Today, this valley is located in the Etzion region, and is surrounded by the Jewish towns of *Carmei Tzur, Bat Ayin, Kfar Etzion* and *Alon Shvut*. The land is truly blessed and is known for its fertile soil. The Gush Etzion Winery, located just outside the town of *Alon Shvut*, has a vineyard in the valley. The grapes grown there are used for their high-end blended red series of wines known as *Emek Beracha*.

The Gush Etzion Winery

29 The terror of *Hashem* seized all the kingdoms of the lands when they heard that *Hashem* had fought the enemies of *Yisrael*.

כט וַיְהִי פַּחַד אֱלֹהִים עַל כָּל־מַמְלְכוֹת הָאֲרָצוֹת בְּשָׁמְעָם כִּי נִלְחַם יְהֹוָה עִם אוֹיְבֵי יִשְׂרָאֵל:

30 The kingdom of *Yehoshafat* was untroubled, and his God granted him respite on all sides.

ל וַתִּשְׁקֹט מַלְכוּת יְהוֹשָׁפָט וַיָּנַח לוֹ אֱלֹהָיו מִסָּבִיב:

31 *Yehoshafat* reigned over *Yehuda*. He was thirty-five years old when he became king, and he reigned in *Yerushalayim* for twenty-five years. His mother's name was Azubah daughter of Shilhi.

לא וַיִּמְלֹךְ יְהוֹשָׁפָט עַל־יְהוּדָה בֶּן־שְׁלֹשִׁים וְחָמֵשׁ שָׁנָה בְּמָלְכוֹ וְעֶשְׂרִים וְחָמֵשׁ שָׁנָה מָלַךְ בִּירוּשָׁלָ͏ִם וְשֵׁם אִמּוֹ עֲזוּבָה בַּת־שִׁלְחִי:

32 He followed the course of his father *Asa* and did not deviate from it, doing what was pleasing to *Hashem*.

לב וַיֵּלֶךְ בְּדֶרֶךְ אָבִיו אָסָא וְלֹא־סָר מִמֶּנָּה לַעֲשׂוֹת הַיָּשָׁר בְּעֵינֵי יְהֹוָה:

33 However, the shrines did not cease; the people still did not direct their heart toward the God of their fathers.

לג אַךְ הַבָּמוֹת לֹא־סָרוּ וְעוֹד הָעָם לֹא־הֵכִינוּ לְבָבָם לֵאלֹהֵי אֲבֹתֵיהֶם:

34 As for the other events of *Yehoshafat*'s reign, early and late, they are recorded in the annals of *Yehu* son of *Chanani*, which were included in the book of the kings of *Yisrael*.

לד וְיֶתֶר דִּבְרֵי יְהוֹשָׁפָט הָרִאשֹׁנִים וְהָאַחֲרוֹנִים הִנָּם כְּתוּבִים בְּדִבְרֵי יֵהוּא בֶן־חֲנָנִי אֲשֶׁר הֹעֲלָה עַל־סֵפֶר מַלְכֵי יִשְׂרָאֵל:

35 Afterward, King *Yehoshafat* of *Yehuda* entered into a partnership with King *Achazyahu* of *Yisrael*, thereby acting wickedly.

לה וְאַחֲרֵיכֵן אֶתְחַבַּר יְהוֹשָׁפָט מֶלֶךְ־יְהוּדָה עִם אֲחַזְיָה מֶלֶךְ־יִשְׂרָאֵל הוּא הִרְשִׁיעַ לַעֲשׂוֹת:

36 He joined with him in constructing ships to go to Tarshish; the ships were constructed in Ezion-geber.

לו וַיְחַבְּרֵהוּ עִמּוֹ לַעֲשׂוֹת אֳנִיּוֹת לָלֶכֶת תַּרְשִׁישׁ וַיַּעֲשׂוּ אֳנִיּוֹת בְּעֶצְיוֹן גָּבֶר:

37 *Eliezer* son of Dodavahu of Mareshah prophesied against *Yehoshafat*, "As you have made a partnership with *Achazyahu*, *Hashem* will break up your work." The ships were wrecked and were unable to go to Tarshish.

לז וַיִּתְנַבֵּא אֱלִיעֶזֶר בֶּן־דֹּדָוָהוּ מִמָּרֵשָׁה עַל־יְהוֹשָׁפָט לֵאמֹר כְּהִתְחַבֶּרְךָ עִם־אֲחַזְיָהוּ פָּרַץ יְהֹוָה אֶת־מַעֲשֶׂיךָ וַיִּשָּׁבְרוּ אֳנִיּוֹת וְלֹא עָצְרוּ לָלֶכֶת אֶל־תַּרְשִׁישׁ:

21 1 *Yehoshafat* slept with his fathers and was buried with his fathers in the City of *David*; his son *Yehoram* succeeded him as king.

א וַיִּשְׁכַּב יְהוֹשָׁפָט עִם־אֲבֹתָיו וַיִּקָּבֵר עִם־אֲבֹתָיו בְּעִיר דָּוִיד וַיִּמְלֹךְ יְהוֹרָם בְּנוֹ תַּחְתָּיו:

2 He had brothers, sons of *Yehoshafat*: *Azarya*, *Yechiel*, *Zecharya*, Azariahu, *Michael*, and Shephatiah; all these were sons of King *Yehoshafat* of *Yisrael*.

ב וְלוֹ־אַחִים בְּנֵי יְהוֹשָׁפָט עֲזַרְיָה וִיחִיאֵל וּזְכַרְיָהוּ וַעֲזַרְיָהוּ וּמִיכָאֵל וּשְׁפַטְיָהוּ כָּל־אֵלֶּה בְּנֵי יְהוֹשָׁפָט מֶלֶךְ־יִשְׂרָאֵל:

3 Their father gave them many gifts of silver, gold, and [other] presents, as well as fortified towns in *Yehuda*, but he gave the kingdom to *Yehoram* because he was the first-born.

ג וַיִּתֵּן לָהֶם אֲבִיהֶם מַתָּנוֹת רַבּוֹת לְכֶסֶף וּלְזָהָב וּלְמִגְדָּנוֹת עִם־עָרֵי מְצֻרוֹת בִּיהוּדָה וְאֶת־הַמַּמְלָכָה נָתַן לִיהוֹרָם כִּי־הוּא הַבְּכוֹר:

⁴ *Yehoram* proceeded to take firm hold of his father's kingdom and put to the sword all his brothers, as well as some of the officers of *Yisrael*.

ד וַיָּקָם יְהוֹרָם עַל־מַמְלֶכֶת אָבִיו וַיִּתְחַזַּק וַיַּהֲרֹג אֶת־כָּל־אֶחָיו בֶּחָרֶב וְגַם מִשָּׂרֵי יִשְׂרָאֵל:

⁵ *Yehoram* was thirty-two years old when he became king, and he reigned in *Yerushalayim* eight years.

ה בֶּן־שְׁלֹשִׁים וּשְׁתַּיִם שָׁנָה יְהוֹרָם בְּמָלְכוֹ וּשְׁמוֹנֶה שָׁנִים מָלַךְ בִּירוּשָׁלָ͏ִם:

⁶ He followed the practices of the kings of *Yisrael* doing what the House of *Achav* had done, for he married a daughter of *Achav*; he did what was displeasing to *Hashem*.

ו וַיֵּלֶךְ בְּדֶרֶךְ מַלְכֵי יִשְׂרָאֵל כַּאֲשֶׁר עָשׂוּ בֵּית אַחְאָב כִּי בַּת־אַחְאָב הָיְתָה לּוֹ אִשָּׁה וַיַּעַשׂ הָרַע בְּעֵינֵי יְהוָה:

⁷ However, *Hashem* refrained from destroying the House of *David* for the sake of the covenant he had made with *David*, and in accordance with his promise to maintain a lamp for him and his descendants for all time.

ז וְלֹא־אָבָה יְהוָה לְהַשְׁחִית אֶת־בֵּית דָּוִיד לְמַעַן הַבְּרִית אֲשֶׁר כָּרַת לְדָוִיד וְכַאֲשֶׁר אָמַר לָתֵת לוֹ נִיר וּלְבָנָיו כָּל־הַיָּמִים:

⁸ During his reign, the Edomites rebelled against *Yehuda*'s rule and set up a king of their own.

ח בְּיָמָיו פָּשַׁע אֱדוֹם מִתַּחַת יַד־יְהוּדָה וַיַּמְלִיכוּ עֲלֵיהֶם מֶלֶךְ:

⁹ *Yehoram* advanced [against them] with his officers and all his chariotry. He arose by night and attacked the Edomites, who surrounded him and the chariot commanders.

ט וַיַּעֲבֹר יְהוֹרָם עִם־שָׂרָיו וְכָל־הָרֶכֶב עִמּוֹ וַיְהִי קָם לַיְלָה וַיַּךְ אֶת־אֱדוֹם הַסּוֹבֵב אֵלָיו וְאֵת שָׂרֵי הָרָכֶב:

¹⁰ Edom has been in rebellion against *Yehuda*, to this day; Libnah also rebelled against him at that time, because he had forsaken God of his fathers.

י וַיִּפְשַׁע אֱדוֹם מִתַּחַת יַד־יְהוּדָה עַד הַיּוֹם הַזֶּה אָז תִּפְשַׁע לִבְנָה בָּעֵת הַהִיא מִתַּחַת יָדוֹ כִּי עָזַב אֶת־יְהוָה אֱלֹהֵי אֲבֹתָיו:

¹¹ Moreover, he built shrines in the hill country of *Yehuda*; he led astray the inhabitants of *Yerushalayim* and made *Yehuda* wayward.

יא גַּם־הוּא עָשָׂה־בָמוֹת בְּהָרֵי יְהוּדָה וַיֶּזֶן אֶת־יֹשְׁבֵי יְרוּשָׁלַ͏ִם וַיַּדַּח אֶת־יְהוּדָה:

¹² A letter from *Eliyahu* the *Navi* came to him which read, "Thus says God of your father *David*: Since you have not followed the practices of your father *Yehoshafat* and the practices of King *Asa* of *Yehuda*,

יב וַיָּבֹא אֵלָיו מִכְתָּב מֵאֵלִיָּהוּ הַנָּבִיא לֵאמֹר כֹּה אָמַר יְהוָה אֱלֹהֵי דָּוִיד אָבִיךָ תַּחַת אֲשֶׁר לֹא־הָלַכְתָּ בְּדַרְכֵי יְהוֹשָׁפָט אָבִיךָ וּבְדַרְכֵי אָסָא מֶלֶךְ־יְהוּדָה:

¹³ but have followed the practices of the kings of *Yisrael*, leading astray *Yehuda* and the inhabitants of *Yerushalayim* as the House of *Achav* led them astray, and have also killed your brothers of your father's house, who were better than you,

יג וַתֵּלֶךְ בְּדֶרֶךְ מַלְכֵי יִשְׂרָאֵל וַתַּזְנֶה אֶת־יְהוּדָה וְאֶת־יֹשְׁבֵי יְרוּשָׁלַ͏ִם כְּהַזְנוֹת בֵּית אַחְאָב וְגַם אֶת־אַחֶיךָ בֵית־אָבִיךָ הַטּוֹבִים מִמְּךָ הָרָגְתָּ:

¹⁴ therefore, *Hashem* will inflict a great blow upon your people, your sons, and your wives and all your possessions.

יד הִנֵּה יְהוָה נֹגֵף מַגֵּפָה גְדוֹלָה בְּעַמֶּךָ וּבְבָנֶיךָ וּבְנָשֶׁיךָ וּבְכָל־רְכוּשֶׁךָ:

¹⁵ As for you, you will be severely stricken with a disorder of the bowels year after year until your bowels drop out."

טו וְאַתָּה בָּחֳלָיִים רַבִּים בְּמַחֲלֵה מֵעֶיךָ עַד־יֵצְאוּ מֵעֶיךָ מִן־הַחֹלִי יָמִים עַל־יָמִים:

16 *Hashem* stirred up the spirit of the Philistines and the Arabs who were neighbors of the Cushites against *Yehoram*.

טז וַיָּעַר יְהוָה עַל־יְהוֹרָם אֵת רוּחַ הַפְּלִשְׁתִּים וְהָעַרְבִים אֲשֶׁר עַל־יַד כּוּשִׁים:

17 They marched against *Yehuda*, breached its defenses, and carried off all the property that was found in the king's palace, as well as his sons and his wives. The only son who remained was *Yehoachaz*, his youngest.

יז וַיַּעֲלוּ בִיהוּדָה וַיִּבְקָעוּהָ וַיִּשְׁבּוּ אֵת כָּל־הָרְכוּשׁ הַנִּמְצָא לְבֵית־הַמֶּלֶךְ וְגַם־בָּנָיו וְנָשָׁיו וְלֹא נִשְׁאַר־לוֹ בֵּן כִּי אִם־יְהוֹאָחָז קְטֹן בָּנָיו:

18 After this, *Hashem* afflicted him with an incurable disease of the bowels.

יח וְאַחֲרֵי כָּל־זֹאת נְגָפוֹ יְהוָה בְּמֵעָיו לָחֳלִי לְאֵין מַרְפֵּא:

19 Some years later, when a period of two years had elapsed, his bowels dropped out because of his disease, and he died a gruesome death. His people did not make a fire for him like the fire for his fathers.

יט וַיְהִי לְיָמִים מִיָּמִים וּכְעֵת צֵאת הַקֵּץ לְיָמִים שְׁנַיִם יָצְאוּ מֵעָיו עִם־חָלְיוֹ וַיָּמָת בְּתַחֲלֻאִים רָעִים וְלֹא־עָשׂוּ לוֹ עַמּוֹ שְׂרֵפָה כִּשְׂרֵפַת אֲבֹתָיו:

20 He was thirty-two years old when he became king, and he reigned in *Yerushalayim* eight years. He departed unpraised, and was buried in the City of *David*, but not in the tombs of the kings.

כ בֶּן־שְׁלֹשִׁים וּשְׁתַּיִם הָיָה בְמָלְכוֹ וּשְׁמוֹנֶה שָׁנִים מָלַךְ בִּירוּשָׁלָ͏ִם וַיֵּלֶךְ בְּלֹא חֶמְדָּה וַיִּקְבְּרֻהוּ בְּעִיר דָּוִיד וְלֹא בְּקִבְרוֹת הַמְּלָכִים:

ben sh'-lo-SHEEM ush-TA-yim ha-YAH v'-mol-KHO ush-mo-NEH sha-NEEM ma-LAKH bee-ru-sha-LA-im va-YAY-lekh b'-LO khem-DAH va-yik-b'-RU-hu b'-EER da-VEED v'-LO b'-kiv-ROT ha-m'-la-KHEEM

22 1 The inhabitants of *Yerushalayim* made *Achazyahu*, his youngest son, king in his stead, because all the older ones had been killed by the troops that penetrated the camp with the Arabs. *Achazyahu* son of *Yehoram* reigned as king of *Yehuda*.

כב א וַיַּמְלִיכוּ יוֹשְׁבֵי יְרוּשָׁלַ͏ִם אֶת־אֲחַזְיָהוּ בְנוֹ הַקָּטֹן תַּחְתָּיו כִּי כָל־הָרִאשֹׁנִים הָרַג הַגְּדוּד הַבָּא בָעַרְבִים לַמַּחֲנֶה וַיִּמְלֹךְ אֲחַזְיָהוּ בֶן־יְהוֹרָם מֶלֶךְ יְהוּדָה:

2 *Achazyahu* was forty-two years old when he became king, and he reigned in *Yerushalayim* one year; his mother's name was *Atalya* daughter of *Omri*.

ב בֶּן־אַרְבָּעִים וּשְׁתַּיִם שָׁנָה אֲחַזְיָהוּ בְמָלְכוֹ וְשָׁנָה אַחַת מָלַךְ בִּירוּשָׁלָ͏ִם וְשֵׁם אִמּוֹ עֲתַלְיָהוּ בַּת־עָמְרִי:

3 He too followed the practices of the house of *Achav*, for his mother counseled him to do evil.

ג גַּם־הוּא הָלַךְ בְּדַרְכֵי בֵּית אַחְאָב כִּי אִמּוֹ הָיְתָה יוֹעַצְתּוֹ לְהַרְשִׁיעַ:

King *David*'s tomb on Mount Zion

21:20 But not in the tombs of the kings
Yehoram does not behave as his forefathers before him did. By marrying into the House of *Achav*, and bringing idol worship into the kingdom, he betrays God. As such, he is punished heavily for his sins, and though he is not stripped of his kingdom, it loses its prominence and power. Upon his death, the people bury him apart from his ancestors. They realize that though he is of the Davidic line, because of his actions he is not a true Davidic king. *Yehoram* teaches us that the Davidic line is not merely an inheritance; it demands a certain code of behavior. So too with all birthrights. The way a person behaves means more than who his ancestors were.

4 He did what was displeasing to *Hashem*, like the house of *Achav*, for they became his counselors after his father's death, to his ruination.

5 Moreover, he followed their counsel and marched with *Yehoram* son of King *Achav* of *Yisrael* to battle against King Hazael of Aram at Ramoth-gilead, where the Arameans wounded *Yoram*.

6 He returned to *Yizrael* to recover from the wounds inflicted on him at *Rama* when he fought against King Hazael of Aram. King *Azarya* son of *Yehoram* of *Yehuda* went down to *Yizrael* to visit *Yehoram* son of *Achav* while he was ill.

7 *Hashem* caused the downfall of *Achazyahu* because he visited *Yoram*. During his visit he went out with *Yehoram* to *Yehu* son of Nimshi, whom *Hashem* had anointed to cut off the house of *Achav*.

8 In the course of bringing the house of *Achav* to judgment, *Yehu* came upon the officers of *Yehuda* and the nephews of *Achazyahu*, ministers of *Achazyahu*, and killed them.

9 He sent in search of *Achazyahu*, who was caught hiding in *Shomron*, was brought to *Yehu*, and put to death. He was given a burial, because it was said, "He is the son of *Yehoshafat* who worshiped *Hashem* wholeheartedly." So the house of *Achazyahu* could not muster the strength to rule.

10 When *Atalya*, *Achazyahu's* mother, learned that her son was dead, she promptly did away with all who were of the royal stock of the house of *Yehuda*.

11 But *Yehoshavat*, daughter of the king, spirited away *Achazyahu's* son *Yoash* from among the princes who were being slain, and put him and his nurse in a bedroom. *Yehoshavat*, daughter of King *Yehoram*, wife of the *Kohen Yehoyada* – she was the sister of *Achazyahu* – kept him hidden from *Atalya* so that he was not put to death.

12 He stayed with them for six years, hidden in the House of *Hashem*, while *Atalya* reigned over the land.

ד וַיַּעַשׂ הָרַע בְּעֵינֵי יְהֹוָה כְּבֵית אַחְאָב כִּי־הֵמָּה הָיוּ־לוֹ יוֹעֲצִים אַחֲרֵי מוֹת אָבִיו לְמַשְׁחִית לוֹ:

ה גַּם בַּעֲצָתָם הָלַךְ וַיֵּלֶךְ אֶת־יְהוֹרָם בֶּן־אַחְאָב מֶלֶךְ יִשְׂרָאֵל לַמִּלְחָמָה עַל־חֲזָאֵל מֶלֶךְ־אֲרָם בְּרָמוֹת גִּלְעָד וַיַּכּוּ הָרַמִּים אֶת־יוֹרָם:

ו וַיָּשָׁב לְהִתְרַפֵּא בְיִזְרְעֶאל כִּי הַמַּכִּים אֲשֶׁר הִכֻּהוּ בְרָמָה בְּהִלָּחֲמוֹ אֶת־חֲזָהאֵל מֶלֶךְ אֲרָם וַעֲזַרְיָהוּ בֶן־יְהוֹרָם מֶלֶךְ יְהוּדָה יָרַד לִרְאוֹת אֶת־יְהוֹרָם בֶּן־אַחְאָב בְּיִזְרְעֶאל כִּי־חֹלֶה הוּא:

ז וּמֵאֱלֹהִים הָיְתָה תְּבוּסַת אֲחַזְיָהוּ לָבוֹא אֶל־יוֹרָם וּבְבֹאוֹ יָצָא עִם־יְהוֹרָם אֶל־יֵהוּא בֶּן־נִמְשִׁי אֲשֶׁר מְשָׁחוֹ יְהֹוָה לְהַכְרִית אֶת־בֵּית אַחְאָב:

ח וַיְהִי כְּהִשָּׁפֵט יֵהוּא עִם־בֵּית אַחְאָב וַיִּמְצָא אֶת־שָׂרֵי יְהוּדָה וּבְנֵי אֲחֵי אֲחַזְיָהוּ מְשָׁרְתִים לַאֲחַזְיָהוּ וַיַּהַרְגֵם:

ט וַיְבַקֵּשׁ אֶת־אֲחַזְיָהוּ וַיִּלְכְּדֻהוּ וְהוּא מִתְחַבֵּא בְשֹׁמְרוֹן וַיְבִאֻהוּ אֶל־יֵהוּא וַיְמִתֻהוּ וַיִּקְבְּרֻהוּ כִּי אָמְרוּ בֶּן־יְהוֹשָׁפָט הוּא אֲשֶׁר־דָּרַשׁ אֶת־יְהֹוָה בְּכָל־לְבָבוֹ וְאֵין לְבֵית אֲחַזְיָהוּ לַעְצֹר כֹּחַ לְמַמְלָכָה:

י וַעֲתַלְיָהוּ אֵם אֲחַזְיָהוּ רָאֲתָה כִּי מֵת בְּנָהּ וַתָּקָם וַתְּדַבֵּר אֶת־כָּל־זֶרַע הַמַּמְלָכָה לְבֵית יְהוּדָה:

יא וַתִּקַּח יְהוֹשַׁבְעַת בַּת־הַמֶּלֶךְ אֶת־יוֹאָשׁ בֶּן־אֲחַזְיָהוּ וַתִּגְנֹב אֹתוֹ מִתּוֹךְ בְּנֵי־הַמֶּלֶךְ הַמּוּמָתִים וַתִּתֵּן אֹתוֹ וְאֶת־מֵינִקְתּוֹ בַּחֲדַר הַמִּטּוֹת וַתַּסְתִּירֵהוּ יְהוֹשַׁבְעַת בַּת־הַמֶּלֶךְ יְהוֹרָם אֵשֶׁת יְהוֹיָדָע הַכֹּהֵן כִּי הִיא הָיְתָה אֲחוֹת אֲחַזְיָהוּ מִפְּנֵי עֲתַלְיָהוּ וְלֹא הֱמִיתָתְהוּ:

יב וַיְהִי אִתָּם בְּבֵית הָאֱלֹהִים מִתְחַבֵּא שֵׁשׁ שָׁנִים וַעֲתַלְיָה מֹלֶכֶת עַל־הָאָרֶץ:

Chronicles

Statue of King *David* in *Yerushalayim*

22:12 Hidden in the House of *Hashem* In her desire to rule, *Atalya* does the unthinkable: She wipes out the entire royal family including her own children and grandchil- dren. There is, however, one exception. Baby *Yoash* is hidden by his aunt, *Yehoshavat*, in the house of God, the *Beit Hamikdash* in *Yerushalayim*. It is this spiritual center of the

vai-HEE i-TAM b'-VAYT ha-e-lo-HEEM mit-kha-BAY SHAYSH
sha-NEEM va-a-tal-YAH mo-LE-khet al ha-A-retz

23 ¹ In the seventh year, *Yehoyada* took courage and brought the chiefs of the hundreds, *Azarya* son of Jeroham, Ishmael son of *Yehochanan*, *Azarya* son of Oved, Maaseiah son of Adaiah, and Elishaphat son of Zichri, into a compact with him.

² They went through *Yehuda* and assembled the *Leviim* from all the towns of *Yehuda*, and the chiefs of the clans of *Yisrael*. They came to *Yerushalayim*

³ and the entire assembly made a covenant with the king in the House of *Hashem*. He said to them, "The son of the king shall be king according to the promise *Hashem* made concerning the sons of *David*.

⁴ This is what you must do: One third of you, *Kohanim* and *Leviim*, who are on duty for the week, shall be gatekeepers at the thresholds;

⁵ another third shall be stationed in the royal palace, and the other third at the Foundation Gate. All the people shall be in the courts of the House of *Hashem*.

⁶ Let no one enter the House of *Hashem* except the *Kohanim* and the ministering *Leviim*. They may enter because they are sanctified, but all the people shall obey the proscription of *Hashem*.

⁷ The *Leviim* shall surround the king on every side, every man with his weapons at the ready; and whoever enters the House shall be killed. Stay close to the king in his comings and goings."

⁸ The *Leviim* and all *Yehuda* did just as *Yehoyada* the *Kohen* ordered: each took his men – those who were on duty that week and those who were off duty that week, for *Yehoyada* the *Kohen* had not dismissed the divisions.

⁹ *Yehoyada* the *Kohen* gave the chiefs of the hundreds King *David*'s spears and shields and quivers that were kept in the House of *Hashem*.

א וּבַשָּׁנָה הַשְּׁבִעִית הִתְחַזַּק יְהוֹיָדָע וַיִּקַּח אֶת־שָׂרֵי הַמֵּאוֹת לַעֲזַרְיָהוּ בֶן־יְרֹחָם וּלְיִשְׁמָעֵאל בֶּן־יְהוֹחָנָן וְלַעֲזַרְיָהוּ בֶן־עוֹבֵד וְאֶת־מַעֲשֵׂיָהוּ בֶן־עֲדָיָהוּ וְאֶת־אֱלִישָׁפָט בֶּן־זִכְרִי עִמּוֹ בַּבְּרִית:

ב וַיָּסֹבּוּ בִּיהוּדָה וַיִּקְבְּצוּ אֶת־הַלְוִיִּם מִכָּל־עָרֵי יְהוּדָה וְרָאשֵׁי הָאָבוֹת לְיִשְׂרָאֵל וַיָּבֹאוּ אֶל־יְרוּשָׁלָ͏ִם:

ג וַיִּכְרֹת כָּל־הַקָּהָל בְּרִית בְּבֵית הָאֱלֹהִים עִם־הַמֶּלֶךְ וַיֹּאמֶר לָהֶם הִנֵּה בֶן־הַמֶּלֶךְ יִמְלֹךְ כַּאֲשֶׁר דִּבֶּר יְהוָה עַל־בְּנֵי דָוִיד:

ד זֶה הַדָּבָר אֲשֶׁר תַּעֲשׂוּ הַשְּׁלִשִׁית מִכֶּם בָּאֵי הַשַּׁבָּת לַכֹּהֲנִים וְלַלְוִיִּם לְשֹׁעֲרֵי הַסִּפִּים:

ה וְהַשְּׁלִשִׁית בְּבֵית הַמֶּלֶךְ וְהַשְּׁלִשִׁית בְּשַׁעַר הַיְסוֹד וְכָל־הָעָם בְּחַצְרוֹת בֵּית יְהוָה:

ו וְאַל־יָבוֹא בֵית־יְהוָה כִּי אִם־הַכֹּהֲנִים וְהַמְשָׁרְתִים לַלְוִיִּם הֵמָּה יָבֹאוּ כִּי־קֹדֶשׁ הֵמָּה וְכָל־הָעָם יִשְׁמְרוּ מִשְׁמֶרֶת יְהוָה:

ז וְהִקִּיפוּ הַלְוִיִּם אֶת־הַמֶּלֶךְ סָבִיב אִישׁ וְכֵלָיו בְּיָדוֹ וְהַבָּא אֶל־הַבַּיִת יוּמָת וִהְיוּ אֶת־הַמֶּלֶךְ בְּבֹאוֹ וּבְצֵאתוֹ:

ח וַיַּעֲשׂוּ הַלְוִיִּם וְכָל־יְהוּדָה כְּכֹל אֲשֶׁר־צִוָּה יְהוֹיָדָע הַכֹּהֵן וַיִּקְחוּ אִישׁ אֶת־אֲנָשָׁיו בָּאֵי הַשַּׁבָּת עִם יוֹצְאֵי הַשַּׁבָּת כִּי לֹא פָטַר יְהוֹיָדָע הַכֹּהֵן אֶת־הַמַּחְלְקוֹת:

ט וַיִּתֵּן יְהוֹיָדָע הַכֹּהֵן לְשָׂרֵי הַמֵּאוֹת אֶת־הַחֲנִיתִים וְאֶת־הַמָּגִנּוֹת וְאֶת־הַשְּׁלָטִים אֲשֶׁר לַמֶּלֶךְ דָּוִיד אֲשֶׁר בֵּית הָאֱלֹהִים:

Land of Israel, the house that *David* longed to build and that was constructed by his son *Shlomo*, which protects the rightful king and preserves the Davidic line. Through *Yehoshavat* and her husband *Yehoyada* the priest, *Hashem* fulfills His promise to *David* that "his line shall continue forever, his throne, as the sun before Me," (Psalms 89:37).

10 He stationed the entire force, each man with his weapons at the ready, from the south end of the House to the north end of the House, at the *Mizbayach* and the House, to guard the king on every side.

י וַיַּעֲמֵד אֶת־כָּל־הָעָם וְאִישׁ שִׁלְחוֹ בְיָדוֹ מִכֶּתֶף הַבַּיִת הַיְמָנִית עַד־כֶּתֶף הַבַּיִת הַשְּׂמָאלִית לַמִּזְבֵּחַ וְלַבָּיִת עַל־הַמֶּלֶךְ סָבִיב:

11 Then they brought out the king's son, and placed upon him the crown and the insignia. They proclaimed him king, and *Yehoyada* and his sons anointed him and shouted, "Long live the king!"

יא וַיּוֹצִיאוּ אֶת־בֶּן־הַמֶּלֶךְ וַיִּתְּנוּ עָלָיו אֶת־הַנֵּזֶר וְאֶת־הָעֵדוּת וַיַּמְלִיכוּ אֹתוֹ וַיִּמְשָׁחֻהוּ יְהוֹיָדָע וּבָנָיו וַיֹּאמְרוּ יְחִי הַמֶּלֶךְ:

va-yo-TZEE-u et ben ha-ME-lekh va-yi-t'-NU a-LAV et ha-NAY-zer v'et HA-ay-DUT va-yam-LEE-khu o-TO va-yim-sha-KHU-hu y'-ho-ya-DA u-va-NAV va-yo-m'-RU y'-KHEE ha-ME-lekh

12 When *Atalya* heard the shouting of the people and the guards and the acclamation of the king, she came out to the people, to the House of *Hashem*.

יב וַתִּשְׁמַע עֲתַלְיָהוּ אֶת־קוֹל הָעָם הָרָצִים וְהַמְהַלְלִים אֶת־הַמֶּלֶךְ וַתָּבוֹא אֶל־הָעָם בֵּית יְהוָה:

13 She looked about and saw the king standing by his pillar at the entrance, the chiefs with their trumpets beside the king, and all the people of the land rejoicing and blowing trumpets, and the singers with musical instruments leading the hymns. *Atalya* rent her garments and cried out, "Treason, treason!"

יג וַתֵּרֶא וְהִנֵּה הַמֶּלֶךְ עוֹמֵד עַל־עַמּוּדוֹ בַּמָּבוֹא וְהַשָּׂרִים וְהַחֲצֹצְרוֹת עַל־הַמֶּלֶךְ וְכָל־עַם הָאָרֶץ שָׂמֵחַ וְתוֹקֵעַ בַּחֲצֹצְרוֹת וְהַמְשׁוֹרֲרִים בִּכְלֵי הַשִּׁיר וּמוֹדִיעִים לְהַלֵּל וַתִּקְרַע עֲתַלְיָהוּ אֶת־בְּגָדֶיהָ וַתֹּאמֶר קֶשֶׁר קָשֶׁר:

14 Then the *Kohen Yehoyada* ordered out the army officers, the chiefs of hundreds, and said to them, "Take her out between the ranks, and if anyone follows her, put him to the sword." For the *Kohen* thought, "Let her not be put to death in the House of *Hashem*."

יד וַיּוֹצֵא יְהוֹיָדָע הַכֹּהֵן אֶת־שָׂרֵי הַמֵּאוֹת פְּקוּדֵי הַחַיִל וַיֹּאמֶר אֲלֵהֶם הוֹצִיאוּהָ אֶל־מִבֵּית הַשְּׂדֵרוֹת וְהַבָּא אַחֲרֶיהָ יוּמָת בֶּחָרֶב כִּי אָמַר הַכֹּהֵן לֹא תְמִיתוּהָ בֵּית יְהוָה:

15 They cleared a passage for her and she came to the entrance of the Horse Gate to the royal palace; there she was put to death.

טו וַיָּשִׂימוּ לָהּ יָדַיִם וַתָּבוֹא אֶל־מְבוֹא שַׁעַר־הַסּוּסִים בֵּית הַמֶּלֶךְ וַיְמִיתוּהָ שָׁם:

16 Then *Yehoyada* solemnized a covenant between himself and the people and the king that they should be the people of *Hashem*.

טז וַיִּכְרֹת יְהוֹיָדָע בְּרִית בֵּינוֹ וּבֵין כָּל־הָעָם וּבֵין הַמֶּלֶךְ לִהְיוֹת לְעָם לַיהוָה:

23:11 And placed upon him the crown and the insignia The Hebrew term for 'insignia' is *aydut* (עדות). According to *Rashi*, this is a reference to the *Torah*, which is called *aydut* or 'testimony' (see Psalms 78:5). Upon being declared king, young *Yoash* is given a *Torah* scroll, since a Jewish king must always carry a copy of the *Torah* with him. Appointing a king is one of the three commandments that

Men kissing a *Torah* scroll during a prayer service on *Sukkot*

the Israelites were instructed to perform after settling the Land of Israel. However, there is a risk that the king will forget the source of his strength and attribute his successes to his own wisdom and power. Therefore, kings were required to carry a *Torah* scroll with them at all times (Deuteronomy 17:14–20) as a constant reminder that all blessing and success in our lives comes not from man but from *Hashem*.

עדות

17 All the people then went to the temple of Baal; they tore it down and smashed its altars and images to bits, and they slew Mattan, the priest of Baal, in front of the altars.

יז וַיָּבֹאוּ כָל־הָעָם בֵּית־הַבַּעַל וַיִּתְּצֻהוּ וְאֶת־מִזְבְּחֹתָיו וְאֶת־צְלָמָיו שִׁבֵּרוּ וְאֵת מַתָּן כֹּהֵן הַבַּעַל הָרְגוּ לִפְנֵי הַמִּזְבְּחוֹת:

18 *Yehoyada* put the officers of the House of *Hashem* in the charge of Levite *Kohanim* whom *David* had assigned over the House of *Hashem* to offer up burnt offerings, as is prescribed in the Teaching of *Moshe*, accompanied by joyful song as ordained by *David*.

יח וַיָּשֶׂם יְהוֹיָדָע פְּקֻדֹּת בֵּית יְהֹוָה בְּיַד הַכֹּהֲנִים הַלְוִיִּם אֲשֶׁר חָלַק דָּוִיד עַל־בֵּית יְהֹוָה לְהַעֲלוֹת עֹלוֹת יְהֹוָה כַּכָּתוּב בְּתוֹרַת מֹשֶׁה בְּשִׂמְחָה וּבְשִׁיר עַל יְדֵי דָוִיד:

19 He stationed the gatekeepers at the gates of the House of *Hashem* to prevent the entry of anyone unclean for any reason.

יט וַיַּעֲמֵד הַשּׁוֹעֲרִים עַל־שַׁעֲרֵי בֵּית יְהֹוָה וְלֹא־יָבֹא טָמֵא לְכָל־דָּבָר:

20 He took the chiefs of hundreds, the nobles, and the rulers of the people and all the people of the land, and they escorted the king down from the House of *Hashem* into the royal palace by the upper gate, and seated the king on the royal throne.

כ וַיִּקַּח אֶת־שָׂרֵי הַמֵּאוֹת וְאֶת־הָאַדִּירִים וְאֶת־הַמּוֹשְׁלִים בָּעָם וְאֵת כָּל־עַם הָאָרֶץ וַיּוֹרֶד אֶת־הַמֶּלֶךְ מִבֵּית יְהֹוָה וַיָּבֹאוּ בְּתוֹךְ־שַׁעַר הָעֶלְיוֹן בֵּית הַמֶּלֶךְ וַיּוֹשִׁיבוּ אֶת־הַמֶּלֶךְ עַל כִּסֵּא הַמַּמְלָכָה:

21 All the people of the land rejoiced, and the city was quiet. As for *Atalya*, she had been put to the sword.

כא וַיִּשְׂמְחוּ כָל־עַם־הָאָרֶץ וְהָעִיר שָׁקָטָה וְאֶת־עֲתַלְיָהוּ הֵמִיתוּ בֶחָרֶב:

24 1 *Yehoash* was seven years old when he became king, and he reigned in *Yerushalayim* forty years. His mother's name was Zibiah of *Be'er Sheva*.

כד א בֶּן־שֶׁבַע שָׁנִים יֹאָשׁ בְּמָלְכוֹ וְאַרְבָּעִים שָׁנָה מָלַךְ בִּירוּשָׁלָ͏ִם וְשֵׁם אִמּוֹ צִבְיָה מִבְּאֵר שָׁבַע:

2 All the days of the *Kohen Yehoyada*, *Yehoash* did what was pleasing to *Hashem*.

ב וַיַּעַשׂ יוֹאָשׁ הַיָּשָׁר בְּעֵינֵי יְהֹוָה כָּל־יְמֵי יְהוֹיָדָע הַכֹּהֵן:

3 *Yehoyada* took two wives for him, by whom he had sons and daughters.

ג וַיִּשָּׂא־לוֹ יְהוֹיָדָע נָשִׁים שְׁתָּיִם וַיּוֹלֶד בָּנִים וּבָנוֹת:

4 Afterward, *Yoash* decided to renovate the House of *Hashem*.

ד וַיְהִי אַחֲרֵיכֵן הָיָה עִם־לֵב יוֹאָשׁ לְחַדֵּשׁ אֶת־בֵּית יְהֹוָה:

5 He assembled the *Kohanim* and the *Leviim* and charged them as follows: "Go out to the towns of *Yehuda* and collect money from all *Yisrael* for the annual repair of the House of your God. Do it quickly." But the *Leviim* did not act quickly.

ה וַיִּקְבֹּץ אֶת־הַכֹּהֲנִים וְהַלְוִיִּם וַיֹּאמֶר לָהֶם צְאוּ לְעָרֵי יְהוּדָה וְקִבְצוּ מִכָּל־יִשְׂרָאֵל כֶּסֶף לְחַזֵּק אֶת־בֵּית אֱלֹהֵיכֶם מִדֵּי שָׁנָה בְּשָׁנָה וְאַתֶּם תְּמַהֲרוּ לַדָּבָר וְלֹא מִהֲרוּ הַלְוִיִּם:

6 The king summoned *Yehoyada* the chief and said to him, "Why have you not seen to it that the *Leviim* brought the tax imposed by *Moshe*, the servant of *Hashem*, and the congregation of *Yisrael* from *Yehuda* and *Yerushalayim* to the Tent of the Pact?"

ו וַיִּקְרָא הַמֶּלֶךְ לִיהוֹיָדָע הָרֹאשׁ וַיֹּאמֶר לוֹ מַדּוּעַ לֹא־דָרַשְׁתָּ עַל־הַלְוִיִּם לְהָבִיא מִיהוּדָה וּמִירוּשָׁלַ͏ִם אֶת־מַשְׂאַת מֹשֶׁה עֶבֶד־יְהֹוָה וְהַקָּהָל לְיִשְׂרָאֵל לְאֹהֶל הָעֵדוּת:

7 For the children of the wicked *Atalya* had violated the House of *Hashem* and had even used the sacred things of the House of *Hashem* for the Baals.

ז כִּי עֲתַלְיָהוּ הַמִּרְשַׁעַת בָּנֶיהָ פָרְצוּ אֶת־בֵּית הָאֱלֹהִים וְגַם כָּל־קָדְשֵׁי בֵית־יְהֹוָה עָשׂוּ לַבְּעָלִים:

8 The king ordered that a chest be made and placed on the outside of the gate of the House of *Hashem*.

ח וַיֹּאמֶר הַמֶּלֶךְ וַיַּעֲשׂוּ אֲרוֹן אֶחָד וַיִּתְּנֻהוּ בְּשַׁעַר בֵּית־יְהֹוָה חוּצָה:

9 A proclamation was issued in *Yehuda* and *Yerushalayim* to bring the tax imposed on *Yisrael* in the wilderness by *Moshe*, the servant of *Hashem*.

ט וַיִּתְּנוּ־קוֹל בִּיהוּדָה וּבִירוּשָׁלַ͏ִם לְהָבִיא לַיהֹוָה מַשְׂאַת מֹשֶׁה עֶבֶד־הָאֱלֹהִים עַל־יִשְׂרָאֵל בַּמִּדְבָּר:

10 All the officers and all the people gladly brought it and threw it into the chest till it was full.

י וַיִּשְׂמְחוּ כָל־הַשָּׂרִים וְכָל־הָעָם וַיָּבִיאוּ וַיַּשְׁלִיכוּ לָאָרוֹן עַד־לְכַלֵּה:

11 Whenever the chest was brought to the royal officers by the *Leviim*, and they saw that it contained much money, the royal scribe and the agent of the chief *Kohen* came and emptied out the chest and carried it back to its place. They did this day by day, and much money was collected.

יא וַיְהִי בְּעֵת יָבִיא אֶת־הָאָרוֹן אֶל־פְּקֻדַּת הַמֶּלֶךְ בְּיַד הַלְוִיִּם וְכִרְאוֹתָם כִּי־רַב הַכֶּסֶף וּבָא סוֹפֵר הַמֶּלֶךְ וּפְקִיד כֹּהֵן הָרֹאשׁ וִיעָרוּ אֶת־הָאָרוֹן וְיִשָּׂאֻהוּ וִישִׁיבֻהוּ אֶל־מְקֹמוֹ כֹּה עָשׂוּ לְיוֹם בְּיוֹם וַיַּאַסְפוּ־כֶסֶף לָרֹב:

12 The king and *Yehoyada* delivered the money to those who oversaw the tasks connected with the work of the House of *Hashem*. They hired masons and carpenters to renovate the House of *Hashem*, as well as craftsmen in iron and bronze to repair the House of *Hashem*.

יב וַיִּתְּנֵהוּ הַמֶּלֶךְ וִיהוֹיָדָע אֶל־עוֹשֵׂה מְלֶאכֶת עֲבוֹדַת בֵּית־יְהֹוָה וַיִּהְיוּ שֹׂכְרִים חֹצְבִים וְחָרָשִׁים לְחַדֵּשׁ בֵּית יְהֹוָה וְגַם לְחָרָשֵׁי בַרְזֶל וּנְחֹשֶׁת לְחַזֵּק אֶת־בֵּית יְהֹוָה:

13 The overseers did their work; under them the work went well and they restored the House of *Hashem* to its original form and repaired it.

יג וַיַּעֲשׂוּ עֹשֵׂי הַמְּלָאכָה וַתַּעַל אֲרוּכָה לַמְּלָאכָה בְּיָדָם וַיַּעֲמִידוּ אֶת־בֵּית הָאֱלֹהִים עַל־מַתְכֻּנְתּוֹ וַיְאַמְּצֻהוּ:

14 When they had finished, they brought the money that was left over to the king and *Yehoyada*; it was made into utensils for the House of *Hashem*, service vessels: buckets and ladles, golden and silver vessels. Burnt offerings were offered up regularly in the House of *Hashem* all the days of *Yehoyada*.

יד וּכְכַלּוֹתָם הֵבִיאוּ לִפְנֵי הַמֶּלֶךְ וִיהוֹיָדָע אֶת־שְׁאָר הַכֶּסֶף וַיַּעֲשֵׂהוּ כֵלִים לְבֵית־יְהֹוָה כְּלֵי שָׁרֵת וְהַעֲלוֹת וְכַפּוֹת וּכְלֵי זָהָב וָכָסֶף וַיִּהְיוּ מַעֲלִים עֹלוֹת בְּבֵית־יְהֹוָה תָּמִיד כֹּל יְמֵי יְהוֹיָדָע:

15 *Yehoyada* reached a ripe old age and died; he was one hundred and thirty years old at his death.

טו וַיִּזְקַן יְהוֹיָדָע וַיִּשְׂבַּע יָמִים וַיָּמֹת בֶּן־מֵאָה וּשְׁלֹשִׁים שָׁנָה בְּמוֹתוֹ:

16 They buried him in the City of *David* together with the kings, because he had done good in *Yisrael*, and on behalf of *Hashem* and His House.

טז וַיִּקְבְּרֻהוּ בְעִיר־דָּוִיד עִם־הַמְּלָכִים כִּי־עָשָׂה טוֹבָה בְּיִשְׂרָאֵל וְעִם הָאֱלֹהִים וּבֵיתוֹ:

va-yik-b'-RU-hu v'-EER da-VEED im ha-m'-la-KHEEM kee a-SAH to-VAH b'-yis-ra-AYL v'-im ha-e-lo-HEEM u-vay-TO

24:16 Because he had done good in *Yisrael*
Yehoyada is buried "with the kings" even though he is not a member of the royal family. He is the only outsider recorded as being buried among the kingly descendants of *David*, something that even some of the actual kings, such as *Yehoram*, did not merit. *Metzudat David* explains that this is part of his reward for having "done good in *Yisrael*" in three ways. He appointed a king from the line of *David*, he brought the people back to *Hashem* and he restored the *Beit Hamikdash*. *Yehoyada* is buried with the kings because he acted in a manner expected of a king, even to the point of risking his own life, and the lives of his family members, for the sake of God and the Nation of Israel.

Introspective religious man at the Mediterranean Sea

120

¹⁷ But after the death of *Yehoyada*, the officers of *Yehuda* came, bowing low to the king; and the king listened to them.

יז וְאַחֲרֵי מוֹת יְהוֹיָדָע בָּאוּ שָׂרֵי יְהוּדָה וַיִּשְׁתַּחֲווּ לַמֶּלֶךְ אָז שָׁמַע הַמֶּלֶךְ אֲלֵיהֶם:

¹⁸ They forsook the House of God of their fathers to serve the sacred posts and idols; and there was wrath upon *Yehuda* and *Yerushalayim* because of this guilt of theirs.

יח וַיַּעַזְבוּ אֶת־בֵּית יְהֹוָה אֱלֹהֵי אֲבוֹתֵיהֶם וַיַּעַבְדוּ אֶת־הָאֲשֵׁרִים וְאֶת־הָעֲצַבִּים וַיְהִי־קֶצֶף עַל־יְהוּדָה וִירוּשָׁלַ͏ִם בְּאַשְׁמָתָם זֹאת:

¹⁹ *Hashem* sent *Neviim* among them to bring them back to Him; they admonished them but they would not pay heed.

יט וַיִּשְׁלַח בָּהֶם נְבִאִים לַהֲשִׁיבָם אֶל־יְהֹוָה וַיָּעִידוּ בָם וְלֹא הֶאֱזִינוּ:

²⁰ Then the spirit of *Hashem* enveloped *Zecharya* son of *Yehoyada* the *kohen*; he stood above the people and said to them, "Thus *Hashem* said: Why do you transgress the commandments of *Hashem* when you cannot succeed? Since you have forsaken *Hashem*, He has forsaken you."

כ וְרוּחַ אֱלֹהִים לָבְשָׁה אֶת־זְכַרְיָה בֶּן־יְהוֹיָדָע הַכֹּהֵן וַיַּעֲמֹד מֵעַל לָעָם וַיֹּאמֶר לָהֶם כֹּה אָמַר הָאֱלֹהִים לָמָה אַתֶּם עֹבְרִים אֶת־מִצְוֹת יְהֹוָה וְלֹא תַצְלִיחוּ כִּי־עֲזַבְתֶּם אֶת־יְהֹוָה וַיַּעֲזֹב אֶתְכֶם:

²¹ They conspired against him and pelted him with stones in the court of the House of *Hashem*, by order of the king.

כא וַיִּקְשְׁרוּ עָלָיו וַיִּרְגְּמֻהוּ אֶבֶן בְּמִצְוַת הַמֶּלֶךְ בַּחֲצַר בֵּית יְהֹוָה:

²² King *Yoash* disregarded the loyalty that his father *Yehoyada* had shown to him, and killed his son. As he was dying, he said, "May *Hashem* see and requite it."

כב וְלֹא־זָכַר יוֹאָשׁ הַמֶּלֶךְ הַחֶסֶד אֲשֶׁר עָשָׂה יְהוֹיָדָע אָבִיו עִמּוֹ וַיַּהֲרֹג אֶת־בְּנוֹ וּכְמוֹתוֹ אָמַר יֵרֶא יְהֹוָה וְיִדְרֹשׁ:

²³ At the turn of the year, the army of Aram marched against him; they invaded *Yehuda* and *Yerushalayim*, and wiped out all the officers of the people from among the people, and sent all the booty they took to the king of Damascus.

כג וַיְהִי לִתְקוּפַת הַשָּׁנָה עָלָה עָלָיו חֵיל אֲרָם וַיָּבֹאוּ אֶל־יְהוּדָה וִירוּשָׁלַ͏ִם וַיַּשְׁחִיתוּ אֶת־כָּל־שָׂרֵי הָעָם מֵעָם וְכָל־שְׁלָלָם שִׁלְּחוּ לְמֶלֶךְ דַּרְמָשֶׂק:

²⁴ The invading army of Aram had come with but a few men, but *Hashem* delivered a very large army into their hands, because they had forsaken God of their fathers. They inflicted punishments on *Yoash*.

כד כִּי בְמִצְעַר אֲנָשִׁים בָּאוּ חֵיל אֲרָם וַיהֹוָה נָתַן בְּיָדָם חַיִל לָרֹב מְאֹד כִּי עָזְבוּ אֶת־יְהֹוָה אֱלֹהֵי אֲבוֹתֵיהֶם וְאֶת־יוֹאָשׁ עָשׂוּ שְׁפָטִים:

²⁵ When they withdrew, having left him with many wounds, his courtiers plotted against him because of the murder of the sons of *Yehoyada* the *kohen*, and they killed him in bed. He died and was buried in the City of *David*; he was not buried in the tombs of the kings.

כה וּבְלֶכְתָּם מִמֶּנּוּ כִּי־עָזְבוּ אֹתוֹ במחליים [בְּמַחֲלֻיִם] רַבִּים הִתְקַשְּׁרוּ עָלָיו עֲבָדָיו בִּדְמֵי בְּנֵי יְהוֹיָדָע הַכֹּהֵן וַיַּהַרְגֻהוּ עַל־מִטָּתוֹ וַיָּמֹת וַיִּקְבְּרֻהוּ בְּעִיר דָּוִיד וְלֹא קְבָרֻהוּ בְּקִבְרוֹת הַמְּלָכִים:

²⁶ These were the men who conspired against him: Zabad son of Shimeath the Ammonitess, and Jehozabad son of Shimrith the Moabitess.

כו וְאֵלֶּה הַמִּתְקַשְּׁרִים עָלָיו זָבָד בֶּן־שִׁמְעָת הָעַמּוֹנִית וִיהוֹזָבָד בֶּן־שִׁמְרִית הַמּוֹאָבִית:

²⁷ As to his sons, and the many pronouncements against him, and his rebuilding of the House of *Hashem*, they are recorded in the story in the book of the kings. His son *Amatzya* succeeded him as king.

כז וּבָנָיו ורב [יֶרֶב] הַמַּשָּׂא עָלָיו וִיסוֹד בֵּית הָאֱלֹהִים הִנָּם כְּתוּבִים עַל־מִדְרַשׁ סֵפֶר הַמְּלָכִים וַיִּמְלֹךְ אֲמַצְיָהוּ בְנוֹ תַּחְתָּיו:

25 ¹ *Amatzya* was twenty-five years old when he became king, and he reigned twenty-nine years in *Yerushalayim*; his mother's name was Jehoaddan of *Yerushalayim*.

כה א בֶּן־עֶשְׂרִים וְחָמֵשׁ שָׁנָה מָלַךְ אֲמַצְיָהוּ וְעֶשְׂרִים וָתֵשַׁע שָׁנָה מָלַךְ בִּירוּשָׁלָ͏ִם וְשֵׁם אִמּוֹ יְהוֹעַדָּן מִירוּשָׁלָ͏ִים:

² He did what was pleasing to *Hashem*, but not with a whole heart.

ב וַיַּעַשׂ הַיָּשָׁר בְּעֵינֵי יְהוָה רַק לֹא בְּלֵבָב שָׁלֵם:

va-YA-as ha-ya-SHAR b'-ay-NAY a-do-NAI RAK LO b'-lay-VAV sha-LAYM

³ Once he had the kingdom firmly under control, he executed the courtiers who had assassinated his father the king.

ג וַיְהִי כַּאֲשֶׁר חָזְקָה הַמַּמְלָכָה עָלָיו וַיַּהֲרֹג אֶת־עֲבָדָיו הַמַּכִּים אֶת־הַמֶּלֶךְ אָבִיו:

⁴ But he did not put their children to death for [he acted] in accordance with what is written in the Teaching, in the Book of *Moshe*, where *Hashem* commanded, "Parents shall not die for children, nor shall children die for parents, but every person shall die only for his own crime."

ד וְאֶת־בְּנֵיהֶם לֹא הֵמִית כִּי כַכָּתוּב בַּתּוֹרָה בְּסֵפֶר מֹשֶׁה אֲשֶׁר־צִוָּה יְהוָה לֵאמֹר לֹא־יָמוּתוּ אָבוֹת עַל־בָּנִים וּבָנִים לֹא־יָמוּתוּ עַל־אָבוֹת כִּי אִישׁ בְּחֶטְאוֹ יָמוּתוּ:

⁵ *Amatzya* assembled the men of *Yehuda*, and he put all the men of *Yehuda* and *Binyamin* under officers of thousands and officers of hundreds, by clans. He mustered them from the age of twenty upward, and found them to be 300,000 picked men fit for service, able to bear spear and shield.

ה וַיִּקְבֹּץ אֲמַצְיָהוּ אֶת־יְהוּדָה וַיַּעֲמִידֵם לְבֵית־אָבוֹת לְשָׂרֵי הָאֲלָפִים וּלְשָׂרֵי הַמֵּאוֹת לְכָל־יְהוּדָה וּבִנְיָמִן וַיִּפְקְדֵם לְמִבֶּן עֶשְׂרִים שָׁנָה וָמַעְלָה וַיִּמְצָאֵם שְׁלֹשׁ־מֵאוֹת אֶלֶף בָּחוּר יוֹצֵא צָבָא אֹחֵז רֹמַח וְצִנָּה:

⁶ He hired 100,000 warriors from *Yisrael* for 100 *kikarim* of silver.

ו וַיִּשְׂכֹּר מִיִּשְׂרָאֵל מֵאָה אֶלֶף גִּבּוֹר חָיִל בְּמֵאָה כִכַּר־כָּסֶף:

⁷ Then a man of *Hashem* came to him and said, "O king! Do not let the army of *Yisrael* go with you, for *Hashem* is not with *Yisrael* – all these Ephraimites.

ז וְאִישׁ הָאֱלֹהִים בָּא אֵלָיו לֵאמֹר הַמֶּלֶךְ אַל־יָבֹא עִמְּךָ צְבָא יִשְׂרָאֵל כִּי אֵין יְהוָה עִם־יִשְׂרָאֵל כֹּל בְּנֵי אֶפְרָיִם:

Chronicles

25:2 But not with a whole heart Why is *Amatzya* hesitant in his service of *Hashem*? Perhaps he had learned idolatry as a child in his father's house. However, he notices that his father, like idolatrous kings before him, was struck down and reaches the conclusion that the worship of the one true God is the safest and most pragmatic course of action. However, when *Amatzya* obeys *Hashem*'s command and sends away his northern mercenaries, they sack his cities in disgust (verse 13). As such, he wonders if his original conclusion was wrong, and perhaps idolatry is the best course after all. We learn from here that it is not enough to serve God out of a desire for advancement. Worship of *Hashem* must be performed "with a whole heart."

"I love Jerusalem" near the Jaffa Gate in *Yerushalayim*

8 But go by yourself and do it; take courage for battle, [else] *Hashem* will make you fall before the enemy. For in *Hashem* there is power to help one or make one fall!"

ח כִּי אִם־בֹּא אַתָּה עֲשֵׂה חֲזַק לַמִּלְחָמָה יַכְשִׁילְךָ הָאֱלֹהִים לִפְנֵי אוֹיֵב כִּי יֶשׁ־כֹּחַ בֵּאלֹהִים לַעְזוֹר וּלְהַכְשִׁיל:

9 *Amatzya* said to the man of *Hashem*, "And what am I to do about the 100 *kikarim* I gave for the Israelite force?" The man of *Hashem* replied, "*Hashem* has the means to give you much more than that."

ט וַיֹּאמֶר אֲמַצְיָהוּ לְאִישׁ הָאֱלֹהִים וּמַה־לַעֲשׂוֹת לִמְאַת הַכִּכָּר אֲשֶׁר נָתַתִּי לִגְדוּד יִשְׂרָאֵל וַיֹּאמֶר אִישׁ הָאֱלֹהִים יֵשׁ לַיהוָה לָתֶת לְךָ הַרְבֵּה מִזֶּה:

10 So *Amatzya* detached the force that came to him from *Efraim*, [ordering them] to go back to their place. They were greatly enraged against *Yehuda* and returned to their place in a rage.

י וַיַּבְדִּילֵם אֲמַצְיָהוּ לְהַגְּדוּד אֲשֶׁר־בָּא אֵלָיו מֵאֶפְרַיִם לָלֶכֶת לִמְקוֹמָם וַיִּחַר אַפָּם מְאֹד בִּיהוּדָה וַיָּשׁוּבוּ לִמְקוֹמָם בׇּחֳרִי־אָף:

11 *Amatzya* took courage and, leading his army, he marched to the Valley of Salt. He slew 10,000 men of Seir;

יא וַאֲמַצְיָהוּ הִתְחַזַּק וַיִּנְהַג אֶת־עַמּוֹ וַיֵּלֶךְ גֵּיא הַמֶּלַח וַיַּךְ אֶת־בְּנֵי־שֵׂעִיר עֲשֶׂרֶת אֲלָפִים:

12 another 10,000 the men of *Yehuda* captured alive and brought to the top of Sela. They threw them down from the top of Sela and every one of them was burst open.

יב וַעֲשֶׂרֶת אֲלָפִים חַיִּים שָׁבוּ בְּנֵי יְהוּדָה וַיְבִיאוּם לְרֹאשׁ הַסָּלַע וַיַּשְׁלִיכוּם מֵרֹאשׁ־הַסֶּלַע וְכֻלָּם נִבְקָעוּ:

13 The men of the force that *Amatzya* had sent back so they would not go with him into battle made forays against the towns of *Yehuda* from *Shomron* to Beth-horon. They slew 3,000 of them, and took much booty.

יג וּבְנֵי הַגְּדוּד אֲשֶׁר הֵשִׁיב אֲמַצְיָהוּ מִלֶּכֶת עִמּוֹ לַמִּלְחָמָה וַיִּפְשְׁטוּ בְּעָרֵי יְהוּדָה מִשֹּׁמְרוֹן וְעַד־בֵּית חוֹרוֹן וַיַּכּוּ מֵהֶם שְׁלֹשֶׁת אֲלָפִים וַיָּבֹזּוּ בִּזָּה רַבָּה:

14 After *Amatzya* returned from defeating the Edomites, he had the gods of the men of Seir brought, and installed them as his gods; he prostrated himself before them, and to them he made sacrifice.

יד וַיְהִי אַחֲרֵי בוֹא אֲמַצְיָהוּ מֵהַכּוֹת אֶת־אֲדוֹמִים וַיָּבֵא אֶת־אֱלֹהֵי בְּנֵי שֵׂעִיר וַיַּעֲמִידֵם לוֹ לֵאלֹהִים וְלִפְנֵיהֶם יִשְׁתַּחֲוֶה וְלָהֶם יְקַטֵּר:

15 *Hashem* was enraged at *Amatzya*, and sent a *Navi* to him who said to him, "Why are you worshiping the gods of a people who could not save their people from you?"

טו וַיִּחַר־אַף יְהוָה בַּאֲמַצְיָהוּ וַיִּשְׁלַח אֵלָיו נָבִיא וַיֹּאמֶר לוֹ לָמָּה דָרַשְׁתָּ אֶת־אֱלֹהֵי הָעָם אֲשֶׁר לֹא־הִצִּילוּ אֶת־עַמָּם מִיָּדֶךָ:

16 As he spoke to him, [*Amatzya*] said to him, "Have we appointed you a counselor to the king? Stop, else you will be killed!" The *Navi* stopped, saying, "I see *Hashem* has counseled that you be destroyed, since you act this way and disregard my counsel."

טז וַיְהִי בְּדַבְּרוֹ אֵלָיו וַיֹּאמֶר לוֹ הַלְיוֹעֵץ לַמֶּלֶךְ נְתַנּוּךָ חֲדַל־לְךָ לָמָּה יַכּוּךָ וַיֶּחְדַּל הַנָּבִיא וַיֹּאמֶר יָדַעְתִּי כִּי־יָעַץ אֱלֹהִים לְהַשְׁחִיתֶךָ כִּי־עָשִׂיתָ זֹּאת וְלֹא שָׁמַעְתָּ לַעֲצָתִי:

17 Then King *Amatzya* of *Yehuda* took counsel and sent this message to *Yoash* son of *Yehoachaz* son of *Yehu*, king of *Yisrael*, "Come, let us confront each other!"

יז וַיִּוָּעַץ אֲמַצְיָהוּ מֶלֶךְ יְהוּדָה וַיִּשְׁלַח אֶל־יוֹאָשׁ בֶּן־יְהוֹאָחָז בֶּן־יֵהוּא מֶלֶךְ יִשְׂרָאֵל לֵאמֹר לְךָ [לְכָה] נִתְרָאֶה פָנִים:

18 King *Yoash* of *Yisrael* sent back this message to King *Amatzya* of *Yehuda*, "The thistle in Lebanon sent this message to the cedar in Lebanon, 'Give your daughter to my son in marriage.' But a wild beast in Lebanon passed by and trampled the thistle.

יח וַיִּשְׁלַח יוֹאָשׁ מֶלֶךְ־יִשְׂרָאֵל אֶל־אֲמַצְיָהוּ
מֶלֶךְ־יְהוּדָה לֵאמֹר הַחוֹחַ אֲשֶׁר בַּלְּבָנוֹן
שָׁלַח אֶל־הָאֶרֶז אֲשֶׁר בַּלְּבָנוֹן לֵאמֹר
תְּנָה־אֶת־בִּתְּךָ לִבְנִי לְאִשָּׁה וַתַּעֲבֹר חַיַּת
הַשָּׂדֶה אֲשֶׁר בַּלְּבָנוֹן וַתִּרְמֹס אֶת־הַחוֹחַ׃

19 You boast that you have defeated the Edomites and you are ambitious to get more glory. Now stay at home, lest, provoking disaster you fall, dragging *Yehuda* down with you."

יט אָמַרְתָּ הִנֵּה הִכִּיתָ אֶת־אֱדוֹם וּנְשָׂאֲךָ
לִבְּךָ לְהַכְבִּיד עַתָּה שְׁבָה בְּבֵיתֶךָ לָמָּה
תִתְגָּרֶה בְּרָעָה וְנָפַלְתָּ אַתָּה וִיהוּדָה
עִמָּךְ׃

20 But *Amatzya* paid no heed – it was *Hashem*'s doing, in order to deliver them up because they worshiped the gods of Edom.

כ וְלֹא־שָׁמַע אֲמַצְיָהוּ כִּי מֵהָאֱלֹהִים הִיא
לְמַעַן תִּתָּם בְּיָד כִּי דָרְשׁוּ אֵת אֱלֹהֵי
אֱדוֹם׃

21 King *Yoash* of *Yisrael* marched up, and he and King *Amatzya* of *Yehuda* confronted each other at *Beit Shemesh* in *Yehuda*.

כא וַיַּעַל יוֹאָשׁ מֶלֶךְ־יִשְׂרָאֵל וַיִּתְרָאוּ פָנִים
הוּא וַאֲמַצְיָהוּ מֶלֶךְ־יְהוּדָה בְּבֵית שֶׁמֶשׁ
אֲשֶׁר לִיהוּדָה׃

22 The men of *Yehuda* were routed by *Yisrael*, and they all fled to their homes.

כב וַיִּנָּגֶף יְהוּדָה לִפְנֵי יִשְׂרָאֵל וַיָּנֻסוּ אִישׁ
לְאֹהָלָיו׃

23 King *Yoash* of *Yisrael* captured *Amatzya* son of *Yoash* son of *Yehoachaz*, king of *Yehuda*, in *Beit Shemesh*. He brought him to *Yerushalayim* and made a breach of 400 *amot* in the wall of *Yerushalayim*, from the *Efraim* Gate to the Corner Gate.

כג וְאֵת אֲמַצְיָהוּ מֶלֶךְ־יְהוּדָה בֶּן־יוֹאָשׁ בֶּן־
יְהוֹאָחָז תָּפַשׂ יוֹאָשׁ מֶלֶךְ־יִשְׂרָאֵל בְּבֵית
שָׁמֶשׁ וַיְבִיאֵהוּ יְרוּשָׁלַםִ וַיִּפְרֹץ בְּחוֹמַת
יְרוּשָׁלַםִ מִשַּׁעַר אֶפְרַיִם עַד־שַׁעַר
הַפּוֹנֶה אַרְבַּע מֵאוֹת אַמָּה׃

24 Then, with all the gold and silver and all the utensils that were to be found in the House of *Hashem* in the custody of *Oved Edom*, and with the treasuries of the royal palace, and with the hostages, he returned to *Shomron*.

כד וְכָל־הַזָּהָב וְהַכֶּסֶף וְאֵת כָּל־הַכֵּלִים
הַנִּמְצְאִים בְּבֵית־הָאֱלֹהִים עִם־עֹבֵד
אֱדוֹם וְאֶת־אֹצְרוֹת בֵּית הַמֶּלֶךְ וְאֵת בְּנֵי
הַתַּעֲרֻבוֹת וַיָּשָׁב שֹׁמְרוֹן׃

25 King *Amatzya* son of *Yoash* of *Yehuda* lived fifteen years after the death of King *Yoash* son of *Yehoachaz* of *Yisrael*.

כה וַיְחִי אֲמַצְיָהוּ בֶן־יוֹאָשׁ מֶלֶךְ יְהוּדָה
אַחֲרֵי מוֹת יוֹאָשׁ בֶּן־יְהוֹאָחָז מֶלֶךְ
יִשְׂרָאֵל חֲמֵשׁ עֶשְׂרֵה שָׁנָה׃

26 The other events of *Amatzya*'s reign, early and late, are recorded in the book of the kings of *Yehuda* and *Yisrael*.

כו וְיֶתֶר דִּבְרֵי אֲמַצְיָהוּ הָרִאשֹׁנִים
וְהָאַחֲרוֹנִים הֲלֹא הִנָּם כְּתוּבִים עַל־סֵפֶר
מַלְכֵי־יְהוּדָה וְיִשְׂרָאֵל׃

27 From the time that *Amatzya* turned from following *Hashem*, a conspiracy was formed against him in *Yerushalayim*, and he fled to *Lachish*; but they sent men after him to *Lachish* and they put him to death there.

כז וּמֵעֵת אֲשֶׁר־סָר אֲמַצְיָהוּ מֵאַחֲרֵי יְהֹוָה
וַיִּקְשְׁרוּ עָלָיו קֶשֶׁר בִּירוּשָׁלַםִ וַיָּנָס
לָכִישָׁה וַיִּשְׁלְחוּ אַחֲרָיו לָכִישָׁה וַיְמִיתֻהוּ
שָׁם׃

28 They brought his body back on horses and buried him with his fathers in the city of *Yehuda*.

כח וַיִּשָּׂאֻהוּ עַל־הַסּוּסִים וַיִּקְבְּרוּ אֹתוֹ עִם־
אֲבֹתָיו בְּעִיר יְהוּדָה׃

26 1 Then all the people of *Yehuda* took *Uzziyahu*, who was sixteen years old, and proclaimed him king to succeed his father *Amatzya*.

כו א וַיִּקְחוּ כָּל־עַם יְהוּדָה אֶת־עֻזִּיָּהוּ וְהוּא
בֶּן־שֵׁשׁ עֶשְׂרֵה שָׁנָה וַיַּמְלִיכוּ אֹתוֹ תַּחַת
אָבִיו אֲמַצְיָהוּ׃

2 It was he who rebuilt Eloth and restored it to
Yehuda after King [*Amatzya*] slept with his fathers.

ב הוּא בָּנָה אֶת־אֵילוֹת וַיְשִׁיבֶהָ לִיהוּדָה אַחֲרֵי שְׁכַב־הַמֶּלֶךְ עִם־אֲבֹתָיו:

3 *Uzziyahu* was sixteen years old when he
became king, and he reigned fifty-two years in
Yerushalayim; his mother's name was Jecoliah of
Yerushalayim.

ג בֶּן־שֵׁשׁ עֶשְׂרֵה שָׁנָה עֻזִּיָּהוּ בְמָלְכוֹ וַחֲמִשִּׁים וּשְׁתַּיִם שָׁנָה מָלַךְ בִּירוּשָׁלָ͏ִם וְשֵׁם אִמּוֹ יְכִילְיָה [יְכָלְיָה] מִן־יְרוּשָׁלָ͏ִם:

4 He did what was pleasing to *Hashem* just as his
father *Amatzya* had done.

ד וַיַּעַשׂ הַיָּשָׁר בְּעֵינֵי יְהֹוָה כְּכֹל אֲשֶׁר־עָשָׂה אֲמַצְיָהוּ אָבִיו:

5 He applied himself to the worship of *Hashem*
during the time of *Zecharya*, instructor in the
visions of *Hashem*; during the time he worshiped
Hashem, *Hashem* made him prosper.

ה וַיְהִי לִדְרֹשׁ אֱלֹהִים בִּימֵי זְכַרְיָהוּ הַמֵּבִין בִּרְאֹת הָאֱלֹהִים וּבִימֵי דָּרְשׁוֹ אֶת־יְהֹוָה הִצְלִיחוֹ הָאֱלֹהִים:

6 He went forth to fight the Philistines, and breached
the wall of Gath and the wall of Jabneh and the
wall of *Ashdod*; he built towns in [the region of]
Ashdod and among the Philistines.

ו וַיֵּצֵא וַיִּלָּחֶם בַּפְּלִשְׁתִּים וַיִּפְרֹץ אֶת־חוֹמַת גַּת וְאֵת חוֹמַת יַבְנֶה וְאֵת חוֹמַת אַשְׁדּוֹד וַיִּבְנֶה עָרִים בְּאַשְׁדּוֹד וּבַפְּלִשְׁתִּים:

7 *Hashem* helped him against the Philistines, against
the Arabs who lived in Gur-baal, and the Meunites.

ז וַיַּעְזְרֵהוּ הָאֱלֹהִים עַל־פְּלִשְׁתִּים וְעַל־הָעֲרְבִיִּים [הָעַרְבִים] הַיֹּשְׁבִים בְּגוּר־בָּעַל וְהַמְּעוּנִים:

8 The Ammonites paid tribute to *Uzziyahu*, and his
fame spread to the approaches of Egypt, for he
grew exceedingly strong.

ח וַיִּתְּנוּ הָעַמּוֹנִים מִנְחָה לְעֻזִּיָּהוּ וַיֵּלֶךְ שְׁמוֹ עַד־לְבוֹא מִצְרַיִם כִּי הֶחֱזִיק עַד־לְמָעְלָה:

9 *Uzziyahu* built towers in *Yerushalayim* on the
Corner Gate and the Valley Gate and on the Angle,
and fortified them.

ט וַיִּבֶן עֻזִּיָּהוּ מִגְדָּלִים בִּירוּשָׁלַ͏ִם עַל־שַׁעַר הַפִּנָּה וְעַל־שַׁעַר הַגַּיְא וְעַל־הַמִּקְצוֹעַ וַיְחַזְּקֵם:

10 He built towers in the wilderness and hewed out
many cisterns, for he had much cattle, and farmers
in the foothills and on the plain, and vine dressers
in the mountains and on the fertile lands, for he
loved the soil.

י וַיִּבֶן מִגְדָּלִים בַּמִּדְבָּר וַיַּחְצֹב בֹּרוֹת רַבִּים כִּי מִקְנֶה־רַּב הָיָה לוֹ וּבַשְּׁפֵלָה וּבַמִּישׁוֹר אִכָּרִים וְכֹרְמִים בֶּהָרִים וּבַכַּרְמֶל כִּי־אֹהֵב אֲדָמָה הָיָה:

11 *Uzziyahu* had an army of warriors, a battle-ready
force who were mustered by Jeiel the scribe and
Maasseiah the adjutant under *Chananya*, one of the
king's officers.

יא וַיְהִי לְעֻזִּיָּהוּ חַיִל עֹשֵׂה מִלְחָמָה יוֹצְאֵי צָבָא לִגְדוּד בְּמִסְפַּר פְּקֻדָּתָם בְּיַד יְעוּאֵל [יְעִיאֵל] הַסּוֹפֵר וּמַעֲשֵׂיָהוּ הַשּׁוֹטֵר עַל יַד־חֲנַנְיָהוּ מִשָּׂרֵי הַמֶּלֶךְ:

12 The clan chiefs, valiants, totaled 2,600;

יב כֹּל מִסְפַּר רָאשֵׁי הָאָבוֹת לְגִבּוֹרֵי חָיִל אַלְפַּיִם וְשֵׁשׁ מֵאוֹת:

13 under them was the trained army of 307,500, who
made war with might and power to aid the king
against the enemy.

יג וְעַל־יָדָם חֵיל צָבָא שְׁלֹשׁ מֵאוֹת אֶלֶף וְשִׁבְעַת אֲלָפִים וַחֲמֵשׁ מֵאוֹת עוֹשֵׂי מִלְחָמָה בְּכֹחַ חָיִל לַעְזֹר לַמֶּלֶךְ עַל־הָאוֹיֵב:

14 *Uzziyahu* provided them – the whole army – with
shields and spears, and helmets and mail, and bows
and slingstones.

יד וַיָּכֶן לָהֶם עֻזִּיָּהוּ לְכָל־הַצָּבָא מָגִנִּים וּרְמָחִים וְכוֹבָעִים וְשִׁרְיֹנוֹת וּקְשָׁתוֹת וּלְאַבְנֵי קְלָעִים:

15 He made clever devices in *Yerushalayim*, set on the towers and the corners, for shooting arrows and large stones. His fame spread far, for he was helped wonderfully, and he became strong.

טו וַיַּעַשׂ בִּירוּשָׁלַ͏ִם חִשְּׁבֹנוֹת מַחֲשֶׁבֶת חוֹשֵׁב לִהְיוֹת עַל־הַמִּגְדָּלִים וְעַל־הַפִּנּוֹת לִירוֹא בַּחִצִּים וּבָאֲבָנִים גְּדֹלוֹת וַיֵּצֵא שְׁמוֹ עַד־לְמֵרָחוֹק כִּי־הִפְלִיא לְהֵעָזֵר עַד כִּי־חָזָק:

16 When he was strong, he grew so arrogant he acted corruptly: he trespassed against his God by entering the Temple of *Hashem* to offer incense on the incense *Mizbayach*.

טז וּכְחֶזְקָתוֹ גָּבַהּ לִבּוֹ עַד־לְהַשְׁחִית וַיִּמְעַל בַּיהוָה אֱלֹהָיו וַיָּבֹא אֶל־הֵיכַל יְהוָה לְהַקְטִיר עַל־מִזְבַּח הַקְּטֹרֶת:

17 The *kohen Azarya*, with eighty other brave *Kohanim* of *Hashem*, followed him in

יז וַיָּבֹא אַחֲרָיו עֲזַרְיָהוּ הַכֹּהֵן וְעִמּוֹ כֹּהֲנִים לַיהוָה שְׁמוֹנִים בְּנֵי־חָיִל:

18 and, confronting King *Uzziyahu*, said to him, "It is not for you, *Uzziyahu*, to offer incense to *Hashem*, but for the Aaronite *Kohanim*, who have been consecrated, to offer incense. Get out of the Sanctuary, for you have trespassed; there will be no glory in it for you from *Hashem*."

יח וַיַּעַמְדוּ עַל־עֻזִּיָּהוּ הַמֶּלֶךְ וַיֹּאמְרוּ לוֹ לֹא־לְךָ עֻזִּיָּהוּ לְהַקְטִיר לַיהוָה כִּי לַכֹּהֲנִים בְּנֵי־אַהֲרֹן הַמְקֻדָּשִׁים לְהַקְטִיר צֵא מִן־הַמִּקְדָּשׁ כִּי מָעַלְתָּ וְלֹא־לְךָ לְכָבוֹד מֵיְהוָה אֱלֹהִים:

19 *Uzziyahu*, holding the censer and ready to burn incense, got angry; but as he got angry with the *Kohanim*, leprosy broke out on his forehead in front of the *Kohanim* in the House of *Hashem* beside the incense *Mizbayach*.

יט וַיִּזְעַף עֻזִּיָּהוּ וּבְיָדוֹ מִקְטֶרֶת לְהַקְטִיר וּבְזַעְפּוֹ עִם־הַכֹּהֲנִים וְהַצָּרַעַת זָרְחָה בְמִצְחוֹ לִפְנֵי הַכֹּהֲנִים בְּבֵית יְהוָה מֵעַל לְמִזְבַּח הַקְּטֹרֶת:

*va-yiz-AF u-zi-YA-hu uv-ya-DO mik-TE-ret l'-hak-TEER uv-za-PO
im ha-ko-ha-NEEM v'-ha-tza-RA-at za-r'-KHA v'-mitz-KHO lif-NAY
ha-ko-ha-NEEM b'-VAYT a-do-NAI may-AL l'-miz-BAKH ha-k'-TO-ret*

20 When the chief *kohen Azarya* and all the other *Kohanim* looked at him, his forehead was leprous, so they rushed him out of there; he too made haste to get out, for *Hashem* had struck him with a plague.

כ וַיִּפֶן אֵלָיו עֲזַרְיָהוּ כֹהֵן הָרֹאשׁ וְכָל־הַכֹּהֲנִים וְהִנֵּה־הוּא מְצֹרָע בְּמִצְחוֹ וַיַּבְהִלוּהוּ מִשָּׁם וְגַם־הוּא נִדְחַף לָצֵאת כִּי נִגְּעוֹ יְהוָה:

21 King *Uzziyahu* was a leper until the day of his death. He lived in isolated quarters as a leper, for he was cut off from the House of *Hashem* – while *Yotam* his son was in charge of the king's house and governed the people of the land.

כא וַיְהִי עֻזִּיָּהוּ הַמֶּלֶךְ מְצֹרָע עַד־יוֹם מוֹתוֹ וַיֵּשֶׁב בֵּית הַחָפְשׁוּת [הַחָפְשִׁית] מְצֹרָע כִּי נִגְזַר מִבֵּית יְהוָה וְיוֹתָם בְּנוֹ עַל־בֵּית הַמֶּלֶךְ שׁוֹפֵט אֶת־עַם הָאָרֶץ:

Ruins of the ancient city of *Beit She'an*, destroyed by earthquake

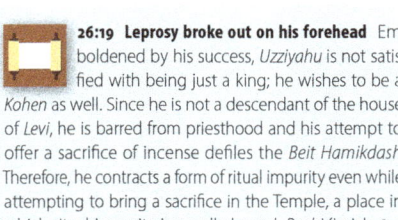

26:19 Leprosy broke out on his forehead Emboldened by his success, *Uzziyahu* is not satisfied with being just a king; he wishes to be a *Kohen* as well. Since he is not a descendant of the house of *Levi*, he is barred from priesthood and his attempt to offer a sacrifice of incense defiles the *Beit Hamikdash*. Therefore, he contracts a form of ritual impurity even while attempting to bring a sacrifice in the Temple, a place in which ritual impurity is usually barred. *Rashi* (Isaiah 6:4) writes that this action causes the earthquake that shook the Land of Israel in the days of *Uzziyahu* (see Amos 1:1 and Zechariah 14:5). This shows the spiritual sensitivity of *Eretz Yisrael*. Not only is *Uzziyahu* punished, but the land itself reacts to the violation of God's command.

22 The other events of *Uzziyahu*'s reign, early and late, were recorded by the *Navi Yeshayahu* son of *Amotz*.

כב וְיֶ֛תֶר דִּבְרֵ֥י עֻזִּיָּ֖הוּ הָרִאשֹׁנִ֣ים וְהָאַחֲרֹנִ֑ים כָּתַ֛ב יְשַׁעְיָ֥הוּ בֶן־אָמֹ֖וץ הַנָּבִֽיא׃

23 *Uzziyahu* slept with his fathers in the burial field of the kings, because, they said, he was a leper; his son *Yotam* succeeded him as king.

כג וַיִּשְׁכַּ֨ב עֻזִּיָּ֜הוּ עִם־אֲבֹתָ֗יו וַיִּקְבְּר֨וּ אֹתֹ֤ו עִם־אֲבֹתָיו֙ בִּשְׂדֵ֤ה הַקְּבוּרָה֙ אֲשֶׁ֣ר לַמְּלָכִ֔ים כִּ֥י אָמְר֖וּ מְצֹורָ֣ע ה֑וּא וַיִּמְלֹ֛ךְ יֹותָ֥ם בְּנֹ֖ו תַּחְתָּֽיו׃

27 1 *Yotam* was twenty-five years old when he became king, and he reigned sixteen years in *Yerushalayim*; his mother's name was Jerushah daughter of *Tzadok*.

כז א בֶּן־עֶשְׂרִ֨ים וְחָמֵ֤שׁ שָׁנָה֙ יֹותָ֣ם בְּמָלְכֹ֔ו וְשֵׁשׁ־עֶשְׂרֵ֣ה שָׁנָ֔ה מָלַ֖ךְ בִּירוּשָׁלָ֑ם וְשֵׁ֣ם אִמֹּ֔ו יְרוּשָׁ֖ה בַּת־צָדֹֽוק׃

2 He did what was pleasing to *Hashem* just as his father *Uzziyahu* had done, but he did not enter the Temple of *Hashem*; however, the people still acted corruptly.

ב וַיַּ֨עַשׂ הַיָּשָׁ֜ר בְּעֵינֵ֣י יְהֹוָ֗ה כְּכֹ֤ל אֲשֶׁר־עָשָׂה֙ עֻזִּיָּ֣הוּ אָבִ֔יו רַ֕ק לֹא־בָ֖א אֶל־הֵיכַ֣ל יְהֹוָ֑ה וְעֹ֥וד הָעָ֖ם מַשְׁחִיתִֽים׃

va-YA-as ha-ya-SHAR b'-ay-NAY a-do-NAI k'-KHOL a-SHER a-SAH u-zi-YA-hu a-VEEV RAK lo VA el hay-KHAL a-do-NAI v'-OD ha-AM mash-khee-TEEM

3 It was he who built the Upper Gate of the House of *Hashem*; he also built extensively on the wall of Ophel.

ג ה֗וּא בָּנָ֛ה אֶת־שַׁ֥עַר בֵּית־יְהֹוָ֖ה הָעֶלְיֹ֑ון וּבְחֹומַ֥ת הָעֹ֖פֶל בָּנָ֥ה לָרֹֽב׃

4 He built towns in the hill country of *Yehuda*, and in the woods he built fortresses and towers.

ד וְעָרִ֥ים בָּנָ֖ה בְּהַר־יְהוּדָ֑ה וּבֶחֳרָשִׁ֣ים בָּנָ֔ה בִּירָנִיֹּ֖ות וּמִגְדָּלִֽים׃

5 Moreover, he fought with the king of the Ammonites and overcame them; the Ammonites gave him that year 100 *kikarim* of silver and 10,000 *kor* of wheat and another 10,000 of barley; that is what the Ammonites paid him, and [likewise] in the second and third years.

ה וְ֠ה֠וּא נִלְחַ֞ם עִם־מֶ֣לֶךְ בְּנֵֽי־עַמֹּון֮ וַיֶּחֱזַ֣ק עֲלֵיהֶם֒ וַיִּתְּנוּ־לֹ֨ו בְנֵֽי־עַמֹּ֜ון בַּשָּׁנָ֣ה הַהִ֗יא מֵאָה֙ כִּכַּר־כֶּ֔סֶף וַעֲשֶׂ֨רֶת אֲלָפִ֤ים כֹּרִים֙ חִטִּ֔ים וּשְׂעֹורִ֖ים עֲשֶׂ֣רֶת אֲלָפִ֑ים זֹ֣את הֵשִׁ֣יבוּ לֹ֗ו בְּנֵ֤י עַמֹּון֙ וּבַשָּׁנָ֣ה הַשֵּׁנִ֔ית וְהַשְּׁלִשִֽׁית׃

6 *Yotam* was strong because he maintained a faithful course before *Hashem* his God.

ו וַיִּתְחַזֵּ֖ק יֹותָ֑ם כִּ֚י הֵכִ֣ין דְּרָכָ֔יו לִפְנֵ֖י יְהֹוָ֥ה אֱלֹהָֽיו׃

7 The other events of *Yotam*'s reign, and all his battles and his conduct, are recorded in the book of the kings of *Yisrael* and *Yehuda*.

ז וְיֶ֨תֶר֙ דִּבְרֵ֣י יֹותָ֔ם וְכָל־מִלְחֲמֹתָ֖יו וּדְרָכָ֑יו הִנָּ֣ם כְּתוּבִ֔ים עַל־סֵ֥פֶר מַלְכֵֽי־יִשְׂרָאֵ֖ל וִיהוּדָֽה׃

A man admires the sunrise at Ramon Crater in the Negev

27:2 The people still acted corruptly While *Yotam* is remembered as a good and righteous king, he fails to influence the people in a significant way. In fact, the people continue their rebellions against *Hashem* and His worship. As is clear throughout *Tanakh*, a king is in a unique position to have significant impact on his subjects. *Chizkiyahu*, for example, is able to create positive change, bringing the nation to a spiritual state that they had not reached since the days of *Shlomo*. *Menashe*, on the other hand, leads the people to a spiritual low point. Therefore, though *Yotam* is considered a good king, he is remembered as a king who failed in his mission to cause the people to repent. Doing what is right is not enough; we must influence and inspire others to do so as well.

8 He was twenty-five years old when he became king, and he reigned sixteen years in *Yerushalayim*.

ח בֶּן־עֶשְׂרִים וְחָמֵשׁ שָׁנָה הָיָה בְמָלְכוֹ וְשֵׁשׁ־עֶשְׂרֵה שָׁנָה מָלַךְ בִּירוּשָׁלָ͏ִם:

9 *Yotam* slept with his fathers, and was buried in the City of *David*; his son *Achaz* succeeded him as king.

ט וַיִּשְׁכַּב יוֹתָם עִם־אֲבֹתָיו וַיִּקְבְּרוּ אֹתוֹ בְּעִיר דָּוִיד וַיִּמְלֹךְ אָחָז בְּנוֹ תַּחְתָּיו:

28 1 *Achaz* was twenty years old when he became king, and he reigned sixteen years in *Yerushalayim*. He did not do what was pleasing to *Hashem* as his father *David* had done,

כח א בֶּן־עֶשְׂרִים שָׁנָה אָחָז בְּמָלְכוֹ וְשֵׁשׁ־עֶשְׂרֵה שָׁנָה מָלַךְ בִּירוּשָׁלָ͏ִם וְלֹא־עָשָׂה הַיָּשָׁר בְּעֵינֵי יְהֹוָה כְּדָוִיד אָבִיו:

2 but followed the ways of the kings of *Yisrael*; he even made molten images for the Baals.

ב וַיֵּלֶךְ בְּדַרְכֵי מַלְכֵי יִשְׂרָאֵל וְגַם מַסֵּכוֹת עָשָׂה לַבְּעָלִים:

3 He made offerings in the Valley of Ben-hinnom and burned his sons in fire, in the abhorrent fashion of the nations which *Hashem* had dispossessed before the Israelites.

ג וְהוּא הִקְטִיר בְּגֵיא בֶן־הִנֹּם וַיַּבְעֵר אֶת־בָּנָיו בָּאֵשׁ כְּתֹעֲבוֹת הַגּוֹיִם אֲשֶׁר הֹרִישׁ יְהֹוָה מִפְּנֵי בְּנֵי יִשְׂרָאֵל:

v'-HU hik-TEER b'-GAY ven hi-NOM va-yav-AYR et ba-NAV
ba-AYSH k'-to-a-VOT ha-go-YIM a-SHER ho-REESH
a-do-NAI mi-p'-NAY b'-NAY yis-ra-AYL

4 He sacrificed and made offerings at the shrines, on the hills, and under every leafy tree.

ד וַיְזַבֵּחַ וַיְקַטֵּר בַּבָּמוֹת וְעַל־הַגְּבָעוֹת וְתַחַת כָּל־עֵץ רַעֲנָן:

5 *Hashem* his God delivered him over to the king of Aram, who defeated him and took many of his men captive, and brought them to Damascus. He was also delivered over to the king of *Yisrael*, who inflicted a great defeat on him.

ה וַיִּתְּנֵהוּ יְהֹוָה אֱלֹהָיו בְּיַד מֶלֶךְ אֲרָם וַיַּכּוּ־בוֹ וַיִּשְׁבּוּ מִמֶּנּוּ שִׁבְיָה גְדוֹלָה וַיָּבִיאוּ דַּרְמָשֶׂק וְגַם בְּיַד־מֶלֶךְ יִשְׂרָאֵל נִתָּן וַיַּךְ־בּוֹ מַכָּה גְדוֹלָה:

6 *Pekach* son of Remaliah killed 120,000 in *Yehuda* – all brave men – in one day, because they had forsaken God of their fathers.

ו וַיַּהֲרֹג פֶּקַח בֶּן־רְמַלְיָהוּ בִּיהוּדָה מֵאָה וְעֶשְׂרִים אֶלֶף בְּיוֹם אֶחָד הַכֹּל בְּנֵי־חָיִל בְּעָזְבָם אֶת־יְהֹוָה אֱלֹהֵי אֲבוֹתָם:

7 Zichri, the champion of *Efraim*, killed Maaseiah the king's son, and Azrikam chief of the palace, and *Elkana*, the second to the king.

ז וַיַּהֲרֹג זִכְרִי גִּבּוֹר אֶפְרַיִם אֶת־מַעֲשֵׂיָהוּ בֶּן־הַמֶּלֶךְ וְאֶת־עַזְרִיקָם נְגִיד הַבָּיִת וְאֶת־אֶלְקָנָה מִשְׁנֵה הַמֶּלֶךְ:

28:3 He made offerings in the Valley of Ben-hinnom Unlike his father and grandfather, *Achaz* was an evil king who reintroduces systematic idol worship and intentionally spreads it to every city in the kingdom (verse 25). In this verse, we are told that he worships *Baal* and burns his children in the Valley of Hinnom. In biblical times this cursed valley was known as the place where the sinful Israelites worshipped the false god *Baal* and offered their children as sacrifices to the fire god *Molech* (Jeremiah 32:35). Therefore, this valley, which is located just outside of the present-day Jerusa-lem Old City walls, was thought to be cursed. Figuratively, it became associated with hell. As the Sages teach (*Eiruvin* 19a), "The gate [to hell] lies between two palm trees in the valley of Hinnom, from which smoke is continually rising." The term 'Gehenna,' referring to hell, is derived from the Hebrew name for the valley, *Gei ben Hinnom* (גיא בן הנום).

Valley of Hinnom

8 The Israelites captured 200,000 of their kinsmen, women, boys, and girls; they also took a large amount of booty from them and brought the booty to *Shomron*.

ח וַיִּשְׁבּוּ בְנֵי־יִשְׂרָאֵל מֵאֲחֵיהֶם מָאתַיִם אֶלֶף נָשִׁים בָּנִים וּבָנוֹת וְגַם־שָׁלָל רָב בָּזְזוּ מֵהֶם וַיָּבִיאוּ אֶת־הַשָּׁלָל לְשֹׁמְרוֹן:

9 A *Navi* of *Hashem* by the name of *Oded* was there, who went out to meet the army on its return to *Shomron*. He said to them, "Because of the fury of God of your fathers against *Yehuda*, He delivered them over to you, and you killed them in a rage that reached heaven.

ט וְשָׁם הָיָה נָבִיא לַיהוָה עֹדֵד שְׁמוֹ וַיֵּצֵא לִפְנֵי הַצָּבָא הַבָּא לְשֹׁמְרוֹן וַיֹּאמֶר לָהֶם הִנֵּה בַּחֲמַת יְהוָה אֱלֹהֵי־אֲבוֹתֵיכֶם עַל־יְהוּדָה נְתָנָם בְּיֶדְכֶם וַתַּהַרְגוּ־בָם בְּזַעַף עַד לַשָּׁמַיִם הִגִּיעַ:

10 Do you now intend to subjugate the men and women of *Yehuda* and *Yerushalayim* to be your slaves? As it is, you have nothing but offenses against *Hashem* your God.

י וְעַתָּה בְּנֵי־יְהוּדָה וִירוּשָׁלַםִ אַתֶּם אֹמְרִים לִכְבֹּשׁ לַעֲבָדִים וְלִשְׁפָחוֹת לָכֶם הֲלֹא רַק־אַתֶּם עִמָּכֶם אֲשָׁמוֹת לַיהוָה אֱלֹהֵיכֶם:

11 Now then, listen to me, and send back the captives you have taken from your kinsmen, for the wrath of *Hashem* is upon you!"

יא וְעַתָּה שְׁמָעוּנִי וְהָשִׁיבוּ הַשִּׁבְיָה אֲשֶׁר שְׁבִיתֶם מֵאֲחֵיכֶם כִּי חֲרוֹן אַף־יְהוָה עֲלֵיכֶם:

12 Some of the chief men of the Ephraimites – *Azarya* son of *Yehochanan*, *Berechya* son of Meshillemoth, Jehizkiah son of *Shalum*, and Amasa son of Hadlai – confronted those returning from the campaign

יב וַיָּקֻמוּ אֲנָשִׁים מֵרָאשֵׁי בְנֵי־אֶפְרַיִם עֲזַרְיָהוּ בֶן־יְהוֹחָנָן בֶּרֶכְיָהוּ בֶן־מְשִׁלֵּמוֹת וִיחִזְקִיָּהוּ בֶּן־שַׁלֻּם וַעֲמָשָׂא בֶּן־חַדְלָי עַל־הַבָּאִים מִן־הַצָּבָא:

13 and said to them, "Do not bring these captives here, for it would mean our offending *Hashem*, adding to our sins and our offenses; for our offense is grave enough, and there is already wrath upon *Yisrael*."

יג וַיֹּאמְרוּ לָהֶם לֹא־תָבִיאוּ אֶת־הַשִּׁבְיָה הֵנָּה כִּי לְאַשְׁמַת יְהוָה עָלֵינוּ אַתֶּם אֹמְרִים לְהֹסִיף עַל־חַטֹּאתֵינוּ וְעַל־אַשְׁמָתֵינוּ כִּי־רַבָּה אַשְׁמָה לָנוּ וַחֲרוֹן אָף עַל־יִשְׂרָאֵל:

14 So the soldiers released the captives and the booty in the presence of the officers and all the congregation.

יד וַיַּעֲזֹב הֶחָלוּץ אֶת־הַשִּׁבְיָה וְאֶת־הַבִּזָּה לִפְנֵי הַשָּׂרִים וְכָל־הַקָּהָל:

15 Then the men named above proceeded to take the captives in hand, and with the booty they clothed all the naked among them – they clothed them and shod them and gave them to eat and drink and anointed them and provided donkeys for all who were failing and brought them to *Yericho*, the city of palms, back to their kinsmen. Then they returned to *Shomron*.

טו וַיָּקֻמוּ הָאֲנָשִׁים אֲשֶׁר־נִקְּבוּ בְשֵׁמוֹת וַיַּחֲזִיקוּ בַשִּׁבְיָה וְכָל־מַעֲרֻמֵּיהֶם הִלְבִּישׁוּ מִן־הַשָּׁלָל וַיַּלְבִּשׁוּם וַיַּנְעִלוּם וַיַּאֲכִלוּם וַיַּשְׁקוּם וַיְסֻכוּם וַיְנַהֲלוּם בַּחֲמֹרִים לְכָל־כּוֹשֵׁל וַיְבִיאוּם יְרֵחוֹ עִיר־הַתְּמָרִים אֵצֶל אֲחֵיהֶם וַיָּשׁוּבוּ שֹׁמְרוֹן:

16 At that time, King *Achaz* sent to the king of Assyria for help.

טז בָּעֵת הַהִיא שָׁלַח הַמֶּלֶךְ אָחָז עַל־מַלְכֵי אַשּׁוּר לַעְזֹר לוֹ:

17 Again the Edomites came and inflicted a defeat on *Yehuda* and took captives.

יז וְעוֹד אֲדוֹמִים בָּאוּ וַיַּכּוּ בִיהוּדָה וַיִּשְׁבּוּ־שֶׁבִי:

18 And the Philistines made forays against the cities of the Shephelah and the *Negev* of *Yehuda*; they seized *Beit Shemesh* and Aijalon and Gederoth, and Soco with its villages, and Timnah with its villages, and Gimzo with its villages; and they settled there.

יח וּפְלִשְׁתִּים פָּשְׁטוּ בְּעָרֵי הַשְּׁפֵלָה וְהַנֶּגֶב לִיהוּדָה וַיִּלְכְּדוּ אֶת־בֵּית־שֶׁמֶשׁ וְאֶת־אַיָּלוֹן וְאֶת־הַגְּדֵרוֹת וְאֶת־שׂוֹכוֹ וּבְנוֹתֶיהָ וְאֶת־תִּמְנָה וּבְנוֹתֶיהָ וְאֶת־גִּמְזוֹ וְאֶת־בְּנֹתֶיהָ וַיֵּשְׁבוּ שָׁם:

19 Thus *Hashem* brought *Yehuda* low on account of King *Achaz* of *Yisrael*, for he threw off restraint in *Yehuda* and trespassed against *Hashem*.

יט כִּי־הִכְנִיעַ יְהוָה אֶת־יְהוּדָה בַּעֲבוּר אָחָז מֶלֶךְ־יִשְׂרָאֵל כִּי הִפְרִיעַ בִּיהוּדָה וּמָעוֹל מַעַל בַּיהוָה:

20 Tillegath-pilneser, king of Assyria, marched against him and gave him trouble, instead of supporting him.

כ וַיָּבֹא עָלָיו תִּלְּגַת פִּלְנְאֶסֶר מֶלֶךְ אַשּׁוּר וַיָּצַר לוֹ וְלֹא חֲזָקוֹ:

21 For *Achaz* plundered the House of *Hashem* and the house of the king and the officers, and made a gift to the king of Assyria – to no avail.

כא כִּי־חָלַק אָחָז אֶת־בֵּית יְהוָה וְאֶת־בֵּית הַמֶּלֶךְ וְהַשָּׂרִים וַיִּתֵּן לְמֶלֶךְ אַשּׁוּר וְלֹא לְעֶזְרָה לוֹ:

22 In his time of trouble, this King *Achaz* trespassed even more against *Hashem*,

כב וּבְעֵת הָצֵר לוֹ וַיּוֹסֶף לִמְעוֹל בַּיהוָה הוּא הַמֶּלֶךְ אָחָז:

23 sacrificing to the gods of Damascus which had defeated him, for he thought, "The gods of the kings of Aram help them; I shall sacrifice to them and they will help me"; but they were his ruin and that of all *Yisrael*.

כג וַיִּזְבַּח לֵאלֹהֵי דַרְמֶשֶׂק הַמַּכִּים בּוֹ וַיֹּאמֶר כִּי אֱלֹהֵי מַלְכֵי־אֲרָם הֵם מַעְזְרִים אוֹתָם לָהֶם אֲזַבֵּחַ וְיַעְזְרוּנִי וְהֵם הָיוּ־לוֹ לְהַכְשִׁילוֹ וּלְכָל־יִשְׂרָאֵל:

24 *Achaz* collected the utensils of the House of *Hashem*, and cut the utensils of the House of *Hashem* to pieces. He shut the doors of the House of *Hashem* and made himself altars in every corner of *Yerushalayim*.

כד וַיֶּאֱסֹף אָחָז אֶת־כְּלֵי בֵית־הָאֱלֹהִים וַיְקַצֵּץ אֶת־כְּלֵי בֵית־הָאֱלֹהִים וַיִּסְגֹּר אֶת־דַּלְתוֹת בֵּית־יְהוָה וַיַּעַשׂ לוֹ מִזְבְּחוֹת בְּכָל־פִּנָּה בִּירוּשָׁלָ͏ִם:

25 In every town in *Yehuda* he set up shrines to make offerings to other gods, vexing God of his fathers.

כה וּבְכָל־עִיר וָעִיר לִיהוּדָה עָשָׂה בָמוֹת לְקַטֵּר לֵאלֹהִים אֲחֵרִים וַיַּכְעֵס אֶת־יְהוָה אֱלֹהֵי אֲבֹתָיו:

26 The other events of his reign and all his conduct, early and late, are recorded in the book of the kings of *Yehuda* and *Yisrael*.

כו וְיֶתֶר דְּבָרָיו וְכָל־דְּרָכָיו הָרִאשֹׁנִים וְהָאַחֲרוֹנִים הִנָּם כְּתוּבִים עַל־סֵפֶר מַלְכֵי־יְהוּדָה וְיִשְׂרָאֵל:

27 *Achaz* slept with his fathers and was buried in the city, in *Yerushalayim*; his body was not brought to the tombs of the kings of *Yisrael*. His son *Chizkiyahu* succeeded him as king.

כז וַיִּשְׁכַּב אָחָז עִם־אֲבֹתָיו וַיִּקְבְּרֻהוּ בָעִיר בִּירוּשָׁלַ͏ִם כִּי לֹא הֱבִיאֻהוּ לְקִבְרֵי מַלְכֵי יִשְׂרָאֵל וַיִּמְלֹךְ יְחִזְקִיָּהוּ בְנוֹ תַּחְתָּיו:

29 ¹ *Chizkiyahu* became king at the age of twenty-five, and he reigned twenty-nine years in *Yerushalayim*; his mother's name was *Aviya* daughter of *Zecharya*.

כט א יְחִזְקִיָּהוּ מָלַךְ בֶּן־עֶשְׂרִים וְחָמֵשׁ שָׁנָה וְעֶשְׂרִים וָתֵשַׁע שָׁנָה מָלַךְ בִּירוּשָׁלָ͏ִם וְשֵׁם אִמּוֹ אֲבִיָּה בַּת־זְכַרְיָהוּ:

2 He did what was pleasing to *Hashem*, just as his father *David* had done.

ב וַיַּעַשׂ הַיָּשָׁר בְּעֵינֵי יְהוָה כְּכֹל אֲשֶׁר־עָשָׂה דָּוִיד אָבִיו:

³ He, in the first month of the first year of his reign, opened the doors of the House of *Hashem* and repaired them.

ג הוּא בַשָּׁנָה הָרִאשׁוֹנָה לְמָלְכוֹ בַּחֹדֶשׁ הָרִאשׁוֹן פָּתַח אֶת־דַּלְתוֹת בֵּית־יְהֹוָה וַיְחַזְּקֵם:

⁴ He summoned the *Kohanim* and the *Leviim* and assembled them in the east square.

ד וַיָּבֵא אֶת־הַכֹּהֲנִים וְאֶת־הַלְוִיִּם וַיַּאַסְפֵם לִרְחוֹב הַמִּזְרָח:

⁵ He said to them, "Listen to me, *Leviim*! Sanctify yourselves and sanctify the House of God of your fathers, and take the abhorrent things out of the holy place.

ה וַיֹּאמֶר לָהֶם שְׁמָעוּנִי הַלְוִיִּם עַתָּה הִתְקַדְּשׁוּ וְקַדְּשׁוּ אֶת־בֵּית יְהֹוָה אֱלֹהֵי אֲבֹתֵיכֶם וְהוֹצִיאוּ אֶת־הַנִּדָּה מִן־הַקֹּדֶשׁ:

⁶ For our fathers trespassed and did what displeased *Hashem* our God; they forsook Him and turned their faces away from the dwelling-place of *Hashem*, turning their backs on it.

ו כִּי־מָעֲלוּ אֲבֹתֵינוּ וְעָשׂוּ הָרַע בְּעֵינֵי יְהֹוָה־אֱלֹהֵינוּ וַיַּעַזְבֻהוּ וַיַּסֵּבּוּ פְנֵיהֶם מִמִּשְׁכַּן יְהֹוָה וַיִּתְּנוּ־עֹרֶף:

⁷ They also shut the doors of the porch and put out the lights; they did not offer incense and did not make burnt offerings in the holy place to the God of *Yisrael*.

ז גַּם סָגְרוּ דַּלְתוֹת הָאוּלָם וַיְכַבּוּ אֶת־הַנֵּרוֹת וּקְטֹרֶת לֹא הִקְטִירוּ וְעֹלָה לֹא־הֶעֱלוּ בַקֹּדֶשׁ לֵאלֹהֵי יִשְׂרָאֵל:

⁸ The wrath of *Hashem* was upon *Yehuda* and *Yerushalayim*; He made them an object of horror, amazement, and hissing as you see with your own eyes.

ח וַיְהִי קֶצֶף יְהֹוָה עַל־יְהוּדָה וִירוּשָׁלָ͏ִם וַיִּתְּנֵם לזועה [לְזַעֲוָה] לְשַׁמָּה וְלִשְׁרֵקָה כַּאֲשֶׁר אַתֶּם רֹאִים בְּעֵינֵיכֶם:

⁹ Our fathers died by the sword, and our sons and daughters and wives are in captivity on account of this.

ט וְהִנֵּה נָפְלוּ אֲבוֹתֵינוּ בֶּחָרֶב וּבָנֵינוּ וּבְנוֹתֵינוּ וְנָשֵׁינוּ בַּשְּׁבִי עַל־זֹאת:

¹⁰ Now I wish to make a covenant with God of *Yisrael*, so that His rage may be withdrawn from us.

י עַתָּה עִם־לְבָבִי לִכְרוֹת בְּרִית לַיהֹוָה אֱלֹהֵי יִשְׂרָאֵל וְיָשֹׁב מִמֶּנּוּ חֲרוֹן אַפּוֹ:

¹¹ Now, my sons, do not be slack, for *Hashem* chose you to attend upon Him, to serve Him, to be His ministers and to make offerings to Him."

יא בָּנַי עַתָּה אַל־תִּשָּׁלוּ כִּי־בָכֶם בָּחַר יְהֹוָה לַעֲמֹד לְפָנָיו לְשָׁרְתוֹ וְלִהְיוֹת לוֹ מְשָׁרְתִים וּמַקְטִרִים:

¹² So the *Leviim* set to – Mahath son of Amasai and *Yoel* son of *Azarya* of the sons of *Kehat*; and of the sons of *Merari*, Keesh son of Abdi and *Azarya* of Jehallelel; and of the Gershonites, Joah son of Zimmah and Eden son of Joah;

יב וַיָּקֻמוּ הַלְוִיִּם מַחַת בֶּן־עֲמָשַׂי וְיוֹאֵל בֶּן־עֲזַרְיָהוּ מִן־בְּנֵי הַקְּהָתִי וּמִן־בְּנֵי מְרָרִי קִישׁ בֶּן־עַבְדִּי וַעֲזַרְיָהוּ בֶּן־יְהַלֶּלְאֵל וּמִן־הַגֵּרְשֻׁנִּי יוֹאָח בֶּן־זִמָּה וְעֵדֶן בֶּן־יוֹאָח:

¹³ and of the sons of Elizaphan, Shimri and Jeiel; and of the sons of *Asaf*, Zecharya and Mattaniah

יג וּמִן־בְּנֵי אֱלִיצָפָן שִׁמְרִי ויעואל [וִיעִיאֵל] וּמִן־בְּנֵי אָסָף זְכַרְיָהוּ וּמַתַּנְיָהוּ:

¹⁴ and of the sons of *Hayman*, Yechiel and *Shim'i*; and of the sons of *Yedutun*, Shemaya and Uzziel –

יד וּמִן־בְּנֵי הֵימָן יחואל [יְחִיאֵל] וְשִׁמְעִי וּמִן־בְּנֵי יְדוּתוּן שְׁמַעְיָה וְעֻזִּיאֵל:

¹⁵ and, gathering their brothers, they sanctified themselves and came, by a command of the king concerning *Hashem*'s ordinances, to purify the House of *Hashem*.

טו וַיַּאַסְפוּ אֶת־אֲחֵיהֶם וַיִּתְקַדְּשׁוּ וַיָּבֹאוּ כְמִצְוַת־הַמֶּלֶךְ בְּדִבְרֵי יְהֹוָה לְטַהֵר בֵּית יְהֹוָה:

16 The *Kohanim* went into the House of *Hashem*
to purify it, and brought all the unclean things
they found in the Temple of *Hashem* out into the
court of the House of *Hashem*; [there] the *Leviim*
received them, to take them outside to Wadi
Kidron.

טז וַיָּבֹאוּ הַכֹּהֲנִים לִפְנִימָה בֵית־יְהוָה
לְטַהֵר וַיּוֹצִיאוּ אֵת כָּל־הַטֻּמְאָה אֲשֶׁר
מָצְאוּ בְּהֵיכַל יְהוָה לַחֲצַר בֵּית יְהוָה
וַיְקַבְּלוּ הַלְוִיִּם לְהוֹצִיא לְנַחַל־קִדְרוֹן
חוּצָה:

17 They began the sanctification on the first day of
the first month; on the eighth day of the month
they reached the porch of *Hashem*. They sanctified
the House of *Hashem* for eight days, and on the
sixteenth day of the first month they finished.

יז וַיָּחֵלּוּ בְּאֶחָד לַחֹדֶשׁ הָרִאשׁוֹן לְקַדֵּשׁ
וּבְיוֹם שְׁמוֹנָה לַחֹדֶשׁ בָּאוּ לְאוּלָם יְהוָה
וַיְקַדְּשׁוּ אֶת־בֵּית־יְהוָה לְיָמִים שְׁמוֹנָה
וּבְיוֹם שִׁשָּׁה עָשָׂר לַחֹדֶשׁ הָרִאשׁוֹן כִּלּוּ:

18 Then they went into the palace of King *Chizkiyahu*
and said, "We have purified the whole House of
Hashem and the *Mizbayach* of burnt offering and
all its utensils, and the table of the bread of display
and all its utensils;

יח וַיָּבוֹאוּ פְנִימָה אֶל־חִזְקִיָּהוּ הַמֶּלֶךְ
וַיֹּאמְרוּ טִהַרְנוּ אֶת־כָּל־בֵּית יְהוָה אֶת־
מִזְבַּח הָעוֹלָה וְאֶת־כָּל־כֵּלָיו וְאֶת־שֻׁלְחַן
הַמַּעֲרֶכֶת וְאֶת־כָּל־כֵּלָיו:

19 and all the utensils that King *Achaz* had befouled
during his reign, when he trespassed, we have made
ready and sanctified. They are standing in front of
the *Mizbayach* of *Hashem*."

יט וְאֵת כָּל־הַכֵּלִים אֲשֶׁר הִזְנִיחַ הַמֶּלֶךְ אָחָז
בְּמַלְכוּתוֹ בְּמַעֲלוֹ הֵכַנּוּ וְהִקְדָּשְׁנוּ וְהִנָּם
לִפְנֵי מִזְבַּח יְהוָה:

20 King *Chizkiyahu* rose early, gathered the officers of
the city, and went up to the House of *Hashem*.

כ וַיַּשְׁכֵּם יְחִזְקִיָּהוּ הַמֶּלֶךְ וַיֶּאֱסֹף אֵת שָׂרֵי
הָעִיר וַיַּעַל בֵּית יְהוָה:

21 They brought seven bulls and seven rams and seven
lambs and seven he-goats as a sin offering for the
kingdom and for the Sanctuary and for *Yehuda*. He
ordered the Aaronite *Kohanim* to offer them on the
Mizbayach of *Hashem*.

כא וַיָּבִיאוּ פָרִים־שִׁבְעָה וְאֵילִים שִׁבְעָה
וּכְבָשִׂים שִׁבְעָה וּצְפִירֵי עִזִּים שִׁבְעָה
לְחַטָּאת עַל־הַמַּמְלָכָה וְעַל־הַמִּקְדָּשׁ
וְעַל־יְהוּדָה וַיֹּאמֶר לִבְנֵי אַהֲרֹן הַכֹּהֲנִים
לְהַעֲלוֹת עַל־מִזְבַּח יְהוָה:

22 The cattle were slaughtered, and the *Kohanim*
received the blood and dashed it against the
Mizbayach; the rams were slaughtered and the
blood was dashed against the *Mizbayach*; the lambs
were slaughtered and the blood was dashed against
the *Mizbayach*.

כב וַיִּשְׁחֲטוּ הַבָּקָר וַיְקַבְּלוּ הַכֹּהֲנִים
אֶת־הַדָּם וַיִּזְרְקוּ הַמִּזְבֵּחָה וַיִּשְׁחֲטוּ
הָאֵלִים וַיִּזְרְקוּ הַדָּם הַמִּזְבֵּחָה וַיִּשְׁחֲטוּ
הַכְּבָשִׂים וַיִּזְרְקוּ הַדָּם הַמִּזְבֵּחָה:

23 The he-goats for the sin offering were presented to
the king and the congregation, who laid their hands
upon them.

כג וַיַּגִּישׁוּ אֶת־שְׂעִירֵי הַחַטָּאת לִפְנֵי הַמֶּלֶךְ
וְהַקָּהָל וַיִּסְמְכוּ יְדֵיהֶם עֲלֵיהֶם:

24 The *Kohanim* slaughtered them and performed
the purgation rite with the blood against the
Mizbayach, to expiate for all *Yisrael*, for the king had
designated the burnt offering and the sin offering
to be for all *Yisrael*.

כד וַיִּשְׁחָטוּם הַכֹּהֲנִים וַיְחַטְּאוּ אֶת־דָּמָם
הַמִּזְבֵּחָה לְכַפֵּר עַל־כָּל־יִשְׂרָאֵל כִּי לְכָל־
יִשְׂרָאֵל אָמַר הַמֶּלֶךְ הָעוֹלָה וְהַחַטָּאת:

25 He stationed the *Leviim* in the House of *Hashem* with cymbals and harps and lyres, as *David* and *Gad* the king's seer and *Natan* the *Navi* had ordained, for the ordinance was by *Hashem* through His *Neviim*.

כה וַיַּעֲמֵד אֶת־הַלְוִיִּם בֵּית יְהֹוָה בִּמְצִלְתַּיִם בִּנְבָלִים וּבְכִנֹּרוֹת בְּמִצְוַת דָּוִיד וְגָד חֹזֵה־הַמֶּלֶךְ וְנָתָן הַנָּבִיא כִּי בְיַד־יְהֹוָה הַמִּצְוָה בְּיַד־נְבִיאָיו:

26 When the *Leviim* were in place with the instruments of *David*, and the *Kohanim* with their trumpets,

כו וַיַּעַמְדוּ הַלְוִיִּם בִּכְלֵי דָוִיד וְהַכֹּהֲנִים בַּחֲצֹצְרוֹת:

27 *Chizkiyahu* gave the order to offer the burnt offering on the *Mizbayach*. When the burnt offering began, the song of *Hashem* and the trumpets began also, together with the instruments of King *David* of *Yisrael*.

כז וַיֹּאמֶר חִזְקִיָּהוּ לְהַעֲלוֹת הָעֹלָה לְהַמִּזְבֵּחַ וּבְעֵת הֵחֵל הָעוֹלָה הֵחֵל שִׁיר־יְהֹוָה וְהַחֲצֹצְרוֹת וְעַל־יְדֵי כְּלֵי דָּוִיד מֶלֶךְ־יִשְׂרָאֵל:

28 All the congregation prostrated themselves, the song was sung and the trumpets were blown – all this until the end of the burnt offering.

כח וְכָל־הַקָּהָל מִשְׁתַּחֲוִים וְהַשִּׁיר מְשׁוֹרֵר וְהַחֲצֹצְרוֹת מַחְצְרִים [מַחְצְרִים] הַכֹּל עַד לִכְלוֹת הָעֹלָה:

29 When the offering was finished, the king and all who were there with him knelt and prostrated themselves.

כט וּכְכַלּוֹת לְהַעֲלוֹת כָּרְעוּ הַמֶּלֶךְ וְכָל־הַנִּמְצְאִים אִתּוֹ וַיִּשְׁתַּחֲווּ:

u-kh'-kha-LOT l'-ha-a-LOT ka-r'-U ha-ME-lekh v'-khol ha-nim-tz'-EEM i-TO va-yish-ta-kha-VU

30 King *Chizkiyahu* and the officers ordered the *Leviim* to praise *Hashem* in the words of *David* and *Asaf* the seer; so they praised rapturously, and they bowed and prostrated themselves.

ל וַיֹּאמֶר יְחִזְקִיָּהוּ הַמֶּלֶךְ וְהַשָּׂרִים לַלְוִיִּם לְהַלֵּל לַיהֹוָה בְּדִבְרֵי דָוִיד וְאָסָף הַחֹזֶה וַיְהַלְלוּ עַד־לְשִׂמְחָה וַיִּקְּדוּ וַיִּשְׁתַּחֲווּ:

31 Then *Chizkiyahu* said, "Now you have consecrated yourselves to *Hashem*; come, bring sacrifices of well-being and thanksgiving to the House of *Hashem*." The congregation brought sacrifices of well-being and thanksgiving, and all who felt so moved brought burnt offerings.

לא וַיַּעַן יְחִזְקִיָּהוּ וַיֹּאמֶר עַתָּה מִלֵּאתֶם יֶדְכֶם לַיהֹוָה גֹּשׁוּ וְהָבִיאוּ זְבָחִים וְתוֹדוֹת לְבֵית יְהֹוָה וַיָּבִיאוּ הַקָּהָל זְבָחִים וְתוֹדוֹת וְכָל־נְדִיב לֵב עֹלוֹת:

32 The number of burnt offerings that the congregation brought was 70 cattle, 100 rams, 200 lambs – all these for burnt offerings to *Hashem*.

לב וַיְהִי מִסְפַּר הָעֹלָה אֲשֶׁר הֵבִיאוּ הַקָּהָל בָּקָר שִׁבְעִים אֵילִים מֵאָה כְּבָשִׂים מָאתָיִם לְעֹלָה לַיהֹוָה כָּל־אֵלֶּה:

Model of the second *Beit Hamikdash* in *Yerushalayim*

29:29 Knelt and prostrated themselves *Chizkiyahu* institutes great reform in the kingdom of *Yehuda*. He abolishes the idolatry established by his father *Achaz*, reopens and cleanses the *Beit Hamikdash*, brings back the *Kohanim* and *Leviim* and reinstitutes the sacrificial offerings to *Hashem*. After the offerings are brought, the people "knelt and prostrated themselves" to *Hashem*. Once the *Beit Hamikdash* has been rededicated to the worship of God through true sacrifices offered with "a willing heart" (verse 31), *Hashem*'s presence returns to the *Beit Hamikdash*, necessitating prostration. Similarly, in our lives, God rests among those who are willing to sacrifice of themselves for Him.

33 The sacred offerings were 600 large cattle and 3,000 small cattle.

לג וְהַקֳּדָשִׁים בָּקָר שֵׁשׁ מֵאוֹת וְצֹאן שְׁלֹשֶׁת אֲלָפִים:

34 The *Kohanim* were too few to be able to flay all the burnt offerings, so their kinsmen, the *Leviim*, reinforced them till the end of the work, and till the [rest of the] *Kohanim* sanctified themselves. (The *Leviim* were more conscientious about sanctifying themselves than the *Kohanim*.)

לד רַק הַכֹּהֲנִים הָיוּ לִמְעָט וְלֹא יָכְלוּ לְהַפְשִׁיט אֶת־כָּל־הָעֹלוֹת וַיְחַזְּקוּם אֲחֵיהֶם הַלְוִיִּם עַד־כְּלוֹת הַמְּלָאכָה וְעַד יִתְקַדְּשׁוּ הַכֹּהֲנִים כִּי הַלְוִיִּם יִשְׁרֵי לֵבָב לְהִתְקַדֵּשׁ מֵהַכֹּהֲנִים:

35 For beside the large number of burnt offerings, there were the fat parts of the sacrifices of well-being and the libations for the burnt offerings; so the service of the House of *Hashem* was properly accomplished.

לה וְגַם־עֹלָה לָרֹב בְּחֶלְבֵי הַשְּׁלָמִים וּבַנְּסָכִים לָעֹלָה וַתִּכּוֹן עֲבוֹדַת בֵּית־ יְהֹוָה:

36 *Chizkiyahu* and all the people rejoiced over what *Hashem* had enabled the people to accomplish, because it had happened so suddenly.

לו וַיִּשְׂמַח יְחִזְקִיָּהוּ וְכָל־הָעָם עַל הַהֵכִין הָאֱלֹהִים לָעָם כִּי בְּפִתְאֹם הָיָה הַדָּבָר:

ל
30 1 *Chizkiyahu* sent word to all *Yisrael* and *Yehuda*; he also wrote letters to *Efraim* and *Menashe* to come to the House of *Hashem* in *Yerushalayim* to keep the *Pesach* for God of *Yisrael*.

א וַיִּשְׁלַח יְחִזְקִיָּהוּ עַל־כָּל־יִשְׂרָאֵל וִיהוּדָה וְגַם־אִגְּרוֹת כָּתַב עַל־אֶפְרַיִם וּמְנַשֶּׁה לָבוֹא לְבֵית־יְהֹוָה בִּירוּשָׁלַ͏ִם לַעֲשׂוֹת פֶּסַח לַיהֹוָה אֱלֹהֵי יִשְׂרָאֵל:

2 The king and his officers and the congregation in *Yerushalayim* had agreed to keep the *Pesach* in the second month,

ב וַיִּוָּעַץ הַמֶּלֶךְ וְשָׂרָיו וְכָל־הַקָּהָל בִּירוּשָׁלָ͏ִם לַעֲשׂוֹת הַפֶּסַח בַּחֹדֶשׁ הַשֵּׁנִי:

3 for at the time, they were unable to keep it, for not enough *Kohanim* had sanctified themselves, nor had the people assembled in *Yerushalayim*.

ג כִּי לֹא יָכְלוּ לַעֲשֹׂתוֹ בָּעֵת הַהִיא כִּי הַכֹּהֲנִים לֹא־הִתְקַדְּשׁוּ לְמַדַּי וְהָעָם לֹא־ נֶאֶסְפוּ לִירוּשָׁלָ͏ִם:

4 The king and the whole congregation thought it proper

ד וַיִּישַׁר הַדָּבָר בְּעֵינֵי הַמֶּלֶךְ וּבְעֵינֵי כָּל־ הַקָּהָל:

5 to issue a decree and proclaim throughout all *Yisrael* from *Be'er Sheva* to *Dan* that they come and keep the *Pesach* for God of *Yisrael* in *Yerushalayim* – not often did they act in accord with what was written.

ה וַיַּעֲמִידוּ דָבָר לְהַעֲבִיר קוֹל בְּכָל־יִשְׂרָאֵל מִבְּאֵר־שֶׁבַע וְעַד־דָּן לָבוֹא לַעֲשׂוֹת פֶּסַח לַיהֹוָה אֱלֹהֵי־יִשְׂרָאֵל בִּירוּשָׁלָ͏ִם כִּי לֹא לָרֹב עָשׂוּ כַּכָּתוּב:

6 The couriers went out with the letters from the king and his officers through all *Yisrael* and *Yehuda*, by order of the king, proclaiming, "O you Israelites! Return to God of your fathers, *Avraham*,

ו וַיֵּלְכוּ הָרָצִים בָּאִגְּרוֹת מִיַּד הַמֶּלֶךְ וְשָׂרָיו בְּכָל־יִשְׂרָאֵל וִיהוּדָה וּכְמִצְוַת הַמֶּלֶךְ לֵאמֹר בְּנֵי יִשְׂרָאֵל שׁוּבוּ אֶל־ יְהֹוָה אֱלֹהֵי אַבְרָהָם יִצְחָק וְיִשְׂרָאֵל

30:6 God of your fathers, *Avraham*, *Yitzchak*, and *Yisrael*
Chizkiyahu invokes the God of *Avraham*, *Yitzchak* and *Yaakov*, the forefathers to whom the Land of Israel was

first promised. He sends his messengers throughout the land to tell those who had inherited the land from their forefathers that if they renew their covenant with *Hashem*

Yitzchak, and *Yisrael,* and He will return to the remnant of you who escaped from the hand of the kings of Assyria.

וְיָשֹׁב אֶל־הַפְּלֵיטָה הַנִּשְׁאֶרֶת לָכֶם מִכַּף מַלְכֵי אַשּׁוּר:

*va-yay-l'-KHU ha-ra-TZEEM ba-i-g'-ROT mi-YAD ha-ME-lekh v'-sa-RAV b'-khol
yis-ra-AYL vee-hu-DAH ukh-mitz-VAT ha-ME-lekh lay-MOR b'-NAY yis-ra-AYL
SHU-vu el a-do-NAI e-lo-HAY av-ra-HAM yitz-KHAK v'-yis-ra-AYL v'-ya-SHOV
el ha-p'-lay-TAH ha-nish-E-ret la-KHEM mi-KAF mal-KHAY a-SHUR*

7 Do not be like your fathers and brothers who trespassed against God of their fathers and He turned them into a horror, as you see.

ז וְאַל־תִּהְיוּ כַּאֲבוֹתֵיכֶם וְכַאֲחֵיכֶם אֲשֶׁר מָעֲלוּ בַּיהֹוָה אֱלֹהֵי אֲבוֹתֵיהֶם וַיִּתְּנֵם לְשַׁמָּה כַּאֲשֶׁר אַתֶּם רֹאִים:

8 Now do not be stiffnecked like your fathers; submit yourselves to *Hashem* and come to His sanctuary, which He consecrated forever, and serve *Hashem* your God so that His anger may turn back from you.

ח עַתָּה אַל־תַּקְשׁוּ עָרְפְּכֶם כַּאֲבוֹתֵיכֶם תְּנוּ־יָד לַיהֹוָה וּבֹאוּ לְמִקְדָּשׁוֹ אֲשֶׁר הִקְדִּישׁ לְעוֹלָם וְעִבְדוּ אֶת־יְהֹוָה אֱלֹהֵיכֶם וְיָשֹׁב מִכֶּם חֲרוֹן אַפּוֹ:

9 If you return to *Hashem,* your brothers and children will be regarded with compassion by their captors, and will return to this land; for *Hashem* your God is gracious and merciful; He will not turn His face from you if you return to Him."

ט כִּי בְשׁוּבְכֶם עַל־יְהֹוָה אֲחֵיכֶם וּבְנֵיכֶם לְרַחֲמִים לִפְנֵי שׁוֹבֵיהֶם וְלָשׁוּב לָאָרֶץ הַזֹּאת כִּי־חַנּוּן וְרַחוּם יְהֹוָה אֱלֹהֵיכֶם וְלֹא־יָסִיר פָּנִים מִכֶּם אִם־תָּשׁוּבוּ אֵלָיו:

10 As the couriers passed from town to town in the land of *Efraim* and *Menashe* till they reached *Zevulun,* they were laughed at and mocked.

י וַיִּהְיוּ הָרָצִים עֹבְרִים מֵעִיר לָעִיר בְּאֶרֶץ־אֶפְרַיִם וּמְנַשֶּׁה וְעַד־זְבֻלוּן וַיִּהְיוּ מַשְׂחִיקִים עֲלֵיהֶם וּמַלְעִגִים בָּם:

11 Some of the people of *Asher* and *Menashe* and *Zevulun,* however, were contrite, and came to *Yerushalayim.*

יא אַךְ־אֲנָשִׁים מֵאָשֵׁר וּמְנַשֶּׁה וּמִזְּבֻלוּן נִכְנְעוּ וַיָּבֹאוּ לִירוּשָׁלָ͏ִם:

12 The hand of *Hashem* was on *Yehuda,* too, making them of a single mind to carry out the command of the king and officers concerning the ordinance of *Hashem.*

יב גַּם בִּיהוּדָה הָיְתָה יַד הָאֱלֹהִים לָתֵת לָהֶם לֵב אֶחָד לַעֲשׂוֹת מִצְוַת הַמֶּלֶךְ וְהַשָּׂרִים בִּדְבַר יְהֹוָה:

13 A great crowd assembled at *Yerushalayim* to keep the Festival of *Pesach* in the second month, a very great congregation.

יג וַיֵּאָסְפוּ יְרוּשָׁלַ͏ִם עַם־רָב לַעֲשׂוֹת אֶת־חַג הַמַּצּוֹת בַּחֹדֶשׁ הַשֵּׁנִי קָהָל לָרֹב מְאֹד:

14 They set to and removed the altars that were in *Yerushalayim,* and they removed all the incense stands and threw them into Wadi Kidron.

יד וַיָּקֻמוּ וַיָּסִירוּ אֶת־הַמִּזְבְּחוֹת אֲשֶׁר בִּירוּשָׁלָ͏ִם וְאֵת כָּל־הַמְקַטְּרוֹת הֵסִירוּ וַיַּשְׁלִיכוּ לְנַחַל קִדְרוֹן:

Table ready for the *Pesach* seder

and rededicate themselves to His service, they can escape foreign domination. He calls on them to bring the *Pesach* sacrifice, which they first brought in Egypt, indelibly identifying them as *Hashem*'s people and symbolizing their freedom. The way to achieve freedom in their land is to renew their loyalty to their Father in Heaven.

15 They slaughtered the paschal sacrifice on the fourteenth of the second month. The *Kohanim* and *Leviim* were ashamed, and they sanctified themselves and brought burnt offerings to the House of *Hashem*.

טו וַיִּשְׁחֲטוּ הַפֶּסַח בְּאַרְבָּעָה עָשָׂר לַחֹדֶשׁ הַשֵּׁנִי וְהַכֹּהֲנִים וְהַלְוִיִּם נִכְלְמוּ וַיִּתְקַדְּשׁוּ וַיָּבִיאוּ עֹלוֹת בֵּית יְהוָה:

16 They took their stations, as was their rule according to the Teaching of *Moshe*, man of *Hashem*. The *Kohanim* dashed the blood [which they received] from the *Leviim*.

טז וַיַּעַמְדוּ עַל־עָמְדָם כְּמִשְׁפָּטָם כְּתוֹרַת מֹשֶׁה אִישׁ־הָאֱלֹהִים הַכֹּהֲנִים זֹרְקִים אֶת־הַדָּם מִיַּד הַלְוִיִּם:

17 Since many in the congregation had not sanctified themselves, the *Leviim* were in charge of slaughtering the paschal sacrifice for everyone who was not clean, so as to consecrate them to *Hashem*.

יז כִּי־רַבַּת בַּקָּהָל אֲשֶׁר לֹא־הִתְקַדָּשׁוּ וְהַלְוִיִּם עַל־שְׁחִיטַת הַפְּסָחִים לְכֹל לֹא טָהוֹר לְהַקְדִּישׁ לַיהוָה:

18 For most of the people – many from *Efraim* and *Menashe*, *Yissachar* and *Zevulun* – had not purified themselves, yet they ate the paschal sacrifice in violation of what was written. *Chizkiyahu* prayed for them, saying, "*Hashem* will provide atonement for

יח כִּי מַרְבִּית הָעָם רַבַּת מֵאֶפְרַיִם וּמְנַשֶּׁה יִשָּׂשכָר וּזְבֻלוּן לֹא הִטֶּהָרוּ כִּי־אָכְלוּ אֶת־הַפֶּסַח בְּלֹא כַכָּתוּב כִּי הִתְפַּלֵּל יְחִזְקִיָּהוּ עֲלֵיהֶם לֵאמֹר יְהוָה הַטּוֹב יְכַפֵּר בְּעַד:

19 everyone who set his mind on worshiping *Hashem*, God of his fathers, even if he is not purified for the sanctuary."

יט כָּל־לְבָבוֹ הֵכִין לִדְרוֹשׁ הָאֱלֹהִים יְהוָה אֱלֹהֵי אֲבוֹתָיו וְלֹא כְּטָהֳרַת הַקֹּדֶשׁ:

20 *Hashem* heard *Chizkiyahu* and healed the people.

כ וַיִּשְׁמַע יְהוָה אֶל־יְחִזְקִיָּהוּ וַיִּרְפָּא אֶת־הָעָם:

21 The Israelites who were in *Yerushalayim* kept the Festival of *Pesach* seven days, with great rejoicing, the *Leviim* and the *Kohanim* praising *Hashem* daily with powerful instruments for *Hashem*.

כא וַיַּעֲשׂוּ בְנֵי־יִשְׂרָאֵל הַנִּמְצְאִים בִּירוּשָׁלַ͏ִם אֶת־חַג הַמַּצּוֹת שִׁבְעַת יָמִים בְּשִׂמְחָה גְדוֹלָה וּמְהַלְלִים לַיהוָה יוֹם בְּיוֹם הַלְוִיִּם וְהַכֹּהֲנִים בִּכְלֵי־עֹז לַיהוָה:

22 *Chizkiyahu* persuaded all the *Leviim* who performed skillfully for *Hashem* to spend the seven days of the festival making offerings of well-being, and confessing to God of their fathers.

כב וַיְדַבֵּר יְחִזְקִיָּהוּ עַל־לֵב כָּל־הַלְוִיִּם הַמַּשְׂכִּילִים שֵׂכֶל־טוֹב לַיהוָה וַיֹּאכְלוּ אֶת־הַמּוֹעֵד שִׁבְעַת הַיָּמִים מְזַבְּחִים זִבְחֵי שְׁלָמִים וּמִתְוַדִּים לַיהוָה אֱלֹהֵי אֲבוֹתֵיהֶם:

23 All the congregation resolved to keep seven more days, so they kept seven more days of rejoicing.

כג וַיִּוָּעֲצוּ כָּל־הַקָּהָל לַעֲשׂוֹת שִׁבְעַת יָמִים אֲחֵרִים וַיַּעֲשׂוּ שִׁבְעַת־יָמִים שִׂמְחָה:

24 King *Chizkiyahu* of *Yehuda* contributed to the congregation 1,000 bulls and 7,000 sheep. And the officers contributed to the congregation 1,000 bulls and 10,000 sheep. And the *Kohanim* sanctified themselves in large numbers.

כד כִּי חִזְקִיָּהוּ מֶלֶךְ־יְהוּדָה הֵרִים לַקָּהָל אֶלֶף פָּרִים וְשִׁבְעַת אֲלָפִים צֹאן וְהַשָּׂרִים הֵרִימוּ לַקָּהָל פָּרִים אֶלֶף וְצֹאן עֲשֶׂרֶת אֲלָפִים וַיִּתְקַדְּשׁוּ כֹהֲנִים לָרֹב:

25 All the congregation of *Yehuda* and the *Kohanim* and the *Leviim* and all the congregation that came from *Yisrael*, and the resident aliens who came from the land of *Yisrael* and who lived in *Yehuda*, rejoiced.

כה וַיִּשְׂמְחוּ כָּל־קְהַל יְהוּדָה וְהַכֹּהֲנִים וְהַלְוִיִּם וְכָל־הַקָּהָל הַבָּאִים מִיִּשְׂרָאֵל וְהַגֵּרִים הַבָּאִים מֵאֶרֶץ יִשְׂרָאֵל וְהַיּוֹשְׁבִים בִּיהוּדָה:

26 There was great rejoicing in *Yerushalayim,* for since the time of King *Shlomo* son of *David* of *Yisrael* nothing like it had happened in *Yerushalayim.*

כו וַתְּהִי שִׂמְחָה־גְדוֹלָה בִּירוּשָׁלֶָם כִּי מִימֵי שְׁלֹמֹה בֶן־דָּוִיד מֶלֶךְ יִשְׂרָאֵל לֹא כָזֹאת בִּירוּשָׁלֶָם:

27 The Levite *Kohanim* rose and blessed the people, and their voice was heard, and their prayer went up to His holy abode, to heaven.

כז וַיָּקֻמוּ הַכֹּהֲנִים הַלְוִיִּם וַיְבָרְכוּ אֶת־הָעָם וַיִּשָּׁמַע בְּקוֹלָם וַתָּבוֹא תְפִלָּתָם לִמְעוֹן קָדְשׁוֹ לַשָּׁמָיִם:

31 1 When all this was finished, all *Yisrael* who were present went out into the towns of *Yehuda* and smashed the pillars, cut down the sacred posts, demolished the shrines and altars throughout *Yehuda* and *Binyamin,* and throughout *Efraim* and *Menashe,* to the very last one. Then all the Israelites returned to their towns, each to his possession.

לא א וּכְכַלּוֹת כָּל־זֹאת יָצְאוּ כָל־יִשְׂרָאֵל הַנִּמְצְאִים לְעָרֵי יְהוּדָה וַיְשַׁבְּרוּ הַמַּצֵּבוֹת וַיְגַדְּעוּ הָאֲשֵׁרִים וַיְנַתְּצוּ אֶת־הַבָּמוֹת וְאֶת־הַמִּזְבְּחֹת מִכָּל־יְהוּדָה וּבִנְיָמִן וּבְאֶפְרַיִם וּמְנַשֶּׁה עַד־לְכַלֵּה וַיָּשׁוּבוּ כָּל־בְּנֵי יִשְׂרָאֵל אִישׁ לַאֲחֻזָּתוֹ לְעָרֵיהֶם:

2 *Chizkiyahu* reconstituted the divisions of the *Kohanim* and *Leviim,* each man of the *Kohanim* and *Leviim* according to his office, for the burnt offerings, the offerings of well-being, to minister, and to sing hymns and praises in the gates of the courts of *Hashem*;

ב וַיַּעֲמֵד יְחִזְקִיָּהוּ אֶת־מַחְלְקוֹת הַכֹּהֲנִים וְהַלְוִיִּם עַל־מַחְלְקוֹתָם אִישׁ כְּפִי עֲבֹדָתוֹ לַכֹּהֲנִים וְלַלְוִיִּם לְעֹלָה וְלִשְׁלָמִים לְשָׁרֵת וּלְהֹדוֹת וּלְהַלֵּל בְּשַׁעֲרֵי מַחֲנוֹת יְהוָה:

3 also the king's portion, from his property, for the burnt offerings – the morning and evening burnt offering, and the burnt offerings for *Shabbatot,* and new moons, and festivals, as prescribed in the Teaching of *Hashem.*

ג וּמְנָת הַמֶּלֶךְ מִן־רְכוּשׁוֹ לָעֹלוֹת לְעֹלוֹת הַבֹּקֶר וְהָעֶרֶב וְהָעֹלוֹת לַשַּׁבָּתוֹת וְלֶחֳדָשִׁים וְלַמֹּעֲדִים כַּכָּתוּב בְּתוֹרַת יְהוָה:

4 He ordered the people, the inhabitants of *Yerushalayim,* to deliver the portions of the *Kohanim* and the *Leviim,* so that they might devote themselves to the Teaching of *Hashem.*

ד וַיֹּאמֶר לָעָם לְיוֹשְׁבֵי יְרוּשָׁלֵַם לָתֵת מְנָת הַכֹּהֲנִים וְהַלְוִיִּם לְמַעַן יֶחֶזְקוּ בְּתוֹרַת יְהוָה:

5 When the word spread, the Israelites brought large quantities of grain, wine, oil, honey, and all kinds of agricultural produce, and tithes of all, in large amounts.

ה וְכִפְרֹץ הַדָּבָר הִרְבּוּ בְנֵי־יִשְׂרָאֵל רֵאשִׁית דָּגָן תִּירוֹשׁ וְיִצְהָר וּדְבַשׁ וְכֹל תְּבוּאַת שָׂדֶה וּמַעֲשַׂר הַכֹּל לָרֹב הֵבִיאוּ:

*v'-khif-ROTZ ha-da-VAR hir-BU v'-NAY yis-ra-AYL ray-SHEET
da-GAN tee-ROSH v'-yitz-HAR ud-VASH v'-KHOL t'-vu-AT
sa-DEH u-ma-SAR ha-KOL la-ROV hay-VEE-u*

A pomegranate field in central Israel

31:5 And tithes of all, in large amounts The gifts and tithes brought to the *Beit Hamikdash* and presented to the *Kohanim* and *Leviim* are examples of biblical commandments that apply only in the Land of Israel. A portion of the crops grown in the land is dedicated to the Creator before we eat from them ourselves, to remind us that no matter how hard we work the land, and despite the tremendous human effort required to produce it, our crops are really a gift from *Hashem.* Additionally, gifts are given to the religious leaders of Israel, to provide physical sustenance in exchange for the spiritual nourishment they offer the people. Since they have no portion of land of their own, the *Kohanim* and *Leviim* are dependent on the rest of the nation for their physical nourishment. In return, their contribution elevates everyone else's existence in the land. Such is life in *Eretz Yisrael* – the physical and spiritual are continuously intertwined.

6 The men of *Yisrael* and *Yehuda* living in the towns of *Yehuda* – they too brought tithes of cattle and sheep and tithes of sacred things consecrated to *Hashem* their God, piling them in heaps.

ו וּבְנֵי יִשְׂרָאֵל וִיהוּדָה הַיּוֹשְׁבִים בְּעָרֵי יְהוּדָה גַּם־הֵם מַעְשַׂר בָּקָר וָצֹאן וּמַעְשַׂר קָדָשִׁים הַמְקֻדָּשִׁים לַיהֹוָה אֱלֹהֵיהֶם הֵבִיאוּ וַיִּתְּנוּ עֲרֵמוֹת עֲרֵמוֹת׃

7 In the third month the heaps began to accumulate, and were finished in the seventh month.

ז בַּחֹדֶשׁ הַשְּׁלִשִׁי הֵחֵלּוּ הָעֲרֵמוֹת לְיִסּוֹד וּבַחֹדֶשׁ הַשְּׁבִיעִי כִּלּוּ׃

8 When *Chizkiyahu* and the officers came and saw the heaps, they blessed *Hashem* and his people *Yisrael*.

ח וַיָּבֹאוּ יְחִזְקִיָּהוּ וְהַשָּׂרִים וַיִּרְאוּ אֶת־הָעֲרֵמוֹת וַיְבָרְכוּ אֶת־יְהֹוָה וְאֵת עַמּוֹ יִשְׂרָאֵל׃

9 *Chizkiyahu* asked the *Kohanim* and *Leviim* about the heaps.

ט וַיִּדְרֹשׁ יְחִזְקִיָּהוּ עַל־הַכֹּהֲנִים וְהַלְוִיִּם עַל־הָעֲרֵמוֹת׃

10 The chief *kohen Azarya*, of the house of *Tzadok*, replied to him, saying, "Ever since the gifts began to be brought to the House of *Hashem*, people have been eating to satiety and leaving over in great amounts, for *Hashem* has blessed His people; this huge amount is left over!"

י וַיֹּאמֶר אֵלָיו עֲזַרְיָהוּ הַכֹּהֵן הָרֹאשׁ לְבֵית צָדוֹק וַיֹּאמֶר מֵהָחֵל הַתְּרוּמָה לָבִיא בֵית־יְהֹוָה אָכוֹל וְשָׂבוֹעַ וְהוֹתֵר עַד־לָרוֹב כִּי יְהֹוָה בֵּרַךְ אֶת־עַמּוֹ וְהַנּוֹתָר אֶת־הֶהָמוֹן הַזֶּה׃

11 *Chizkiyahu* then gave orders to prepare store-chambers in the House of *Hashem*; and they were prepared.

יא וַיֹּאמֶר יְחִזְקִיָּהוּ לְהָכִין לְשָׁכוֹת בְּבֵית יְהֹוָה וַיָּכִינוּ׃

12 They brought in the gifts and the tithes and the sacred things faithfully. Their supervisor was Conaniah the *Levi*, and *Shim'i* his brother was second in rank.

יב וַיָּבִיאוּ אֶת־הַתְּרוּמָה וְהַמַּעֲשֵׂר וְהַקֳּדָשִׁים בֶּאֱמוּנָה וַעֲלֵיהֶם נָגִיד כונניהו [כָּנַנְיָהוּ] הַלֵּוִי וְשִׁמְעִי אָחִיהוּ מִשְׁנֶה׃

13 *Yechiel* and Azaziah and Nahath and *Asael* and Jerimoth and *Yozavad* and Eliel and Ismachiah and Mahath and Benaiah were commissioners under Conaniah and *Shim'i* his brother by appointment of King *Chizkiyahu*; *Azarya* was supervisor of the House of *Hashem*.

יג וִיחִיאֵל וַעֲזַזְיָהוּ וְנַחַת וַעֲשָׂהאֵל וִירִימוֹת וְיוֹזָבָד וֶאֱלִיאֵל וְיִסְמַכְיָהוּ וּמַחַת וּבְנָיָהוּ פְּקִידִים מִיַּד כונניהו [כָּנַנְיָהוּ] וְשִׁמְעִי אָחִיו בְּמִפְקַד יְחִזְקִיָּהוּ הַמֶּלֶךְ וַעֲזַרְיָהוּ נְגִיד בֵּית־הָאֱלֹהִים׃

14 Kore son of Imnah the *Levi*, the keeper of the East Gate, was in charge of the freewill offerings to *Hashem*, of the allocation of gifts to *Hashem*, and the most sacred things.

יד וְקוֹרֵא בֶן־יִמְנָה הַלֵּוִי הַשּׁוֹעֵר לַמִּזְרָחָה עַל נִדְבוֹת הָאֱלֹהִים לָתֵת תְּרוּמַת יְהֹוָה וְקָדְשֵׁי הַקֳּדָשִׁים׃

15 Under him were Eden, Miniamin, *Yeshua*, *Shemaya*, Amariah, and *Shechanya*, in offices of trust in the priestly towns, making allocation to their brothers by divisions, to great and small alike;

טו וְעַל־יָדוֹ עֵדֶן וּמִנְיָמִן וְיֵשׁוּעַ וּשְׁמַעְיָהוּ אֲמַרְיָהוּ וּשְׁכַנְיָהוּ בְּעָרֵי הַכֹּהֲנִים בֶּאֱמוּנָה לָתֵת לַאֲחֵיהֶם בְּמַחְלְקוֹת כַּגָּדוֹל כַּקָּטָן׃

16 besides allocating their daily rations to those males registered by families from three years old and up, all who entered the House of *Hashem* according to their service and their shift by division;

טז מִלְּבַד הִתְיַחְשָׂם לִזְכָרִים מִבֶּן שָׁלוֹשׁ שָׁנִים וּלְמַעְלָה לְכָל־הַבָּא לְבֵית־יְהֹוָה לִדְבַר־יוֹם בְּיוֹמוֹ לַעֲבוֹדָתָם בְּמִשְׁמְרוֹתָם כְּמַחְלְקוֹתֵיהֶם:

17 and in charge of the registry of *Kohanim* by clans, and of the *Leviim*, from twenty years old and up, by shifts, in their divisions;

יז וְאֵת הִתְיַחֵשׂ הַכֹּהֲנִים לְבֵית אֲבוֹתֵיהֶם וְהַלְוִיִּם מִבֶּן עֶשְׂרִים שָׁנָה וּלְמָעְלָה בְּמִשְׁמְרוֹתֵיהֶם בְּמַחְלְקוֹתֵיהֶם:

18 and the registry of the dependents of their whole company – wives, sons, and daughters – for, relying upon them, they sanctified themselves in holiness.

יח וּלְהִתְיַחֵשׂ בְּכָל־טַפָּם נְשֵׁיהֶם וּבְנֵיהֶם וּבְנוֹתֵיהֶם לְכָל־קָהָל כִּי בֶאֱמוּנָתָם יִתְקַדְּשׁוּ־קֹדֶשׁ:

19 And for the Aaronite *Kohanim*, in each and every one of their towns with adjoining fields, the above-named men were to allocate portions to every male of the *Kohanim* and to every registered *Levi*.

יט וְלִבְנֵי אַהֲרֹן הַכֹּהֲנִים בִּשְׂדֵי מִגְרַשׁ עָרֵיהֶם בְּכָל־עִיר וָעִיר אֲנָשִׁים אֲשֶׁר נִקְּבוּ בְּשֵׁמוֹת לָתֵת מָנוֹת לְכָל־זָכָר בַּכֹּהֲנִים וּלְכָל־הִתְיַחֵשׂ בַּלְוִיִּם:

20 *Chizkiyahu* did this throughout *Yehuda*. He acted in a way that was good, upright, and faithful before *Hashem* his God.

כ וַיַּעַשׂ כָּזֹאת יְחִזְקִיָּהוּ בְּכָל־יְהוּדָה וַיַּעַשׂ הַטּוֹב וְהַיָּשָׁר וְהָאֱמֶת לִפְנֵי יְהֹוָה אֱלֹהָיו:

21 Every work he undertook in the service of the House of *Hashem* or in the Teaching and the Commandment, to worship his God, he did with all his heart; and he prospered.

כא וּבְכָל־מַעֲשֶׂה אֲשֶׁר־הֵחֵל בַּעֲבוֹדַת בֵּית־הָאֱלֹהִים וּבַתּוֹרָה וּבַמִּצְוָה לִדְרֹשׁ לֵאלֹהָיו בְּכָל־לְבָבוֹ עָשָׂה וְהִצְלִיחַ:

32 1 After these faithful deeds, King Sennacherib of Assyria invaded *Yehuda* and encamped against its fortified towns with the aim of taking them over.

לב א אַחֲרֵי הַדְּבָרִים וְהָאֱמֶת הָאֵלֶּה בָּא סַנְחֵרִיב מֶלֶךְ־אַשּׁוּר וַיָּבֹא בִיהוּדָה וַיִּחַן עַל־הֶעָרִים הַבְּצֻרוֹת וַיֹּאמֶר לְבִקְעָם אֵלָיו:

2 When *Chizkiyahu* saw that Sennacherib had come, intent on making war against *Yerushalayim*,

ב וַיַּרְא יְחִזְקִיָּהוּ כִּי־בָא סַנְחֵרִיב וּפָנָיו לַמִּלְחָמָה עַל־יְרוּשָׁלָ͏ִם:

3 he consulted with his officers and warriors about stopping the flow of the springs outside the city, and they supported him.

ג וַיִּוָּעַץ עִם־שָׂרָיו וְגִבֹּרָיו לִסְתּוֹם אֶת־מֵימֵי הָעֲיָנוֹת אֲשֶׁר מִחוּץ לָעִיר וַיַּעְזְרוּהוּ:

4 A large force was assembled to stop up all the springs and the wadi that flowed through the land, for otherwise, they thought, the king of Assyria would come and find water in abundance.

ד וַיִּקָּבְצוּ עַם־רָב וַיִּסְתְּמוּ אֶת־כָּל־הַמַּעְיָנוֹת וְאֶת־הַנַּחַל הַשּׁוֹטֵף בְּתוֹךְ־הָאָרֶץ לֵאמֹר לָמָּה יָבוֹאוּ מַלְכֵי אַשּׁוּר וּמָצְאוּ מַיִם רַבִּים:

5 He acted with vigor, rebuilding the whole breached wall, raising towers on it, and building another wall outside it. He fortified the Millo of the City of *David*, and made a great quantity of arms and shields.

ה וַיִּתְחַזַּק וַיִּבֶן אֶת־כָּל־הַחוֹמָה הַפְּרוּצָה וַיַּעַל עַל־הַמִּגְדָּלוֹת וְלַחוּצָה הַחוֹמָה אַחֶרֶת וַיְחַזֵּק אֶת־הַמִּלּוֹא עִיר דָּוִיד וַיַּעַשׂ שֶׁלַח לָרֹב וּמָגִנִּים:

6 He appointed battle officers over the people; then, gathering them to him in the square of the city gate, he rallied them, saying,

ו וַיִּתֵּן שָׂרֵי מִלְחָמוֹת עַל־הָעָם וַיִּקְבְּצֵם אֵלָיו אֶל־רְחוֹב שַׁעַר הָעִיר וַיְדַבֵּר עַל־לְבָבָם לֵאמֹר:

7 "Be strong and of good courage; do not be frightened or dismayed by the king of Assyria or by the horde that is with him, for we have more with us than he has with him.

ז חִזְקוּ וְאִמְצוּ אַל־תִּירְאוּ וְאַל־תֵּחַתּוּ מִפְּנֵי מֶלֶךְ אַשּׁוּר וּמִלִּפְנֵי כָּל־הֶהָמוֹן אֲשֶׁר־עִמּוֹ כִּי־עִמָּנוּ רַב מֵעִמּוֹ:

8 With him is an arm of flesh, but with us is *Hashem* our God, to help us and to fight our battles." The people were encouraged by the speech of King *Chizkiyahu* of Yehuda.

ח עִמּוֹ זְרוֹעַ בָּשָׂר וְעִמָּנוּ יְהוָה אֱלֹהֵינוּ לְעָזְרֵנוּ וּלְהִלָּחֵם מִלְחֲמֹתֵנוּ וַיִּסָּמְכוּ הָעָם עַל־דִּבְרֵי יְחִזְקִיָּהוּ מֶלֶךְ־יְהוּדָה:

9 Afterward, King Sennacherib of Assyria sent his officers to *Yerushalayim* – he and all his staff being at *Lachish* – with this message to King *Chizkiyahu* of Yehuda and to all the people of Yehuda who were in *Yerushalayim*:

ט אַחַר זֶה שָׁלַח סַנְחֵרִיב מֶלֶךְ־אַשּׁוּר עֲבָדָיו יְרוּשָׁלַיְמָה וְהוּא עַל־לָכִישׁ וְכָל־מֶמְשַׁלְתּוֹ עִמּוֹ עַל־יְחִזְקִיָּהוּ מֶלֶךְ יְהוּדָה וְעַל־כָּל־יְהוּדָה אֲשֶׁר בִּירוּשָׁלַם לֵאמֹר:

10 "Thus said King Sennacherib of Assyria: On what do you trust to enable you to endure a siege in *Yerushalayim*?

י כֹּה אָמַר סַנְחֵרִיב מֶלֶךְ אַשּׁוּר עַל־מָה אַתֶּם בֹּטְחִים וְיֹשְׁבִים בְּמָצוֹר בִּירוּשָׁלָ͏ִם:

11 *Chizkiyahu* is seducing you to a death of hunger and thirst, saying, '*Hashem* our God will save us from the king of Assyria.'

יא הֲלֹא יְחִזְקִיָּהוּ מַסִּית אֶתְכֶם לָתֵת אֶתְכֶם לָמוּת בְּרָעָב וּבְצָמָא לֵאמֹר יְהוָה אֱלֹהֵינוּ יַצִּילֵנוּ מִכַּף מֶלֶךְ אַשּׁוּר:

12 But is not *Chizkiyahu* the one who removed His shrines and His altars and commanded the people of Yehuda and Yerushalayim saying, 'Before this one *Mizbayach* you shall prostrate yourselves, and upon it make your burnt offerings'?

יב הֲלֹא־הוּא יְחִזְקִיָּהוּ הֵסִיר אֶת־בָּמֹתָיו וְאֶת־מִזְבְּחֹתָיו וַיֹּאמֶר לִיהוּדָה וְלִירוּשָׁלַם לֵאמֹר לִפְנֵי מִזְבֵּחַ אֶחָד תִּשְׁתַּחֲווּ וְעָלָיו תַּקְטִירוּ:

13 Surely you know what I and my fathers have done to the peoples of the lands? Were the gods of the nations of the lands able to save their lands from me?

יג הֲלֹא תֵדְעוּ מֶה עָשִׂיתִי אֲנִי וַאֲבוֹתַי לְכֹל עַמֵּי הָאֲרָצוֹת הֲיָכוֹל יָכְלוּ אֱלֹהֵי גּוֹיֵ הָאֲרָצוֹת לְהַצִּיל אֶת־אַרְצָם מִיָּדִי:

14 Which of all the gods of any of those nations whom my fathers destroyed was able to save his people from me, that your God should be able to save you from me?

יד מִי בְּכָל־אֱלֹהֵי הַגּוֹיִם הָאֵלֶּה אֲשֶׁר הֶחֱרִימוּ אֲבוֹתַי אֲשֶׁר יָכוֹל לְהַצִּיל אֶת־עַמּוֹ מִיָּדִי כִּי יוּכַל אֱלֹהֵיכֶם לְהַצִּיל אֶתְכֶם מִיָּדִי:

15 Now then, do not let *Chizkiyahu* delude you; do not let him seduce you in this way; do not believe him. For no god of any nation or kingdom has been able to save his people from me or from my fathers – much less your God, to save you from me!"

טו וְעַתָּה אַל־יַשִּׁיא אֶתְכֶם חִזְקִיָּהוּ וְאַל־יַסִּית אֶתְכֶם כָּזֹאת וְאַל־תַּאֲמִינוּ לוֹ כִּי־לֹא יוּכַל כָּל־אֱלוֹהַּ כָּל־גּוֹי וּמַמְלָכָה לְהַצִּיל עַמּוֹ מִיָּדִי וּמִיַּד אֲבוֹתָי אַף כִּי אֱלֹהֵיכֶם לֹא־יַצִּילוּ אֶתְכֶם מִיָּדִי:

16 His officers said still more things against *Hashem* and against His servant *Chizkiyahu*.

טז וְעוֹד דִּבְּרוּ עֲבָדָיו עַל־יְהוָה הָאֱלֹהִים וְעַל יְחִזְקִיָּהוּ עַבְדּוֹ:

17 He also wrote letters reviling God of *Yisrael*, saying of Him, "Just as the gods of the other nations of the earth did not save their people from me, so the God of *Chizkiyahu* will not save his people from me."

יז וּסְפָרִים כָּתַב לְחָרֵף לַיהוָה אֱלֹהֵי יִשְׂרָאֵל וְלֵאמֹר עָלָיו לֵאמֹר כֵּאלֹהֵי גּוֹיֵ הָאֲרָצוֹת אֲשֶׁר לֹא־הִצִּילוּ עַמָּם מִיָּדִי כֵּן לֹא־יַצִּיל אֱלֹהֵי יְחִזְקִיָּהוּ עַמּוֹ מִיָּדִי:

¹⁸ They called loudly in the language of *Yehuda* to the people of *Yerushalayim* who were on the wall, to frighten them into panic, so as to capture the city.

יח וַיִּקְרְאוּ בְקוֹל־גָּדוֹל יְהוּדִית עַל־עַם יְרוּשָׁלַ͏ִם אֲשֶׁר עַל־הַחוֹמָה לְיָרְאָם וּלְבַהֲלָם לְמַעַן יִלְכְּדוּ אֶת־הָעִיר:

¹⁹ They spoke of the God of *Yerushalayim* as though He were like the gods of the other peoples of the earth, made by human hands.

יט וַיְדַבְּרוּ אֶל־אֱלֹהֵי יְרוּשָׁלָ͏ִם כְּעַל אֱלֹהֵי עַמֵּי הָאָרֶץ מַעֲשֵׂה יְדֵי הָאָדָם:

²⁰ Then King *Chizkiyahu* and the *Navi Yeshayahu* son of *Amotz* prayed about this, and cried out to heaven.

כ וַיִּתְפַּלֵּל יְחִזְקִיָּהוּ הַמֶּלֶךְ וִישַׁעְיָהוּ בֶן־אָמוֹץ הַנָּבִיא עַל־זֹאת וַיִּזְעֲקוּ הַשָּׁמָיִם:

²¹ *Hashem* sent an angel who annihilated every mighty warrior, commander, and officer in the army of the king of Assyria, and he returned in disgrace to his land. He entered the house of his god, and there some of his own offspring struck him down by the sword.

כא וַיִּשְׁלַח יְהוָה מַלְאָךְ וַיַּכְחֵד כָּל־גִּבּוֹר חַיִל וְנָגִיד וְשָׂר בְּמַחֲנֵה מֶלֶךְ אַשּׁוּר וַיָּשָׁב בְּבֹשֶׁת פָּנִים לְאַרְצוֹ וַיָּבֹא בֵּית אֱלֹהָיו וּמִיצִיאֵו [וּמִיצִיאָיו] מֵעָיו שָׁם הִפִּילֻהוּ בֶחָרֶב:

²² Thus *Hashem* delivered *Chizkiyahu* and the inhabitants of *Yerushalayim* from King Sennacherib of Assyria, and from everyone; He provided for them on all sides.

כב וַיּוֹשַׁע יְהוָה אֶת־יְחִזְקִיָּהוּ וְאֵת יֹשְׁבֵי יְרוּשָׁלַ͏ִם מִיַּד סַנְחֵרִיב מֶלֶךְ־אַשּׁוּר וּמִיַּד־כֹּל וַיְנַהֲלֵם מִסָּבִיב:

va-yo-SHA a-do-NAI et y'-khiz-ki-YA-hu v'-AYT yo-sh'-VAY
y'-ru-sha-LA-im mi-YAD san-khay-REEV me-lekh a-SHUR
u-mi-yad KOL vai-na-ha-LAYM mi-sa-VEEV

²³ Many brought tribute to *Hashem* to *Yerushalayim*, and gifts to King *Chizkiyahu* of *Yehuda*; thereafter he was exalted in the eyes of all the nations.

כג וְרַבִּים מְבִיאִים מִנְחָה לַיהוָה לִירוּשָׁלַ͏ִם וּמִגְדָּנוֹת לִיחִזְקִיָּהוּ מֶלֶךְ יְהוּדָה וַיִּנַּשֵּׂא לְעֵינֵי כָל־הַגּוֹיִם מֵאַחֲרֵי־כֵן:

²⁴ At that time, *Chizkiyahu* fell deathly sick. He prayed to *Hashem*, who responded to him and gave him a sign.

כד בַּיָּמִים הָהֵם חָלָה יְחִזְקִיָּהוּ עַד־לָמוּת וַיִּתְפַּלֵּל אֶל־יְהוָה וַיֹּאמֶר לוֹ וּמוֹפֵת נָתַן לוֹ:

²⁵ *Chizkiyahu* made no return for what had been bestowed upon him, for he grew arrogant; so wrath was decreed for him and for *Yehuda* and *Yerushalayim*.

כה וְלֹא־כִגְמֻל עָלָיו הֵשִׁיב יְחִזְקִיָּהוּ כִּי גָבַהּ לִבּוֹ וַיְהִי עָלָיו קֶצֶף וְעַל־יְהוּדָה וִירוּשָׁלָ͏ִם:

 32:22 *Hashem* delivered *Chizkiyahu* and the inhabitants of *Yerushalayim* *Chizkiyahu* was one of the greatest Jewish kings of all time. He abolished idolatry and improper worship and brought the people back to *Hashem*. The Sages teach that *Chizkiyahu* was so great that God considered making him the *Mashiach*, but decided not to, since *Chizkiyahu* failed to sing songs of praise to *Hashem* after being miraculously saved from Sennacherib's siege of *Yerushalayim*. Surely *Chizkiyahu* recognized and appreciated the miracle that

Date palms flourish in the Israeli desert

God had done for him and the people. Yet his faith in *Hashem* was so strong, and he was so confident in God's salvation, that he was not surprised by the miracle and therefore not moved to sing songs of praise. This failure to sing to *Hashem* in praise of the great miracle was the reason he forfeited the possibility of becoming the Messiah. God performs miracles on a daily basis in the personal lives of every individual and for the Nation of Israel living in the Land of Israel. We must never take His blessings for granted.

²⁶ Then *Chizkiyahu* humbled himself where he had been arrogant, he and the inhabitants of *Yerushalayim*, and no wrath of *Hashem* came on them during the reign of *Chizkiyahu*.

²⁷ *Chizkiyahu* enjoyed riches and glory in abundance; he filled treasuries with silver and gold, precious stones, spices, shields, and all lovely objects;

²⁸ and store-cities with the produce of grain, wine, and oil, and stalls for all kinds of beasts, and flocks for sheepfolds.

²⁹ And he acquired towns, and flocks of small and large cattle in great number, for *Hashem* endowed him with very many possessions.

³⁰ It was *Chizkiyahu* who stopped up the spring of water of Upper *Gichon*, leading it downward west of the City of *David*; *Chizkiyahu* prospered in all that he did.

³¹ So too in the matter of the ambassadors of the princes of Babylon, who were sent to him to inquire about the sign that was in the land, when *Hashem* forsook him in order to test him, to learn all that was in his mind.

³² The other events of *Chizkiyahu*'s reign, and his faithful acts, are recorded in the visions of the *Navi Yeshayahu* son of *Amotz* and in the book of the kings of *Yehuda* and *Yisrael*.

³³ *Chizkiyahu* slept with his fathers, and was buried on the upper part of the tombs of the sons of *David*. When he died, all the people of *Yehuda* and the inhabitants of *Yerushalayim* accorded him much honor. *Menashe*, his son, succeeded him.

33 ¹ *Menashe* was twelve years old when he became king, and he reigned fifty-five years in *Yerushalayim*.

² He did what was displeasing to *Hashem*, following the abhorrent practices of the nations that *Hashem* had dispossessed before the Israelites.

כו וַיִּכָּנַע יְחִזְקִיָּהוּ בְּגֹבַהּ לִבּוֹ הוּא וְיֹשְׁבֵי יְרוּשָׁלָםִ וְלֹא־בָא עֲלֵיהֶם קֶצֶף יְהֹוָה בִּימֵי יְחִזְקִיָּהוּ:

כז וַיְהִי לִיחִזְקִיָּהוּ עֹשֶׁר וְכָבוֹד הַרְבֵּה מְאֹד וְאֹצָרוֹת עָשָׂה־לוֹ לְכֶסֶף וּלְזָהָב וּלְאֶבֶן יְקָרָה וְלִבְשָׂמִים וּלְמָגִנִּים וּלְכֹל כְּלֵי חֶמְדָּה:

כח וּמִסְכְּנוֹת לִתְבוּאַת דָּגָן וְתִירוֹשׁ וְיִצְהָר וְאֻרָוֹת לְכָל־בְּהֵמָה וּבְהֵמָה וַעֲדָרִים לָאֲוֵרוֹת:

כט וְעָרִים עָשָׂה לוֹ וּמִקְנֵה־צֹאן וּבָקָר לָרֹב כִּי נָתַן־לוֹ אֱלֹהִים רְכוּשׁ רַב מְאֹד:

ל וְהוּא יְחִזְקִיָּהוּ סָתַם אֶת־מוֹצָא מֵימֵי גִיחוֹן הָעֶלְיוֹן וַיַּישְּׁרֵם לְמַטָּה־מַּעְרָבָה לְעִיר דָּוִיד וַיַּצְלַח יְחִזְקִיָּהוּ בְּכָל־מַעֲשֵׂהוּ:

לא וְכֵן בִּמְלִיצֵי שָׂרֵי בָּבֶל הַמְשַׁלְּחִים עָלָיו לִדְרשׁ הַמּוֹפֵת אֲשֶׁר הָיָה בָאָרֶץ עֲזָבוֹ הָאֱלֹהִים לְנַסּוֹתוֹ לָדַעַת כָּל־בִּלְבָבוֹ:

לב וְיֶתֶר דִּבְרֵי יְחִזְקִיָּהוּ וַחֲסָדָיו הִנָּם כְּתוּבִים בַּחֲזוֹן יְשַׁעְיָהוּ בֶן־אָמוֹץ הַנָּבִיא עַל־סֵפֶר מַלְכֵי־יְהוּדָה וְיִשְׂרָאֵל:

לג וַיִּשְׁכַּב יְחִזְקִיָּהוּ עִם־אֲבֹתָיו וַיִּקְבְּרֻהוּ בְּמַעֲלֵה קִבְרֵי בְנֵי־דָוִיד וְכָבוֹד עָשׂוּ־לוֹ בְמוֹתוֹ כָּל־יְהוּדָה וְיֹשְׁבֵי יְרוּשָׁלַםִ וַיִּמְלֹךְ מְנַשֶּׁה בְנוֹ תַּחְתָּיו:

לג א בֶּן־שְׁתֵּים עֶשְׂרֵה שָׁנָה מְנַשֶּׁה בְמָלְכוֹ וַחֲמִשִּׁים וְחָמֵשׁ שָׁנָה מָלַךְ בִּירוּשָׁלָםִ:

ב וַיַּעַשׂ הָרַע בְּעֵינֵי יְהֹוָה כְּתוֹעֲבוֹת הַגּוֹיִם אֲשֶׁר הוֹרִישׁ יְהֹוָה מִפְּנֵי בְּנֵי יִשְׂרָאֵל:

va-YA-as ha-RA b'-ay-NAY a-do-NAI k'-to-a-VOT ha-go-YIM a-SHER ho-REESH a-do-NAI mi-p'-NAY b'-NAY yis-ra-AYL

33:2 Following the abhorrent practices of the nations
Before entering the Land of Israel, *Hashem* tells the Children of Israel that remaining in the land is dependent upon their moral character. He

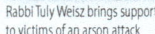

Rabbi Tuly Weisz brings support to victims of an arson attack

³ He rebuilt the shrines that his father *Chizkiyahu* had demolished; he erected altars for the Baals and made sacred posts. He bowed down to all the host of heaven and worshiped them,

ג וַיָּשָׁב וַיִּבֶן אֶת־הַבָּמוֹת אֲשֶׁר נִתַּץ יְחִזְקִיָּהוּ אָבִיו וַיָּקֶם מִזְבְּחוֹת לַבְּעָלִים וַיַּעַשׂ אֲשֵׁרוֹת וַיִּשְׁתַּחוּ לְכָל־צְבָא הַשָּׁמַיִם וַיַּעֲבֹד אֹתָם:

⁴ and he built altars [to them] in the House of *Hashem*, of which *Hashem* had said, "My name will be in *Yerushalayim* forever."

ד וּבָנָה מִזְבְּחוֹת בְּבֵית יְהוָה אֲשֶׁר אָמַר יְהוָה בִּירוּשָׁלַם יִהְיֶה־שְׁמִי לְעוֹלָם:

⁵ He built altars for all the host of heaven in the two courts of the House of *Hashem*.

ה וַיִּבֶן מִזְבְּחוֹת לְכָל־צְבָא הַשָּׁמָיִם בִּשְׁתֵּי חַצְרוֹת בֵּית־יְהוָה:

⁶ He consigned his sons to the fire in the Valley of Ben-hinnom, and he practiced soothsaying, divination, and sorcery, and consulted ghosts and familiar spirits; he did much that was displeasing to *Hashem* in order to vex Him.

ו וְהוּא הֶעֱבִיר אֶת־בָּנָיו בָּאֵשׁ בְּגֵי בֶן־הִנֹּם וְעוֹנֵן וְנִחֵשׁ וְכִשֵּׁף וְעָשָׂה אוֹב וְיִדְּעוֹנִי הִרְבָּה לַעֲשׂוֹת הָרַע בְּעֵינֵי יְהוָה לְהַכְעִיסוֹ:

⁷ He placed a sculptured image that he made in the House of *Hashem*, of which *Hashem* had said to *David* and to his son *Shlomo*, "In this House and in *Yerushalayim*, which I chose out of all the tribes of *Yisrael*, I will establish My name forever.

ז וַיָּשֶׂם אֶת־פֶּסֶל הַסֶּמֶל אֲשֶׁר עָשָׂה בְּבֵית הָאֱלֹהִים אֲשֶׁר אָמַר אֱלֹהִים אֶל־דָּוִיד וְאֶל־שְׁלֹמֹה בְנוֹ בַּבַּיִת הַזֶּה וּבִירוּשָׁלַם אֲשֶׁר בָּחַרְתִּי מִכֹּל שִׁבְטֵי יִשְׂרָאֵל אָשִׂים אֶת־שְׁמִי לְעֵילוֹם:

⁸ And I will never again remove the feet of *Yisrael* from the land that I assigned to their fathers, if only they observe faithfully all that I have commanded them – all the teaching and the laws and the rules given by *Moshe*."

ח וְלֹא אוֹסִיף לְהָסִיר אֶת־רֶגֶל יִשְׂרָאֵל מֵעַל הָאֲדָמָה אֲשֶׁר הֶעֱמַדְתִּי לַאֲבֹתֵיכֶם רַק אִם־יִשְׁמְרוּ לַעֲשׂוֹת אֵת כָּל־אֲשֶׁר צִוִּיתִים לְכָל־הַתּוֹרָה וְהַחֻקִּים וְהַמִּשְׁפָּטִים בְּיַד־מֹשֶׁה:

⁹ *Menashe* led *Yehuda* and the inhabitants of *Yerushalayim* astray into evil greater than that done by the nations that *Hashem* had destroyed before the Israelites.

ט וַיֶּתַע מְנַשֶּׁה אֶת־יְהוּדָה וְיֹשְׁבֵי יְרוּשָׁלָם לַעֲשׂוֹת רָע מִן־הַגּוֹיִם אֲשֶׁר הִשְׁמִיד יְהוָה מִפְּנֵי בְּנֵי יִשְׂרָאֵל:

¹⁰ *Hashem* spoke to *Menashe* and his people, but they would not pay heed,

י וַיְדַבֵּר יְהוָה אֶל־מְנַשֶּׁה וְאֶל־עַמּוֹ וְלֹא הִקְשִׁיבוּ:

¹¹ so *Hashem* brought against them the officers of the army of the king of Assyria, who took *Menashe* captive in manacles, bound him in fetters, and led him off to Babylon.

יא וַיָּבֵא יְהוָה עֲלֵיהֶם אֶת־שָׂרֵי הַצָּבָא אֲשֶׁר לְמֶלֶךְ אַשּׁוּר וַיִּלְכְּדוּ אֶת־מְנַשֶּׁה בַּחֹחִים וַיַּאַסְרֻהוּ בַּנְחֻשְׁתַּיִם וַיּוֹלִיכֻהוּ בָּבֶלָה:

¹² In his distress, he entreated *Hashem* his God and humbled himself greatly before the God of his fathers.

יב וּכְהָצֵר לוֹ חִלָּה אֶת־פְּנֵי יְהוָה אֱלֹהָיו וַיִּכָּנַע מְאֹד מִלִּפְנֵי אֱלֹהֵי אֲבֹתָיו:

warns them not to learn from or mimic the abominations of the peoples already living there, since doing so will lead to expulsion from the land, just as the nations originally living there were expelled (Deuteronomy 18:9–12). King *Menashe* explicitly violates this command, causing the People of Israel to follow "the abhorrent practices of the nations." As such, God responds by declaring that He will send away the remainder of the Nation of Israel and allow their enemies to defeat them (II Kings 21:14).

13 He prayed to Him, and He granted his prayer, heard his plea, and returned him to *Yerushalayim* to his kingdom. Then *Menashe* knew that *Hashem* alone was *Hashem*.

14 Afterward he built the outer wall of the City of *David* west of *Gichon* in the wadi on the way to the Fish Gate, and it encircled Ophel; he raised it very high. He also placed army officers in all the fortified towns of *Yehuda*.

15 He removed the foreign gods and the image from the House of *Hashem*, as well as all the altars that he had built on the Mount of the House of *Hashem* and in *Yerushalayim*, and dumped them outside the city.

16 He rebuilt the *Mizbayach* of *Hashem* and offered on it sacrifices of well-being and thanksgiving, and commanded the people of *Yehuda* to worship God of *Yisrael*.

17 To be sure, the people continued sacrificing at the shrines, but only to *Hashem* their God.

18 The other events of *Menashe*'s reign, and his prayer to his God, and the words of the seers who spoke to him in the name of God of *Yisrael* are found in the chronicles of the kings of *Yisrael*.

19 His prayer and how it was granted to him, the whole account of his sin and trespass, and the places in which he built shrines and installed sacred posts and images before he humbled himself are recorded in the words of Hozai.

20 *Menashe* slept with his fathers and was buried on his palace grounds; his son *Amon* succeeded him as king.

21 *Amon* was twenty-two years old when he became king, and he reigned two years in *Yerushalayim*.

22 He did what was displeasing to *Hashem*, as his father *Menashe* had done. *Amon* sacrificed to all the idols that his father *Menashe* had made and worshiped them.

23 He did not humble himself before *Hashem*, as his father *Menashe* had humbled himself; instead, *Amon* incurred much guilt.

24 His courtiers conspired against him and killed him in his palace.

יג וַיִּתְפַּלֵּל אֵלָיו וַיֵּעָתֶר לוֹ וַיִּשְׁמַע תְּחִנָּתוֹ וַיְשִׁיבֵהוּ יְרוּשָׁלַ͏ִם לְמַלְכוּתוֹ וַיֵּדַע מְנַשֶּׁה כִּי יְהֹוָה הוּא הָאֱלֹהִים:

יד וְאַחֲרֵי־כֵן בָּנָה חוֹמָה חִיצוֹנָה לְעִיר־דָּוִיד מַעְרָבָה לְגִיחוֹן בַּנַּחַל וְלָבוֹא בְשַׁעַר הַדָּגִים וְסָבַב לָעֹפֶל וַיַּגְבִּיהֶהָ מְאֹד וַיָּשֶׂם שָׂרֵי־חַיִל בְּכָל־הֶעָרִים הַבְּצֻרוֹת בִּיהוּדָה:

טו וַיָּסַר אֶת־אֱלֹהֵי הַנֵּכָר וְאֶת־הַסֶּמֶל מִבֵּית יְהֹוָה וְכָל־הַמִּזְבְּחוֹת אֲשֶׁר בָּנָה בְּהַר בֵּית־יְהֹוָה וּבִירוּשָׁלָ͏ִם וַיַּשְׁלֵךְ חוּצָה לָעִיר:

טז ויכן [וַיִּבֶן] אֶת־מִזְבַּח יְהֹוָה וַיִּזְבַּח עָלָיו זִבְחֵי שְׁלָמִים וְתוֹדָה וַיֹּאמֶר לִיהוּדָה לַעֲבוֹד אֶת־יְהֹוָה אֱלֹהֵי יִשְׂרָאֵל:

יז אֲבָל עוֹד הָעָם זֹבְחִים בַּבָּמוֹת רַק לַיהֹוָה אֱלֹהֵיהֶם:

יח וְיֶתֶר דִּבְרֵי מְנַשֶּׁה וּתְפִלָּתוֹ אֶל־אֱלֹהָיו וְדִבְרֵי הַחֹזִים הַמְדַבְּרִים אֵלָיו בְּשֵׁם יְהֹוָה אֱלֹהֵי יִשְׂרָאֵל הִנָּם עַל־דִּבְרֵי מַלְכֵי יִשְׂרָאֵל:

יט וּתְפִלָּתוֹ וְהֵעָתֶר־לוֹ וְכָל־חַטָּאתוֹ וּמַעְלוֹ וְהַמְּקֹמוֹת אֲשֶׁר בָּנָה בָהֶם בָּמוֹת וְהֶעֱמִיד הָאֲשֵׁרִים וְהַפְּסִלִים לִפְנֵי הִכָּנְעוֹ הִנָּם כְּתוּבִים עַל דִּבְרֵי חוֹזָי:

כ וַיִּשְׁכַּב מְנַשֶּׁה עִם־אֲבֹתָיו וַיִּקְבְּרֻהוּ בֵּיתוֹ וַיִּמְלֹךְ אָמוֹן בְּנוֹ תַּחְתָּיו:

כא בֶּן־עֶשְׂרִים וּשְׁתַּיִם שָׁנָה אָמוֹן בְּמָלְכוֹ וּשְׁתַּיִם שָׁנִים מָלַךְ בִּירוּשָׁלָ͏ִם:

כב וַיַּעַשׂ הָרַע בְּעֵינֵי יְהֹוָה כַּאֲשֶׁר עָשָׂה מְנַשֶּׁה אָבִיו וּלְכָל־הַפְּסִילִים אֲשֶׁר עָשָׂה מְנַשֶּׁה אָבִיו זִבַּח אָמוֹן וַיַּעַבְדֵם:

כג וְלֹא נִכְנַע מִלִּפְנֵי יְהֹוָה כְּהִכָּנַע מְנַשֶּׁה אָבִיו כִּי הוּא אָמוֹן הִרְבָּה אַשְׁמָה:

כד וַיִּקְשְׁרוּ עָלָיו עֲבָדָיו וַיְמִיתֻהוּ בְּבֵיתוֹ:

Chronicles

144

25 But the people of the land struck down all who had conspired against King *Amon*; and the people of the land made his son *Yoshiyahu* king in his stead.

כה וַיַּכּוּ עַם־הָאָרֶץ אֵת כָּל־הַקֹּשְׁרִים עַל־הַמֶּלֶךְ אָמוֹן וַיַּמְלִיכוּ עַם־הָאָרֶץ אֶת־יֹאשִׁיָּהוּ בְנוֹ תַּחְתָּיו:

34 1 *Yoshiyahu* was eight years old when he became king, and he reigned thirty-one years in *Yerushalayim*.

א בֶּן־שְׁמוֹנֶה שָׁנִים יֹאשִׁיָּהוּ בְמָלְכוֹ וּשְׁלֹשִׁים וְאַחַת שָׁנָה מָלַךְ בִּירוּשָׁלָ͏ִם:

2 He did what was pleasing to *Hashem*, following the ways of his father *David* without deviating to the right or to the left.

ב וַיַּעַשׂ הַיָּשָׁר בְּעֵינֵי יְהֹוָה וַיֵּלֶךְ בְּדַרְכֵי דָּוִיד אָבִיו וְלֹא־סָר יָמִין וּשְׂמֹאול:

3 In the eighth year of his reign, while he was still young, he began to seek the God of his father *David*, and in the twelfth year he began to purge *Yehuda* and *Yerushalayim* of the shrines, the sacred posts, the idols, and the molten images.

ג וּבִשְׁמוֹנֶה שָׁנִים לְמָלְכוֹ וְהוּא עוֹדֶנּוּ נַעַר הֵחֵל לִדְרוֹשׁ לֵאלֹהֵי דָּוִיד אָבִיו וּבִשְׁתֵּים עֶשְׂרֵה שָׁנָה הֵחֵל לְטַהֵר אֶת־יְהוּדָה וִירוּשָׁלַ͏ִם מִן־הַבָּמוֹת וְהָאֲשֵׁרִים וְהַפְּסִלִים וְהַמַּסֵּכוֹת:

4 At his bidding, they demolished the altars of the Baals, and he had the incense stands above them cut down; he smashed the sacred posts, the idols, and the images, ground them into dust, and strewed it onto the graves of those who had sacrificed to them.

ד וַיְנַתְּצוּ לְפָנָיו אֵת מִזְבְּחוֹת הַבְּעָלִים וְהַחַמָּנִים אֲשֶׁר־לְמַעְלָה מֵעֲלֵיהֶם גִּדֵּעַ וְהָאֲשֵׁרִים וְהַפְּסִלִים וְהַמַּסֵּכוֹת שִׁבַּר וְהֵדַק וַיִּזְרֹק עַל־פְּנֵי הַקְּבָרִים הַזֹּבְחִים לָהֶם:

5 He burned the bones of *Kohanim* on their altars and purged *Yehuda* and *Yerushalayim*.

ה וְעַצְמוֹת כֹּהֲנִים שָׂרַף עַל־מִזְבְּחוֹתִים [מִזְבְּחוֹתָם] וַיְטַהֵר אֶת־יְהוּדָה וְאֶת־יְרוּשָׁלָ͏ִם:

6 In the towns of *Menashe* and *Efraim* and *Shimon*, as far as *Naftali*, [lying] in ruins on every side,

ו וּבְעָרֵי מְנַשֶּׁה וְאֶפְרַיִם וְשִׁמְעוֹן וְעַד־נַפְתָּלִי בהר בתיהם [בְּחַרְבֹתֵיהֶם] סָבִיב:

7 he demolished the altars and the sacred posts and smashed the idols and ground them into dust; and he hewed down all the incense stands throughout the land of *Yisrael*. Then he returned to *Yerushalayim*.

ז וַיְנַתֵּץ אֶת־הַמִּזְבְּחוֹת וְאֶת־הָאֲשֵׁרִים וְהַפְּסִלִים כִּתַּת לְהֵדַק וְכָל־הַחַמָּנִים גִּדַּע בְּכָל־אֶרֶץ יִשְׂרָאֵל וַיָּשָׁב לִירוּשָׁלָ͏ִם:

8 In the eighteenth year of his reign, after purging the land and the House, he commissioned *Shafan* son of Azaliah, Maaseiah the governor of the city, and Joah son of Joahaz the recorder to repair the House of *Hashem* his God.

ח וּבִשְׁנַת שְׁמוֹנֶה עֶשְׂרֵה לְמָלְכוֹ לְטַהֵר הָאָרֶץ וְהַבָּיִת שָׁלַח אֶת־שָׁפָן בֶּן־אֲצַלְיָהוּ וְאֶת־מַעֲשֵׂיָהוּ שַׂר־הָעִיר וְאֵת יוֹאָח בֶּן־יוֹאָחָז הַמַּזְכִּיר לְחַזֵּק אֶת־בֵּית יְהֹוָה אֱלֹהָיו:

9 They came to the *Kohen Gadol Chilkiyahu* and delivered to him the silver brought to the House of *Hashem*, which the *Leviim*, the guards of the threshold, had collected from *Menashe* and *Efraim* and from all the remnant of *Yisrael* and from all *Yehuda* and *Binyamin* and the inhabitants of *Yerushalayim*.

ט וַיָּבֹאוּ אֶל־חִלְקִיָּהוּ הַכֹּהֵן הַגָּדוֹל וַיִּתְּנוּ אֶת־הַכֶּסֶף הַמּוּבָא בֵית־אֱלֹהִים אֲשֶׁר אָסְפוּ־הַלְוִיִּם שֹׁמְרֵי הַסַּף מִיַּד מְנַשֶּׁה וְאֶפְרַיִם וּמִכֹּל שְׁאֵרִית יִשְׂרָאֵל וּמִכָּל־יְהוּדָה וּבִנְיָמִן וישבי [וַיָּשֻׁבוּ] יְרוּשָׁלָ͏ִם:

10 They delivered it into the custody of the overseers who were in charge at the House of *Hashem*, and the overseers who worked in the House of *Hashem* spent it on examining and repairing the House.

11 They paid it out to the artisans and the masons to buy quarried stone and wood for the couplings and for making roof-beams for the buildings that the kings of *Yehuda* had allowed to fall into ruin.

12 The men did the work honestly; over them were appointed the *Leviim* Jahath and *Ovadya*, of the sons of *Merari*, and *Zecharya* and Meshullam, of the sons of *Kehat*, to supervise; while other *Leviim*, all the master musicians,

13 were over the porters, supervising all who worked at each and every task; some of the *Leviim* were scribes and officials and gatekeepers.

14 As they took out the silver that had been brought to the House of *Hashem*, the *Kohen Chilkiyahu* found a scroll of *Hashem*'s Teaching given by *Moshe*.

15 *Chilkiyahu* spoke up and said to the scribe *Shafan*, "I have found a scroll of the Teaching in the House of *Hashem*"; and *Chilkiyahu* gave the scroll to *Shafan*.

16 *Shafan* brought the scroll to the king and also reported to the king, "All that was entrusted to your servants is being done;

17 they have melted down the silver that was found in the House of *Hashem* and delivered it to those who were in charge, to the overseers."

18 The scribe *Shafan* also told the king, "The *Kohen Chilkiyahu* has given me a scroll"; and *Shafan* read from it to the king.

19 When the king heard the words of the Teaching, he tore his clothes.

20 The king gave orders to *Chilkiyahu*, and *Achikam* son of *Shafan*, and *Avdon* son of *Micha*, and the scribe *Shafan*, and Asaiah the king's minister, saying,

21 "Go, inquire of *Hashem* on my behalf and on behalf of those who remain in *Yisrael* and *Yehuda* concerning the words of the scroll that has been found, for great indeed must be the wrath of *Hashem* that has been poured down upon us because our fathers did not obey the word of *Hashem* and do all that is written in this scroll."

י וַיִּתְּנוּ עַל־יַד עֹשֵׂה הַמְּלָאכָה הַמֻּפְקָדִים בְּבֵית יְהוָה וַיִּתְּנוּ אֹתוֹ עוֹשֵׂי הַמְּלָאכָה אֲשֶׁר עֹשִׂים בְּבֵית יְהוָה לִבְדּוֹק וּלְחַזֵּק הַבָּיִת:

יא וַיִּתְּנוּ לֶחָרָשִׁים וְלַבֹּנִים לִקְנוֹת אַבְנֵי מַחְצֵב וְעֵצִים לַמְחַבְּרוֹת וּלְקָרוֹת אֶת־הַבָּתִּים אֲשֶׁר הִשְׁחִיתוּ מַלְכֵי יְהוּדָה:

יב וְהָאֲנָשִׁים עֹשִׂים בֶּאֱמוּנָה בַּמְּלָאכָה וַעֲלֵיהֶם מֻפְקָדִים יַחַת וְעֹבַדְיָהוּ הַלְוִיִּם מִן־בְּנֵי מְרָרִי וּזְכַרְיָה וּמְשֻׁלָּם מִן־בְּנֵי הַקְּהָתִים לְנַצֵּחַ וְהַלְוִיִּם כָּל־מֵבִין בִּכְלֵי־שִׁיר:

יג וְעַל הַסַּבָּלִים וּמְנַצְּחִים לְכֹל עֹשֵׂה מְלָאכָה לַעֲבוֹדָה וַעֲבוֹדָה וּמֵהַלְוִיִּם סוֹפְרִים וְשֹׁטְרִים וְשׁוֹעֲרִים:

יד וּבְהוֹצִיאָם אֶת־הַכֶּסֶף הַמּוּבָא בֵּית יְהוָה מָצָא חִלְקִיָּהוּ הַכֹּהֵן אֶת־סֵפֶר תּוֹרַת־יְהוָה בְּיַד־מֹשֶׁה:

טו וַיַּעַן חִלְקִיָּהוּ וַיֹּאמֶר אֶל־שָׁפָן הַסּוֹפֵר סֵפֶר הַתּוֹרָה מָצָאתִי בְּבֵית יְהוָה וַיִּתֵּן חִלְקִיָּהוּ אֶת־הַסֵּפֶר אֶל־שָׁפָן:

טז וַיָּבֵא שָׁפָן אֶת־הַסֵּפֶר אֶל־הַמֶּלֶךְ וַיָּשֶׁב עוֹד אֶת־הַמֶּלֶךְ דָּבָר לֵאמֹר כֹּל אֲשֶׁר־נִתַּן בְּיַד־עֲבָדֶיךָ הֵם עֹשִׂים:

יז וַיַּתִּיכוּ אֶת־הַכֶּסֶף הַנִּמְצָא בְּבֵית־יְהוָה וַיִּתְּנוּהוּ עַל־יַד הַמֻּפְקָדִים וְעַל־יַד עוֹשֵׂי הַמְּלָאכָה:

יח וַיַּגֵּד שָׁפָן הַסּוֹפֵר לַמֶּלֶךְ לֵאמֹר סֵפֶר נָתַן לִי חִלְקִיָּהוּ הַכֹּהֵן וַיִּקְרָא־בוֹ שָׁפָן לִפְנֵי הַמֶּלֶךְ:

יט וַיְהִי כִּשְׁמֹעַ הַמֶּלֶךְ אֵת דִּבְרֵי הַתּוֹרָה וַיִּקְרַע אֶת־בְּגָדָיו:

כ וַיְצַו הַמֶּלֶךְ אֶת־חִלְקִיָּהוּ וְאֶת־אֲחִיקָם בֶּן־שָׁפָן וְאֶת־עַבְדּוֹן בֶּן־מִיכָה וְאֵת שָׁפָן הַסּוֹפֵר וְאֵת עֲשָׂיָה עֶבֶד־הַמֶּלֶךְ לֵאמֹר:

כא לְכוּ דִרְשׁוּ אֶת־יְהוָה בַּעֲדִי וּבְעַד הַנִּשְׁאָר בְּיִשְׂרָאֵל וּבִיהוּדָה עַל־דִּבְרֵי הַסֵּפֶר אֲשֶׁר נִמְצָא כִּי־גְדוֹלָה חֲמַת־יְהוָה אֲשֶׁר נִתְּכָה בָנוּ עַל אֲשֶׁר לֹא־שָׁמְרוּ אֲבוֹתֵינוּ אֶת־דְּבַר יְהוָה לַעֲשׂוֹת כְּכָל־הַכָּתוּב עַל־הַסֵּפֶר הַזֶּה:

22 *Chilkiyahu* and those whom the king [had ordered] went to the *Neviah Chulda*, wife of *Shalum* son of Tokhath son of Hasrah, keeper of the wardrobe, who was living in *Yerushalayim* in the Mishneh, and spoke to her accordingly.

כב וַיֵּלֶךְ חִלְקִיָּהוּ וַאֲשֶׁר הַמֶּלֶךְ אֶל־חֻלְדָּה הַנְּבִיאָה אֵשֶׁת שַׁלֻּם בֶּן־תּוֹקְהַת [תָּקְהַת] בֶּן־חַסְרָה שׁוֹמֵר הַבְּגָדִים וְהִיא יוֹשֶׁבֶת בִּירוּשָׁלַ͏ִם בַּמִּשְׁנֶה וַיְדַבְּרוּ אֵלֶיהָ כָּזֹאת:

23 She responded to them: "Thus said God of *Yisrael*: Say to the man who sent you to Me,

כג וַתֹּאמֶר לָהֶם כֹּה־אָמַר יְהֹוָה אֱלֹהֵי יִשְׂרָאֵל אִמְרוּ לָאִישׁ אֲשֶׁר־שָׁלַח אֶתְכֶם אֵלָי:

24 'Thus said *Hashem*: I am going to bring disaster upon this place and its inhabitants – all the curses that are written in the scroll that was read to the king of *Yehuda* –

כד כֹּה אָמַר יְהֹוָה הִנְנִי מֵבִיא רָעָה עַל־הַמָּקוֹם הַזֶּה וְעַל־יוֹשְׁבָיו אֵת כָּל־הָאָלוֹת הַכְּתוּבוֹת עַל־הַסֵּפֶר אֲשֶׁר קָרְאוּ לִפְנֵי מֶלֶךְ יְהוּדָה:

25 because they forsook Me and made offerings to other gods in order to vex Me with all the works of their hands; My wrath shall be poured out against this place and not be quenched.'

כה תַּחַת אֲשֶׁר עֲזָבוּנִי וַיְקַטְּרוּ [וַיְקַטְּרוּ] לֵאלֹהִים אֲחֵרִים לְמַעַן הַכְעִיסֵנִי בְּכֹל מַעֲשֵׂי יְדֵיהֶם וְתִתַּךְ חֲמָתִי בַּמָּקוֹם הַזֶּה וְלֹא תִכְבֶּה:

26 But say this to the king of *Yehuda* who sent you to inquire of *Hashem*: 'Thus said God of *Yisrael*: As for the words which you have heard,

כו וְאֶל־מֶלֶךְ יְהוּדָה הַשֹּׁלֵחַ אֶתְכֶם לִדְרוֹשׁ בַּיהֹוָה כֹּה תֹאמְרוּ אֵלָיו כֹּה־אָמַר יְהֹוָה אֱלֹהֵי יִשְׂרָאֵל הַדְּבָרִים אֲשֶׁר שָׁמָעְתָּ:

27 since your heart was softened and you humbled yourself before *Hashem* when you heard His words concerning this place and its inhabitants, and you humbled yourself before Me and tore your clothes and wept before Me, I for My part have listened, declares *Hashem*.

כז יַעַן רַךְ־לְבָבְךָ וַתִּכָּנַע מִלִּפְנֵי אֱלֹהִים בְּשָׁמְעֲךָ אֶת־דְּבָרָיו עַל־הַמָּקוֹם הַזֶּה וְעַל־יֹשְׁבָיו וַתִּכָּנַע לְפָנַי וַתִּקְרַע אֶת־בְּגָדֶיךָ וַתֵּבְךְּ לְפָנָי וְגַם־אֲנִי שָׁמַעְתִּי נְאֻם־יְהֹוָה:

YA-an rakh l'-va-v'-KHA va-ti-ka-NA mi-lif-NAY e-lo-HEEM b'-shom-a-KHA et di-va-RAV al-ha-ma-KOM ha-ZEH v'-al yo-sh'-VAV va-ti-ka-NA l'-fa-NAI va-tik-RA et b'-ga-DE-kha va-TAYVK l'-fa-NAI v'-gam a-NEE sha-MA-tee n'-UM a-do-NAI

28 Assuredly, I will gather you to your fathers, and you will be laid in your grave in peace; your eyes shall see nothing of the disaster that I will bring upon this place and its inhabitants.'" They reported this back to the king.

כח הִנְנִי אֹסִפְךָ אֶל־אֲבֹתֶיךָ וְנֶאֱסַפְתָּ אֶל־קִבְרֹתֶיךָ בְּשָׁלוֹם וְלֹא־תִרְאֶינָה עֵינֶיךָ בְּכֹל הָרָעָה אֲשֶׁר אֲנִי מֵבִיא עַל־הַמָּקוֹם הַזֶּה וְעַל־יֹשְׁבָיו וַיָּשִׁיבוּ אֶת־הַמֶּלֶךְ דָּבָר:

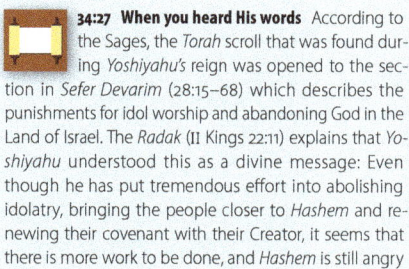

34:27 When you heard His words According to the Sages, the *Torah* scroll that was found during *Yoshiyahu's* reign was opened to the section in *Sefer Devarim* (28:15–68) which describes the punishments for idol worship and abandoning God in the Land of Israel. The *Radak* (II Kings 22:11) explains that *Yoshiyahu* understood this as a divine message: Even though he has put tremendous effort into abolishing idolatry, bringing the people closer to *Hashem* and renewing their covenant with their Creator, it seems that there is more work to be done, and *Hashem* is still angry with His people. Instead of giving up, *Yoshiyahu* is motivated to redouble his efforts to bring the people back to God. Hearing *Hashem's* "words concerning this place and its inhabitants," meaning that God is still planning to punish the people and exile them from *Eretz Yisrael*, is enough to motivate *Yoshiyahu* to intensify his efforts and to humble himself before *Hashem*.

Open *Torah* scroll

<table>
<tr>
<td>29 Then the king sent word and assembled all the elders of *Yehuda* and *Yerushalayim.*</td>
<td>כט וַיִּשְׁלַח הַמֶּלֶךְ וַיֶּאֱסֹף אֶת־כָּל־זִקְנֵי יְהוּדָה וִירוּשָׁלָ͏ִם:</td>
</tr>
</table>

30 The king went up to the House of *Hashem* with all the men of *Yehuda* and the inhabitants of *Yerushalayim* and the *Kohanim* and the *Leviim* – all the people, young and old – and he read to them the entire text of the covenant scroll that was found in the House of *Hashem.*

ל וַיַּעַל הַמֶּלֶךְ בֵּית־יְהוָה וְכָל־אִישׁ יְהוּדָה וְיֹשְׁבֵי יְרוּשָׁלַ͏ִם וְהַכֹּהֲנִים וְהַלְוִיִּם וְכָל־הָעָם מִגָּדוֹל וְעַד־קָטָן וַיִּקְרָא בְאָזְנֵיהֶם אֶת־כָּל־דִּבְרֵי סֵפֶר הַבְּרִית הַנִּמְצָא בֵּית יְהוָה:

31 The king stood in his place and solemnized the covenant before *Hashem*: to follow *Hashem* and observe His commandments, His injunctions, and His laws with all his heart and soul, to fulfill all the terms of the covenant written in this scroll.

לא וַיַּעֲמֹד הַמֶּלֶךְ עַל־עָמְדוֹ וַיִּכְרֹת אֶת־הַבְּרִית לִפְנֵי יְהוָה לָלֶכֶת אַחֲרֵי יְהוָה וְלִשְׁמוֹר אֶת־מִצְוֹתָיו וְעֵדְוֹתָיו וְחֻקָּיו בְּכָל־לְבָבוֹ וּבְכָל־נַפְשׁוֹ לַעֲשׂוֹת אֶת־דִּבְרֵי הַבְּרִית הַכְּתוּבִים עַל־הַסֵּפֶר הַזֶּה:

32 He obligated all the men of *Yerushalayim* and *Binyamin* who were present; and the inhabitants of *Yerushalayim* acted in accord with the Covenant of *Hashem*, God of their fathers.

לב וַיַּעֲמֵד אֵת כָּל־הַנִּמְצָא בִירוּשָׁלַ͏ִם וּבִנְיָמִן וַיַּעֲשׂוּ יֹשְׁבֵי יְרוּשָׁלַ͏ִם כִּבְרִית אֱלֹהִים אֱלֹהֵי אֲבוֹתֵיהֶם:

33 *Yoshiyahu* removed all the abominations from the whole territory of the Israelites and obliged all who were in *Yisrael* to worship *Hashem* their God. Throughout his reign they did not deviate from following God of their fathers.

לג וַיָּסַר יֹאשִׁיָּהוּ אֶת־כָּל־הַתּוֹעֵבוֹת מִכָּל־הָאֲרָצוֹת אֲשֶׁר לִבְנֵי יִשְׂרָאֵל וַיַּעֲבֵד אֵת כָּל־הַנִּמְצָא בְּיִשְׂרָאֵל לַעֲבוֹד אֶת־יְהוָה אֱלֹהֵיהֶם כָּל־יָמָיו לֹא סָרוּ מֵאַחֲרֵי יְהוָה אֱלֹהֵי אֲבוֹתֵיהֶם:

35 1 *Yoshiyahu* kept the *Pesach* for *Hashem* in *Yerushalayim*; the *Pesach* sacrifice was slaughtered on the fourteenth day of the first month.

לה א וַיַּעַשׂ יֹאשִׁיָּהוּ בִירוּשָׁלַ͏ִם פֶּסַח לַיהוָה וַיִּשְׁחֲטוּ הַפֶּסַח בְּאַרְבָּעָה עָשָׂר לַחֹדֶשׁ הָרִאשׁוֹן:

2 He reinstated the *Kohanim* in their shifts and rallied them to the service of the House of *Hashem.*

ב וַיַּעֲמֵד הַכֹּהֲנִים עַל־מִשְׁמְרוֹתָם וַיְחַזְּקֵם לַעֲבוֹדַת בֵּית יְהוָה:

3 He said to the *Leviim*, consecrated to *Hashem*, who taught all *Yisrael*, "Put the *Aron Kodesh* in the House that *Shlomo* son of *David*, king of *Yisrael*, built; as you no longer carry it on your shoulders, see now to the service of *Hashem* your God and His people *Yisrael*,

ג וַיֹּאמֶר לַלְוִיִּם הַמְּבוֹנִים [הַמְּבִינִים] לְכָל־יִשְׂרָאֵל הַקְּדוֹשִׁים לַיהוָה תְּנוּ אֶת־אֲרוֹן־הַקֹּדֶשׁ בַּבַּיִת אֲשֶׁר בָּנָה שְׁלֹמֹה בֶן־דָּוִיד מֶלֶךְ יִשְׂרָאֵל אֵין־לָכֶם מַשָּׂא בַּכָּתֵף עַתָּה עִבְדוּ אֶת־יְהוָה אֱלֹהֵיכֶם וְאֵת עַמּוֹ יִשְׂרָאֵל:

4 and dispose yourselves by clans according to your divisions, as prescribed in the writing of King *David* of *Yisrael* and in the document of his son *Shlomo,*

ד וְהָכוֹנוּ לְבֵית־אֲבוֹתֵיכֶם כְּמַחְלְקוֹתֵיכֶם בִּכְתָב דָּוִיד מֶלֶךְ יִשְׂרָאֵל וּבְמִכְתַּב שְׁלֹמֹה בְנוֹ:

5 and attend in the Sanctuary, by clan divisions, on your kinsmen, the people – by clan divisions of the *Leviim.*

ה וְעִמְדוּ בַקֹּדֶשׁ לִפְלֻגּוֹת בֵּית הָאָבוֹת לַאֲחֵיכֶם בְּנֵי הָעָם וַחֲלֻקַּת בֵּית־אָב לַלְוִיִּם:

6 Having sanctified yourselves, slaughter the *Pesach* sacrifice and prepare it for your kinsmen, according to the word of *Hashem* given by *Moshe*."

7 *Yoshiyahu* donated to the people small cattle – lambs and goats, all for *Pesach* sacrifices for all present – to the sum of 30,000, and large cattle, 3,000 – these from the property of the king.

8 His officers gave a freewill offering to the people, to the *Kohanim*, and to the *Leviim*. *Chilkiyahu* and *Zecharya* and *Yechiel*, the chiefs of the House of *Hashem*, donated to the *Kohanim* for *Pesach* sacrifices 2,600 [small cattle] and 300 large cattle.

9 Conaniah, *Shemaya*, and Nethanel, his brothers, and Hashabiah and Jeiel and Yozavad, officers of the *Leviim*, donated 5,000 [small cattle] and 500 large cattle to the *Leviim* for *Pesach* sacrifices.

10 The service was arranged well: the *Kohanim* stood at their posts and the *Leviim* in their divisions, by the king's command.

11 They slaughtered the *Pesach* sacrifice and the *Kohanim* [received its blood] from them and dashed it, while the *Leviim* flayed the animals.

12 They removed the parts to be burnt, distributing them to divisions of the people by clans, and making the sacrifices to *Hashem*, as prescribed in the scroll of *Moshe*; they did the same for the cattle.

13 They roasted the *Pesach* sacrifice in fire, as prescribed, while the sacred offerings they cooked in pots, cauldrons, and pans, and conveyed them with dispatch to all the people.

14 Afterward they provided for themselves and the *Kohanim*, for the Aaronite *Kohanim* were busy offering the burnt offerings and the fatty parts until nightfall, so the *Leviim* provided both for themselves and for the Aaronite *Kohanim*.

15 The Asaphite singers were at their stations, by command of *David* and *Asaf* and *Hayman* and *Yedutun*, the seer of the king; and the gatekeepers were at each and every gate. They did not have to leave their tasks, because their Levite brothers provided for them.

ו וְשַׁחֲטוּ הַפָּסַח וְהִתְקַדְּשׁוּ וְהָכִינוּ לַאֲחֵיכֶם לַעֲשׂוֹת כִּדְבַר־יְהֹוָה בְּיַד־מֹשֶׁה:

ז וַיָּרֶם יֹאשִׁיָּהוּ לִבְנֵי הָעָם צֹאן כְּבָשִׂים וּבְנֵי־עִזִּים הַכֹּל לַפְּסָחִים לְכָל־הַנִּמְצָא לְמִסְפַּר שְׁלֹשִׁים אֶלֶף וּבָקָר שְׁלֹשֶׁת אֲלָפִים אֵלֶּה מֵרְכוּשׁ הַמֶּלֶךְ:

ח וְשָׂרָיו לִנְדָבָה לָעָם לַכֹּהֲנִים וְלַלְוִיִּם הֵרִימוּ חִלְקִיָּה וּזְכַרְיָהוּ וִיחִיאֵל נְגִידֵי בֵּית הָאֱלֹהִים לַכֹּהֲנִים נָתְנוּ לַפְּסָחִים אַלְפַּיִם וְשֵׁשׁ מֵאוֹת וּבָקָר שְׁלֹשׁ מֵאוֹת:

ט וְכָנַנְיָהוּ [וְכָנַנְיָהוּ] וּשְׁמַעְיָהוּ וּנְתַנְאֵל אֶחָיו וַחֲשַׁבְיָהוּ וִיעִיאֵל וְיוֹזָבָד שָׂרֵי הַלְוִיִּם הֵרִימוּ לַלְוִיִּם לַפְּסָחִים חֲמֵשֶׁת אֲלָפִים וּבָקָר חֲמֵשׁ מֵאוֹת:

י וַתִּכּוֹן הָעֲבוֹדָה וַיַּעַמְדוּ הַכֹּהֲנִים עַל־עָמְדָם וְהַלְוִיִּם עַל־מַחְלְקוֹתָם כְּמִצְוַת הַמֶּלֶךְ:

יא וַיִּשְׁחֲטוּ הַפָּסַח וַיִּזְרְקוּ הַכֹּהֲנִים מִיָּדָם וְהַלְוִיִּם מַפְשִׁיטִים:

יב וַיָּסִירוּ הָעֹלָה לְתִתָּם לְמִפְלַגּוֹת לְבֵית־אָבוֹת לִבְנֵי הָעָם לְהַקְרִיב לַיהֹוָה כַּכָּתוּב בְּסֵפֶר מֹשֶׁה וְכֵן לַבָּקָר:

יג וַיְבַשְּׁלוּ הַפֶּסַח בָּאֵשׁ כַּמִּשְׁפָּט וְהַקֳּדָשִׁים בִּשְּׁלוּ בַּסִּירוֹת וּבַדְּוָדִים וּבַצֵּלָחוֹת וַיָּרִיצוּ לְכָל־בְּנֵי הָעָם:

יד וְאַחַר הֵכִינוּ לָהֶם וְלַכֹּהֲנִים כִּי הַכֹּהֲנִים בְּנֵי אַהֲרֹן בְּהַעֲלוֹת הָעוֹלָה וְהַחֲלָבִים עַד־לָיְלָה וְהַלְוִיִּם הֵכִינוּ לָהֶם וְלַכֹּהֲנִים בְּנֵי אַהֲרֹן:

טו וְהַמְשֹׁרְרִים בְּנֵי־אָסָף עַל־מַעֲמָדָם כְּמִצְוַת דָּוִיד וְאָסָף וְהֵימָן וִידֻתוּן חוֹזֵה הַמֶּלֶךְ וְהַשֹּׁעֲרִים לְשַׁעַר וָשָׁעַר אֵין לָהֶם לָסוּר מֵעַל עֲבֹדָתָם כִּי־אֲחֵיהֶם הַלְוִיִּם הֵכִינוּ לָהֶם:

16 The entire service of *Hashem* was arranged well that day, to keep the *Pesach* and to make the burnt offerings on the *Mizbayach* of *Hashem*, according to the command of King *Yoshiyahu*.

טז וַתִּכּוֹן כָּל־עֲבוֹדַת יְהֹוָה בַּיּוֹם הַהוּא לַעֲשׂוֹת הַפֶּסַח וְהַעֲלוֹת עֹלוֹת עַל מִזְבַּח יְהֹוָה כְּמִצְוַת הַמֶּלֶךְ יֹאשִׁיָּהוּ:

17 All the Israelites present kept the *Pesach* at that time, and the festival of *Pesach* for seven days.

יז וַיַּעֲשׂוּ בְנֵי־יִשְׂרָאֵל הַנִּמְצְאִים אֶת־הַפֶּסַח בָּעֵת הַהִיא וְאֶת־חַג הַמַּצּוֹת שִׁבְעַת יָמִים:

18 Since the time of the *Navi Shmuel*, no *Pesach* like that one had ever been kept in *Yisrael*; none of the kings of *Yisrael* had kept a *Pesach* like the one kept by *Yoshiyahu* and the *Kohanim* and the *Leviim* and all *Yehuda* and *Yisrael* there present and the inhabitants of *Yerushalayim*.

יח וְלֹא־נַעֲשָׂה פֶסַח כָּמֹהוּ בְּיִשְׂרָאֵל מִימֵי שְׁמוּאֵל הַנָּבִיא וְכָל־מַלְכֵי יִשְׂרָאֵל לֹא־עָשׂוּ כַּפֶּסַח אֲשֶׁר־עָשָׂה יֹאשִׁיָּהוּ וְהַכֹּהֲנִים וְהַלְוִיִּם וְכָל־יְהוּדָה וְיִשְׂרָאֵל הַנִּמְצָא וְיוֹשְׁבֵי יְרוּשָׁלָ͏ִם:

v'-LO na-a-SAH FE-sakh ka-MO-hu b'-yis-ra-AYL mee-MAY sh'-mu-AYL ha-na-VEE v'-khol mal-KHAY yis-ra-AYL lo a-SU ka-PE-sakh a-SHER a-SAH yo-shi-YA-hu v'-ha-ko-ha-NEEM v'-hal-vi-YIM v'-khol y'-hu-DAH v'-yis-ra-AYL ha-nim-TZA v'-yo-sh'-VAY y'-ru-sha-LA-im

19 That *Pesach* was kept in the eighteenth year of the reign of *Yoshiyahu*.

יט בִּשְׁמוֹנֶה עֶשְׂרֵה שָׁנָה לְמַלְכוּת יֹאשִׁיָּהוּ נַעֲשָׂה הַפֶּסַח הַזֶּה:

20 After all this furbishing of the Temple by *Yoshiyahu*, King Neco of Egypt came up to fight at Carchemish on the Euphrates, and *Yoshiyahu* went out against him.

כ אַחֲרֵי כָל־זֹאת אֲשֶׁר הֵכִין יֹאשִׁיָּהוּ אֶת־הַבַּיִת עָלָה נְכוֹ מֶלֶךְ־מִצְרַיִם לְהִלָּחֵם בְּכַרְכְּמִישׁ עַל־פְּרָת וַיֵּצֵא לִקְרָאתוֹ יֹאשִׁיָּהוּ:

21 [Neco] sent messengers to him, saying, "What have I to do with you, king of *Yehuda*? I do not march against you this day but against the kingdom that wars with me, and it is *Hashem*'s will that I hurry. Refrain, then, from interfering with *Hashem* who is with me, that He not destroy you."

כא וַיִּשְׁלַח אֵלָיו מַלְאָכִים לֵאמֹר מַה־לִּי וָלָךְ מֶלֶךְ יְהוּדָה לֹא־עָלֶיךָ אַתָּה הַיּוֹם כִּי אֶל־בֵּית מִלְחַמְתִּי וֵאלֹהִים אָמַר לְבַהֲלֵנִי חֲדַל־לְךָ מֵאֱלֹהִים אֲשֶׁר־עִמִּי וְאַל־יַשְׁחִיתֶךָ:

22 But *Yoshiyahu* would not let him alone; instead, he donned [his armor] to fight him, heedless of Neco's words from the mouth of *Hashem*; and he came to fight in the plain of Megiddo.

כב וְלֹא־הֵסֵב יֹאשִׁיָּהוּ פָּנָיו מִמֶּנּוּ כִּי לְהִלָּחֵם־בּוֹ הִתְחַפֵּשׂ וְלֹא שָׁמַע אֶל־דִּבְרֵי נְכוֹ מִפִּי אֱלֹהִים וַיָּבֹא לְהִלָּחֵם בְּבִקְעַת מְגִדּוֹ:

35:18 No *Pesach* like that one Like his great-grandfather *Chizkiyahu*, *Yoshiyahu* incorporates the *Pesach* ritual into the process of renewing the covenant with *Hashem*. However, the verse implies that the *Pesach* celebration in the time of *Yoshiyahu* was even greater than that of *Chizkiyahu*, stating that there had not been a Passover celebration like it since the days of *Shmuel*. Radak suggests that what made *Yoshiyahu*'s celebration greater than *Chizkiyahu*'s was the fact that it was celebrated by "all *Yehuda* and *Yisrael* there present." Whereas many of the remaining members of the king-dom of *Yisrael* had scorned *Chizkiyahu*'s invitation to celebrate the *Pesach* holiday together with the kingdom of *Yehuda* in *Yerushalayim* (II Chronicles 30:10), in *Yoshi-yahu*'s time, members of both kingdoms came together wholeheartedly in the service of *Hashem*. The unity of the Children of Israel is what enhanced the celebration beyond any that had taken place throughout the entire period of the kings.

Hands uniting for Israel

150

²³ Archers shot King *Yoshiyahu*, and the king said to his servants, "Get me away from here, for I am badly wounded."

²⁴ His servants carried him out of his chariot and put him in the wagon of his second-in-command, and conveyed him to *Yerushalayim*. There he died, and was buried in the grave of his fathers, and all *Yehuda* and *Yerushalayim* went into mourning over *Yoshiyahu*.

²⁵ *Yirmiyahu* composed laments for *Yoshiyahu* which all the singers, male and female, recited in their laments for *Yoshiyahu*, as is done to this day; they became customary in *Yisrael* and were incorporated into the laments.

²⁶ The other events of *Yoshiyahu*'s reign and his faithful deeds, in accord with the Teaching of *Hashem*,

²⁷ and his acts, early and late, are recorded in the book of the kings of *Yisrael* and *Yehuda*.

36 ¹ The people of the land took *Yehoachaz* son of *Yoshiyahu* and made him king instead of his father in *Yerushalayim*.

² *Yehoachaz* was twenty-three years old when he became king and he reigned three months in *Yerushalayim*.

³ The king of Egypt deposed him in *Yerushalayim* and laid a fine on the land of 100 silver *kikarim* and one gold *kikar*.

⁴ The king of Egypt made his brother Eliakim king over *Yehuda* and *Yerushalayim*, and changed his name to *Yehoyakim*; Neco took his brother Joahaz and brought him to Egypt.

⁵ *Yehoyakim* was twenty-five years old when he became king, and he reigned eleven years in *Yerushalayim*; he did what was displeasing to *Hashem* his God.

⁶ King Nebuchadnezzar of Babylon marched against him; he bound him in fetters to convey him to Babylon.

כג וַיֹּרוּ הַיֹּרִים לַמֶּלֶךְ יֹאשִׁיָּהוּ וַיֹּאמֶר הַמֶּלֶךְ לַעֲבָדָיו הַעֲבִירוּנִי כִּי הָחֳלֵיתִי מְאֹד:

כד וַיַּעֲבִירֻהוּ עֲבָדָיו מִן־הַמֶּרְכָּבָה וַיַּרְכִּיבֻהוּ עַל רֶכֶב הַמִּשְׁנֶה אֲשֶׁר־לוֹ וַיּוֹלִיכֻהוּ יְרוּשָׁלִַם וַיָּמָת וַיִּקָּבֵר בְּקִבְרוֹת אֲבֹתָיו וְכָל־יְהוּדָה וִירוּשָׁלִַם מִתְאַבְּלִים עַל־יֹאשִׁיָּהוּ:

כה וַיְקוֹנֵן יִרְמְיָהוּ עַל־יֹאשִׁיָּהוּ וַיֹּאמְרוּ כָל־הַשָּׁרִים ׀ וְהַשָּׁרוֹת בְּקִינוֹתֵיהֶם עַל־יֹאשִׁיָּהוּ עַד־הַיּוֹם וַיִּתְּנוּם לְחֹק עַל־יִשְׂרָאֵל וְהִנָּם כְּתוּבִים עַל־הַקִּינוֹת:

כו וְיֶתֶר דִּבְרֵי יֹאשִׁיָּהוּ וַחֲסָדָיו כַּכָּתוּב בְּתוֹרַת יְהוָֹה:

כז וּדְבָרָיו הָרִאשֹׁנִים וְהָאַחֲרֹנִים הִנָּם כְּתוּבִים עַל־סֵפֶר מַלְכֵי־יִשְׂרָאֵל וִיהוּדָה:

לו א וַיִּקְחוּ עַם־הָאָרֶץ אֶת־יְהוֹאָחָז בֶּן־יֹאשִׁיָּהוּ וַיַּמְלִיכֻהוּ תַחַת־אָבִיו בִּירוּשָׁלָ͏ִם:

ב בֶּן־שָׁלוֹשׁ וְעֶשְׂרִים שָׁנָה יוֹאָחָז בְּמָלְכוֹ וּשְׁלֹשָׁה חֳדָשִׁים מָלַךְ בִּירוּשָׁלָ͏ִם:

ג וַיְסִירֵהוּ מֶלֶךְ־מִצְרַיִם בִּירוּשָׁלָ͏ִם וַיַּעֲנֹשׁ אֶת־הָאָרֶץ מֵאָה כִכַּר־כֶּסֶף וְכִכַּר זָהָב:

ד וַיַּמְלֵךְ מֶלֶךְ־מִצְרַיִם אֶת־אֶלְיָקִים אָחִיו עַל־יְהוּדָה וִירוּשָׁלַ͏ִם וַיַּסֵּב אֶת־שְׁמוֹ יְהוֹיָקִים וְאֶת־יוֹאָחָז אָחִיו לָקַח נְכוֹ וַיְבִיאֵהוּ מִצְרָיְמָה:

ה בֶּן־עֶשְׂרִים וְחָמֵשׁ שָׁנָה יְהוֹיָקִים בְּמָלְכוֹ וְאַחַת עֶשְׂרֵה שָׁנָה מָלַךְ בִּירוּשָׁלָ͏ִם וַיַּעַשׂ הָרַע בְּעֵינֵי יְהוָֹה אֱלֹהָיו:

ו עָלָיו עָלָה נְבוּכַדְנֶאצַּר מֶלֶךְ בָּבֶל וַיַּאַסְרֵהוּ בַּנְחֻשְׁתַּיִם לְהֹלִיכוֹ בָּבֶלָה:

7 Nebuchadnezzar also brought some vessels of the House of *Hashem* to Babylon, and set them in his palace in Babylon.

ז וּמִכְּלֵי בֵּית יְהֹוָה הֵבִיא נְבוּכַדְנֶאצַּר לְבָבֶל וַיִּתְּנֵם בְּהֵיכָלוֹ בְּבָבֶל:

8 The other events of *Yehoyakim*'s reign, and the abominable things he did, and what was found against him, are recorded in the book of the kings of *Yisrael* and *Yehuda*. His son *Yehoyachin* succeeded him as king.

ח וְיֶתֶר דִּבְרֵי יְהוֹיָקִים וְתֹעֲבֹתָיו אֲשֶׁר־עָשָׂה וְהַנִּמְצָא עָלָיו הִנָּם כְּתוּבִים עַל־סֵפֶר מַלְכֵי יִשְׂרָאֵל וִיהוּדָה וַיִּמְלֹךְ יְהוֹיָכִין בְּנוֹ תַּחְתָּיו:

9 *Yehoyachin* was eight years old when he became king, and he reigned three months and ten days in *Yerushalayim*; he did what was displeasing to *Hashem*.

ט בֶּן־שְׁמוֹנֶה שָׁנִים יְהוֹיָכִין בְּמָלְכוֹ וּשְׁלֹשָׁה חֳדָשִׁים וַעֲשֶׂרֶת יָמִים מָלַךְ בִּירוּשָׁלָ͏ִם וַיַּעַשׂ הָרַע בְּעֵינֵי יְהֹוָה:

10 At the turn of the year, King Nebuchadnezzar sent to have him brought to Babylon with the precious vessels of the House of *Hashem*, and he made his kinsman *Tzidkiyahu* king over *Yehuda* and *Yerushalayim*.

י וְלִתְשׁוּבַת הַשָּׁנָה שָׁלַח הַמֶּלֶךְ נְבוּכַדְנֶאצַּר וַיְבִאֵהוּ בָבֶלָה עִם־כְּלֵי חֶמְדַּת בֵּית־יְהֹוָה וַיַּמְלֵךְ אֶת־צִדְקִיָּהוּ אָחִיו עַל־יְהוּדָה וִירוּשָׁלָ͏ִם:

11 *Tzidkiyahu* was twenty-one years old when he became king, and he reigned eleven years in *Yerushalayim*.

יא בֶּן־עֶשְׂרִים וְאַחַת שָׁנָה צִדְקִיָּהוּ בְמָלְכוֹ וְאַחַת עֶשְׂרֵה שָׁנָה מָלַךְ בִּירוּשָׁלָ͏ִם:

12 He did what was displeasing to *Hashem* his God; he did not humble himself before the *Navi Yirmiyahu*, who spoke for *Hashem*.

יב וַיַּעַשׂ הָרַע בְּעֵינֵי יְהֹוָה אֱלֹהָיו לֹא נִכְנַע מִלִּפְנֵי יִרְמְיָהוּ הַנָּבִיא מִפִּי יְהֹוָה:

13 He also rebelled against Nebuchadnezzar, who made him take an oath by *Hashem*; he stiffened his neck and hardened his heart so as not to turn to God of *Yisrael*.

יג וְגַם בַּמֶּלֶךְ נְבוּכַדְנֶאצַּר מָרָד אֲשֶׁר הִשְׁבִּיעוֹ בֵּאלֹהִים וַיֶּקֶשׁ אֶת־עָרְפּוֹ וַיְאַמֵּץ אֶת־לְבָבוֹ מִשּׁוּב אֶל־יְהֹוָה אֱלֹהֵי יִשְׂרָאֵל:

14 All the officers of the *Kohanim* and the people committed many trespasses, following all the abominable practices of the nations. They polluted the House of *Hashem*, which He had consecrated in *Yerushalayim*.

יד גַּם כָּל־שָׂרֵי הַכֹּהֲנִים וְהָעָם הִרְבּוּ לִמְעֹל־מַעַל כְּכֹל תֹּעֲבוֹת הַגּוֹיִם וַיְטַמְּאוּ אֶת־בֵּית יְהֹוָה אֲשֶׁר הִקְדִּישׁ בִּירוּשָׁלָ͏ִם:

15 God of their fathers had sent word to them through His messengers daily without fail, for He had pity on His people and His dwelling-place.

טו וַיִּשְׁלַח יְהֹוָה אֱלֹהֵי אֲבוֹתֵיהֶם עֲלֵיהֶם בְּיַד מַלְאָכָיו הַשְׁכֵּם וְשָׁלוֹחַ כִּי־חָמַל עַל־עַמּוֹ וְעַל־מְעוֹנוֹ:

16 But they mocked the messengers of *Hashem* and disdained His words and taunted His *Neviim* until the wrath of *Hashem* against His people grew beyond remedy.

טז וַיִּהְיוּ מַלְעִבִים בְּמַלְאֲכֵי הָאֱלֹהִים וּבוֹזִים דְּבָרָיו וּמִתַּעְתְּעִים בִּנְבִאָיו עַד עֲלוֹת חֲמַת־יְהֹוָה בְּעַמּוֹ עַד־לְאֵין מַרְפֵּא:

17 He therefore brought the king of the Chaldeans upon them, who killed their youths by the sword in their sanctuary; He did not spare youth, maiden, elder, or graybeard, but delivered all into his hands.

יז וַיַּעַל עֲלֵיהֶם אֶת־מֶלֶךְ כַּשְׂדִּיים [כַּשְׂדִּים] וַיַּהֲרֹג בַּחוּרֵיהֶם בַּחֶרֶב בְּבֵית מִקְדָּשָׁם וְלֹא חָמַל עַל־בָּחוּר וּבְתוּלָה זָקֵן וְיָשֵׁשׁ הַכֹּל נָתַן בְּיָדוֹ:

18 All the vessels of the House of *Hashem*, large and small, and the treasures of the House of *Hashem* and the treasures of the king and his officers were all brought to Babylon.

יח וְכֹל כְּלֵי בֵית הָאֱלֹהִים הַגְּדֹלִים וְהַקְּטַנִּים וְאֹצְרוֹת בֵּית יְהֹוָה וְאֹצְרוֹת הַמֶּלֶךְ וְשָׂרָיו הַכֹּל הֵבִיא בָבֶל:

19 They burned the House of *Hashem* and tore down the wall of *Yerushalayim*, burned down all its mansions, and consigned all its precious objects to destruction.

יט וַיִּשְׂרְפוּ אֶת־בֵּית הָאֱלֹהִים וַיְנַתְּצוּ אֵת חוֹמַת יְרוּשָׁלָ͏ִם וְכָל־אַרְמְנוֹתֶיהָ שָׂרְפוּ בָאֵשׁ וְכָל־כְּלֵי מַחֲמַדֶּיהָ לְהַשְׁחִית:

20 Those who survived the sword he exiled to Babylon, and they became his and his sons' servants till the rise of the Persian kingdom,

כ וַיֶּגֶל הַשְּׁאֵרִית מִן־הַחֶרֶב אֶל־בָּבֶל וַיִּהְיוּ־לוֹ וּלְבָנָיו לַעֲבָדִים עַד־מְלֹךְ מַלְכוּת פָּרָס:

21 in fulfillment of the word of *Hashem* spoken by *Yirmiyahu*, until the land paid back its *Shabbatot*; as long as it lay desolate it kept *Shabbat*, till seventy years were completed.

כא לְמַלֹּאות דְּבַר־יְהֹוָה בְּפִי יִרְמְיָהוּ עַד־רָצְתָה הָאָרֶץ אֶת־שַׁבְּתוֹתֶיהָ כָּל־יְמֵי הָשַּׁמָּה שָׁבָתָה לְמַלֹּאות שִׁבְעִים שָׁנָה:

22 And in the first year of King Cyrus of Persia, when the word of *Hashem* spoken by *Yirmiyahu* was fulfilled, *Hashem* roused the spirit of King Cyrus of Persia to issue a proclamation throughout his realm by word of mouth and in writing, as follows:

כב וּבִשְׁנַת אַחַת לְכוֹרֶשׁ מֶלֶךְ פָּרַס לִכְלוֹת דְּבַר־יְהֹוָה בְּפִי יִרְמְיָהוּ הֵעִיר יְהֹוָה אֶת־רוּחַ כּוֹרֶשׁ מֶלֶךְ־פָּרַס וַיַּעֲבֶר־קוֹל בְּכָל־מַלְכוּתוֹ וְגַם־בְּמִכְתָּב לֵאמֹר:

23 "Thus said King Cyrus of Persia: God of Heaven has given me all the kingdoms of the earth, and has charged me with building Him a House in *Yerushalayim*, which is in *Yehuda*. Any one of you of all His people, *Hashem* his God be with him and let him go up."

כג כֹּה־אָמַר כּוֹרֶשׁ מֶלֶךְ פָּרַס כָּל־מַמְלְכוֹת הָאָרֶץ נָתַן לִי יְהֹוָה אֱלֹהֵי הַשָּׁמַיִם וְהוּא־פָקַד עָלַי לִבְנוֹת־לוֹ בַיִת בִּירוּשָׁלַ͏ִם אֲשֶׁר בִּיהוּדָה מִי־בָכֶם מִכָּל־עַמּוֹ יְהֹוָה אֱלֹהָיו עִמּוֹ וְיָעַל:

koh a-MAR KO-resh ME-lekh pa-RAS kol mam-l'-KHOT ha-A-retz
NA-tan LEE a-do-NAI e-lo-HAY ha-sha-MA-yim v'-HU fa-KAD
a-LAI liv-NOT LO VA-yit bee-ru-sha-LA-im a-SHER bee-hu-DAH
mee va-KHEM mi-kol a-MO a-do-NAI e-lo-HAV i-MO v'-YA-al

36:23 Let him go up The last verse in the *Tanakh* calls upon the Jewish people to ascend to *Eretz Yisrael*. After decades of Babylonian rule, Cyrus grants permission for the exiled Jews to return to their land and rebuild the *Beit Hamikdash* in *Yerushalayim*. This was a fulfillment of the prophecy of *Yirmiyahu*, that after seventy years *Hashem* would return the Jewish people home (Jeremiah 29:10). Just as He fulfilled His word to return the People of Israel to the Land of Israel after the first exile, today as well God has begun to fulfill His promise to gather the exiles from the four corners of the earth and to bring the ultimate redemption (Deuteronomy 30:3–5). Since the establishment of the State of Israel, millions of Jews have returned home from over one hundred different countries. How fortunate are we to witness the beginning stages of the tremendous miracle of the ingathering of the exiles. May we soon merit the final fulfillment of the complete redemption of Israel and the entire world.

New immigrants at Ben Gurion airport

List of Transliterated Words in *The Israel Bible*

The following is a list of nouns which have been transliterated into Hebrew in the English translation and commentary of *The Israel Bible*:

Hebrew Name	English Name	Pronunciation	Hebrew
Achan	Achan	a-KHAN	עָכָן
Achav	Ahab	akh-AV	אַחְאָב
Achaz	Ahaz	a-KHAZ	אָחָז
Achazyahu	Ahaziah	a-khaz-YA-hu	אֲחַזְיָהוּ
Achiezer	Ahiezer	a-khee-E-zer	אֲחִיעֶזֶר
Achihud	Ahihud	a-khee-HUD	אֲחִיהוּד
Achikam	Ahikam	a-khee-KAM	אֲחִיקָם
Achilud	Ahilud	a-khee-LUD	אֲחִילוּד
Achimelech	Ahimelech	a-khee-ME-lekh	אֲחִימֶלֶךְ
Achira	Ahira	a-khee-RA	אֲחִירַע
Achisamach	Ahisamach	a-khee-sa-MAKH	אֲחִיסָמָךְ
Achitofel	Ahithophel	a-khee-TO-fel	אֲחִיתֹפֶל
Achituv	Ahitub	a-khee-TUV	אֲחִיטוּב
Achiya	Ahijah	a-khi-YAH	אֲחִיָּה
Adam	Adam	a-DAM	אָדָם
Adar	Adar	a-DAR	אֲדָר
Adoniyahu	Adonijah	a-do-ni-YA-hu	אֲדֹנִיָּהוּ
Adulam	Adullam	a-du-LAM	עֲדֻלָּם
Agur	Agur	a-GUR	אָגוּר
Aharon	Aaron	a-ha-RON	אַהֲרֹן
Amasa	Amasa	a-ma-SA	עֲמָשָׂא
Amatzya	Amaziah	a-matz-YAH	אֲמַצְיָה
Amen	Amen	a-MAYN	אָמֵן
Amiel	Ammiel	a-mee-AYL	עַמִּיאֵל
Aminadav	Amminadab	a-mee-na-DAV	עַמִּינָדָב
Amitai	Amittai	a-mi-TAI	אֲמִתַּי
Amnon	Amnon	am-NON	אַמְנוֹן

Hebrew Name	English Name	Pronunciation	Hebrew
Amon	Amon	a-MON	אָמוֹן
Amos	Amos	a-MOS	עָמוֹס
Amotz	Amoz	a-MOTZ	אָמוֹץ
Amram	Amram	am-RAM	עַמְרָם
Anatot	Anathoth	a-na-TOT	עֲנָתוֹת
Aron	Ark	a-RON	אָרוֹן
Aron HaBrit	Ark of the Covenant	a-RON ha-b'-REET	אָרוֹן הַבְּרִית
Arpachshad	Arpachshad	ar-pakh-SHAD	אַרְפַּכְשַׁד
Asa	Asa	a-SA	אָסָא
Asael	Asahel	a-sah-AYL	עֲשָׂהאֵל
Asaf	Asaph	a-SAF	אָסָף
Ashdod	Ashdod	ash-DOD	אַשְׁדוֹד
Asher	Asher	a-SHAYR	אָשֵׁר
Ashkelon	Ashkelon	ash-k'-LON	אַשְׁקְלוֹן
Atalya	Athaliah	a-tal-YAH	עֲתַלְיָה
Avdon	Abdon	av-DON	עַבְדּוֹן
Avichayil	Abihail	a-vee-KHA-yil	אֲבִיחַיִל
Avidan	Abidan	a-vee-DAN	אֲבִידָן
Avigail	Abigail	a-vee-GA-yil	אֲבִיגַיִל
Avihu	Abihu	a-vee-HU	אֲבִיהוּא
Avimelech	Abimelech	a-vee-ME-lekh	אֲבִימֶלֶךְ
Avinadav	Abinadab	a-vee-na-DAV	אֲבִינָדָב
Aviram	Abiram	a-vee-RAM	אֲבִירָם
Avishai	Abishai	a-vee-SHAI	אֲבִישַׁי
Aviya	Abijah	a-vi-YAH	אֲבִיָּה
Aviyam	Abijam	a-vi-YAM	אֲבִיָּם
Avner	Abner	av-NAYR	אַבְנֵר
Avraham	Abraham	av-ra-HAM	אַבְרָהָם
Avram	Abram	av-RAM	אַבְרָם
Avshalom	Absalom	av-sha-LOM	אַבְשָׁלוֹם
Azarya	Azariah	a-zar-YAH	עֲזַרְיָה
Azeika	Azekah	a-zay-KAH	עֲזֵקָה
Azza	Gaza	a-ZAH	עַזָּה

Hebrew Name	English Name	Pronunciation	Hebrew
B'nei Yisrael	The Children of Israel	b'-NAY yis-ra-AYL	בְּנֵי יִשְׂרָאֵל
Barak	Barak	ba-rakh-AYL	בָּרָק
Baruch	Baruch	ba-RUKH	בָּרוּךְ
Barzilai	Barzillai	bar-zi-LAI	בַּרְזִלַּי
Basha	Baasa	ba-SHA	בַּעְשָׁא
Batsheva	Bath-sheba	bat-SHE-va	בַּת־שֶׁבַע
Be'er Sheva	Beer-sheba	b'-AYR SHE-va	בְּאֵר שֶׁבַע
Be'eri	Beeri	b'-ay-REE	בְּאֵרִי
Beit Aven	Beth-aven	bayt A-ven	בֵּית אָוֶן
Beit El	Beth-el	bayt el	בֵּית אֵל
Beit Hamikdash	Temple	bayt ha-mik-DASH	בֵּית הַמִּקְדָּשׁ
Beit Lechem	Beth-lehem	bayt LE-khem	בֵּית לָחֶם
Beit Shean	Beth-shean	bayt sh'-AN	בֵּית שְׁאָן
Beit Shemesh	Beth-shemesh	bayt SHE-mesh	בֵּית שָׁמֶשׁ
Berechya	Berechiah	be-rekh-YAH	בֶּרֶכְיָה
Betzalel	Bezalel	b'-tzal-AYL	בְּצַלְאֵל
Bilha	Bilhah	bil-HAH	בִּלְהָה
Binyamin	Benjamin	bin-ya-MIN	בִּנְיָמִין
Boaz	Boaz	BO-az	בֹּעַז
Buki	Bukki	bu-KEE	בֻּקִּי
Buzi	Buzi	bu-ZEE	בּוּזִי
Carmel	Carmel	kar-MEL	כַּרְמֶל
Chachalya	Hacaliah	kha-khal-YAH	חֲכַלְיָה
Chagai	Haggai	kha-GAI	חַגַּי
Chana	Hannah	kha-NAH	חַנָּה
Chanamel	Hanamel	kha-nam-AYL	חֲנַמְאֵל
Chanani	Hanani	kha-NA-nee	חֲנָנִי
Chananya	Hananiah	kha-nan-YAH	חֲנַנְיָה
Chaniel	Hanniel	kha-nee-AYL	חַנִּיאֵל
Chanoch	Enoch	kha-NOKH	חֲנוֹךְ
Chava	Eve	kha-VAH	חַוָּה
Chavakuk	Habakkuk	kha-va-KUK	חֲבַקּוּק
Chermon	Hermon	kher-MON	חֶרְמוֹן

Hebrew Name	English Name	Pronunciation	Hebrew
Chetzron	Hezron	khetz-RON	חֶצְרוֹן
Chever	Heber	KHE-ver	חֶבֶר
Chevron	Hebron	khev-RON	חֶבְרוֹן
Chilkiyahu	Hilkiah	khil-ki-YA-hu	חִלְקִיָּהוּ
Chizkiyahu	Hezekiah	khiz-ki-YA-hu	חִזְקִיָּהוּ
Chofni	Hophni	khof-NEE	חָפְנִי
Chogla	Hoglah	khog-LAH	חָגְלָה
Chulda	Hulda	khul-DAH	חֻלְדָּה
Chur	Hur	Khur	חוּר
Dan	Dan	Dan	דָּן
Daniel	Daniel	da-ni-YAYL	דָּנִיֵּאל
Datan	Dathan	da-TAN	דָּתָן
David	David	da-VID	דָּוִד
Devora	Deborah	d'-vo-RAH	דְּבוֹרָה
Dina	Dinah	DEE-nah	דִּינָה
Doeg Ha'adomi	Doeg the Edomite	do-AYG ha-a-do-MEE	דּוֹאֵג הָאֲדֹמִי
Efraim	Ephraim	ef-RA-yim	אֶפְרַיִם
Efrat	Ephrat	ef-RAT	אֶפְרָתָה
Efrat	Ephrathah	ef-RA-tah	אֶפְרָתָה
Ehud	Ehud	ay-HUD	אֵהוּד
Eila	Elah	AY-lah	אֵלָה
Eilon	Elon	ay-LON	אֵילוֹן
Ein Gedi	En-gedi	ayn GE-dee	עֵין גֶּדִי
Elazar	Eleazar	el-a-ZAR	אֶלְעָזָר
Elchanan	Elhanan	el-kha-NAN	אֶלְחָנָן
Eli	Eli	ay-LEE	עֵלִי
Eliav	Eliab	e-lee-AV	אֱלִיאָב
Elidad	Elidad	e-lee-DAD	אֱלִידָד
Eliezer	Eliezer	e-lee-E-zer	אֱלִיעֶזֶר
Elimelech	Elimelech	e-lee-ME-lekh	אֱלִימֶלֶךְ
Elisha	Elisha	e-lee-SHA	אֱלִישָׁע
Elishama	Elishama	e-lee-sha-MA	אֱלִישָׁמָע
Elisheva	Elisheba	e-lee-SHE-va	אֱלִישֶׁבַע

Hebrew Name	English Name	Pronunciation	Hebrew
Elitzafan	Eli-zaphan	e-lee-tza-FAN	אֱלִיצָפָן
Elitzur	Elizur	e-lee-TZUR	אֱלִיצוּר
Eliyahu	Elijah	ay-li-YA-hu	אֵלִיָּהוּ
Elkana	Elkanah	el-ka-NAH	אֶלְקָנָה
Elyasaf	Eliasaph	el-ya-SAF	אֶלְיָסָף
Elyashiv	Eliashib	el-ya-SHEEV	אֶלְיָשִׁיב
Enosh	Enosh	e-NOSH	אֱנוֹשׁ
Er	Er	ayr	עֵר
Eshtaol	Eshtaol	esh-ta-OL	אֶשְׁתָּאֹל
Esther	Esther	es-TAYR	אֶסְתֵּר
Eved Melech	Ebed-melech	E-ved ME-lekh	עֶבֶד־מֶלֶךְ
Even Ha-Ezer	Eben-Ezer	E-ven ha-E-zer	אֶבֶן הָעֵזֶר
Ever	Eber	AY-ver	עֵבֶר
Evyatar	Abiathar	ev-ya-TAR	אֶבְיָתָר
Ezra	Ezra	ez-RA	עֶזְרָא
Gad	Gad	gad	גָּד
Gadi	Gaddi	ga-DEE	גַּדִּי
Gadiel	Gaddiel	ga-dee-AYL	גַּדִּיאֵל
Gamliel	Gamaliel	gam-lee-AYL	גַּמְלִיאֵל
Gedalia	Gedaliah	g'-dal-YA (hu)	גְּדַלְיָהוּ
Gedera	Gederah	g'-day-RAH	גְּדֵרָה
Gershom	Gershom	gay-r'-SHOM	גֵּרְשׁוֹם
Gershon	Gershon	gay-r'-SHON	גֵּרְשׁוֹן
Geshem	Geshem	GE-shem	גֶּשֶׁם
Geuel	Geuel	g'-u-AYL	גְּאוּאֵל
Gidon	Gideon	gid-ON	גִּדְעוֹן
Gilad	Gilead	gil-AD	גִּלְעָד
Gilgal	Gilgal	gil-GAL	גִּלְגָּל
Giva	Gibeah	giv-AH	גִּבְעָה
Givon	Gibeon	giv-ON	גִּבְעוֹן
Hadassa	Hadassah	ha-da-SAH	הֲדַסָּה
Har Eival	Mount Ebal	ay-VAL	הַר עֵיבָל
Har Gerizim	Mount Gerizim	g'-ri-ZEEM	הַר גְּרִזִים

Hebrew Name	English Name	Pronunciation	Hebrew
Har HaBayit	Temple Mount	har ha-BA-yit	הַר הַבַּיִת
Har HaZeitim	the Mount of Olives	har ha-zay-TEEM	הַר הַזֵּיתִים
Hashem	Lord/God		
Hayman	Heman	hay-MAN	הֵימָן
Hoshea	Hosea	ho-SHAY-a	הוֹשֵׁעַ
Ido	Iddo	i-DO	עִדּוֹ
Imanu-El	Immanuel	i-MA-nu ayl	עִמָּנוּ אֵל
Ish-boshet	Ish-bosheth	eesh BO-shet	אִישׁ־בֹּשֶׁת
Itamar	Ithamar	ee-ta-MAR	אִיתָמָר
Itiel	Ithiel	ee-tee-AYL	אִיתִיאֵל
Ivtzan	Ibzan	iv-TZAN	אִבְצָן
Iyov	Job	i-YOV	אִיּוֹב
Kadmiel	Kadmiel	kad-mee-AYL	קַדְמִיאֵל
Kalev	Caleb	ka-LAYV	כָּלֵב
Keesh	Kish	keesh	קִישׁ
Kehat	Kohath	k'-HAT	קְהָת
Keinan	Kenan	kay-NAN	קֵינָן
Kemuel	Kemuel	k'-mu-AYL	קְמוּאֵל
Keruvim	Cherubim	k'-ru-VEEM	כְּרוּבִים
Kilyon	Chilion	kil-YON	כִּלְיוֹן
Kiryat Arba	Kiriath-arba	keer-YAT AR-bah	קִרְיַת אַרְבַּע
Kiryat Sefer	Kiriath-sepher	keer-YAT SAY-fer	קִרְיַת־סֵפֶר
Kiryat Ye'arim	Kiriath-jearim	keer-YAT y'-a-REEM	קִרְיַת יְעָרִים
Kislev	Chislev	kis-LAYV	כִּסְלֵו
Kohanim	Priests	ko-ha-NEEM	כֹּהֲנִים
Kohelet	Koheleth	ko-HE-let	קֹהֶלֶת
Kohen	Priest	ko-HAYN	כֹּהֵן
Kohen Gadol	High Priest	ko-HAYN ga-DOL	כֹּהֵן גָּדוֹל
Korach	Korah	KO-rakh	קֹרַח
Kushi	Cushi	ku-SHEE	כּוּשִׁי
Lachish	Lachish	la-KHEESH	לָכִישׁ
Leah	Leah	lay-AH	לֵאָה
Lemech	Lamech	LE-mekh	לֶמֶךְ

160

Hebrew Name	English Name	Pronunciation	Hebrew
Lemuel	Lemuel	l'-mu-AYL	לְמוֹאֵל
Levi	Levi	lay-VEE	לֵוִי
Leviim	Levites	l'-vee-IM	לְוִים
Machla	Mahlah	makh-LAH	מַחְלָה
Machlon	Mahlon	makh-LON	מַחְלוֹן
Machseya	Mahseiah	makh-say-YAH	מַחְסֵיָה
Malachi	Malachi	mal-a-KHEE	מַלְאָכִי
Manoach	Manoah	ma-NO-akh	מָנוֹחַ
Mashiach	Messiah	ma-SHEE-akh	מָשִׁיחַ
Mefiboshet	Mephibosheth	m'-fee-VO-shet	מְפִיבֹשֶׁת
Mehalalel	Mahalalel	ma-ha-lal-AYL	מַהֲלַלְאֵל
Menachem	Menahem	m'-na-KHAYM	מְנַחֵם
Menashe	Menasseh	m'-na-SHEH	מְנַשֶּׁה
Menorah	Candlestick	m'-no-RAH	מְנֹרָה
Merari	Merari	m'-ra-REE	מְרָרִי
Metushelach	Methusaleh	m'-tu-SHE-lakh	מְתוּשָׁלַח
Micha	Micah	mee-KHAH	מִיכָה
Michael	Michael	mee-kha-AYL	מִיכָאֵל
Michaihu	Micaiah	mee-KHAI-hu	מִיכָיְהוּ
Michal	Michal	mee-KHAL	מִיכַל
Milka	Milcah	mil-KAH	מִלְכָּה
Miriam	Miriam	mir-YAM	מִרְיָם
Mishael	Mishael	mee-sha-AYL	מִישָׁאֵל
Mishkan	Tabernacle	mish-KAN	מִשְׁכָּן
Mitzpa	Mizpah	mitz-PAH	מִצְפָּה
Mizbayach	Altar	miz-BAY-akh	מִזְבֵּחַ
Mordechai	Mordecai	mor-d'-KHAI	מָרְדְּכַי
Moriah	Moriah	mo-ri-YAH	מוֹרִיָּה
Moshe	Moses	mo-SHEH	מֹשֶׁה
Nachbi	Nahbi	nakh-BEE	נַחְבִּי
Nachor	Nahor	na-KHOR	נָחוֹר
Nachshon	Nahshon	nakh-SHON	נַחְשׁוֹן
Nachum	Nahum	na-KHUM	נַחוּם

Hebrew Name	English Name	Pronunciation	Hebrew
Nadav	Nadab	na-DAV	נָדָב
Naftali	Naphtali	naf-ta-LEE	נַפְתָּלִי
Naomi	Naomi	na-o-MEE	נָעֳמִי
Natan	Nathan	na-TAN	נָתָן
Naval	Nabal	na-VAL	נָבָל
Navi	Prophet	na-VEE	נָבִיא
Navot	Naboth	na-VAL	נָבָל
Nechemya	Nehemiah	n'-khem-YAH	נְחֶמְיָה
Negev	Negeb	NE-gev	נֶגֶב
Nerya	Neriah	nay-ri-YAH	נֵרִיָּה
Netanel	Nethanel	n'-tan-AYL	נְתַנְאֵל
Neviah	Prophetess	n'-vee-AH	נְבִיאָה
Neviim	Prophets	n'-vee-EEM	נְבִיאִים
Nisan	Nisan	nee-SAN	נִיסָן
Noa	Noah	no-AH	נֹעָה
Noach	Noah	NO-akh	נֹחַ
Nov	Nob	nov	נֹב
Nun	Nun	nun	נוּן
Oded	Oded	o-DAYD	עוֹדֵד
Ohola	Oholah	a-ho-LAH	אָהֳלָה
Oholiav	Oholiab	o-ha-lee-AV	אָהֳלִיאָב
Oholiva	Oholibah	a-ho-lee-VAH	אָהֳלִיבָה
Omri	Omri	om-REE	עָמְרִי
Onan	Onan	o-NAN	אוֹנָן
Otniel	Othniel	ot-nee-AYL	עָתְנִיאֵל
Ovadya	Obadiah	o-vad-YAH	עֹבַדְיָה
Oved	Obed	o-VAYD	עוֹבֵד
Oved Edom	Obed Edom	o-VAYD e-DOM	עוֹבֵד אֱדֹם
Pagiel	Pagiel	pag-ee-AYL	פַּגְעִיאֵל
Palti	Palti	pal-TEE	פַּלְטִי
Paltiel	Paltiel	pal-tee-AYL	פַּלְטִיאֵל
Pekach	Pekah	PE-kakh	פֶּקַח
Pedael	Pedahel	p'-da-AYL	פְּדַהְאֵל

162

Hebrew Name	English Name	Pronunciation	Hebrew
Pekachya	Pekahiah	p'-kakh-YAH	פְּקַחְיָה
Peleg	Peleg	PE-leg	פֶּלֶג
Penina	Peninnah	p'-ni-NAH	פְּנִנָּה
Peretz	Perez	PE-retz	פֶּרֶץ
Petuel	Pethuel	p'-tu-AYL	פְּתוּאֵל
Pinchas	Phinehas	peen-KHAS	פִּינְחָס
Rachel	Rachel	ra-KHAYL	רָחֵל
Ram	Ram	ram	רָם
Rama	Ramah	ra-MAH	רָמָה
Re'u	Reu	r'-U	רְעוּ
Rechovam	Rehoboam	r'-khav-AM	רְחַבְעָם
Reuven	Reuben	r'-u-VAYN	רְאוּבֵן
Rivka	Rebecca	riv-KAH	רִבְקָה
Rut	Ruth	rut	רוּת
Salma	Salmon/Salmah	sal-MAH	שַׂלְמָה
Salmon	Salmon	sal-MON	שַׂלְמוֹן
Sara	Sarah	sa-RAH	שָׂרָה
Sarai	Sarai	sa-RAI	שָׂרַי
Selah	Selah	SE-lah	סֶלָה
Seraya	Seraiah	s'-ra-YAH	שְׂרָיָה
Serug	Serug	s'-RUG	שְׂרוּג
Setur	Sethur	s'-TUR	סְתוּר
Shaarayim	Shaaraim	sha-a-RA-yim	שַׁעֲרַיִם
Shabbat	Sabbath	sha-BAT	שַׁבָּת
Shabbatot	Sabbaths	sha-ba-TOT	שַׁבָּתוֹת
Shafan	Shaphan	sha-FAN	שָׁפָן
Shafat	Shaphat	sha-FAT	שָׁפָט
Shalem	Salem	sha-LAYM	שָׁלֵם
Shalum	Shallum	sha-LUM	שַׁלּוּם
Shamgar	Shamgar	sham-GAR	שַׁמְגַּר
Shamua	Shammua	sha-MU-a	שַׁמּוּעַ
Shaul	Saul	sha-UL	שָׁאוּל
Shealtiel	Shealtiel	sh'-al-tee-AYL	שְׁאַלְתִּיאֵל

Hebrew Name	English Name	Pronunciation	Hebrew
Shear Yashuv	Shear-Jashub	sh'-AR ya-SHUV	שְׁאָר יָשׁוּב
Shechanya	Shecaniah	sh'-khan-YAH	שְׁכַנְיָה
Shechem	Shechem	sh'-KHEM	שְׁכֶם
Sheila	Shelah	shay-LAH	שֵׁלָה
Shelach	Shelah	SHE-lakh	שֶׁלַח
Shelumiel	Shelumiel	sh'-lu-mee-AYL	שְׁלֻמִיאֵל
Shem	Shem	Shaym	שֵׁם
Shemaya	Shemaiah	sh'-ma-YAH	שְׁמַעְיָה
Sheshbatzar	Sheshbazzar	shaysh-ba-TZAR	שֵׁשְׁבַּצַּר
Shet	Seth	Shayt	שֵׁת
Shevat	Shebat	sh'-VAT	שְׁבָט
Shilo	Shiloh	shi-LOH	שִׁלֹה
Shim'i	Shimei	shim-EE	שִׁמְעִי
Shimon	Simeon	shim-ON	שִׁמְעוֹן
Shimshon	Samson	shim-SHON	שִׁמְשׁוֹן
Shlomo	Solomon	sh'-lo-MOH	שְׁלֹמֹה
Shmuel	Samuel	sh'-mu-AYL	שְׁמוּאֵל
Shofar	Horn	sho-FAR	שׁוֹפָר
Shofarot	Horns	sho-fa-ROT	שׁוֹפָרוֹת
Shomron	Samaria	sho-m'-RON	שֹׁמְרוֹן
Sivan	Sivan	see-VAN	סִיוָן
Tamar	Tamar	ta-MAR	תָּמָר
Tanakh	Hebrew Bible	ta-NAKH	תָּנָ"ךְ
Tapuach	Tappuah	ta-PU-akh	תַּפּוּחַ
Tavor	Tabor	ta-VOR	תָּבוֹר
Tekoa	Tekoa	t'-KO-a	תְּקוֹעָה
Terach	Terah	TE-rakh	תֶּרַח
Teveria	Tiberias	t'-ver-YAH	טְבֶרְיָה
Tevet	Tebeth	tay-VAYT	טֵבֵת
Tirtza	Tirzah	tir-TZAH	תִּרְצָה
Tola	Tola ˈ	to-LA	תּוֹלָע
Tzadok	Zadok	tza-DOK	צָדוֹק
Tzefanya	Zephaniah	tz'-fan-YAH	צְפַנְיָה

164

Hebrew Name	English Name	Pronunciation	Hebrew
Tzelofchad	Zelophehad	tz'-lo-f-KHAD	צְלָפְחָד
Tzeruya	Zeruiah	tz'-ru-YAH	צְרוּיָה
Tzfat	Safed	tz'-FAT	צְפַת
Tzidkiyahu	Zedekiah	tzid-ki-YA-hu	צִדְקִיָּהוּ
Tziklag	Ziklag	tzi-k'-LAG	צִקְלַג
Tzion	Zion	tzi-YON	צִיּוֹן
Tzipora	Zipporah	tzi-po-RAH	צִפֹּרָה
Tzora	Zorah	tzor-AH	צָרְעָה
Tzuriel	Zuriel	tzu-ree-AYL	צוּרִיאֵל
Ukal	Ucal	u-KAL	אֻכָל
Uri	Uri	u-REE	אוּרִי
Uriya	Uriah	u-ri-YAH	אוּרִיָּה
Utz	Uz	Utz	עוּץ
Uzziyahu	Uzziah	u-zi-YA-hu	עֻזִּיָּהוּ
Yaakov	Jacob	ya-a-KOV	יַעֲקֹב
Yachaziel	Jahaziel	ya-kha-zee-AYL	יַחֲזִיאֵל
Yael	Jael	ya-AYL	יָעֵל
Yaffo	Joppa/Jaffa	ya-FO	יָפוֹ
Yair	Jair	ya-EER	יָאִיר
Yakeh	Jakeh	ya-KEH	יָקֶה
Yarden	Jordan	yar-DAYN	יַרְדֵּן
Yarmut	Jarmuth	yar-MUT	יַרְמוּת
Yechezkel	Ezekiel	y'-khez-KAYL	יְחֶזְקֵאל
Yechiel	Jehiel	y'-khee-AYL	יְחִיאֵל
Yechonya	Jeconiah	y'-khon-YAH	יְכָנְיָה
Yedutun	Jeduthun	y'-du-TUN	יְדוּתוּן
Yehoachaz	Jehoahaz	y'-ho-a-KHAZ	יְהוֹאָחָז
Yehoash	Jehoash	y'-ho-ASH	יְהוֹאָשׁ
Yehochanan	Jehohanan	y'-ho-kha-NAN	יְהוֹחָנָן
Yehonatan	Jonathan	y'-ho-na-TAN	יְהוֹנָתָן
Yehoram	Jehoram	y'-ho-RAM	יְהוֹרָם
Yehoshafat	Jehoshaphat	y'-ho-sha-FAT	יְהוֹשָׁפָט
Yehoshavat	Jehoshabeath	y'-ho-shav-AT	יְהוֹשַׁבְעַת

Hebrew Name	English Name	Pronunciation	Hebrew
Yehosheva	Jehosheba	y-ho-SHE-va	יְהוֹשֶׁבַע
Yehoshua	Joshua	y'-ho-SHU-a	יְהוֹשֻׁעַ
Yehotzadak	Jehozadak	y'-ho-tza-DAK	יְהוֹצָדָק
Yehoyachin	Jehoiachin	y'-ho-ya-KHEEN	יְהוֹיָכִין
Yehoyada	Jehoiada	y'-ho-ya-DA	יְהוֹיָדָע
Yehoyakim	Jehoiakim	y'-ho-ya-KEEM	יְהוֹיָקִים
Yehu	Jehu	yay-HU	יֵהוּא
Yehuda	Judah	y'-hu-DAH	יְהוּדָה
Yehudi	Jew	y'-hu-DEE	יְהוּדִי
Yehudim	Jews	y'-hu-DEEM	יְהוּדִים
Yered	Jared	YE-red	יֶרֶד
Yericho	Jericho	y'-ree-KHO	יְרִיחוֹ
Yerovam	Jeroboam	ya-rov-AM	יָרָבְעָם
Yerubaal	Jerubbaal	y'-ru-BA-al	יְרֻבַּעַל
Yerushalayim	Jerusalem	y'-ru-sha-LA-yim	יְרוּשָׁלַיִם
Yeshayahu	Isaiah	y'-sha-YA-hu	יְשַׁעְיָהוּ
Yeshua	Jeshua	yay-SHU-a	יֵשׁוּעַ
Yiftach	Jephthah	yif-TAKH	יִפְתָּח
Yigal	Igal	yig-AL	יִגְאָל
Yirmiyahu	Jeremiah	yir-m'-YA-hu	יִרְמְיָהוּ
Yishai	Jesse	yi-SHAI	יִשַׁי
Yisrael	Israel	yis-ra-AYL	יִשְׂרָאֵל
Yissachar	Issachar	yi-sa-KHAR	יִשָׂשכָר
Yitzchak	Issac	yitz-KHAK	יִצְחָק
Yizrael	Jezreel	yiz-r'-EL	יִזְרְעָאל
Yoash	Joash	yo-ASH	יוֹאָשׁ
Yoav	Joab	yo-AV	יוֹאָב
Yochanan	Johanan	yo-kha-NAN	יוֹחָנָן
Yocheved	Jochebed	yo-KHE-ved	יוֹכֶבֶד
Yoel	Joel	yo-AYL	יוֹאֵל
Yona	Jonah	yo-NAH	יוֹנָה
Yonadav	Jonadab	yo-na-DAV	יוֹנָדָב
Yonatan	Jonathan	yo-na-TAN	יוֹנָתָן

Hebrew Name	English Name	Pronunciation	Hebrew
Yoram	Joram	yo-RAM	יוֹרָם
Yosef	Joseph	yo-SAYF	יוֹסֵף
Yoshiyahu	Josiah	yo-shi-YA-hu	יֹאשִׁיָּהוּ
Yotam	Jotham	yo-TAM	יוֹתָם
Yotzadak	Jozadak	yo-tza-DAK	יוֹצָדָק
Yozavad	Jozabad	yo-za-VAD	יוֹזָבָד
Zanoach	Zanoah	za-NO-akh	זָנוֹחַ
Zecharya	Zechariah	z'-khar-YAH	זְכַרְיָה
Zerach	Zerah	ZE-rakh	זֶרַח
Zerubavel	Zerubbabel	z'-ru-ba-VEL	זְרֻבָּבֶל
Zevulun	Zebulun	z'-vu-LUN	זְבוּלֻן
Zilpa	Zilpah	zil-PAH	זִלְפָּה
Zimri	Zimri	zim-REE	זִמְרִי

Jewish Holidays

Chanukah	Hanukkah	kha-nu-KAH	חֲנוּכָּה
Pesach	Passover	PE-sakh	פֶּסַח
Purim	Purim	pu-REEM	פּוּרִים
Rosh Hashana	Jewish New Year	rosh ha-sha-NAH	רֹאשׁ הַשָּׁנָה
Shavuot	Feast of Weeks	sha-vu-OT	שָׁבוּעוֹת
Shemini Atzeret	Eight Day of Assembly	sh'-mee-NEE a-TZE-ret	שְׁמִינִי עֲצֶרֶת
Sukkot	Feast of Tabernacles	su-KOT	סֻכּוֹת
Yom Kippur	Day of Atonement	yom kee-PUR	יוֹם כִּיפּוּר

Biblical Measurements

Amah	Cubit	a-MAH	אַמָּה
Amot	Cubits	a-MOT	אַמּוֹת
Bat	Bath	bat	בַּת
Batim	Baths	ba-TEEM	בָּתִּים
Beka	half-shekel	BE-ka	בֶּקַע
Chomarim	Homers	kho-ma-REEM	חֳמָרִים
Chomer	Homer	KHO-mer	חֹמֶר
Efah	Ephah	ay-FAH	אֵיפָה
Geira	Gerah	gay-RAH	גֵּרָה

Hebrew Name	English Name	Pronunciation	Hebrew
Gomed	Gomed	GO- med	גֹּמֶד
Hin	Hin	heen	הִין
Kav	kab	kav	קַב
Kesita	kesitah	k'-see-TAH	קְשִׂיטָה
Kikar	talent	ki-KAR	כִּכָּר
Kikarim	talents	ki-ka-RIM	כִּכָרִים
Kor	kor	kor	כֹּר
Letek	lethech	LE-tek	לָתֶךְ
Log	Log	log	לֹג
Maneh	Mina	ma-NEH	מָנֶה
Manim	Minas	ma-NEEM	מָנִים
Omer	Omer	O-mer	עֹמֶר
Pim	Pim	peem	פִּים
Se'ah	Seah	say-AH	סְאָה
Se'eem	Seahs	s'-EEM	סְאִים
Shekalim	Shekels	sh'-ka-LEEM	שְׁקָלִים
Shekel	Shekel	SHE-kel	שֶׁקֶל
Tefach	Handbreadth	TE-fakh	טָפַח
Zeret	Span	ZE-ret	זֶרֶת

Photo Credits

I Chronicles

1:43 Ilan Ejzykowicz/Shutterstock.com, **2:4** Courtesy of Israel365, **4:40** Alexandre Rotenberg/Shutterstock.com, **5:20** Yuri Yavnik/Shutterstock.com, **6:16** Leonid Andronov/Shutterstock.com, **7:31** Mark Neyman, Government Press Office (Israel), **8:28** John Theodor/Shutterstock.com, **9:3** Mark Neyman, Government Press Office (Israel), **11:4** Barbarajo/Shutterstock.com, **12:16** Protasov AN/Shutterstock.com, **13:2** kavram/Shutterstock.com, **14:10** vvvita/Shutterstock.com, **15:3** VanderWolf Images/Shutterstock.com, **16:42** Faruk, Wikimedia Commons, **17:12** Mikhail Semenov/Shutterstock.com, **19:2** John Theodor/Shutterstock.com, **20:1** Seth Aronstam/Shutterstock.com, **21:24** John Theodor/Shutterstock.com, **22:5** Sarit Richerson/Shutterstock.com, **23:26** By U.S. Embassy Tel Aviv – Flickr: Visit to Meah She'arim_113, CC BY-SA 2.0, https://commons.wikimedia.org/w/index.php?curid=32606244, **24:2** MyStarHeimwerker/Shutterstock.com, **25:8** Government Press Office (Israel), **26:1** John Theodor/Shutterstock.com, **27:1** KrispelSlaven/Shutterstock.com, **28:6** John Theodor/Shutterstock.com, **29:22** By Proesi at German Wikipedia – Self-photographed, CC BY-SA 2.0 de, https://commons.wikimedia.org/w/index.php?curid=16231918

II Chronicles

1:10 Israel Tourism, Wikimedia Commons, **2:3** S1001/Shutterstock.com, **3:10** Moshe Milner, Government Press Office (Israel), **4:20** Amos Ben Gershom, Government Press Office (Israel), **5:14** John Theodor/Shutterstock.com, **6:27** John Theodor/Shutterstock.com, **7:14** Protasov AN/Shutterstock.com, **8:12** Andrew Shiva, Wikimedia Commons, **9:1** Courtesy of Israel365, **10:6** Noam Armonn/Shutterstock.com, **11:4** Evgeny Pylayev/Shutterstock.com, **13:8** MWPHOTOS55/Shutterstock.com, **14:10** Moshe Milner, Government Press Office (Israel), **15:15** Noam Chen via goisrael.com, **16:7** Liron-Afuta/Shutterstock.com, **17:10** By U.S. Department of State – Ambassador Shapiro Visits the Mir Yeshiva, Public Domain, https://commons.wikimedia.org/w/index.php?curid=38511675, **18:2** Wikimedia Commons, **20:26** Michaeli, Wikimedia Commons, **19:5** Moshe Milner, Government Press Office (Israel), **21:20** By SHARONGABAY2 – Own work, CC BY-SA 3.0, https://commons.wikimedia.org/w/index.php?curid=36216075, **22:12** Lenar Musin/Shutterstock.com, **23:11** Avi Ohayon, Government Press Office (Israel), **24:16** Max Zalevsky/Shutterstock.com, **25:2** KiyechkaSo/Shutterstock.com, **26:19** Shimon Bar/Shutterstock.com, **27:2** GotovyyStock/Shutterstock.com, **28:3** John Theodor/Shutterstock.com, **29:29** Mikhail Semenov/Shutterstock.com, **30:6** David Cohen 156/Shutterstock.com, **31:5** Yuri Dondish/Shutterstock.com, **32:22** Sergei25/Shutterstock.com, **33:2** Courtesy of Israel365, **34:27** Chameleons Eye/Shutterstock.com, **35:18** Rawpixel.com/Shutterstock.com, **36:23** Mark Neyman, Government Press Office (Israel)

Map of Modern-Day
Israel and its Neighbors

The following is a map of modern-day Israel and the surrounding countries

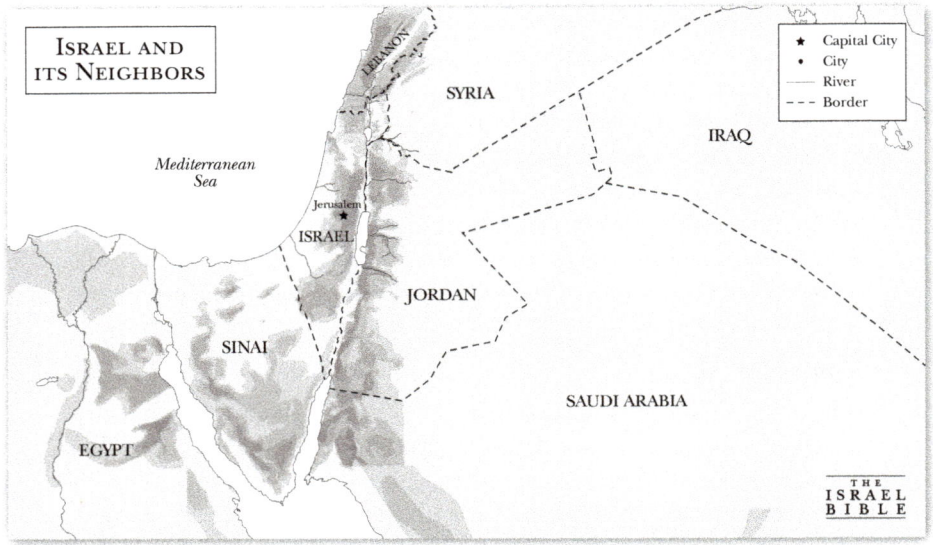

NOTES

NOTES

NOTES

NOTES

NOTES

For more inspiring commentary,
interactive maps, educational videos,
vivid photographs and more,
please visit our website

www.TheIsraelBible.com

THE
ISRAEL
BIBLE